Life in the Spirit

BOOKS BY THOMAS C. ODEN

Life in the Spirit

SYSTEMATIC THEOLOGY:
VOLUME THREE

Thomas C. Oden

HarperSanFrancisco
A Division of HarperCollins*Publishers*

For my major mentors,
Jewish and Christian,
without whom this series would never
have been conceived —
Will Herberg and Albert Outler

All quotations from the Bible, unless otherwise noted, are from The New International Version.

LIFE IN THE SPIRIT, *Systematic Theology: Volume Three*. Copyright © 1992 by Thomas C. Oden. All rights reserved. Printed in the United States of America. No part of this book may be used or reproduced in any manner whatsoever without written permission except in the case of brief quotations embodied in critical articles and reviews. For information address HarperCollins Publishers, 10 East 53rd Street, New York, NY 10022.

FIRST EDITION

Library of Congress Cataloging-in-Publication Data
Oden, Thomas C.
  Life in the Spirit / Thomas C. Oden. — 1st ed.
    p.   cm. — (Systematic theology ; v. 3)
  Includes bibliographical references and indexes.
  ISBN 0–06–066349–9 (alk. paper)
  1. Holy Spirit. 2. Salvation. 3. Church. 4. Eschatology.
  I. Title. II. Series: Oden, Thomas C. Systematic theology ; v. 3.
  BT121.2.036 1992
  230—dc20   90–55805
                                                                CIP

92 93 94 95 96 RRD (H) 10 9 8 7 6 5 4 3 2 1

This edition is printed on acid-free paper that meets the American National Standards Institute Z39.48 Standard.

Contents

Preface

As Basil observed, "The athlete does not so much complain of being wounded in the struggle as of not being able even to secure admission into the stadium" (Basil, *On the Holy Spirit* III.29, *NPNF* 2 VIII, p. 48). I am grateful for admission into this theological stadium, where a lengthy race is now coming to its last round.

Modest Reaffirmations. At the end of this journey I reaffirm solemn commitments made at its beginning:

- To make no new contribution to theology
- To resist the temptation to quote modern writers less schooled in the whole counsel of God than the best ancient classic exegetes
- To seek quite simply to express the one mind of the believing church that has been ever attentive to that apostolic teaching to which consent has been given by Christian believers everywhere, always, and by all—this is what I mean by the Vincentian method (Vincent of Lérins, *Comm., LCC* VII, pp. 37–39, 65–74; for an accounting of this method, see *LG,* pp. 322–25, 341–51)

I am dedicated to unoriginality. I am pledged to irrelevance if relevance means indebtedness to corrupt modernity. What is deemed relevant in theology is likely to be moldy in a few days. I take to heart Paul's admonition: "But even if we or an angel from heaven should preach a gospel *other than* the one we preached to you, let him be eternally condemned! As we [from the earliest apostolic kerygma] had already said, so now I say again: If anybody is preaching to you a gospel other than what you accepted [*par o parelabete,* other than what you received from the apostles], let him be eternally condemned [*anathema esto*]!" (Gal. 1:8, 9, NIV, italics added).

My purpose is to set forth the teachings of the person and work of the Holy Spirit, saving grace, the called-out people, and the consummation of history, on which there has been substantial agreement between traditions of East and West, Catholic, Protestant, and Orthodox. I will listen intently for the historic ecumenical consensus received by believers of widely varied languages, social locations, and cultures, whether of East or West, African, or Asian, whether expressed by women or men of the second or first Christian millennium, whether European or decisively pre-European, post- or pre-Constantinian.

My aim has not been to survey the bewildering varieties of *dis*sent, but to identify and plausibly set forth the cohesive central tradition of general lay *con*sent to apostolic teaching, not through its centrifugal variations but in its centripetal centering. I will spend little time trying to knock down others' cherished views. The focus is upon setting forth plausible layers of argument traditionally employed in presenting in connected order the most commonly held points of biblical teaching of the saving work of the Spirit in persons and community, within and beyond history, as classically exegeted by the leading teachers of its first five centuries.

Theological innovators who still doubt that the scriptural textuary is the crucial wellspring of Christian existence and reflection will always be disappointed in such an effort. But all who wear this festive wedding garment are warmly welcomed to the feast.

My intention is not to try to satisfy the finicky appetites of naturalistic skeptics who will always remain hungry. Nor is it to find a clever way of making the way of salvation conveniently acceptable to the prejudices of modernity. I am pledged not to become fixated upon the ever-spawning species of current critical opinion, but instead to focus single-mindedly upon early consensual assent to apostolic teaching of how God the Spirit works to fulfill the mission of God the Son on behalf of God the Father.

That the Holy Spirit is fulfilling the mission of the Son is less an argument than a historical fact. My purpose is not to seek to establish by argument that the Spirit is God, but rather to show that this has indeed been believed by Christians of countless cultural settings, times, and social locations.

I do not assume that my reading partner already affirms classic Christian teaching, but only ask that he or she is willing to give fair hearing to the ways in which classic Christian teaching has reasoned about its own grounding and empowerment. I will not evade or eviscerate the traditional language of the church, or seek constantly to substitute diluted terms congenial to modernity. The tested language of the church speaks in its own unrelenting ways to modern minds struggling with the follies and limits of modernity. Deteriorating modern ideologies must now catch up with the ever-new forgings of classic Christianity, not the other way around.

Whether one breathes easiest at a high liturgical or at a down-to-earth, socially engaged, pragmatic altitude, whether one's imagination is awakened more by theoretical or by practical interests, whether one enters the fray with Eastern or Western sympathies, whether one feels more comfortable with an Enlightenment or pietistic vocabulary, I hope that each one of these varied partners may recognize the best of their own recent traditions as already at home and included within the embrace of classical Christian exegesis. Christian orthodox exegesis deserves advocates who try to do what Rachel Carson did for birds or what Archie Carr did to advocate the cause of endangered sea turtles.

The Reference System.   Theological argument does well to view itself modestly as merely an introduction to its annotations. I earnestly wish more attention to be paid to notes than text, more to primary sources than my arrangement of them, more to the substance of the references than to the particular frame in which one observer beholds, places, or organizes them. If it is possible for an author sincerely to ask a reader to rivet radical attention upon the sources to which he points and relatively less to the sequence and structure of his own inventions, I would indicate from the outset that as my true intention. Picture me as on my knees begging you to do just this one thing.

Over fifteen thousand specific primary source references to consensus-bearing exegetes are offered in this series. The weighting of references may be compared to a pyramid of sources, with canonical scripture as foundational base, then the early Christian writers, first pre-Nicene then post-Nicene, as the supporting mass or trunk, then the best of medieval followed by centrist Reformation writers at the narrowing center, and more recent interpreters at the smaller, tapering apex— but only those who grasp and express the anteceding mind of the believing historical church. I am pledged not to try heroically to turn that pyramid upside down, as have those guild theologians who most value only what is most recent or most outrageous. Earlier rather than later sources are cited where possible, not because older is sentimentally prized, but because they have had longer to shape historical consensus. Consent-expressing exegetes are preferred to those whose work is characterized more by individual creativity, controversial brilliance, stunning rhetoric, or speculative genius.

Complaints about proof-texting must not lead one to ignore the very canonical textuary upon which classic Christian teaching thrives. The modern form of historical exegesis that sincerely intends at every step to place every scriptural reference in its historical context risks becoming a long string of historical excursi on modern commentators so as to inadvertently forget the apostolic text itself. In this way the well-motivated attempt at historical critical exegesis may take a heavy toll on both catechesis and morality.

The history of orthodox Christian teaching is primarily a history of exegesis. It would be absurd to provide references to early exegetes but fail to mention the texts themselves. Most common points of consensual Christian exegesis on the Spirit, the church, and the meaning of history were reasonably well formulated by the fifth century. Upon these we will focus.

Like Kierkegaard, I now reach out energetically only for my one reader—you. To you I wish to offer the full energy of my life insofar as a black-and-white page can convey it. Like Gregory Nazianzen, I know that "I am a little shepherd, and preside over a tiny flock, and I am among the least of the servants of the Spirit. But Grace is not narrow, or circumscribed by place. Wherefore let freedom of speech be given even to the small—especially when the subject matter is of such great importance" (Gregory Nazianzen, *Letters* XLI, *NPNF* 2 VII, p. 450).

Is this project intransigently antiquarian and reactionary? I can think of nothing more forward-looking than taking the risk of allowing ourselves to be addressed by the texts of scripture and tradition. I am drawn to the living tradition, not dead archaisms. I hope rather to treat solidly conserving forms of Christian tradition with an attentiveness to their own originally fresh sense of imagination. Where highly imaginative forms of Christian traditioning have received general lay consent, I seek to be attentive to their deeper rootage in ancient tradition. It is not impossible to do both, for this is what the classic exegetes did consistently—they treated conserving forms of Christian tradition with lively imagination, and imaginative forms of Christian experience with a celebration of their antecedents.

Theology attempts to be *systematic* insofar as it looks for a cohesive, internally consistent grasp of the whole of Christian teaching so as to view each part in relation to the whole. As for those points where the meaning of the apostolic witness is contested or remains ambiguous, the subject will be left open for further inquiry, acknowledging principal viewpoints remaining in tension.

For the reader who is paying the detailed attention to embedded annotations for which I am hoping, several technical conventions may help locate references: References to Migne (*MPG, Patrologia Graeca, MPL, Patrologia Latina*) cite column numbers. In some cases I have made my own translations of a text, and in other cases referenced alternative translations. Where a Latin or Greek document is unavailable in full in standard English translation but well quoted by another source, I have referenced that source. At times two translations or editions of a text may be cited when both carry pertinent nuances of the original, with the first to be taken as the primary reference. Where *cf.* occurs, I am signaling the reader to compare.

From welcome feedback from friendly critics I have become aware that some wish that references might pursue more fully the context of the quote, while others wish that the references would be less detailed. I have tried to strike a balance between excess in either direction. If upon searching for a reference a reader finds that some sections deal with subjects other than those under discussion, please look for particular portions of the larger discussion that pertain to the subject at hand. I have sought to make page references neither too long or short, hoping not to weigh down the reader with historical complexities and hoping not to withhold from the reader any pertinent information about where the ideas are best found. A short reference may be embedded in a longer discussion necessary to provide its context, in which case I have usually referenced the larger context. If anything, I have erred on the side of brevity. Where an extended number of pages is referenced, it is deemed useful that the reader grasp the context of the constellation of ideas referenced.

The Thread of Life—A Personal Word of Gratitude.   The recurring theme that has held this series together since its inception a decade ago is *life*—its source, its appearing as incarnate Word, and the gift of Life in the Spirit. I did not know then that my own life would be gravely threatened, hanging by a thread for several days after heart surgery just before completion of this last volume. I am grateful to God that I fully recovered to continue this study of the Giver, Redeemer, and Consummator of life. I am especially thankful for my physician Carlos Garces, cardiologist Stephen Guss, heart surgeon Grant Parr, and the nurses at Morristown Hospital and Execor Rehabilitation Center, who kept this body alive under trying circumstances. The experience has intensified my love of life and my sense of the value of the unrepeatable gift that God has given each person, and deepened my awareness of how God's strength is made perfect through human weakness.

Paul expressed his ongoing confidence that "he who began a good work in you will carry it on to completion" (Phil. 1:6). This volume is all about the life-enabling, maturing, completing, consummating work of the Spirit. It brings to completion, amid real hazards, a journey I set out upon long ago. If Michelangelo could invest eleven years on the Rondanini *Pietà*, I do not regret spending a decade hammering and polishing this argument.

For rabbinics partners in dialogue, especially Rabbi Judah Goldin, my colleague Peter Ochs, and the late Will Herberg, I am inexpressibly grateful. To Joseph Cardinal Ratzinger I remain especially indebted for his critical insight and caring concern. To superb Protestant, Catholic, and Jewish partners in dialogue in the New York circle of theologians in the Avery Dulles duodecim I am truly appreciative. Especially for the extended ministry of friendship of Richard John Neuhaus and Father C. John McCloskey, I give thanks.

Orthodox theologians to whom I am most deeply indebted include Thomas Hopko, John Breck, Vigen Guroian, and David Ford. Among Catholic thinkers upon whom I have most depended are Hans Urs von Balthasar, Louis Bouyer, Michael Novak, and George Weigel. Evangelical scholars to whom I continue to be indebted include Carl F. H. Henry, David Wells, Timothy Smith, Ward Gasque, James I. Packer, Clark Pinnock, and Stanley Gundry. Other Protestant partners in dialogue upon whom I have long depended are Reinhold and H. Richard Niebuhr, Wolfhart Pannenberg, and Albert C. Outler. Recently I have benefited from expository teaching ministries of John McArthur, Charles Swindoll, Warren Wiersbe, Robert A. Cook, Donald Barnhouse, David Hocking, and J. V. McGee, who have enriched my awareness of traditional Reformed and Baptist exegesis, and from the writings of H. Vinson Synon, W. J. Hollenweger, Gary B. McGee, and Frederick Dale Bruner.

I have been rescued from innumerable blunders, gaffes, and academic misdemeanors by astute manuscript readers. I am grateful for the steady covenant friendship of colleagues who undertook a careful critique of portions of this manuscript, some of whom are cherished members of my own family (Bishop William B. Oden, the Rev. James Hampson, Professor Amy Oden, the Rev. Robert Stuart Jummonville), and others treasured members of my extended family of former students. To Daniel Clendenin and Alan Padgett, who took on the special burden of thoroughly critiquing the entire manuscript, I am incalculably indebted for dozens of helpful suggestions. Among Drew colleagues, I note special thanks to James M. O'Kane, John F. Ollom, George deStevens, Robert Corrington, Donald Dayton, and Alister McGrath. Among others to whom I owe special gratitude who responded critically to major parts of the manuscript are Bishop Dan Solomon, Chancellor Dennis Kinlaw, and Professors David Buschart, Young Ho Chun, Kenneth Collins, Daniel Davies, David Eaton, Robert Jenson, Roderick Leupp, Fred Norris, Darius Salter, Donald Thorsen, John Tyson, William Ury, Charles Villa-Vicencio, Woodrow Whidden, Robert Wilken, and Ben Witherington. Innumerable hours have been selflessly devoted by these colleagues to this project. I have valued thoughtful critical responses from Pastors Michael Graef, Gregory Johansen, Paul Stallsworth, and James Heidinger, and from my highly esteemed graduate teaching assistants at various stages: Kent Branstetter, Kenneth Brewer, Christopher Hall, and Paul Sparacio. To each one of the above, who collectively and unpretentiously constitute something of a continuing seminar and postcritical theological connection, I offer a deeply felt personal word of thanks. With each of these colleagues I have felt the freedom to debate, respectfully differ, painstakingly argue, and hear rigorous argument, and from each I have learned. This far-flung circle of collaborators stretching from Africa to the Far East and to Oxford, Tübingen, and Rome means all the world to me.

I am grateful to have been permitted to live in such momentous times as these, when both church and university stand at a decisive crossroads. I am grateful for being given an academic home in a university of the evangelical heritage where just such issues as *pneuma, ekklēsia,* and *eschaton* could be pursued on the (elsewhere) almost comic premise that they are just as crucial to the university as those of the hard sciences.

Only at the end of this lengthy process am I becoming aware of some surprising feedback. Some of my readers are telling me that even if they cannot join in the premises of Christian teaching, they nonetheless find it beautiful, aesthetically whole, and of immense interest merely as a historical exercise. Though I welcome this kind of reader, it has been clear in my mind from the outset that this work is addressed primarily to the *ekklēsia,* not to the secularizing culture. If the *saeculum* finds it beautiful or edifying, I can only invite further inquiry into the truth of why.

Introduction

Some of the most intriguing and difficult questions of theology lie straight ahead under the topics of the work of the Holy Spirit in the renewal of persons in community.

The Saving Work of the Spirit

The Living God, first volume of this series, set forth the ancient ecumenical Christian understanding of God, creation, and providence. *The Word of Life,* volume 2 of *Systematic Theology,* asked whether the Word became flesh, and whether that has saving significance for us. *Life in the Spirit* asks how the work of God in creation and redemption is being brought to consummation by the Holy Spirit in persons, through communities, and in the full range of human destiny. Though grounded in this larger sequence, this volume can be read as a self-contained argument. It points toward but does not require the reading of its companion volumes.

The issues ahead have been more prone than others to defensive polemics and special institutional memories. There is an understandable reason why these practical, churchly, and end questions of theology are at sensitive points more resistant to consensual interpretation, for they take the theological task ever closer to the varieties of personal experience, concrete variables of social and political order, ideologies and competing worldviews, histories of church polities, and particular ways of engaging in the mission of the Spirit. Despite these obstacles, this study hopes to find an audience with Catholics without offense to Baptists, with charismatics without losing touch with Eastern Orthodox communicants, with social liberationists without demeaning pietists. How? By seeking the shared rootage out of which each has grown.

Defining Sources of Classic Consensual Teaching. Who are the "principal consensual exegetes" to whom the argument so frequently turns? Above all, they are the ecumenical councils and early synods that came to be often quoted as representing the mind of the believing church; the four standard ecumenical teachers of the Eastern church tradition (Athanasius, Basil, Gregory Nazianzen, John Chrysostom) and of the West (Ambrose, Jerome, Augustine, and Gregory the Great), as well as others who have been perennially valued for accurately stating certain points of ecumenical consensus: Cyril of Jerusalem, Cyril of Alexandria, Hilary, Leo, John of Damascus, and Thomas Aquinas. "Classic" in this definition includes classic Reformation sources from Luther, Melanchthon, and Calvin through Chemnitz and Ursinus to Wesley and Edwards and consensus-bearing Protestant formularies consistent with ancient consensual exegesis. I do not hesitate to quote at times relatively nonconsensual writers like Origen, Tertullian, Novatian, and Menno Simons, but I do so on those points at which they generally have confirmed or articulated or refined consensual views, not on points where

1

they diverge into idiosyncratic thinking (Vincent of Lérins, *Comm.* 17, 18, *NPNF* 2 XI, pp. 143–45).

Because the exegetical questions grow increasingly controverted and technical in these contested theological battlefields, more explanatory detail is required to establish irenic argument. It would be possible to set forth a much briefer summary of these issues, but I am assuming that my reader would prefer to be guided just to that depth that is required for a clear and adequate grasp of the subject matter without unnecessary excursions (Leo, *Letters* I, *NPNF* 2 XII, p. 1).

Whether the Intent of Classic Ecumenic Referencing Differs from Modern. The religion-teaching guild functions with an underlying value premise that is best termed modern chauvinism. Modern chauvinism holds that whatever is premodern is likely to be relatively worthless; that whatever worth might be encased in premodern sources must be translated in terms that are acceptable to moderns before its worth can be extracted; and that whatever is newer is predictably superior intellectually and morally. Accordingly, a major function of footnoting in guild religious studies, fixated as it is upon novelty, is the identification of the most recent sources that achieve presumably *new* perspectives and transcend the supposed limits of the old. Regrettably, the premise is as common as it is arrogant.

The major function of referencing in the classical ecumenical tradition, by contrast, is the identification of ancient, tried, and consensually reliable formularies and authorities for articulating the mind of the believing church, especially under idiosyncratic or heterodox challenge. The purpose is to set forth sources that have been repeatedly and reliably quoted by the believing community to point to shared affirmations and assumptions (Vincent of Lérins, *Comm.* 1–3, *FC* 7, pp. 267–72).

Hence the ethic of footnoting that pervades the ethos of modern scholarship must be transmuted by classical Christian scholarship, which has always had little desire to state wholly original ideas or to pretend to identify the first pristine occurrence or expression of an idea in time, aware that all ideas in history live in an organic continuum of historical consciousness and gradual development.

The church is approaching its third millennium. It is beyond the capacity of any writer to reference all such sources, especially where the history of exegesis has a multimillennia trajectory. The purpose is not an absolute completeness of reference (the entire project would then turn comically into an endless series of footnotes) but rather a spare and fitting *selection* of those references that proximately express the mind of the believing church throughout all its history. This has been a variegated history personally unified in Christ, whose oneness is contextually enabled by the Spirit. For the principles underlying this selection, I refer the reader to the prefaces and methodological epilogues to the two previous volumes in the series.

Introducing the Study of the Spirit

Pneumatology is the systematic analysis and interpretation of the texts of scripture and tradition that deal with the regenerating and consummating work of the Holy Spirit (*pneuma hagion*). Like Christology, it has been typically structured around the distinction between the person (identity) and work (activity) of the Holy Spirit—the overarching subject of this volume. So vast is the subject matter that it requires careful reasoning to establish a fitting route of approach to its range and consequences.

The Necessity and Importance of the Doctrine of the Holy Spirit. All that we understand of the Father and the Son, we understand through the illumining work of the Spirit (John 16; Ignatius, *Eph.*, *ANF* I, pp. 49–58). Whatever grasp one may have of God's revelation is always enabled by the Spirit. In whatever ways sinners are empowered to overcome the corrupting aspects of the world, the flesh, and the adversary, they do so by the power of the Spirit. The Spirit leads the faithful into all truth by pointing constantly toward the truth embodied in Jesus (John 16:13; Ignatius, *Eph.* 9, *ANF* I, p. 53).

The Father and Son have given the church no greater gift than the outpouring of God's own Spirit. "God does not give a Gift inferior to Himself" (Augustine, *Faith and the Creed* 9.19, *FEF* III, 1561, p. 44). The Son promised that the Spirit would follow his ministry on earth, and that incomparable blessings would ensue with the ministry of the Spirit. Having once been given the gift of the Spirit at Pentecost, the believing community has never been left without this Comforter (John 14:18; John Chrysostom, *Hom. on John* LXXV, *NPNF* 1 XIV, pp. 274–75).

The Neglect of the Teaching of the Holy Spirit. The work of the Spirit has been less studied and consensually defined than the work of the Son. When Paul asked his hearers at Ephesus, "Did you receive the Holy Spirit when you believed?" they answered, "No, we have not even heard that there is a Holy Spirit" (Acts 19:2). Even now many think it possible to teach the gospel of Jesus without awareness of the work of the Spirit. John Paul II has rightly called for renewed study of the Holy Spirit in the last decade of this millennium (*Dominum et Vivificantem*).

The modern tendency is to depersonalize the Spirit, to treat God the Spirit as reducible to an idea of spirituality or an attribute of God, rather than God's own personal meeting with persons living in history. This has contributed to the neglect and misunderstanding of this subject.

Perennial distortions associated with naturalistic spiritualism, pantheism, excessive subjectivism, and crude views of faith healing probably would not have burgeoned so abundantly in the history of the church had more thorough attention been given to the systematic understanding of the mission of the Holy Spirit (Augustine, *Faith and the Creed* 9.19, *FEF* III, 1561, p. 44).

It is a scandal to modern "critical" scholarship that standard discussions of the Holy Spirit often make no inquiry whatever into the great early treatises on the Holy Spirit by Didymus, Basil, Gregory of Nyssa, Gregory Nazianzen, and Ambrose. It remains a mixed blessing that modern charismatic and Pentecostal voices have so stressed special aspects of the work of the Spirit that some other Protestant voices have tended to back away completely from all teaching concerning the Spirit. The texts of scripture, however, leave no doubt in our minds of the importance of teaching of and by the Spirit.

"The subject of the Holy Spirit presents a special difficulty," wrote Gregory Nazianzen, because by the time we get to it, "worn out by the multitude of questions," we may become like those who have "lost their appetite, who having taken a dislike to some particular kind of food, shrink from all food; so we in like manner have an aversion from all discussion" (Gregory Nazianzen, *Orat.* XXXI, *Of the Holy*

Spirit, NPNF 2 VII, p. 318). The laity have a right to be scripturally instructed, but the clergy remain ill prepared.

The Pivot of Pneumatology: From "for Us" to "in Us."   We stand at a crucial pivot of Christian theology, shifting the focus from the work of the Son to the work of the Spirit in the church in applying the benefits of the work of the Son. "It is the peculiar office and work of the Holy Ghost to reveal and glorify Christ, and to testify concerning Him" (Luther, *Lectures on John* 7:39; Jacobs, *SCF,* p. 185).

In volume two of this series we have spoken chiefly of God *for* us. Now we speak more deliberately of God working *in* us. We speak not of events addressing us as it were from the outside of our experience (*extra nos*) but more deliberately of active inward processes and events by which persons in community are convicted, transformed, regenerated, justified, and brought into union with Christ, one by one. This is God's work within humanity (*intra nos*) viewed individually and socially.

The forgiveness of God the Son, having been once for all offered on the cross, must be ever again received, and at each stage we must be freshly enabled to receive it. In Christ we learn what God has done on our behalf. By the Spirit we are being enabled to *reshape our doing* in response to what God has done, to reform our loves in relation to God's incomparable love, to allow God's redeeming work to touch every aspect of our broken lives. With this pivot, our own decisions and actions now become a crucial part of the salvation story, the history of the body of Christ (for the transition from "for us" to "in us," see pivot between Books 1 and 2 of Calvin's *Institutes* or J. Wesley "On Working out Our Salvation," *WJWB, Sermon* 85, *WJW* VI, pp. 506–13).

God not only forgives sin through the Son but through the Spirit works to overturn the power of sin in actual daily interpersonal behavior and life in community. The gospel not only announces the death and resurrection of Christ but calls us to die to sin and live to God by the power of the Spirit. Thus by death we receive true life (Ignatius, *Rom.* 6, *ANF* I, p. 76). By the Spirit we ourselves consciously and unconsciously, actively and passively, enter the sphere of God's saving work.

Consensual Christian teaching does not consider the work of the Spirit incidental or ancillary. For here the work of God enters deeply into personal existence to meet and redeem existing persons. Neglect of this part of Christian teaching leads to forgetfulness of how God accomplishes the salvation of humanity.

The Lord and Giver of Life.   The Spirit is "Lord and Giver of Life" (*to kurion,* [*kai*] *to zōopoion,* Nicene-Constantinopolitan Creed, *COC* II, p. 57; 1 Cor. 15:45). "The Spirit gives life" (John 6:63; 2 Cor. 3:6). "God our life is the life of all" (Hildegard of Bingen, *Symphonia,* p. 143).

The new life involves entry into a family, into sonship and daughterhood (Rom. 8:12–17; Gal. 4:6) in relation to an incomparably caring parent (*Abba,* "Papa"). The Spirit bears witness within our spirits that we are children of this *Abba* in this family (Rom. 8:16).

All who have lived out of the history of sin are said to be born of the flesh. Flesh (*sarx*) refers not merely to the physical body but to the whole person under the power of sin who compulsively pursues works of the flesh (Gal. 5:19–21). All who faithfully receive the Spirit are born anew, given a new spiritual beginning and called to grow in grace (John 3:1–8). The new person in Christ is born of the Spirit to faith active in love (Rom. 8:1–7). Those newly born of God are no longer idolatrously enslaved by the elemental spirits of this world (Gal. 4:3). Regenerated life need not any longer be lived out in bondage to psychological scripts from parents and siblings and social influences, or skewed political interests or economic forces of poverty or exploitation. It is lived out in freedom for the neighbor, freeing persons to fulfill their original human purpose whatever the historical conditions, to enjoy all things in God, to receive life day by day from the eternal Giver (Gal. 5; Calvin, *Inst.* 3.10; 3.23.12).

The Third Article of the Creed. All baptismal creeds confess in this or similar language: I believe in the Holy Spirit (*pneuma hagion;* Lat: *Spiritum Sanctum, COC* II, p. 55; Der-Balyzeh Papyrus, *SCD* 1, p. 3; *Roman Symbol, Psalter of Rufinus, SCD* 2, p. 5). "We believe in one Holy Spirit the Paraclete" (Eastern Form of the Apostles' Creed, Cyril of Jerusalem, *Catecheses, SCD* 9, p. 8). This article of baptismal faith became expanded through a history of exposition and controversy into the doctrine of the Holy Spirit.

In learning by heart the Creed of Epiphanius (c. A.D. 374, second formula), the catechumen rehearsed twelve clauses that summarily set forth the work of the Spirit:

> We believe in the Holy Spirit who
> spoke in the law,
> and taught by the prophets,
> and descended to the Jordan,
> spoke by the Apostles,
> and lives in the saints;
> thus we believe in him: that he is the Holy Spirit,
> the Spirit of God,
> the perfect Spirit,
> the Spirit Paraclete,
> uncreated [*aktiston*],
> proceeding from the Father [*ek tou Patros ekporeuomenon*]
> and receiving of the Son [*ek tou huiou lambanomenon*], in whom we
> believe.
>
> (*SCD* 13, p. 10; cf. *COC* II, p. 37)

Key points of the third article were concisely summarized as in the Statement of Faith of the United Church of Christ:

> He *bestows* upon us his Holy Spirit,
> creating and renewing the Church of Jesus Christ,
> binding in covenant faithful people of all ages,
> tongues, and races,
> He *calls* us into his Church
> to accept the cost and joy of discipleship,
> to be his servants in the service of men,
> to proclaim the gospel to all the world
> and resist the powers of evil,
> to share in Christ's baptism and eat at his table,

to join him in his passion and victory.
He *promises* to all who trust him
forgiveness of sins and fullness of grace,
courage in the struggle for justice and peace,
his presence in trial and rejoicing, and eternal life in his kingdom
which has no end.

(*CC*, p. 697, italics added)

The Continuum of Testimony.   The primitive rule of faith as recorded by Irenaeus (c. A.D. 190) shows the prominent role of the Holy Spirit recognized by the
early Christian community. Salvation history is placed within the context of the
work of the triune God. It is the Spirit who bears testimony in the present age to
the Father and the Son. The one *ekklēsia* believes:

in one God, the Father Almighty, Maker of heaven, and earth, and the
sea, and all things that are in them;
and in one Christ Jesus, the Son of God, who became incarnate for our
salvation;
and in the Holy Spirit, who proclaimed through the prophets the dispensations of God, and the advents, and the birth from a virgin, and the
passion, and the resurrection from the dead, and the ascension into heaven.

(Irenaeus, *Ag. Her.* I, x, 1; *CC*, p. 21)

Pre-Nicene writers understood that this rule of faith had been passed along by
apostolic testimony from Jesus to the present. Less than 150 years after Paul
(around A.D. 200), Tertullian countered the novelties of Praxeas with this recollection of the primitive confession of the Spirit as sanctifier who engenders holiness: God "sent from the Father the Holy Spirit the Paraclete, the sanctifier of the
faith of those who believe in the Father and the Son and the Holy Spirit. That *this
Rule has come down from the beginning of the Gospel,* even before all former heretics,
not to speak of Praxeas of yesterday, will be proved as well by the comparative
lateness of all heretics as by the very novelty of Praxeas of yesterday" (*Ag. Praxeas*
2; *CC*, p. 22, italics added; cf. Bull, *DNF;* William Beveridge, *Synodikon*).

The Second Ecumenical Council (Constantinople I) settled the question of the
deity of the Spirit as firmly as Nicaea had defined the deity of Christ and triunity
of God. The Nicene-Constantinopolitan Creed (381) set forth an ecumenically
received definition of the person and work of God the Spirit in these terms: "We
believe in the one God . . . And in the Holy Spirit, the Lord and life-giver, Who
proceeds from the Father, Who is worshiped and glorified together with the Father and Son, Who spoke through the prophets" (Creed of the 150 Fathers, *CC*,
p. 33; *SCD* 86, p. 36). To this day the Eastern traditions adhere to this language
(that the Spirit proceeds from the Father, not from Father and Son; John 15:26;
John of Damascus, *OF* I.11.4; *Longer Catech.*, Eastern Orthodox Church, 242,
COC II, p. 482).

The Personal Pronoun

If Not "It," Is the Spirit "He," or "She"?   In acknowledging the prevailing form
of address as "he" in the Christian tradition, it is useful to ask whether it is appro-

priate within the bounds of classic Christian assumptions to address the Spirit in the feminine gender.

The issue is difficult to settle on grammatical grounds: *Ruach* in Hebrew is feminine. *Pneuma* in Greek is a neuter, yet even when the neuter is used, masculine pronouns may accompany it. Even in the New Revised Standard Version, whose mandate specified that "masculine-oriented language should be eliminated as far as this can be done without altering passages that reflect the historical situation of ancient patriarchal culture," crucial passages could not be rendered in the neuter: "When the Spirit of truth comes, he will guide you into all the truth; for he will not speak on his own, but will speak whatever he hears [*akouei lalēsei*], and he will declare to you the things that are to come" (John 16:13, NRSV). God is named as *Abba* (Father); the messianic Son (*ben, huios*) stands in the male line of David; the Spirit is *ruach* or *pneuma* (feminine or neuter). Grammatical gender, however, does not necessarily imply sexual distinctions. It is hazardous to appeal either "to Hebrew or Greek to determine the choice of English pronouns for the Holy Spirit" (Kimel, *NLG,* p. 8).

Gregory Nazianzen was long ago amused by those who insistently held "God to be a male," which he regarded as a misplaced analogy. Just as one cannot say that God because Father is therefore male, so one cannot conclude that "Deity is feminine from the gender of the word, and the Spirit neuter," since the designation "has nothing to do with generation. But if you would be silly enough to say, with the old myths and fables, that God begat the Son by a marriage with His own Will, we should be introduced to the Hermaphrodite god of Marcion and Valentinus who imagined these newfangled Aeons" (Gregory Nazianzen, *Orat.* XXXI.7, *On the Holy Spirit, NPNF* 2 VII, p. 320, translation amended).

God has become self-revealed in scripture largely but not exclusively in masculine terms such as king, lord, husband, judge, master, and father. The work of the Spirit is at times compared to mothering and nurturing actions: "As a mother comforts her child, so will I comfort you" (Isa. 66:13). But still it is the Spirit of one regularly addressed as "he": "Where is he who set his Holy Spirit among them" (Isa. 63:11b). God the Spirit is not named Mother but compared to a mother (R. Frye, *Language for God and Feminist Language,* pp. 17–22; cf. Virginia R. Mollenkott, *The Divine Feminine*).

Elizabeth Achtemeier has persuasively shown that the prophets did not suffer from a failure of imagination to grasp God as female, for they were surrounded by cultures dominated by feminine deities, but they chose not to use feminine language "because they knew and had ample evidence from the religions surrounding them that the female language for the deity results in a basic distortion of the nature of God and of his relation to his creation" (in D. Miller, ed., *The Hermeneutical Quest,* p. 109)—namely, the deification of nature, pantheism, and immanental religion. "When you have a Goddess as the creator, it's her own body that is the universe. She is identical with the universe" (J. Campbell, *The Power of Myth,* p. 167).

Grammatical heroics that attempt a complete withdrawal from masculine language are often rhetorically awkward, contorted, and unwieldy, especially where nouns are repeated to avoid the pronoun regarded as offensive, where verbs are preferred that require no object, where the odd repetition of the word "God" is used as a substitute for "he," and direct address is shifted to "you."

The exegete is sorely tempted to rewrite scripture to gain a more attractive position with a modern audience. But no one prays to an "it," even if steeped in modernity. Liturgical "reforms" that systematically expunge the name Father from all acts of worship are especially unconscionable. That Jesus repeatedly named God Father (*Abba*) is a singular feature of his teaching. God is not merely like a father; God is Father, named as such by the Son. It is God the Spirit who teaches us to cry out *"Abba"* (Rom. 8:16). The church is that community that celebrates God as *Abba* (Irenaeus, *Ag. Her.* V.8, *ANF* I, pp. 533–34; Barth, *The Christian Life*, p. 51). Christian worshipers reluctant to address God by the name Jesus specifically taught them to speak can hardly be said to have learned how to pray. "We are bound to be baptized in the terms we have received and to profess belief in the terms in which we have been baptized" (Basil, in Torrance, *The Trinitarian Faith*, Edinburgh: T & T Clark, 1988, p. 193).

Neither Sex Adequate to God—Both Sexes Honored by God.   Neither male nor female language adequately grasps the fullness of the divine reality (Gregory Nazianzen, *Orat.* XXVII, *NPNF* 2 VII, pp. 284–88; John of Damascus, *OF* I.4–8, *FC* 37, pp. 170–85). Consistent with its purpose in allowing classical Christian texts to speak for themselves, irenic theology maintains faithfulness to the historic language of the church but, in doing so, seeks fairness and balance in the contemporary use of language.

If both sexes are to be honored and blessed in the incarnation, and if the one giving birth must be female, then the one born must be male (Augustine, *EDQ* 11, *FC* 70, p. 42). This is an argument carefully considered in the previous volume on Christology: *if the mother of the Savior must of necessity be female, since only females are mothers, the Savior would logically have to be male if both sexes are significantly involved in the salvation event.* The only alternative would be to have a female mother of the Savior and a female Savior. For an androgynous or hermaphroditic Savior would fail to share in the specific nature of our sexual human condition. Surely the female birth-enabler is no less an intrinsic part of the divine economy than the Messiah in the male line of David as promised (cf. *LG*, pp. 7–9, 222–23; *WL*, pp. 117–18, 148).

Augustine summed up that God "was not ashamed of the male nature, for He took it upon Himself; or of the female, for He was born of a woman." Hence we are "liberated by the agency of both sexes" (*The Christian Combat* 22, *FC* 21, pp. 338–39). God's "temporal plan ennobled each sex, both male and female. By possessing a male nature and being born of a woman He further showed by this plan that God has concern not only for the sex He represented but also for the one through which He took upon Himself our nature" (*On Faith and the Creed* 4.9, *FC* 27, p. 326).

To denude language of all gender reference is ideological bias reflecting an antihistorical mentality. It is also a denial of our very createdness. No woman or man I know wishes to be called an "it." If so, how can one be satisfied with "it" language addressed to God? The scandal of particularity remains. God meets us in specific times and places amid people with specific names and genders and of particular parents of a particular race and culture. To back away wholly from gender reference is to stand offended at the gospel of a man born of woman, and the Spirit who transcends the gender differences between *ruach* and *pneuma*.

Caveats on the Study of the Spirit

The Spirit's own guidance is requisite to the study of the Spirit, "not that we may speak what is worthy of Him, for this is impossible" but that we may not fail to speak altogether; hence it belongs to "grace itself to grant both to us to speak without deficiency and to you [the learner] to hear with discretion" (Cyril of Jerusalem, *Catech. Lect.* XVI.1, *NPNF* 2 VII, p. 115).

Incorporeality of the Spirit.   Whereas the incarnate Lord is revealed in the flesh, the Spirit tends more to be unpretentiously concealed, hidden in the silent depths of the heart and the quiet hedgings of history. The incarnate Lord was seen; the Word of Life "handled," "touched," personally addressed (1 John 1:1, 2). When the Spirit moves, the mover is silent and invisible. In the incarnation we meet God's own personal coming, the attested personal embodiment of God in time. In life in the Spirit we deal with God's coming in us in a silent, growing, inconspicuous embodiment of the body of Christ in time as enlivened by the unseen Spirit (Basil, *On the Spirit*, NPNF 2 VIII, pp. 33–39). What is most important in this inquiry is often least empirically quantifiable.

The Appeal to Mystery.   The Spirit is intrinsically a mystery, like the wind, whose movements are too complex and hidden to predict (John 3:8; Barth, *CD* IV/2, pp. 339 ff.). It is easy to know that the wind is moving, but difficult to tell precisely from where to where, even on a vast scale with the best electronic measuring devices, as every meteorologist knows. However evident may be the work of the Spirit to the heart, it is not visible to the eye or audible to the ear or tangible to the touch. The fact that we cannot see the wind does not mean that it does not exist. We hear it, feel it, observe its results. At times the unseen wind is capable of uprooting giant trees and swelling vast ocean waves—visible effects of a less visible operation. It was by a strong wind (*ruach*, Spirit) that the Red Sea was divided at the Exodus (Exod. 14:21).

The work of the Spirit everywhere leaves footprints, traces, signs, and symbols. These are best expressed not in flat empirical descriptions but in powerful metaphors as indirect and hidden as the work itself: breath, dove, fire, oil.

Some works of the Spirit apparently are intended to remain veiled, whereas other works of the Spirit have been openly revealed in history, recorded and recalled in scripture. Among matters known to faith but consensually regarded as finally remaining mysterious and unexplained are the eternal generation of the Son, the procession of the Spirit, the melding of grace and human freedom, and the triune God. "We say, three persons, not in order to express it, but in order not to be silent" (Augustine, *Trin.* V.9, *NPNF* 1 III, p. 92; *FC* 45, p. 187). Though it may seem "undignified to give any answer at all to the statements that are foolish," the mute alternative is more dangerous "lest through our silence error may prevail" (Gregory of Nyssa, *On the Holy Spirit*, NPNF 2 V, p. 315).

No rational thought exceeds the deeper rationality of the Trinity: "God, who creates, is Himself the highest of the objects of thought, both for those who think, and that which is thought of, the power of thinking and being thought of, in Whom every desire finds its bourne, beyond Whom it can no further go" (Gregory Nazianzen, *Orat.* XXI.1, *NPNF* 2 VII, pp. 269–70, translation amended).

The Limits of Scientific Inquiry into the Spirit.   To the skeptical gaze of naturalistic reductionism, little seems to evidence the silent footprints of the Spirit—hardly a trace, hardly an aroma. Tenderly God touches, breathes upon human history. What is revealed of the Spirit is more whispered than spoken (Job 26:13–14; John 3:8; John Chrysostom, *Hom. on John* 26, *FC* 33, pp. 250–59; Kuyper, *WHS*, pp. 3–7). "Truth is always a quarry hard to hunt, and therefore we must look everywhere for its tracks" (Basil, *On the Holy Spirit* I.1, *NPNF* 2 VIII, p. 2).

It should not be surprising therefore that the novice in religious studies may become soon impatient with this mystery, the sinner skeptical, and the hardened cynic repulsed by all talk of it. The Spirit withholds disclosure from the objectivizing gaze of the scientist who wishes chiefly to measure, graph, control, and submit reports. Hence "the gate is narrow and the way is hard, that leads to life, and those who find it are few" (Matt. 7:14, RSV).

This does not mean that research is impossible, but rather that it must conform attentively to its subject: "The Spirit is breath. The wind sings in the trees. I would like, then, to be an Aeolian harp and let the breath of God make the strings vibrate and sing. Let me stretch and tune the strings—that will be the austere task of research. And let the Spirit make them sing a clear and tuneful song of prayer and life!" (Congar, *IBHS* I, p. x).

The teacher of orthodoxy must be "not, like our modern wise men, yielding to the spirit of the age, nor defending our faith by indefinite and sophistical language, as if they had no fixity of faith" (Gregory Nazianzen, *Orat.* XVIII.16, *NPNF* 2 VII, p. 259).

Whether the Spirit Remains Inaccessible to Objective Investigation.   The ancient church teachers thought that there must be some hidden purpose in the vast *withholding* of specific empirical information concerning the work of the Spirit (Gregory Nazianzen, *Orat.* XXXI.5; Cyril of Jerusalem, *Catech. Lect.* XVI.23). They were convinced, with Paul, that all would ultimately be revealed (1 Cor. 13:12, 13). Under present conditions of finitude and moral blindness amid the history of sin, no one is able fully to grasp whence and whither this wind, God's Spirit, comes and goes. The providential purpose of the hiddenness of the Spirit is to awaken and engender that trust which walks by faith, not sight (2 Cor. 5:7).

Scripture must guide vulnerable, subjective experience at every step along this way, since each individual's personal experience is prone to self-deception and interest-laden distortions. No subject of Christian teaching is more prone to fanaticism and novelty and subjectivism than the Holy Spirit. Social, political, and cultural variables inevitably shape our imaginings of the active work of God in our hearts (Ezek. 13; R. Niebuhr, *NDM* I; H. R. Niebuhr, *RMWC*).

In no other precinct of theology are we more prone to make confident appeals to personal experience, yet these appeals do not guarantee that our feelings will be apostolically grounded. The work of the Spirit deserves especially careful attention precisely because it is so prone to subjective manipulation and ideological abuse. It remains as insufficiently treated as it is exceedingly important.

On Not Being Wise Above Scripture.   In studying the Spirit the consensual tradition has sought not to be wise above scripture, not to try to exceed the ways in which God's own Spirit has become self-attested through holy writ (1 Cor. 1:18–

31). "It is not our duty to indulge in conjecture" (Irenaeus, *Ag. Her.* II.28.6, *ECF,* p. 75; cf. *ANF* I, p. 401).

In receiving the Spirit we have "not received the spirit of the world but the Spirit who is from God, that we may understand what God has freely given us. This is what we speak, not in words taught us by human wisdom but in words taught by the Spirit, expressing spiritual truths in spiritual words" (1 Cor. 2:12, 13; John Chrysostom, *Hom. on 1 Cor.* VII, *NPNF* 1 XIII, pp. 33–43).

Faith "sees *something* of that which it does *not see entire*, nor is it permitted to *ignore* what it is *not allowed to comprehend*" (Hugh of St. Victor, *SCF,* p. 53, italics added). Christian teaching does well to speak modestly of the Spirit as the Spirit has become self-revealed in the history attested by scripture (Cyril of Jerusalem, *Catech. Lect.* XVI.2, XVII.1, *NPNF* 2 VII, pp. 115, 124).

The Cohesive Sequence from Saving Spirit Through Church to Consummation. The classic tradition has reasoned by means of an orderly progression of interconnected topics from pneumatology to soteriology through ecclesiology toward eschatology. Here is the essential movement: The reality of the church emerges out of the saving action of God in Christ through the Spirit; the church is the providential means and sphere through which persons are enabled to receive eternal life. The genesis of the church is the regenerating Spirit. The nurture of the church occurs by grace through Word and Sacraments. The present church shares in the communion of saints in time and eternity. This sequence draws all post-Ascension topics of theology into coherent order.

These topics are inseparably bound. "Where the Spirit of God is, there is the Church and every kind of grace" (Irenaeus, *Ag. Her.* III.24.1, *ECF,* p. 83). To elect to live without the grace offered in the church is like a neonate refusing nourishment from the mother's breast.

Whether Spirit Is Logically Prior to Church. In systematic study we proceed not chronologically but logically, economically, methodically. We are listening for consensual, ecumenical voices, not in order of their historical sequence, but by means of a reasonable unfolding and fitting organization of Christian teaching.

According to consensual reasoning, the inquiry into the Spirit logically precedes and conditions the inquiry into the church, and points toward the end time. The study of the Holy Spirit remains an indispensable, nonnegotiable locus of Christian teaching. At key turning points along the way of systematic theology we regularly check and reset our bearings, seeking a sense of right location and due categorization of topics, in this case Spirit and church within the whole scope of Christian teaching.

The order of the Nicene Creed and early baptismal catechetics sets the sequence of topics by moving from *Spiritum Sanctum* through *ecclesiam* toward the *vitam venturi seculi* ("life of the world to come," *COC* II, p. 59). As early as Novatian, Cyril of Jerusalem, and Hilary, the topics of salvation, grace, and the church were being located within the "third article" sequence of teachings on the work of the Spirit (Novatian, *Trinity* XXIX–XXXI, *ANF* IV, pp. 640–44; Cyril, *Catech. Lect.,* *NPNF* 2 VII, pp. 115 ff.; Hilary, *On the Trinity, FC* 25). We follow the steps of patristic and centrist Catholic and Protestant teaching, as seen in Augustine, Thomas Aquinas, Peter Lombard, and Calvin, in reserving the discussion of church and the human future to a position following the doctrines of the Spirit, repentance, faith, and justification.

This order resists the premise that individual faith chronologically precedes the church, that the church is merely a secondary product of individual faith, and that the *ekklēsia* is ancillary to the real work of the Holy Spirit in personal conversion. Church and sacraments are not merely supplementary, external supports of faith (*externum subsidium fidei*, Zwingli, *Comm. True and False Religion, WZ* 3, pp. 176 ff.; Brunner, *Dogmatics* III, p. 19) but intrinsic to faith (Calvin, *Inst.* 4.14).

Classic exegetes reasoned about salvation always from within the premises of *koinonia*, never without a community of memory and testimony. One believes only from within a community of belief, not in a vacuum. It is unthinkable that faith could be considered without the church. The Spirit is the life of the community— *anima ecclesiae*, uniting God with humanity and the faithful with each other. The newborn cannot lisp God as *Abba* without *ekklēsia* as mamma (Cyprian, *Letters* 39, *ANF* V, pp. 316–19; cf. Schleiermacher, *The Christian Faith* II.123, part 3, pp. 572–74, cf. 116.3, p. 536; 121.2, p. 563; 170.1, p. 738).

The Spirit's Presence as Datum of History.   It is a matter of historical record that the church has been created, that *ekklēsia* has been called out. The Spirit is active in history wherever sent by the Father as the Gift that the Son is making to the called out people. The Son explicitly promised that the Spirit will abide until the Son returns (John 14:15–24; 16:5–15).

The central motif of the work of the Spirit is attesting and bringing into lively historical embodiment the work of the Son (Luke 24:44–49; John 15:26; Acts 1:4–8). This does not imply a unilateral divine accomplishment by absolute fiat or simple decree, for the Spirit works patiently through human wills, engaged lives, concrete actions, and the foolishness of preaching (1 Cor. 1:18–31). The cross is a once-for-all event; the Spirit-enabled reception of the Word it speaks does not occur once for all in one time or place, but again and again in myriad times and places until the Lord's coming again (John 20:22; Acts 19:2; John Chrysostom, *Hom. on John* LXXXVI, *NPNF* 2 XIV, p. 325; Schmaus, *Dogma* 4, pp. 50–60). No human organization is more intriguing as a social process than the *ekklēsia* called forth by the Spirit of Jesus. It both embraces and transcends antiquity and modernity, East and West, Hebraic, Greek, Roman, European, African, Asian, and American civilizations.

No one has better expressed this than Macaulay writing on the continuity of the apostolic tradition: "No other institution is left standing which carries the mind back to the times when the smoke of sacrifice rose from the Pantheon, and when cameleopards and tigers bounded in the Flavian amphitheater." The most grandiose royal dynasties are but of yesterday compared with the apostolic tradition. Compared with the ecumenical councils, the great monarchies of France and Germany are of recent origin—monarchies now gone, while the ancient ecumenical definitions remain with full vitality. The church saw "the commencement of all the governments and of all the ecclesiastical establishments that now exist in the world; and we feel no assurance that she is not destined to see the end of them all. She was great and respected before the Saxon had set foot in Britain, before the Frank had passed the Rhine, when Grecian eloquence still flourished at Antioch, when idols were still worshipped in the temple of Mecca" (Macaulay, "Essay on L. von Ranke's History").

PART I

The Holy Spirit

The Spirit indwells in human history to attest God the Father and God the Son; to draw together the called-out people for celebration and proclamation; to reveal the truth to those yielded to the Spirit's promptings; to equip for service; to seal the promise of things to come; to elicit faith, hope, and love; and to redress the history of sin.

1 The Person of the Holy Spirit

THE DEITY AND PERSONAL
IDENTITY OF THE HOLY SPIRIT

The Deity of the Holy Spirit

To God the Spirit are ascribed attributes that belong to God alone: omniscience (Isa. 40:13; 1 Cor. 2:10–12), omnipresence (Ps. 139:7–10), omnipotence (Job 33:4; Ps. 104:30; Rom. 15:18, 19), eternality (Heb. 9:14; *LG*, pp. 199–201).

The Spirit Is God.   The Spirit is rightly called God (Acts 5:3, 4). The names of the Spirit make clear the deity of the Spirit (1 Cor. 2:11–14; 2 Cor. 3:17, 18; cf. Matt. 12:28, Luke 11:20). Scripture attests the Spirit as eternal (Heb. 9:14), life giving (Rom. 8:2), incomparably one (Eph. 4:4), of one essence with God, "the Lord, who is the Spirit" (2 Cor. 3:18; Basil, *On the Spirit* I.9–12, *NPNF* 2 VIII, pp. 15–18; Calvin, *Inst.* 1.13.14–15).

It is by the Spirit that demons were cast out by the Son (Matt. 12:28), sinners entered the kingdom of God (John 3:5), the Son was raised from the dead (Rom. 8:11). The Spirit who raises from the dead and has life within himself must be God.

God is called "the Spirit" because incomparably spiritual; "Holy Spirit" because incomparably holy (Rom. 1:4); "the Spirit of God" (Gen. 1:2; Matt. 3:16) because he is truly God; and "the Spirit of Christ" (Rom. 8:9; 1 Pet. 1:11) because he is sent by the Son to execute the Son's mission to the world (Ursinus, *Comm. Heid. Catech.*, p. 271). These references confirm the deity of the Spirit, who is nothing less than "the Spirit of the Lord" (Luke 4:18; Acts 5:9), "his Spirit" (Rom. 8:11), "the Spirit of the living God" (2 Cor. 3:3), "Spirit of our God" (1 Cor. 6:11). The Spirit is ascribed as author of revelation, bestower of truth (John 14:17), "the Spirit of wisdom and understanding, the Spirit of counsel and of power, the Spirit of knowledge and of the fear of the Lord" (Isa. 11:2; cf. Exod. 28:3; Eph. 1:17), who gives grace and enables supplication (Zech. 12:10; Heb. 10:29).

Gregory brilliantly summarized that God's is the only Spirit who

> always existed, and exists, and always will exist,
> who neither had a beginning, nor will have an end . . .
> ever being partaken, but not partaking;
> perfecting, not being perfected;
> sanctifying, not being sanctified;
> deifying, not being deified . . .
> Life and Lifegiver;
> Light and Lightgiver;
> absolute Good, and Spring of Goodness . . .

15

> by Whom the Father is known and the Son is glorified. . . . Why make
> a long discourse of it? All that the Father has the Son has also,
> except the being Unbegotten; and all that the Son has the Spirit
> has also, except the Generation.
>
> (Gregory Nazianzen, *Orat.* XLI.9, *NPNF* 2 VII, p. 382, amended)

The Worship of God the Spirit.   The Spirit is called Lord (1 Cor. 12:4–6) because
he is God, entitled to the same worship rightly offered up to the Father and the
Son (Basil, *On the Spirit* VIII.44–XXI.52, *NPNF* 2 VIII, pp. 27–34). The Spirit's
name is placed on equal terms with the Lord in the apostolic benediction (2 Cor.
13:14). The Spirit's equality with Father and Son is clear from the great commission (Matt. 28:19), an equality that does not erase distinguishability (Athanasius,
LCHS IV.3–4; cf. Gregory of Nyssa, *On the Holy Spirit*, *NPNF* 2 IV, p. 325). "The
Spirit is jointly worshipped in God, when God is worshipped in the Spirit"
(Ambrose, *Of the Holy Spirit* III.X.82, *NPNF* 2 X, p. 147). By diminishing the Spirit
one does not exalt Father or Son: "If ever there was a time when the Son was not,
then there was a time when the Spirit was not. If the One was from the beginning,
then the Three were so too. If you throw down the One, I am bold to assert that
you do not set up the other Two" (Gregory Nazianzen, *Orat.* XXXI.4, *On the Holy
Spirit*, *NPNF* 2 VII, p. 319).

The Holy Spirit is supplicated as "perfecting all other things, but Himself lacking in nothing; living not as needing restoration, but as Supplier of life; not growing by additions, but straightway full, the self-established, omnipresent, source of
sanctification" (Basil, *On the Holy Spirit*, I.9, *NPNF* 2 VIII, p. 15, amended). Daily
prayer has begun for centuries in the Orthodox tradition with this prayer: "O
Heavenly King, the Comforter, the Spirit of Truth, who art everywhere and fillest
all things, Treasury of blessings and Giver of Life, Come and abide in us, and
cleanse us from every impurity, and save our souls, O Good One."

The Many Names of the One Spirit.   Though called by many names, the Spirit is
one (Tho. Aq., *ST* I–I, Q36, I, pp. 182–85): Only the Spirit of life could be the
Spirit of holiness. Only the Holy Spirit could be the one Spirit of the Church.
Only the Spirit of love could be at once the sacramental and charismatic Spirit.
Though any systematic discussion of the Holy Spirit must be divided into sequential parts, God the Spirit remains undivided, and "we preach faith undivided towards Him" (Cyril of Jerusalem, *Catech. Lect.* XVII.2, *NPNF* 2 VII, p. 124).

The work of the one Spirit is indicated by varied names ascribed in scripture.
As compassionate Lord, the Spirit is Comforter (John 14:16), as reclaimer, the
Spirit of adoption (Rom. 8:15), as regenerator, the Spirit of Life (Rom. 8:2), as
life giver, the Spirit who awakens faith (2 Cor. 4:13), as merciful One, the Spirit
of Grace (Heb. 10:29), as teacher, the Spirit of Truth (John 14:17), as counselor,
the Spirit of Wisdom (Eph. 1:17), as sanctifier, the Spirit of holiness (Rom. 1:14;
Cyril of Jerusalem, *Catech. Lect.* XV.5, *NPNF* 2 VII, p. 125; Calvin, *Inst.* 3.1.3).

Jesus himself chose the expression "Holy Breath" to designate the comforter to
follow him (John 20:22; M. Sheeben, *The Mysteries of Christianity*, pp. 97 f.). "Christ
breathed the Spirit in a corporeal fashion and thus showed that as from the
mouth of a man comes the corporeal breath, so from the divine substance in a
way that befits it comes the breath that proceeds from it" (Cyril of Alexandria,

Comm. on John 14.16, tractate IX, MPG 74.258; cf. Letters 55.40–43, FC 77, pp. 34–36). "The Greeks have compared the Spirit to the breathing forth of an outer breath, the Latins to the breathing forth of an inner love" (Bonaventure, Comm., Book I of Lombard's Sentences, XI, Q1; Heron, HS, p. 87).

Faith's privilege is not merely to believe that the Spirit is the third person of the Trinity but to "take him for Christ's Agent or Advocate with our souls, and for our Guide, Sanctifier, and Comforter" (Baxter, Christian Directory I.3.3). Holy Spirit is "the third name of divinity, the proclaimer of the one monarchy, and at the same time the interpreter of the economy . . . the 'leader into all truth'" (Tertullian, Ag. Praxeas 30, ECF, p. 131). The Holy Spirit is "the Inspirer of the Faith, the Teacher of Knowledge, the Fount of Love, the Seal of Chastity, and the Cause of all Power" (Leo, Sermons LXXV, NPNF 2 XII, p. 191).

The Oneness of God the Spirit.   The Spirit is none other than the One God who has met Israel as Yahweh, the God of Israel, God of Hosts, Spirit of Yahweh (Num. 11:29; Judg. 3:10; Ps. 139:7; Isa. 61:1). "For the Holy Spirit is not subject to any foreign power or law, but is the Arbiter of His own freedom, dividing all things according to the decision of His own will to each" (Ambrose, Of the Holy Spirit, prologue.18, NPNF 2 X, p. 96). It is not "allowable to suppose that there are many Holy Spirits, Who come into being by as it were a daily production" (Ambrose, Of the Holy Spirit II.VI.52, NPNF 2 X, p. 121; cf. Athanasius, LCHS III.2–4).

Since the Spirit manifests the love of the Father for the Son, and of the Son for the Father, the Spirit is their common gift. The three proper names for the third person of the Trinity were Holy Spirit, Love, and Gift (Peter Lombard, Sent. I.xvii.6; Tho. Aq., ST I–I, Q36–38, I, pp. 189–93). "For he is called properly what they are called in common, because the Father is a spirit and the Son is a spirit, and the Father is holy and the Son is holy. In order that the communion between them might be signified by a name which is appropriate to both, the Holy Spirit is called the gift of both" (Augustine, Trin. V.11, FC 45, p. 190).

The Multicultural Self-offering of the One Spirit.   The ascription of God as Spirit is not the exclusive possession of Christians and Jews. Through his omnipresence God the Spirit moves among all peoples, all cultures, all times and places.

God the Spirit is received through the means of grace by which God has chosen to meet all humanity: not only conscience and moral reasoning, prayer, prophecy, sacrifice, and the protosacramental life, but also covenant history, recalled through the proclaimed and written Word and enacted in the Sacraments.

New life in the Spirit is offered quintessentially through church and sacraments, yet intended for all. As the Word is made flesh in the Son, so the Spirit is being embodied in the church. As God tabernacled with humanity in the flesh through the Son, so does God after his earthly ministry dwell with humanity through the Spirit. The disciples are regarded as "a holy temple in the Lord," the Spirit dwelling within them: "And in him you too are being built together to become a dwelling in which God lives by his Spirit" (Eph. 2:22).

The Omnipresence of the One Spirit.   The premise of the omnipresence of God the Spirit is celebrated in Psalm 139: "Where can I go from your Spirit? Where can I flee from your presence? If I go up to the heavens, you are there; if I make my bed in the depths, you are there" (Ps. 139:7, 8). There is no place where the

Spirit is not. There is no time when the Spirit was not. "It is the nature of the Holy Spirit to be both over all and in all," both transcendent and working immanently in human hearts (Ambrose, *Of the Holy Spirit* III.XIX.150, *NPNF* 2 X, p. 156). This is counterpantheistic because in all the concreteness of personal engagement, God the Spirit remains God.

The implication is not that the omnipresent One in "coming" to one place "leaves" another. God the Spirit can be said to "descend," "indwell," and "fill" without changing place or emptying from some other place. Such statements are grounded in the premises of omnipresence and eternality—attributes ascribed properly only to God.

In dwelling on earth the Spirit does not cease to remain eternally with the Father and the Son (Ambrose, *Of the Holy Spirit* I.VII.81, 82, *NPNF* 2 X, p. 104). "The Spirit is not, then, sent as it were from a place, nor does He proceed as from a place." We are left with the impression that the Spirit is coming down to us, while in truth our minds by grace are being enabled to ascend to the Spirit (Ambrose, *Of the Holy Spirit* I.XI.119–21, *NPNF* 2 X, p. 109). "Spirit cannot be cabined or confined," since "omnipresent in space and time, and under all conditions present in its fulness" (Hilary, *Trin.* II.31, *NPNF* 2 IX, p. 60; cf. Athanasius, *LCHS* I.26).

God's Spirit and the Human Spirit. "God *is* Spirit, man *has* spirit" (Brunner, *Dogm.* II, p. 63). "Man has spirit, as one who is possessed by" Spirit (Barth, *CD* III/2, 46.2, p. 354). God the Spirit breathes into life the souls of human persons (Tertullian, *Apology* 48, *APT*, p. 100). Since God is addressed as Thou, not it, those who image or mirror God are rightly addressed as you, not it (M. Buber, *I and Thou;* Brunner, *The Divine Human Encounter*).

The *ruach* of God is not separable from God, even as your own spirit is not separable from you. Nothing less than God is present when God's Spirit is present. When God chooses to become particularly present, reaching out to humanity, God does not cease being holy (2 Chron. 5–7; John 1). God's own Spirit is shared with other spirits without ceasing to be entire, as a "sunbeam whose kindly light falls on him who enjoys it as though it showed for him alone, yet illumines land and sea and mingles with the air" (Basil, *On the Holy Spirit* I.9, *NPNF* 2 VIII, p. 15).

It was the Hebrew word for breath (*ruach*) that became translated into Latin as *anima* and Greek as *psuche* (animated life or animal soul). All who are alive breathe. Breath is an indicator of aliveness. *Nephesh* (soul, life, blood soul) names the power of life, pointing also to the root metaphor of breathing, especially in older strands of the Old Testament. Later the language shifted toward *ruach* as center of personal life and selfhood. "Into your hands I commit my spirit" (Ps. 31:5), my *ruach,* my distinctively personal life of thinking, feeling, awareness, and activity.

If in scripture "every thing which has not a solid body is in a general way called spirit," it is not surprising to hear angelic and demonic powers referred to as spirit, and to the human person as spirit, to soul as spirit, and even to virtue as spirit. The Holy Spirit differs from all these forms of created spirit, being God who "beholds the beginning of the world, and knows the end" (Cyril of Jerusalem, *Catech. Lect.* XVI. 15, *NPNF* 2 VII, p. 119).

The Personal Identity of the Holy Spirit

The Spirit is addressed as a person, less "it" than "Thou." Not impersonal but personal pronouns are regularly used to refer to the Spirit—"I will send him to you" (John 16:7).

This personalization was taken for granted when the council at Jerusalem declared, "It seemed good to the Holy Ghost and to us" (Acts 15:28) that a particular action was to be taken, as if to say that Peter and James and John and others were there, and the Holy Spirit was also there in the conversation, personally sharing with them, dwelling with them as incomparable partner in their effort (Calvin, *Comm.* XIX, pp. 77–80; cf. Luther, *Answer to Emser, LW* 39, pp. 175–78, 197–99).

The properties of a person are those that are continually attributed to that person. The properties continually attributed by scripture to the Holy Spirit are teaching, comforting, guiding, giving, calling, and sending. "Thus it is said that [the Holy Spirit] teaches, comforts and guides us in all truth, that he distributes gifts as he will; that he calls and sends apostles" (Ursinus, *Comm. Heid. Catech.,* p. 272).

The Spirit Acts Personally.   God the Spirit is attested as acting as persons act. The apostolic testimony applied intensely personal analogies: guiding (Rom. 8:14), convicting (John 16:8), interceding (Rom. 8:26), calling (Acts 13:2), commissioning (Acts 20:28).

Like a person, the Spirit can be resisted (Acts 7:51), avoided, or responsively answered (Acts 10:19–21). Only a person can be vexed (Isa. 63:10) or grieve (Eph. 4:30). Only one with intelligence and the capacity for communication can speak from heart to heart. These are qualities of personhood. Only a person can teach, talk, reveal his will to other persons, become angry (Isa. 63:10). As persons speak and communicate, so does the Holy Spirit speak in scripture to the faithful (Mark 13:11; Acts 8:29; 21:11; 1 Tim. 4:1; Rev. 2:7) to disclose his will and listen responsively to creatures.

Only a person can be lied to—no one can lie to a stone or vegetable. Ananias was condemned not for lying to Peter but for lying to the Holy Spirit. Those who lie to the Holy Spirit, lie to God (Acts 5:3–9; Calvin, *Inst.* XVIII, pp. 197–99).

The Spirit is found actively directing the mission of the apostolate, setting aside Paul and Barnabas for their specific work (Acts 13:2), selecting overseers for the flock (Acts 20:28; Ambrose, *Of the Holy Spirit* II.XIII.145, *NPNF* 2 X, p. 133), bearing witness (Acts 5:32; Rom. 8:16), distributing gifts freely as he chooses (1 Cor. 12:11).

These functions imply intelligence, will, feeling, purpose—all characteristics of personhood, which God possesses in incomparable measure (2 Cor. 12:8, 11). The Spirit searches our hearts (1 Cor. 2:10–11), teaching human persons individually and within community (Rom. 8:12–27).

If the Holy Spirit is not God but an activity of God, then "He will be effected, but will not effect, and will cease to exist as soon as He has been effected, for this is the nature of an activity. How is it then that He acts and says such and such things, and defines, and is grieved, and is angered, and has all the qualities which belong clearly to one that moves" freely (Gregory Nazianzen, *Orat.* XXXI.6, *On the Holy Spirit, NPNF* 2 VII, p. 319).

If "the Israelites could not look steadily at the face [*prosōpon*] of Moses because of its glory, fading though it was, will not the ministry of the Spirit be even more glorious?" (2 Cor. 3:7, 8). If he speaks, forbids, appoints, witnesses, is lied to, and resisted, the Spirit must be personal and free, for only a person can do these things. So the Spirit is not merely a metaphor of Jesus himself, but as much a living person (*prosōpon*, personal face) as Jesus himself (Nicetas of Remesiana, *Power of the Holy Spirit*, FC 7, pp. 28 ff.). The Spirit in scripture is God himself. The Christian community confesses its belief not merely about but *in* God the Spirit. "Belief in" is directed to a person; "belief about" is directed to things (Gregory Nazianzen, *Orat.* XXXI.6, *On the Holy Spirit*, NPNF 2 VII, p. 319).

The Interpersonal Mystery.   God works person to person, within human wills and consciousness, in the heart, through language. God the Spirit relates interpersonally to apostles on an intimate basis, while maintaining His own distinctive pretemporal relation to God the Father and God the Son in the eternal mystery of the communion of the triune God (Cyril, *Catech. Lect.*, NPNF 2 VII, pp. 115 ff.).

God must be a speaking person, John of Damascus argued, unless we posit the droll premise that God is less a person than we ourselves. For it is through our own personal spirit that we breathe out words. God the Spirit is experienced as a person is experienced, as "endowed with free volition, and energy . . . as the companion of the Word and the revealer of His energy . . . proceeding from the Father and resting in the Word, and shewing forth the word . . . endowed with life, free volition, independent movement, energy, ever willing that which is good . . . having no beginning and no end. For never was the Father at any time lacking in the Word, nor the Word in the Spirit" (John of Damascus, *OF* I.7, *NPNF* 2 IX, p. 5). The Spirit is God's own quiet coming to execute the Father's plan, to attest the Son's saving work, to enlighten, counsel, strengthen, and enable life until the Son's return.

The Depersonalization of the Spirit.   Although the work of the Spirit may be spoken of in the neuter tense, God the Spirit is not properly addressed as "it" or "object" or "impersonal being" or by any expression that suggests that God the Spirit has no proper name as a person. "Holy Spirit" is that proper name, which by analogy to human proper names is best spoken of either as he or she. To persistently think of God the Spirit as "it" (not as Thou) is to apply a mistaken analogy (Basil, *On the Holy Spirit;* Buber, *I and Thou;* Brunner, *Dogm.* III). *The Faith of Damasus* ecumenically defined that "the proper name for the Father is Father, and the proper name for the Son is Son, and the proper name for the Holy Spirit is Holy Spirit" (*SCD* 15, p. 11).

The depersonalization of God the Spirit has occurred in the period of philosophical idealism. Hegel reduced the Spirit to a logic of history. Tillich reduced the Spirit to an existential category of being itself. Process theology reduced the Spirit to creative energy. Much liberation theology reduced the Spirit to political praxis. Each reduction is tempted by unconstrained application of a mistaken impersonal analogy to the person of the Spirit.

Since the word *person* has been "sanctioned by the usage of more than 1,500 years, and there is no other word which would really be better, more generally understandable and less exposed to misconception," Christian teaching continues to speak of God the Spirit as person (Rahner, *TI* IV, pp. 101–2). Without personal language, God the Spirit soon becomes reduced to a symbolic generalized "dimension of depth" (Tillich, *ST* I, p. 113). Nor does it stand as an improvement to replace the term *person* with an alternative expression like "mode of being" (Barth, *CD* I/1, p. 407).

There can be no objection to speaking of the Spirit in objective terms as divine Subject, just as we speak of other persons not always by personal naming but as "the doctor" or "the trumpet player," provided that when one does so one remembers that the One addressed in objective terms as Other remains free as persons are free, and more free than finite persons are free, hence finally is never reducible to an "it." Scriptural exegetes are therefore ill advised to consistently address the Spirit as "it" with the avowed intent of pointing to the Spirit's self-effacing presence (Heron, *HS*, p. 176), for it is precisely the free personal God who is becoming self-effacing, and the cause is not well served by calling the Spirit "it." Though some have argued that the Cappadocians went awry in describing the Spirit in personal ways parallel to the Son (Lampe, *God as Spirit*), irenic theology sees this tendency as merely following the lead of scripture texts that themselves insist upon doing so.

Whether the Holy Spirit Is Reducible to the General Attribute of Spirituality. Although spirituality is an attribute of God, for "God is spirit," it is misleading to assume that the Holy Spirit can be reduced to a characteristic of God alongside other divine attributes like eternity and omniscience. That would be to deny to the Spirit that personhood which scripture attests. Rather the Spirit is a distinctive divine person who possesses these characteristics and qualities ascribed as divine attributes. The Holy Spirit is not merely a quality or attribute or emanation of God, but rather a distinct person within the Godhead (Basil, *On the Spirit* I.21–23, *NPNF* 2 VII, pp. 33–35).

Baptism is administered in the name of the Holy Spirit, as well as Father and Son. One cannot baptize in the name of an abstract quality, or an attribute, but only in the name of a living, authorizing person. To baptize in the name of the Father and Son and the attribute of spirituality would be a curious and inconsistent use of language. So the Spirit is a divine person and not merely spirituality as a divine attribute (Ambrose, *Of the Holy Spirit* I.13 ff., *NPNF* 2 X, pp. 110 ff.). "There are three in God to whom we can say 'You'" (Lonergan, Fortman, *AHS*, p. 162).

On Sinning Against the Spirit

One may sin against the Spirit in two ways, by "grieving the Spirit," and by "blaspheming the Spirit," a distinction that must neither be overstated nor neglected.

Grieving the Spirit. There is not one single sin against the Spirit, but many. The Spirit may be ignored or refused, having been once accepted, as the Galatians had turned from grace back to law (Gal. 3:2, 3). The Spirit may be resisted (Acts 7:51). The convicting work of the Spirit may be quenched, choked, and virtually extinguished by our resistances (1 Thess. 5:19). A work may be begun in the Spirit that is later threatened with apostasy or defection (1 Tim. 1:19).

When the covenant people rebel against Yahweh through their neglect, egoism, and faithlessness, rejecting the offer of God's tender mercies, they grieve the Holy Spirit (Isa. 63:10). Paul implored his hearers to "not grieve the Holy Spirit" (Eph. 4:30). One may grieve the Spirit without blaspheming the Spirit.

Blaspheming the Holy Spirit. In Levitical law, blasphemy implied an explicit abuse and rejection of the divine name, hence of the divine reality. Jesus amazed his hearers when he said, "Every sin and blasphemy will be forgiven men, but the blasphemy against the Spirit will not be forgiven. Anyone who speaks a word against the *Son* of Man *will* be forgiven, but anyone who speaks against the Holy *Spirit* will *not* be forgiven, either in this age or in the age to come" (Matt. 12:31, 32, italics added; cf. Mark 3:27, 28; Luke 10:12; Nicetas of Remesiana, *The Power of the Holy Spirit, FC* 7, p. 37). This was said in response to "teachers of the law who came down from Jerusalem" to trap him, who predictably concluded, "He is possessed by Beelzebub!" (Mark 3:22; cf. Matt. 12:24).

The blasphemy referred to is that of directly ascribing to the power of evil the coming of God into history through the Son and the Spirit (Mark 3:28, 29, and parallels). This sin instantly places the self beyond the range of forgiveness, because every step toward repentance and faith is enabled by the Holy Spirit (Gregory of Nyssa, *On the Holy Spirit, NPNF* 2 IV, pp. 321–34). To blaspheme the Holy Spirit is gravely to misunderstand oneself in God's presence (Athanasius, *Ag. Arians, NPNF* 2 IV, pp. 335, 336).

Unpardonable? Paul's life offers ample evidence that blasphemy as such is forgivable (1 Tim. 1:13). Blasphemy against the Spirit is not unforgivable in the sense that God is powerless or unwilling to forgive, but in the sense that the sinner is militantly unwilling to receive forgiveness. The sin is not unpardonable because the atoning work of the Son is not sufficient for that sin, but because that sufficient work is willfully demeaned, blocked, and detested by those for whom it would otherwise be entirely sufficient (Heb. 6:4–6). This sin is said to be unforgivable because as long as we are so deluded that we cannot repent, we cannot be forgiven, having closed off the possibility of being forgiven by closing ourselves to the Spirit. Those guilty of such sin are in the nature of the case unable to receive forgiveness (Cyprian, *Letters, FC* 51, pp. 46–49, 252, 287–91; Tho. Aq., *ST* II–II, Q14, III, pp. 1233–37).

For those who obstinately leave behind the help of the Spirit, there is nothing more left. There is no further help to be given beyond the help God offers for salvation. It is possible for persons to pass beyond that limit and become so hardened to God's saving action that no further recourse is to be expected. Those who absolutely turn from the work of the Spirit are left by their own choice "without hope and without God in the world" (Eph. 2:12). One who persists in the Macedonian heresy (that the Spirit is not God) will be found "unpardonable because it cuts him off from Him by Whom he could confess: nor will he ever attain to healing pardon who has no Advocate" (Leo, *Sermons* LXXV, *NPNF* 2 XII, p. 191, italics added).

Those who persist in denying the Spirit should not wonder that the Christian life remains to them an enigma (Winslow, *The Work of the Holy Spirit*, pp. 27–30). For to deny the Spirit is to deny God who searches the heart and tries the reins of the human spirit (Cyprian, *Letters, FC* 51, pp. 47–49; Calvin, *Inst.* 1.13.14–15;

3.3.21–24; 4.20). Meanwhile God is never defeated by our blasphemies, only we (Calvin, *Inst.* 3.3.21–24).

HOLY SPIRIT IN HOLY TRIAD

The living God offers life. *The Word of life* takes responsibility for humanity. *Life in the Spirit* brings to consummation the embodied speech of the Word.

God the Father engenders the plan of salvation, offering to send the Son by the power of the Spirit. God the Son embodies and executes the atoning, redemptive plan to save humanity. God the Spirit applies the benefits of redemption under conditions of continuing historical development to empower the actual salvation of the faithful.

Triune Premise: From the Father, Through the Son, by the Spirit

The power to bring into being proceeds from the Father. The power to mediate bodily the saving act belongs to the Son. The power to consummate and realize God's saving work belongs to the Spirit. This is not a tritheism that posits three Gods, for in all these powers the faithful speak strictly of the one and only almighty God. "With the Holy Ghost through One Son, we preach one God" (Cyril of Jerusalem, *Catech. Lect.* XVI.4, *NPNF* 2 VII, p. 116). Abraham "saw Three and worshipped One" (Ambrose, *Of the Holy Spirit* II.intro.4, *NPNF* 2 X, p. 115).

It is fitting to view the administration of the Spirit within a firmly received triune premise. God the Father, Son, and Spirit is inseparably one *ousia* (essence). Within the one God are distinguishable three equal coeternal *hupostases* (persons, *LG*, pp. 181–225; *WL*, 77–82).

Inseparable, Distinguishable, Coeternal.   Only within the triune premise can numerous vexations, perplexities, and errors be resolved. Whatever is said of God is rightly said of Son and Spirit. "Anyone who has seen me has seen the Father" who sends "the Spirit of truth" (John 14:9, 16). Christ's ministry of reconciliation in the atonement (2 Cor. 5:18) and the work of the Spirit in the administration of redemption (2 Cor. 3:6–11) are a single ministry through distinguishable personal agents of the Godhead (Nicetas of Remesiana, *Power of the Holy Spirit*, FC 7, pp. 23 ff.; Calvin, *Inst.* 1.9.3; cf. E. J. Fortman, *The Triune God;* R. W. Jenson, *The Triune Identity*).

"The Spirit works, the Son fulfills his ministry, and the Father approves"; thus humanity is "brought to full salvation" wherein "the whole grace of the Spirit" is offered to "make us like him" so to "perfect in us the Father's will" (Irenaeus, *Ag. Her.* IV.20.6; V.8.1, *ECF,* p. 84). "Through the Spirit we rise to the Son; through the Son we rise to the Father" (Irenaeus, *Ag. Her.* V.36.2, *ECF,* p. 85; cf. Origen, *De Principii* I.3.5, *ANF* IV, p. 253).

The Spirit enables that access to the Father which is merited by the Son: "For through him we both have access to the Father by one Spirit" (Eph. 2:18). As there is no second Father or second Son, so there is no second Spirit equal to him who is the unsearchable "sanctifying principle of all things," who "illuminates the souls

of the just" (Cyril of Jerusalem, *Catech. Lect.* XVI.1, *NPNF* 2 VII, p. 115). Merely
to name Christ is already to imply "God the Father by Whom the Son was anointed, and the Son Himself Who was anointed, and the Holy Spirit with Whom He
was anointed" (Ambrose, *Of the Holy Spirit* I.III.44, *NPNF* 2 X, p. 99).

Triunity is not an invention of postapostolic teaching, but embedded so deeply
in apostolic testimony as to be inseparable from it: "How much more, then will
the blood of *Christ* [the Son], who through the eternal *Spirit* offered himself unblemished to God [the Father], cleanse our consciences from acts that lead to
death, so that we may serve *the living God*" (Heb. 9:14, italics added). God the
Spirit proceeds from (*ek*) the Father through (*dia, per*) the Son, as coessential (*hom-
oousios*), coeternal, and coequal with God the Father and God the Son (Tertullian,
Ag. Praxeas IV, *ANF* III, pp. 598–99; Gregory Nazianzen, *Orat.* XXXI.4; Basil, *On
the Holy Spirit* I.3; X; XI; *Hom.* XV.3).

Any exegetical attempt can be examined with respect to the adequacy or inepti-
tude of its Trinitarian understandings. One God meets us as Father, incarnate Son,
and Spirit fulfilling the mission of the Son. The Fourth Lateran Council summarized
for the Western church generations of exegetical refinement of the triune relation:
"the Father from no one, the Son from the Father alone, and the Holy Spirit equally
from both; and without beginning, always, and without end; the Father generat-
ing, the Son being born, the Holy Spirit proceeding; consubstantial, co-equal, co-
omnipotent and co-eternal; one origin of all things" (Fourth Lateran Council, 1,
TGS, pp. 122–23; cf. Rufinus, *Comm. on Apostles' Creed* 35, *NPNF* 2 III, p. 557). By
the Spirit the work of the triune God is being consummated, perfected, bonded in
love (Cyril of Alexandria, *Thesaurus* 34; *MPG* 75.612; Bermejo, *SL,* pp. 102–23). By
the Spirit's illumination and guidance the faithful grow from grace to grace.

The Spirit Proceeding.   The Advocate Spirit is "uncreated, proceeding from the
Father, and receiving from the Son" (Creed of Epiphanius, Second Formula, *COC*
II, pp. 37, 38). "Good, then, is the Spirit, but good, not as though acquiring but
as imparting goodness," not receiving goodness from creatures but offering goodness to creatures, for the Spirit is not sanctified by creatures but creatures by the
Spirit. The absolute holiness of the Spirit cannot be attained by us directly, because of the divine nature, but can be received by participative grace because the
divine goodness chooses to become sharable (Ambrose, *Of the Spirit* I.V.72–74,
NPNF 2 X, pp. 102–3).

The relation of Father and Spirit is described not as generation, as in the case
of the Son, but as a sending-forth (*pempō,* John 14:26) and a procession (*ekporeu-
omai,* John 15:26). Basil drew from Paul the summary formula: "From the Father
through the Son" (*Ag. Eunomians* III.6).

Athanasius provided the decisive analogy: "As a river is generated from its
source, and is not separated from it, although there are two forms and two
names. . . . As the source is not the river, nor the river the source, but each is one
and the same water." "For like as the well is not a river, nor the river a well, but
both are one and the same water which is conveyed in a channel from the well
to the river," so the Father's deity proceeds into the Spirit without division
(Athanasius, *Ekthesis* 2, *ECF,* p. 298; cf. *NPNF* 2 IV, p. 84; *LCHS* I.19).

Dual Procession in the West.   The procession of the Holy Spirit from the Father
and the Son was defined in the West at the Third Synod of Toledo (A.D. 589),

adding "proceeding from the Father *and the Son*" (*Filioque*) to the Nicene Creed, an addition never accepted by the East. The Western tradition thus confessed a dual procession, wherein the "Spirit proceeds eternally from the Father and the Son, yet not as from two origins, but as from one origin, not by two breathings but by a single breathing" (Council of Lyons II, *SCD* 460, p. 182). This became the chief theological cause of the major division in the history of the church of East and West. The *Filioque* was generally chanted in masses of the Frankish empire. Frankish monks in late ninth-century Jerusalem aroused strong opposition from those who confessed the original Nicene Creed (without the *Filioque*), a controversy that has continued for over a millennium.

Protestant formularies generally reflect the Western tradition, as do the Anglican articles: "The Holy Ghost, proceeding from the Father and the Son, is of one substance, majesty, and glory, with the Father and the Son, very and eternal God" (Thirty-nine Articles, V, *CC*, p. 267). The Eastern tradition considered the *Filioque* as tending toward a Sabellian subordination and depersonalization of the Spirit (Lossky, *MTEC*). These two positions appear to be gradually converging in current ecumenical dialogue.

The Triune Ground and Work of Salvation.   The Father is moved with love toward fallen humanity to send the Son. The Son assumed human nature, suffered, died, and was resurrected to redeem humanity. The Holy Spirit provides the means by which recipients of this good news can appropriate and apply it.

The rudimentary underpinning of this teaching is arguably embedded in the Petrine salutation to God's scattered elect, "who have been chosen according to the foreknowledge of God the Father, through the sanctifying work of the Spirit, for obedience to Jesus Christ and sprinkling by his blood" (1 Pet. 1:2).

The sequence of salvation proceeds *from* the benevolence of God the Father toward humanity, *through* the atoning death of the Son in offering redemption, *toward* the grace of the Spirit in applying and enabling redemption. The whole triune God works toward salvation: "The Father loves those who have fallen, the Son redeems those who have been loved, and the Holy Ghost calls and teaches those who have been redeemed" (Quenstedt, *TDP* 1; Schmid, *DT*, p. 269).

The same triune reasoning was expressed by the Scholastics in terms of the causes of salvation—the original cause of salvation as the love of God the Father, the meritorious cause of justification as the sacrifice of the Son, the efficient cause of actually received salvation as the power of the Spirit eliciting by grace the response of the free will of the redeemed sinner (Tho. Aq., *ST* II–I, Q112, II, pp. 1140–43; Tillett, *PS*, pp. 129, 130).

The Economy of Triune Teaching.   The work of the Holy Spirit is best beheld through a history that can be narrated by remembered events. The outworking of revelation as expressed in these events occurs in clusters or periods or eras of special outworkings of grace. The danger of exaggerated dispensationalisms and modalisms lies in overstating discontinuities between these periods, or hyperperiodizing the work of grace. The one God must not be separated into three or more discontinuous parts of history (modalism, Sabellianism). The triune God works variously in various historical outworkings.

Gregory Nazianzen counseled that healthy triune reasoning must tend neither toward "Sabellianising as to the One, nor Arianising as to the Three, either by contracting and so atheistically annihilating the Godhead, or by tearing It asunder by distinctions of unequal greatness or nature" (*Orat.* XVIII.16, *NPNF* 2 VII, p. 260).

In this way it is possible without offense to the unity of God to ascribe creation primarily but not exclusively to the Father (Gen. 1–3), justification primarily but not exclusively to the Son (John 3:17; Gal. 4:4, 5), and sanctification primarily but not exclusively to the Spirit (2 Thess. 2:13; Titus 3:3). "Those operations in which eternal determination and origination are prominent are ascribed to the Father, those in which mediation and agency appear are referred to the Son, and those of efficiency, quickening and perfecting are attributed to the Spirit" (Hall, *DT* VIII, p. 7; cf. Owen, *Works* 3, pp. 9–17).

The time *before* the incarnation features the work of the one God chiefly but not exclusively as the creative and providential work of the *Father*. The time *between* incarnation and ascension focuses intensely but not restrictively upon the redemptive work of the one God through the *Son*. The present period of history following the ascension focuses primarily but not exclusively upon the consummating, finishing work of the one God through the *Spirit*. Such generalizations, however true, must be hedged carefully against modalistic excess, where the unity of God becomes misplaced in the earnest effort to make distinctions. The primary premise of any such reflection is that the *one* God is present in all triune acts and outworkings (Athanasius, *LCHS* IV.5).

Spirit as Personal Relation.   In the Western tradition, the persons of the Trinity are defined by their relations to each other. If each person is "a subsisting *relation*," the Trinity is relational by definition (Tho. Aq., *ST* I, Q29.4, italics added). The Spirit is especially beheld in the relation of love between Father and Son, the "bond of love" (*vinculum caritatis*) between Father and Son (Augustine, *Trin.* XV.17–20, *NPNF* 1 III, pp. 215–20). The Spirit is the inwardly enlivening principle of union, hiddenly uniting soul and body, inwardly uniting Christ and the church, and quietly uniting the church itself (Richard of St. Victor, *Trin.* III.11, *CWS*, pp. 384–85; cf. *MPL* 196.887–992; Bermejo, *SL*, pp. 85–96).

The image of God in humanity is revealed in the traces of the Trinity (*vestigia Trinitatis*) in the human capacity to remember, understand, and love God. As human personhood exists as a *relation* between memory, intelligence, and will, so does the triune God exist as a relation of the Father as divine mind or memory, the Son as his expressed knowledge or Word or understanding, and the Spirit as the will or bond of love between Father and Son (Augustine, *Trin.* XIV.15– XV.28). The correlated Augustinian triune analogies of mind, knowledge, and love (*mens, notitia, amor*) and memory, intelligence, and will (*memoria, intellectus, voluntas*) frequently reappeared in medieval discussions of the Trinity (Alexander of Hales, *Summa Universae Theologiae* I, Q46; Tho. Aq., *ST* I, Q27.4; Alan of Lille, *De Arte* I, sent. 25), which later would come to form the "very rhythm of reality in the Hegelian Idealism of the 19th century" (Heron, *HS*, p. 92).

The Need to Distinguish the Work of the Spirit from Father and Son.   "We acknowledge the Holy Spirit to be indeed *from* God, and *of* Christ. . . . Since he is not ingenerate, he is not to be confused with the Father; nor with the Son, since he is not the Only-begotten" (Gregory of Nyssa, *On the Holy Spirit* 2, *LCF*, p. 150; cf. *NPNF* 2 V, p. 315). "No one is his own spirit, no more than he is his own father or his own son," even as "no one is sent of himself" (Ursinus, *Comm. Heid. Catech.*, pp. 272–73; John 14:16, 26; 15:26).

The entire work of grace is ordered and directed by the one triune God who works as Spirit through varied administrations and gifts, "but the same God works all of them in all" (1 Cor. 12:4–6). The precise distinctions between the three persons of the one triune God are constantly reflected in texts of scripture, yet remained exegetically somewhat undeveloped, though not ignored, in the first two centuries.

By the second century, the need was more generally felt to state clearly the reasons why scripture required speaking of the Spirit as a distinct divine person, and how that related to the unity and triunity of God. "The grace of the Holy Spirit is added that those creatures which are not holy by virtue of their own being may be made holy by participation in the Spirit. Thus they derive existence from God the Father, rationality from the Word, sanctity from the Holy Spirit" (Origen, *Principles* I.III.8, in Heron, *HS*, p. 72; cf. *ANF* IV, p. 255). It was not until heterodox voices had to be answered that these matters were forced to gain wider consensual clarity. The councils thought that the Spirit was providentially allowing heterodoxy to challenge the truth of scripture in order that the Spirit would lead the church to search scripture more deliberately to discover a more cohesive reflection upon the triunity of God.

These exegetical distinctions were soon formulated into perennial ecumenical teaching: Wherever the one God, Father, Son, and Spirit, is working so as to generate or bring forth, that work proceeds from the Father. Wherever the one God, Father, Son, and Spirit, works to declare his will and speak his Word and order his mission, that work is said to be more properly the work of the Son. Wherever the one God, Father, Son, and Spirit, works to realize, accomplish, and consummate what God has begun and continued, that work is more properly the work of the Spirit (Gregory Nazianzen, *Orat.*, XXX, XXXI, *NPNF* 2 VII, pp. 309–28; Augustine, *Trin.* VI, *FC* 45, pp. 199–215).

If sent by the Father (John 14:26), the Spirit must be in some sense distinguishable from the Father. If "another Paraclete" (John 14:16) sent in the name of the Son (John 14:26), the Spirit must be distinct from the Son. The names *Parakletos* and "Holy Spirit" (*hagiou pneumatos*) distinguish this "(invisible) advocate from Christ the other (visible) advocate" (Fortman, *AHS,* p. 167; cf. p. 158).

The Prepositions "from Whom," "through Whom," and "by Whom" of 1 Corinthians 8:6, 7, and Romans 11:36.   Paul wrote to Corinth that "for us there is but one God, the Father, from whom all things came and for whom we live; and there is but one Lord, Jesus Christ, through whom all things came, and through whom we live" (1 Cor. 8:6b–7a). A distinction appears to be operative between "from whom" and "through whom," arguably as distinguishing the work of the Father from the Son. In speaking of the Spirit of God whose judgments are unsearchable, the counselor whose paths are "beyond tracing out," the received kerygma took Paul one step further toward an implicit triune premise: "For *from* [*ek*] him and *through* [*di*] him and *to* [*eis*] him are all things. To him be the glory forever! Amen" (Rom. 11:36, italics added). These particles "signify each other" (Ambrose, *The Holy Spirit, FC* 44, p. 127, italics added).

The work of God is therefore said to be threefold in these passages: God is the One God *from* whom all things come to be. God is the One God *through* whom all things are put rightly in order and when awry brought to a coherence consistent with the divine purpose. God is the One God *into* whom all things are coming to their fitting conclusion or perfection.

It is this cohesive apostolic thinking that in due time, under the challenge of heretical views, became further defined as the triune Christian teaching assented to by the ecumenical church: God the Spirit is the same God we know in creation and redemption, willing what the Father wills, sent on behalf of the Son, uttering inner testimony to the work of the triune God in creation, redemption, and consummation. "The Father creates all things *through* the Word, *in* the Spirit" (Athanasius, *LCHS* III.4, *ECF*, p. 296). "The Father through the Son, with the Holy Ghost, is the giver of all grace, the gifts of the Father are none other than those of the Son, and those of the Holy Ghost; for there is one Salvation, one Power, one Faith; One God, the Father; One Lord, His only-begotten Son; One Holy Ghost, the Comforter" (Cyril of Jerusalem, *Catech. Lect.* XVI.24, *NPNF* 2 VII, p. 121). The work of the Spirit is to bring to fulfillment that holy love which has been abundantly poured forth from the Father and offered through the Son (John 1:1–7; Rom. 11:36; 1 Cor. 8:6). That work of the one God which brings creaturely things to their proper fulfillment and destiny is the work of the Holy Spirit.

Glorious Refractions of the Three-One Light. In refining these distinctions, the ecumenical tradition could not help but resort to poetic utterance: We proclaim "concisely and simply the doctrine of God the Trinity, comprehending out of Light (the Father), Light (the Son), in Light (the Holy Ghost) . . . Was and Was and Was, but Was One Thing, Light thrice repeated; but One Light. . . . In Thy Light shall we see Light" (Gregory Nazianzen, *Orat.* XXXI.3, *NPNF* 2 VII, p. 318; Ps. 36:9).

Precise language must bend toward metaphor when pointing to personal mystery: "While there is one Person of the Sent, another of the Sender, and another of the Promiser, both the Unity and the Trinity are at the same time revealed to us." "The mercy of the Trinity divided for Itself the work of our restoration in such a way that the Father should be propitiated, the Son should propitiate, and the Holy Ghost enkindle" (Leo, *Sermons* LXXVII, *NPNF* 2 XII, p. 192).

From this premise the Helvetic Consensus could affirm that "the sphere of the Father's election (*Patris eligentis*), the Son's redemption (*Filii redimentis*), and the Spirit's sanctification (*Spiritus Sanctus sanctificantis*) is one and the same (*aequalis pateat)" (CC,* p. 315), and the Baltimore Catechism could attest that "the Father is entirely in the Son and in the Holy Ghost; the Son is entirely in the Father and in the Holy Ghost; and the Holy Ghost is entirely in the Father and in the Son . . . none precedes the other in eternity, nor surpasses the other in power" (p. 78).

We have the Son "in us through the Spirit," and "similarly, we have in us also the Father through the Son" (Cyril of Alexandria, *Comm. on John* IX; *MPG* 74.279–80). "The Spirit exists from him by nature, and being sent from him upon creation, effects the renovation" (Cyril of Alexandria, *Thesaurus, LCF*, p. 266).

Correctives of Key Historical Errors

Luther and Calvin held close to the Trinitarian arguments of Augustine. Calvin stressed the clear and certain testimony of the Spirit through the written Word. Wesley stressed the assurance of the Spirit in the heart of the renewed person.

Nineteenth-century developments were strongly shaped by Kantian moralism, Hegelian idealism, and Schleiermacher's emphasis upon religious experience. Twentieth-century Protestant and Catholic developments have been strongly influenced by Pentecostal and charismatic views. Their elaboration reaches beyond the range of this inquiry. It remains a pious Protestant exaggeration to insist that "the developed doctrine of the work of the Holy Spirit is an exclusively Reformation doctrine, and more particularly a Reformed doctrine, and more particularly still a Puritan doctrine" (Warfield, "Introductory Note," Kuyper, *WHS*, p. xxxiii).

The following discussion will be confined largely to conciliar decisions of the first four centuries, when it became necessary for the church to reject several distorted exegetical approaches:

Simony as an Offense to the Spirit.   The first heresy to arise against the Holy Spirit was the simoniacal heresy, or simony, which *used the Spirit instrumentally to make money*, after the pattern of Simon the sorcerer, who tried to purchase the incomparable Gift of God with money (Acts 8:18, 19), who wanted power "that he might sell to others that which could not be sold, and which he did not himself possess" (Cyril of Jerusalem, *Catech. Lect.* XVI.10, *NPNF* 2 VII, p. 117). One who is "promoted to any sacred order for a price, being already corrupted in the very root of his advancement, is the more ready to sell to others what he has bought" (Gregory the Great, *Letters* LIII, *NPNF* 2 XII, p. 182). Ordained ministers obsessively anxious for upward mobility flirt with simony.

Nominalism and Modalism.   Another early serious error was to regard the Holy Spirit as little more than *the name that the church decided to give to the gifts bestowed upon the apostles*, a nominalism that tended to reduce God the Spirit to our act of naming God in a particular mode (modalism, Sabellianism, Paul of Samosata, Praxeas, Noetus, cf. Kelly, *ECD*, p. 118). The heart of this misconception was that the Spirit is a part or role played by God (Sabellianism, A.D. 215), or that there are three distinct separable chronological modes or conceptions of God: creation, redemption, sanctification—"one of them infinite both in essence and power, and the second in power but not in essence, and the third circumscribed in both" (Gregory Nazianzen, *Orat.* XXXI.5, *On the Holy Spirit*, *NPNF* 2 VII, p. 319), thus denying the eternality of the three persons. The work of the triune God must not be conceived modalistically as a series of separable stages in which the Father first generates, then stops and then the Son begins to speak and reveal the will of the Father, then stops, and then turns over the world to the Spirit to apply the Word in the hearts of creatures.

Montanism.   Another problem emerged with the late second-century Montanists, who spoke in tongues, who thought that *the Paraclete was speaking directly through themselves*, yet in such a way as to teach nonconsensual conclusions (Hippolytus, *Refutation of All Heresies*, v. 12, *ANF* V, p. 123). They taught that the Spirit in the last days had come upon postapostolic prophets like Montanus and his followers, Priscilla and Maximilla (Montanism, Phrygianism, Cataphrygians), who thought that the Paraclete was delivering new revelations through them and that additional revelations beyond apostolic testimony were needed for faith (Athanasius, *De Synodis*, *NPNF* 2 IV, p. 452). Montanus "dared to say that he was himself the Holy Ghost,—he, miserable man," who crazily named the tiny hamlet of Pepuza in Phrygia "Jerusalem," yet continued calling himself by the shared name "Christian" (Cyril of Jerusalem, *Catech. Lect.* XVI.8, *NPNF* 2 VII, p. 117). Similarly, Manes (c. 215–275) had illusions of himself as Paraclete, the One whom Christ promised would come.

Marcionism and Sadduceeanism.   Another early heresy of the Spirit was that of Marcion, who argued that *the Old Testament was not inspired by the Holy Spirit,* but only parts of the New. The Sadducees had long before rejected the Holy Spirit on the grounds that he was not attested in the books of Moses (Gregory Nazianzen, *Orat.* XXXI.5, *On the Holy Spirit, NPNF* 2 VII, p. 319). Hence in the creeds it became necessary to counter by saying that the Spirit "spake by the prophets" (Creed of the 150 Fathers, *COC* II, p. 59).

The Arian, Tropici, and Macedonian Distortions.   A more widespread heresy was that of the Tropici or Metaphoricals, and the Semi-Arian Macedonians, who taught that *the Spirit was created by the Son, hence less than God,* analogous to the Arian view that the Son is less than the eternal God (Athanasius, *LCHS* 1.21, 30; cf. T. Torrance, *Theology in Reconstruction,* chap. 12). Deposed from the See of Constantinople in A.D. 360, Macedonius defined the Holy Spirit as a divine energy diffused throughout the universe (anticipating modern process theology), not a person distinct from the Father and the Son (Socrates, *Ecclesiastical History* II.45, *NPNF* 2 II, p, 74; Sozomen, *Ecclesiastical History* IV.27, *NPNF* 2 II, p. 322; cf. Gregory of Nyssa, *On the Holy Spirit, NPNF* 2 V, pp. 315–25). The Macedonian heresy, also called the Pneumatomachi party ("murderers of the spirit"), ascribed equality to the Father and the Son, but thought the Spirit of lower rank (Council of Constantinople I, Canon 1, *NPNF* 2 IV, p. 172; Leo, *Sermons* LXXV, *NPNF* 2 XII, p. 191).

Athanasius set forth classic arguments for the consubstantiality of the Spirit with the Father and the Son, showing that the Spirit is indeed to be worshiped as God (*LCHS* 1.20–27; 3:1–6; John Chrysostom, *Baptismal Instructions,* ACW 31, pp. 64–65). The Tropici, intensely preoccupied with typological or figurative language of the scripture, maintained that Spirit is a creature (as Arianism had said of the Son), perhaps an angel of the highest rank. Ecumenical teaching countered that the Holy Spirit is not an angel as if "sent forth to minister," but rather the true God who sends and is himself sent without ceasing to be God, and able to search the deep things of God (Cyril of Jerusalem, *Catech. Lect.* XVI.23, *NPNF* 2 VII, p. 121; 1 Cor. 2:10, 11). To those who wished to applaud Jesus without the Holy Spirit (the Macedonians and Arians), Ambrose wrote tersely: "The Lord will answer them: You set forward My Name, and deny My Substance. . . . That is not My Name which is divided from the Father, and separated from the Spirit. . . . I do not recognize My Name where I do not recognize My Spirit" (Ambrose, *Of the Holy Spirit* XVII.131, *NPNF* 2 X, pp. 153, 154).

By A.D. 382 the Council of Rome had consensually defined it as sacrilegious to say "that the Holy Spirit was made" or is a creature (*SCD* 58, 61, pp. 30, 31). Here the scriptural maxim applies: "Those who honor me I will honor, but those who despise me will be disdained" (1 Sam. 2:30).

Eunomianism (Anomoeanism).   The Arian bishop Eunomius taught a single supreme ungenerated Being (*agennesia*) whose simplicity was *opposed to all distinction.*

The Holy Spirit was thought to be a created being, created by the Son. Consubstantiality was denied. He was answered by Basil (*On the Holy Spirit*), Gregory of Nyssa (*Against Eunomius, NPNF* 2 IV, pp. 58–66), and Gregory Nazianzen (*Orat.* XXXI.12), who argued that the Holy Spirit was worthy of worship as God, and that the Spirit proceeds from the Father (John 15:26).

Tritheism.   Tritheism misunderstands the Father, Son, and Spirit as if they were separate and distinct Gods, denying the unity of substance of the three divine persons, thereby separating the Holy Spirit from the intimacy of the Trinity (Gregory Nazianzen, *Orat.* XXXI, *On The Holy Spirit, NPNF* 2 VII, p. 318). Discussions by Basil, Gregory of Nyssa, Cyril of Jerusalem, Ambrose, and Augustine on the work of the Holy Spirit remain the crucial consensual answers to this charge. "So, then, the Father is holy, the Son is holy, and the Spirit is holy, but they are not three Holies. . . . Cherubim and Seraphim with unwearied voices praise Him and say: 'Holy, Holy, Holy, is the Lord God of Sabaoth.' They say it, not once, lest you should believe that there is but one; not twice, lest you should exclude the Spirit; they say not holies [in the plural], lest you should imagine that there is plurality, but they repeat thrice and say the same word, that even in a hymn you may understand the distinction of Persons in the Trinity, and the oneness of the Godhead" (Ambrose, *Of the Holy Spirit* III.XVI.109–10, *NPNF* 2 X, pp. 150–51).

Though many others could be named, these seven deviations constituted the major offenses against the doctrine of the Spirit in early Christian teaching, thereafter perennially being remembered as heresies. Insofar as these views have twisted and dislocated exegesis of passages pertaining to the Spirit, ecumenical Christianity has been forced from its early centuries to follow the maxim "Drink water from your own cistern," (Prov. 5:15)—the teaching of the One who truly offers the water of life (John 4:14)—unpolluted by counterapostolic fantasies (Clement of Alexandria, *Stromata*, I.1, *ANF* II, p. 301; Cyril of Jerusalem, *Catech. Lect.* XVI.10, *NPNF* 2 VII, p. 117).

2   The Work of the Spirit

God has chosen humanity to be the special object of divine grace, the unique vessel through which the divine glory is to be revealed. According to the Nicene-Constantinopolitan Creed, it is *for us* humans and our salvation that God came. The salvation event occurred "for us men [i.e., for humanity, *anthrōpous*] and for our salvation"—*propter nos homines et propter salutem nostram* (Gk. *di emas tous anthrōpous kai dia ton hemeteran soterian,* Creed of 150 Fathers, *COC* II, p. 57; Cyril of Alexandria, *Letters* 55, *FC* 77, pp. 115 ff.).

Why *for us?* What moved God to act on behalf of the salvation of humanity? Nothing but God's own good pleasure (*eudokia,* Eph. 1:5, 9; Phil. 2:13) in saving sinners by grace. God was not externally bound to save some or all by a higher will imposed by some external necessity. Peace on earth is offered to those "on whom his favor rests" (Luke 2:14). This is why the work of grace is a central feature of the doctrine of the Holy Spirit.

This divine person is everywhere found engendering new persons, as if enabling them to be born anew to reflect the goodness of God. It is the Spirit who is forever giving new life to persons (John 6:63), quickening the life of faith, preaching, sealing in baptism, and revealing "what is yet to come" (John 16:13). The Spirit is preeminently at work where new life in Christ is being elicited, the truth of the Son attested, and the community of faith engendered. Vitality, authority, and community are continuing evidences of the work of the Spirit.

BEFORE THE COMING OF THE SON

The *Oikonomia* of the Holy Spirit in the Administration of Redemption Before the Incarnation

Administration is what the Spirit does to make effective the benefits of Christ (Barth, *CD* II/1, pp. 141 ff.; III/4, pp. 320 ff.). "Surely you have heard about the administration [*oikonomian*] of God's grace that was given to me for you" (Eph. 3:2). Though the term *administration* has the ring of a modern jargon for business management, it has for centuries been used to refer to a central aspect of the classic Christian teaching of the Holy Spirit. "What then, is the Paraclete's administrative office but this: the direction of discipline, the revelation of the Scriptures, the re-formation of the intellect.... First comes the grain, and from the grain arises the shoot, and from the shoot struggles out the shrub: thereafter boughs and leaves gather strength, and the whole that we call a tree expands: then follows the swelling of the germen, and from the germen bursts the flower, and from the flower the fruit opens: that fruit itself, rude for a while, and unshapely, little by little, keeping the straight course of its development, is trained to the mellowness of its flavour" (Tertullian, *On the Veiling, ANF* IV, pp. 27–28).

It is perplexing to organize systematically the themes of the work of the Spirit because they are so vast in scriptural testimony. It is virtually impossible to reduce this complexity to a simple sequence, yet systematic reflection upon scripture requires that certain overarching points not be missed (cf. G. B. Stevens, *TNT*, pp. 213–23, 431–45; W. Beyschlag, *NTT* II, pp. 204–28; A. M. Fairbairn, *PCMT*, pp. 487–92; W. N. Clarke, *OCT*, pp. 369–427; J. J. van Oosterzee, *CD* II, pp. 633–95).

The Christian teaching of salvation deals first with the general features of the Spirit's administration of redemptive grace and only then with the specific teachings of call, repentance, justification by grace through faith, regeneration, adoption, sanctification, and union with Christ. These we seek to cover.

A Preliminary Survey of the Economy of Redemption. The scriptures reveal an economy of redemption—the overall ordering of God's saving activity toward humanity. Through this broad-ranging design, God has "made known to us the mystery of his will according to his good pleasure, which he purposed in Christ, to be put into effect [*oikonomian*] when the times will have reached their fulfillment—to bring all things in heaven and on earth together under one head" (Eph. 1:9, 10).

It is crucial to grasp what such an economy requires, and in what sense God eternally grasps and foreknows the entire plan, yet by foreknowing does not unilaterally (monergistically, noncooperatively) decree the plan so as to make human responsiveness irrelevant. Only God knows how it can be that the plan is characterized by contingency, yet finally certain in its outcome, even while specific outworkings remain obscure to finite human knowing. It is the triune God who coordinately initiates, embodies, enables, and consummates the plan (Augustine, *CG* V.9–1, *NPNF* 1 II, pp. 90–96; Nicetas of Remesiana, *Power of the Holy Spirit*, *FC* 7, p. 32).

This economy or plan of salvation requires an envisioned *end* or purpose for history, appropriate *means* fitting to that end, and the effective *application* of these means to accomplish this purpose. To make all these work together is to economize them, or administer them as an *oikonomia* (ordered arrangement).

An *oikonomia* is best viewed not as a period of time but as an ordering and providing for the divine-human covenant relation as a whole from beginning to end. What the Greeks called *oikonomia*, the Latins rendered *dispensatio* (Tertullian, *Ag. Praxeas* 2, *ANF* III, p. 598).

Salvation Rendered Sure, Not Merely Potential.   In this plan God did not merely render salvation hypothetically possible while leaving the outcome entirely dependent upon whether other finite wills might or might not respond to grace. The salvation of which the Bible speaks is by faith known to be ultimately secured and made certain by God's own determination, even though at present it is still penultimately being worked out.

There is little final ambiguity in the phrase "I give them eternal life and they shall never perish; no one can snatch them out of my hand" (John 10:27), though many hazards remain yet ahead before the full accomplishment of God's saving purpose on the last day. On the rock of Peter's confession ("You are the Christ") the community of faith is being built so securely that "the gates of hell cannot prevail" against it (Matt. 16:18, kjv).

The saving intention of God is made known in the history of salvation attested by scripture. Although essentially accomplished already in Jesus Christ, its historical outworking is still in process. Meanwhile the faithful are assured by the Spirit that what has begun in Jesus Christ will be consummated in future history in a fitting way.

To speak of the saving work of the Spirit, it is necessary first to speak of the eternal purpose of God as that purpose has become manifested through historical events. The eternally envisioned divine purpose has gradually unfolded through a series of economies or providences, which from the postresurrection viewpoint may be seen as times of preparation. Through providence, God coordinates the divine purposes with distortable acts of human freedom so as to govern fallen history without coercing the liberty of creatures.

The Pretemporal Divine Decree: The Son Chosen Before the Creation to Redeem Whatever Might Fall.   Salvation is offered according to the eternal counsel of God's pretemporal will (Eph. 1:11, *thelema*). Christ came to fulfill in time the eternal intentionality of the divine will. When the Son came into the world, he said to the Father, "I have come to do your will" (Heb. 10:5, 9). The intent to reconcile whatever might fall was present in the triune God prior to creation. The Son could therefore be aptly described as "the Lamb that was slain from the creation of the world" (Rev. 13:8).

An intrinsic connection is assumed in the New Testament between creation, redemption, and consummation (Rom. 5). This eternal foreknowing did not woodenly imply that all companionate wills are reduced to nothing by the divine will. That God permits other finite wills to exercise choice is evident from their actual creation. Redemptive love is thus the primordial purpose and norm preceding creation. Its manifestation is the reason God creates (Irenaeus, *Ag. Her.,* III.18, *ANF* I, pp. 446–48).

The Eternal Being of the Spirit as Premise of the Temporal Work of the Spirit. The being of God the Spirit is eternal. The Spirit's work in nature and history occurs in time. The being of God must be posited before any working can be evidenced. The premise of God's visible activity is God's invisible being prior to any action. What God does is formed by who God is and what God wills. It is not as though God first does something and then that is subsequently called God's will. God *is* Spirit eternally prior to any consequent activity as Spirit. As we see the rays of the sun, yet not by looking at the sun itself, so when we see God's outward works, we posit God as ground and giver of those works (Athanasius, *Defence of the Nicene Definition* III.12, *NPNF* 2 IV, p. 158).

In the hidden counsels of God, the One who speaks in creation may seem to be without any interpersonal distinction, yet classical theology posits love and intercommunion within the triune God prior to creation. "Let *us* make humankind in *our* image" (Gen. 1:26, NRSV, italics added; John Chrysostom, *Hom. on Gen.* 8.8, *FC* 74, p. 109). "A stream is one until it falls over the precipice and divides into many drops. So is the life of God one and undivided while hidden within Himself; but when it is poured out into created things its colors stand revealed" (Kuyper, *WHS,* pp. 14, 15).

The Work of the Spirit in Creation and Providence

The arena of the work of the Spirit is celebrated in liturgy and common prayer as manifested throughout all creation, not stingily, but abundantly through every phase and field of cosmic and human history. The work of the Spirit does not begin belatedly with Pentecost, but is found profusely in all creation and its continuing providences, and especially in the entire history of salvation, which in due time comes to fulfillment in the incarnation and the Spirit's enabling of the body of Christ, to be finally consummated at the general resurrection.

General and Special Operations of the Spirit.   As the Son is said to be coworking with the Father in creation and with the Spirit in consummation, so the Spirit coworks with the Father in creation and the Son in redemption (Athanasius, *LCHS* I.22–27). These are viewed as general operations shared in the divine triad.

In this sense it is celebrated that God's Spirit creates (Gen. 1:2; Ps. 104:30; Job 33:4), redeems (Isa. 44:3, 23), and offers gifts to creatures (Gen. 2:7; 41:38; Exod. 28:3; 31:3). The Spirit illumines reason, enables political order, and restrains the capacity for humanity to destroy itself. Among those "general operations" of the Spirit shared with the Father and the Son are the offering of life, supporting of life newly given, nurturing continuing life, strengthening life nurtured, and guiding life strengthened. This applies to all forms of life, whether plant, animal, or human.

The spiritual kingdom that begins in creation, and becomes self-disclosed in Christ, is being brought to completion finally at the end of history. God the Spirit is at work throughout this whole world-historical process. "It is right to recognize along with these more general activities a special range of peculiarly personal relationships between God and those men who actually respond to His presence in conscious trust. Through such men, God is able to perform works of power that are not possible in lives ruled by unbelief. This is in a special way the distinctive work of the Holy Spirit" (Federal Council of Churches, *Relation of the Church to the War, CC*, p. 540).

The Work of the Spirit in Creation.   The biblical narrative begins with the work of the Spirit in creating: "Now the earth was formless and empty, darkness was over the surface of the deep, and the Spirit of God was hovering over the waters. And God said, 'Let there be light'" (Gen. 1:2, 3; Tertullian, *On Baptism* 3, 4, *ANF* III, pp. 670–71; Tho. Aq., *ST* I Q67, I, pp. 334–37).

The Spirit of God moved to bring order from chaos, elegance from emptiness, making beautiful in its own way each creature touched, garnishing the heavens. "There can be nothing which the Holy Spirit can be said not to have made" (Ambrose, *Of the Holy Spirit* I.V.37, *NPNF* 2 X, p. 119). "By his breath [*ruach*] the skies became fair," exclaimed Job, acknowledging that "these are but the outer fringe of his works," which only bespeak "the whisper we hear of him" in his full glory (Job 26:13–14). "Who has measured the waters in the hollow of his hand, or with the breadth of his hand marked off the heavens? Who has held the dust of the earth in a basket, or weighed the mountains on the scales and the hills in a balance? Who has understood the mind of the Lord, or instructed him as his counselor?" (Isa. 40:12, 13).

No gift reaches creation without the Spirit (Basil, *On the Holy Spirit* I.IX.24–26, *NPNF* 2 VIII, 16, 17). "By the word of the Lord were the heavens made, their starry host by the breath [*ruach*] of his mouth" (Ps. 33:6).

The Spirit works through providence to sustain all that is created (Ps. 104:10–14, 30; Lactantius, *DI, FC* 49, pp. 227 ff.). The Spirit filled Bezalel and the craftsmen as they worked on the temple (Exod. 31:3; 35:31), awakening the artistic spirit in humanity (Exod. 28:3). By the Spirit the enormous diversity of creation is brought into a single meaningful whole. Even the sins of the fallen, for which God is not responsible, are in time made serviceable to the whole (Origen, *Ag. Celsus* IV.54, 70; *Comm. on Numbers*, homily 14.2). "Winds take wing from you, dashing rain against stone; and ever-fresh springs well from you, washing the evergreen globe" (Hildegard of Bingen, *Symphonia*, p. 151).

The Presence of the Spirit in Historical Processes.   Only One who is "God of the spirits of all flesh" (Num. 16:22) could work to unify all diverse human purposes (Job 32:8), inspiring not only the civil lawgivers and sages but also the poets, and above all the prophets (Num. 1:7, 25, 26; 2 Sam. 23:2; 1 Kings 22:24; Ezek. 2:2; 11:5; Dan. 4:8, 11; Mic. 3:8); commissioning magistrates, judges, kings, and prophets; restraining evil; and enabling good. The Spirit works in universal human history, striving with persons (Gen. 6:3), witnessing to all of God's own coming (John 15:26, 27), convicting of sin (Acts 2:36), attesting God's righteousness, making sure the promises of God (Acts 2:32, 33),

By the Spirit "Othniel judged; Gideon waxed strong; Jephtha conquered; Deborah, a woman, waged war; and Samson, so long as he did righteously and grieved Him not, wrought deeds above man's power" (Cyril of Jerusalem, *Catech. Lect.* XVI.28, *NPNF* 2 VII, p. 122). The Spirit's guidance occurred from the outset not by obstructing but by allowing the people of God to meet and deal with changing historical conditions. The dynamics of grace emerge under extremely variable historical conditions through the guidance of the Spirit (*Common Catech.*, p. 642).

There is no work or thought or achievement of humanity that can be called good, true, or beautiful that is not premised by the Spirit's gift (Jer. 31:35; Ps. 136:25; 2 Cor. 3:3–11; John 3:34; Wisd. 7:17–20). The Spirit guides human insight in literature, the arts, the sciences, philosophy, poetry, and political life. Renaissance art at times portrayed Socrates as teaching on the porch of the temple (cf. Justin Martyr, *Address to the Greeks* 20–33, *ANF* I, pp. 281–87). Justin Martyr was convinced that Plato knew of the Holy Spirit (*Exhortation to the Greeks* 32–38, pp. 414–23), and Nemesius regarded him as the philosopher nearest the truth of providence (Nemesius, *On the Nature of Man, LCC* IV, pp. 432–45). Not yet as personal indwelling, the Spirit was nonetheless present in preparing all humanity for God's own coming in the Son.

The Spirit Gives Life.   Merely to be alive is to be endowed with life by the Spirit of God. This was assumed by Job when he declared that he would hold on to his integrity "as long as I have life within me, the breath [*ruach*] of God in my nostrils" (Job 27:3). Life is wholly dependent upon its being received from God the Spirit. The withdrawal of the Spirit could mean only death. "The Spirit of God has made me; the breath of the Almighty gives me life" (Job 33:4). If God would withdraw "his spirit [*ruach*] and breath [*neshamah*], all mankind would perish" (Job 34:14, 15). "When you send your Spirit [*ruach*], they are created, and you renew the face of the earth" (Ps. 104:30). "When you take away their breath [*ruach*], they die and return to the dust" (Ps. 104:29; cf. Gen. 2:7; Ezek. 37:9).

In giving life to humanity, the Spirit is preparing to bring persons into communion with God. Only in this way could the vast, silent, otherwise unperceiving creation respond to God in conscious, knowing companionship and relationship (Gen. 2:7). "Just as the Word of Life is Life, so the Spirit of life is Life" (Ambrose, *The Holy Spirit, FC* 44, p. 89). The Spirit bestows life; creatures receive life. He is unction and seal; they are sealed and anointed (Athanasius, *LCHS* I.22–23). Though death is a necessary terminus of all finite life under the conditions of sin, "The Spirit which speaks and sends is a living Spirit" (Cyril of Jerusalem, *Catech. Lect.* XVII.28, *NPNF* 2 VII, p. 131). "As the movement flowing from the soul to the body is the life of the body, so the movement whereby the universe is moved by God is, so to speak, a certain life of the universe" (Tho. Aq., *Compend.* 147, p. 157).

Though God may be greatly glorified by the vast speechless cosmic and natural creation, the scriptures speak more clearly of the delight that comes to God from conscious, rational, free creatures who love God in and through all creation. The work of the Spirit is indeed diffusely present in cosmic creation, but more intensely, intimately, and decisively present in human creation and redemption. Here the question turns upon how erring children of the divine Father might be made able to glorify the incomparably holy God. How could sinners magnify God? How could self-determining creatures prone to fall come to that maturity of moral character that reflects the goodness of God? This could occur only by the power of the Spirit. The plan of the triune God for redemption is accomplished only when God's own Spirit dwells in the fallen human heart so as to refashion it.

It is unthinkable that a prize offered to parents for the talent of their children might suddenly become more important to them than the joy of actually touching and embracing their children. The token is hardly in the same class with that which it betokens. So it is with God's delight in the life of human creatures made and restored in the divine image. God's experience of humanity is in itself God's delight, whatever their products or achievements or results.

The Creating and Recreating Power of the Spirit.   The primordial work of God in creation is a pattern and type of the work of God in regeneration or re-creation of the soul dead in sin (Eph. 2:1–10; Athanasius, *LCHS* I.9). As the heavens were made by the breath [*ruach*] of the Lord (Ps. 33:6), so the fallen creature is remade by God's Word through the Spirit as if breathing new life into sinners. The Spirit accompanies the Word as breath speech (Gregory of Nyssa, *The Great Catechism* II, III, *NPNF* 2 IV, p. 477). "The same Spirit who in the beginning moved upon the waters has in the dispensation of grace given us the holy Scripture, the Person of Christ, and the Christian Church" (Kuyper, *WHS*, p. 25; Athanasius, *LCHS* I.19–22).

Through directly touching, meeting, and indwelling within the human spirit, God the Spirit gives new life to the sinner, sustains the soul through the hazards of moral bankruptcy, and works to draw human freedom without coercion back to its original purpose of refracting the goodness of God. Whether the freedom of the creature remains alienated or redeemed, the Spirit continues to work within the inner sphere of personal freedom to glorify God in whatever ways possible by drawing freedom persuasively toward its true ground. God is at work in the soul from the beginning of its creation to its final restoration.

When the Lord "gave his life for our life," he poured "out the Spirit of the Father to unite us and reconcile God and man, bringing God down to man through the Spirit, and raising man to God through his incarnation," "attaining his purpose not by force . . . but by way of persuasion" (Irenaeus, *Ag. Her.* V.1.1–2, *ECF*, pp. 79–80).

A modalist spin on salvation history tends to limit and relegate the work of the Spirit exclusively to the latter-day completion of redemption, forgetting those texts that refer to the Spirit as present in creation and incarnation. This is countered by consensual exegesis that celebrates the work of the Spirit as intrinsic to the entire eternal plan of the triune God, known before history, working incessantly throughout the entirety of history, before, during, and after the coming of the Son. "If the work of the Spirit were confined to the sanctification of the redeemed, He would be absolutely inactive if sin had not entered into the world" (Kuyper, *WHS*, p. 12).

The Holy Spirit in Prophecy and Messianic Expectation

Prefiguring of the Covenant Calling of the Spirit in the History of Israel.   The Hebraic idea of the called people of God (*qahal*) is that of a people brought by Yahweh into covenant, elected not for superiority but for service, God's own people, a holy nation (Exod. 19:3–6; Deut. 7:6; 1 Sam. 12:22; Ps. 135:4; Rom. 1:6;

Eph. 1:4, 5; 1 Pet. 2:9). An exclusively racial definition of the covenant people was not to remain God's final disclosure, even in the promise to Abraham. For the promise was that through the seed of Abraham "all nations on earth will be blessed, because you obeyed me" (Gen. 22:18). The rite of circumcision, the crucial importance of sacrifice, and the threefold order of Aaronic ministry (high priest, priests, and Levites) were already staples of Jewish community life that were to become transmuted in Christianity (Ignatius, *Philadelphians* 10, *AF*, p. 107; Hall, *DT* VII 41; Stone, *EVO*, chap. 2; John Owen, *Works* 3, pp. 105–25).

When Paul wrote that his forefathers were "all baptized into Moses in the cloud and the sea" (1 Cor. 10:2), he was describing "an imitative anticipation of the future," "an exhibition of things expected," as "represented by the rough and shadowy outlines of the types" prefigured in Moses' time. Thus the manna was regarded by the patristic writers as "a type of the living bread," the exodus a type of baptism; "the blood of the sheep is a type of the blood of Christ," the sea and the cloud "prefigured the grace to be," "the sea is typically a baptism," and "the cloud is a shadow of the gift of the Spirit" (Basil, *On the Holy Spirit* I.14, *NPNF* 2 VIII, p. 19; Gregory of Nyssa, *The Life of Moses, CWS*, pp. 38–41).

God Spoke by the Prophets Through the Spirit.   In the creed the church confesses that God the Spirit "spoke through the prophets" (Creed of the 150 Fathers, *CC*, p. 33; Eastern Form of the Apostolic Creed, Cyril of Jerusalem, *SCD* 9, p. 8; Heb. 1:1; 1 Cor. 12:8–10). In the sackcloth prayer of the people of Israel upon returning from bondage, according to Nehemiah, the people confessed to Yahweh, "For many years you were patient with them. *By your Spirit you admonished them through your prophets*" (Neh. 9:30, italics added; Theophilus, *To Autolycus* II.9, *ANF* II, p. 97).

The Spirit is present in the called out people of God in the old covenant. Micah attested being "filled with power, with the Spirit of the Lord" (Mic. 3:8). In their rebellion the people of Israel "grieved his Holy Spirit" (Isa. 63:10). The psalmist prayed to God, "Do not cast me from your presence or take your Holy Spirit from me. Restore to me the joy of your salvation and grant me a willing spirit, to sustain me" (Ps. 51:11, 12).

God the Spirit is both author and subject of prophecy. God remains free to use human speech to declare to humanity his revelation, which no finite mind could invent. The Spirit is active throughout the history of Israel in law, psalm, and proverb (2 Sam. 23:2; Ps. 51:11; Prov. 1:23). Patriarchs, prophets, priests, and all before and after them who sought the way of holiness were being quickened by the same Spirit (Leo I, *Sermons* XXVI, *NPNF* 2 XII, p. 137; *MPL* 54.405). The Spirit came upon Enos, Enoch, Noah, Abraham, Isaac, Jacob, Joseph, Moses, Huldah, Deborah, Job, Bezaleel, Samuel, David, and the prophets. "My Spirit remains among you" (Hag. 2:5).

Joel specifically told of a future time when the Spirit would be poured out upon all flesh (Joel 2:28, 29). Peter preached that Joel's prophecy (2:30, 31) had been explicitly fulfilled at Pentecost (Acts 2:14–21; Kuyper, *WHS*, pp. 112–16).

The Called Out People Made One by One Calling

The Unity of the Called Out People of All Times.   The covenant community that appears in the Old Testament as seed of Abraham reappears in the New Testament as *ekklēsia* (Irenaeus, *Ag. Her.* IV.5, *ANF* I, p. 467). From the remnant of

Israel comes the promise of the new Israel. The church universalizes the life of Israel (Gal. 6:16). The chosen seed bears fruit for all humanity.

As God never left himself without witness in the world, so God never left the world without some anticipatory form of the calling and ingathering of the people of God, now being fulfilled and embodied in the life of the church. Before the incarnation this covenant people was being gathered in the form of expectation; after the incarnation in the form of fulfillment (Hippolytus, *On the Consummation of the Word, MPG*, 10:903–52).

The Spirit came to humanity in the form of figurative types and shadows of that which was to come—the incarnate Lord whose coming as the light of the world bathed all previous shadows of revelation in pure light (1 John 1:4–9; Kuyper, *WHS*, p. 53). Seen in terms of the continuous history of covenant, there is only one called out people of God, made one by their one calling, yet this one people has journeyed through many stages of historical development. Amid astonishing varieties of complex history, there remains a distinct thread of continuity in the economy of salvation history (Irenaeus, *Ag. Her.* IV.33.7, *COC* II, p. 16).

Whether the Earlier Ingathering Is Viewed from the Vantage Point of the Later. The way the Spirit worked before the incarnation was anticipated by those Spirit-led communities who implicitly or explicitly looked toward the event of God's own coming. Much of the outward form and aspect of those anticipations (temple sacrifice, feast days, the codification of Levitical law, the ordering of priesthood) continued to have transmuted relevance to the new people of God, viewed in the light of the resurrection (Heb. 7:1–23). After the resurrection, the searching of scripture became a spiritual exercise of seeking to understand the typic anticipations of God's own coming.

In this way, the work of God the Spirit prior to the incarnation had an anticipatory meaning for those who experienced it and a hermeneutical meaning for those who remembered these anticipations. In due time each of these preliminary meanings would be seen from the vantage point of their fulfillment and completion in Christ. From the latter vantage point, there is no need for the Gentiles to be circumcised, because the Christ has come, where by faith they too may become circumcised of heart.

The One Ekklēsia Before and After the Incarnation. If God from the beginning has willed that all should be saved (1 Tim. 2:4), then "it is necessary that there always should have been, and should be at this day, and to the end of the world, a Church" (Second Helvetic Confession, *CC*, p. 141). Melanchthon argued that there has always been and always will be a true church, in the sense of those who either proleptically or actually hold to true faith (*Corpus Reformatorum* XII.481–83), yet this church is always mixed with hypocrites while in history (*SHD* II, pp. 340, 354; Melanchthon, XXI.834). Gregory the Great argued that the "one, holy universal church" has embraced believers from the time of Abel onward (*Hom. on Ezek.* I.8.28; II.3.17; Irenaeus, *Ag. Her.* IV.18, *ANF* I, p. 485).

In the ceremonies of the Mosaic tradition, Christians found the prototypes of their own worship. Christians continue to be instructed by the Decalogue, now most fully fulfilled in the active and passive obedience of Christ. Christians continue to be edified by the faith of Abraham, Sarah, Isaiah, Ruth, Job, David, Amos, Esther, and Joel (Rom. 4, 9; Heb. 11).

The history of the people of Israel has become Christianity's own history, without which the fabric of the story of God's coming in Jesus would be vacuous and ephemeral. Marcion's attempt to "tear away" the Old from the New Testament (Cyril of Jerusalem, *Catech. Lect.* I, *NPNF* 2 VII, p. 116) and to dismiss the old covenant as if irrelevant to the new was considered dangerous (Irenaeus, *Ag. Her.* IV.7, *ANF* I, p. 470).

The Spirit "used this gentle treatment, fitted for our needs, gradually accustoming us to see first the shadows of objects, and to look at the sun in water, to save us from dashing against the spectacle of pure unadulterated light, and being blinded. Just so the Law, having a shadow of things to come . . . [became the] means to train the eyes of the heart" (Basil, *On the Holy Spirit* I.14, *NPNF* 2 VIII, p. 21).

The Continuity of Old and New.   The anticipative form of the called out people of God before Christ prefigures the fulfilled form of the church after Pentecost. This continuity is unclear without the prophetic witness. The purpose of prophecy is clearly set forth in John's Gospel: "I have told you now before it happens, so that when it does happen you will believe" (John 14:29; cf. 13:19). These anticipations must not be forgotten but by the power of the Spirit savored and remembered in Christian proclamation, that faith may be engendered (Isa. 41:23; 42:9; 43:19; Heb. 11:3–38).

As the called out community prior to the incarnation shared in God's coming salvation by way of hope in God's promise, so does the called out community after the incarnation share in God's accomplished salvation in the form of accurate recollection, testimony, remembrance, and celebration of God's own coming, which is even yet awaiting God's coming again (Anon., *Reply to Marcion* II, III, *ANF* IV, pp. 146–56).

This is the centering dynamic of the unity of the church: God's own Spirit awakening the one body of Christ, which was not ready to exist in the form of historical fulfillment until the fullness of time had come. This new called out people began to exist when after the ascension the Head of the body, sitting at the right hand of the Father, was ready to form the body through the indwelling Spirit. "God placed all things under his feet and appointed him to be head over everything for the church, which is his body, the fullness of him who fills everything in every way" (Eph. 1:22, 23).

It was the same Holy Spirit who spoke through the prophets who also worked in the ministry of Jesus and the Church (Acts 7:51; (Cyril of Jerusalem, *Catech. Lect.* XVII.5, *NPNF* 2 VII, p. 125). The New Testament makes it abundantly clear that the Old Testament references to *ruach Yahweh* are to the same One who is later personally called the Holy Spirit, the Comforter (Acts 2:16–21).

Believers in Hope Prior to Christ.   Believers who quietly expected God's coming prior to the incarnation shared in the promise, and in this way they shared in the church in the form of expectation and anticipative trust, patiently awaiting the formation of the body of Christ after the ascension. The creation of the fulfilled *ekklēsia* at Pentecost was a once-for-all occurrence. There the transition was made in history between the community of expectation and the community of God's own coming.

Prior to the incarnation, the Spirit was omnipresently working in and beyond Israel to call forth the community of faith in the form of expectation. After the incarnation, the Spirit was omnipresently working in and beyond Israel to call forth the community of faith in the form of fulfillment, indwelling within that community to enable each member of the community to be united with the living Lord.

The Pivot of History. The rapid succession of events following the crucifixion set the stage for the coming of the Spirit. Christ, having died for our sins, was buried, descended, raised, ascended to the right hand of the Father in heavenly intercession. The new covenant was ratified, the great commission given, and all this was immediately followed by

> The outpouring of the Spirit at Pentecost
>
> The calling out of the new people of God
>
> The forming of the body of Christ
>
> The introduction of the new law of love, a new rule of life fit for these momentous changes
>
> The gospel beginning to be preached to the whole world

All this happened within weeks after the death of Jesus. This intense series of events is called the pivot of history, the inauguration of the new aeon.

This pivot must be seen in relation to another expected pivot of time yet ahead, the end of the present age. That will be treated later as the subject of eschatology, but again in that case, the expected series of concluding events is expected to be swift and stupendous:

> The regathering of Israel
>
> The return of Christ
>
> Final judgment
>
> The binding of Satan
>
> The messianic kingdom
>
> The Bride of Christ reigning with the Son in eternity

This vast body of scriptural material becomes blended in the single notion of God's salvation (*yeshuah, soteria*) of humanity, the history of the divine-human covenant (Isa. 51:6–8; Luke 19:9; Acts 16:17; Rom. 1:16; 1 Pet. 1:9; Barth, *CD* IV/1; Chafer, *ST* VI, pp. 101, 102).

Types and Symbols of the Holy Spirit in Scripture

God's indwelling Spirit was first revealed under anticipatory types or prefigurations of what was to come. Symbols of the promise of the coming of the Holy Spirit that recur in the Hebrew Bible include wind, fire, water, dove, and the oil of anointing.

These types and metaphors dramatically coalesce in the event of Pentecost: "Suddenly a sound like the blowing of a violent wind came from heaven and filled the whole house where they were sitting," and "all of them were filled with the Holy Spirit," who appeared to them as flaming tongues parting asunder so as to settle upon each one of them (Acts 2:2–4); they received the promised "baptism with the Spirit and with fire" (Matt. 3:11), after which they preached the baptism of repentance (Acts 13:24); and they received the anointing of the Spirit that was promised to be poured out in the last days (Acts 2:17, 33; Titus 3:5, 6).

Spirit as Invisible Wind.   No words can be said without wind moving through the flexing chambers of our voices. As we use invisible wind to speak words and convey meanings, so God's unseen Spirit is moving by silent means to convey God's revelation. Wind is not discernible to the visual sense, though one can feel it on one's skin. The breath of God is like wind (Athanasius, *LCHS* I.7–8).

In speaking with Nicodemus, Jesus compared the Spirit to the wind that moves where it wills. One cannot ever account precisely from where it comes or goes or why. Similarly we are born of God from above by the Spirit (John 3:8). The Spirit of God is that invisible enabling agent by which God's power is manifested while remaining unseen. *Ruach* is the outbreathing, the proceeding, the going forth of the life of God (Athanasius, *LCHS* I.15–19).

What seemed to be a violent wind from heaven signified the inrushing presence of the One who was ready to grant to all humanity power to receive the kingdom of God, whereupon "the whole house became the vessel of the spiritual water. . . . Thus they were entirely baptized according to the promise, and invested soul and body with a divine garment of salvation" (Cyril of Jerusalem, *Catech. Lect.* XVII.15, *NPNF* 2 VII, p. 128).

Spirit as Cleansing Water.   The Spirit is typified by water, a symbol for cleansing, reviving, and refreshing, without which life does not long continue (Cyril of Jerusalem, *Catech. Lect.* XVI.12, *NPNF* 2 VII, p. 118; Hildegard of Bingen, *Symphonia*, p. 141). Water is "a perfect, gladsome, simple material substance, pure in itself" that "supplied a worthy vehicle to God" (Tertullian, *On Baptism* 3, *ANF* III, p. 670; Cyprian, *Letters*, *FC* 51, pp. 255 ff.). As the Son, the living water, cleanses the faithful from all unrighteousness (1 John 1:9), so is cleansing from sin enabled by the Spirit, who like a deep source of spring water renews the believer steadily (John 4:14; Athanasius, Defence of Dionysius, *NPNF* 2 IV, pp. 182–85).

The Spirit, like water, is life-giving, revitalizing (*Apostolic Constitutions* VII.IV.43, *ANF* VII, p. 477; Athanasius, *LCHS* I.19). Ezekiel saw a river flowing from the temple of God, which, beginning with a mere trickle, broadened into a vast river that would sustain the trees along its banks, finally sweetening the sea (Ezek. 47:1–12). In the very sea that had been dead, "swarms of living creatures will live wherever the river flows" (Ezek. 47:9; cf. Rev. 22:1, 2; Ambrose, *Of the Holy Spirit* III.XX.153–57, *NPNF* 2 X, p. 156).

Water as a type of the Spirit becomes most explicit in John's Gospel, where during the first seven days of the Feast of Tabernacles, the people brought water from the Pool of Siloam to the altar. On the eighth day, "the last and greatest day of the feast, Jesus stood and said in a loud voice, 'If anyone is thirsty, let him come to me and drink. Whoever believes in me, as the Scripture has said, streams of living water will flow from within him.' By this he meant the Spirit, whom those who believed in him were later to receive. Up to that time the Spirit had not been given, since Jesus had not yet been glorified" (John 7:37, 38; John Chrysostom, *Hom. on John* 51, *FC* 41, pp. 33–37).

The gifts at Pentecost were confirmed by baptism in cleansing, purifying, life-giving water. In time the dew of the Paraclete's gifts, which had previously descended only on the fleece of Israel, would fall abundantly on the whole earth through the mission of the church to the world (Ambrose, *On the Spirit* I.preface, *NPNF* 2 X, pp. 93–96).

Spirit as Purging Fire.   Divine revelation was often experienced as accompanied by light, fire, radiance, or brightness. Moses' burning bush, Elijah on Mount Carmel, Paul on the road to Damascus, and John on Patmos all attest the presence of light or fire in divine disclosure (1 Kings 18:38; Rev. 22:5; Athanasius, *Defence of the Nicene Definition, NPNF* 2 IV, pp. 164–66). Hildegard sang,

> Praise to you
> Spirit of fire!
> to you who sound the timbrel
> and the lyre.
> Your music sets our minds
> ablaze!
>
> (Hildegard of Bingen, *Symphonia*, p. 143)

Fire could symbolize both the coming of God's grace toward those who were responsive and the rejection of sin by the holiness of God (Exod. 3:2; 14:20; 24:17), whose anger against sin is like a consuming fire (Heb. 12:29; Ephraim Syrus, *Hymns, NPNF* 2 XIII, p. 277). Fire both "improves good deeds like gold, and consumes sins like stubble" (Ambrose, *Of the Holy Spirit* I.XIV.169, *NPNF* 2 X, p. 112). By fire the dross is burned away and the purer elements conserved (Theodotus, XXV, *Excerpts, ANF* VIII, p. 46). His gold needs his flame (John Chrysostom, *Hom. on the Statues, NPNF* 1 IX, p. 332).

As fire warms, so does the Spirit. As fire ignites, so is human speech and action ignited by the Spirit (Cyprian, *Treatises XII, ANF* V, p. 555). Jeremiah wrote of Yahweh's address, "I will make my words in your mouth a fire, and these people the wood it consumes" (Jer. 5:14). When Jeremiah tried not to mention the word he heard from the Lord, he found that "his word is in my heart like a fire, a fire shut up in my bones" (Jer. 20:9).

When fire passes into iron the whole of it becomes fire, "so that what was cold becomes burning and what was black is made bright"—in this way "the Holy Ghost enters into the very inmost recesses of the soul" by a saving fire which burns away the thorns of sin (Cyril of Jerusalem, *Catech. Lect.* XVII.14, *NPNF* 2 VII, p. 128).

The fire of the Spirit can symbolize protection, as in the pillar of fire that guided Israel in the desert (Exod. 13:21; Zech. 2:5), or purifying discipline, as in a refiner's fire (Mal. 3:3; Titus 2:14). Those who attest the Spirit's life are destined to "suffer grief in all kinds of trials. These have come so that your faith—of greater worth than gold, which perishes even though refined by fire—may be proved genuine" (1 Pet. 1:6, 7; Wm. Penn, *No Cross, No Crown*). Zealous service of the Spirit is likened to fire, where love is flaming into human warmth and fervent prayer (Ambrose, *Duties* III.18, *NPNF* 2 X, p. 84). With the memory of such metaphors in the background, the gifts at Pentecost were described as "tongues of fire that separated and came to rest on each of them" (Acts 2:3).

The Spirit desires to kindle this fire with all speed, "for He longs for speed in doing us good"; hence the Spirit "moves with speed like the speed of light." Yet the demonic imitates the Spirit by appearing as an angel of light, "pretending to be that light, that it may cheat us by its appearance" (Gregory Nazianzen, *Orat.* XL.36–37, *NPNF* 2 VII, p. 373; Athanasius, *LCHS* I.19).

Spirit as Guileless Dove.   At Jesus' baptism the Spirit descended upon him in the form of a dove (Matt. 3:16; Mark 1:10; Luke 3:22; John 1:32) from heaven to earth, resting upon him (Gregory of Nyssa, *FGG*, pp. 189 ff., 284 ff.). John the Baptist had testified, "'The man on whom you see the Spirit come down and remain is he who will baptize with the Holy Spirit.' I have seen and I testify that this is the Son of God" (John 3:33, 34).

The dove that returned to the ark with an olive leaf furnished Noah the proof that God's judgment of humanity was ending and that the renewal of humanity was occurring. The dove was a figure or type of the Spirit suggesting peace, gentleness, grace, beauty, and guilelessness (Cyprian, *On the Unity of the Church*, *ACW* 25, pp. 51 f.; *Letters, FC* 51, pp. 304–5; Tertullian, *On Baptism* 8, *ANF* III, p. 673; *Ag. Valentinians*, 3, p. 504). The dove of Noah prefigured the dove of Jesus' baptism: "For as in his time by means of word and of water there came salvation to themselves, and the beginning of a new generation, and the dove returned to him towards evening with an olive branch; thus, say [the apostles], the Holy Ghost also descended upon the true Noe, the Author of the second birth, who draws together into one the wills of all nations, of whom the various dispositions of the animals in the ark were a figure:—Him at whose coming the spiritual wolves feed with the lambs . . . that He might shew that it is He who by the wood of the Cross saves them who believe" (Cyril of Jerusalem, *Catech. Lect.* XVII.10, *NPNF* 2 VII, p. 126). Cyril argued that this prophecy was being fulfilled in his own historical period when warring nations were feeding together in post-Constantinian peace.

The Anointing of the Spirit

The figure of anointing embraced metaphors of consecrating, setting apart, giving gifts and blessings, and making fit for service. Anointing was a dramaturgical expression of the Spirit's comforting presence, seal, and blessing. Prophets were anointed that God's own Spirit might address the people directly (1 Kings 19:16). Priests were anointed that the Spirit might minister to the people through worship and sacrifice (Lev. 8:12). Governors and judges were anointed that the Spirit might rightly govern the people and judge justly (1 Sam. 15:1, 17; Barth, *CD* II/2, pp. 438 ff.).

Anointing with Oil as a Type of the Spirit.   Oil [*shemen,* Gk: *elaion*] was considered useful not only as a source of nutrition (Rev. 6:6) but also as a medicine (Mark 6:13; James 5:14; Hildegard of Bingen, *Symphonia*, p. 141), as well as having sacrificial and ceremonial functions (Ambrose, *Letters* 52, *NPNF* 2 X, p. 448). Oil was employed for many uses in healing, illuminating, comforting, and anointing (Num. 4:9, 6:15; Matt. 25:3–8; Methodius, *Banquet of the Ten Virgins* VI.4,

ANF VI, p. 330). Similarly, God the Spirit works by healing, illumining, comforting, and anointing (*Apostolic Constitutions* VII.IV.42, *ANF* VII, p. 476; cf. Calvin, *Inst.* 4.19).

As oil was used to light up the tabernacle (Exod. 25:6), the faithful are called to walk according to the light provided by the Spirit. The lamp of the Word that guides our path through the dark is kept burning by the Spirit (Ps. 119:105; John Chrysostom, *Baptismal Instructions, ACW* 31, pp. 51–52, 71–74).

As Christ was anointed not with material oil but with the incomparable oil of gladness, even the Holy Spirit, "so ye were anointed with ointment, having been made partakers and fellows of Christ." But this is not plain ointment, any more than eucharistic bread is merely bread after the invocation, for then it becomes Christ's gift that by the Spirit is being "made fit to impart His Divine Nature. Which ointment is symbolically applied to thy forehead and thy other senses; and while thy body is anointed with the visible ointment, thy soul is sanctified by the Holy and Life-giving Spirit" (Cyril of Jerusalem, *Catech. Lect.* XXI.2, *NPNF* 2 VII, p. 149).

Calling, Empowering, Anointing. Oil was used in the setting apart of holy places, offices, and duties (Exod. 40:9–16; Lev. 8). The Spirit works to anoint prophetic, priestly, and governance ministries. The Spirit anoints the prophet to speak the Word unfailingly (1 Kings 19:16), the priest to be set apart for holiness unto the Lord (Lev. 8:12), the governing powers that justice may rest upon them (1 Sam. 15:1).

Servants of the old covenant shared in God's plan of redemption by this anointing of the Spirit. As oil makes one's face shine, so does the Spirit make the believer radiant with the "oil of joy" (Ps. 45:7). As the Spirit effectively anointed prophetic, priestly, and governance ministries in the Old Testament, so does the Spirit anoint the varied ministries of the *ekklēsia*.

The Spirit bestowed upon key leaders special gifts. Saul prophesied (1 Sam. 10:10). When David was anointed, the "Spirit of the Lord came mightily upon David from that day forward" (1 Sam. 16:13, RSV). Samson was filled with enormous strength when the Spirit came upon him (Judg. 14:19). God's *ruach* came upon Gideon, Jephthah, and Saul amid combat (Judg. 5:34; 11:29; 1 Sam. 11:6).

The Spirit anoints and empowers those whom he calls to special service. As the Spirit empowered Joseph's administrative skill (Gen. 41:38, 39), so the Spirit enabled the skill of artisans to enhance the beauty of the temple (Exod. 31:2–4; 1 Kings 7:14), and so blessed Aaron's garments of consecration (Exod. 28:3). The Spirit was in Joshua in leading Israel to the promised land (Num. 27:18), in Gideon's stunning triumph (Judg. 6:34), in David's calling and guidance (1 Sam. 16:12, 13).

The Spirit called and enabled Ezekiel to speak to a troubled, rebellious nation (Ezek. 2:2, 3). The Spirit "entered into me," said Ezekiel, and "I heard him speaking to me" (Ezek. 2:2, RSV). The prophets foresaw that the Spirit would in the fullness of time be poured out "on all people" (Joel 2:28) to inaugurate the messianic kingdom (Isa. 32:15; 44:3; 59:21; Zech. 12:10), which would extend even to the Gentiles (Isa. 60:3–11; Acts 2:16, 17). The turn of history finally came when John the Baptist announced that one would come after him baptizing with the Holy Spirit and with fire (Luke 3:16).

First Bathing, Then Anointing.   Oil was applied in a special sequence in cere-monial cleansing (as in the case of the leper, Lev. 14:10–32): first to the ear that one would be ready to hear, then to the thumb of the right hand that it might become an instrument of righteousness, then to the great toe of the right foot that one might walk in the way of holiness. The remainder was poured on the head so the whole soul might be consecrated to God in an act of overflowing grace. This Levitical use of oil became the pattern for rites of healing through the Spirit and for final passage (*viaticum*).

In the early church those baptized were anointed on the forehead, that they might be delivered from sin, so with unveiled face they might reflect as a mirror the glory of God (2 Cor. 3:18). Then they were anointed on the ears to be "quick to hear the Divine Mysteries," on the nostrils to be ready to savor the sweet smell of Christ, and on the breast, that having put on the breastplate of righteousness they might stand against the adversary. "For as Christ after His Baptism, and the visitation of the Holy Ghost, went forth and vanquished the adversary, so likewise ye, after Holy Baptism and the Mystical Chrism, having put on the whole armor of the Holy Ghost, are to stand against the power of the adversary" (Cyril of Jerusalem, *Catech. Lect.* XXI.4, *NPNF* 2 VII, p. 150), knowing that "I can do every-thing through him who gives me strength" (Phil. 4:13). Once having received this anointing, this chrism, they were ready to be named by Christian names and called into the Christian life, having received new birth into a new family.

The relation of bathing and anointing is seen in the Mosaic covenant where Aaron was first bathed in water and then anointed. On this basis Cyril could rea-son that "Aaron was called Christ or Anointed, evidently from the typical Chrism." So also was Solomon first bathed in Gihon and then anointed (1 Kings 1:30). "To them however these things happened in a figure, but to you [catechumens] not in a figure, but in truth; because ye were truly anointed by the Holy Ghost" (Cyril of Jerusalem, *Catech. Lect.* XXI.6, *NPNF* 2 VII, p. 150).

Anointing Spirit, Anointed Son.   It is God the Spirit who anoints (*mashach*, Lev. 8; 1 Sam. 16; Athanasius, *LCHS* I.22–4). The Spirit is the active agent in the rite of anointing by oil. Aaron became the model of one who being first anointed was then qualified to anoint others, a pattern that was followed by the high priest anointing priests and the apostles anointing the apostolate (Exod. 40; 1 John 2:27).

The archetype of the anointed One (*Mashiach, Christos*) is the Son of whom it would be said that "the Spirit of the Lord is on me, because he has anointed me to preach good news to the poor" (Luke 4:18; cf. Isa. 61:1, 2). Peter recalled "how God anointed Jesus of Nazareth with the Holy Spirit and power" (Acts 10:38). The Spirit remained active in every activity of the Son (Athanasius, *LCHS* I.19–20).

Unity of the Spirit's Ministry.   All these types and figurative images complement each other in speaking of the one ministry of the Holy Spirit. All major aspects of the work of the Spirit in the New Testament are anticipated in Old Testament types. The believer is clothed with power, born from above, anointed, and set apart for service by the work of the Spirit.

"Thus with divine accuracy did even the types anticipate the two-fold provision for the Christian life, cleansing by the blood and hallowing by the oil—justification in Christ, sanctification in the Spirit" (A. J. Gordon, *MS*, p. 95). Adoption into the family of God is given by the grace of baptism, and the empowerment of the Christian life is given by the filling of the Spirit. As faith is the only prerequisite for receiving justifying grace in baptism, so is that same faith (yieldedness, obedience, complete submission, entire consecration) the sole precondition of being baptized and filled by the Spirit.

AFTER THE COMING OF THE SON

Pivot of Pneumatology: The Work of the Spirit in the Life of the Incarnate Son

A methodological preface to what follows: Earnest attempts have been made to set forth the varieties of pneumatology (Pauline, Johannine, Lucan, and others) in the New Testament in their developments and redactions (R. Bultmann, H. Conzelmann, E. Schweizer, C. K. Barrett, G. T. Montague, et al.). Respecting these efforts, the subject matter of irenic systematic theology is different—not the comparative-developmental account of varieties of Christian teaching (a historical exercise employing historical method primarily), but the search for consensual reception of consensually received texts that reflect the one mind of the believing church (a theological exercise using theological method primarily). Given the limits of this study, we leave many ancillary questions of development to historians, except as those varieties of developments can be shown to be consensually received within some cohesive whole. If no such whole exists, there is no systematic theology and no irenic pneumatology possible. It is the whole that we now seek to identify, using all major textual sources of the New Testament canon.

The Life of the Holy Spirit in the Life of Son.   To the Son "whom God has sent," the Father has given "the Spirit without limit" (John 3:34). As a man, Jesus walked day by day in radical dependence upon God the Spirit, prayed and spoke by the power of the Spirit. In portraying Jesus as constantly dependent upon the Spirit, the Gospels were not challenging or questioning his deity or divine Sonship. Rather, as eternal Son the theandric person already was truly God, while as a man, Jesus was truly human, bone of our bone, flesh of our flesh, seed of Abraham, whose humanity was continually replenished by the Spirit (Luke 4:14; Heb. 2:14–17). He did not walk or speak by his own independent human power, but by the power of the Spirit.

Every gift requisite to the Son's mission was provided by the Spirit. "Jesus, full of the Holy Spirit, returned from the Jordan and was led by the Spirit" (Luke 4:1). It was "the Son, who as to his human nature was a descendant of David," who was "through the Spirit of holiness," according to Paul, "declared with power to be the Son of God by his resurrection from the dead" (Rom. 1:4).

The Ministry of the Holy Spirit in the Ministry of the Son.   Mary trusted the word of annunciation, "The Holy Spirit will come upon you" (Luke 1:35), and Joseph was not afraid, because the child "conceived in her is from the Holy Spirit" (Matt. 1:20). The earthly ministry of the Son was brought to fruition step-by-step through the power of the Spirit, who was active from the Son's very conception and birth (Luke 1:28–35; Matt. 1:18–23).

The Spirit filled the growth of the Son with grace (John 3:34), descending in the form of a dove at his baptism, anointing him to messianic mission, equipping him for mission (Mark 1:10; Luke 2:40, 52; Matt. 3:13–17), guiding and strengthening him amid temptation (Matt. 4:1–13; Luke 4:1, 2), empowering his proclamation and wonderful deeds of mercy and healing (Luke 4:14–18; Matt. 12:18, 28). The baptism of John was destined to be superseded by one who would baptize with the Holy Spirit (Mark 1:8; Matthew and Luke add "and with fire," Matt. 3:11; Luke 3:16).

When Jesus began preaching, he pointedly announced, "The Spirit of the Lord is upon me" (Luke 4:18). Peter preached that "God anointed Jesus of Nazareth with the Holy Spirit and with power" and "he went around doing good and healing all who were under the power of the devil, because God was with him" (Acts 10:38). The disciples were taught that the Holy Spirit would be received in answer to earnest prayer (Luke 11:13).

Even in death it was "through the eternal Spirit" that Jesus "offered himself unblemished to God" (Heb. 9:14). The Spirit accompanied him on the cross. The Spirit is found guiding Jesus even after the grave (Act 1:1, 2), empowering his resurrection and ascension (Rom. 1:4; 1 Tim. 3:16; John 16:13–15). "He was put to death in the body but made alive by the Spirit, through whom also he went and preached to the spirits in prison" (1 Pet. 3:18, 19). "And if the Spirit of him who raised Jesus from the dead is living in you, he who raised Christ from the dead will also give life to your mortal bodies through his Spirit, who lives in you" (Rom. 8:11).

After Jesus had finished his earthly journey, the Father sent the Spirit to fulfill the mission of the Son, who ascended to heaven, retaining his humanity, being exalted and seated at the right hand of the Father without ceasing to be human, still bearing the wounds of his crucifixion. So his intercessory work in the presence of the Father is as our wounded human brother and advocate. The Father in receiving Jesus receives those who are united with Jesus through the Spirit.

God's Own Spirit.   The Comforter who came at Pentecost was distinguishable but not separable from the Son who came in holy nativity. "The teachings of Christ and of the Holy Ghost are not different, but the same" (Cyril of Jerusalem, *Catech. Lect.* XVI.14, *NPNF* 2 VII, p. 119; 1 John 2:1; John 14:16, 26). "The words I have spoken to you are spirit and they are life" (John 6:63). Christ is called the Spirit of God (*pneuma theou*, 2 Clem. 9.5; Irenaeus, *Ag. Her.* V.1.2; Theophilus, *To Autolycus* II.10; Tertullian, *Apology* 21). "And if anyone does not have the Spirit of Christ, he does not belong to Christ" (Rom. 8:9).

The Spirit works to enable the faithful to hear and respond to Christ's living personal presence. The Spirit makes effectual the work of the Son in ways beyond our ken, at a depth that cannot be uttered (Rom. 8:26), and not merely with words but with a demonstration of the Spirit and power (1 Cor. 2:4). This is what Calvin called the secret operation of the Holy Spirit (*arcana operatio spiritus sancti, Inst.* 3.1.1; 4.14–19).

In expanding on the theme "the Spirit gives life" (2 Cor. 3:6), Paul compared the fading of the ceremonial law (symbolized by Moses' veil, Exod. 34:29–35) to the radiance of the new covenant: "Now the Lord of whom this passage speaks is the Spirit; and where the Spirit of the Lord is, there is liberty. And because for us there is no veil over the face, we all reflect as in a mirror the splendour of the Lord; thus we are transfigured into his likeness, from splendour to splendour; such is the influence of the Lord who is Spirit" (2 Cor. 3:17, 18, NEB). He was not thereby reducing Spirit to incarnation, or vice versa, but rather consenting to the implicit triune premise of the early kerygma that the one God was truly incarnate Lord without ceasing to offer life now as active Spirit.

The Mission of the Holy Spirit in the Administration of Redemption After the Incarnation: The Present Age

The Spirit comes to attest the Son so as to guide the faithful into all truth, put doubt to flight, magnify the power of God, remember accurately the events of the Son's coming, provide for its accurate transmission, and assure the faithful of their adoption as sons and daughters in the family of God. The Spirit is given as a seal or stamp that God places upon his own, an earnest or pledge of what is to come in the final consummation.

The present age extends from ascension to Parousia, wherein the Spirit is working to awaken, engender, and sustain the continuing body of Christ, to restore humanity as a whole. We now experience the age between the first and second advent of Christ. The work of the Spirit will be crowned by the return of the Son and the judgment of history. "This Gift [the Holy Spirit] is with us unto the end of the world, the solace of our waiting . . . the light of our minds, the sun of our souls" (Hilary, *Trin.* II.35, *NPNF* 2 IX, p. 61).

The New Age.   The notion of a *new age* (a new creation, Gal. 6:15; new covenant, 2 Cor. 3:6; new life, Rom. 6:4; a new and living way, Heb. 10:20) is recurrent in the New Testament. This makes ironic the fact that the term *new age* has been recently seized and distorted by pantheistic, naturalistic spiritualists and paranormal experimenters. It is precisely amid declining modernity that "New Age" has come to mean "the old paganism." But that irony gives no sufficient reason why Christian orthodoxy should abandon a term long offered by apostolic teaching. The apostolic language is better defended against distortion than abandoned.

The present age is the age of the Spirit, to whom has been committed the work of applying the redemption of the Son to the lives of persons by calling, justifying, and sanctifying them. The new age or dispensation of the Spirit is given to comfort and guide the witnessing community following Christ's ascension. The present age is now continuing in our present history, and at some point it will be completed with the return of the Son. The time of the Spirit is from Pentecost to Parousia.

The Personal Direction of the Spirit.   The *ekklēsia* is now under the personal direction of the third person of the Trinity just as directly as the apostles were under the personal direction of the Son during his earthly ministry (Acts 8:29, 39; 10:19; 11:12; H. E. Manning, *The Temporal Mission of the Holy Ghost*). As in baptism when the whole person is drenched with the love of God, so in the coming of the Spirit the whole of present history is being flooded with the revelation of that love.

The Spirit is given in the place of Christ's bodily presence. Before the pivot of history, the Spirit was not yet unreservedly self-offered as indwelling. Afterward, when the risen Lord ascended, he promised that the Spirit would come as helper and abiding companion of the people of God, and that the Spirit would accompany the witnessing community until he personally returned.

The Spirit reproves and challenges the faithful to accountability to the holy God, and comforts the faithful in their sin. "His coming is gentle; the perception of Him is fragrant. his burden most light. . . . He comes to save, and to heal, to teach, to admonish, to strengthen, to exhort, to enlighten" (Cyril of Jerusalem, *Catech. Lect.* XVI.16, *NPNF* 2 VII, p. 119).

The History of the Acts of the Spirit.   As the earthly history of the Son is available for historical inquiry, so may we also examine the earthly history of the Spirit. We may apply, so far as they will go, the same methods of historical inquiry to attest the Spirit as we employed to inquire into the incarnate, theàndric Mediator (John of Damascus, *OF* III.19, *NPNF* 2 IX, pp. 67–68; cf. *WL*, pp. 197–212, 220–29). The Son had a time of ministry on earth that he came to fulfill, and having finished it returned to the Father. So does the Spirit have a time of ministry on earth, which begins with a particular event, Pentecost.

The Spirit has never altogether left fallen human history, but the ministry of the Spirit glimpsed through law and prophets was proleptic, occasional, special, and anticipatory of full indwelling of the Spirit to be clarified through future events. The Holy Spirit is the coordinator and economizer of the gift of redemption both before and after the resurrection. The indwelling of the Spirit becomes a historical event only after the ascension of the Son.

The Present Age an Allowed Time to Attest to the World.   Israel bore testimony to the unity of God (Deut. 6:4). The Spirit-led church bears testimony to the triune God. Israel had not yet been called to a cross-cultural mission. Christianity became the new Israel with that new mission (Gal. 6:16; Rom. 9–11).

The present age is the age of Gentile inclusion, not Gentile hegemony or superiority, but inclusion in the salvation history into which Israel has been covenanted from the time of Abraham. The present age is providentially given to allow time for the gathering-scattering community to attest God's saving action through the Son and the Spirit. In the time remaining in world history, God intends to restore whatever might have fallen through sin so as to apply the work of the Son fittingly to humanity. After this present age, ending in final judgment, we expect the age to come in which the restoration of all things will at long last appear in a new heaven and a new earth.

Before Jesus, Israel had attested the one holy God to all who would hear, but Israel had no deliberate mission to declare God's reconciling Word to the whole world, no great commission, no gospel. Prior to his ascension, even Jesus did not actively extend his mission beyond Israel, for he explicitly said at this preresurrection stage, "I was sent only to the lost sheep of Israel" (Matt. 15:24). And when he sent the disciples out on their early mission, they were instructed, "Do not go among the Gentiles or enter any town of the Samaritans. Go rather to the lost sheep of Israel" (Matt. 10:5, 6).

After his ascension, however, the disciples were commanded to go into all the world and preach the gospel to every creature until Christ's return. The Gentiles were privileged to enter into the sphere of divine reconciliation just as much as the Jews. Paul reminded Gentile hearers that "formerly" (before the present age of the gospel) "at that time you were separate from Christ, excluded from citizenship in Israel and foreigners to the covenants of the promise, without hope and without God in the world. But now in Christ Jesus you who once were far away have been brought near through the blood of Christ" (Eph. 2:12, 13).

This is why the entire present age from ascension to Parousia is an age of testimony, proclamation, self-giving *marturia,* so as to fulfill Israel's calling to become a blessing for all humanity, so that "all people on earth will be blessed through you" (Gen. 12:3). "When the Counselor comes, whom I will send to you from the Father, the Spirit of truth who goes out from the Father, he will testify about me. And *you also must testify*" (John 15:26, 27a, italics added). The Spirit continues to teach that which can only be revealed in due time, bearing witness to "the whole design of God," revealing "many things which relate to discipline" (Tertullian, *On Monogamy* 2, 4, *ECF,* pp. 131–32).

A Slightly Revised Judaism? Why a New Institution?   The *ekklēsia* was called out to embody the spiritual benefits of Christ's life and work. The gifts of the Spirit required a new institution and a reconceived liturgy to express the enriched spirituality offered in Christ. Why weren't the institutions of Judaism adequate to this new reality? Why were a new era and a new community required?

Jewish religion was shaped to serve a particular ethos, out of a particular history. Because Judaism was provincially grounded, focused as it was upon the temple in Jerusalem, and racially self-defined as children of Abraham, it could not be the vocation of Judaism in its Levitic form to expand and serve and transmute the whole of humanity. From Judaism had to come something other than Judaism— a religion with a universal mission, capable of being adapted to all races, all cultures, all particular histories, all stages of human development. If the decisive spatial category of Judaism was "the land," for Christianity it was "the world" (Justin Martyr, *Dialogue with Trypho, ANF* I, pp. 194–272).

The sacrificial system that had been maintained in late Judaism was not adequate to universal human needs. By means of the Eucharist, Son and Spirit found fit means for remission of human sin and sanctification of persons, so as to apply Christ's sacrifice for sin to all who repent and believe. Jesus brought a newness that could not be confined in the old forms. New wine must be poured into new wineskins (Mark 2:22). "No one sews a patch of unshrunk cloth on an old garment. If he does, the new piece will pull away from the old, making the tear worse" (Mark 2:21).

Evil in the Present Age.   In the eyes of New Testament writers the present age is not only being ultimately shaped by the power of the Spirit but also penultimately by the continuing remnants of the power of evil. The "present evil age" from which Christ came to rescue us would remain an age of sin, which would continue until the final days, though its ultimate defeat has already occurred on the cross and begun in human hearts (Eph. 5:13–16; 6:12–16; 2 Tim. 3:12, 13).

Believers expect to be engaged in a continuing struggle with the world, the flesh, and the devil, to test and strengthen their faith. They are called to "put on the full armor of God so that you can take your stand against the devil's schemes. For our struggle is not against flesh and blood, but against the rulers, against the authorities, against the powers of this dark world and against the spiritual forces of evil in the heavenly realms" (Eph. 6:10–12).

The Work of the Spirit in Birthing, Nurturing, and Consecrating.   Amid these challenging conditions, the Spirit continues to give birth, nurture, and sanctify. The Spirit in the present age is *giving birth* to the called out community, quickening its life, adding to its common life by converting persons one by one. As Christ has life in himself, so does the Spirit breathe life into the church. A single member of the church has no sufficient power to give or deny life to the church, though a member may fail in a particular mission and thus cause misery in the whole body. Since life is given to the church by God the Spirit, life is not taken away by the discrete members of the body. Not only is the social organism given life, but it is continually sustained in life by Word and Sacrament, by the power of the Spirit. The church is not only engendered, but also *nurtured* by the Spirit, its walk daily illumined by the Spirit through the written and preached Word attesting the revealed Word. The believing church is protected from utter failure by the Spirit, who has promised not to abandon the church, though the church may temporarily fall into error.

The Spirit continues to work to consecrate, *sanctify*, and perfect the church, setting it apart from the world for its special mission and ministry within the world, abiding in this community "as source of grace, operating in its sacramental ministrations, and guaranteeing their efficacy and sanctifying benefit to all who worthily use them. The sins of Churchmen, indeed, reduce these benefits, but the Spirit continues to retain sinners within the Church, in order that He may make the grace of repentance available to them" (Hall, *DT* VIII, pp. 22, 23).

The Spirit's Work in Applying the Work of the Son

The Spirit works as personal agent of the mission of the Son to reveal the Son and bring his redemptive work to consummation (Hilary, *Trin.* VIII.19, *NPNF* 2 IX, p. 142).

The Spirit Accurately Remembers the Son.   The Spirit is sent by the Father in the name of the Son: "But the Counselor, the Holy Spirit, whom the Father will send in my name, will teach you all things and will remind you of everything I have said to you" (John 14:26; cf. 1 John 2:27). From this text derive classic interpretations of the inspiration of scripture (John Chrysostom, *Hom. on John* XXIII, *NPNF* 1 XIV, pp. 82–83). It is by this canonically received holy writ that the Spirit teaches "all things"—all that is necessary for salvation, brought to accurate and sufficient remembrance. The Spirit assists our recollection of the history of salvation, both by inspiring a written record of it and making certain that record is sufficiently reliable to be an adequate memory of the salvation event (Augustine, *Hom. on John* CIV, *NPNF* 1 VII, pp. 391–93).

Theories of inspiration of scripture founder in the attempt to locate the authority of scripture autonomously in the text itself or the writer while neglecting the Spirit who inspires, transmits, and rightly recalls the text. The inspiration of scripture is essentially a doctrine of the work of the Holy Spirit, and only secondarily therefore a doctrine of authority, reliable transmission, and textual adequacy (Calvin, *Inst.* 3.2).

It is not an alternative revelation different from that declared in Jesus that the Spirit is bringing, but rather the ever-fuller clarification of the revelation Jesus brought from the Father (Gregory Nazianzen, *Orat.* XXXI, *NPNF* 2 VI, pp. 318–

22; Fortman, *AHS,* p. 16). The Spirit does not speak independently of the triune God as if functioning as an autonomous authority, but always speaks and recalls so as to enable the mission of the Son—the reconciliation of humanity with the Father. As the Son attests the Father, so the Spirit attests the Son (John 15:26). "For he who does not believe the Spirit does not believe in the Son, and he who has not believed in the Son does not believe in the Father . . . for it is impossible to worship the Son save by the Holy Ghost; impossible to call upon the Father save by the Spirit of adoption" (Basil, *On the Spirit* I.11, *NPNF* 2 VIII, p. 18). It is precisely what the Son conveys from the Father that the Spirit speaks, attests, and conveys from the Son, who promised that "when he, the Spirit of truth, comes, he will guide you into all truth. He will not speak on his own; he will speak only what he hears, and he will tell you what is yet to come. He will bring glory to me by taking from what is mine and making it known to you" (John 16:13, 14; C. Wesley, *Hymns of Petition and Thanksgiving for the Promise of the Father, WHNS*).

The Spirit elicits not only accurate memory of salvation but active confession of Christ: "Therefore I tell you that no one who is speaking by the Spirit of God says, 'Jesus be cursed,' and no one can say, 'Jesus is Lord,' except by the Holy Spirit" (1 Cor. 12:3; cf. Ambrose, *Of the Holy Spirit* III.XXII.167, *NPNF* 2 X, p. 158).

The truth into which the faithful are being Spirit-guided is the truth of saving faith. It is this truth that the Spirit is speaking to the church. "He who has an ear, let him hear what the Spirit says to the churches" (Rev. 2:17). The apostolic witnesses were specifically instructed under persecution, "Just say whatever is given you at the time, for it is not you speaking, but the Holy Spirit" (Mark 13:11).

The Intercession of the Son for the Life of the World. The Son tasted death for all humanity (Heb. 2:9). Before the Comforter came to dwell in the present age, however, it was necessary that the Son first appear before the heavenly Father to attest the sacrifice he offered for humanity's sin as sufficient for their salvation. Entering in the Father's presence as humanity's advocate, mediator, priest, and brother, the ascended Son sat at the Father's right hand, where he was restored to the position of equality he had enjoyed before the humbling descent of the incarnation. The artistic imagination of Renaissance Christianity soared dramatically in portraying this reconciling event of the Son showing his wounded hands and feet to the Father as the basis of his intercession: "Father, I want those that you have given me to be with me where I am" (John 17:24).

The Son's ascension to the Father signified a refilling with that majesty of which he had been emptied. The Spirit's humble descent now works quietly to advocate and complete the Son's mission throughout the earth (Clare of Assisi, *Rule, CWS,* pp. 218–29). It was expedient that the Son go away, for only if he went to intercede with the Father could he send the Spirit to comfort the body of believers.

The Son's acceptance by the Father was thus the basis of the Spirit's pledge or seal or earnest of our acceptance by the Father. When Jesus was accepted by the Father, those whose lives are hid in him through the Spirit were also accepted by the Father (Eph. 1:7). God's acceptance of penitent sinners is thus settled once for all on the cross. What remains is for each hearer to make a full personal and moral response to the Spirit's witness.

Only after the Son's earthly ministry could the Spirit begin in earnest to communicate and apply his work to humanity. His heavenly intercession is presupposed in the table set for the Eucharist. "Without the expiatory work of Christ for us, the sanctifying work of the Spirit in us were impossible; and on the other hand, without the work of the Spirit within us, the work of Christ for us were without avail. . . . The fact that the Comforter is here is proof that the Advocate is there in the presence of the Father" (Gordon, *MS*, p. 38).

Peter's preaching at Pentecost clarified the Father, Son, and Spirit relation: "God has raised this Jesus to life, and we are all witnesses of the fact. Exalted to the right hand of God, he has received from the Father the promised Holy Spirit and has poured out what you now see and hear" (Acts 2:32, 33). Pentecost was the triune God's clear signal that redemption had been accomplished by the Son and was now being administered by the Spirit (Proclus, *Orat.* 16, *MPG* 65, pp. 805–8; T. Goodwin, *Works* VI, pp. 7–10).

There is an intrinsic connection between Jesus' proclamation of the expected divine governance and the actual divine governance that has in fact come in the indwelling of the Spirit: "Luke makes it plain that the intention of the clause 'Thy kingdom come' is to implore the aid of the Holy Spirit. For in his gospel, in the place of 'Thy kingdom come,' he says 'Let the Holy Spirit come upon us and purify us,'" hence "Matthew uses 'kingdom' where Luke speaks of 'Holy Spirit'" (Gregory of Nyssa, *De oratio dominica* 3, *LCF*, p. 149; *MPG* 46.1109; *ACW* 18, p. 53).

Descending Spirit and Ascending Son.   As the Son ascended to the Father, the Spirit descended to the disciples. This humbling descent of the Spirit did not amount to a diminution of power but its expression, just as the "self-emptying, which [the Lord] underwent for man's restoration, was the dispensation of compassion, not the loss of power" (Leo, *Sermons* LXXII, *NPNF* 2 XII, p. 186). Political theologies that rightly stress serving care for the poor may inadvertently, in the process of desperately seeking temporal power, turn away from the lowering, descending, humbling, yielding, self-submissive motifs of baptism and crucifixion.

Jesus had promised the disciples that they would see "the angels of God ascending and descending on the Son of Man" (John 1:51; John Chrysostom, *Hom. on John*, *FC* 33, p. 203). In this present age of the Spirit, the kingdom of God is being freely opened up to us, as was shown to Stephen (Acts 7:55). God is communicating "himself to us to be our life" (Calvin, *Comm.* XVII, pp. 80–81). The angels are ministering in reference to the Son, in relation to whom we are becoming fellow citizens of the saints (Eph. 2:19). Jacob's ladder to heaven (Gen. 28:12) is now being ascended and descended freely, with open communication between formerly estranged sinners and the reconciling God (Athanasius, *Festal Letters* III, XIX, *NPNF* 2 IV, pp. 512–15; 544–48).

While tarrying in Jerusalem, the disciples were not yet authorized to set out on their mission to the world, until the Spirit had come to indwell with them to empower their testimony. The descent of the Spirit was the signal that the atoning work had been fully accepted by the Father, and that the Son was reigning with the Father in heaven (Matt. 3:16, 17; Calvin, *Comm.* XVI, pp. 202–6; *WL*, pp. 236–38).

The Triune Work Economized.   The Spirit "is given to those who believe, coming for comfort, and sanctification, and initiation" (Council of Antioch, 2, *CCC*, p. 13; Athanasius, *Councils of Ariminum and Seleucia* 23, *NPNF* 2, IV, p. 461). The Anglican Catechism viewed the saving work of the one God as proceeding through a sequence of economies: the work of the Father in creation; the work of the Son in reconciliation; and the work of the Spirit in sanctification (*BCP*). Though distinguishable, these ages or economies must not be inordinately abstracted as if modalistically separable from one another, for they flow from one to the other organically and historically (Heron, *HS*, p. 52).

There is a cohesive economy of succession in the history of revelation: First the law is given, with its ordering of sacrifice, to bring the people of God under its tutelage; then Christ comes to culminate all sacrifice on the cross so as to do for us what the law could not do; then the Spirit communicates and applies to humanity the finished work of the cross (Rom. 8:1–4; Augustine, *Spirit and Letter*, *LCC* VII, pp. 226–50; John of Damascus, *OF* III.1, *NPNF* 2 IX, pp. 45 ff.).

Distinguishing Son and Spirit.   As God the Son is sent to do the work of the Father, so God the Spirit is sent to human hearts to accomplish the work of the Son. Each person of the Trinity refers to the others. The Son's words were not his own but his Father's (John 14:10, 24; 17:14). The Spirit is the Spirit of the Son as well as the Spirit of the Father, "proceeding [*ektoreuomenon*] from the Father and receiving [*laubanomenon*] from the Son" (Epiphanius, Creed, Second Formula, *COC* II, pp. 37–38; Hall, *DT* VIII, p. 5). It was the Son who died for us and rose again, not the Spirit. The Spirit did not perform any high priestly function, as did the Lamb of God. The work of the Spirit in us is distinct from that of the Son for us. For "the Holy Spirit could not be crucified, Who had not flesh and bones, but the Son of God was crucified, Who took flesh and bones" (Ambrose, *Of the Holy Spirit* I.IX.107, *NPNF* 2 X, p. 107).

"As Christ is represented as the ambassador of the Father, so the Holy Spirit is represented as the ambassador of the Son, coming vested with his authority, as the interpreter and executor of his will" (A. Clarke, *CT*, p. 157). "As the Father revealed himself through the Son, so the Son by the Holy Spirit now reveals himself through the church; as Christ was the image of the invisible God, so the church is appointed to be the image of the invisible Christ; and his members, when they are glorified with him, shall be the express image of his person" (Gordon, *MS*, p. 32). "What the presence of Christ was in the Gospels, the Head without a corporate body, the presence of the Spirit is, representing the Invisible Head of a body now visible" (Pope, *Compend.* III, pp. 264, 265).

The Inwardness of the Spirit's Work.   The scene of the Spirit's work of grace is amid the most inward dimensions of human consciousness. There is nothing too subtle or dense for the Spirit to penetrate or too sinful for the Spirit to cleanse or too weary for the Spirit to refresh or too dark for the Spirit to understand or too dead for the Spirit to breathe life into again. The Spirit strives with us, prays for us, groans with us.

The Spirit has missional requirements distinguishable from the Son. The Spirit must penetrate our motives, the springs of thought, the nuances of character, the dynamics of will. Yet this inwardness is not lacking in social consequence: "Souls wherein the Spirit dwells, illuminated by the Spirit, themselves become spiritual, and send forth their grace to others," whereby, "the weak are held by the hand, and they who are advancing are brought to perfection" (Basil, *On the Spirit* I.9, *NPNF* 2 VIII, p. 15).

The Community-Creating Spirit.   At Pentecost the Spirit who is eternally present to all was poured out in an exceptional indwelling upon the apostles. After Pentecost the Spirit was found constantly to be forming actual living communities of grace and testimony. All those united to Christ by faith are united with the called out community by the Spirit (Cyprian, *The Unity of the Catholic Church, LCC* V, pp. 124–42).

The Holy Spirit after the incarnation was not creating a conglomerate of isolated regenerated persons but rather a community, a family of the regenerated, an ordered household, an organic body. *Ekklēsia* is called to be a bonded, caring community, a *koinonia,* a new social creation of grace, the resurrection of the people of God raised up in the light of God's own coming, a peculiar people (Kuyper, *WHS,* pp. 119, 120).

God the Spirit is love. This love is working to elicit a new community of trust, forgiveness, and faith active in love. God the Spirit is not imprisoned in the buildings and institutional structures we call the church, but is free to awaken and teach and renew by these appointed means the called out people who assemble in these buildings.

The Spirit in the Church.   The Spirit works in the church to form the *ekklēsia* (1 Cor. 12:13), to dwell in the body of believers (2 Cor. 6:16), to build up the community of faith (Acts 2:47; Eph. 2:21, 22; 1 Pet. 2:5, 6), to elicit true worship (Phil. 3:3, John 4:24; Athanasius, *LCHS* I.32–33; T. Goodwin, *Works* VI, pp. 13–39). The Spirit empowers the church's witness amid a hazardous and fallen world (Acts 1:8). The Spirit calls living persons to specific vocational tasks and responsibilities and missional challenges (Acts 13:2), unifying diverse gifts in the one body of Christ (Phil. 2:2–4).

The Son placed under the governance of the Spirit not merely redeemed individuals one by one but also the redeemed community together. The Spirit works in the community to offer new life, birthing, regenerating (John 3:3; Titus 3:5), baptizing believers into the body (1 Cor. 12:13), indwelling in their hearts (1 Cor. 3:16), freeing from guilt, sin, and death (Rom. 7:9–8:2), strengthening the inner life amid hardships and challenges (Eph. 3:16–19), bearing witness to their daughterhood and sonship with the Father (Rom. 8:16), sealing believers until the day of redemption (Eph. 4:30), bearing fruits of faith active in love (Gal. 5:19–23; Rom. 14:17; 15:13), guiding into all truth (John 16:13), directing the life of prayer (Rom. 8:26, 27; 1 Cor. 14:15; Eph. 6:18; Jude 20), bringing into accurate recollection the words of Christ (John 14:26), enabling fitting proclamation of the good news of God's own coming (Acts 1:8; 1 Cor. 2:1–5), revealing the deep things of God through spiritual discernment. For "'No eye has seen, no ear has heard, no mind conceived what God has prepared for those who love him'—but God has revealed it to us by his Spirit" (1 Cor. 2:9).

The Spirit is attested in healings, exorcisms, tongues (Acts 2:4–6; 10:46), proclamation (4:8, 31), power (6:10), prophecy (11:28; 21:4, 11), martyrdom (7:55), counsel (8:29; 10:19), mission (13:4), hedgings of the way (16:6, 7), warnings (20:23), and in the authorization of overseers to watch over the flock (20:28).

The Spirit-Enabled Prayers of the Called People.   When we are unable to pray rightly, "the Spirit helps us in our weakness. We do not know what we ought to pray for, but the Spirit himself intercedes for us with groans that words cannot express. And he who searches our hearts knows the mind of the Spirit, because the Spirit intercedes for the saints in accordance with God's will" (Rom. 8:26, 27). No one is so devoid of grace that he cannot pray for grace.

In the East the central moment of the Eucharist was the *epiklesis*, which invoked the Father to send his Spirit upon the *ekklēsia* and upon the bread and wine. This prayer for the Spirit is beautifully expressed by Simeon:

> Come, for you continue always unmoved,
>   yet at every instant you are wholly in movement;
> you draw near to us who lie in hell,
>   yet you remain higher than the heavens.
> Come, for your name fills our heart with longing
>   and is ever on our lips;
> yet who you are and what your nature is, we cannot say or know.
> Come, Alone to the alone;
> Come, for you yourself are the desire that is in me.
> Come, my breath and my life.
>
> (Simeon the New Theologian, in K. Ware, "The Holy Spirit in the
>   Personal Life of the Christian," in *Unity in the Spirit* [Geneva:
>   WCC, 1979], pp. 139–69)

THE PERSONAL INDWELLING OF THE SPIRIT

As the Messiah is the personal Word of redemption, the Spirit is the personal administrator of the Word. The central role of the Spirit in the economy of salvation could not be fully clear, though anticipated, until the act of atonement was complete on the cross and confirmed in the resurrection. Only then was the time fulfilled for the Spirit's outpouring on the day of Pentecost. Then the coming fire that had been anticipated in the Shekinah (the ancient symbol of the glory of the tabernacling of God with humanity) became poured out in tongues of fire, attesting the resurrection in all human languages.

The Counselor

The Personal Naming of the Spirit. *Parakletos* is more than a descriptive noun. It is the personal name chosen by the Son by which the faithful were privileged to address God's own Spirit in the new age (Hilary, *Trin.* VIII.19–27, *NPNF* 2 IX, pp. 142–45). Variously translated as Comforter, Advocate, Helper, Counselor, or Guide, the literal meaning of *parakaleo* is to call to one's aid (Nicetas of Remesiana, *Power of the Holy Spirit*, FC 7, p. 36). *Parakletos* is one called to another's side to take his or her part, as a friend, a counselor, always lending aid, a partaker in another's cause (John 16:7; cf. 1 John 2:1).

God the Spirit was not named *Parakletos* by the apostles but by the Son himself. The full meaning of this name would be revealed only through a history of the Spirit's activity. *Parakletos* is the One called to breathe life into the community of faith, sent personally to fill the void that otherwise would have been left by

Christ's departure (Origen, *OFP*, pp. 116–19). "Unless I go away, the Counselor will not come to you, but if I go, I will send him to you" (John 16:7).

Before and during the incarnation, the Spirit had been cooperating with the Father and the Son in the plan of salvation. After the incarnation, the Spirit became the principal advocate to speak of and for Christ, to enliven and dwell in the body of Christ, to make his atoning work effective in history (Tertullian, *Ag. Praxeas* 27–30, *ANF* III, pp. 623–27). The Spirit's presence in the church was understood as God's own real presence, promised to abide till the end of history, making the Son's presence real, making the Father's love known. "He is called Comforter, because He comforts and encourages," and "makes intercession," prompting supplicants to "scorn wealth," turn away from temptation, and endure martyrdom (Cyril of Jerusalem, *Catech. Lect.* XVI.19, 20, *NPNF* 2 VII, p. 120).

Why Another Advocate?   In the present age following the ascension, the Holy Spirit is "another Counselor to be with you forever," fulfilling the ministry of the Son. On this triune premise it could be said paradoxically that the Paraclete is both sent by the Son (John 14:26) and the coming of the Son in a new form. "I will not leave you as orphans; I will come to you" (John 14:18).

As long as Christ was on earth, he was the comforter, guide, and guardian of the disciples. After his ascension he promised to give them *"another* Counselor." Why *"another"* if the first was sufficient?—"that you might acknowledge His co-equality. For this word Another marks an Alter Ego, a name of equal Lordship, not of inequality" (Gregory Nazianzen, *Orat.* XLI.12, *NPNF* 2 VII, p. 383). In this way *Parakletos* became a name applied by apostolic rememberers first to the Son and then to the Spirit (Ambrose, *Of the Holy Spirit* I.XIII.157, *NPNF* 2 X, p. 111).

The *ascended Son* continues in heavenly intercession as an advocate to "speak to the Father in our defense" (1 John 2:1; Origen, *Principles*, II.7, *ANF* IV, p. 286). The *descended Spirit* is here to counsel the world of *sin*, of the *righteousness* of the Son who intercedes with the Father, and of future *judgment* of the idolatries of this world (John 16:8–11). *Parakletos* thus plays a continuing servant role to further enable the mission of the servant Messiah. "He will bring glory to me by taking from what is mine and making it known to you" (John 16:14). By the Son's death "the inheritance becomes available, and when he had ascended into heaven he sent down the Holy Spirit to distribute the estate among those who were joint heirs with him" (A. J. Gordon, *MS*, pp. 49, 50).

The Personal Coming of the Spirit.   Through the Son human history was brought into concrete meeting with the incarnate God, who felt our human infirmities, afflictions, and death. Through the Spirit, this encounter comes to even closer quarters by indwelling in our hearts and attesting the work of the Son in our hearts (Barth, *CD* II/2, pp. 344 ff.; F. D. Bruner, *A Theology of the Holy Spirit*).

As a person enfleshed in history, Jesus could only be one place at one time. As present in the Spirit, the Son could be present to the church in all places and times. In his flesh he dwelt with humanity for a particular time. By his Spirit he would come to dwell with humanity for all times. By the Spirit the triune God would become accessible to all, thus nearer to the far-flung body of believers than had he remained on the earth endlessly.

Why This Time for the Coming of the Spirit?   The Spirit is not best understood merely as a surrogate of one absent or as a secondary substitute for the vitality of Christ or an acceptable compensation for what was missing. Rather, the coming of the Spirit is the coming of the triune God in the time of fulfillment, whose outpouring follows directly upon the ministry of the Son. Christ himself is present in and through the gifts of the Spirit (John 16:12–33). God's own coming in the Son is intrinsically related to God's own coming in the Spirit. Both manifest God's own coming to humanity.

Even before the resurrection, the gift of the Spirit was ready to be bestowed by the Father. Yet before the resurrection, the disciples were still unprepared for this gift, as was all humanity. It was not until the Son had said, "It is finished," that the prophetic expectation could be fulfilled (John 19:30; Augustine, *Comm. on John* CXIX.6, *NPNF* 1 VII, p. 434; John Chrysostom, *Hom. on John* 85, *FC* 41, p. 434). Only after the resurrection could the gospel be proclaimed as a finished series of saving events. Before the resurrection, the mission of the Son was clouded with controversy and despair. After the resurrection, the mission of the Son became clear and vindicated. "Looking at Calvary we say, This love deserved to conquer; looking to the risen Lord we add, And in fact it *has* conquered" (Mackintosh, *PJC*, p. 375; cf. Hogg, *Christ's Message of the Kingdom*, p. 213).

Before Pentecost there existed a visible community of believers united with God the Son. There can be little doubt that the sacrament of *holy communion* came before Pentecost. Arguably this implied that the Lord's Supper was given to create, enable, and nurture the church, not merely to be nurtured by it. The grace that flows through the sacraments brings the church into being, awakening faith, hope, and love.

Pentecost: The Outpouring of the Holy Spirit

After Passover and the Feast of the Unleavened Bread in the Jewish calendar came the Feast of the Firstfruits (a liturgical type of the resurrection; Lev. 23:17–20; Rom. 8:23; 1 Cor. 15:20–23). It was followed fifty days later by *pentecostē*, the Greek term for "fifty days," celebrated a week of weeks after Firstfruits (Exod. 23:16; Tho. Aq., *ST* I–II Q102.5, I, pp. 1067–69), which presented the firstfruits of harvest, the Hebraic type of the firstfruits of the ingathering of the reign of God. Fifty days after firstfruits, two loaves of bread were offered, the yeast of which prefigured the formation of the church on the day of Pentecost (Lev. 23:15–21).

Tarrying in Jerusalem for a Week of Weeks.   The Lord had instructed the disciples to wait in Jerusalem for the Spirit. This was an auspicious moment for a new beginning in the history of salvation. The feast of Pentecost had gathered large numbers of people to Jerusalem only a short time after Jesus' death and resurrection (Acts 2; Calvin, *Comm.* VIII, pp. 73–74). They had come from remote parts of the known world. It was to this gathering that the Spirit came and was poured out with such power. The key text of Levitical instruction for Pentecost was, "From the day after the Sabbath, the day you brought the sheaf of the wave offering, count off seven full weeks. Count off fifty days up to the day after the seventh Sabbath, and then present an offering of new grain in the Lord" (Lev. 23:15, 16).

The Christian Pentecost referred backward to the Levitical Feast of Weeks and forward to the celestial banquet in the general resurrection. The disciples did not wait an indefinite period for the descent of the Spirit, but precisely fifty liturgically prescribed days after the resurrection. "For as of old, when the Hebrew nation were released from the Egyptians, on the fiftieth day after the sacrificing of the lamb the Law was given on Mount Sinai, so after the suffering of Christ, where the true Lamb of God was slain, on the fiftieth day from His Resurrection, the Holy Ghost came down upon the Apostles and the multitude of believers" (Leo, *Sermons*, LXXV, *NPNF* 2 XII, p. 190). Pentecost is "the sequel and completion of the Paschal feast" (Leo, *Letters* XV, *NPNF* 2 XII, p. 28). "Pentecost is a reminder of the resurrection expected in the age to come," for eternity is symbolized by seven times seven, and as a circle that begins again on the same point that it ends (Basil, *On the Spirit*, *NPNF* 2 VIII, p. 42).

The resurrected Lord had instructed the disciples that after the resurrection, "repentance and forgiveness of sins will be preached in his name to all nations, beginning at Jerusalem. You are witnesses of these things. I am going to send you what the Father has promised, but stay in the city until you have been clothed with power from on high" (Luke 24:47–49; cf. Matt. 24:19, 20).

The Spirit No Longer a Transient Visitor. At Pentecost the *ekklēsia* became indwelt as temple of God, a renewed holy temple for intercession, prophecy, celebration of the sacraments, and praise (Jude 20). The one Holy Spirit who before had called, anointed, and visited chosen vessels sporadically came to abide with the faithful community and, anticipatively, with the whole of humanity (Heb. 8:10; John 14:15–19). At Pentecost the Holy Spirit "descended into the temple of his apostles, which he has prepared for himself, as a shower of sanctification, appearing no more as a transient visitor, but as a perpetual Comforter and as an eternal inhabitant" (Augustine, quoted in A. J. Gordon, *MS*, p. 26).

As the preexistent Son had anteceded the incarnation, so the eternal Spirit had anteceded Pentecost. As the mediator between the holy God and sinful humanity was born in nativity at Bethlehem, so the distributor of the gifts of the Son gave birth to the new people of God. It is as if God the Spirit were taking up residence in the *ekklēsia* at the point at which God the Son ascended to intercede with the Father. This indwelling was promised to continue until the end of time.

The One who is to take up residence with the church is the "Holy *Spirit,* whom the *Father* will send in *my* name" (John 14:25, italics added). With this Johannine recollection, the triune teaching is already in place. "If anyone loves me he will obey my teaching. My Father will love him, and we will come to him and *make our home* [*monēn*] with him" (John 14:23, italics added). Father, Son, and Spirit are all taking up abode in the faithful through the indwelling Spirit. More precisely, "the first two Persons of the Godhead now hold residence in the church through the Third. The Holy Spirit during the present time is in office on earth; and all spiritual presence and divine communion of the Trinity with men are through him" (A. J. Gordon, *MS*, p. 28; Leo the Great, Sermon 76, *MPL* 54, 405).

The Quickening Sequence of Events. Jesus had already breathed upon the disciples saying, "Receive the Holy Spirit." They had already confessed his Lordship and repented and believed in him. In what sense, then, is it said that the Holy

Spirit was personally and incomparably received at Pentecost? How are we to understand the signs (tongues, fire, wind) that accompanied Pentecost?

Here is the quickening sequence of the work of the Spirit immediately following Christ's earthly ministry: Christ had prayed that the Spirit would be a continuing, abiding, indwelling presence with his own (John 14:16–17). The disciples were instructed to tarry until they were imbued with power by the Spirit (Luke 24:49). After repeated promises of the coming of the Spirit (John 14:17, 26; 15:26; 16:7, 13), Jesus breathed the Spirit upon his disciples after his resurrection (John 20:22). The Spirit was poured in fullness on the whole gathered community at Pentecost (Acts 2).

This was the beginning of a steady chain of remarkable disclosures: The Spirit again came through the laying on of hands of Peter and John in Samaria (Acts 8:14–17) and again fell on Gentile believers in the house of Cornelius: "While Peter was still speaking these words, the Holy Spirit came on all who heard the message. The circumcised believers who had come with Peter were astonished that the gift of the Holy Spirit had been poured out even on the Gentiles. For they heard them speaking in tongues and praising God" (Acts 10:44–46). When Paul baptized the Ephesians "the Holy Spirit came on them, and they spoke in tongues and prophesied" (Acts 19:6). After Pentecost, "They devoted themselves to the apostles' teaching and to the fellowship, to the breaking of bread and to prayer" (Acts 2:42). "And the Lord added to their number daily those who were being saved" (Acts 2:47). After Pentecost the charismata were diversely distributed by the Spirit to the whole church. Those who had been timid, quarrelsome, and confused before receiving the Spirit, afterward went out illumined, united, courageous, and determined (Hilary, *Trin.* XIII.31–35, *NPNF* 2 IX, pp. 146–48).

After Pentecost it becomes clearer that the Spirit is essential to every moment and each specific phase of the manifestation of God's salvation to and for humanity. The Spirit works thereafter to reveal the Son, to bring his work to consummation, to work externally in bearing testimony through the written and preached word, and inwardly within the hearts of both the resistant and the faithful, and to exercise guidance over the church so as to provide the gifts of the Spirit to the community of faith (Tertullian, *Flight in Time of Persecution* 1, 14, *FC* 40, pp. 275, 307).

The Spirit's work was aptly summarized by the Augsburg Confession as ruling, comforting, enlivening, and protecting: "Afterward He ascended into heaven, that He might sit at the right hand of the Father, and forever reign and have dominion over all creatures, and sanctify them that believe in Him, by sending the Holy Ghost into their hearts, to rule, comfort, and quicken them, and to defend them against the devil and the power of sin" (Augsburg Conf., art. III).

The Early and Latter Rain.   Rain had long been a symbol of the refreshing, life-giving outpouring of the Spirit (Ps. 72:6, 7). "Be glad, O people of Zion, rejoice in the Lord your God, for he has given you the autumn rains in righteousness. He sends you abundant showers, both autumn and spring rains, as before. The threshing floors will be filled with grain; the vats will overflow with new wine and oil" (Joel 2:23, 24). "So if you faithfully obey the commands I am giving you today—to love the Lord your God and to serve him with all your heart and with all your soul—then I will send rain on your land in its season, both autumn and spring rains, so that you may gather in your grain, new wine and oil" (Deut. 11:13, 14).

The comparison of the Spirit's coming with rain was easily grasped by all who knew the two rainy seasons of Palestine, fall and spring, early and late, the first at the time of planting when the seeds were just sown in fallow ground, and the latter rain in the spring when the grain was ripening for harvest. Similarly it was promised to occur in the economy of salvation that the Comforter would come both early and late, but with special power and efficacy at the latter time. The Spirit was working both in planting and harvest. One tradition of exegesis has viewed the early rain as prophetic expectation and the latter rain as prophetic fulfillment. Another tradition viewed the early rain as Pentecost and the latter rain as the outpouring of the Spirit in the end time. In either case the Spirit comes both early and late, preveniently and cooperatively.

In the Paraclete, God the Spirit came silently, as gentle rain, invisibly within the ambiguous conditions of human history. In the Parousia, the Son will return gloriously and openly under unambiguous conditions of the final judgment of history. The Comforter is promised from Pentecost to Parousia to work as "Guardian and Sanctifier of the Church, the Ruler of souls, the Pilot of the tempest-tossed, leading wanderers to the light" (Cyril of Jerusalem, *Catech. Lect.* XVII.13, *NPNF* 2 VII, p. 127).

The Spirit Will Do Greater Things Than These. Only on this basis can we understand one of the most astonishing statements reported of Jesus: "I tell you the truth, anyone who has faith in me will do what I have been doing. He [*Parakletos*] will do even greater things than these, because I am going to the Father" (John 14:12). The Paraclete as third person of the Godhead teaches nothing other than Christ taught, yet as administrator and fulfiller of Christ's mission He contextually teaches and applies the truth more concretely than Christ's earthly teaching alone (Augustine, *Comm. on John* 72–73, *NPNF* 1 VII, pp. 330–33; A. J. Gordon, *MS*, pp. 53, 54; Tophel, *The Work of the Holy Spirit in Man*, p. 32).

The Tongues at Pentecost and After

The Spirit "came in the form of Tongues because of His close relation to the Word" (Gregory Nazianzen, *Orat.* XLI.11, *NPNF* 2 VII, p. 383). A word in my mind requires a tongue to be spoken. Thoughts without tongues remain unknown. With the distribution of fiery tongues, the Spirit came not in the form of occasional energy, but fully indwelling, coming as God "associating with us, and dwelling in us. For it was fitting that as the Son had lived with us in bodily form— so the Spirit too should appear in bodily form; and that after Christ had returned to His own place, He should have come down to us—*Coming* because He is the Lord; *Sent* because He is not a rival God" (Gregory Nazianzen, *Orat.* XLI.11, *NPNF* 2 VII, p. 383).

Tongues at Pentecost. Those who received the Spirit at Pentecost spoke in the languages of many nations. What happened was not that the visitors in Jerusalem all spoke the same language or babbled meaninglessly. Rather, the Jews gathering from diaspora spoke numerous Gentile languages as an anticipatory indication that the Spirit was intending to make the gospel known to all nations. "All of them were filled with the Holy Spirit and began to speak in other tongues as the Spirit enabled them" (Acts 2:4). There remain broad analogies between what liturgical traditions call Epiphany, Pentecostals call glossolalia, and social liberationists call inclusiveness. However disparate in symbol systems, all coalesce in the core idea of the mission of the Word to the world through the Spirit.

The sounds the apostles heard at the Feast of Weeks were at first foreign to the Aramaic and Greek they spoke. They may have experienced these utterances previously as indiscriminate gibberish. But many present at Pentecost attested hearing God the Spirit speak to them in their own indigenous languages. To the Greeks, the speech of God at Pentecost was in Greek, to Romans in Latin, to local inhabitants in Aramaic (Acts 2:5–12). The persons named among those present at Pentecost (Galileans, Parthians, Medes, Elamites; Mesopotamians, Judeans, Cappadocians, persons from Pontus, Asia, Phrygia, Pamphylia, Egypt, Libya, and Crete) symbolically spanned all known countries in every direction from Jerusalem (Cyril of Jerusalem, *Catech. Lect.* XVII.16, *NPNF* 2 VII, p. 126).

Imagine a gathering of a dozen people from different countries speaking different languages at the same time. It would be difficult to discern anything at all. But what was being experienced by these hearers was understanding in their own language. An awesome consequence is implied: the Word spoken in Christ was now being empowered by the Spirit to be spoken everywhere in every language. It thenceforth became imperative for the remembering, proclaiming community to attest God's own coming in all languages. The Spirit was actively promising to help facilitate this difficult process (Basil, *On the Spirit* I.27, *NPNF* 2 VIII, p. 42; Congar, *IBHS* II, pp. 145 ff.).

None of the languages of Acts 2 were "unknown tongues." Someone knew how to speak each one of those languages. The purpose of this cross-cultural, international gift was to enable the mission of the Son to be realized through the mission of the Spirit, through clear communication of the gospel to the whole world, with its many languages. Each person was hearing the speech of the disciples "in his own native language," whether "Parthians, Medes, Elamites" (Acts 2:8). The reference was not simply to ecstatic utterance without translatable meaning. There is an enormous difference between disconnected speech patterns that have no meaning and the gift of hearing the gospel clearly in one's own native tongue that was reported at Pentecost. Some modern glossolalia implies the former, not the latter. It may be that speaking in tongues at Pentecost simply meant that the Aramaic of the disciples of Galilee was assisted by the Spirit so that Jerusalem visitors of all languages began immediately to understand it. The disciples had no time or opportunity or learning to acquire immediately the capacity to speak in all these languages. The Holy Spirit demonstrated the divine intent to communicate to all in the church's first miracle. Though conceivable as a miracle of hearing, leading exegetes have generally understood it as a miracle of speaking (Gregory Nazianzen, *Orat.* XLI.15, *NPNF* 2 VII, p. 384). Three thousand were saved.

The Road from Jerusalem. The early church quickly went from Jerusalem to the cosmopolitan centers of trade, at major crossroads of humanity, from Antioch to Ephesus to Athens, Corinth, and Rome, to attest this incomparable truth. The church was from the outset composed of many persons speaking different languages. It became an important task for the church to learn quickly to speak and translate into many different languages, otherwise the speech of others would simply sound like gibberish. "The Holy Spirit taught them many languages at once, languages which in all their life they never knew," in sharp contrast with their previous unlearned condition (Cyril of Jerusalem, *Catech. Lect.* XVII.16, *NPNF* 2 VII, p. 128).

In 1 Corinthians 14, Paul placed strong emphasis upon the translation of tongues so that prophetic utterances could be rightly understood, not simply viewed as meaningless utterance. Contemporary worldwide print, broadcast, preaching, and discipling ministries are among the Spirit-enabled modern forms of speaking in the varied tongues of humanity. The King James Version translated the Greek as "unknown tongues," but the term "unknown" is not in the Greek of 1 Corinthians 14:2–19. At Pentecost "the languages peculiar to each nation became common property in the mouth of the church. And therefore from that day the trumpet of the Gospel-preaching has sounded loud; from that day the showers of gracious gifts, the rivers of blessings, have watered every desert" (Leo, *Sermons* LXXV, *NPNF* 2 XII, p. 190).

Beyond Babel: The Renewal of Broken Human Speech.   Classic exegetes loved to contrast Babel and Pentecost (Origen, *On Genesis,* chap. 1; Cyril of Jerusalem, *Catech. Lect.* XVII. 17, *NPNF* 2 VII, p. 128; Gregory Nazianzen, *Orat.* XLI.16; John Chrysostom, *Homily 2 on Pentecost* 2; *MPG* 50, 467): as the idolatry of Babel had resulted in the breaking down of international communication through divine judgment on sin, now the grace of God was reaching out to all nations in the midst of their egocentric incapacity to communicate (John Chrysostom, *Demons Do Not Govern the World, NPNF* 1 IX, pp. 181–83).

Pentecost was an international event signaling that God's peace was not limited exclusively to the Jews but that God was pouring out his own Spirit upon all flesh, as long ago promised (Joel 2:28). The Spirit of God speaks all languages (Augustine, sermons 267, 268, 269, *MPL* 38, 1225–57; John Chrysostom, *Homily 35 on First Corinthians, MPG* 61, 296), hence "supersedes the divisiveness of Babel" (*Doc. Vat. II, Mis.* 4).

Classic exegetes viewed the fall of language as an expression of the fall of humanity (Gen. 11:5–9; Ps. 55:9–11; James 3:5–8; John Chrysostom, *Hom. on Gen.* 30, *FC* 82, pp. 220–36). If one thinks of what the world might have been like if wholly unstained by sin, language would be used only to attest truth. Language in the innocent state of original righteousness would display complete accord between God's own Spirit and the human spirit. Under the conditions of the history of sin, however, language became Babel—distorted, deceptive, misshapen, skewed. When the heart is self-deceived, language cannot bring truth to accurate expression (Calvin, *Comm.* I, pp. 320–39).

God is not content to allow sin to have the last word. Pentecost restores the congruence of human speech with the divine address. Pentecost is anticipative of the end time, when all human speech will finally be redeemed and brought back to unblemished truth in the celestial community. In the midst of the babbling of the nations of the world, divided and conquered by sin, the Holy Spirit at Pentecost comes to unite all humanity by making all human languages congruent with God's address (Calvin, *Comm.* XVIII, pp. 77 ff.; Kuyper, *WHS,* pp. 136–38).

One may think without a tongue but not speak. *Logos* (word, thought) is attested only by means of *glōssa* (tongue). The tongue gives the mind a palpable means of expression. Without a tongue one cannot speak one's mind. The coming renewal of broken human language is a dramatic expression of the Spirit's overarching mission of human renewal (Phil. 2:11; Rev. 5:9–13; Augustine, *Narration on Psalm 54* 11, *MPL* 36, 636; Sermon 271; Gregory the Great, *Homily on the Gospels,* bk. 2, hom. 30, 4, *MPL* 76, 1222.

The Grace of Baptism Requires Speaking All the World's Languages.   The gift of tongues at Pentecost assumes the baptism of the Spirit. When filled with the Spirit they spoke in all languages. The context was freighted with a special need for assurance of the truth of the gospel and the power to attest it. Later, in the conversion of the Gentile Cornelius, Peter said, "As I began to speak, the Holy Spirit came on them as he had come on us at the beginning. Then I remembered what the Lord had said, 'John baptized with water, but you will be baptized with the Holy Spirit'" (Acts 11:15, 16). The implication was not that baptism must be inevitably connected with ecstatic utterance, but that the special ministry of the Spirit was present to point the emergent church toward the Gentile world, the world of many tongues, to proclaim the gospel to all nations in all languages (Cyril of Jerusalem, *Catech. Lect.* XVII.14, *NPNF* 2 VII, p. 127).

Speaking in Tongues Not Confined to Pentecost.   Does spirit-filled utterance enabling all linguistic groups to hear the word remain a distinguishing mark of the church today? Jesus had indicated to the disciples in the Markan epilogue that they would "speak in new tongues" (Mark 16:17), in varied languages. Among the gifts of the Spirit in Paul's view was the gift of "speaking in different kinds of tongues" (*heterō gene glossōn*) and to others "the interpretation of tongues" (1 Cor. 12:10). This need not mean exclusively ecstatic or unknown utterance but may also refer to proclaiming the gospel in other known human languages.

At Pentecost the tongues were apparently intelligible to many of different native languages. After Pentecost these utterances were understood only by some, perhaps only a few, and needed *hermēneia*, "interpretation," a process that itself was a gift of the Spirit (1 Cor. 12:10). The miracle of Pentecost pointed the way toward the laborious and practical task ahead for the church: to learn the world's languages.

Paul did not hesitate to remind his hearers that he had spoken "in tongues more than all of you" (1 Cor. 14:18). He then qualified this by warning that "in the church I would rather speak five intelligible words to instruct others than ten thousand in a tongue" (1 Cor. 14:19). Shortly thereafter Paul would warn the great international Christian community at Corinth of abuses of this gift: "If anyone speaks in a tongue, two—or at the most three—should speak, one at a time, and someone must interpret. If there is no interpreter, the speaker should keep quiet in the church and speak to himself and God" (1 Cor. 14:27, 28). Isaiah had earlier warned against "spiritists, who whisper and mutter" (Isa. 8:19). The Spirit wishes to communicate accurately God's merciful will to save. "Tongues, then, are a sign, not for believers but for unbelievers" (1 Cor. 14:22), namely, the Gentiles with their many languages, awaiting the plausible declaration of the Word of life.

Aware that the first Pentecost had taken place quite near the very spot he was preaching, Cyril reminded his hearers that it is not only "in our time have multitudes of strangers first begun to assemble here from all quarters, but they have done so since that time" (Cyril of Jerusalem, *Catech. Lect.* XVII.18, *NPNF* 2 VII,

p. 128). For this reason, not a frivolous one, Jerusalem is called "mother of cities," for from there the good news would go out to all the world (Cyril of Jerusalem, *Catech. Lect.* XVIII.34, *NPNF* 2 VII, p. 142).

Pentecost and Corinth Contrasted.   With Jerusalem's tongues of Pentecost, the Spirit was offering gifts that granted understanding, resolved confusions, and reordered lives. With Corinth's tongues, the pattern at times reverted to sounding more like Babel; tongues became a serious pastoral problem for Paul, who admonished that "everything should be done in a fitting and orderly way" (1 Cor. 14:40).

Paul did not forbid the Corinthians to speak in tongues but reminded them that there are greater gifts, the more excellent way of faith, hope, and love (1 Cor. 13). If one speaks in tongues without love it sounds merely like "a resounding gong or a clanging cymbal" (1 Cor. 13:1).

It appears that many in Corinth were speaking in tongues at the same time with no understanding or upbuilding occurring (1 Cor. 14:2, 6, 14). If "everyone speaks in tongues, and some who do not understand or some unbelievers come in, will they not say you are out of your mind?" (1 Cor. 14:23).

Discerning the Spirits

Whether Tongues Are a Sign of Spiritual Fullness.   Modern advocates of glossolalia argue that the gift of ecstatic utterance is nowhere forbidden, and far from censuring it, Paul quarrels only with perversions of it, not with its proper use, noting, "I thank God that I speak in tongues more than all of you" (1 Cor. 14:18), and urging the faithful to "eagerly desire spiritual gifts" (1 Cor. 14:1).

Opponents of glossolalia argue that the original purpose of speaking in tongues was to attest the outpouring of the Spirit at the first Pentecost, and that purpose having been fulfilled, there is now little further purpose for this gift. The gift of ecstatic utterance seems to have been only rarely (not normatively) given during the two millennia of the church's history. It is not self-evident that all who think they have received this gift have actually received it.

If the Spirit freely and sovereignly bestows *charismata* of the Spirit, then it is not fitting for recipients to set their hearts upon receiving particular special gifts. Rather, they do well to receive gratefully whatever the Spirit offers (1 Cor. 12:11). We are commanded to be filled with the Holy Spirit (Eph. 5:18), not to seek to acquire particular gifts (Origen, *De Principii* I.3, *ANF* IV, pp. 254–55).

It seems a telling hint that the fiery tongues were portrayed in early Christian art and exegesis as located not in the mouth but crowning the head, as if "spiritual diadems," reminiscent of the fiery swords of paradise: "A fiery sword barred of old the gates of Paradise; a fiery tongue which brought salvation restored the gift" (Cyril of Jerusalem, *Catech. Lect.* XVII.15, *NPNF* 2 VII, p. 128). By this means the Spirit was teaching "truths which cannot be uttered in words"(Origen, *De Principii* II.7, *ANF* IV, p. 285; 2 Cor. 12:4). "The tongues were *cloven* [divided], because of the diversity of Gifts; and they *sat* to signify His Royalty and Rest among the saints," and the tongues *came down* to us that we might go up to Him (Gregory Nazianzen, *Orat.* XLI.12, *NPNF* 2 VII, p. 383, italics added).

On Testing the Spirits to See Whether They Are of God.   The apostles were aware that false claims would be made concerning the Spirit: "The Spirit clearly says that in later times some will abandon the faith and follow deceiving spirits and things taught by demons" (1 Tim. 4:1). We are specifically warned by the apostles not to "believe every spirit, but test the spirits to see whether they are from God, because many false prophets have gone out into the world. This is how you can recognize the Spirit of God: Every spirit that acknowledges that Jesus Christ has come in the flesh is from God, but every spirit that does not acknowledge Jesus is not from God" (1 John 4:1–3). It is necessary to test the spirits by checking all claims against the prophetic and apostolic history of God's own self-disclosure. Hence the maxim "To the law and to the testimony! If they do not speak according to this word, they have no light of dawn" (Isa. 8:19, 20).

The revealed Word of God as consensually and canonically received by this transgenerational community thus becomes the trustworthy standard by which divers spirits can be tested. Anyone may make a reasonable test of the claims of the competing "spirits" to see if they are of God by examining whether they are consistent with what is historically and reliably known of the revealed God. God the Spirit is always meeting us in a new way, yet always in continuity with the ways in which the triune God has already become self-revealed in the histories of Israel, Jesus, and the church.

Of the apostles at Pentecost it was said, "Some, however, made fun of them, and said, 'They have had too much wine'" (Acts 2:13). Cyril astutely commented, "They spoke truly, though in mockery," for they were filled with the new wine from the spiritual Vine. Before Pentecost, attentive souls only occasionally partook of the Spirit, but now "they were baptized completely" in the Spirit, in a "sober drunkenness, deadly to sin and life-giving to the heart" (Cyril of Jerusalem, *Catech. Lect.* XVII.18, 19, *NPNF* 2 VII, p. 128).

The Continuing Need for Discernment.   The Spirit assists in this discernment process. "God is not the author of confusion, but of peace" (1 Cor. 14:33, KJV). "We are witnesses of these things, and so is the Holy Spirit, whom God has given to those who obey" (Acts 5:32). Meanwhile the Adversary continues to disguise every genuine good, offering lesser goods as if better, and evil as good. Hence Jesus warned, "Watch out that no one deceives you. For many will come in my name" (Matt. 24:4, 5). "For false Christs and false prophets will appear and perform great signs and miracles to deceive even the elect—if that were possible. See, I have told you ahead of time" (Matt. 24:24). "For such men are false apostles, deceitful workmen, masquerading as apostles of Christ. And no wonder, for Satan himself masquerades as an angel of light" (2 Cor. 11:13, 14).

Spirit as Author of Scripture

"All Scripture is God-breathed [*theopnuestos*] and is useful for teaching, rebuking, correcting and training in righteousness, so that the man of God may be thoroughly equipped for every good work" (2 Tim. 3:16, 17; Theophilus, *To Autolycus* II.22.9; III.11–14; Irenaeus, *Ag. Her.* III.16.2, 9). Scripture is breathed out by God, the product of God's Word or speech, as breathing is intrinsically connected with human speech (Ambrose, *Of the Holy Spirit* III.XIV.112, *NPNF* 2

X, p. 151). Although "inspiration of scripture" is commonly used to describe this doctrine, *theopneustos* focuses upon the simple spiration (breathing) of God's own life into the written word, rather than upon an autonomous process of *in*spiration as if separable from the Speaker-Breather-Inspirer.

God's Own Word Breathed into the Written Word.   The Paraclete is the Spirit of truth, who brings Christ's words to reliable remembrance and bears witness to him (John 14:16, 26; 15:26). The Holy Spirit not only "subsists and lives," but also "speaks and foretells" (Cyril of Jerusalem, *Catech. Lect.* XVII. 33, *NPNF* 2 VII, p. 132).

God the Spirit enabled the revelation that is faithfully remembered in the form of canonical scripture. The list or canon of scriptural texts was repeatedly received consensually as God the Spirit's own address, who bestowed upon the writers the gift of rightly remembering the events through which God became revealed (Athanasius, *Festal Letters* XXXIX, *NPNF* 2 IV, pp. 551–52).

In their original form and language, prior to any possibility of copyist errors or glossings, the canonical scriptures, according to ecumenical teaching, constituted the address of God to humanity enabled by the Holy Spirit working through attentive, reliable attestors. The believing church ecumenically consents to the premise that the Spirit has so reliably protected this recollection and transmission of scripture that no truth essential to salvation has been lost. The account of God's saving action toward humanity is in this way available to be read wherever canonical scripture is rightly recalled, translated, understood, and reappropriated.

Holy Spirit Speaking Through Scripture.   Among the last words of David recorded in 2 Samuel were these: "The Spirit of the Lord spoke through me; his word was on my tongue." The New Testament repeatedly acknowledges God's Spirit as author of Hebrew scripture. Jesus regarded Psalm 110 as written by David but given by the Spirit (Matt. 22:43). Peter assumed that Psalm 2 had been spoken "by the Holy Spirit through the mouth of our father David" (Acts 4:25; cf. 1:16).

Paul told the Jewish leaders of Rome that "the Holy Spirit spoke the truth to your forefathers when he said through Isaiah the prophet" that they were prone to be "ever hearing but never understanding" (Acts 28:25, 26; Isa. 6:9, 10). When the author of Hebrews quoted Psalm 95:7–11, he did not hesitate to say, "So, as the Holy Spirit says" (Heb. 3:7; cf. 10:15, 16).

Theandric Analogy to the Authorship of God the Spirit Through Human Writers. The theandric analogy (see *WL*, pp. 165 ff.) was cautiously applied by classic exegetes to thinking about the address of scripture. Just as Jesus Christ was truly human and truly God, so the address of God the Spirit in scripture is truly human—in the sense that it is "fleshed out" in human language, in a historical setting by actual persons living finite lives—without ceasing to be truly God's own Word that abides forever (Rom. 1:3, 4; 8:3; 2 Cor. 2:8; Phil. 2:2–8).

God the Spirit is viewed by the consensual tradition as author of scripture (Origen, *Ag. Celsus* 5:60; Basil, *Hom. on Ps. 1*). The authors wrote or spoke as moved by God's own Spirit. Their consciousness, peculiarities of language, personalities, and psyches became fittingly adapted instruments of the divine address (Calvin, *Inst.* 4.8.5–9).

This does not imply that these finite writers were suddenly made morally infallible, or that they were geniuses or possessed extrasensory or paranormal powers. The Spirit did, however, find their particular psyches, their intelligence, their language, their social location, their historical placement, useful to the divine plan and purpose, and spoke through them to and for all.

Nor does this necessarily imply that the writers themselves always understood fully the import of their own writings. Daniel specifically articulated this ambiguity when he, "exhausted" and "ill," wrote of his vision recorded in scripture: "I was appalled by the vision; it was beyond understanding" (Dan. 8:27). It was while Balaam was intending to curse Israel that he was inadvertently led by the Spirit to offer Israel a beautiful blessing (Num. 22–24). Even Balaam's ass became a useful means for the divine address (Num. 22:28).

"For prophecy never had its origin in the will of man, but men spoke from God as they were carried along by the Holy Spirit" (2 Pet. 1:21). Prophecy was not understood by ancient ecumenical exegesis as a product of the human imagination, but of human agency being gloriously transfigured by God's own Spirit, wherein human egocentricity did not interrupt or distort what God sought to communicate.

That the address of God is clothed in the language of a particular writer with a particular style does not diminish the force of the moving Spirit that enables the writing. These sentences remain as truly God's own address as if spoken audibly from Sinai's burning bush.

Theophilus provided an early statement of the doctrine of God-breathed scripture: "Men of God carrying in them a holy spirit and becoming prophets, being inspired and made wise by God, became God-taught," being deemed worthy to become "instruments of God, and contain the wisdom that is from Him," attested accurately what God had been doing before their own time, in their own time, and would yet do in the future (Theophilus, *To Autolycus* II.9, *ANF* II, p. 97).

The Appeal to Christ and the Apostles.   Amid controversy, the precise words of Christ as apostolically attested were the final court of appeal. "Unless I find it in the originals in the gospel, I do not believe, and when I said to them, 'It is written,' they answered me, 'That settles it'" (Ignatius, *Philadelphians* 8.2; cf. *Smyrnaeans* 7.2).

The apostles repeatedly appealed to Christ's own precise words as having binding authority (1 Thess. 4:15; Gal. 6:2; 1 Cor. 7:10–25; Acts 20:35) and often assumed that their readers would regard their own utterances as having similar binding authority insofar as they were consistent with those of the risen Lord (2 Thess. 2:15; 2 Cor. 2:9; 7:15; cf. *Barnabas* 9.9 ff.; Ignatius, *Philadelphians* 7.1). Already by the time of the writing of Second Peter, the letters of Paul were being read, along with the Hebrew Bible, as comparable with "the other scriptures" (*loitas graphas*, 2 Pet. 3:16). The Gospels and epistles were regularly read in services of worship (1 Thess. 5:7; Col. 4:16; James 1:1; 1 Pet. 1:1; Clement of Rome, *Corinth* 47.1; Justin Martyr, *Apology* I.67; Irenaeus, *Ag. Her.* II.27.2; Muratorian Canon). Clement of Rome thought that the communications he had exchanged with the church at Corinth had been "written through the Holy Spirit" (Clement, *Corinth* 63; *SCD* 41, p. 19; Tertullian, *Prescription Ag. Her.* 36, *APT*, p. 486).

Prior to the formal firming up of the apostolic canon, other writings besides the New Testament writings were also being read and highly esteemed, especially

Hermas, Barnabas, Didache, Clement of Rome, which were at times read in public along with the others (Hermas, *Vis.* II.4.3; Dionysius of Corinth and Hegesippus as reported in Eusebius, *CH* IV.23.11). After formal canonization (Council of Carthage III, *SCD* 92, p. 39), these other writings, though revered, were not considered first-generation apostolic testimony.

Whether There Is a Consensual Theory of Inspiration. Though no consistent theory of inspiration of scripture was ecumenically received, certain metaphors recur in the earliest apologetics. Athenagoras spoke of the prophets as elevated to a state of ecstasy wherein the Holy Spirit breathed upon them like a musician might play a flute (*A Plea for the Christians* 7–9, *ANF* II, pp. 132–33). Augustine acknowledged that the writers brought to bear their own memory and imagination and will in the report of revelatory events, yet the Holy Spirit elicited these recollections so as to ensure the accuracy of their reporting, transcription, and reception. He made detailed inquiry into seeming inconsistencies and discrepancies of the Gospel narratives (*Harmony of the Gospels, NPNF* 1 VI, pp. 73 ff.). The commonly received assumption was that the Spirit so guided the writers that without circumventing their human willing, knowing, language, personal temperaments, or any other distinctly personal factors, God's own Word was recalled and transmitted with complete adequacy and sufficiency.

There is never in scripture an attempt rationally to demonstrate the inspiration of scripture, as if rational demonstration might take on more importance than the divine address itself. Rather it is assumed that God the Spirit is acting sufficiently to guarantee the authenticity and adequacy of scripture (John of Damascus, *OF* IV.17, *NPNF* 2 IX, p. 89). Although the scriptures do not provide logical arguments for the proof of their being breathed out by God, they assert and assume this as a premise.

The Conveyance of the Written Word Is Spirit-guided. The same Spirit who calls forth the canon of sacred scripture protects it from distortion and illumines our minds in the reading of it (Origen, *Principles,* preface, *ANF* IV, p. 239). The Spirit gives special gifts to human authorship to guarantee an adequate and sufficiently reliable conveyance of the divine address (John 16:14; John Chrysostom, *Hom. on John* 78, *FC* 41, pp. 338–51).

The Spirit continues to sustain the memory of revelation, to "give you grace to preserve that which he has given you to preach" that you "may set forth that one truth which the Spirit himself has taught you, although with divers voices" (Ecumenical Councils, Ephesus, *Letter of Celestine, NPNF* 2 XIV, p. 221).

Holy Spirit in Holy Writ

The principal role of the Spirit is to make known the Son after his ascension, for "no one can say, 'Jesus is Lord,' except by the Holy Spirit" (1 Cor. 12:3).

Called Out People Under the Norm of Canon. Protestants often argue that "the church did not produce the Scriptures; but the Scriptures gave birth to the church" (Ursinus, *Comm. on Heid. Catech.,* p. 290). That is especially true after the writing of the New Testament, but what of the decades before (A.D. 30–50)?

Anglican, Catholic, and Orthodox writers are correct to argue (in a way that predates form-criticism by centuries) that the remembering church by the power of the Spirit gave birth to scripture. The earliest church delivered the scriptures so that the scriptures could deliver subsequent generations of the church.

The church from its beginnings has been shaped by a received tradition of holy writ. By holy writ we mean first the Hebrew scriptures. Then, as the New Testament became consensually canonized, the church understood itself to stand under the norm of the apostolic proclamation, for apostolicity was the chief criterion of the New Testament canon. Future proclamation must be shaped in correspondence with the testimony of the written Word of Old and New Testaments (Decree of Damasus, Roman Synod, A.D. 382, SCD 84, p. 34). The definition of the commonly received canon is an act of the consenting church, but an act in which the church paradoxically places itself precisely under the authority of the apostolic testimony (Tertullian, *Prescription Ag. Her.* 19–21, ANF III, pp. 251–52; Hilary, *Trin.* IV.14–19, NPNF 2 IX, pp. 75–77). "Sacred Scripture is thus the *norma normans* of the Church's tradition, and the tradition must be seen as the *norma normata*" (Küng, *TC*, p. 16).

"The apostles, like a rich man depositing his money in a bank, delivered into her [the church's] hands in the fullest measure the whole truth. . . . Suppose there arise a dispute relative to some important question among us, should we not have recourse to the most ancient churches with which the apostles held constant intercourse, and learn from them what is certain and clear on the question at issue?" (Irenaeus, *Ag. Her.* III.4.1, *NE,* p. 120).

Historical Revelation Requires a Written Word.   Christianity proclaims a Savior who meets us personally. The saving act of God is an event that occurred through the life and death of Jesus in history. Hence the recollection of the salvation event always has the character of historical and personal recollection. This constant historical reference of faith runs counter to a rationalism that seeks to formulate unhistorical ideas, or a mysticism that wishes to merge self in God (Origen, *OFP*, pp. 29, 116). Both seek timeless truth, not the truth that is personally made known in time through a personal history.

The reason the *ekklēsia* reveres the canonical list of received scriptures today is the same reason they were specified in the early centuries: to preserve accurately the apostolic memory through changing historical circumstances. If revelation occurs in history and calls for continued recollection amid subsequent histories, it cannot proceed safely to transmit this memory without a written word.

Suppose there were no written Word whatever, but only a remembered oral tradition. Wouldn't the hazards of history soon require that such an oral tradition be transmitted carefully in writing? That is precisely what happened in the middle decades of the first century. It was unimaginable that an oral tradition of such worth would remain forever unwritten.

It was precisely while explaining why he was *"writing* these things to you" that the author of the First Letter of John, resisting Gnostic views that the apostolic teaching needed to be supplemented with a higher *gnosis,* said, "The anointing you [already] received from him [the Holy One, v. 20] remains in you, and you do not need anyone [else] to teach you. But as his anointing teaches you about all things and as that anointing is real, not counterfeit—just as it has taught you, remain in him" (1 John 2:26, 27, italics added). John is not rejecting all human teachers, but is rejecting those who would expect new revelations that transcend the anointing, recollecting, and teaching ministry of the Holy Spirit through the remembered and written word.

Signs of Divine Address.   The signs by which the written word is recognized as God's own address are the power of the word to change lives, the moral excellence of its teaching, which could not have been invented by corrupted human reason and imagination, the incomparable once-for-all events to which it testifies, and its "mighty effect" upon hearts, as seen in the fact that "twelve Apostles, taken from among poor and unlearned people, of the lowest class, by this doctrine overcame and subdued to Christ the mighty, the wise, and the rich" (Longer Catech., Eastern Orthodox Church, *COC* II, pp. 454, 455; cf. J. Wesley, *A Clear and Concise Demonstration of the Divine Inspiration of the Holy Scriptures, WJW* XI, p. 484).

Spirit Works Through the Word in the Heart to Persuade

The Spirit both inspires the scripture and convinces the hearer of its truth. The power by which the Word becomes hearable is itself the same power that breathed forth the scriptural testimony (Calvin, *Inst.* 1.9.2; 2.15.2). "The Spirit is the uniter of inner and outer, past and present, written Word and faith's hearing, Christ and ourselves" (Heron, *HS*, p. 106).

If the scriptures were wholly unambiguous and always plain, then Peter would not have written that some of Paul's letters contain some things hard to understand, and there would be no need to follow the Lord's command to search the scriptures, and Paul would have said without reason that God has given the gift of teaching to the church (Conf. of Dositheus, XVIII, *CC*, p. 507).

The Personal Hearing of the Written Word.   The Spirit does not work only objectively or externally through scripture and preaching. The Spirit also works inwardly: in the heart of the unconverted to elicit repentance and faith, and in the heart of the believer to dispense the gifts of the Spirit in faith, hope, and love. In this way the Spirit works to bring the saving grace of the triune God to realization by eliciting full response to the unalloyed message of salvation, the whole counsel of God.

Two steps are implied: the Holy Spirit works in the administration of redemption first to speak *to* the human spirit through scripture and preaching, and then *within* the human spirit to elicit repentance and faith. The Spirit thus works both *externally* in bearing the objective testimony of scripture and preaching and *inwardly* within the hearts of the resistant as well as the faithful. It is through the work of the Spirit that humanity has come to hear of the work of the Son.

Elihu reasoned that "it is the spirit in a man, the breath of the Almighty, that gives him understanding" (Job 32:8). Only the inwardly personal spirit of a man or woman is able to hear the intensely personal disclosure of the Spirit of Yahweh. God's own Spirit enables the human spirit to understand the word itself, and that the word comes from God. As one reads scripture, one gradually comes to the personal awareness that "I have experienced that!" (Zwingli, *Werke*, 1828 German ed., I.79, 81, 389).

Scripture is despised by the intelligentsia for its simplicity. To elitists, "those things which appear humble are considered anile [old-womanish], foolish, and common. So entirely do they regard nothing as true except that which is pleasant to the ear; nothing as credible, except that which can excite pleasure; no one estimates a subject by its truth but by its embellishment" (Lactantius, *DI* V.1, *ANF* VII, p. 136). Such has been the way of the guild scripture scholars. Meanwhile scripture remains its own best interpreter, by means of the analogy of faith (Tertullian, *Ag. Praxeas* 17–21, *ANF* III, pp. 612–15). Simplicity is the first defense of Christian truth (1 Cor. 1:18–21; 3:18–23; Tertullian, *Ag. Valentinians* 3, p. 504–5, *ANF* III, p. 505).

Hearing as Spirit-Enabled. The Author of the divine address helps the hearer to understand the address itself. The Spirit assists hearers to "understand what God has freely given us" (1 Cor. 2:12). Unless the Spirit is active to penetrate our self-deceptions, how could we, trapped in a history of sin, recognize this address? The Spirit works preveniently to make the mind receptive, to enable openness to the divine address, and to prepare the believer to be unafraid of receiving the truth (John of Damascus, *OF* IV.17, *NPNF* 2 IX, p. 89).

This receiving occurs by the internal testimony of the Holy Spirit (*testimonium internum spiritus sancti*), for only God the Spirit can authenticate the Father's own address to the heart (Calvin, *Inst.* 1.7.4). Scripture conveys the living Word of God to us only as the Spirit makes us able to hear (Augustine, *Spirit and Letter* 28–45, *NPNF* 1 V, pp. 95–102). "For the word of God is living and active. Sharper than any double-edged sword, it penetrates even to dividing soul and spirit, joints and marrow; it judges the thoughts and attitudes of the heart" (Heb. 4:12).

It is the Spirit of truth who is Himself the truth (John 14:17; 1 John 5:7). Now we see as if dimly through a mirror. The Holy Spirit works to make the image clearer. Ultimately we will come closer to a more perfect knowledge (1 Cor. 13). Meanwhile, in the growing experience of the worshiping community, "the words of the Lord are flawless, like silver refined in a furnace of clay, purified seven times" (Ps. 12:6).

The Guarding and Reappropriating of This Recollection. The recollection of the saving action of God in Christ could not be carelessly passed along like other memories. It dealt with God's own self-communication through a person. It recollected a series of events that constituted the incomparable salvation event.

This history recollected, however, is never merely past event, but always received as relevant and beneficial in the present, occurring now in the life of the believer, attested by the Spirit through the written Word (Kierkegaard, *TC,* cf. *PF, CUP*).

The Spirit works by writing the image of Christ upon the hearts of the faithful. Hence each one who shares Christ's risen life is like a letter written to all who are daily met: "You are a letter from Christ, the result of our ministry, written not with ink but with the Spirit of the living God, not on tablets of stone but on tablets of human hearts" (2 Cor. 3:2, 3).

The Power of the Word. Wherever this word of scripture is read attentively, it transforms human lives, affects human societies, changes political structures, redeems human fallenness. When Paul left the elders of Ephesus, he committed them "to God and to the word of his grace, which can build you up and give you an inheritance among all those who are sanctified" (Acts 21:32).

The omnipotent God is not lacking in ability to deliver his Word to humanity accurately through the writers of scripture "without waiving their human intelligence, their individuality, their literary style, their personal feelings, or any other human factor" (Walvoord, *HS*, p. 60). "For though we live in the world, we do not wage war as the world does. The weapons we fight with are not the weapons of the world. On the contrary, they have divine power to demolish strongholds. We demolish arguments and every pretension that sets itself up against the knowledge of God, and we take captive every thought to make it obedient to Christ" (2 Cor. 10:4, 5).

The Spirit in Preaching and Sacrament.   The Spirit ensures that the writing and transmission of the apostolic witnesses are sufficiently accurate to deliver the testimony of salvation to subsequent generations. Hence the next generation already has in hand a written testimony to which preaching becomes accountable: an account of the history of salvation sufficient to depend upon, not merely hearsay tales or abstract theories, but historical reports of eyewitnesses. The Spirit works in preaching, seeking to elicit through the preacher's speech an accurate attestation to the salvation event, and in the hearers a sufficiently accurate reception. Both the written and preached word are addressed to the unconverted to awaken their desire for the truth, and to the faithful to bring them into closer personal union with the truth (Calvin, *Inst.* 3.1–2; Barth, *CD* I/1, pp. 51 ff., 88 ff.).

Inward Testimony.   Luther resisted the individualistic notion of a direct, unmediated operation of the Spirit, as if apart from written word, sacrament, and community. As the Son comes in the flesh within the historical continuum of a particular people, so does the Spirit meet us in community through bodily signs, water, poured-out wine, the heard words of preaching, and the written word. The Spirit "has determined to give the inward part to no man except through the outward part" (Luther, *EA* 21.208, 212). "And so Paul preached the Word outwardly to Lydia, a purple-seller among the Philippians; but the Lord inwardly opened the woman's heart" (Second Helvetic Confession, *CC*, p. 134; cf. Acts. 16:14). The Spirit's illumination occurs "with and through the word" (Schmaldcald Articles, cf. Luther, *Babylonian Captivity, MLS*, pp. 265–69; cf. *EA* 14.188).

Through Word and Sacrament the Spirit comes to us and operates within our hearts (*intus operans*, Luther, *EA* 29.108; 9.210) to apply the chief miracle that Christ operates upon the soul—the giving of life. When the word of God goes out in preaching, it does not come back empty (Luther, *WA* 2.112; *EA* 29.208). In doing so, the Spirit does not enlarge or add to the apostolic testimony, but adapts that word to the individual contextually (Athanasius, *Ag. Arians, NPNF* 2 IV, pp. 351–52).

The Spirit assists the community of faith in accurately remembering, rightly interpreting, and practically applying the scripture (John 14:26; 1 Cor. 2:13; 2 Tim. 1:5). This is why the clearest and surest expositions of the scripture are to be found in the community of faith guided by the Spirit and not among individualistic inquirers (Irenaeus, *Ag. Her.* V.26, *ANF* I, pp. 496–97).

Opposite Errors: Overfamiliarity and Skepticism.   Two errors tend to elicit exaggerations in the Christian teaching of the Spirit speaking through the written word. One is an overfamiliarity that leads to fanaticism, the other an excessive skepticism that leads to impotence and indecision.

Some tend to substitute for canonical scripture their own private forms of inspiration. So intent are they upon hearing God's private address to them that they forget or neglect the Spirit's address through apostolic teaching. They imagine that God is speaking to them in specific detail, presuming an extraordinary familiarity with the mind of the Godhead as revealed to them individualistically. So authoritative do they imagine their private inspiration that any suggestion that it might be in any way colored by their own projections is taken as opposed to faith itself. The remedy for privatistic excess lies in listening for the address of the Spirit inwardly in a way that corresponds with the written Word received and celebrated in the historic Christian community (Hilary, *Trin.* I.37, 38, *NPNF* 2 IX, pp. 50–51).

If this error is based upon too gullible a readiness to believe on inadequate grounds, the opposite error is a skepticism that hesitates to receive any creditable testimony at all. Compulsive skepticism is always asking for more evidence, never satisfied with any testimony given, hence remaining blocked from full enjoyment of the assurance of the Spirit. A healthy skepticism is commended that modestly seeks, doggedly asks tough questions, and probes in honest self-examination. But this can come to excess in the persistent habit of setting obstacles of suspicion in the way of otherwise plausible testimony (S. Kierkegaard, *On Self-Examination;* Merrill, *ACE*, pp. 173–89).

We do well to expect neither too much nor too little from the inward witness of the Spirit with our spirits. Each tendency must be judged by its fruits. Aware that some Latin codices of the New Testament had been falsified by heretics, Ambrose appealed to his reader to "look at the Greek codices" (*Of the Holy Spirit* II.V.46, *NPNF* 2 X, p. 120). From intertestamental times, the study of the written word has assumed linguistic and philological skills, if the divine address is to be treated seriously.

Gregory offered a memorable picture of the biblical exegete in his fond description of Athanasius: "From meditating on every book of the Old and New Testament, with a depth such as none else has applied even to one of them, he grew rich in contemplation, rich in splendour of life, combining them in wondrous sort by that golden bond which few can weave; using life as the guide of contemplation, contemplation as the seal of life" (Gregory Nazianzen, *Orat.* XXI.6, *NPNF* 2 VII, p. 271).

PART II

Salvation

Salvation denotes the action of God in delivering humanity. It is the divine work of rescuing sinners.

In the salvation of humanity, God offers the recovery of what unfallen man and woman were originally made capable—daily trusting response to God. By descending to humanity, God has accomplished what human effort could not do in its attempt to ascend to righteousness by moral endeavor. Those willing to hear are being saved *from* sin, despair, and death and saved *for* new life and union with the Son through the Spirit (Acts 16:30–31; Rom. 5:9, 10; Eph. 2:5–8).

3 The Way of Repentance

INTRODUCTION TO THE STUDY OF SALVATION

The Terms of Salvation

The terms of salvation are conditions of the personal appropriation of God's saving action—repentance and faith. They are the simple terms of the earliest Christian preaching: repent and believe.

John the Baptist preached, "Repent, for the kingdom of heaven is near" (Matt. 3:2). Jesus' public ministry commenced with the call to "repent and believe the good news" (Mark 1:15). When the disciples were sent to proclaim the coming kingdom, they preached repentance (Luke 24:47). Peter's first sermon and subsequent apostolic testimony consistently called first for repentance (Acts 2:38; cf. 3:19; 26:17, 18; Cyril of Jerusalem, *Catech. Lect.* II, *NPNF* 2 VII, pp. 7–13; Melanchthon, *Loci, LCC* XIX, pp. 140 ff.).

The Purpose of Preaching.   To make the call to repentance and faith plausible is the perennial task of Christian preaching. When it is neglected, every other aspect of the mission of the church stands imperiled. Preaching that lacks the courage to call hearers to repent is limp and timid. Theology that lacks the capacity for admonition smells of hypocrisy (Ambrose, *Letters* 46, *FC* 26, pp. 233–34).

The purpose of preaching is to draw the hearer caringly toward saving faith in God. That faith can only begin with repentance. It is in the repentance of one sinner that heaven rejoices (Luke 15:10; 13:5). This is not a narrow or dated subject.

There reigns in the broken human heart a feeling of discord, a lack of congruence between who one is and who one ought to be (Augustine, *Conf.* V, *NPNF* 1 I, pp. 79–89). Christian preaching does not circumvent this feeling of incongruence but exposes and addresses it openly. The crushed heart must be empathically felt. The longing for peace, the earnest desire for truth, the penetration of self-deceptions, the hunger for freedom from a life of sin is the direct concern of Christian testimony (Cyprian, *Treatise* X, *ANF* V, p. 491–93). Every resource of rhetoric is employed to make the requirement of God as clear as possible and the eventful love of God as palpable and real (2 Cor. 5:20; Augustine, *Chr. Doctrine* 4, *NPNF* 1 II, pp. 575–76; W. B. Pope, *Compend.* II, pp. 367–76; J. Miley, *ST* II, pp. 100 ff.; N. Burwash, *MCT* II, pp. 227–35).

The Order of the Terms of Salvation.   The characteristic order of the apostolic teaching of the call to salvation is as follows:

Repent
Be baptized
For the remission of sins
Receive the gift of the Holy Spirit

Having initiated the reversal of conversion, the Spirit abides to continue as comforter, guide, witness, to bring every thought captive to the Son, and to bring all our redeemed powers to maturity in all spiritual graces (Cyril of Jerusalem, *Catech. Lect.* II–V, *NPNF* 2 VII, pp. 8–33; S. Merrill, *ACE*, pp. 164–68).

In baptism we come to share in the life that corresponds with Christ who "died for all, that those who live should no longer live for themselves but for him" (2 Cor. 5:15), in whom "you were washed, you were sanctified, you were justified in the name of the Lord Jesus Christ and by the Spirit of our God" (1 Cor. 6:11).

What Is Meant by Being "Saved"?

To be saved is to be delivered from bondage, brought into freedom, rescued from death, given a new lease on life. That which is reclaimed by God's saving action is life—abundant life, eternal life, life in the Spirit (John 5, 6; Rom. 8:1–10; 1 John 5). The technical term *soteriology,* derived from the Greek *sōtēria* (salvation) and *logos* (word), refers to an academic discipline that inquires into God's saving action. The term *conversion,* discussed later, refers to the whole process of reversal in all its components, with special focus upon its early stages. Though *conversion* and *salvation* are in English deeply intermeshing terms, they come from different Latin root words: *convertere* (to turn around, turning toward) and *salvare* (to securely save), from *salvus* (safe, unhurt, sound, healthy).

The Premise of Lostness.   Regrettably the term *salvation* has been cheapened by an extensive history of abuse. To understand what it means to be saved, one must first understand what it means to be lost (*appolu,* Matt. 18:1; Tertullian, *On Chastity* 7–9, *AEG* IV, pp. 125–26).

The metaphor of lostness comes from Jesus himself, who spoke of the lost son, the lost sheep, the lost coin. His parables set forth the power of being found, saved from lostness. A faraway pigsty was not where the prodigal truly belonged. Only when he returned home to the father was he saved. The lost sheep were saved not because they found their own way back but because the shepherd went out and diligently searched for them. The difference between the sheep and the prodigal is that the sheep were passively brought back, but the prodigal had actively to decide to risk coming back home. To be saved, the human person must decide and want to be saved and must respond to the grace that enables one to come home (Luke 15).

Suppose one could imagine a perpetually unfallen humanity. It would require no Savior. Fallen humanity, however, lives out of an actual history of sin. Fallen humanity requires a Savior (the Son) and an Enabler (the Spirit) to make it possible that the Savior be received. No human renewal is possible without a *Sōtēr* (Savior), who makes the atoning work possible, and God's own Spirit, who makes the saving act of the Son appropriable (1 John 4:13–14; Augustine, *Hom. on Epist. of John* VIII, *NPNF* 1 VII, pp. 506–13).

The obstacles being overcome in God's saving action are those "of nature by His incarnation, of sin by His death, and of death by His resurrection" (Nicholas Cabasilas, *Quaestiones ad Thalassium,* 60, *MPG,* 90.621). Through the divine descent to become human, humanity is being raised by the Spirit to enter into union with God, which is "the final end for which the world has been created out of nothing" (Lossky, *MTEC,* p. 136).

The Way of Salvation.   The salvation prepared for the world can only become subjectively appropriated when one repents, trusts in God's pardoning grace, and follows the narrow way. The concern of the study of salvation is the clarification of the steps along this way, problems associated with these steps, and the grace that enables each step (Calvin, *Inst.* 2.6.1, Pope, *Compend.* II, pp. 55 ff.; A. A. Hodge, *OOT,* pp. 338 ff.). The salvation of which Christianity speaks distinguishes it from other religions. No other religious tradition speaks of salvation by a messianic, theandric mediator who died on a cross to save sinners, then rose to intercede for them. In receiving this salvation, humanity is offered an undeserved gift that cannot be earned, purchased, or morally merited. The way of salvation is narrow. The paths are wide and many that lead to ruin (Matt. 7:14).

A Complex Matrix of Doctrinal Loci Integrated

The Hebrew and Greek words for salvation (*yeshuah, teshuah, sōtēria*) convey a complex matrix of meanings: deliverance, rescue, safety, preservation, soundness, restoration, and healing (Pss. 3:8; 51:12; Isa. 51:5–8; Eph. 1:13; 2 Tim. 2:10). The term *salvation* is best not employed in a strictly individualistic sense, for it includes the whole history of God's saving activity and the history of human reception of it. The code question, Are you saved? is an intense personalizing of the question of salvation that may inadvertently tend to neglect the broader scope of salvation history (Luke 1:69; Rom. 13:11; 1 Pet. 1:1–10).

Salvation Teaching Summarized.   Salvation teaching may be broadly summarized as follows: In the justifying work of the Son, the obstacles to divine-human reconciliation are overcome. In the Spirit's regeneration of new life, grace to live by faith is actually being imparted and received (Luke 3:6; 2 Cor. 5:2).

This means: The Father fulfilled his saving purpose by sending his only Son to save sinners, to inaugurate the Reign of God through his birth, life, teaching, ministry, death, resurrection, ascension, and heavenly intercession. The events of Jesus' last days of earthly ministry constituted the accomplished salvation occurrence. In the term *salvation,* the New Testament referred to the totality of this event in all its component aspects and sequences and to the consequences emerging out of Jesus' person and work and to God's sending of the Spirit to create the new Israel to proclaim this salvation worldwide (Acts 16:17; Hunter, *Introducing New Testament Theology.* Philadelphia: Westminster, 1978, p. 9).

Luther's *Large Catechism* nailed down this connection: "Neither you nor I could ever know anything of Christ, or believe in him and take him as our Lord, unless these were first offered to us and bestowed on our hearts through the preaching of the Gospel by the Holy Spirit. . . . In order that this treasure might not be buried but put to use and enjoyed, God has caused the Word to be published and proclaimed, in which he has given the Holy Spirit to offer and apply to us this treasure of salvation. Therefore to sanctify is nothing else than to bring us to the Lord Christ to receive this blessing, which we could not obtain by ourselves" (Third Article, *TGS,* p. 169).

Salvation as Pivotal, Cohering Theme of Scripture.   Salvation is one of the most comprehensive terms of Christian teaching, gathering into a single word-picture a broad range of theological loci crucial to the Christian life: redemption, reconciliation, atonement, propitiation, predestination, calling, covenant, grace, conviction, repentance, forgiveness, justification, adoption, faith, conversion, regeneration, sanctification, and perseverance (*TDNT, sōtēria*).

Suppose we strike *salvation* from the Christian vocabulary in a reactionary attempt to curb abuses of the way it has been taught. Then we must begin searching anew for terms of proximately analogous meaning—*liberation, ego strength, freedom, revolution, the overcoming of estrangement*—none of which are precise equivalents, though each may enrich the vocabulary of salvation. It is difficult even to say what Christianity is without using the term *salvation* (*sōtēria*) and its cognates (save, *yasha, sōzō,* Savior, *sōtēr;* Calvin, *Inst.,* 3.14–18).

Admittedly, these same verbs (*save, rescue, preserve, restore*) all are used to freight nonreligious meanings. One may save a pizza slice or rescue a lost computer file or preserve a political party or restore a painting. Though the English noun *salvation* may have numerous nonreligious uses, these tend to be derived by analogy from religious uses (*TDNT; OED; WNUUD*).

Defining Soteriology in Relation with Companion Systematic Disciplines.   The study of salvation embraces the dynamics of *sōtēria* based on the person of the *Sōtēr*—what the theandric person did and suffered as applied by the Holy Spirit to the hearts of believers. Soteriology is a bridge discipline between the study of the Son and of the Spirit, between justification and sanctification, between God for us and God in us. Whereas the work of the Son inquires into those texts that set forth who Christ is, the work of the Spirit inquires into those texts that show how the eternal purpose of God is being inwardly appropriated through a succession of events—creation, fall, call, exile, redemption—grounded in the history of Israel, fulfilled in Christ, shared in by the church, and brought finally to full consummation in and beyond history (Tho. Aq., *ST* III, Q1 ff., II, pp. 2025 ff.).

*Soter*iology (Savior study) is not finally reducible to *anthropo*logy (which studies the humanity rescued by God's action). Anthropological reductionism (as seen in L. Feuerbach, S. Freud, F. Buri, H. Braun) assumes that theology is anthropology writ large, and that all talk of God's action finally amounts merely to references to human action (Feuerbach, *The Essence of Christianity,* chap. 2). Soteriology is not bereft of a subject (*soter*).

The Work of Application.   The *application* of the work of the Son is accomplished through Spirit. The Son merits our salvation; the Spirit applies the redeeming work to our temporal lives. What is accomplished for us in Christ remains to be embodied in us through the Spirit (Rom. 8; Gal. 3:1–5).

The special mission of the Spirit is to make real the fruits and benefits of Christ in believers. God the Son has already done the saving mediatorial work. God the Spirit is now enabling that saving work to be appropriated in human community. Salvation is brought to full effect "not by might nor by power, but by my Spirit, says the Lord Almighty" (Zech. 4:6). It is the Spirit's work fittingly to mature and complete the process of salvation, to bring to serviceable application and reception the work of the Son on the cross for our justification (Gal. 5:16–26).

The mission of God, anticipated in prophecy and embodied in God's own incarnate coming, does not come to an immediate completion on the cross, but continues and extends palpably after Christ's resurrection and ascension: "Up to that time the Spirit had not been given, since Jesus had not yet been glorified" (John 7:39). While the work of the Son continues in intercession with the Father, the work of the Spirit continues in the church and world through common grace, preaching, sacraments, prayer, and conscience (Cyril of Jerusalem, *Catech. Lect.* XIV–XVIII, *NPNF* 2 VII, pp. 115–44).

Ministries of the Spirit in Personal Salvation

The work of the Spirit in administering personal redemption is seen in a sequence of stages.

The Sequential Elements of Personal Salvation Teaching. The Spirit works to restrain, convict, regenerate, indwell, baptize, seal, and fill (Owen, *Works,* vol. 4, bk. VIII, pp. 352 ff.; Chafer, *ST* VI, p. 103). The study of salvation seeks to grasp the sequence of these outworkings as received by consensual exegetes. The familiar sequence is as follows:

- The restraint of sin, by which the Spirit provides time for repentance
- The conviction of sin, by which Spirit awakens the sinner to the awareness of sin
- Repentance, by which the Spirit leads the penitent to godly sorrow for sin, reform of behavior, reparation for harm done to others, revulsion against sin, and confession of sin
- Faith, by which the Spirit enables one to place personal trust in the Savior
- Regeneration, by which the Spirit quickens life spiritually so as to begin a new life born of God, born by adoption into the family of God
- The indwelling of the Spirit, by which the Spirit comes to reside in the heart of the believer
- Baptism of the Spirit, by which the new person becomes dead to the old way and alive to the new
- The sealing of the Holy Spirit, by which the Spirit confirms the living Word in the heart
- Assurance, by which the Holy Spirit witnesses inwardly to the spirit of the believer that he or she is a son or daughter of God, pardoned and adopted, enabling a firm conviction that the believer is reconciled to God
- The filling of the believer by the Holy Spirit, by which the Spirit comes more and more fully to express the way of holiness in the life of the believer
- Sanctification, by which the Spirit works to bring the regenerate spirit into full participation in the life of God through union with Christ

The Overarching Order of Salvation. The varied ministries of the Spirit were astutely summarized by Basil: "Through the Holy Spirit comes our restoration to paradise, our ascension into the kingdom of heaven, our return to the adoption of sons, our liberty to call God our Father, our being made partakers of the grace of Christ, our being called children of light, our sharing in eternal glory, and, in a word, our being brought into a state of all 'fullness of blessing'" (*On the Holy Spirit* 15.36, *NPNF* 2 VIII, p. 22).

Similarly Ambrose argued that the Spirit moves from the providential ordering of life to the saving work of redemption, "from the grace of giving life to that of sanctification, to translate us from earth to heaven, from wretchedness to glory, from slavery to a kingdom" (*Of the Holy Spirit* I.XI.122, *NPNF* 2 X, p. 109).

Gradually these points came under more deliberate discussion under the topic of soteriology arranged as an order of salvation (*ordo salutis*). The Anglican order of salvation held that the faithful "through Grace obey the calling; they be justified freely; they be made sons of God by adoption; they be made like the image of his only begotten Son Jesus Christ; they walk religiously in good works, and at length, by God's mercy, they attain to everlasting felicity" (Thirty-nine Articles, XVII, *CC*, p. 272). The Lutheran order is similar: "The Holy Spirit has called me through the Gospel, enlightened me with his gifts, and sanctified and preserved me in the true faith, just as he calls, gathers, enlightens, and sanctifies the whole Christian church on earth and preserves it in union with Jesus Christ in the one true faith" (Luther, *Small Catech.*, creed, art. III, *CC*, p. 116). In sum, "The office of the Holy Spirit may be said to embrace the following: to instruct, to regenerate, to unite to Christ and God, to rule, to comfort and strengthen us" (Ursinus, *Comm. Heid. Catech.*, p. 277).

Each stage is premised upon God's justifying grace in Jesus Christ. Through these ministries the Spirit wishes to draw and persuade, not force, the human will; to convince, not coerce, in order to enable the deepest possible experience of God's saving action. God is not willing that any should perish but that all should willingly come to repentance (2 Pet. 3:9). The sinner is not compelled to come to grace but offered grace as a gift to be received (Augustine, *On Nature and Grace* 81–84, *NPNF* 1 V, pp. 149–51; A. Clarke, *CT*, pp. 149–81; N. Burwash, *MCT* II, pp. 200–211; W. Tillett, *PS*, pp. 125–40; D. Whedon, *ERD*, pp. 109–45).

Past, Present, and Future Salvation

Salvation is gradually being received through a linear progression of historic events. Jesus had promised that the kingdom would come gradually: "first the stalk, then the head, then the full kernel in the head" (Mark 4:28). The converting-saving grace of God is often found to work especially in crisis moments of personal reversal, which are then followed by a continuing work of grace that develops over time. We have been saved from the penalty of sin in justification; we are being saved from the power of sin in sanctification; and we shall be saved finally from the presence of sin in glorification.

Having Been Saved.   Salvation is not merely an abstract idea but an actual series of historical events. If salvation were merely an idea in our minds and never an event, it is doubtful that it would be significant enough to become a subject of study. Hence, to understand the salvation of humanity, we must think eventfully and historically of what God is doing in the real world. Salvation includes the whole range of the divine activity on behalf of humanity in past, present, and future history. The Greek verb *to save* (*sōzō*) may be used in a punctiliar or durative sense, as a point in time, or as duration in time, or as a series of overlapping processes, or as a continuous process with distinguishable components (*TDNT, sōzō;* Erickson, *CT* 3, p. 889).

The worshiping community speaks in the past tense of God's saving activity as having already pardoned sinners, cleansed them from sin, justified them by grace, and freed them for a life of accountable love. Salvation in this sense has already occurred, and is understood as a finished work in Christ on the cross (Eph. 2:1–10).

Present Salvation.   At the same time the worshiping community is aware that God the Spirit is acting in the present to bind up the demonic powers, currently forgiving sin, now raising the dead, and cleansing from corruption (Rom. 6; Gal. 2:20). When Paul spoke of believers being "sealed for the day of redemption" (Eph. 4:30), he was looking toward a coming consummation of a redemption that was already being experienced in the present in an anticipative way, grounded in a past event of redemption, the cross. "For he has rescued us from the dominion of darkness and brought us into the kingdom of the Son he loves, in whom we have redemption, the forgiveness of sins" (Col. 1:14).

The tenses flow together when those who already "have the first fruits of the Spirit" wait eagerly for their adoption as sons and daughters, for "the redemption of their bodies," while the whole of creation still is groaning for redemption (Rom. 8:23). All that needs to be done from God's side for divine-human reconciliation has already occurred on the cross, awaiting our responsive action, to be fittingly brought to consummation by the work of the Spirit.

This deliverance has come to a vast cloud of individual believers amid and through their own specific developing personal histories. Each autobiography could be told as a personal narrative. This focus on personal testimony became the hallmark of piety both Catholic (Augustine, *Conf.;* Teresa of Avila, *Life;* Thérèse of Lisieux, *Story of a Soul)* and Protestant (J. Edwards, *Faithful Narrative;* Wesley, *Journals;* Phoebe Palmer, *The Way of Holiness*).

The Coming Salvation.   The *ekklēsia* is looking toward a consummation of God's saving activity at the end of history. God's design to save humanity includes all time, not just part of history. The fulfillment of God's purpose in creation is awaiting a final consummation in the end of days (1 Pet. 1:3–5; 1 John 3:1–3).

In some key salvation texts all three tenses interfuse: "For the grace of God *has appeared* [past tense], bringing salvation to all, training us to renounce impiety and worldly passions, and in the *present* age to live lives that are self-controlled, upright, and godly, while we *wait for* the blessed [future] hope" (Titus 2:11, 12, NRSV, italics added; Luther, *LW* 29, pp. 64–67). Paul wrote to the Philippians that he was confident that God "who began a good work in you will carry it on to completion until the day of Christ Jesus" (Phil. 1:6).

THE NARROW WAY OF REPENTANCE

Repentance remains a central Christian teaching "to be preached by every minister" (Westminster Conf. XV, *CC,* p. 209). From the outset it has been regarded among "the elementary teachings about Christ" (Heb. 6:1). Repentance is a grace of the Holy Spirit that puts one's feet on the way to the mercy of Christ. It is a work of preaching: "Come hither to me, He says to Daniel; young though thou be, convict old men infected with the sins of youth" (Cyril of Jerusalem, *Catech. Lect.* XVI.27–31, *NPNF* 2 VII, pp. 122, 123).

The narrow way to salvation must begin with repentance: "Godly sorrow brings repentance that leads to salvation" (2 Cor. 7:10). Narrow (compressed, *thlibō*) is the way that leads to life (Matt. 7:14; Clement of Rome, *Corinth* 7:1–8.5; Newman, *PPS* VII, p. 115; Kierkegaard, *TC; CDisc*).

The Nature of Repentance

True contrition cannot be feigned. Nor can it lack the intent to forsake sin altogether.

Defining Repentance.   Though the English word *repentance* carries the nuance of sorrow for what one has done, it does not adequately imply reformation of character; hence it is a less powerful term than the Greek *metanoia,* which implies a fundamental behavioral reversal (Matt. 3:8; Acts 26:20; Heb. 6:1, 6; Tertullian, *On Repentance, ANF* III, pp. 657–66; Calvin, *Inst.* 3.3.5). *Metanoia* denotes a radical change of mind and heart followed by a behavioral reformation of a sinful life, a sorrowing for sin so as to forsake sin altogether. Repentance is a "coming to oneself" (Luke 15:10), a voluntary change of mind, heart, and will of the sinner in turning away from sin (Clement of Alexandria, *Who Is the Rich Man That Shall Be Saved?* XXXIX, *ANF* II, p. 602; Beyschlag, *NTT* I, pp. 282–87). Genuine repentance occurs only when one earnestly calls to mind one's own misdeeds so as to elicit profound sorrow for sin so as to renounce and forsake sin (Fletcher, *Works* III, pp. 112–31; Watson, *TI* II, ch. 19; Tillett, *PS*, pp. 155–74). "By repentance I mean conviction of sin, producing real desires and sincere resolutions of amendment" (J. Wesley, *WJWB*, sermon 7, *WJW* V, p. 76; *Wesleyan Methodist Catech.;* Field, *HCT*, p. 13; A. A. Hodge, *OOT*, pp. 487–95). Repentance assumes a full commitment of heart and mind to the mortification of those sins that so easily beset us, and to the Spirit's vivification of a new life (Calvin, *Inst.* 3.3.8). Lacking deep hunger for a fundamental change of life, mind, heart, self-understanding, and behavior, a surface repentance only becomes a new temptation to hypocrisy. Repentance is incomplete or insincere that does not resolve to lead a new life (2 Cor. 7:10; A. H. Strong, *ST*, p. 462).

Repentance Distinguished from Loss of Ego Strength.   Repentance does not ask for false humility, but for true and accurate recollection of misdeeds (Goodwin, *Works,* VI, pp. 359–89). It does not suggest loss of appropriate self-esteem but rather requires a higher valuing of oneself by becoming radically honest before God so as to put one's feet on the way (pp. 489–97). It does not imply a diminishing of personal identity but an honoring and clarifying of one's personal identity through candid self-confrontation (Ephraim Syrus, *Nisibene Hymns, NPNF* 2 XIII, pp. 170–71).

In repentance one not only loathes one's own guilt *intra*personally, but does so in the personal presence of the holy, merciful God, hence *inter*personally, and in corporate worship, and in meeting with the neighbor. Repentance includes both contrition and reformation—not only a genuine sorrow for sin, but also a desire to make reparation for sin to counteract the consequences of our previous decisions so as to show forth fruits fitting to repentance (Luke 19:8; Cyprian, *The Lapsed, ACW* 25, pp. 24–26). As an act of penitence, Fabiola (d. 399) "founded a hospital, into which she might gather sufferers out of the streets, and where she might nurse the unfortunate victims of sickness and want" (Jerome, *Letters* 77.6, *CCC,* p. 183).

Mind, Heart, and Will Join in Repentance.   Repentance requires a decisive reversal of the previous sin-laden course of *mind, heart,* and *will.*

Repentance requires moral reasoning enabled by prevening grace to penetrate self-deceptions and attend realistically to the claims of conscience (H. R. Niebuhr, "On Faith in God," *RMWC*). Penitential reasoning focuses nonevasively upon the sinner's actual condition in relation to the holiness of God (John Chrysostom, *Baptismal Instructions, ACW* 31, pp. 126–27, 286–88). The requirement of God as illumined by scripture and tradition becomes more intensely experienced as one compares God's justice and love with one's own personal implication in social sin (Calvin, *Inst.* 3.4.17–18; 4.17). The reversal does not occur without first a *change of mind,* a revised conception of oneself, utilizing one's own best moral reasoning to recognize the intolerable cost of sin.

Where the reversal touches the mind, but not the heart and will, the despair of sin deepens. Repentance requires a *change of heart,* a deep sorrowing for sin, aware that sin, whether personal or social, is at heart sin against God (Ps. 51:4). Far more than a mode of analytical reasoning, repentance is a deeply felt remorse and emotively experienced regret over wrongs done voluntarily against others, offending one's own integrity and dignity and finally offending God. There is a deeply emotive aspect in true penitence, a grieving over one's alienated self and broken relationships, a loathing of sin and godly sorrow for irresponsibility, a heavy feeling of condemnation that intends to have a constructive effect by changing character and habit (Rom. 7; Second Clement 9.8; J. Wesley *WJWB* I, sermon 9; *WJW* V, pp. 98–111).

Repentance requires a *change of will,* a redirected disposition to seek a new life of forgiveness and grateful responsibility. This change is not fully accounted for as an act of knowing or feeling. It is a grace-enabled act of willing, a determination to turn the whole self around. Having recognized and grieved over his sin, David prayed, "Restore to me the joy of your salvation and grant me a willing spirit, to sustain me" (Ps. 51:12, 13; Luther, *LW* 12, pp. 382–84). The change of mind and heart makes way for a volitional change of behavior reaching habitually into the depths of moral character. The inward feeling of remorse moves toward outward acts of turning away from the life of sin (Apostolic Constitutions II.22–24, *ANF* VII, pp. 406–8).

The Dynamics of Repentance

The deeper purpose of the Spirit's work in and through conscience is not merely to accuse or excuse behavior by attesting moral wrong or right within but to bring the human spirit back into an originally congruent relation of trust in God by leading through repentance to faith (Rom. 2:15; 1 Cor. 8:7–12; 1 Pet. 3:16, 21).

Before God.   Psalm 51 is traditionally understood as a penitential prayer after David had committed adultery with Bathsheba and had been confronted with his sin by the prophet Nathan. He prayed for mercy: "According to your great compassion, blot out my transgressions. Wash away all my iniquity and cleanse me from my sin" (Ps. 51:1, 2). Unrepented sin only intensifies the syndrome of guilty recollection: "For I know my transgressions, and my sin is always before me." (Ps. 51:3). Only one thing is needful: "Surely you desire truth in the inner parts; you teach me wisdom in the inmost place" (Ps. 51:6). "Cleanse me with hyssop, and I will be clean; wash me, and I will be whiter than snow" (v. 7). "Hide your face from my sins and blot out all my iniquity. Create in me a pure heart, O God, and renew a steadfast spirit within me" (Ps. 51:9, 10; Luther, *LW* 12, pp. 303–84).

Sin, whether against neighbor or commonweal, finally must be understood in God's presence. "Against you, you only, have I sinned and done what is evil in your sight" (Ps. 51:4). Why is one guilty before God because of a wrong done to another human being? Because God has given the freedom that one has abused. It is finally to God that abused freedom experiences itself as responsible (Calvin, *Comm.* V, pp. 281–99; S. Kierkegaard, *Stages on Life's Way*). Though conscience teaches that something is wrong, it also points transcendently to God as source of moral accountability. Conscience functions not only in relation to society or neighbor or oneself but ultimately in relation to the Giver of life (Jer. 3:11–13; Rom. 2:15).

The Grace of Repentance.   The orientation of the fallen will is toward persisting in sin and away from any recognition of possible salvation. The fallen will tends toward unawareness of God's holiness, having no intent to change. The earliest, most preliminary, gift of the grace of repentance is an acknowledgment of the radical need of sinners for a new life, awakening the earnest desire for salvation from sin (Ambrose, *Jacob and the Happy Life, FC* 65, pp. 119 ff.).

Scripture abounds in descriptions of radical repentance (Ps. 119:58–60; Ezek. 36:31; Isa. 57:15; 66:2), prayers of contrition (Ps. 130:1–4; Dan. 9:4–7; Ezra 9:5, 6), and typic accounts of decisive reversal (the prodigal, Luke 15:17–21; the publican, Luke 18:13, 14; Saul of Tarsus, Acts 9:5–11).

After repeated admonitions, Ezekiel called Israel to "Repent! Turn away from all your offenses; then sin will not be your downfall. Rid yourselves of all the offenses you have committed, and get a new heart and a new spirit. Why will you die, O house of Israel? For I take no pleasure in the death of anyone, declares the Sovereign Lord. Repent and live!" (Ezek. 18:30–32; Tertullian, *On Repentance* IV, *ANF* III, p. 659).

John the Baptist's call to repentance stood in this prophetic-penitential tradition, intensified by messianic expectation. John called for the baptism of repentance and demanded evidences of authentic conversion, fruits fitting to a life of decisive reversal (Matt. 3:9–10). His preaching pointed toward a coming forgiveness of sins (Mark 1:4; Luke 3:3). He set the stage for Jesus' preaching of repentance, which is bound intrinsically with the gospel call (Justin Martyr, *Dialogue with Trypho,* 50, 51, *ANF* I, pp. 220–21).

Evangelical Repentance.   Evangelical repentance is that repentance required by the gospel, a godly sorrow elicited in the heart by the Holy Spirit, by which the sinner becomes intensely aware of sin as an offense to divine holiness and loathes sin's power. One becomes keenly aware of the burden and skewed power of one's own freedom. One turns away from sin in grief over the misdeeds done, and toward God seeking pardon (John Chrysostom, *Baptismal Instructions*, ACW 31, pp. 50–53; Wesley, *WJWB*, sermon 9).

Evangelical repentance embraces these interpenetrating dimensions of spiritual and moral reversal: conviction of sin, godly sorrow, heartfelt contrition (*paenitere ex animo*) for sin, a resolution to forsake all sin, confession (*exomologesis* to God and where pertinent to offended persons), and moral reformation, including amendment of life and acts of reparation (*Homily Ascribed to Clement* 13.11; 8.3, 4; Tertullian, *On Repentance* 9–12, ANF III, pp. 664–66; Irish Articles 38, *COC* III, p. 534).

There is an implicit psychological order in this progression: convicting grace elicits a sense of anguish about the power and cost of sin, which requires self-examination, followed by an act of contrition and confession of sin, requiring a decision to renounce all sin, out of which comes a reformation of moral behavior, accompanied by a growing recognition of the offer of grace in the gospel (Tho. Aq., *ST* supp., Q1, III, pp. 2573–75). In walking this path, penitents are cautioned against either presumptive self-righteousness or despair over the intractable loss of righteousness.

Five landmarks on the way of repentance were set forth by John Chrysostom: openly declaring one's sins, forgiving the sins of others indebted to us, diligent prayer, acts of loving-kindness, and unfeigned humility, as in the case of the publican (*Resisting the Temptations of the Devil*, NPNF 1 IX, p. 190).

The Second Helvetic Confession further refined this progression: "By repentance we understand (1) the recovery of a right mind in sinful man awakened by the Word of the Gospel and the Holy Spirit, and received by true faith, by which the sinner immediately acknowledges his innate corruption and all his sins accused by the Word of God; and (2) grieves for them from his heart, and not only bewails and frankly confesses them before God with a feeling of shame, but also (3) with indignation abominates them and (4) now zealously considers the amendment of his ways and constantly strives for innocence and virtue in which conscientiously to exercise himself all the rest of his life" (XIV, *BOC* 5.093). Some classic writers simplified this process as a threefold act of conviction, contrition, and reformation. We will discuss each of these phases sequentially, with special attention to self-examination and reparation.

All aspects of this interrelated sequence are to be viewed as a single, whole act of reversal. If one feels conviction without any act of contrition, repentance remains stillborn. If one seeks to reform one's moral behavior without profoundly sorrowing (*lupē, dolor*) over one's sins or confessing them to God (*homologeō, confessio*), then repentance has not matured. If one confesses one's sins and engages in no acts of reparation or no attempt to right the wrongs done, then repentance has not borne sufficient moral fruit. The doctrine of repentance seeks to grasp the whole sequence integrally and consistently, rather than partially and in pieces (Cyril of Jerusalem, *Catech. Lect.* II, *NPNF* 2 VII, pp. 8–13; Rabanus Maurus, *De institutione clericorum* II.30; cf. *Abstract of Principles* IX, CC, p. 341).

Conviction of Sin

Conviction is that emergent personal awareness that one's own life is imprisoned in sin (Rom. 7:23; Gal. 3:23; Barth, *CD* I/2, pp. 768 ff.). In order to repent one must first be enabled to recognize the power and destructiveness of sin in oneself and feel the moral bruise sin has left. This recognition is no easy matter, since willed sin develops elaborate resistances to beholding its own dynamics (Pastor of Hermas, *Similitude* 5, *ANF* II, pp. 37, 38; Outler, *Psychotherapy and the Christian Message* 2; Menninger, *Whatever Became of Sin?*).

The Recognition by the Will of Its Own Slavery.   To be convicted is to discover personally that one is rightly under the condemnation of one's own conscience and, through conscience, God's own holy address. One feels that one's "hands are full of blood" (Isa. 1:15). Under conviction, the "whole head is injured," the "whole heart afflicted. From the sole of your foot to the top of your head there is no soundness" (Isa. 1:5, 6). Under conviction one is aware that the syndromes of anxiety, guilt, boredom, and death, intensified by the law (which is spiritual but distorted by sin), have so increased that the human condition is plausibly described as "sold as a slave to sin" (Rom. 7:14)!

Human existence is so inclined to evil that each one of the descendants of Adam and Eve are said to be personally and willfully implicated in the sin that has pervaded human history east of Eden. Before any sin can be enacted, it must be willed by some free personal agent, for that which is not willed is not sin (Tatian, *Address to the Greeks* XI, *ANF* II, p. 69). "Sinful volitions make sinful acts; sinful acts often repeated make sinful habits; sinful habits long continued in make sinful character; and sinful character at length determines and fixes unalterably the sinner's destiny" (Tillett, *PS*, p. 143).

Unclean Lips.   Conviction of sin came upon Isaiah in the temple filled with smoke: "'Woe to me!' I cried. 'I am ruined! For I am a man of unclean lips, and I live among a people of unclean lips, and my eyes have seen the King, the Lord Almighty.' Then one of the seraphs flew to me with a live coal in his hand, which he had taken with tongs from the altar. With it he touched my mouth and said, 'See, this has touched your lips; your guilt is taken away and your sin atoned for.'" (Isa. 6:5–7, cf. Dan. 4:32–36; Tertullian, *On Repentance* 12, *APT*, p. 370).

Peter boldly confronted his hearers with their acquiescence to the sin of the whole covenant community in the crucifixion: "God has made this Jesus, whom you crucified, both Lord and Christ." Their conviction was immediate: "When the people heard this, they were *cut to the heart.*" They "said to Peter and the other apostles, 'Brothers, *what shall we do?*' Peter replied, 'Repent and be baptized, every one of you, in the name of Jesus Christ for the forgiveness of your sins. And you will receive the gift of the Holy Spirit'" (Acts 2:36–38, italics added; Ambrose, *Of the Holy Spirit* I.XII.127, *NPNF* 2 X, p. 110).

It Is the Spirit Who Convicts.   Conviction is the work of the Spirit in which one grows in awareness of one's lost condition. Through convicting grace the Spirit works to awaken the realization of how deeply one is personally trapped in intergenerational patterns of sin, unable to break free (Exod. 20:5; Num. 14:18; cf. Jer. 31:29, 30). "The man without the spirit does not accept the things that come from God, for they are foolishness to him, and he cannot understand them, because they are spiritually discerned" (1 Cor. 2:14).

If it is the Spirit who convicts, it is the Spirit who prepares the time and conditions of conviction. Often this time occurs under conditions of true worship, guided by ordered ministries ordained of the Spirit, attesting the written and revealed

Word, placed in the frame of reference of the sacramental life quickened by the Spirit.

Felt emotive remorse is a consequence of conviction but not in itself conviction, which is primarily the work of the Spirit, not finally reducible to a human emotion (T. Goodwin, *Works*, VI, pp. 361–66). Amid the grace of repentance, "No one has anything of his own except falsehood and sin" (Augustine, *On the Gospel of St. John* 5.1, *NPNF* 1 VI, p. 31).

The Spirit Convinces the World of Sin, Righteousness, and Judgment. The Spirit penetrates the self-deceptions, evasions, defensive ploys, and indifference of the world. The Spirit works to change the lowered awareness of sin into heightened awareness, making the unrighteous hungry for righteousness, as if already facing final judgment (*An Ancient Homily by an Unknown Author* [Second Clement], 16– 20, *AF*, pp. 68–70). "And when he comes," said Jesus of the Holy Spirit, "he will prove the world wrong about sin and righteousness and judgment; about sin, be- cause they do not believe in me; about righteousness, because I am going to the Father and you will see me no longer; about judgment, because the ruler of this world has been condemned" (John 16:8–11, NRSV).

The Spirit points both to God's present judgment of idolatry in history, and to God's final judgment of all human folly (Cyprian, *Treatise* VI, *ANF* V, pp. 465– 69). This judging activity is already beheld upon the cross, where all humanity would be justly under the sentence of death and ready for execution except for the Advocate Son who takes upon himself the penalty, so that "the sinner is placed on the other side of his own execution. Though alive and uninjured, the believing sinner may look back upon his own execution as accomplished" (Chafer, *ST* VI, p. 98; cf. Rom. 8:1; 2 Cor. 5:14).

The self-righteous find it extremely difficult to believe that on the cross God has taken their sin upon himself. The Advocate Spirit enables this belief. As the Son is openly revealing the righteousness of God on the cross, so the Spirit is quietly illumining the righteousness of God as benefiting each sinner.

The Convicting Spirit Does Not Choose to Work Irresistibly. Conviction does not inevitably lead to repentance. Though Felix visibly trembled when Paul "dis- coursed on righteousness, self-control and the judgment to come," he did not move to conviction, but evasion: "That's enough for now! You may leave. When I find it convenient, I will send for you" (Acts 24:25). The convenient time never came.

That the Spirit may be resisted is evident from Stephen's last words upon being stoned to death: "You stiff-necked people, with uncircumcised hearts and ears! You are just like your fathers: You always resist the Holy Spirit! Was there ever a prophet your fathers did not persecute?" (Acts 7:51, 52).

The Spirit does not coerce conviction but quietly persuades and educes respon- sive cooperation in human wills (J. Watson, *Doctrines of Grace*, pp. 25–40; Pope, *Compend.* II, pp. 361–76; Burwash, *MCT* II, pp. 224–27). The silent inward work occurs "Not by might nor by power, but by my Spirit" (Zech. 4:6; cf. Ambrose, *Duties, NPNF* 2 X, pp. 1 ff.). "The Spirit gives life; the flesh counts for nothing" (John 6:63).

It is a gift with which recipients are enabled to work cooperatively: "For it is God who works in you to will and to act according to his good purpose"; hence you are to "continue to work out your salvation with fear and trembling" (Phil. 2:12, 13). God who made you without you and atoned for you without you is determined to save you only with your free consent (Eph. 2:8–10; John Chrysostom, *Hom. on Phil.* VIII, *NPNF* 1 XIII, pp. 219–23; Augustine, *On Grace and Free Will* 31–37, *NPNF* 1 V, pp. 457–58).

True repentance is never easy, for "the god of this age has blinded the minds of unbelievers, so that they cannot see the light of the gospel" (2 Cor. 4:4). Those most penitent are most aware that had the Spirit not drawn them toward the mercy of God, they would never have reversed course on their own. "No one can come to me unless the Father who sent me draws him" (John 6:44). Precisely when walking "through the valley of the shadow of death," one may be freed to recall how "goodness and mercy" have followed "all the days of my life" (Ps. 23:4, 6). Meanwhile the idolatrous world remains blinded to God's mercy until illumined by the Spirit (Cyprian, *Treatise* V, *ANF* V, pp. 457 ff.).

The Dynamics of Resistance.   "So far from co-operating with the Spirit in the new creation, the natural man presents every *resistance* and *opposition* to it. There is not only a passive *aversion* but an active *resistance* to the work. . . . Oh let no individual be so deceived as to believe that when God the eternal Spirit enters the soul, He finds the temple swept and garnished, and prepared for His reception" (Winslow, *WHS*, pp. 58–59, italics added; cf. Menno Simons, *Foundation of Chr. Doctrine, CWMS*, p. 161).

Even while one resists it, this intensified consciousness may break through. It is precisely while one is desperately fighting against conviction that one may come to feel it most intensely. Just then it becomes most "hard for you to kick against the goads" (Acts 26:14). Such conviction stunned Paul as he journeyed to Damascus to persecute Christians and "take them as prisoners to Jerusalem"—"a light from heaven flashed around him. He fell to the ground and heard a voice say to him, 'Saul, Saul, why do you persecute me?' 'Who are you, Lord?' Saul asked. 'I am Jesus, whom you are persecuting,' he replied." When he got up from the ground and opened his eyes, "he could see nothing. So they led him by the hand into Damascus. For three days he was blind, and did not eat or drink anything" (Acts 9:3–9). Later when he recalled his previous alienation, he exclaimed, "What a wretched man I am! Who will rescue me from this body of death?" The answer was at hand: "Thanks be to God" that "there is now no condemnation for those who are in Christ Jesus" (Rom. 7:24, 25; 8:1).

Illuminating Grace Elicits Rigorous Self-examination.   Spiritual directors of classic pastoral care have counseled penitents to meditate upon the goodness of God in preparation for the most searching forms of self-examination, contrition, and moral redirection (Tertullian, *Exomologesis* 9, 10, *ACW* 28, pp. 31–32). Those who appear cleverly to avoid self-examination will finally be "weighed on the scales and found wanting" (Dan. 5:27). "We are instructed about our own sin and not about our neighbors'" (Juliana of Norwich, *Revelations of Divine Love*, p. 225).

The intent of self-examination is to take the risk of probing hidden faults, not masochistically but realistically, to behold their tenacity and power, the complexity of secret sin, the layers of distorted perception. "Sin is a monster of such frightful mien, Which, to be hated, needs but to be seen" (A. Pope). The extent of the self-examination required hinges upon the nature and depth of misdeeds and the deceptions that cover them. "Where there is purifying there is Illumination; and Illumination is the satisfying of desire to those who long for the greatest things, or the Greatest Thing, or That Which surpasses all greatness" (Gregory Nazianzen, *Orat.* XXXIX.8, *NPNF* 2 VII, p. 354).

Charles Wesley prayed for the grace of repentance:

> O that I could repent!
>   O that I could believe!
> Thou, by thy voice the marble rent,
>   The rock in sunder cleave.
> Thou, by thy two-edged sword,
>   My soul and spirit part;
> Strike with the hammer of thy word,
>   And break my stubborn heart.

(C. Wesley, WHNS 105)

The Refusal of Cheap Grace.   True repentance refuses to be comforted until the work of conviction is thoroughly experienced. It is a radical act of self-examination reaching into every chamber of the house of willed experience (John Cassian, *Conferences, On Mortification, NPNF* 2 XI, pp. 531–50; D. Bonhoeffer, *Cost of Discipleship*).

To those who appeal to "the natural weakness of their own minds, the unfavorable circumstances in which they were placed, etc., etc., are all pleaded as excuses for their sins . . . the possibility of repentance is precluded" until one comes to take full responsibility for one's own choices (Clarke, *CT,* p. 123; S. Kierkegaard, *Either/Or* II).

Intensely personal repentance is only deepened and complicated by social and political sin, which may require lengthy societal inquiry and reexamination to discern the patterns of its emergence, how reparations may be made, and how repentance may bear fruits (Matt. 3:8; Acts 17:30). More important than length in penitential time is depth of penitential candor.

The Evangelical Pedagogy of Law.   The Spirit works both through judging sins and through promising forgiveness. The Spirit awakens in consciousness the knowledge of offenses against the law and makes plausible the pardon of the gospel. The law teaches us to recognize our sin and our need of grace, while the gospel shows us how God has come to humanity to provide mercy for our sins (John Chrysostom, *Hom. on the Statues, NPNF* 1 IX, pp. 362 ff.; Luther, *The Freedom of a Christian, MLS,* pp. 52 ff.).

The sick must take seriously their illness before they feel the urgent need of a physician. The Spirit works through the law to accomplish this recognition. The law rigorously attests the holiness of God (Ps. 19:7; Rom. 7:12). The Spirit works through conscience to bring the requirement to sharper moral awareness. Sinners see in the light of the law how inadequate are their own stunted virtues (Hodge, *OOT,* pp. 487–95; Wakefield, *CT,* pp. 471–78; Miley, *ST* II, p. 100). "Those who preach only the gospel to sinners, at best, only heal the hurt of the daughter of my people slightly. The law, therefore, is the grand instrument in the hands of a faithful minister to alarm and awaken sinners" (Clarke, *CT,* p. 128).

By the law comes increased awareness of sin (Rom. 3:20). It is the schoolmaster who brings us gradually to grace in Christ (Gal. 3:24). We would not have known sin clearly except in the light of the law (Rom. 7:7). It is like a mirror into which we look to see our true condition revealed (James 1:22–25).

The faithful keep the law because they have been redeemed, not in order to be redeemed. They do all things through Christ who gives them strength (Eph. 3:16; Phil. 4:13). Faith does not make void the law but establishes it (J. Wesley, *The Law Established Through Faith* I,II, *WJW* V, pp. 447–67, *WJWB*, sermons 35, 36).

> Convince us first of unbelief,
> And freely then release;
> Fill every soul with sacred grief,
> And then with sacred peace.
>
> Impov'rish, Lord, and then relieve,
> And then enrich the poor;
> The knowledge of our sickness give,
> The knowledge of our cure.
>
> That blessed sense of guilt impart,
> And then remove the load;
> Trouble, and wash the troubled heart
> In the atoning blood.
>
> (C. Wesley, "Come O Thou All-victorious Lord," *PS*, p. 153).

Contrition

Contrition is brokenness of heart, awareness of radical moral poverty in God's presence, the crushed spirit. The contrite heart prays for the gift of clear discernment of one's sins, seeking to penetrate and clearly expose self-deceptions and the innumerable ways that sin seeks to cover its tracks with pretended righteousness (Isa. 57:14–21; Mark 13:5, 6; Heb. 3:13).

The Sinner's Prayer.   The essential prayer of the penitent is "God be merciful to me a sinner" (Luke 18:13, KJV). Anyone can pray the sinner's prayer except one who imagines that such a prayer does not apply to oneself. But no one can repent without the grace-enabled gift of penitence, and for that the sinner earnestly prays (Mark 2:17). Prayer is the sinner's refuge.

It is doubly ironic that only sinners can repent. If repentance is a condition of saving faith, then salvation is offered to sinners only. "For I have not come to call the righteous, but sinners" (Matt. 9:13). Since all who flow through the history of sin are sinners, all are called to repentance.

"The Lord is close to the brokenhearted and saves those who are crushed in spirit" (Ps. 32:18). The penitent lapsed are never to be denied mercy (Cyprian, *On the Lapsed, ANF* V, pp. 437 ff.; Dionysius, *Exegetical Fragments, ANF* VI, p. 120).

Approaching with Confidence.   There is a paradox of humble contrition and boldness in faith: Some glimpse of faith is anticipatively present in every preliminary step toward penitence: "Let us therefore approach the throne of grace with confidence, so that we may receive mercy and find grace to help us in our time of need" (Heb. 4:16). This boldness (*parrhēsia*, openness, confidence, Eph. 3:12; 1 John 4:17) is grounded in the Father's love: "Which of you, if his son asks for bread, will give him a stone? Or if he asks for a fish, will give him a snake? If you, then, though you are evil, know how to give good gifts to your children, how much more will your Father in heaven give good gifts to those who ask him!" (Matt. 7:9–11). Jesus instructed his disciples, "Ask and it will be given to you; seek and you will find; knock and the door will be opened to you" (Matt. 7:7).

Salvation draws near to those who, like Isaiah and Luther, most deeply experience the impossibility of standing in God's presence. Salvation remains furthest from those who imagine sin a small matter easily dealt with, or repentance a quick fix, who routinely assume their own uprightness (Kierkegaard, *SD*).

True and False Repentance. However earnestly qualified, like all Christian teachings, repentance is liable to be misunderstood:

- As a human accomplishment by which one seems to make oneself worthy of grace
- As an autonomous attempt at self-reform
- As if reducible to a public or social act of outward profession of misdeeds, rather than an earnest inward act occurring essentially in the presence of God
- As an intellectual change of mind without a change of will or heart, as if repentance were essentially the acceptance of the idea of sin, rather than that one is personally a sinner oneself
- As a wrenching emotional experience involving grief over sin and catharsis, yet without moral reformation or fundamental spiritual redirection

These misconceptions lead to false repentance (Calvin, *Inst.* 3.3.24). They recur historically, either in a Pelagianism that views the will as so capable of turning itself around that the grace of repentance becomes virtually unnecessary or in a quietism that does not regard repentance as an active change but monergistically as a unilateral divine gift that may only be passively waited for, or in an enthusiasm that reduces repentance to an emotion, substituting the passion of remorse for grace-enabled godly sorrow, or in a Pharisaic legalism that turns the grace of repentance into a new law (Tertullian, *ANF* III, pp. 657–64; cf. Tillett, *PS*, pp. 155–74; van Oosterzee, *CD* p. 649).

The Blessing of True Repentance. The first four beatitudes of the Sermon on the Mount set forth the essence of true repentance: *Poverty of spirit* recognizes how lacking is our righteousness and how great the need for God's righteousness. Those who *mourn* their offenses, sorrowing over sins voluntarily committed and omitted, are made happy by God's forgiveness. The *meek* are willing early to surrender their own pride to God's saving purpose and accept the tendered offer of God's mercy. Those who *hunger and thirst for righteousness*, earnestly desiring to receive the bread and water of life, will be filled (Matt. 5:3–6; Clement of Alexandria, *Who Is the Rich Man That Shall Be Saved?* 16, *AEG* II, p. 183).

With true repentance the love of sin is already beginning to die in one's heart. It may not be fully conquered, but the power of sin has been delivered a crippling,

deathly blow, even while sin struggles to remain (Rom. 7). "Real repentance consists in the heart's being broken *for* sin and *from* sin" (John Nevin, in Weaver, *CT*,
p. 151).

Joy in the Reversal of Sin.   Rightly understood, repentance is a source of joy in
the freed, renewed life (Luke 15:7, 10). Luther told his spiritual mentor, Staupitz,
that the very word that had once been so terrible—repentance—had become the
most fragrant of words (*WML* I, p. 40). The special joy of repentance is that no
matter how far one may have fallen, the way remains open to receive God's forgiveness (Kierkegaard, *CDisc.*). "Though your sins are like scarlet, they shall be as
white as snow" (Isa. 1:18).

Precisely when our hearts most loudly attest guilt, God is greater than our
hearts. The most that conscience can do toward salvation is reveal moral inade-
quacy, leading to despair, pointing beyond itself to convicting grace. "We set our
hearts at rest in his presence whenever our hearts condemn us. For God is greater
than our hearts, and he knows everything" (1 John 3:19, 20). Only when the sickness worsens sufficiently to drive one to the physician does healing draw near.

Worldly Sorrow, Godly Sorrow.   Worldly sorrow is idolatrous regret that does not
understand how profoundly sin offends God, whose holiness requires the plenary
renunciation of sin (John Chrysostom, *Instruction to Catechumens*, *NPNF* 1 IX,
pp. 170–71; John Cassian, *Conferences*, *NPNF* 2 XI, pp. 230 ff.). Worldly sorrow
ironically may bind one more closely into the syndromes of guilt by engendering
the pretense that some fundamental change is taking place when it is not (Kierkegaard, *E/O* II). Worldly sorrow, however, may be used by the Spirit to awaken
godly sorrow, to increase the desire to escape the consequences of sin (Jer. 31:12;
2 Cor. 7:7).

Godly sorrow, on the other hand, feels revulsion in the presence of sin, not
merely fear of the consequences of sin. It takes ownership of personal guilt, holds
the whole desperate human situation up before God, and feels the radical brokenness of the best human intentions. In godly sorrow, we "bewail our manifold
sins and wickedness" (*BCP*), trembling before the holiness of God. "The sacrifices
of God are a broken spirit; a broken and contrite heart, O God, you will not despise" (Ps. 51:17).

Paul hoped that grief over sin would have its intended effect by leading to repentance: "Even if I caused you sorrow by my letter, I do not regret it. Though I
did regret it—I see my letter hurt you, but only for a little while—yet now I am
happy, not because you were made sorry, but because your sorrow led you to
repentance. For you became sorrowful as God intended and so were not harmed
in any way by us." (2 Cor. 7:8, 9). He then stated this crucial maxim: "Godly sorrow brings repentance that leads to salvation and leaves no regret, but worldly
sorrow brings death" (2 Cor. 7:10).

A worldly sorrow seeks to escape punishment. A godly sorrow seeks to deal with
the cause of guilt. Paul knew that godly sorrow would elicit a health-giving series
of reversals: the earnest desire to do good (*spoudēn*), eagerness to clear one's conscience (*apologian*), indignation over sin (*aganaktesin*), alarm over judgment (*pho-
bon*), longing for reconciliation (*epipothesin*), zealous concern (*zēlon*), readiness to
see justice done (*ekdikēsin*, 2 Cor. 7:11; Calvin, *Comm.* XX, pp. 271–78).

A worldly sorrow may exhibit regret for sin, but the regret is focused upon the loss of created values and this-worldly relationships, not of the living God. Its dread and shame come from offending creaturely powers and goods, not God. This is the sorrow that "brings death" by driving one further toward despair absent divine forgiveness and in some cases to deep depression or even suicide (Tertullian, *On Repentance, APT,* pp. 350–66).

Has modernity lost the capacity for godly sorrow? Indeed, repentance may be that act that runs most directly counter to prevailing modern assumptions—progress in history, the essential goodness of humanity, the social determination of murder, rape, and plunder. Taking personal responsibility for sin is the heart of evangelical repentance. Sin is not caused by parents or siblings or bad teachers or heredity or physiological temperament or the stars, but finally by one's own freedom that has entered decisively into self-determined collusion with wickedness, determining oneself toward bondage to sinful habituation and demeaned character. Modernity has not lost the capacity for godly sorrow, but the assumptions of modernity have made ever more difficult the repentance that has always been hard (Oden, *AMW,* pp. 12 ff.).

Resolution to Forsake All Sin

Repentance calls for not only a change of the mind and a confession from the mouth but also a corrective work of the hands to redo what sin has undone (*conversio mentis, confessio oris, et vindicta peccati*).

The Ax at the Root.   Repentance is an act aimed at the root of sin. This is powerfully indicated by the metaphor of John the Baptist: "The ax is already at the root of the trees" (Matt. 3:10). One does not repent by trimming leaves one at a time, or even by cutting off an entire branch. The whole life of sin must go, must be renounced altogether, and peremptorily (Ambrose, *On the Mysteries* 1–3, *NPNF* 2 X, pp. 317–18). Essential to godly sorrow is an overarching decision to renounce a corrupted life altogether and to forsake all sin.

The psalmist knew that "if I had cherished sin in my heart, the Lord would not have listened" (Ps. 66:18). "The Lord detests the sacrifice of the wicked" (Prov. 15:8), because they remain wicked precisely amid the hypocrisy of appearing to repent (Barth, *CD* I/2, pp. 768 ff.; IV/2, pp. 557 ff.). It may only complicate matters to strike a halfway covenant with sin and learn to compromise with clever self-deceptions. The penitent act must have the intent of finality, unlike that of sailors who desperately throw their belongings overboard in a storm but long for them in the calm that follows (Luther, *How Confession Should be Made, LW* 39, pp. 30–33; Hugh of St. Victor, *SCF,* pp. 271 ff.; Weaver, *CT,* p. 151). True repentance requires the abandonment of the life of sin (Clement of Alexandria, *Who Is the Rich Man That Shall Be Saved?* XXXIX, *ANF* II, p. 602). It leads to the reshaping of behavior (Calvin, *Inst.* 3.4). It is not a hedged bet that tries to both repent and cling to sin.

Behavioral Amendment, Reparation, and Reformation.   Genuine repentance calls for a fitting act of restitution, the restoration of whatever has been wrongly acquired, in which practical amends are made for injustices inflicted upon others insofar as that is reasonably possible (Cyprian, *Letters, FC* 51, pp. 46–55, 146 ff.).

God "requires him to make restitution to the person injured if it lie in the compass of his power. . . . No man should expect mercy at the hand of God who, having wronged his neighbour, refuses, when he has it in his power, to make restitution" (A. Clarke, *CT*, p. 124).

Reparation seeks to repair, so far as feasible, whatever has been wrongly done or previously injurious. If one has defrauded or harmed or offended or stolen, one must make fair restoration for the injury. Zacchaeus had spent his life cheating others. Called to repentance by the servant Messiah, he "stood up and said to the Lord, 'Look Lord! Here and now I give half of my possessions to the poor, and if I have cheated anybody out of anything, I will pay back four times the amount.' Jesus said to him, 'Today salvation has come to this house'" (Luke 19:5–9). Since reparation was immediate and generous, Zacchaeus became a prototype of earnest repentance (Tertullian, *Ag. Marcion* IV.37, *ANF* III, p. 412).

It may seem impossible to make up for wrongs done to others, but this must nonetheless be proportionally attempted. Such acts of reparation are not repentance *per se*, but fruits of repentance (Matt. 3:8). Repentance itself is not primarily a self-initiated work but an act of receiving the grace of penitence, a receptive act that readies the self to receive the grace of pardon.

It is necessary to "put aside the deeds of darkness" if we are to "put on the armor of light" (Rom. 13:12). "Amendment of life and the forsaking of sin should then follow" (Augsburg Conf. XII, *CC*, p. 71).

One is not saved *in* one's sin, but *from* one's sin. When genuine repentance puts on Christ, it makes "no provision for the flesh" (Rom. 13:14, KJV).

In acts of reparation, while relying upon Christ's juridical righteousness, one is also participating in Christ's active obedience, seeking justice for the harmed neighbor. It is not as if reparation is something we do in which God's own doing has ceased; rather, it remains God's doing and enabling of our willing, which takes the form of taking responsibility for the neighbor as Christ took responsibility for us on the cross (Calvin, *Inst.* 3.3.16–20).

Aversion to Sin.   The revulsion is not toward sin in general or in the abstract, but to one's own actual besetting sins. My sin is loathed as my own, made by me, offending the One who granted me the very freedom that has gone awry. "The memory of them is grievous unto us," states the prayer of confession (*BCP*). If the sense of loathing my own sin is lacking or ephemeral, then the expected new life can hardly go very deep. However intensified by idolatry, actual sin is always at some level a voluntary, collusive transgression of a known moral requirement. Hence genuine conviction is directed not merely toward neurosis or imaginary sin but toward actually willed sin (John 8:6b-11; J. Wesley, *WJWB, Sermons*, 3:204).

There is a determination in true repentance to disavow what had been wrongly worshiped and to resist what had been inordinately loved. Proportionally as one's eyes are opened to sin, the determination to combat sin is intensified. Earnest repentance is manifested by abhorring one's hurtful past, not delaying responsiveness to grace, seeking counsel for casting off doubt, and breaking off unseemly company (Cyprian, *Letters*, FC 51, pp. 86–89, 183–86; Clementina, *Recognitions* X.43, *ANF* VIII, p. 203). When we willfully cling to sin, we reinforce the choice to deaden our awareness of the enormity of sin and its baleful consequences, and thereby distance ourselves from the active outreach of God's mercy.

ISSUES OF PENITENCE AND CONFESSION

Exegetical Issues of Penitential Practice

Whether Repentance Must Recur Daily.   Repentance continues daily in the life of the faithful, sustained by Word and Sacrament. "Once for all we have the washing in Baptism; every day we have washing in prayer" (Augustine, *On the Creed* 1:7, 15, *NPNF* 1 III, p. 374). Sacramentally viewed, baptism is the appointed means by which the Spirit regenerates persons and incorporates them into covenant community. The grace of baptism offers a regenerating gift. Confirmation, or reaffirmation of baptism, offers growth in the graces begun in baptism (Hugh of St. Victor, *SCF*, pp. 302–4). The Spirit may work within or apart from ordinary means. Evangelical repentance is not an everyday experience but may come at a critical juncture that affects every subsequent day of one's life.

Falling away from the first baptismal repentance was regarded as such a serious matter that the letter to the Hebrews wonders if any recovery would be possible: "It is impossible for those who have once been enlightened, who have tasted the heavenly gift, who have shared in the Holy Spirit, who have tasted the goodness of the word of God and the powers of the coming age, if they fall away, to be brought back by repentance" (Heb. 6:4–6). Here the author seems to be arguing that one's faith must either grow or die (Heb. 6:7–8; Calvin, *Comm.* XXII, pp. 135–44). Other passages make it clear that repentance remains a recurring act within the Christian life. Faith requires a continuing self-denial, confession, reparation, and ongoing penitence (Rev. 2:5, 16; 3:3, 19).

The renewing of repentance remains a continuing necessity, so long as sin remains in believers (*Homily Ascribed to Clement, ANF* VII, p. 519). The first of Luther's Ninety-five Theses is that the whole life of believers is repentance. Paul directed his exhortations to repentance to the whole Christian community (Rom. 12:2; Eph. 4:23, 24; cf. Rev. 2:5),

Repentance is pertinent to the Christian life inasmuch as sin stubbornly remains in the life of the regenerate. Out of repentance and faith comes a life seeking to glorify God. Continuing repentance is enabled by grace (*Heid. Catech.*, answers 88–90).

Augustine distinguished three levels or dimensions of repentance: repentance for sins committed before baptism that call for the repentance of baptismal faith; repentance after baptism for the lighter daily sins, requiring daily repentance as medicine of forgiveness; and repentance after baptism in the more serious sense in which he referred to penitents (*poenitentes*) in the church who are struggling with grave sins (Conf. 10; cf. Ambrose, *On Repentance, NPNF* 2 X, pp. 329–59).

Whether Repentance of Itself Secures Forgiveness.   Pelagian writers tended to assume that upon repentance one is necessarily forgiven by a moral necessity grounded in God. There is little support in scripture for the notion that repentance of itself is sufficient to secure pardon, for that would essentially make divine pardon a debt owed to human sincerity. Though many passages connect pardon with repentance, pardon always remains a free gift (Eph. 2:4–10).

Among penitential innovations introduced by medieval Scholastics and rejected by Protestant critics were substitution of private for public penance; the external-

ization of religion by the theory of *opus operatum:* the payment of *Wergeld* or penance moneys for penalties; and the connection of works of satisfaction with
deliverance from purgatory (Luther, *The Pagan Servitude of the Church, MLS,*
pp. 249 ff.; *SHD* II 47).

Whether Deathbed Repentance Is Efficacious.   A deathbed repentance is always
possible, as the thief on the cross suggests, but hazardous insofar as it tends to
promote the antinomian temptation that one may sin now, for there will always
be time to repent. But will there always be time? As long as one lives there is always
time to repent, but if one's life is cut short unexpectedly, precisely then there
remains no time (Matt. 6:19–24; Luke 12:16–21). It is always possible to repent
at any point "before the last day of life," but delay is not recommended "because
we cannot place limits to God's mercy nor fix times for Him with whom conversion
suffers no delay." To persons *in extremis* "the grace of absolution must not be refused even when it can be asked for only by signs" (Leo, *Letters* CVIII, *NPNF* 2
XII, p. 80; John Chrysostom, *Baptismal Instructions, ACW* 31, pp. 132–35).

Whether Repentance Is a Duty.   Psychologically viewed, repentance is the premise of healthy catharsis, having profound therapeutic consequences, even if one
does not posit a relation to God as decisive for moral reversal. Morally viewed,
repentance is a duty. Convicting grace is not an incidental or optional idea that
can be received or ignored depending upon how one feels about it (*Homily Ascribed
to Clement* VII, *ANF* VII, p. 519). Rather it has an imperative quality.

Scripture moves beyond psychological description, while including it. Scripture
portrays repentance as a divine command. God "commands all people everywhere
to repent" (Acts 17:30). This requires sincere awareness of one's own personal
collusion in the actual history of sin. Jesus said, "Unless you repent, you too will
all perish" (Luke 13:3). Under Jesus' instruction, the disciples "went out and
preached that people should repent" (Mark 6:12).

Whether It May Be Said That God Repents.   Certain passages of scripture speak
anthropomorphically of God as so moved with grief as to relent from a former
judgment, or to "repent" (KJV, *nacham,* to pity, to be comforted, eased) from a
previous resolve (Ps. 106:45; Jer. 18:8–10), when upon hearing their earnest
prayers Yahweh does not execute a threatened judgment. In the story of Noah,
"The Lord saw how great man's wickedness on the earth had become, and that
every inclination of the thoughts of his heart was only evil all the time. The Lord
was *grieved* [repented himself, KJV] that he had made man on the earth, and his
heart was filled with pain" (Gen. 6:5, 6, italics added). Yahweh is said to have
"grieved that I have made Saul king" (1 Sam. 15:11). These are anthropomorphic
expressions inasmuch as they speak as though God were *anthropos,* humanly motivated, like ordinary persons in their capacity for grief (Barth, *CD* IV/1, p. 561).

These passages do not imply that God did wrong or that God's character became altered, but that God freely responds to human alienation in ways that correspond to changed circumstances, relenting, reconsidering accordingly (Ezek.
18:24–32). Having dealt with the people mercifully, Yahweh grieves over bungled
human freedom, or having judged severely now offers mercy (Amos 7:3, 6; Jer.
18:8–10; Exod. 32:14).

When we say, "Now the sun is shining," and "Now it is not shining," we do not mean that the sun changes, but that our perception of it changes (Athanasius, *Defence of the Nicene Definition* V, *NPNF* 2 IV, pp. 164–66, cf. pp. 366 ff.). Similarly, what seem to be changes in God are historical changes to which God is compassionately responsive. "Every good and perfect gift is from above, coming down from the Father of the heavenly lights, who does not change like shifting shadows" (James 1:17). The grief analogy breaks down at the point where it is recognized that God "is not a man, that he should change his mind" (1 Sam. 15:29; Heb. 7:21).

Conversion

To convert (*epistrephō*, Lat. *convertere*) is to turn around, to pivot, to change from one course to another (Acts 3:19). A conversion is a change from unfaith to faith. It is Torah that converts the soul (Ps. 19:7). Calling a little child to stand among his disciples, Jesus said, "Unless you change [*straphō*, KJV, be converted] and become like little children, you will never enter the kingdom of heaven" (Matt. 18:3).

Defining Conversion.   Conversion is a reversal of disposition and personal moral direction. Conversion involves a turning away from sin (repentance) and a turning to Christ (faith), two phases of a single act of turning (Calvin, *Inst.* 3.3). Repentance is a principle part, but not the whole, of conversion. Conversion is a part, but not the whole, of the doctrine of reconciliation (Watson, *TI* II, chap. XIX).

Conversion is the trajectory from repentance to regeneration. If repentance is a revulsion against the dying life of slavery to sin, regeneration is a new birth, in which new spiritual life is imparted. To be born again, one must repent. In repenting, one may be born again. Repentance is retrospective, regeneration prospective. Repentance looks back in regret and remorse toward sin. Regeneration looks forward to a new life that has emerged out of a new birth of faith (Fletcher, *Works* III, pp. 112–31; Clarke, *CT*, pp. 122–28). The process considered together is conversion.

The conversion from sin to faith requires that one first become aware of one's distance from God and repent, aware that God is reaching out for sinners in the atoning work of the cross, and that the sinner must earnestly seek God and his favor in Christ by confession of sin and trust in God (Goodwin, *Works* VI, pp. 117–40).

The Grace of Conversion Works by Persuasion.   The hidden spring of this entire reversal of mind, heart, and will is the love of God. This turning of mind, heart, and will is awakened in persons through the power of the Holy Spirit. The Spirit does not coerce or overleap or overpower human self-determination, but persuades, coaxes, challenges, pries loose, and invites freedom. Were it strictly a matter of the Spirit overpowering the human will, then there could be no call to any duty of repentance, as in scripture: "Repent, then, and turn to God, so that your sins may be wiped out, that times of refreshing may come from the Lord" (Acts 3:19). Such an appeal assumes that the hearer may or may not decide to repent.

Enabled by grace, freedom is called to examine itself, its deceptions and evasions. God will not do the repenting for us. Throughout the whole sequence of developing penitential consciousness, grace elicits voluntary repentance. Contrition is never self-initiated, but responsive to God's gift, so as to require a definite task. Only on this cooperative basis can repentance be viewed simultaneously as a gift of God (Acts 5:31; 11:18) and a command to the human will (Mark 5:12; Luke 13:3; Acts 8:22; 17:30; Calvin, *Inst.* 3.3).

Pastoral care of the impenitent is a gradual, delicate, uncoercive process of nurture and encouragement: "The Lord's servant must not quarrel; instead, he must be kind to everyone, able to teach, not resentful. Those who oppose him he must gently instruct, in the hope that God will grant them repentance leading them to a knowledge of the truth" (2 Tim. 2:25).

Whether Faith and Repentance Are Experienced in a Sequence.   Repentance in one sense goes before faith, in another sense accompanies faith, and in still another sense issues from and necessarily follows faith. As godly sorrow for sin, repentance precedes and makes way for faith. Repentance and faith exist in an interactive relation inasmuch as repentance is turning away from sin whereas faith is turning toward Christ in a single turning (Gregory of Nyssa, *FGG*, pp. 219–20). Because sin remains in believers, the act of penitence must be daily renewed (Calvin, *Inst.* 3.3.5, 6). In this sense one may say that repentance necessarily follows from the earliest steps of faith (Van Oosterzee, *CD*, p. 648).

Repentance is a turning away from sin, faith a turning toward grace, yet both constitute a single, decisive turning. Repentance and faith are negative and positive aspects of a single conversion away from sin toward God. Repentance presupposes faith, and faith cannot proceed without repentance; hence to preach faith is necessarily to preach repentance (Matt. 3:1–12; Acts 19:4; 20:21).

This dialectic helps explain why some New Testament texts describe faith as the only condition of salvation ("everyone who believes in him receives forgiveness," Acts 10:43), while others appear to imply that only repentance is required for salvation—"Repent, then, and turn to God, so that your sins may be wiped out" (Acts 3:19). There are other passages that closely interweave repentance and faith: "Repent and believe the good news" (Mark 1:15).

Some anticipatory faith in God's mercy is presupposed in taking the first steps in penitence, for "without faith it is impossible to please God, because anyone who comes to him must believe that he exists and that he rewards those who earnestly seek him" (Heb. 11:6). In this way repentance and faith are so inextricably joined together in scripture that it is impossible to assign to one or the other a temporal or logical priority (Melanchthon, *Loci, LCC* XIX, pp. 88 ff.; cf. *CR* XXI.427 ff.).

Faith is, strictly speaking, the only condition of conversion. Repentance in itself does not atone, but begins to open the recipient to the benefits of Christ's atonement. Even amid repentance, God remains offended by the sins of humanity. God's holiness does not become indifferent to sin even among penitents. Only in the theandric mediator is the ransom for sin made and the penalty for sin once for all paid. God does not forgive sin indiscriminately without repentance and serious amendment of life. By repentance and faith in God's atoning action, divine forgiveness is not made an arbitrary matter or an act contrary to the divine holiness but an act consistent with God's holy love (Melanchthon, *Loci, LCC* XIX, pp. 131–33).

The Order of Conversion.   Jesus called hearers to "repent and believe the good news" (Mark 1:15). This order is implicit in John the Baptist's call for all to be baptized with the baptism of repentance and in this way prepare the way for God's own coming. "John's baptism was a baptism of *repentance*. He told the people to *believe* in the one coming after him, that is, in Jesus" (Acts 19:4, italics added).

Systematically viewed, the order of conversion is textually grounded in the terms of salvation: "Repent and be baptized, every one of you, in the name of Jesus Christ for the forgiveness of your sins" (Acts 2:38). Paul told the elders at Miletus, "I have declared to both Jews and Greeks that they must turn to God in repentance and have faith in our Lord Jesus" (Acts 20:21).

Some exegetes view regeneration as prior to faith, and faith as the consequence of regeneration. Though there is truth embedded in both views, the prevailing logical-consensual order in interpreting the sense of scripture is that faith's first work is repentance, and penitent faith is the condition of regeneration. This is less a chronological than a logical order or systematic arrangement of loci.

Confession of Sin

Confession is used in two complementary ways in the New Testament: as the confession of sin and the confession of Christ. "If we confess our sins, he is faithful and just and will forgive us our sins and purify us from all unrighteousness" (1 John 1:9). "If anyone acknowledges that Jesus is the Son of God, God lives in him and he in God" (1 John 4:15). One is hardly prepared to confess Christ who has not confessed one's sin (Clement of Rome, *Corinth* 51, 52, *ANF* I, p. 19).

The Nature of Confession of Sin.   Confession of sin is personal acknowledgment of one's own violation of moral law, including participation in societal injustices, before God (Cyprian, *The Lapsed, ACW* 25, pp. 35–36; L. L. Hamline, *Works of Rev. L. L. Hamline.* 2 vols. Cincinnati: Hitchcock and Walden, 1869–1871; I, pp. 29–52; C. Hodge, *The Way of Life,* pp. 240–85; Tillett, *PS,* pp. 199–210). Although confession to oneself and the neighbor are significant and should not be neglected, the act of confession of sin is not addressed primarily to oneself or to society or to one's neighbor or therapist, but is finally made in the presence of God (Calvin, *Inst.* 3.3–4; Barth, *CD,* IV/4, pp. 57 ff.). Since it is with God-given freedom that one sins, it is necessarily the living God with whom the confessor finally has to deal (Clarke, *CT,* pp. 479–85).

Genuine repentance is evidenced by the confession of sin to God, as in the case of the tax collector who "stood at a distance. He would not even look up to heaven, but beat his breast, and said, 'God, have mercy on me, a sinner'" (Luke 18:13). Without confession (*exomologesis*), the power of sin continues to mount (Tertullian, *On Repentance* 10–11, *ANF* III, pp. 664–65; Mark the Ascetic, *Letter to Nicolas, Philokalia* I, p. 149). "If we claim to be without sin, we deceive ourselves and the truth is not in us. If we confess our sins, he is faithful and just and will forgive us our sins, and purify us from all unrighteousness. If we claim we have not sinned, we make him out to be a liar and his word has no place in our lives" (1 John 1:8–10). One who "conceals his sins" cannot expect to grow spiritually, "but whoever confesses and renounces them finds mercy" (Prov. 28:13).

Whether to Despair over Sin Is to Confess Sin.   Psalm 32 powerfully described the transition from despairing guilt to freeing confession: "When I kept silent, my bones wasted away through my groaning all day long." The awareness of guilt did not go away as he sought sleep. The silence had a physical effect, a wasting away. "For day and night your hand was heavy upon me; my strength was sapped as in the heat of the summer" (Ps. 32:3, 4). Grace came in the convicting form of heaviness, draining that strength that would resist a healing transformation (cf. Pss. 38:4; 69:20; Prov. 25:20; 1 Pet. 1:6).

"Then I acknowledged my sin to you and did not cover up my iniquity. I said, 'I will confess my transgressions to the Lord.'" Confession is contrasted with continuing to "cover up" in God's presence. "And you forgave the guilt of my sin. . . . Rejoice in the Lord and be glad, you righteous; sing, all you who are upright in heart!" (Ps. 32:3–11). What the sinner had attempted to cover up now becomes covered by divine forgiveness: "Blessed is he whose transgressions are forgiven, whose sins are covered. Blessed is the man whose sin the Lord does not count against him and in whose spirit is no deceit" (Ps. 32:1, 2).

The relief and joy experienced in confession is viewed as an unburdening of conscience and a cleansing from the stain of guilt (John Cassian, *On the Holy Fathers of Sketis, Philokalia* I, pp. 103, 140; Peter of Damaskos, *Treasury, Philokalia* II, pp. 199–200). Repentance is a cleansing bath for the soul (John Chrysostom, *Baptismal Instructions, ACW* 31, pp. 135–39). Spiritual beauty and health return to the soul by repentance (p. 91).

The Character of Sincere Confession.   To be genuine, confession must be sincere, definite, and unconditional, not ambivalent or vague, and it must not secretly cling to sin. "As there is no sin so small but it deserves damnation, so there is no sin so great that it can bring damnation upon those who truly repent. Men ought not to content themselves with a general repentance" (Westminster Conf. XV, *CC*, p. 210).

The particular way one makes confession is not prescribed by scripture, but evangelical repentance assumes some form of confession fitting to the need for behavioral reversal (Calvin, *Necessity of Reforming the Church, LCC* XXII, pp. 211–16). There remains a dual danger of making confession either needlessly hard or all too easy, the latter being the modern temptation. The former was an exaggeration of the church under conditions of persecution in the second century, when only one act of postbaptismal repentance was permitted, as when Tertullian wrote that God "has stationed in the vestibule a second penitence to open to them that knock; but only once, because it is for the second time; it can never open again, because the last time it opened in vain" (Tertullian, *On Repentance* 7, *ECF,* p. 153; cf. *ANF* III, p. 663).

The consensual tradition is more fitly expressed by Leo: "The manifold mercy of God so assists men when they fall, that not only by the grace of baptism, but also by the remedy of penitence is the hope of eternal life revived, in order that they who have violated the gifts of the second birth, condemning themselves by their own judgment, may attain to remission" (*Letters* CVIII, *NPNF* 2 XII, p. 80).

Confession to Whom?   Confession may occur in the presence of a trusted pastor or a Christian brother or sister. But confession is primarily to God, even when it seeks to communicate its transcendent significance interpersonally. "For that confession is sufficient, which is first offered to God, then also to a priest who serves as an intercessor" (Leo the Great, *SCD* 145, p. 59). Thus it is commended that each one find another, whether clerical or lay, whose life is shaped by the

Spirit, through whom the soul may be unburdened and hear the forgiving word (Luther, *Lectures on Gen.* 31–37, 1544, *LW* 6, pp. 297–98; *SHD* I, pp. 158–59).

Some texts suggest that confession of sin requires not only a private confession to God but a public or interpersonal confession to the Christian community in order to authenticate and make sharable the private transaction of the sinner with God (Ambrose, *On Repentance* 9–11, *NPNF* 2 X, pp. 355–59). Whether "private or public," to one or many, whether "to those that are offended" (Westminster Conf. XV, *CC*, p. 210; Tertullian, *APT*, pp. 367–69), confession is ultimately offered in the presence of God, the true physician of souls, even if penultimately to another human being (Origen, *Hom. on Ps. 36;* hom. 1.5). Contrition may be undermined if one is proudly unwilling to make relevant public confession for sins that harm the commonweal or body of Christ. The truly penitent are ready to confess to whomever is most pertinent their misdeeds and need of divine mercy.

Public Confession. The confession must be as public or interpersonal as the offense or harm has been (Luke 7; 1 Cor. 5:2; 2 Cor. 2:7). "The repentance of those whose sins are public should be in public" (Rabanas Maurus, *De institutione clericorum* II.30; Council of Rheims II, A.D. 813, *DUCC* II, p. 436; cf. Hefele, *HC* III.758).

There is a danger that a public act of confession may harm someone else; a person drawn involuntarily into a sequence of sordid events reported might find that his or her reputation has been harmed by well-intended confession. Honest confession does not require that one publicly or compulsively rehearse all one's sins in specific detail (how boring!—hearing confession in a convent, said one priest, seems like being bombed incessantly with flower petals).

Private Confession. Private offenses are dealt with according to the scriptural instructions of Matthew 18:15–17 and James 5:19, 20. Public offenses are dealt with according to the guidelines found in 1 Corinthians 5:3–5; 1 Thessalonians 5:14; and 2 Thessalonians 3:6.

The penitential practices of Irish Christianity were introduced into Scotland and France by Columba and Columbanus in the sixth century, and within a few generations private repentance had become the norm in place of public repentance (Columbanus, *Penitential, MPL* 130.209–84; McNiell, *HCS*). After the Council of Chalons, A.D. 813, penitential books began to appear to give pastors instructions for examining penitents and applying appropriate acts of reparation (*SCD* 894–96, 1111, 1411–17).

A balanced statement was set forth by the Second Helvetic Confession: "But we believe that this sincere confession which is made to God alone, either privately between God and the sinner, or publicly in the Church where the general confession of sin is said, is sufficient. . . . Therefore it is necessary that we confess our sins to God our Father, and be reconciled with our neighbor if we have offended him. Concerning this kind of confession, the Apostle James says: 'Confess your sins to one another' [James 5:16]. If, however, anyone is overwhelmed by the burden of his sins and by perplexing temptations, and will seek counsel, instruction and comfort privately, either from a minister of the Church, or from any other brother who is instructed in God's law, we do not disapprove; just as we also fully approve of that general and public confession of sins which is usually said in Church" (chap. XIV, *BOC* 5.095; cf. Tho. Aq., *ST* supp., Q6, III, pp. 2586–91).

By regular confession "genuine self-knowledge is increased, Christian humility grows, bad habits are corrected, spiritual neglect and tepidity are countered, the conscience is purified, the will strengthened, a salutary self-control is attained and grace is increased" (Pius XII, *Mystici Corporis* 86, p. 54). The spiritual adviser is urged to "be discreet and cautious, so that he may pour wine and oil into the wounds of the injured person like a skilled physician, diligently inquiring into the circumstances both of the sinner and of the sin, so that he may wisely understand what advice he should give him and what remedy he should apply" (Fourth Lateran Council, *CC*, p. 59).

Confession of Christ

Absolution completes confession of sin and joins it with confession of Christ. Having confessed, the faithful are then to "receive absolution or forgiveness from the confessor as from God himself" (Luther, *Small Catechism, CC*, p. 121).

Confessing Christ with the Mouth from the Heart.   Paul taught that "if you *confess* with your mouth, 'Jesus is Lord,' and *believe* in your heart that God raised him from the dead, you will be saved. For it is with your *heart* that you believe and are justified, and it is with your *mouth* that you confess and are saved" (Rom. 10:9–11, italics added).

To confess Christ is to acknowledge him as he is and makes himself known: as Son of God, servant Messiah, risen Lord, Savior of humanity. To merely breathe this acknowledgment inwardly is not sufficient. It must be breathed in speech, articulated in sentences to fellow human beings, fitting to the occasion. Especially it must be spoken where necessary among the enemies of Christ, precisely where it brings reproach and danger (Polycarp, *Martyrdom, ANF* I, p. 41; Hodge, *The Way of Life,* pp. 259 ff.; Tillett, *PS*, p. 198).

The good confession need not be woodenly stereotyped as occurring in a public act of worship, but it does require that believers speak openly as Christ's ambassadors under his Lordship even when put at hazard. If under safe circumstances one publicly confesses Christ yet fails to confess Christ at a risk-laden moment of *status confessionis* when confession is required in order to maintain and demonstrate faith, then one has not rightly confessed (Barth, *CD* III/4, pp. 87 f.; D. Bonhoeffer, *Cost of Discipleship*). One who insists upon confessing Christ purely inwardly and silently and unpublicly has not yet learned what it means to confess with one's mouth (Rom. 10:10; Ambrose, *On Repentance* 7–9, *NPNF* 2 X, pp. 352–56). Yet under persecution, even silence may become a powerful confession of Christ (Ignatius, *Eph.* 15, *ANF* I, p. 55).

If We Deny Him.   Jesus taught plainly, "Whoever acknowledges me before men, I will also acknowledge from before my Father in heaven. But whoever disowns me before men, I will disown from before my Father in heaven" (Matt. 10:32, 33).

It is hardly possible to conceive of a saving faith that fails to confess Christ openly. Those who wish to believe yet anxiously hide their confession are thereby declaring what they most love: "Yet at the same time many even among the leaders believed in him. But because of the Pharisees *they would not confess their faith for fear* they would be put out of the synagogue; for they loved praise from men more than praise from God" (John 12:42, 43, italics added). "If we deny him, he also will deny us" (2 Tim. 2:12, KJV). "If anyone is ashamed of me and my words in this adulterous and sinful generation, the Son of Man will be ashamed of him when he comes in his Father's glory with the holy angels" (Mark 8:38).

Whether Sins Are Enumerable. The Augsburg Confession taught that private confession and declaration of pardon should be retained, yet noted that "in confession it is not necessary to enumerate all trespasses and sins, for this is impossible: Ps. 19:12, 'Who can discern his errors?'" (XI, *CC*, p. 71). "Our wretched human nature is so deeply submerged in sins that it is unable to perceive or know them all, and if we were to be absolved only from those which we can enumerate we would be helped but little" (XXV, *CC*, p. 87; see Melanchthon, *Loci*, *LCC* XIX, pp. 141–44).

Whether Sacraments Are Acts of Confession. Baptism and Eucharist are modes of confession that Christ himself authorized and instituted. By baptism we confess and share in his death and resurrection. By partaking of the Lord's Table, we confess his living presence and Lordship. By these appointed means, the church is called regularly to confess Christ until the final reckoning (Tho. Aq., *ST* supp., Q4, III, pp. 2582–84; Barth, *CD* IV/4, pp. 3 ff.).

Confession and Character. In cultures where it is commonly assumed that Christ is a legitimate guide, confession may seem so routinized as to become virtually meaningless. In cultures where the confession of Christ is viewed as treason or blasphemy or idolatry or insurrection (as under Nazi or Stalinist or Maoist persecution), the confessing act becomes most compelling and powerful. Yet even in predominately Christian cultures (Christendom, so-called), confession is hardly a routine matter and sometimes requires courage (S. Kierkegaard, *Attack upon "Christendom"*; Barth, *CD* III/4, pp. 52 ff.).

Where a painful break with culture is required, where confession is costly, where it may involve social rejection or persecution, confessing Christ is accompanied by that special grace by which the faithful are enabled to be clear about their confession. This is why richer faith may paradoxically emerge amid apparently poorer or repressed civilizations, where to confess Christ requires a severe break with the world, its support structures, police security operations, and idolatries (Ambrose, *On the Mysteries*, *NPNF* 2 X, pp. 317–23). So it is today that Christianity flourishes in Eastern Europe, Asia, Latin America, and Africa, but languishes North and West.

Moral cowardice detracts from the credibility of faith, however well trained doctrinally. Nothing betrays weak faith more than lack of courage. One whose faith has not been tested by confession has not ventured deeply into faith (Cyprian, *Letters*, *FC* 51, pp. 94–103). Peter lacked courage at the crucifixion but was given the grace of boldness thereafter in the presence of the rulers of Israel (Acts 4:1–22).

Martyrdom. Martyr (*martus*, witness) referred in the first instance to the apostles as witnesses to Christ's life and resurrection. Amid persecution, *martus* became reserved for those who had suffered for the faith, and especially those who had died for the faith (Cyprian, *Letters*, *FC* 51, pp. 24–28, 49–70, 197 ff.). The baptism of blood was viewed as equivalent of the grace of baptism where normal baptism had been unreceived. The anniversary of the death of a martyr was considered a heavenly birthday (*natalis*), and an annual celebration at his or her tomb was a familiar part of early church practice of prayer, as early as the second century (*Martyrdom of Polycarp* 18, *LCC* I, p. 156; Tertullian, *ANF* III, pp. 693–96; Anon., *Acts and Martyrdom of St. Matthew, ANF* VIII, p. 530; *The Revelation of Moses, ANF* VIII, p. 669).

"By martyrdom a disciple is transformed into an image of his Master by freely accepting death for the salvation of the world—as well as his conformity to Christ in the shedding of his blood," an act that few may be called upon to do, yet "all must be prepared to confess Christ before men" (*Ch.* 42, *Doc. Vat. II*). No one offers his or her own life for Jesus' sake without the Holy Spirit, who teaches in the very hour of martyrdom what ought to be said and done (Cyril of Jerusalem, *Catech. Lect.* XVI.21, *NPNF* 2 VII, p. 121).

Where Christianity is popularly accepted, yet inwardly despised, there is great peril to faith (Wesley, *A Farther Appeal*). Martyrs' blood seeds great trees of faith, deeply rooted and prepared for harsh winters (Calvin, *Inst.* 1.8.12, 13; S. Kierkegaard, *Two Ages;* Tillett, *PS,* p. 201).

4 Justification by Grace Through Faith

JUSTIFICATION BY GRACE

Justification

Justification is essential to peace of conscience. No evangelical teaching is more crucial. The Christian life hinges upon its proper understanding (Calvin, *Inst.* 3.11). Rightly received, it vitalizes and consecrates all the energies of the redeemed community. It has been known to engender intrepid responses in those from whom such responses might otherwise have been least expected.

Justification Defined.   Justification is the declaration of God that one, however sinful, who trusts in Christ's atoning work is treated or accounted as righteous, insofar as in Christ one has entered into an uprighted relation with God (Barth, *CD* II/2, pp. 125 ff.; cf. Clarke, *OCT*, p. 406; Stevens, *TNT*, pp. 417 ff.). This is not a legal fiction but a merciful divine action historically enacted on the cross.

Justification is the reversal of God's judgment against the sinner whereby the sinner is declared to be no longer exposed to the penalty of the law, which is ultimately spiritual death, but restored to divine favor (Tho. Aq., *ST* II–I, Q113, III, pp. 1144–52; Strong, *ST,* pp. 471–83, 849). Justification is that divine act whereby one stands in right relation with God, an act of God's free grace through which the sinner is absolved from guilt and accepted as righteous on account of the Son's atoning work (Luther, *The Freedom of a Christian, MLS*, pp. 55–68; Wakefield, *CT* II, p. 406).

Juridical Uprighting. Justification in its biblical sense does not imply that one is already behaviorally or in practice ethically made righteous. Rather it means to declare or deem upright so as to acquit from guilt and punitive liability (*TDNT, dikaiōsis;* Calvin, *Inst.* 3.11–14). It is not an act by which the sinner's nature is changed or by which one is already subjectively made righteous. That is the subject of sanctification. Nowhere in scripture does "justify" imply the direct infusion of a fully matured, fully habituated behavioral quality in the recipient (Augustine, *justum facere, On Trin.* 13.18; *Spirit and Letter,* chap. 26; *Contra Julian* II.168). Rather it refers to an actual declaration through which one is accredited right before the law and Lawgiver.

Justification does not result from higher commitment to greater ideals or more advanced actualization of good character or better performance of the demands of the law. It is solely due to a verdict rendered that reveals God's attitude toward the sinner whose life is hid in Christ. *Justification* is a term that derives from the legal sphere; hence it is called a *forensic* or judicial metaphor. Accordingly, one is justified who is made upright with the Lawgiver (Apology of the Augsburg Conf. IV, *BOC,* pp. 107 ff.).

In taking up the question of justification, we are asking exclusively about what God has done to acquit sin, not yet about what persons do in response. Only after dealing with the new juridical position of humanity in Christ is it possible to take up responsive concerns, which will follow in subsequent discussions of faith active in love, regeneration, adoption, union with Christ, and sanctification (Westminster Conf., *CC,* pp. 207 ff.).

The Decisive Baseline of Evangelical Teaching. Luther wrote in the Smalcald Articles, "Nothing in this article can be given up or compromised. . . . On this article rests all that we teach. . . . Therefore we must be quite certain and have no doubts about it. Otherwise all is lost" (II.1, *BOC,* p. 292).

Justification is not the summit but the ground of the Christian life, not the end but the beginning of the journey of evangelical faith. So pivotal is it to Christian preaching that if it is unbalanced in any way, reverberations are felt in the whole edifice of faith. Many pitfalls must be avoided in preaching this word and presenting this teaching wisely.

Clarification of justification teaching includes the definition of its nature, author, and ground, the sole condition upon which its reception depends, and the ordinary means by which it is received (Pope, *Compend.* II, pp. 402–51; Miley, *ST* II, pp. 309–24; Merrill, *ACE,* pp. 76–116). Also due for examination are the peculiar paradoxes and dilemmas of this teaching, and its potential misconceptions.

Put summarily: Justification's nature is pardon, its condition is faith, its ground is the righteousness of God, and its fruits and evidences are good works (J. Wesley, *WJW* V, pp. 55, 56; Fletcher, *Works* II, pp. 304–8; Watson, *TI* II, chap. 23). The Augsburg Confession defined justification normatively for Protestant theology: "It is also taught among us that we cannot obtain forgiveness of sin and righteousness before God by our own merits, works, or satisfactions, but that we receive forgiveness of sin and become righteous before God by grace, for Christ's sake, through faith, when we believe that Christ suffered for us and that for his sake our sin is forgiven, and righteousness and eternal life are given to us. For God will regard and reckon this faith as righteousness, as Paul says in Romans 3:21–26 and 4:5" (*CC*, p. 69).

Justification Under the Law

Hebraic Roots of the Justification Teaching. Righteousness (*tsedeq, tsedaqa;* LXX: *dikaiosune*) does not so much point to a personal ethical quality, as a right relationship with God (1 Kings 8:32). The righteous one (*tsaddiq*) stands in a right relation with God, restraining the tendency toward evil (*yetzer hara*) and following the divine leading toward good (*yetzer hatob*) through Torah and almsgiving (Exod. 23:7; Deut. 25:1; cf. Melanchthon, *Loci,* XIX, pp. 89 ff., 126 ff.; Guthrie, *NTT,* p. 495).

Two Ways of Justification. Justification may either be viewed as justification by just deeds or justification by grace through faith in Christ (Justin Martyr, *Dialogue with Trypho* XC–XCV, *ANF* I, pp. 244–47). One may be conceived as just or upright in one of two senses—under the law or under the gospel. One may stand in right relation with God either by absolutely doing right or by faith in the One who embodies the right and who does and is what is right (Ps. 119; Gal. 3; cf. Luther, *Comm. on Galatians*).

These two ways are summarized under the terms *law* and *gospel.* "The former is the method of justifying man perfect; but the latter, of justifying man a sinner and corrupt" by "the righteousness of another, even of Christ our Surety, imputed by grace to him that believes in the Gospel" (Helvetic Consensus Formula, *CC,* p. 320).

Whether It Is Possible to Be Upright Before the Law. As to the righteousness of the law, it is said that "if we are careful to obey all this law before the Lord our God, as he has commanded us, that will be our righteousness" (Deut. 6:25). Note, however, that under the strict definition of justification by just deeds, no sin can be overlooked. Under law, Yahweh does not justify the sinner, only the just: "I will not acquit the guilty" (Exod. 23:7). The just judge is required by justice to justify the righteous and condemn the wicked (Deut. 25:1). Conscience does not reassure the sinner.

Insofar as justification by law is theoretically possible but practically unlikely due to the history of sin, there remains only justification by grace as a plausible definition of the justification of a sinner. We are discouraged by scripture from imagining that anyone can actually fulfill the law perfectly apart from grace (Rom. 1:18–2:29; Gal. 2:16; Luther, *Two Kinds of Righteousness, LW* 31, pp. 293 ff.; Calvin, *Inst.* 3.11). Bildad's plaintive question to Job—"How then can a man be righteous before God?"—is the same desperate cry of all who are deeply aware of how distorted human history has become by sin. The psalmist groaned in awareness that "no one living is righteous before you" (Ps. 143:3). The apostles had absorbed this tradition: "There is not a righteous man on earth who does what is right and never sins" (Eccles. 7:20). "There is no one who does not sin" (2 Chron. 6:36). "There is no one who does good, not even one" (Rom. 3:12; Pss. 14:1–3; 53:1–3).

Justification Under Grace

An entirely different premise for approaching justification is made possible by the gospel: "Justification is not paid for deserts, but simply given as a free gift" (Leo, *Sermons* XLIX, *NPNF* 2 XII, p. 161).

God's Way of Recovering a Right Relation with the Sinner.   In the New Testament, as in the Old, to justify is to vindicate an action as right, or to stand in a right relation with God (Rom. 3:24). There is now another way of justification: God's unmerited favor toward sinners.

Justification before the law is conceptually possible but, amid the history of sin, extremely unlikely. "For it is not those who hear the law who are righteous in God's sight, but it is those who obey the law who will be declared righteous" (Rom. 2:13). The only basis upon which one may stand in right relation with God in terms of the law is absolute rectitude, complete innocence. A charge can be erased under law only if one is not guilty. The more honestly we stand before God, the clearer it is that "all have sinned" (Rom. 3:23). The entire history of sin awaits the sentence of the final judge (Rom. 3:19–23).

Precisely amid the history of sin, however, good news has come: one may come into a right relation with God by being "justified freely by his grace" (Rom. 3:24; Calvin, *Catech. of Church of Geneva, LCC* XXII, pp. 103–7).

Anticipations of Uprighting by Grace.   Even as early as Abel, some had come to know that one may stand upright before God by grace through faith, for "by faith he [Abel] was commended as a righteous man" (Heb. 11:4). So also did Noah become "heir of the righteousness that comes by faith" (Heb. 11:7).

Abraham was the decisive type: "By faith Abraham, when called to go to a place he would later receive as his inheritance, obeyed and went, even though he did not know where he was going" (Heb. 11:8). His faith "was credited to him as righteousness" (Gen. 15:6; Rom. 4:3; Calvin, *Inst.* 3.11). Habakkuk grasped the heart of the matter, that "the righteous will live by his faith" (2:4).

Isaiah anticipated the justification that would come through the suffering of the messianic Servant who "makes his life a guilt offering"; "after the suffering of his soul, he will see the light of life, and be satisfied; by his knowledge my righteous servant will justify many, and he will bear their iniquities" (Isa. 53:10, 11). This expected one appeared in Jesus.

The Coming Kingdom Where Righteousness Reigns.   Jesus announced the coming righteousness of God. Those who enter his kingdom, where God's own righteousness personally comes and reigns, participate in a righteousness that exceeds that of the scribes and Pharisees (Matt. 5:20).

In his presence even the obnoxious tax-collector who was grieving over his sins could go "home justified" (Luke 18:14). Those who pretend to merit righteousness or desperately justify themselves in resistance to the coming of God's forgiving love are not ready for this kingdom (Luke 10:29; 16:15; Barth, *CD* IV/1, pp. 219 ff.). The righteous (*dikaio*) on the last day are those who constantly offer acts of compassion to the needy neighbor, yet in doing so are unaware that their kindness has been shown to the unrecognized Son of God (Matt. 25:37, 46).

The Difficulty of Hearing the Word of Justification: The Habit of Self-justification in Modernity.   It is characteristic of modern consciousness that persons assume that they must be justified by their own individual works. Culture-bound, stereotyped sex-role assumptions play heavily into modern forms of works-righteousness. Men commonly justify their existence by their physical or athletic ability or prowess or production or jobs or wealth; women commonly justify their existence by their beauty or nurturance. The message of justification is difficult to accept because it seems too good to be true. It says, Stop trying to justify yourself. You do not need to. There is no way to buy or deserve God's love or acceptance. You are already being offered God's love on the cross, without passing any tests. The word of the cross is not, I will love you *if* you jump this hoop, but "while we were yet helpless, at the right time, Christ died for the ungodly" (Rom. 5:6–8, RSV). God who penetrates all subterfuges and masks knows already our failures and loves us anyway, just as we are. Luther grasped with deep personal conviction that on the basis of the works of the law, the holy God would not let sin go unpunished, yet on the basis of the gospel God is merciful precisely toward penitent sinners (Luther, *Lectures on Romans, LW* 25).

Righteousness from God

Even though justification is a highly refined interest of the Pauline letters, it is found generally in scripture. Paul's view must be understood in relation to Mosaic law, the psalms, prophets, and the proclamation of Jesus on righteousness (Irenaeus, *Ag. Her.* IV.34.2, *ANF* I, p. 511). Paul's emphasis upon juridical uprighting needs to be kept in tension with the writing of others in the New Testament who speak further in a complementary way about the intrinsic relation of justification and sanctification (1 Pet. 2:24; 3:14; 2 Pet. 1:1; 3:13; 1 John 2:29; 3:7, 10).

Romans 3:22–26 summarized Paul's justification teaching: "This righteousness from God comes through faith in Jesus Christ to all who believe. There is no difference, for all have sinned and fall short of the glory of God, and are justified freely by his grace through the redemption that came by Christ Jesus. God presented him as a sacrifice of atonement, through faith in his blood. He did this to demonstrate his justice, because in his forbearance he had left the sins committed beforehand unpunished—he did it to demonstrate his justice at the present time, so as to be just and the one who justifies those who have faith in Jesus" (cf. Clement of Alexandria, *Instructor* I.8–10, *ANF* II, pp. 225–33, Luther, *LW* 33, pp. 263–65; Calvin, *Comm.* XIX, pp. 134–47). It is understandable that pious Jews would resist the teaching that God has chosen to justify ungodly pagans (Rom. 4:5) apart from the works of the law by faith alone (Rom. 3:26; Gal. 2:16).

Righteousness Revealed.   The righteousness of God is now fully made known. "For in the gospel a righteousness from God is revealed, a righteousness that is by faith from first to last, just as it is written: 'The righteous will live by faith'" (Rom. 1:17). This "righteousness from God" means the quality of righteousness that can stand uprightly in God's presence (Calvin, *Comm.* XX, Rom., pp. 63–66; Ridderbos, *Paul,* p. 163).

The Courtroom Metaphor.   The heart of the idea of uprighting cannot be penetrated without exploring the metaphor of the courtroom. God's justifying action is analogous to a judicial act by which God declares the sinner free from guilt and acquitted. God forgives the penitent believer and, based on this pardon, declares that person right with the divine Judge. God acquits the ungodly who believe in Christ and declares them just. Condemned before, they are now acquitted; previously rejected, now accepted personally (*acceptatio personae*, Melanchthon, *Loci*, XIX, pp. 88 ff.; cf. *CR* XXI.742) into the presence of God. The expected condemnation has been reversed to acquittal.

In this court, God is judge whose judgments are right and sure (Gen. 18:25), and the law is the historical expression of what God requires. God does not act subservient to a law above God. Rather the origin of all right law is in the righteous One alone. What God requires of us is conformity to God's own way of acting—righteously. It is in this law that the faithful "delight" and "meditate day and night" (Ps. 1:2).

All the elements of the courtroom situation are presupposed. The judge is God: "You have come to God, the judge of all" (Heb. 12:23). The defendant is everyone who has become tragically enmeshed in the history of sin: "the whole world" being "held accountable to God" (Rom. 3:19). "Everyone who sins breaks the law; in fact, sin is lawlessness" (1 John 3:4). The plaintiff or accuser is personified as Moses, or generalized as "the law": "Your accuser is Moses" (John 5:45). The internal witness is conscience, the moral testimony of the heart, or moral reasoning: "the requirements of the law are written on their [the Gentiles'] hearts . . . their consciences also bearing witness, and their thoughts now accusing, now even defending them" (Rom. 2:15).

In this court an indictment is being read according to "the written code, with its regulations, that was against us and that stood opposed to us" (Col. 2:14). A sentence is being delivered: "Indeed, in our hearts we felt the sentence of death" (2 Cor. 1:9). The defendant is as good as dead: "As for you, you were dead in your transgressions and sins" (Eph. 2:1; J. Wesley, "The Great Assize," *WJWB* I, sermon 15; *WJW* V, pp. 171–85).

The Advocate.   There is, however, in this courtroom an incomparable Advocate: "We have one who speaks to the Father in our defense—Jesus Christ, the Righteous One" (1 John 2:1). A satisfaction is offered, substituting another's suffering of the penalty for sinners: "He is the atoning sacrifice for our sins" (1 John 2:2). The sacrifice of one is accepted for many: "Through the obedience of the one man the many will be made righteous" (Rom. 5:19). On this basis the judge reverses the judgment, grants a full acquittal, and justifies the accused: "Therefore, there is now no condemnation for those who are in Christ Jesus" (Rom. 8:1).

"God made him who had no sin to be sin for us, so that in him we might become the righteousness of God" (2 Cor. 5:21). Our righteousness does not imply an already actualized or perfectly just ethical behavior. This is clear by analogy with Christ's seeming "sin," which is his real act of becoming "sin for us," which is a substitutional or forensic "sinfulness" on our behalf, not a behavioral sinfulness (John Chrysostom, *Hom. on 2 Cor.* XI, *NPNF* 1 XII, pp. 333–35; Ladd, *TNT*, p. 446). Christ had no sin ethically, but became sin for us in a substitutionary sense, so that we might share really in his righteousness.

The Final Reversal.   In a civil court, there are in sequence three possible ways of being justified: *upon arraignment,* by sufficiently answering a specific accusation showing oneself by the facts to be not guilty; *after arraignment*, by demonstrating that regardless of what one may be accused of, however damaging the evidence, the law itself protects one from penalty, hence one is justified; and *after a trial* in which one is found guilty, by executive clemency remitting the penalty, on the principle of *pardon*.

It is in this third sense that the New Testament most often employs the idea of justification. For all are guilty as charged of sin (before and after arraignment); hence there is no other ground left except clemency or pardon. Such clemency implies not an abrogation of the law, but an exercise of judicial prerogative. The law is being personally applied to a particular case by a particular judge as a decision rightly made whereby the law itself is reestablished and magnified (Tho. Aq., *ST* II–II, Q157, II, pp. 1834–47; Ralston, *ED*, pp. 367–413).

Justification is the very last event of reversal in this extended courtroom drama. It depends for its context and meaning upon the previous events of litigation. It is amid this metaphorical theater that the biblical terms are understood: *Dikaiosis* is a judicial decision or sentence of acquittal. *Dikaios* (righteous), *dikaioma* (judgment), *dikaioo* (to declare righteous, to justify), *logizomai* (to reckon or credit the account of), and *dikaisune* (righteousness) all derive from the same courtroom premise. Forgiveness is not offered to declare sinners behaviorally innocent, but to remove their liability to punishment. Such terms are applied not literally but analogically to God's declarative action of pardon. Analogies are not equations but similarities amid remaining differences (as God's righteousness is not in the simple sense reduced to human righteousness).

The Acquittal.   The salvation event is like an act of acquittal: the defendant is instantly relieved of all charges. It is that act by which a judge officially declares one to stand upright in the presence of the judge.

When justification, as a judicial term, is applied to God's act toward the penitent hid in Christ, it becomes understood as full pardon from all guilt and a new reckoning of the sinner as righteous (*Epistle to Diognetus* 9, *ECW*, p. 180). As in a court of law one may be declared released from charges, so in the presence of God one may be declared righteous so that one's sin no longer counts against one.

The bare metaphor of acquittal, taken abstractly, is insufficient to express God's saving action. Acquittal declares that one has *done no wrong*. Justification is the acceptance of the sinner, united in Christ by faith, precisely while it remains clear that he or she *has done wrong*. It is while the conscience-stricken sinner is disclaiming his innocence and openly declaring his guilt that acquittal is announced. If such a condemned person is to be delivered from guilt, it must be by a just cancellation of the charge or blotting out from the record any charge against him or her.

No Condemnation.   Gospel justification views the convicted offender as suddenly pardoned in a way that destroys the connection between a behavior and its penal consequence (Apology of the Augsburg Conf., *BOC*, pp. 100 ff.; Field, *HCT*, p. 157). Pardon reverses the sentence of condemnation (Rom. 8:1).

Justification is best understood in direct contrast with condemnation. Those justified are not condemned; those not justified are condemned. There is no middle way (Matt. 12:37). To justify is to liberate the offender precisely when condemnation seemed evident. Under the law the sinner is condemned. Under the gospel the sinner is justified (Melanchthon, *Loci* XIX, pp. 61 ff.; Küng, *Justification*, pp. 93 ff.).

"It is God who justifies. Who is he that condemns?" (Rom. 8:33b, 34a). If God "shall say that thou art a sinner, say thou: 'Lord, I interpose the death of our Lord Jesus Christ between my sins and thee'" (Anselm, *Consolatio, MPL* 158.687; Strong, *ST*, p. 849). This is why justification can be offered to sinners only. Those who assume they are not sinners assume they do not need it.

Whether Justification Is an End-of-History Event. The final-day character of justification is evident in Jesus' proclamation: "But I tell you that men will have to give account on the day of judgment for every careless word they have spoken. For by your words you will be acquitted, and by your words you will be condemned" (Matt. 12:36, 37). The concluding act of the justification drama is the last day. The same word for justification that is used in courts of law (Isa. 5:23; Deut. 25:1) is also used of God's judgment in the last day (Matt. 12:37; Rom. 2:13, 16). This future justifying act of God, having already been established on the cross, is looking toward its end-time completion: "Since we have now been justified by his blood, how much more shall we be saved from God's wrath through him!" (Rom. 5:9). Justification is a presently experienced reality, assuming union with Christ by faith, anticipatory of the final day of judgment.

The verdict of this final-day court has already been announced, though history continues. Justification is an end-time event in which the believer stands already in an anticipative sense. Those united to Christ are justified from all guilt—past, present, and future. Those who die believing will not be condemned in final judgment, but justified. God's final justifying action awaits the end of history, though the verdict is already known.

Christ Our Righteousness. Jeremiah prophesied of a coming One who would be called "the Lord our Righteousness" (Jer. 23:6). Isaiah expected One Anointed to "preach good news to the poor" (Isa. 61:1), who would clothe sinners "with garments of salvation" and array them "in a robe of righteousness" (Isa. 61:10; John Chrysostom, *Baptismal Instructions, ACW* 31, pp. 71, 135–39). Christ is attested as "king of righteousness" (Heb. 7:2).

The idea that Christ is our righteousness is distortable in an antinomian direction. The notion that one's sins are unconditionally covered by another's righteousness may invite license. It is indeed through faith that Christ's righteousness is accounted to us (Rom. 3:24, 25), but it is misleading to conclude from this that personal qualities of Christ's actual obedience are being directly or immediately imparted (given) or infused (poured in) to the believer without faith that freely becomes active in love (Clement of Alexandria, *Stromata* II.6, *ANF* II, p. 354). The faith that saves is faith that so trusts in Christ as to work in love (Calvin, *Inst.* 3.16–18).

The one God who justifies may be at one point referred to as Father (Rom. 8:33), at another point as Son (Matt. 9:6), and elsewhere as Spirit (1 Cor. 6:11; Augustine, *Trin.* I.8–12, *NPNF* 1 III, pp. 26–31). The triune premise allows and requires the interconnected affirmation that the Son justifies by the Spirit according to the will of the Father. "It is God who justifies" (Rom. 8:33), for it is God the Father who sent the Son and "presented him as a sacrifice of atonement, through faith in his blood" (Rom. 3:25; 8:30–32; Gal. 3:8).

As If Righteous?

Whether the Justified Sinner Is Immediately Made Morally Upright in Actual Behavior. The moral problem of justification teaching is to understand how the sinner can be viewed by God "as if" righteous without morally exhibiting any righteousness. How can one be treated as if justified while one still remains unrighteous? In what sense is one "really righteous" in an actualized ethical sense, and in what sense merely regarded as if righteous?

Justification does not mean that the sinner immediately possesses, by virtue of Christ's justifying grace, a just disposition or holy moral character, but rather that one is freed from the obligation to suffer the penalty of law, treated as if one had fulfilled the law by virtue of Christ's fulfillment of the law on one's behalf. Our righteousness is not attained by the direct ethical infusion or literal transfer of Christ's behavior to our behavior, but rather by a lifelong, active appropriation through faith of God's pardoning grace (Calvin, *Inst.* 3.4.5, 12).

Christ has endured the penalty already for the sinner, who is united to Christ by faith. New life in Christ is invited by grace to grow gradually in behavioral conformity with the requirement of God. Even if this conformity is incomplete in this life, it lives in hope of its being completed by grace in the final judgment. "When he appears, we shall be like him" (1 John 3:2).

"We, who with unveiled faces all reflect the Lord's glory, *are being transformed into his likeness* with ever-increasing glory, which comes from the Lord, who is the Spirit" (2 Cor. 3:18, italics added). This assumes a mirror metaphor whereby the faithful are being transformed into the same image, the image of God, "changed from one form into another, and we pass from an obscure form to a bright form, for though obscure, yet it is the image of God. . . . And when this nature, the most excellent in created things, is justified from its impiety by its own Creator, it is transferred from a deformed form into a beautiful form" (Augustine, *Trin.* XV.8.14, *FC* 45, p. 470).

In What Sense One Is Clothed in Christ's Righteousness. Zechariah had a series of visions that early church exegetes viewed as anticipatory of the coming of Christ. In the third of these, "Joshua was dressed in filthy clothes as he stood before the angel. The angel said to those who were standing before him, 'Take off his filthy clothes.' Then he said to Joshua, 'See, I have taken away your sin, and I will put rich garments on you'" (Zech. 3:4). This prophetic metaphor was taken by classic exegetes to be an anticipatory reference to repentance and restoration to favor that only became fully knowable in Christ (John Chrysostom, *Baptismal Instructions, ACW* 31, pp. 135–39, 162–63).

This clothing metaphor (Isa. 61:10; 2 Cor. 5:1–21; 1 Pet. 5:5; Rev. 4:4; 7:9) augments the courtroom metaphor. To declare sinners upright before God is to deal with them as if they were clothed in Christ's goodness, accepting them as if they were perfect doers of the law, absolved from guilt, released from debt, discharged from any penalty due, despite past unrighteousness (Cyprian, *Letters, FC* 51, pp. 272 ff.).

The benefits of Christ's obedience (active and passive) are accounted or reckoned to the believer, but this does not imply that the believer actually and immediately lives with perfect uprightness or acts precisely as Christ acted. The proximate participation of the believer in deeds that reflect the goodness of Christ requires a further work of the Spirit in fully applying the benefits of justification to the sinner. That is the subject of sanctification. Justification remains a declarative act of God external to human willing, as distinguished from sanctification, which is an efficacious act of God the Spirit within the sinner's will, to change that will (Calvin, *Inst.* 3.16; J. Wesley, *WJW* VI, pp. 65–77, *WJWB* 45; *WJW* V, pp. 212–23; *WJWB* 18; Pope, *Compend.* III, pp. 3–36; Hodge, *ST* III, pp. 213–30; Strong, *ST*, p. 849).

Whether There Is a Real Annihilation of Guilt.   Though remitted sins cease to exist in God's eyes, their consequences persist in the history of sin. Just because I repent of my sin does not mean that the hurt I caused another is suddenly no longer felt or other consequences obliterated. That is why reparation is such an important part of the moral follow-through for forgiveness.

But from God's eyes, the sin is forever blotted out, removed, crossed off the list of indebtedness (Isa. 1:18; Mic. 7:18–19). "I, even I, am he who blots out your transgressions, for my own sake, and remembers your sins no more" (Isa. 43:25). "As far as the east is from the west, so far has he removed our transgressions from us" (Ps. 103:12). On this basis the psalmist could meaningfully pray, "Blot out my transgressions. Wash away all my iniquity, and cleanse me from my sin" (Ps. 51:1, 2). "Repent, then," Peter preached, "and turn to God, so that your sins may be wiped out" (Acts 3:19).

God's justifying action on the cross calls for a continuing reception of sanctifying grace by which sin is gradually uprooted from personal habituation. It is precisely justifying grace, the once offered "blood of Christ," that seeks continually to cleanse us "from all sin" (1 John 1:7), having "freed us from our sins by his blood" (Rev. 1:5).

> His blood atoned for all our race,
> And sprinkles now the throne of grace . . .
> Before the throne my Surety stands;
> My name is written on his hands.
>
> (C. Wesley, in Tillett, *PS*, p. 225; cf. *WHNS* 726)

The Causes of Justification

Four movements are embraced by God's justifying action, according to Thomas Aquinas: the offer of justifying grace; the grace-enabled movement of the free will toward God through faith; the movement of the freed will against sin; and the remission of guilt (Tho. Aq., *ST* I–II, Q113, I, pp. 1144–53; cf. Bonaventure, *Breviloquium* 5.3). Protestant exegesis tends to conflate these into a single declarative judgment.

The grace of baptism is the means provided by which this justifying grace is initiated and declared as beginning, as if with a new birth. The reception of justifying grace is like moving from death to life, from darkness to light (1 John 3:14; Col. 2:13; Eph. 5:8).

The causality of justification has been a complex argument in the history of exegesis, especially as treated in Scholastic and Counter-Reformation teaching (Calvin, *Inst.* 3.14; cf. Heppe, *RD; Trent* VI, pp. 33, 34; *SCD* 799, 804, pp. 248,

255). The several levels of the cause of justification have been at various times sorted out as one or more of the following:

- Grace as *originating* cause, source, and fountain of justification. By grace alone the plan of redemption is foreknown and executed: The Father's offer of mercy is by grace; Christ's atoning work for us is by grace; the Spirit's work in us is by grace. The opening, emerging, maturing, and completing movements of repentance, faith, and obedience are all by grace. So it is exclusively by grace that one is saved through faith.

- The love of God the Father for fallen humanity is sometimes said to be the *procuring* cause—the reason why the plan of salvation was ordered and initiated. This is sometimes described as the moving cause, the grace and love of the Father that those who have faith should be redeemed (John 4:16; Rom. 5:8; Col. 2:16).

- The atoning value or merit of Christ on the cross is sometimes said to be the *meritorious* cause of justification (Rom. 5:19; 2 Cor. 5:19–21; Heb. 10:10–14), the sole reason why sinners are regarded as justified. The Son is the only meriting cause of justification.

- The grace of repentance is sometimes said to be the *preparatory* cause of justification, awakened and elicited by prevening grace. God's own Spirit is the efficient cause, the working agent who applies the justifying action of the Son to responding hearts, regenerating, enabling faith and obedience (Rom. 8:30–33; Eph. 1:13, 14).

- The *instrumental* cause is baptism, by which this faith is received and life in the Spirit is born anew (Col. 2:12; Titus 3:5; John 3:5).

- The *receiving* cause (sometimes called the subjective or conditional cause in the subject self) is saving faith, itself enabled by grace (Rom. 3:26–4:25; Gal. 3:8, 9). Faith as receiving cause of justification is the sole instrumentality through which justification comes to each one, the hand by which we reach out and receive the proffered blessing to make it our own, and in this sense its sole condition (Luther, *LW* 31, pp. 346–49; Merrill, *ACE*, p. 104).

- The *formal* cause is the justice or uprightness of God, as adapted to the human condition, which wills to make creatures also upright (*Trent,* session VI.7, p. 33; Hall, *DT* VIII, p. 263).

- The glory of God is the *final* cause (Tho. Aq., *ST;* Weaver, *CT,* p. 166; Gamertsfelder, *ST,* p. 499).

These levels of causality are combined, subdivided, or their sequence rearranged by various traditions. What is consensually agreed upon is that the central nexus at which human decision is touched by all these levels of causality is saving faith, the grace-enabled human responsiveness by which sinners receive the justifying grace of Christ and become united with him (Second Helvetic Conf., chap. 15 ff., *COC* III, pp. 266 ff.; *Westminster Catech., CC,* pp. 207 ff.).

The Blessings of Justification

Justification as Christian Theodicy.   In daily experience we are met with perplexing questions of why good people suffer. Life does not long permit an evasion of this query: Why does God permit sin, especially sin that causes suffering to innocent parties? In *The Living God* I addressed this question in some detail; the gist of it is: Only a primordially good freedom can fall into sin. In the goodness of creation, God wants to give us that freedom. Evil could be completely prevented only by absolutely preventing freedom or protecting freedom from all possibility of being distorted or falling, and that would then be inconsistent with God's purpose in offering humanity freedom (*LG,* pp. 279–315; John of Damascus, *OF* II.24, 25, *NPNF* 2 IX, pp. 38–40).

Classic pastoral reasoning about suffering returns often to the well of justification teaching, where the whole question of theodicy is itself being transformed. At the cross it becomes no longer a question of why God permits sin and evil. Rather, more radically, God takes fallen freedom and blots out its transgressions, giving freedom a new start! In this way the language of justification responds profoundly to the perennial quandary of why human suffering is permitted in God's world (Luther, *Sermons on St. John, LW* 23, p. 81; Barth, *CD* II/3, pp. 292 ff.).

Justification teaching takes the theodicy dilemma much further than philosophical reasoning by framing the question from the cross where God's holy love suffers to upright historical wrongs. In justification, God gives a new birth of freedom. Pardon does not end suffering, but cleans the slate for freedom to begin anew. Fallen freedom cannot redeem itself. God acts justly and as justifier of fallen freedom (Rom. 3:26; Clement of Alexandria, *Instructor* I.8, *ANF* II, pp. 225–28; Calvin, *Comm.* XX, Rom., pp. 139–46). Just as sin is "not known except by the pain it causes," so is the making of satisfaction "more pleasing to God and more valuable for man's salvation than ever Adam's sin was harmful" (Dame Juliana of Norwich, *RDL,* pp. 125, 127).

Why a Comforting Doctrine.   Justification is one of the proffered blessings that belong to the emerging age of God's own coming. The psalmist pronounced one blessed "whose transgressions are forgiven, whose sins are covered. Blessed is the man whose sin the Lord does not count against him and in whose spirit is no deceit" (Ps. 32:1; Callistus, *Epistles* II, *ANF* VIII, p. 618).

If it were possible for one to provide complete restitution for all those wrongs one has done to others, then one might imagine that the grace of justification and forgiveness might be somehow less necessary. But the problem remains: one cannot go back and undo all that one has wrongly or harmfully done. No restitution can ever be adequate. We have all caused harm for which we can never make full restitution. This is why we stand in such dire need of forgiveness (Tho. Aq., *ST* II–II, Q62, II, pp. 1455–61; E. Lewis, *Great Christian Teachings,* p. 41).

The Anglican Articles of Religion underscore the comfort and benefit of justification teaching: "We are accounted righteous before God, only for the merit of our Lord and Savior Jesus Christ by faith, and not for our own works or deservings; wherefore, that we are justified by faith only is a most wholesome doctrine, and very full of comfort" (Thirty-nine Articles, XI, *BCP;* cf. *Heid. Catech.* 1, *COC* III, pp. 307–8).

With paradoxical vivacity, Luther wrote, "As often as you insist that I am a sinner, just so often do you call me to remember the benefit of Christ my Redeemer, upon whose shoulders, and not upon mine, lie all my sins. . . . So, when you say that I am a sinner, you do not terrify, but comfort me immeasurably" (Luther, *Comm. on Galatians,* Middleton translation amended, pp. 21, 22).

Elements of Justification Teaching: Forgiving, Pardoning, Reckoning, and Reconciling

These overlapping metaphors mesh together in the scriptural teaching of justifying grace: the offender is forgiven, the accused is pardoned, the offense is remitted, the lost child welcomed home. In these ways, justifying grace reveals a subtle cohesion of divine attributes. The single turn from repentance to faith is variably symbolized as

an act of forgiveness that encourages,

an acquittal that remits,

a new mode of accounting that crosses out the penalty, and

a divine-human reconciliation that embraces the lost.

The scriptural metaphors are more mixed and complicated than this fourfold sequence, but their complexity is encompassed and summarized by it (Ursinus, *Comm. on the Heid. Catech.*, pp. 325 ff.; Gamertsfelder, *ST*, p. 494). Though distinguishable, forgiveness and pardon will be considered together.

Whether Pardon and Forgiveness Are Distinguishable Terms.   Forgiveness of sins is the earliest blessing of saving faith. It necessarily precedes the reception of other benefits. It remains an article of the Apostles' Creed to confess, "I believe in the forgiveness of sins" (*SCD* 2, p. 5; cf. Rufinus, *Comm. on Apostles' Creed* 40, *NPNF* 2 III, p. 559; Baxter, *PW* XIX, pp. 102–8).

Forgiveness and pardon are related metaphors belonging to different spheres: The act of forgiveness belongs to the family metaphor, while the act of pardon belongs to the courtroom metaphor. The judge can pardon but not forgive. The loving parent can forgive where such forgiveness would be inappropriate in a courtroom. Though distinguishable, they are complementary, and in the New Testament the two metaphors are intensely conflated: it is through divine forgiveness that an acquittal is offered. It is not that those free from condemnation are then forgiven—that would reverse the order. Rather those forgiven are thereby freed from condemnation (John 3:16; Rom. 4:5; 5:1, 16; Gal. 2:16; John Chrysostom, *Comm. on Gal., NPNF* 1 XIII, pp. 1 ff.).

In this way the forgiveness of sins and the declaration of the sinner as pardoned and united with Christ's righteousness are different angles of vision upon the same event. Each correlated verb amplifies the meaning of the other: give, forgive, justify, pardon, remit, cover sin, and reckon faith for righteousness.

Distinguishing Pardon and Justification.   Though it is divine mercy that pardons, it is divine justice that justifies (Anselm, *CDH;* Field, *HCT*, p. 198; Hare, *On Justification*). "To *pardon* is, in the exercise of sovereign prerogative, to waive the execution of the penal sanctions of the law; to *justify* is to declare that the demands of the law are satisfied, not waived. Pardon is a sovereign act; justification is a judicial act" (C. Hodge, *The Way of Life*, p. 154, italics added; Tillett, *PS*, p. 219; cf. *Trent, SCD* 792, 799, pp. 248–52; Pius V, *Errors of Michael du Bay, SCD* 1031 ff., pp. 395 ff.). Pardon refers to a juridical declaration by which that remission is formally announced and accomplished (Justin Martyr, *Dialogue with Trypho*

XIII–XIV, *ANF* II, pp. 200–202). One who is justified is declared just or upright on the basis of the pardon through which guilt is remitted.

In law, when pardon is granted it is not, strictly speaking, according to the law but above the law, mercifully transcending the demands of the law. Mercy alone may pardon. Not so with justification, for *only mercy and justice in unison can justify.* Justification is that key moment in the history of salvation in which the righteousness of God is declared in relation to the history of sin, yet without offense to the justice of God (Calvin, *Inst.* 3.11–15; Pope, *Compend.* II, pp. 253–316).

In Christ, pardon and justification intertwine, so that one whom God pardons is justified and one whom God justifies is pardoned. Even if not strictly equivalent, they are inseparable. Where one is mentioned, the other is usually implied (Mark 1:4; Luke 1:77; 3:3; Acts 2:38; 5:31; 10:43; Eph. 1:7; Rom. 3:24; Titus 3:7). For this reason *pardon* and *justification* at times appear in scripture as virtually synonymous terms: "Therefore, my brothers, I want you to know that through Jesus the forgiveness of sins is proclaimed to you. Through him everyone who believes is justified from everything you could not be justified from by the law of Moses" (Acts 13:38, 39; Luke 18:13, 14; Rom. 4:5, 8; cf. Ralston, *ED* II, pp. 292–94).

Only the theandric mediator could justly pardon without demeaning justice. Only the crucified Lord could at the same time remain "just" and "forgive us our sins" (1 John 1:9; Rom. 3:26), so that grace might reign through merciful righteousness and not by mercy alone as if disengaged from justice. Forgiveness is consistent with God's righteous character: "If we confess our sins, he is faithful and just and will forgive us our sins and purify us from all unrighteousness" (1 John 1:9).

The Moral Difficulty of Receiving Pardon from Another. There are times when the word of pardon is extremely difficult to hear and make plausible. Even when most urgently thirsted for, it may seem wholly out of reach. Then it is "out of the depths" that the cry for reconciliation comes (Ps. 130:1).

One cannot reason one's way from conviction to pardon. It is exclusively an act of grace offered and revealed by the incomparable One who pardons. It is not merely willed from within oneself. No matter how much one may look for naturalistic correlates of divine mercy, my word of pardon to myself is always finally hollow and insufficient. Admittedly, there may indeed be times when I need to permit myself to forgive myself or to be forgiven by another. But it is finally by Another that one is forgiven, not by oneself. Hence pardon is intrinsically interpersonal (Ps. 25:11; Isa. 40:1, 2; Barth, *CD* I/2, pp. 433 ff.).

Nature does not pardon. Reason can only analyze the need for pardon, as in psychoanalysis. Through reason we may learn that God is just, but it is hardly a reasonable deduction that God would justify sinners precisely while they were yet ungodly (Rom. 5:8). Conscience is the last of all human faculties to pardon sin. Its main constructive function in the presence of sin is to accuse.

One cannot believe one is forgiven without having received the grace of readiness to be forgiven (Kierkegaard, *PF*, pp. 16–22). Christians learn of pardon through searching scripture, coming to table with the risen Lord to receive Holy Communion, hearing the inner testimony of the Spirit attest scripture as true. "If you, O Lord, kept a record of sins, O Lord, who could stand? But with you there is forgiveness" (Ps. 130:3, 4).

The Mystery of Pardon.   Since sin is against God, only God can remove it or blot out the charge. Christ's sacrificial death expiates sin. Faith receives the gift. Without faith the gift is given but unreceived. When his detractors asked Jesus, "Who can forgive sins but God alone?" (Luke 5:21), they were asking a profound question, but without recognition that it was God indeed who was standing in their midst announcing to the paralytic, "Friend, your sins are forgiven" (Luke 5:20).

The relation of atonement and pardon is among the great mysteries of faith, as are triunity, incarnation, and resurrection. All theories pale in relation to the experienced fact that pardon is known in a lively way in the Christian community at the Lord's Table and in the hearing of the Word (Luke 24:35; Luther, *Large Catech.* V, *BOC*, pp. 447 ff.; Thirty-nine Articles, XIX, *CC*, p. 273). Faith simply receives this revelation gratefully, rejoicing in the gift rather than pretending to penetrate this mystery with infinite curiosity (Ambrose, *The Mysteries, FC* 44, pp. 6 ff.).

The apostles expected a final, history-ending, transtemporal disclosure of meaning, which could hardly be fitted into the assumptions of the history of sin. Yet enough had been revealed to them that they could confidently celebrate that atonement meant pardon, even if they could not specify precisely how except to point to the mystery of grace. However beyond our ken, the reality of forgiveness is to be preached without delay or apology (Ambrose, *On Repentance* 5–10, *NPNF* 2 X, pp. 332–37). The risen Lord taught that "repentance and forgiveness of sins will be preached in his name to all nations, beginning at Jerusalem" (Luke 24:47). This is just what Peter did when the Spirit was given at Pentecost (Acts 2:38; 3:19).

Forgiveness as Given.   The central feature of for*give*ness is its radical gift character. For*give*ness can only occur when freely given away (Anglo-Saxon: *for-,* away, and *giefan,* to give; Gk. *aphesis,* a letting go). Anyone who forgives another who has deeply offended is engaging in a gracious act, thereby sharing in God's own grace (Barth, *CD* I/2, pp. 433 ff.).

Forgiveness is a costly gift, since the one forgiving cancels the debt and forfeits that which is due, taking responsibility for any liability or deficit (Calvin, *Inst.* 3.18–20; 4.1). God's forgiveness of our sins involves and requires God's taking our sins upon himself, bearing them on the cross, taking the penalty for us, being punished where sinners justly should have been punished under law (Justin Martyr, *Dialogue with Trypho* 13, *ANF* I, p. 201).

Where forgiveness pervades a relationship, it is no longer dominated by aggressive charges, counterclaims, and legalistic attempts to recover damages, but by overflowing love, acceptance, reconciliation, and grace. Love covers a multitude of sins (James 5:20). In forgiving, one graciously gives up the nursing of resentment, as well as all debts and charges against the other (Leo, *Sermons* XLIX, *NPNF* 2 XII, pp. 160, 161).

Justification is a gift of God to which the human recipient has no inherent right or claim (Eph. 1:6, 7; 2:7, 8; Rom. 4:4; John 3:16; Titus 2:11). If divine forgiveness had been humanly merited, there would have been nothing to forgive, for merit then would replace the need for forgiveness. Lack of merit is a primary assumption of forgiveness (Second Council of Orange, *SCD* 176 ff., pp. 75 ff.).

The Lord's Prayer makes it clear that one is bound to share with others the forgiveness received of God (Tertullian, *On Prayer* 7, *ANF* III, p. 684). The two dimensions of the prayer are inseparable: God is forgiving us while we in turn are forgiving others (Luke 11:4). Jesus held the connection rigorously: "if you do not forgive men their sins, your Father will not forgive your sins" (Matt. 6:15).

The New Accounting

Imputed Righteousness. The apostles made heavy use of the bookkeeping analogy: imputing or crediting to another's account. To impute (*logizomai*) is to ascribe good or evil to a person as coming from another, to credit as a virtue to another or to charge as a fault to another.

The language of imputation has entered importantly into justification teaching as seen in Paul's crucial phrase "faith is credited [*logizetai*] as righteousness" (Rom. 4:5). Our sins are charged to Christ. Christ's obedience is offered for our account (Calvin, *Inst.* 2.16.6; 17.4, 5). "Faith may be said to be imputed to us for righteousness, as it is the sole condition of our acceptance" (J. Wesley, *NUNT*, Rom. 4:9, *NB*, p. 499; Watson, *TI* II, p. 587).

The imputation metaphor is multidimensional: Adam's sin has been reckoned to flow into the history of all humanity, so Adam's debt is "charged to our account." Human sin has been reckoned or accounted to Christ, so Christ paid the penalty for human sin generally, becoming a curse for us. Human sin is mercifully not being counted against or imputed to the sinner who trusts Christ (Rom. 4:22–24; 2 Cor. 5:19). Christ's righteousness is reckoned to that believer (Calvin, *Inst.* 3.11–15).

Complementary Sides of Imputation. Justification teaching employs a twofold reversal in the bookkeeping metaphor—it means both the discharging (nonimputation) from sin and the crediting (imputation) of Christ's righteousness (Clement of Alexandria, *Stromata* V.5, *ANF* II, pp. 444–46; Calvin, *Inst.* 4.16–17; Wakefield, *CT* II, p. 407). Debt is discharged; substitutionary payment is credited. This the *Epistle to Diognetus* called "the sweet exchange" (9, *ECW*, p. 180).

Paul's teaching made both levels explicit: (1) that sin is not charged against the believing sinner, for "God was reconciling the world to himself in Christ, *not counting* men's sins against them" (2 Cor. 5:19), and (2) that Christ's righteousness is accredited to the believing sinner, who is "found in him, not having a righteousness of my own that comes from the law, but that which is through faith in Christ—the *righteousness that comes from God and is by faith*" (Phil. 3:9, italics added). Righteousness is thus reckoned to one "who does not work but trusts God," whose "faith is credited as righteousness" (Rom. 4:5).

The accounting metaphor accords believers the standing of uprightness that they do not reach by their own deeds. The believer is treated as actually righteous in relation to God. Since one cannot on one's own achieve an adequate righteousness, God mercifully provides it. This is why one's ethical deeds are not the basis for gaining standing in God's presence. Only in the cross is it possible to see that sin is forgiven without offending God's own righteousness (Anselm, *CDH;* Calvin, *Inst.* 3.11.21–23).

But how can God remain holy if sin is easily dismissed? That is just the point: it is not an easy dismissal. It required a cross, a death, a burial. The cross is a sacrificial offering substituting Christ's goodness for our sin. The burden of our sin is transferred directly from our shoulders to Christ's cross (Rom. 3:21–15; 2 Cor. 5:21).

A related business metaphor, *remission*, was pressed to the service of proclaiming justifying grace. Remission refers to that act by which debt or guilt or penalty is set aside (literally, sent back; Lat. *remittere*). To remit is to cancel a debt or refrain from enforcing a requirement, so that "everyone who believes in him receives forgiveness [*aphesis*] of sins" (Acts 10:43).

The apostles were authorized to proclaim freedom from the ceremonial observances of ancient Israel, to teach that law as a "shadow of the good things that are coming—not the realities themselves. For this reason it can never, by the same sacrifices repeated endlessly year after year, make perfect those who draw near to worship" (Heb. 10:1, 2). On the cross was "effected a transfer from the Law to the Gospel, from the Synagogue to the Church, from many sacrifices to one Victim" (Leo the Great, sermon LXVIII.3, *MPL* LIV.374).

On Correcting Exaggerations in the Dialectic of Imputation and Impartation.
When preaching applies the forensic language of imputation to imply the formal, juridical declaration of God's act for us as God's righteousness imputed to us (Rom. 4:5), it does not thereby imply that this forensic act nullifies all need for growth in behavioral righteousness. Paul's own language forbids this. Paul never suggested that we are saved *in* our sins but *despite* our sins and *from* our sins (Rom. 6). Christ's righteousness does not exempt believers from responsibility to reflect that righteousness in their behavior (Rom. 5:17–21; 8:5–13; Sanday and Headlam, *Epist. to the Romans*, pp. 148–52). Such texts do not imply that the imputed declaration has no effect or consequence upon human behavior. Rather the declaration intends to change human behavior (Calvin, *Inst.* 3.11–12).

God "calls things that are not as though they were" (Rom. 4:17). God deals with the baptized faithful as though they were saints, even if they are not yet fully responsive to God's goodness.

By analogy, the child is valued by the parent not only in the form of actual behavior but also in the form of potentiality, even when the maturity is not yet actual but present already in acornlike, seminal form. "We are valued in the light of what by the grace of Christ we have begun to become. . . . God regards us *non quales sumus, sed quales futuri sumus*," not as we are but as we shall in the future be. "If they fail to grow in righteousness, they will necessarily cease to be accounted righteous . . . justification means our being accounted righteous, rather than our being made so; but in its Pauline context it postulates our being made righteous, and implies a real inception of this making by an imparting to us of regenerating and sanctifying grace" (Hall, *DT* VIII, pp. 261–63) so as to enable us to grow up in righteousness (Eph. 4:15; Augustine, *Comm. on John*, tractate XXVI.1, *NPNF* 1 VII, p. 168).

Justifying faith is not simply the covering over of immorality, for an immoral life as such cannot be imputed for righteousness if it remains buried in sin. So justifying faith must mean also a responsive life of growing upright actions and habituation that makes for righteousness, even though these do not merit God's pardon—for that has already been merited by the cross (Matt. 7:16–25; Rom. 10:10; 12:1–5).

That grace "not only pronounces, but makes us righteous" (Chrestos Androutsos, *Dogmatike.* Athens: Kratous, 1907, p. 267; Merrill, *ACE,* p. 229) is a point that (however true) risks making grace cheap (D. Bonhoeffer, *The Cost of Discipleship;* cf. Cyprian, treatise XI, *ANF* V, p. 499). As the sin that flowed from Adam's fall was a real event with real consequences, so does the righteousness that flows from the cross have real behavioral consequences. Justification in due course calls for an actual renewal of the inner person (Tertullian, *Ag. Marcion* I.28; Basil, *On the Holy Spirit* 15, 35; Gregory Nazianzen, *Orat.* XL.3).

The faith that uprights the sinner must involve a moral response to grace that becomes fruitful in good works (Eph. 2:8; 6:23; Heb. 12:2). The faith that precedes good works will in due course bear the fruit of good works (John 6:44; Acts 18:27; Rom. 12:3). It is hardly genuine faith if it lacks the disposition to love (Clement of Rome, *Cor.* 50.5). If one's faith is to be imputed to one for righteousness, one must repent and turn around one's behavior and be converted and born anew (Luke 24:47; Acts 2:38; 20:21), a turning that is only possible by grace (Gal. 5:6; James 2:14–26; Heb. 11:6; George Bull, *Some Important Points of Primitive Christianity.* 3 vols. Oxford: Parker, 1816, I.4; II.5; Newman, *Lectures on Justification* I, X).

The purity of heart that will see God finally is an absolutely imputed and proximately imparted righteousness that reflects God's own righteousness and thereby reveals the hidden similarity between the image of God and unfallen human freedom. The righteousness of God is imagable in human willing by grace through faith. Whatever righteousness is shared by the faithful is grounded in and akin to God's own righteousness (Goodwin, *Works* VI, pp. 459–522).

Whether Sola Fidism *Requires a Moral Corrective.*   It is at this point that a caveat is needed against an exaggerated *sola fidism*. The tendency to view sin as merely "covered over" by the merits of Christ or by an external imputation of the righteousness of Christ may run an antinomian risk. If so, it becomes necessary to point out that God's righteousness is truly imparted on the cross and sins actually blotted out precisely in order that the justified person may become in some measure uprighted in behavioral responses (Luther, *Good Works*, SWML I, pp. 105–96).

Justifying faith is at once a faith in Christ that is imputed to us for righteousness and a faith in Christ that seeks to impart and draw forth righteousness (Augustine, *Spirit and Letter* 18.31; 26.45; *Grace and Free Will* 6.13). God "graciously imparts to me the righteousness of Christ" (*Heid. Catech.* Q56, COC III, p. 325).

Justifying grace offers us a new relation to God, while sanctifying grace works to make that relation real in our behavior. By justifying grace the new birth begins. By sanctifying grace the neonate is nurtured, sustained, and enabled to grow in grace (J. Wesley, *NB; Salvation by Faith*, WJWB I, sermon 1; WJW V, pp. 1–6).

Justification is "not that by which the Lord is just, but that by which He justifies those who from unrighteous He makes righteous" (Augustine, sermon 131; Pohle *DT* VII, p. 320). The love of God shed abroad in our hearts is "that by which he makes us his lovers; like the righteousness of God by which we are made righteous through his gift, or the salvation of the Lord by which he causes us to be saved" (Augustine, *Spirit and Letter* 56, LCC VIII, p. 241).

The Stress on Imparted Righteousness in Post-Tridentine Teaching.   Roman Catholic teaching has considered it a limitation of Protestant teaching that justification seems to be restricted to the remission of sins only or to a purely forensic imputation of the righteousness of Christ, as if putting a cloak over continuing actual sin (Fifth Lateran Council, SCD 742, pp. 240–43; Trent, SCD 792, 804, 820 f., pp. 248–58). Catholic teaching has stressed the sanctifying sacramental work of grace that begins at justification to elicit an actual righteousness in which persons are made just and friends of God and taken behaviorally into a state of adoption (Trent, *SCD* 792–99, pp. 248–52), made holy through sanctifying grace as a "permanent principle of supernatural life" (Pius XI, *SCD* 2237, p. 583), with an infusion of faith, hope, and charity (Innocent III, *SCD* 410, p. 160; cf. Joyce, *CDG*, pp. 202 ff.; Newman, *Lectures on Justification;* Otten, *MHD* II, pp. 464–71). This theme indeed found moderated expression in various Protestant and pietistic circles, in the teachings both of Anglican centrism and Wesleyan revivalism, which sought a via media between Rome and Wittenberg.

The Council of Trent held that justification is accomplished through the infusion of sacramental sanctifying grace, which elicits an actual residual or inhering grace that seeks to meld habitually with the believer's behavior (Trent, IV.6–10, pp. 32–36). Sanctification is that union with God by which the soul is enabled to reflect God's own holiness through actual behavior. Sanctifying grace is more than an ornament or cloak for sin; it has the intent of making holy that which had heretofore lived in sin (Tho. Aq., *ST* I–II, Q113.7–10; Bellarmine, *De Iustificatione, Opera* [1873], VI, pp. 208 ff.). Christ's righteousness does not exempt the faithful from the moral task of transforming their behavior so as to become ready for God's own righteousness (Rom. 5:17–21; 8:5–13; 10:10; Phil. 2:12). That faith is credited for righteousness does not mean that we need not grow any further in our capacity to reflect God's righteousness. Rather it means that justifying faith is a new birth that grows in the grace that enables one better to mirror God's righteousness. Insofar as righteousness enters the soul, sin must exit. There remains an antinomian temptation in talk of "sinning bravely" (*pecca fortiter*) and imputed righteousness that covers over sin absolutely (Westminster Conf., XVI, *CC*, pp. 210–12; J. Wesley, *Free Grace, WJW* VII, pp. 373–86; *WJWB*, sermon 110, 3:542–63). In the Tridentine decree on justification, the order of salvation begins with prevenient grace, by means of the calling and awakening of the sinner. Here there is some measure of cooperation with grace before justification, and works preceding justification are not altogether sinful (Trent, VI, canons 4–7, pp. 42, 43). Justification follows this prepared inclination (*dispositio*), not as a bare remission of sin, but also as "sanctification and renewal of the inner man through the voluntary reception of grace and of gifts, whence the man from unrighteous becomes righteous" (Trent, Sixth Session, canon 7; *SHD* II 435, 436). "Though 'he died for all,' yet all do not receive the benefit of his death, but only those to whom the merit of his Passion is communicated." By "predisposing grace" and "without any merits," sinners are called, "so that, while God touches the heart of man through the illumination of the Holy Spirit, man himself neither does absolutely nothing while receiving that inspiration, since he can also reject it, nor yet is he able by his own free will and without the grace of God to move himself to justice in his sight" (Trent, VI.3, 5, pp. 30–32). "Hence when it is said in the sacred writings: *Turn ye to me, and I will turn to you* [Zach. 1:3], we are reminded of our liberty; and when we reply: *Convert us, O Lord, to thee, and we shall be converted* [Lam. 5:21], we confess that we need the grace of God" (Trent, V.5, pp. 31, 32, italics added).

Some of these terms and expressions were challenged in specific detail by Protestant theologians (Chemnitz, *Examination of the Council of Trent;* Heppe, *RD*), who wisely resisted any hint of a natively inhering grace or merit by works. In our century, Protestant and Catholic traditions of justification teaching have grown much closer to being on speaking terms (Küng, *Justification;* McGrath, *Justitia Dei*).

The Search for Ecumenic Balance in General Lay Consent.   Christians of all centuries employ the metaphor of being accounted righteous, following Paul who spoke of faith being "credited as righteousness" (Rom. 4:5), hence imputed. But this must not be taken to mean "an unconditional pledge of final salvation regardless of our actual growth in righteousness" (Hall, *DT* VIII, p. 260; cf. Tho. Aq., *ST* I–II, Q113; Newman, *Lectures on Justification*).

By justifying grace we are accounted righteous and enabled to begin to grow in a new birth of righteousness toward fuller behavioral righteousness. This juridical act is accompanied by but not conflated with the imparting of sanctifying grace that enables daily growth in righteousness. Hence in its narrow sense justification means being accounted righteous, but in its broader Pauline usage it implies the task of responsiveness, in which we are in the process of being made behaviorally righteous by receiving the graces that enable our sanctification. Augustine wisely argued that "grace assists in both ways—by remitting the evil things that we have done, and by aiding us to depart from the evil and do the good" (*SHD* I, p. 349).

A blatantly immoral faith cannot be imputed for righteousness if it continues to wallow in immorality (Luther, *Two Kinds of Righteousness, MLS*, pp. 86–98). Justifying faith enables and makes for behavioral righteousness, not merely juridical or abstract or hypothetical righteousness. Once faith is imputed to us for righteousness, we must then behaviorally manifest the life of growth in grace in order to authenticate and continue and daily nurture this gift, but in no sense is the resultant behavior as such meritorious (Calvin, *Inst.* 4.16, 17).

There remain duties specific to me that no other person can fulfill for me. My duty to my children remains mine, and the work of the Son does not circumvent my coworking with grace. Christ does not directly pay my insurance bill or vote for me or pass my driver's license test or review a book for me or protect my wife when she is endangered. Rather, Christ furnishes grace sufficient for me to fulfill these duties, and pardons me when I fail, when I contritely repent in faith with sincere determination to walk in the way of holiness (Field, *HCT*, pp. 199, 200).

Restoration to Favor

The prodigal was not merely pardoned, but to his astonishment received back into the family with full rights of sonship (Luke 15:22–31). Remission of sin is followed by the reconciling embrace of the Father. Justification is not merely a cold announcement of nonliability but a warm welcome from the waiting Father (Melanchthon, *Loci*, XIX, pp. 71 ff., 106–8).

Reconciliation to the Family of God.   Restoration to divine favor is called reconciliation (*katallagē*), whereby alienated covenant partners are brought back together into their original pacific relation. Whereas the cool, distant language of the courtroom speaks of justification, the warm and intimate family metaphor speaks of gracious adoption into the family of God (2 Cor. 5:18–20).

The Westminster Confession shows how the two metaphors mesh effortlessly: "All those that are justified God vouchsafeth, in and through His only Son Jesus Christ, to make partakers of the grace of adoption, by which they are taken into the number, and enjoy the liberties and privileges of the children of God, have his name put upon them, receive the Spirit of adoption" (XII, *CC*, p. 208).

The Fatherly Embrace.   By means of the family metaphor, justification takes on a much more personal and interpersonal meaning. Here one meets not a judge but a parent, not a piece of paper but an embrace, not a release from charges but an empowering, enabling, supporting family. Here one is not only released from prison but brought into the protection and discipline of caring parents and family. The new focus is not upon the disencumbrance of the charge of sin, but upon an inheritance.

Peace with God.   Justification implies that the war between sinners and God is over, that we approach the holy God freely, assured of our participation in the family of God and its inheritance of salvation. "Therefore, since we have been justified through faith, we have peace with God through our Lord Jesus Christ, through whom we have gained access by faith into this grace in which we now stand" (Rom. 5:1, 2). "The fruit of righteousness will be peace; the effect of righteousness will be quietness and confidence forever" (Isa. 32:17).

   Nemesius offered a stunning comparison between laughter and justification. Freedom from guilt is the proper spiritual and moral laughter of penitent humanity. "Laughter is a peculiar mark of man's being, because it is something that pertains to him only, to every single man, and to all men at all times, so, in like fashion, it is peculiar to man that he, in distinction from all other creatures, endowed with reason, should, by God's grace, be released, upon repentance, from the guilt of former transgressions. This, too, pertains to man only, to every single man, and to all men at all times" (Nemesius, *On the Nature of Man, LCC* IV, p. 244).

FAITH IN CHRIST

   The benefits of Christ's mediatorial work are applied by the Spirit and appropriated by the believer *through faith.* "For it is by grace you have been saved, through faith—and this is not from yourselves, it is the gift of God—not by works, so that no one can boast" (Eph. 2:8, 9). It is this faith that God declares as righteousness (Rom. 3:1–4:21; Augsburg Conf., art. IV).

   Faith is the reception of grace. The familiar phrase "justification by faith" may become misleading insofar as it suggests that our faith rather than God's grace saves (Calvin, *Inst.* 3.11–12). *The faithful are justified by grace, not by their own faith* (Melanchthon, *Loci,* XIX, pp. 89 ff.).

The Single Turning

Away and Toward.   In the turn that is conversion, the turning away and the turning toward are one turn. As repentance turns away from the past, the old Adam, the failed era of despairing freedom, so faith turns toward God's future, the new Adam, the emerging era of redeemed freedom amid the governance of God made known in Christ (Rom. 5:12–17). As repentance grieves over its lack of accountability to the law, faith rejoices over God's becoming accountable for us in the

gospel (Ambrose, *On Repentance* II.9, *NPNF* 2 X, pp. 355–56). In receiving justifying grace, the mind "must, by a movement of its free-will withdraw from sin
and draw near to justice. . . . Hence in the justification of the ungodly there must
be two acts of the free-will—one, whereby it tends to God's justice; the other
whereby it hates sin" (Tho. Aq., *ST* I–II, Q113.5; I, p. 1148).

There is an intimate inner correlation between each of the major phases of the
order of salvation, whose topics include call, repentance, justification, faith, regeneration, adoption, sanctification, and union with Christ. To lack any of these
exegetical motifs would be to leave something deficient in the teaching of salvation. Though distinguishable, they cannot artificially be separated and are united
in the one Spirit (Augustine, *Trin.*, *FC* 45, pp. 251–52; 374–76).

Whether the Simplicity of Faith May Become a Theological Topic.   Faith's capacity to articulate its own ground in grace is always less adequate than that ground
itself. In seeking to explain faith, defensive theological reasoning historically has
tended to elaborate fine distinctions that convey the impression that faith is obscure, complex, and difficult.

Yet in apostolic teaching, faith is utterly simple and direct in its radical decisive-
ness. Christian teaching can do no better than convey that profound simplicity
(Cyprian, treatise XII, *ANF* V, p. 547). Mercifully salvation depends upon grace-
enabled faith, not the absolute clarity of faith's attempted definitions of itself.
Salvation depends upon it. "God was pleased through the foolishness of what was
preached to save those who believe" (1 Cor. 1:21).

Finding Out by Choosing to Do.   When the religious professionals were astonished that Jesus had such extraordinary learning "without having studied," the
theandric mediator made this extraordinary response: "If anyone *chooses* to do
God's will, *he will find out* whether my teaching comes from God or whether I speak
on my own" (John 7:17, italics added). The implication: Only one who is willing
to risk following the Lord by doing what he says will then learn his doctrine (John
Chrysostom, *Hom. on John* XLIX, *NPNF* 1 XIV, p. 177; Augustine, *Comm. on John*,
tractate XXIX.6, *NPNF* 1 VII, p. 184).

Active, choosing, risk-taking trust is the premise of understanding whether
Jesus is the Christ (Calvin, *Inst.* 1.14). Without choosing to follow the Christ, without committing oneself to do God's will, one is not likely to be sufficiently ready
for saving grace to be rightly received and understood (J. Wesley, *The Way to the
Kingdom*, *WJWB*, sermon 7, vol. 1, pp. 217–32). Hence the study of faith does well
first to pray for the grace to study faith's simplicity (Augustine, *Conf.* I.1; *NPNF*
1 I, pp. 45 ff.).

Faith

Faith (*pistis*) is the means by which salvation is appropriated through personal
trust in the Son as Savior.

Faith Defined.   Faith is the firm conviction (*persuasio*) of the grace of God, secured by a sense of repose enabled by this conviction, a firm "confidence (*fiducia*)
of the heart, by which we *securely acquiesce* in the mercy of God promised to us
through the gospel" (Calvin, *CR* XXXIII.333; *SHD* II 402; cf. *Inst.* 3.1.1–7).

Faith is that habitual act of the penitent which by grace trusts in Christ's righteousness (Cyprian, *Letters, FC* 51, pp. 22–24, 122 ff., 162 ff.; Fulgentius, *De Fide seu Regula Verae Fidei ad Petrum,* prologue, *MPL* 140.103 ff.). Such faith is accompanied inwardly by the Spirit's assurance and outwardly by works of love in relation to the neighbor. Faith is the primary condition set forth in scripture for receiving justification (Stevens, *TNT,* pp. 419 ff.; Hodge, *OOT,* pp. 465–81; Strong, *ST,* p. 465; Clarke, *OCT,* pp. 401–5).

Personal Trust.   To trust a person is a more decisive, risk-laden act than to trust empirical evidence. We say that one believes in a fact when one is assured of its truth, but one believes in another *person* only when one is sufficiently assured of that person's trustworthiness. Faith as trust is implied even in the etymology of the Hebrew verb *ʾaman* (to believe), to remain steadfast, to stay, to make the heart firm (Ps. 31:23; Neh. 7:2; Dan. 6:4).

Saving faith is *personal trust*—trust in a person, Jesus Christ, the one mediator between God and humanity. The Greek terms that translate *faith (pistis, pisteuō)* imply reliance upon and trust in another who is viewed as trustworthy (root meaning: binding, putting faith in, relying upon). Faith is not about Christ or merely toward Christ, but in Christ. "Everyone who believes *in him* [*eis auton*] receives forgiveness" (Acts 10:43, italics added). The jailer at Philippi was told by Paul, "Believe in the Lord Jesus, and you will be saved" (Acts 16:31).

This personal trust is grounded in the conviction of the credibility of the apostolic testimony to him, as witnessed by the Spirit. "Anyone who believes in [*pisteuōn eis*] the Son of God has this testimony in his heart" (1 John 5:10)—the historical testimony has already been heard and assimilated (Luther, *SML* VII, pp. 231 ff.). Faith in God implies that God's declarations and disclosures about and of himself in the history of Jesus are true and sufficient for faith (Calvin, *Inst.* 2.6). There is an intrinsic connection between the self-evidencing of revelation and faith.

Faith According to Hebrews 11:1.   The most direct definition of faith in the New Testament requires careful examination: "Now faith is being sure of what we hope for and certain of what we do not see" (Heb. 11:1). Faith is confidence in and assurance of the truth of what we hope for, and the evidence or conviction (*elenchos*) of that which cannot be seen (Luther, *Lectures on Hebrews, LW* 29, pp. 229 ff.).

Our faith is the proof of the reality of the things we cannot see, making us certain of what lies beyond empirical sight. Faith requires laying hold of that which cannot be attained by sense perception or logic alone, either inductively or deductively (John Chrysostom, *Hom. on Heb.* XXII, *NPNF* 1 XIV, p. 465). Accordingly, faith is the joyful, consenting affirmation of mind, heart, and will to the truth of what is not empirically seen: God's self-disclosure. "Faith is the eye, and revelation the window through which the soul looks up to God" (Merrill, *ACE,* p. 52).

Faith's Evidences.   The consensually received testimony of prophets, martyrs, saints, inspired writers, and revered exegetes is viewed as primary evidence of truth in the Christian community. Faith is different from conjecture, supposition, fantasy, imagination, or premature assumption. It is based upon the evidences of faith—revelation in history (John of Damascus, *OF* III.9, *NPNF* 2 IX, p. 78).

To believe without evidence is gullibility. Faith is not gullibility, because it does not require belief without evidence. The task of reason is to assess the quality of evidence.

Faith reaches for evidences beyond hard empirical data, seeking evidences of God's promise. The biblical prototypes of persons of faith are recounted in Hebrews 11. This sort of evidentiary search is in part historical, and to that extent must be approached in the way that historical evidence is rightly and appropriately established. Yet the best historians are well aware of the limits of historical method. The evidences of faith are also moral, hence the inquiry proceeds by moral reasoning that cannot remain bound to the rules of empirical evidence. But the evidences of faith are preeminently spiritual, requiring reliable testimony that corresponds with faith's less visible referent, grace (Calvin, *Inst.* 3.2). Faith's evidences cannot remain trapped within a straitjacket of empirical premises (Clementina, *Recognitions* II.69, *ANF* VIII, p. 116).

Neither Sight nor Doubt.   Faith is distinguished from sight, on the one hand, and doubt, on the other. Believers walk by faith, not by either empirically certain sight or spiritually uncertain doubt. By grace believers are made inwardly certain of what they cannot see or quantify empirically, because God is not a visible object of sense (John 1:18; Acts 17:29; Gregory Nazianzen, *Orat., NPNF* 2 VII, pp. 288–91).

"We live by faith, not by sight" (2 Cor. 5:7). Yet faith is not a spiritual blindness but a spiritual seeing (John 6:40; Heb. 11:27) of that which is concealed from the sensory apparatus, a beholding of the invisible, "a trust in the unseen as though it were seen, in that which is hoped and waited for as if it were present" (Longer Catech., Eastern Orthodox Church, 6, *COC* II, p. 446).

Even though specific operations and outcomes of God's promise may remain partially obscure, faith relies on the trustworthiness of God for the right unfolding of these outcomes. It is in this sense that the letter to Hebrews celebrated the faith of Abel, Enoch, Noah, Abraham, and Moses: "All these people were still living by faith when they died. They did not receive the things promised; they only saw them and welcomed them from a distance" (Heb. 11:13). It is essential to living faith to trust what is unseen, or not completely seen, but revealed in such a way as to be understood as trustworthy even if not fully seen (Chemnitz, *TNC,* pp. 411–19, 450, 451). The truth of faith is veiled in symbols since faith is not directly accessible to empirical knowing (Clement of Alexandria, *Stromata* V.1–10, *ANF* II, pp. 445–60).

The Necessity and Possibility of Faith.   Faith is the only condition requisite to a reconciled relation to the Giver of Life. Without faith no one can receive God's saving gifts. Nothing will substitute. Faith is the primary condition for the reception of every subsequent stage of God's saving activity, the inward pivot of the Christian teaching of salvation (Luther, *Freedom of a Christian, MLS,* pp. 56–61). At no point is it possible to say that having discussed faith, we can now turn to other theological subjects so as to leave faith behind (Calvin, *Inst.* 3.2).

The necessity of faith had been grasped clearly in the Old Testament. Habakkuk had already understood that "the righteous will live by his faith" (Hab. 2:4). Before him Jehosaphat had received the tradition that affirmed, "Have faith in the Lord your God and you will be upheld" (2 Chron. 20:20).

Faith could not be required as a duty or unbelief condemned as sinful if it were not possible to believe in God. Wherever a duty is seriously enjoined, the power to perform that duty must be reasonably implied (Tho. Aq., *SCG* III.90, II, p. 39; Kant, *Prolegomena to the Metaphysics of Morals*). That cannot be necessary which is impossible. Faith is made possible by grace.

The power to believe is supplied not by the fallen nature, not by the alienated will acting autonomously, but by grace enabling freedom. Were it not preveniently enabled, then there could be no meaningful call to faith or guilt due to unbelief (Aphrahat, *Demonstrations, On Faith, NPNF* 2 XIII, pp. 350–52). Though faith is not the first grace, since justifying is preceded by preparing grace (Tho. Aq., *ST* I–II, Q109, I, pp. 1123–31; Clement XI, *SCD* 1376 ff., pp. 348 ff.), it is the beginning and necessary foundation of that life which is being justified (Council of Orange II, *SCD* 178, p. 76).

Faith's Part in Justification Teaching.

If justification were a material gift, it could be offered regardless of the attitude or trust or spiritual readiness of the recipient. But justification is a spiritual gift: a new start at life offered to the human spirit through God's own Spirit (J. Wesley, *The Way to the Kingdom, WJWB*, sermon 7, vol. 1, pp. 217–32). It is a personal gift that must be received by a personal agent.

Trusting God's Word in faith is the only way by which the benefit of justification can be received. This is why faith is sometimes called the instrumental or conditional cause of justification, since we are justified by means of faith alone, upon the condition of receiving justifying grace by faith. Faith's part is simply to acknowledge the rightness of God's act by receiving it trustingly (Athanasius, *Resurrection Letters* 12, pp. 183 ff.; Ambrose, *Of Christian Faith* I.1 ff., *NPNF* 2 X, pp. 201 ff.). Faith praises the Justifier by taking seriously the justifying action. Repentance is not, strictly speaking, a condition of justification, but rather that turning from evil that is presupposed in faith's reception of God's justifying action (Tertullian, *On Repentance, ANF* III, pp. 657 ff.).

Without Faith It Is Impossible to Please God.

If trusting God's Word is the absolute and irreplaceable condition of entering into the realm of God's governance, then the opposite holds; lack of faith is viewed in the New Testament as a pivotal rejection of God's veracity: "Whoever does not believe stands condemned already" (John 3:18; John Chrysostom, *Hom. on John* XXVIII, *NPNF* 1 VII, p. 97). The world is being convicted of guilt "because men do not believe on me" (John 16:9; Augustine, *Comm. on John*, tractate XCV, *NPNF* 1 VII, pp. 368–71).

By refusing to trust and receive God's revealed mercy on the cross, we place an insuperable obstacle in the way of our justification. By rejecting God's free gift, we leave ourselves alienated from God. Without faith in Christ, there is no forgiveness of sins (Heb. 11:6; Acts 16:31; Mark 16:16). "Whoever rejects the Son will not see life" (John 3:36; John Chrysostom, *Hom. on John* XXXI, *NPNF* 1 XIV, p. 106). Every human action lacking trust in God, however well intended, is fundamentally misguided—off the mark (*hamartia*). For what could be more offensive to God than to doubt the truth of God's costly self-disclosure? Hence James instructs us to ask in faith, not double-mindedness (James 1:6–8).

Always flawed is any human action that comes out of the self-righteous presumption that human goodness can proceed without trust in the One who gives life. The consequent language seems harsh to modern hearers: "Without faith it is impossible to please God, because anyone who comes to him must believe that he exists and that he rewards those who earnestly seek him" (Heb. 11:6). Yet upon closer examination, this very text shows that those who have not heard of Christ can be justified by implicit, anticipatory faith in God (Clement of Alexandria, *Stromata* II.1–6, *ANF* II, pp. 347–54; Calvin, *Comm.* XXII, pp. 270–82). It is difficult to imagine how one could approach God without believing that God exists and that he rewards those who seek him. These two premises may be anticipatively believed by animists, Hindus, and Muslims without their ever hearing of the history of Jesus, as was the case with Abel. Without belief in the reality and justice of God, one can hardly further approach the mercy of God revealed.

Faith as Power. The metaphor of seed was used by Jesus dramatically to attest the power of faith: "If you have faith as small as a mustard seed, you can say to this mountain, 'Move from here to there' and it will move. Nothing will be impossible for you" (Matt. 17:20). What does seed have that makes it analogous to the kingdom of God? Readiness to receive the conditions of growth (Calvin, *Comm.* XVI, p. 326).

The gospel is "the power of God for the salvation of everyone who believes" (Rom. 1:16). The greatness of God's power manifests itself in bringing life from death (1 John 4:7–21). Paul's preaching did not proceed "with wise and persuasive words, but with a demonstration of the Spirit's power, so that your faith might not rest on men's wisdom, but on God's power" (1 Cor. 2:5; Goodwin, *Works* VI, pp. 405–55).

Distinctions Within the Study of Faith

Classically, several types of distinction have been employed concerning faith: The faith that is believed is distinguished from faith as believing. Faith as a particular act is distinguished from faith as habitual; implicit from explicit faith; immature from mature faith active in love. Human faith (including historical faith and intellectual assent) is distinguished from divine faith made possible by grace. The study of faith (discursive faith) is distinguished from the act of faith (or direct faith). These distinctions have been found useful in the attempt to formulate the relation between dimensions of Christian faith and the general concepts and phenomena of faith in the history of religions (Calvin, *SW*, pp. 274; 381–84; Heppe, *RD*, pp. 526–36).

Faith as Believing and Believed. The faith that is believed is the apostolic testimony, the consensually received objective truth of the Christian faith (*fides quae creditur*). It is this sense of the term *faith* that Jude meant when he urged his hearers to "contend for the faith that was once for all entrusted to the saints" (Jude 3).

That is conceptually distinguishable from the personal *act of believing* that truth subjectively, or faith that actively believes (*fides qua creditur*, faith as existentially trusting in another). Faith both is believed and believes. Faith can believe because it has heard of the faith that is believed (Jude 3; Irenaeus, *Fragments* XXXVI, *ANF* I, p. 574).

Faith as Act and Habit.   One may engage in a *particular act* of faith without having established faith as a matter of *habitual action* or *character*. The life of faith
commended in the New Testament is not simply a single fleeting act, but rather
an entire way of life, a way of walking by trusting in God continually, by repeatedly
layered actions that reinforce habituation (Gal. 5:25; 1 John 1:6, 7). Similarly, the
love a child has for a parent or the confidence one has in a friend is not simply a
matter of a single momentary action, but rather an enduring, habituated pattern
of behavior upon which another may count.

Faith as Explicit and Implicit.   *Fides explicita* is an express belief in the truth of
revelation, while *fides implicita* is a virtual belief, when one implicitly affirms what
the church teaches. For catechumens or confirmands, it is necessary to express
explicit faith in relation to the Apostles' Creed, Decalogue, and Lord's Prayer,
while other revealed truths may be held *fide implicita* (Tho. Aq., *ST* II–II, Q2.7;
cf. Luther, *On the Creed, Commandments and Lord's Prayer*). When the theologian
seeks to affirm heartily whatever it is that God has revealed as consensually received by the ecumenical tradition, that is an act of implicit faith that trusts the
consensus even when it does not adequately grasp it, while hoping to grasp it ever
better (Vincent of Lérins, *Comm., NPNF* 2 XI, pp. 132 ff.; Beveridge, *On the Consent of the Church, CVL*, pp. 141–53).
     It is said that the saints and prophets of the Old Testament experienced an
implicit faith (Calvin, *Inst.* 3.2.3), while Christian believers are invited to experience a clearer, more well-defined basis for belief, or *explicit faith*. Explicit faith
knows the ground upon which it believes because the salvation event has been
revealed. Those who lived before Christ or who have not explicitly heard the good
news may share in an implicit faith in the promise of God's coming without grasping particulars of historical revelation. Such faith is efficacious, or "counted for
righteousness," as in the case of Abraham (Rom. 4:5; Heb. 11:8–19).
     The ancient patriarchs and prophets had implicit faith in Christ and were jus-
tified without explicit faith in the Trinity and incarnation and without baptism.
They believed by way of desire (*fides in voto*) in a way that anticipated explicit faith
even when it was not available to them (Tho. Aq., *ST* II–II, Q2.7.3).
     Implicit assent to at least two teachings is presupposed in Hebrews 11:6: the
existence and justice of God, to the extent a given person is capable of assent. A
similar distinction is that between unformed or *inchoate faith* and *mature faith,* or
saving faith active in love (Calvin, *SW,* 381–84; *Inst.* 3.2.10). The faculty of faith
that is inchoately present in every human spirit is gradually, in God's own time,
being awakened by God's own Spirit. "Faculties of the human body, if denied their
exercise, will lie dormant. The eye without light, natural or artificial, cannot fulfill
its office; the ear will be ignorant of its functions unless some voice or sound be
heard; the nostrils unconscious of their purpose unless some scent be breathed.
Not that the faculty will be absent, but that there will be no experience of its
existence. So, too, the soul of man, unless through faith it has appropriated the
gift of the Spirit, will have the innate faculty of apprehending God, but be destitute of the light of knowledge" (Hilary, *Trin.* II.35, *NPNF* 2 IX, p. 61).

Human Faith and Saving Faith.   Faith as trust is familiar to human experience
of all cultures and not an exclusive possession of Christianity. Children have faith
in their parents, quite apart from any deliberate thought of divine revelation. A

wife trusts her husband. A voter may have faith in a political party. Such is called *human faith* to distinguish it from that faith in Christ that is enabled by saving grace, which is termed *saving faith* (*fides salvifica*), or divine faith.

Faith in the general sense is the faculty of accepting the unseen as true, as illuminating, as existing. Such a general faith knows what it knows without the empirical evidence ordinarily expected of knowledge of the material, physical world. This is a common human capacity. No culture is without it (Luther, *Large Catechism* I, *BOC*, p. 365; cf. M. Eliade; W. H. Smith; H. Kraemer).

Such general human faith necessarily involves the whole person: knowing, feeling, and willing. Hence saving faith does not require a new faculty of the self. Rather, prevening grace works within human knowing, feeling, and willing to move the self toward that saving faith that knows, feels, and wills in relation to God's own personal coming. The capacity for personal trust is preveniently enabled by common grace, so that every human being—as in the case of conscience—has a latent sufficient capacity of intellect, sensibility, and will to be able to respond to grace when grace becomes known through the Word (Augustine, *Conf.* I.1, *LCC* VII, p. 7). "To whatever extent the truths of religion are known and embraced, faith in them is the healthy and legitimate exercise of the human mind, receiving the evidence, internal and external, which authenticates revelation" (Pope, *Compend.* II, p. 377).

Conscience is a faculty of human consciousness that is formed universally, yet may become transformed by converting grace. Similarly, faith is a faculty of belief in what is unseen that is found universally in some form in the human condition, which may become enlivened by converting grace (J. Wesley, *On Faith*, *WJW* VII, pp. 195 ff.; cf. VII, pp. 231 ff., *WJWB*, sermon 117, vol. 4, pp. 28 ff.). "Accordingly, the *capacity to have faith*, as the capacity to have love, belongs to men's nature; but *to have faith*, even as to have love, belongs to the grace of believers" (Augustine, *On the Predestination of the Saints* 5:10, *NPNF* 1 V, p. 503, italics added).

Saving faith is full and unconditional reliance on Christ for salvation, an act of personal trust in the Mediator (Clarke, *CT*, pp. 479–85; Watson, *TI* II, chap. 23). Saving faith believes and personally trusts "that Jesus is the Christ, the Son of God" (John 10:21). Saving faith is faith in Christ, renouncing all gods but the living God, disavowing all Lords but the crucified-resurrected Lord, willing to take up one's cross and follow (Pope, *Compend.* II, pp. 376–90; cf. Miley, *ST* II, pp. 318–26; Burwash, *MCT* II, pp. 236–44). Saving faith in Christ must be distinguished from projection of human need or imagination. The Freudian teaching that some ideas of God are a projection of human needs (borrowed by him from Feuerbach) had been long before anticipated by Luther: "Faith is not man's opinion and dream, which some take to be faith. . . . When they hear the Gospel, they immediately devise from their own powers the imagination in their hearts to which they give expression in the words 'I believe.' This they regard the right faith. Nevertheless it is nothing but man's thought and imagination" (*SCF*, p. 188; projection is an idea frequently anticipated in classic exegesis, see Lactantius, *DI* II.7, *ANF* VII, p. 50; Athenagoras, *A Plea in Defense of the Faith*, 27, 28, *LCC* I, pp. 330–31; Luther, *Large Catechism* I, *BOC*, p. 365).

General Faith and the History of Religions. Faith in God (in an implicit, discursive, human, or inchoate sense) belongs not just to the history of revelation but more generally to the history of religions. For God has not left himself without witness in the world. Faith in God is experienced in an anticipatory sense in the worship that devout persons of all times have sought to offer to God, who has become known in creation and providence and general revelation in anticipation of God's particular self-disclosure to Israel and through Christ.

"By faith we understand that the universe was formed at God's command, so that what is seen was not made out of what was visible" (Heb. 11:2). Such faith enters into a general human and rational understanding without direct dependence upon a special history of revelation. It was "by faith" that "Abel offered God a better sacrifice," hence "by faith he still speaks, even though he is dead" (Heb. 11:4). "By faith Enoch was taken from this life" (v. 5).

Scripture is clearly signaling that those who lived prior to Christ and without historical knowledge of the yet-to-unfold narrative of salvation still could be saved by faith in the promise of that unfolding, insofar as God's mercy had been set before them anticipatively through reason, conscience, sacrificial acts, and human religious traditions.

Abraham's faith was implicitly a faith in the promise of God's future deliverance (Gregory of Nyssa, *FGG,* pp. 119–21). When Yahweh who had promised Abraham that all nations were to be blessed through his son, Isaac, commanded Abraham to go to Mount Moriah and offer Isaac as a sacrifice, Abraham trusted God, made necessary preparations, and immediately set out on the journey. His readiness to trust in God's promise made him the prototype for all persons of faith in the Bible (Heb. 11:8–19; Kierkegaard, *F&T*).

The faith of non-Israelites appeared to be a special concern of Jesus: "Other sheep I have, which are not of this fold" (John 10:16, KJV). Commenting upon the faith of the Roman Centurion, Jesus said, "I tell you the truth, I have not found anyone in Israel with such great faith. I say to you that many will come from the east and the west, and will take their places at the feast with Abraham, Isaac and Jacob in the kingdom of heaven" (Matt. 8:10, 11; Irenaeus, *Ag. Her.* IV.58.10, *AEG* II, p. 311).

The Faith That Is Studied and the Study of Faith

Saving faith can become the subject of academic definition or debate or public discourse. When faith is temporarily taken out of its own realm of active trust in God and subjected to rational analysis and reflection, in the way that any other subject can be investigated, it is termed *discursive faith,* or faith as a subject of intelligent discourse. Faith in this sense is sometimes distinguished from a *direct faith* that actively trusts. It is direct faith that is being investigated, but in the process of investigation it temporarily becomes discursive faith.

Faith as a Premise of Scientific Inquiry.   Faith in the general sense is a premise of all human knowing, all empirical inquiry, all deductive reasoning (Clement of Alexandria, *Stromata* II.4, *ANF* II, p. 350). For one cannot make a scientific investigation without assuming the intelligibility of the natural order, an axiom that cannot be empirically proven (Tho. Aq., *ST* II–II, Q9, III, pp. 1210–12). Hence *credo ut intelligam* (whereby one believes in order to know) is a scientific axiom. "For a farmer does not plow a furrow in the earth without faith, nor a merchant entrust his life to a bit of wood on the raging high seas. Neither are marriages contracted nor anything else in life done without faith" (John of Damascus, *OF* IV.11, *FC* 37, p. 349).

The Relation of Faith and Argument.   Saving faith is distinguished from intellectual conviction that arises out of argument concerning Christian teaching. One may be reasonably convinced that God is holy and loving, yet not trust that God in Christ has personally loved and saved "even me" from sin (J. Wesley, *JJW*, May 24, 1738). It is possible to believe certain aspects of Christian teaching of forgiveness, yet not personally trust God from the heart for the forgiveness of one's own sins. "For it is with your heart that you believe and are justified, and it is with your mouth that you confess and are saved. As the Scripture says, 'Anyone who trusts in him will never be put to shame'" (Rom. 10:10, 11; Calvin, *On Reform*, *SW*, pp. 163–70). What the mouth rightly confesses must come deeply from the heart.

Historical Faith and Intellectual Assent.   Saving faith in Christ is distinguishable from historical faith (*fides historica*), that faith which is convinced by historical evidence that an event occurred. One may, for example, believe on the basis of historical testimony that Christ in fact died on the cross, and yet not believe that his death was a ransom for one's own sin. Saving faith "is not merely a knowledge of historical events, but is a confidence in God" (Augsburg Conf., XX, *CC*, p. 77).

Nor is faith as personal trust sufficiently understood as a historical belief in the facts reported in scripture (*fides historica*), yet faith willingly hears the evidences of God's self-disclosure. One cannot affirm that Christ died for me without first understanding that Christ died. That is in part a matter of historical evidence. Hence some historical knowledge or confidence in the reporting of the history of Jesus is requisite to saving faith, though such "historical faith" (*fides historica*) cannot in itself have saving effect or substitute for faith. The bare minimum of what is knowable of Jesus may be grossly underestimated, as in the case of Bultmann, who argued that "nothing needs to be taught about Jesus except 'that,' nothing except *that* in his historical life the event had its beginning and the event continues in the preaching of the community" (*Faith and Understanding*, p. 309).

Faith does not conclude that historical evidence is unimportant: "We did not follow cleverly invented stories when we told you about the power and coming of our Lord Jesus Christ, but we were eyewitnesses of his majesty" (2 Pet. 1:16; cf. 1 John 1:1 ff.). The proper rules of eyewitnesses were assumed, as confirmed in the case of the Transfiguration: "We ourselves heard this voice that came from heaven when we were with him on the sacred mountain" (2 Pet. 1:18).

Complementary Elements of Faith: Assent, Trust, and Decision.   The faith that saves embraces a belief of the mind, a trust of the heart, and a decision of the will. Every act of sincere faith wells up from the whole person as knowing, feeling, and willing (Augustine, *Trin.* IX–X, *NPNF* 1 III, pp. 125–43). Three structural elements are traditionally thought to be combined in saving faith: a fully convinced affirmation of the truth of God's self-disclosure; a reversal of one's emotive energies, so that all loves are understood in relation to the love of God; and a voluntary, personal surrender of one's will to God's will. These three dimensions are correlated with the fundamental human faculties of knowing, feeling, and willing (J. Bunting, *Sermon on Justification by Faith;* Field, *HCT*, pp. 204, 205). "Faith is the

assent of the mind, the consent of the will and the choice of trust of the heart"
(J. M. Shaw, *Christian Doctrine,* London: Lutterworth Press, 1953, p. 235).

The Assent of the Mind

One cannot be saved by that which is not true. The Greek word *pistis* means at
one level simply belief in the truth, or that persuasion by which something is received as true. Thus one crucial element of Christian faith is the conviction that
what is believed (God's word addressed on the cross) is true and worthy of confidence (Heb. 6:18; Augustine, *On the Profit of Believing* XXXIV, *NPNF* 1 III,
pp. 363–64).

The Dimension of Knowing in Faith.   If faith is believing God's promises, then
faith presupposes a kind of knowing. Saving faith does not function altogether
without or against reason, though it reaches beyond reason. Faith embraces an
intellectual aspect—recognition of the truth of God's self-disclosure and of the
plan of salvation fulfilled in Christ. Faith cannot proceed confidently without the
conviction that the history of divine self-disclosure is reliable and reported with
sufficient reliability to be believed (Tho. Aq., *ST* II–II, Q8, III, pp. 1204–9).

The New Testament itself was deeply concerned to establish the authenticity of
its witnesses to the events of revelation, as in John's explicit report of the breaking
of Jesus' legs in the crucifixion shows: "The man who saw it has given testimony,
and his testimony is true. He knows that he tells the truth, and he testifies so that
you also may believe" (John 19:35). Reliable, accredited eyewitnesses attest the
truth, and it is on this basis that faith becomes possible (John 20:31). "This salvation, which was first announced by the Lord, was confirmed to us by those who
heard him. God also testified to it by signs, wonders and various miracles, and
gifts of the Holy Spirit" (Heb. 2:3, 4; Calvin, *Comm.* XXII, pp. 53–56).

This is why teaching the facts concerning revelation and providing plausible
interpretations of those facts is a premise of teaching faith and making way for
faith. If faith is at one level a kind of knowing, then it must be known and taught
in the same way that other forms of knowing are known and taught: through
accurate data gathering and presentation, logical organization and deduction,
and critical rational analysis (J. Wesley, *An Earnest Appeal to Men of Reason and
Religion, WJW* VII, pp. 1–45; Pannenberg, *RAH*).

Christ Takes Every Thought Captive.   Jesus urged a critical spirit: "If I am not
doing the works of my Father, then do not believe me; but if I do them, even
though you do not believe me, believe the works, that you may know and understand that the Father is in me" (John 10:37, RSV; Augustine, *Comm. on John,* tractate XLVIII, *NPNF* 1 VII, pp. 266–69).

The intellectual side of belief is deepened through personal trust in God the
Son. Personal trust may be strengthened by the rigor of Christian intellectual inquiry that emerges out of it when its inner identity and commitment are firmly in
place. It is this side of faith to which Paul referred when he sought to "take captive
every thought to make it obedient to Christ" (2 Cor. 10:5).

Intellectual assent is not the whole of faith, but remains one of its elementary
aspects, and is rejected by piety at its peril. Speculative rationalistic inquiry that
studies philosophy may enrich faith, though it does not do so necessarily. Histor-

ical knowledge rightly should enhance and clarify faith, which is and remains essentially the gift of God, yet it may also destabilize and thwart the growth of faith when operating out of philosophical premises alien to faith (Clement of Alexandria, *Stromata* V.1, *ANF* II, pp. 445 f.; Irenaeus, *Ag. Her.* I, *ANF* I, pp. 315 ff.).

Although Christians walk by faith, not by sight, faith is not a blind assent contrary to reason (Vatican Council I, *SCD* 1790, p. 445). Rather it is *"a well grounded conviction, and a reasonable confidence, based upon good and sufficient evidence.* God has never enjoined upon man the duty of faith without first presenting before him a reasonable foundation for the same. Christ never arbitrarily assumed the prerogatives of the Messiahship, but he appealed, for the confirmation of his claims, to honorable and weighty testimony, nor are we required to believe the gospel, independent of the evidence it affords of its own divinity" (Ralston, *ED* II, p. 284).

The Interlocking Nexus of Assent and Saving Faith.   John's Gospel was written for this specific purpose: "that you may believe *that* Jesus is the Christ, the Son of God, and that by believing you may have life in his name" (John 20:31, italics added). The belief is primarily *in* Jesus personally, but this presupposes *that* Jesus is the Son of God. Assent to an objective confession must accompany internal trust in order for the circle of faith to be complete (Augustine, *Enchiridion,* 7–9, *NPNF* 1 III, pp. 238–39; *Conf.* VI.5, *NPNF* 1 I, pp. 92–93).

Faith is "ordinarily wrought by the ministry of the Word, by which also, and by the administration of the sacraments and prayer, it is increased and strengthened. By this faith a Christian believeth to be true whatsoever is revealed in the Word" (Westminster Conf., XIV, *CC,* p. 209). The usual way of coming to faith is through believable hearing of the word of Christ as it becomes mediated through scripture, preaching, and sacrament (John of Damascus, *OF* III.10, *NPNF* 2 IX, p. 79). The Spirit elicits faith by means of the plausibly preached, written, and heard Word. "Faith comes from hearing the message, and the message is heard through the word of Christ" (Rom. 10:17). The authority of God speaks in "each particular passage" in different ways, "yielding obedience to the commands, trembling at the threatenings, and embracing the promises of God" (Westminster Conf., XIV, *CC,* p. 209).

When adequate evidence is laid out, it is expected that by grace one is being made able to believe, or may pray for such grace. Such evidence has been set forth in the life, death, and resurrection of Jesus. "Faith is when my heart and the Holy Ghost in the heart says, The promise of God is true and certain" (Apology of the Augsburg Conf., sec. 103, p. 122, Jacobs, *SCF,* p. 188). The Westminster Confession spoke unitively of the "principal acts of saving faith" as "accepting, receiving, and resting upon Christ alone for justification" (XIV, *CC,* p. 209).

Distinguishing Assent from Saving Faith.   Saving faith is distinguished from the convergence of probabilities, from purely private experience, and from a direct infusion of knowledge from God (Innocent XI, *SCD* 1242, p. 333; Pius X, *SCD* 2025 ff., pp. 510–16). It is the act of the will by which one offers free submission to God's revelation (Pius IX, *SCD* 1637, p. 411; Vatican Council I, *SCD* 1791, p. 445).

Lacking personal trust, bare intellectual assent is hardly sufficient for salvation. "You believe that there is one God. Good! Even the demons believe that—and shudder" (James 2:19). Such belief is not likely to survive skeptical inquiry, much less cross-bearing.

Simon the sorcerer apparently at an elementary level heard the preaching of Philip and, assenting, "believed and was baptized," but his subsequent manipulative behavior indicates that his assent was not enduring, saving faith, for he remained "captive to sin" (Acts 8:9–25). Though formally convinced that Jesus was "a teacher who has come from God," Nicodemus had not yet come to saving faith, for later Jesus called him to a new birth that enables a new seeing (John 3:3).

Melanchthon summed up this point: "Faith signifies to *assent* to the promise of God (which is in the *intellect*), and with this assent is necessarily connected *confidence* (which is the will, willing and accepting the promised reconciliation" (*CR* XXI.790; in *SHD* II 361).

More poignantly the great mathematician Pascal wagered, "Who then will blame Christians for inability to give a reason for their belief, professing as they do a religion for which they can give no reason? When they expound it they declare it to be folly, *stultitiam*, and then you complain that they do not prove it! If they proved it they would belie themselves," for either "God is or is not. But which way shall we lean? Reason can settle nothing here; there is an infinite gulf between us. A game is on, at the other end of this infinite distance, and heads or tails will turn up. What will you wager? According to reason you cannot do either; according to reason you cannot leave either undone. . . . but wager you must; there is no option. . . . if you win, you win all; if you lose, you lose naught. Then do not hesitate, wager that He is" (*Pensées, TGS*, p. 216).

Trust of the Heart

Job's trust in God points to the radical character of risk in faith: "Though he slay me, yet will I trust in him" (Job 13:15).

Trust of the Whole Person in Saving Grace.   Faith requires the assent of the whole heart, the confident affirmation of the whole person, not of the mind only. Through personal assent, the facts of revelation become graciously applied to one's own personal situation. One comes to trust that the One whom one believes is able to deliver from anxiety, guilt, sin, death, and despair. This act of the heart is the faith by which salvation is received (Calvin, *Inst.* 1.14; 3.2; J. Edwards, *Religious Affections, WJE* I, pp. 236 ff.).

The central element of faith is an act of confidence (Eph. 3:12; *pepoithesis,* Clement of Rome, *Cor.* 26.1; 35.2) or reliance upon what is believed (John Chrysostom, *Baptismal Instructions, ACW* 31, pp. 171–72, 245–46). "Justifying faith implies, not only a Divine evidence or conviction that God was in Christ reconciling the world unto Himself, but a sure trust and confidence that Christ died for *my* sins, that He loved me and gave Himself for me" (Wesley, *WJWB* I, sermon V, *WJW* V, pp. 53–64).

From the Heart.   The receiver in faith's receptivity and actor in faith's activity is not separable from the person's mind, or the person's sensory apparatus, or the person's will, but altogether faith belongs to the unifying center of the human person. This is what is signified by the metaphor of the heart. "For it is with your heart that you believe [*kardia gar pisteuetai*] and are justified" (Rom. 10:10).

Amid persecution when the creed risked saying, "I believe" (*pisteuō, credo*), it required an utterance from the heart. The whole person—not just the mind or affections—is saying, "I believe." No human act more completely engages and embraces the whole person than the act of believing (Clement of Rome, *Corinth* 22–39, *ANF* I, pp. 11–15).

Luther defined true faith as "that assured trust and firm assent of heart by which Christ is laid hold of" (*Commentary on Luke,* in Gamertsfelder, *ST,* p. 495). Similarly, the Anglican Homily of Salvation spoke of faith as "a sure trust and confidence in God's merciful promises, to be saved from everlasting damnation by Christ: whereof doth follow a loving heart to obey his commandments" (*A Sermon on the Salvation of Mankind, CC,* p. 249).

Beyond intellectual assent, personal trust embraces an emotive dimension, a centered passionate leap of the whole person toward the mercy of God (Kierkegaard, *CUP,* pp. 90–97, 340 ff., *TC,* pp. 26–39). Faith is consent from the heart, laying hold of the truth of God's mercy as it addresses the soul. "Faith is that by which we rest immovably, firmly, and undistractedly upon the mercy of God" (Zwingli, *Werke* [1828], III, p. 231; *On True and False Religion, WZ,* pp. 98 ff.). Paul prayed that each believer would be "strengthened in your inner being, so that Christ may dwell in your hearts through faith" (Eph. 3:16).

Decision of the Will

Faith is a radical willing by which the person renounces other gods and pretended saviors. Faith is finally an unfettered kind of willing—a willing to trust the incomparably good will of Another.

The Volitional Element in Faith. This volitional element of faith is not merely a momentary surrender to God, but a determination to walk daily trusting in God, responsible to the divine requirement. Faith awakens a distinctive type of volition that is willing to forgo other forms of trust in favor of personal trust in the Source and End of all finite values (John Chrysostom, *None Can Harm Him Who Does Not Injure Himself, NPNF* 1 IV, pp. 280–84; H. R. Niebuhr, "On Faith in God," *RMWC*). In that yes is necessarily implied a no toward final trust in lesser values. The volitional element of faith is the will to trust God above all else, abandoning all competing idolatrous sources of reliance, excluding all other claims of gods that pretend to bestow the final meaning upon life, cleaving only to One worthy of absolute trust, the triune God.

Faith as trust surrenders the whole mind and heart and soul to God (Clement of Rome, *Cor.* 10.1, 11), receiving and appropriating Christ's justifying action and participating in Christ's obedience as the source of pardon and renewal (Luther, *On the Councils, LW* 41, pp. 110–13; Calvin, *Inst.* 3.2; 3.11).

Faith as Renunciation and Decision Freely Resolving a Life of Righteousness. The will that must take this decisive step of renunciation is a will that is by its fallen nature distrustful, self-assertive, egocentric, and idolatrous. This is why the broken will cannot begin to repent and have faith without grace enabling it (Augustine, *On Forgiveness of Sins, and Baptism* II.5, *NPNF* 1 VI, pp. 44–45). Despite this impotence, conscience and reason continue to attest that the person is constituted for communion with the eternal, invisible One.

Faith in Christ is therefore a decision. "I stand at the door and knock. If anyone hears my voice and opens the door, I will come in and eat with him, and he with me" (Rev. 3:20). The choice is ours, for "to all who received him, to those who believed in his name, he gave the right to become children of God" (John 1:12). Faith answers yes to the invitation to "come to me" (Matt. 11:28), to drink from "a spring of water welling up to eternal life" (John 4:14), to "trust in God, trust also in me" (John 14:1).

Trust may become a habit of will enabled by God the Spirit wherein one personally relies on the merit of the crucified Lord. In personal trust in the living Lord, the will rests in God as its chief present good and its future hope of good. While idolaters rely upon their absolutized finite values, faith in God trusts in God (Luther, *Large Catechism, BOC,* pp. 365–71).

The Obedience of Faith.   In faith one submits to Christ's lordship. The very word *disciple* implies that one is undergoing discipline, training in attentiveness, becoming as a little child (Matt. 18:1–4). The truth is revealed to babes, to those teachable and ready for learning, not those who feel no need of learning. Entering into the school of Christ is like taking up a yoke in the spirit of meekness, submitting to discipline under authority (Matt. 11:29, 30). Paul spoke candidly of the "obedience that accompanies your confession of the gospel" (2 Cor. 9:13).

The lordship of Christ comes before one's father, daughter, mother, brother, sister, wife, family members, property, or even life itself (Matt. 10:34–39; Luke 14:26). One does not become a disciple without being willing to forsake contrary idolatrous loyalties (Luke 14:33). Jesus demanded of the rich young ruler that he sell all (Mark 10:21). Those who wish first to bury their dead or bid farewell to their loved ones have not yet understood the radical nature of the impending reign of God (Luke 9:57–62; Origen, *Comm. on Luke, AEG* III, p. 256). Obedience to Jesus' teaching is the only reliable foundation for the Christian life; otherwise one builds on sand. Not those who merely say "Lord, Lord," but "only he who does the will of my Father" will enter the kingdom of heaven (Matt. 7:21, 24–27).

Paul spoke of the obedience that is of faith (Rom. 1:5), which calls for complete yielding of one's life as servant of righteousness, in obedience to the gospel (Rom. 6:18; 2 Thess. 1:8; 1 Pet. 4:17). Those who obey do not describe themselves as degraded or demeaned or weakened or enslaved, but as freed, honored to be included in God's own redeeming purposes, raised to glory, and strengthened by grace to meet whatever task may come. "It is for freedom that Christ has set us free. Stand firm, then, and do not let yourselves be burdened again by a yoke of slavery" (Gal. 5:1).

Faith is of God precisely while being fully willed by human will. The tension of this dialectic is seen in the prayer "Lord, I believe, help thou mine unbelief" (Mark 9:24, kjv). "Now if faith is simply of free will, and is not given by God, why do we pray for those who will not believe? This it would be absolutely useless to do, unless we believe, with perfect propriety, that Almighty God is able to turn to believe wills that are perverse and opposed to faith" (Augustine, *On Grace and Free Will,* chap. 14:29, *NPNF* 1 V, p. 455).

The New Nature.   The birth of faith is accompanied by the birth of a new spiritual nature that revolts against sin and cannot ever again be content to live under its tyranny. With God's own Spirit aiding in the battle against temptation, even if the conflict of spirit and flesh persists, the new spiritual life is confident of finally overcoming (2 Cor. 5:6–10; 1 John 2:28).

Even if the flesh is not able to be struck with a once-for-all blow that will end all sin's historical consequences, still one understands that the old sin nature has been crucified with Christ (Gal. 2:20). The power of evil is broken in the life of all who receive and trust in the atoning work of the cross, whose faith becomes active in love (Thecla, *ANF* VIII, p. 490).

Whether the Struggle Continues. The regenerate are called to "Be self-controlled and alert. Your enemy the devil prowls around like a roaring lion looking for someone to devour. Resist him, standing firm in the faith" (1 Pet. 5:8, 9a). The adversary continues to test the faithful, as Jesus remarked to Peter: "Simon, Simon, Satan has asked to sift you as wheat. But I have prayed for you, Simon, that your faith may not fail" (Luke 22:31, 32).

The faithful are urged to "Resist the devil, and he will flee from you. Come near to God and he will come near to you" (James 4:7). The full armor of God allows the believer to "stand against the devil's schemes. For our struggle is not against flesh and blood, but against the rulers, against the authorities, against the powers of this dark world and against the spiritual forces of evil in the heavenly realms" (Eph. 6:11, 12).

Faith in the Son. Faith trusts in "the living God" who has "appeared in a body," and now is being "vindicated by the Spirit" (1 Tim. 3:15, 16). In attaching faith to the eternal Son, one attaches faith to the triune God. Hence Christian teaching speaks personally of the object of saving faith as Jesus Christ. Faith trusts in the person of Christ as truly God, truly human, mediator between God and humanity. "Salvation is found in no one else, for there is no other name under heaven given to men by which we must be saved" (Acts 4:12).

To trust in the Son is to trust in the Father by the Spirit. Paul was "sent not from men nor by man, but by Jesus Christ and God the Father, who raised him from the dead" (Gal. 1:1). The One who raised Jesus from the dead and Christ himself are one—the one triune God. "No one who denies the Son has the Father" (1 John 2:23). Personal trust in the Son can be referred to the Father who by the Spirit raised up the Son from death. "God will credit righteousness" to those "who believe in him who raised Jesus our Lord from the dead" (Rom. 4:24).

One cannot separate trust in this person from trust in his work. In personally trusting in Christ, faith at the same time trusts in the testimony to the work of Christ—his incarnate coming, his obedience to law, his proclamation and teaching, his life and ministry, his death and resurrection and promised coming again.

Some still "demand miraculous signs," and others "look for wisdom, but we preach Christ crucified" (1 Cor. 1:23). To those who hesitated to personally trust in him, he retorted, "You do not know me or my Father," for, "If you knew me, you would know my Father also" (John 8:19; Origen, *Comm. on John*, AEG III, pp. 268–72).

The Gift of Faith and Human Agency

The relation of faith and grace is explicitly set forth in Paul's summary formula: "By grace you have been saved, through faith" (Eph. 2:8). "Therefore, the promise comes by faith, so that it may be by grace" (Rom. 4:16; Prosper of Aquitaine, *Call of All Nations* I.24, *ACW,* p. 76).

Faith as Gift Requiring Response.   One cannot posit faith without a believer any more than one can posit thought without a thinker. "For as a writing-reed or a dart has need of one to use it, so grace also has need of believing minds. . . . It is God's to grant grace, but yours to receive and guard" (Cyril of Jerusalem, *Catech. Lect.* I:3, *NPNF* 2 VII, pp. 6, 7).

In response to all that God has done, the hearer is invited to act so as to rely upon God's act. It is not asserted that faith can act by itself, but that it does act responsively. Faith's sufficiency is from God, yet so as to enable freedom, action, trust. "This righteousness from God comes through faith in Jesus Christ to all who believe." All who have sinned "are justified freely by his grace through the redemption that came by Christ Jesus" (Rom. 3:22–24; Tertullian, *Ag. Marcion* V.13, *ANF* III, pp. 457–48).

Hence faith is simultaneously a gift of God and a free human act. God works in us that we may have a good will, and with us when we have a good will, offering both "the truth to be believed" and "the Savior to be trusted" (Merrill, *ACE,* p. 53; Augustine, *On Nature and Grace, NPNF* 1 V, pp. 121 ff.). Since "it is God who works in you," you are asked to "continue to work out your salvation" (Phil. 2:12, 13).

The Author of Faith.   That faith is the gift of God does not imply the absence of human agency. If faith is an act of trust, it requires a willing human agent—one made capable of trust. The One trusted is a Person, God's own incomparably personal coming into our midst. This person is faith's author (*archēgon*) and perfecter (*teleiotēn*) upon whom our eyes are fixed, "who for the joy set before him endured the cross" (Heb. 12:2).

As we receive food by eating, we receive Christ by believing (Second Helvetic Conf., XV, *BOC* 5.110). God does not believe for us, but enables our believing, just as God does not walk for us, eat for us, see for us. As we may refuse to walk, eat, or see, so we may refuse to believe. But when we believe, it is truly our own action, yet always enabled by grace, exercising the gracious ability God has given us to trust in the eventful Word spoken in Jesus Christ (John of Damascus, *OF* IV.10, *FC* 37. pp. 348–51).

Faith as Passive and Active.   Accordingly, faith is neither indolently waiting so as to lack activity or compulsively acting so as to lack receptivity; faith is a receptivity that acts responsively and energetically and an activity that answers. As *activity* in response to grace, faith acts through its receptivity, gives through receiving, walks through being held up, speaks through being spoken to. As *receptivity*, the whole person stands in full readiness as if emptied of arbitrary self-will to receive and follow the Way of life. This readiness is premised in the account of Peter's confession, "You are the Christ, the Son of the living God." For Jesus replied, "Flesh and blood hath not revealed it unto thee, but my Father which is in heaven" (Matt. 16:17, KJV).

One emptied of arbitrary self-will is most readied for becoming filled of the love of God to be shed abroad in human history. One fully receptive to God's Spirit becomes fully active in relation to neighbor. Faith is an activity that lives out of

Christ, knows and wills in Christ, a life of union with Christ (Quenstedt, *TDP* III, pp. 619 ff.; Heppe, *RD,* p. 511; Schmid, *DT,* pp. 480–86).

The balanced dialectic between receptivity and activity repeatedly appears in the Pauline epistles: "So then, just as you received Christ Jesus as Lord, continue to live in him, rooted and built up in him, strengthened in the faith as you were taught" (Col. 2:6). "But whatever was to my profit I now consider loss. . . . that I may gain Christ and be found in him, not having a righteousness of my own that comes from the law, but that which is through faith in Christ—the righteousness that comes from God and is by faith" (Phil. 3:7–9).

The receiving/acting equilibrium was rightly grasped by Luther: "Christ as a Gift nourishes your faith and makes you a Christian; but Christ as an Example exercises your works. These do not make you a Christian but are performed by you, who have previously been made a Christian" (Luther, *WLS* I, p. 199; *WA* 10 I, 1, 11 f.). "Christ is set before us and given to us as an example and pattern which we are to follow. For when we possess Christ through faith as a free gift, we should go on and do as He has done for us and imitate Him in our entire life and sufferings" (Luther, *Sermon on 1 Pet. 4,* 1523, *WLS* I, p. 199; *WA* 12, 372).

Benefits of Salvation.   The three key benefits of salvation are justification (receiving the pardon of God canceling our sin), regeneration (receiving new life in the Spirit and participation in the family of God), and sanctification (receiving the growth-enabling, completing, maturing, perfecting grace of God that leads toward holiness of heart and life). Each tends increasingly toward the experiential actualization of life in Christ, toward concrete participation in the body of Christ.

These benefits—God's mercy, justification by grace, rebirth from above, and entrance into the family of God—were summarized in the letter to Titus in this way: "He saved us through the washing of rebirth and renewal by the Holy Spirit, whom he poured out on us generously through Jesus Christ our Savior, so that, having been justified by his grace, we might become heirs having the hope of eternal life" (Titus 3:4; cf. Goodwin, *Works* VI, pp. 73–85).

All benefits occur by grace through faith. Faith in Christ brings all things good (Clement of Rome, *Cor.* 22.1, *SHD,* p. 57). Salvation is redemption actualized in human life, where the Word of Life dwells in us to become our own life (1 John 1:1–7).

FAITH WORKING THROUGH LOVE

Whether Faith Works or Works Believe

Faith is the sole condition of salvation. No merit is needed on our part, since the merit offered on the cross is sufficient. One is justified by faith alone, yet faith is not alone but accompanied by the Spirit's fruits of good works (Leo, *Sermons* XC, *NPNF* 2 XII, p. 201). Faith is "the alone instrument of justification; yet it is not alone in the person justified, but is ever accompanied with all other saving graces, and is no dead faith, but worketh by love" (Westminster Conf., XI, *CC,* p. 207; cf. Augustine, *Faith and Works* 16.27; *Hom. on John,* tractate 6.21).

Faith is known by its works as a tree is known by its fruit (Luther, *The Freedom of a Christian, MLS,* pp. 71–80). As the tree lives out of the interconnected difference between its fruits and its roots, so the Christian life lives out of the interconnected difference between faith and works (Calvin, *Inst.* 2.2).

Faith Elicits Good Works, Not Merit.   Faith bears fruit through responsive love toward the next one we see. "For in Christ Jesus neither circumcision nor uncircumcision has any value. The only thing that counts is faith expressing itself through love" (Gal. 5:6). Trust in God translates ethically into responsiveness to God's address. Faith acts by means of love (Melanchthon, *Loci, LCC* XIX, pp. 110–18). Those who are to share God's life eternally are being readied for that sharing by learning to walk in the way of holiness.

Faith is the basis of the Christian life, moral responsiveness, redeemed ethical behavior (Tho. Aq., *ST* II–II, Q4, III, pp. 1189–97). "Faith receives, love gives" (Luther, *WA* 8.355, 362 ff.; *EA* 9.280 f.). "Faith remains the doer and love remains the deed" (Luther, *EA* 8.63; *SHD* II, p. 275). "Faith brings man to God; love brings God to men. Through faith man allows God to do him good; through love God does good to men." The Christian is therefore through faith a free lord subject to none and through love a ministering servant responsive to all (Luther, *Freedom of the Christian, MLS*, pp. 79–81; *EA* 14.40; 27, pp. 181–85).

"Faith is the beginning, love the end. And these two in union are divine. All other things relating to a holy life are consequences of these" (Ignatius, *Eph.* 14.1; *SHD,* p. 66). Other virtues are daughters of faith (Hermas, *Vis.* 3.8.3, 4; *Mand.* 5.2.3). Faith and love are the whole sum of the Christian life (Ignatius, *Smyrna* 6.1).

Dead Faith.   The faith by which one lives in union with Christ is vitally active. It walks. Unattended by good works, it proves to be not a living but a dead faith. "As the body without the spirit is dead, so faith without deeds is dead" (James 2:26). "But someone will say, 'You have faith; I have deeds.' Show me your faith without deeds, and I will show you my faith by what I do" (James 2:18). It is a "dead faith" that fails to lead to the obedience of faith, the life of works of love, for it lacks our appropriation of Christ's reconciling ministry. This is why "faith without deeds is useless" (James 2:20). It is unthinkable that justification could occur without some dimension of repentance (Luke 13:3). "In the same way, faith by itself, if it is not accompanied by action, is dead" (James 2:17).

To Faith Is Added Hope and Love.   Faith is characteristically accompanied by hope and love (1 Cor. 13:13). As the receptive act of responding to promised grace, faith is intrinsically connected with hope (Heb. 11:1; *Barnabas* 1.4–6; 4.8). As the active process of sharing grace, faith is intrinsically related to love toward the neighbor (*Barnabas* 2.2; 11.8–11). Faith, the "mother of us all," is characteristically "accompanied by hope, and led by love to God and Christ and our neighbor" (Polycarp, *Phil.* 3, *LCC* I, p. 132).

Hope is that excellent habituation by which one securely trusts that God will be faithful to his promise and will provide the faithful with fit means to receive it. The ground of hope is the almighty power of God, and confidence that God will provide means to save. The apostle prayed, "May the God of hope fill you with all joy and peace as you trust in him, so that you may overflow with hope by the power of the Holy Spirit" (Rom. 15:13). "For in this hope we are saved. But hope that is seen is no hope at all. Who hopes for what he already has? But if we hope for what we do not yet have, we wait for it patiently" (Rom. 8:24, 25). In this way hope becomes "an anchor for the soul, firm and secure" (Heb. 6:19).

"To faith, therefore, must be added hope, and to hope, love" (Augustine, *Sermons* XVI.6; cf. Gregory the Great, *Hom. on the Gospel* 29). Faith works precisely through love (Gal. 5:6). "Faith working by love, not faith without love, is the means and condition of man's justification before God" (Fourteen Theses, Old Catholic Union Conference, *CC* II, p. 546). When Paul wrote that one is "justified without the works of the law," he did not mean that faith is sufficient precisely when it "leads a bad life and has no good deeds to allege. It is impossible that such a character should be deemed a 'vessel of election'" (Augustine, *Grace and Free Will* VII.18, Pohle *DT* VII, p. 289; cf. *FC* 59, p. 269).

Both Jesus and Paul used dramatic rhetoric to make this point: "Not everyone who says to me, 'Lord, Lord,' will enter the kingdom of heaven, but only he who does the will of my Father who is in heaven" (Matt. 7:21). "If I have a faith that can move mountains, but have not love, I am nothing" (1 Cor. 13:2). Love delights in the good of the beloved (John Chrysostom, *Hom. on the Statues, NPNF* 1 IX, pp. 453, 464). "If a stranger fall at your feet, homeless and a foreigner, welcome Him who for your sake was a stranger, and that among His own" (Gregory Nazianzen, *Orat.* XL.31, *NPNF* 2 VII, p. 371, translation amended).

Meanwhile, the arrogant idea of "works of supererogation" (presuming to do more than God requires) is strongly rejected (Thirty-nine Articles, XIV, *CC*, p. 271). Christ taught, "So you also, when you have done everything you were told to do, should say, 'We are unworthy servants'" (Luke 17:10).

Whether It Is Adequate to Speak of "Faith Only."   As the embryo has no part whatever in its conception, so the recipient of saving grace makes no self-initiated contribution to justifying grace. Those dead in sin can have no part whatever in the initiation of their regeneration. We are not justified by *our* loving or cleaving but only by divine grace to which faith responds in the trust that loves (Eph. 2:1–10).

When Christians speak of "faith alone," using the "exclusive particles"—"without works," "without law"—this is done in order to exclude any hint that we may be justified by our own works or actions, intentions or deeds. These precise exclusions do not intend to deny that good works follow faith as its expected fruits (Calvin, *Inst.* 3.11–17). They merely seek to exclude all human boasting, all self-righteousness. The intent is "that neither renewal, sanctification, virtues, nor other good works are our righteousness before God, nor are they to be made and posited to be a part or a cause of our justification, nor under any kind of pretense, title, or name are they to be mingled with the article of justification as pertinent or necessary to it. The righteousness of faith consists solely in the forgiveness of sins by sheer grace, entirely for the sake of Christ's merit" (Formula of Concord, p. 546; cf. Melanchthon, *Loci*, 3d ed., *CR* XXI, 753–55).

Only is an excluding term. What does it exclude, when we say "faith alone" or "faith only"? It surely does not exclude grace or the cross or obedience. For it comes by grace through the cross and elicits obedience (Creed of Dositheus, XIII, *CC*, pp. 496, 497). One might say more precisely that we are justified by grace alone, or the blood of Christ alone, than to say too simply that we are justified by faith alone. "Faith alone" rightly understood means that nothing else is required as a subjective condition than faith as the receiving cause of justification. God the

Son offers sufficient sacrifice on the cross, faith accepts and trusts it, and the outcome is justification by grace through faith (Thirty-nine Articles of Religion, XI, CC, p. 270). The reason these explicit disclaimers have seemed so necessary is that some have set forth a skewed teaching in which good works appeared to be requisite to faith or a teaching of justification conditioned upon works of satisfaction (Augustine, *Spirit and Letter* 50–60, *NPNF* 1 V, pp. 104–10; cf. Sermon 151).

Melanchthon concluded that only faith justifies, but faith is not alone (*Sola fides justificat, sed fides non est sola*). Faith can never be "alone" in the sense of being "without works." Against the thesis of George Major that works are necessary to salvation, the Formula of Concord concluded that good works voluntarily performed are commanded and commended, and that faith brings with it good works (art. IV, 625–37; cf. Luther, *Instructions for Visitors*, *LW* 40, p. 280).

Faith Not Because of Works, but Faith Must Work.   Faith does not remain vitally healthy without doing good works. Faith is active in love. Yet faith does no good in which it can boast as having satisfied God's requirement. The Augsburg Confession taught that "faith is bound to bring forth good fruits, and that it is necessary to do good works commanded by God, because of God's will, but not that we should rely on those works to merit justification before God" (art. VI, Jacobs, *SCF*, p. 199; cf. *CC*, p. 69). Faith does not justify because it works, for that would shift the justifier from God to human faith (Calvin, *Inst.* 3.11–14).

God commands good works not merely of those under the law, but of those redeemed by Christ (Isa. 1:16, 17; Matt. 3:8; John 15:8; Titus 3:8). Good works are an expression of genuine faith in the sense that good works make evident the sincerity of faith (Matt. 5:14–16; Rom. 2:22–24; 12:1, 2; Titus 2:14; James 1:25). "We confess him by our works" (*2 Clement* 4.3).

No Justification on Account of Faith.   It is misleading to suggest that we are justified *on account of* our faith. Rather we are justified through faith, in the sense that faith is the only means by which Christ's work is rightly received. Faith does not in and of itself justify. No one is saved *on account of (propter)* faith, but *by (per)* faith. It is not bare faith of itself that saves, but Christ who saves through faith. The saving efficacy lies not in the response—not in the disconnected act of faith itself—but in the One to whom faith responds (Chemnitz, *TNC*, pp. 411–20, 450–51).

This is why justification teaching requires precise statement: It is not our faith that is accepted by God, but Christ's work. It is Christ's work on our behalf that faith receives and trusts, and thereby is reconciled to God. Faith is rendered possible by grace—it is not that faith renders grace possible (Calvin, *Inst.* 3.14–17). Faith becomes responsive in obedient love, but it is not our obedience that makes us worthy of being declared upright in God's presence.

This teaching was prototypically defined in the Reformed tradition by the Westminster divines that God justifies "not by imputing faith itself, the act of believing, or any other evangelical obedience to them, as their righteousness; but by imputing the obedience and satisfaction of Christ unto them, they receiving and resting on him and his righteousness by faith; which faith they have not of themselves, it is the gift of God" (Westminster Conf., XI, *CC*, p. 207; cf. Athanasius, *Resurrection Letters*, 5, pp. 86–92).

It is not as working but as trusting that sinners enter into union with Christ by faith and receive pardon. Faith does not justify in the sense that it would assume itself to be the source of righteousness. Rather faith is a renunciation of all claims of righteousness, trusting in Christ's righteousness (Rom. 4; Phil. 3:9).

Faith Made Complete in Works of Love: James and Paul

The absence of works indicates that faith is not working actively; hence itself is lacking. In distinguishing between active (true) and inactive (false) faith, James was not contradicting Paul, who viewed saving faith as the condition of the sinner's being made whole. For works are reliable evidences or proof or demonstration that faith is working actively. Faith alone justifies, but faith without works of love is not the basis upon which the person will be long preserved in a justified life. The grace that justifies, as received through faith, prompts the person to a disposition to love the neighbor (Irenaeus, *Ag. Her.* IV.6.5). Faith is perfected and given form through love (Tho. Aq., *ST* II–II, Q4.3). James exposed the false piety of those who claimed to have faith yet showed no behavioral evidences of faith active through compassion. "Was not our ancestor Abraham considered righteous for what he did when he offered his son Isaac on the altar? You see that his faith and his actions were working together, and *his faith was made complete* by what he did" (James 2:21, 22, italics added; Clement of Rome, *Corinth*, 32, 33).

On What Principle May James and Paul Be Reconciled?   James at first glance seems to press the matter beyond Paul when he writes, "You see that a person is justified by what he does and not by faith alone" (James 2:24). How is that to be understood in the light of the Pauline teaching of justification by grace through faith?

Where a teaching of scripture is treated in detail in one letter, and briefly in another, the hermeneutical principle that applies is to give relatively more weight to the extended argument. Since Paul deals with justification by faith extensively in Galatians and Romans, these passages are to be taken as the formative spring of the teaching (*sedes doctrinae*) of justification, which is supplemented by James.

It is difficult to establish that there is a genuine conflict between Paul and James, for Paul is dealing primarily with the justification that God declares with respect to human sin as viewed in Christ, whereas James is dealing primarily with the way the justified life is made recognizable through acts of love. James is describing the life of those who have already been justified through faith, whereas Paul is focused more particularly upon the entrance into the life of faith through justifying grace.

Their Systematic Affinities.   James was not arguing that faith as such is meritorious, for he makes explicit that "even the demons believe" (James 2:19). James's formula that faith is completed by works (James 2:22) has deep affinities with the Pauline formula that faith is active in love (Gal. 5:6; 1 Cor. 13). The dead "faith" that James was resisting was not trust in Christ's righteousness but merely a mouthing of faith that "does nothing" (James 2:16), which is even less than that of the demons, who at least believe there is one God "—and shudder" (James 2:19).

Paul's challenge was to defend faith against boasting and legalism, while James's challenge was equally valid: to defend faith against license and lethargy. James sought to lead the believer away from self-centered idleness and presumption. Paul sought to rescue the sinner from despair and pride. Paul aimed the arrow of faith at works-righteousness, while James aimed it at apathy.

James was just as ready as Paul to affirm, "'Abraham believed God, and it was credited to him as righteousness,' and he was called God's friend" (James 2:23, referring to Gen. 15:6). Trust in God's righteousness was the basis upon which Abraham was restored to friendship with the holy God. Hence there is not in James an absence of the teaching of faith, but an assumption of it.

Whether Justification Sets One Free from the Law.   Paul like James condemned false teachers who would make grace a warrant for continuing in sin (Rom. 3:8). "Shall we go on sinning so that grace may increase? By no means! We died to sin; how can we live in it any longer?" (Rom. 6:1, 2; Calvin, *On Reform, SW*, pp. 96–98; 172–77; 204–5). For these reasons it is incorrect to pit Paul against James on justification and works (Shaw, *CT*, p. 256).

Christ did not come to free us *from* but *for* obedience (Newman, *Parochial Sermons* VIII, pp. 203, 204). When faith is credited for righteousness, the law is not nullified, but upheld (Rom. 3:31; cf. Calvin, *Inst.* 2.7.1).

Luther resisted the antinomianism that would exalt license so as to neglect the divine command: "Christ did not so die for sinners that we might continue to live in sins. He did not come to confirm sin. This is not the purpose He came to serve. Rather He came to redeem men from sin" (Luther, *Good Friday Sermon on Luke 23:34–43*, 1534, *WLS* I, p. 196). The antinomian principle in our time has most flagrantly been made an axiom by Tillich: "Where there is New Being, there is no commandment and no judgment" (*ST* II, p. 119).

The Increase of Faith

Whether There Are Degrees of Faith.   That there are degrees of faith is evident from Jesus' distinction between those of "little faith" (Matt. 6:30) and those of "great faith" (Matt. 8:10; Archelaus, *Disputation with Manes* 42, *ANF* VI, pp. 216–18).

Faith may increase. Its intellectual vitality may deepen, its emotive and volitional strength grow. "Your faith is growing more and more, and the love every one of you has for each other is increasing" (2 Thess. 1:3). The disciples pled with the Lord, "Increase our faith!" (Luke 17:5). Faith may grow in love, peace, hope, and joy. "Our hope is that, as your faith continues to grow, our area of activity among you will greatly expand" (2 Cor. 10:15; John Chrysostom, *The Paralytic, NPNF* 1 IX, pp. 215–16).

Since faith is an act that assumes knowing, feeling, and willing, and since intellect, passion, and volition may grow stronger by exercise and habituation, faith may increase (Tho. Aq., *ST* I–II, Q52.1, I, pp. 806–10; II–II, Q1–7, II, pp. 1169–1204). The Spirit does not work only for a moment upon the human person, but, because the person develops, the Spirit works through personal growth. Faith acquires increasing strength by enduring trials, bearing the cross, walking in the way (James 1:2; 1 Pet. 1:6; 2 John 4, 6).

Whether Faith May Be Lost.   That faith can be lost is evident from Jesus' own description of those who "believe for a while, but in the time of testing they fall away" (Luke 8:13; Augustine, *Trin.*, *FC* 45, pp. 372). Timothy was instructed to "hold on to faith," aware that some had entirely "shipwrecked their faith" (1 Tim. 1:19). Paul specifically named two shipwrecks—Hymenaeus and Alexander—and elsewhere we learn of others (Demas, Philetus).

Even "if you think you are standing firm," Paul warned the Corinthian believers, "be careful that you don't fall!" (1 Cor. 10:12). Some may "fall away," having "tasted the heavenly gift," having once "shared in the Holy Spirit, who have tasted the goodness of the word of God and the powers of the coming age" (Heb. 6:4, 5).

The leaven can lose its efficacy (Matt. 16:6). The salt can lose its taste (Matt. 5:13). Faith is not lost, however, by any sin except the lack of faith (Trent VI, *SCD* 808, p. 255). Among biblical metaphors and parables that assume the vulnerability of faith are horticultural images: the barren tree (Luke 13:6–9); the broken shoots of the olive (Rom. 11:17–21); the dead branch of the vine (John 15:6); the fruitless tree (Matt. 3:10).

When faith is lost having been held, its being lost does not occur through the direct willing of God but through the recalcitrance of sin. "The Lord is not slow in keeping his promise, as some understand slowness. He is patient with you, not wanting anyone to perish, but everyone to come to repentance" (2 Pet. 3:9). That this is written to the faithful is evident from the opening passage of the letter (2 Pet. 1:1–11). Patience in well-doing is an expression of habitual reception of grace (Cyprian, *Treatises* IX, *ANF* V, pp. 484 ff.).

Whether Pardon May Be Forfeited.   Humanity cannot undo what God has done on the cross. One or another may fail to accept it, but that does not quiet the Word finally spoken there or negate the act accomplished for all. Yet insofar as a particular believer is concerned, is it possible, once having received pardon, to cast it back, forget it, or negate it? No and yes. Never in the sense of undoing God's act. Those who live in Christ are promised sufficient grace to carry them to completion of God's intention (Phil. 3:12–14). But yes in the sense that if they forsake trusting and once again choose death and throw themselves back into self-justifying syndromes of sin and despair under the law, they then live as if the pardon were forfeited, negating its benefits. The parable of the unmerciful servant tells this story exactly of one who having received pardon forfeited it (Matt. 18; Oden, *SA*, pp. 107–16).

Systemic sins against faith occur either by heresy or by apostasy. In heresy one who is baptized holds to the name Christian yet denies the apostolic faith. He "either gives birth to, or follows, false and new opinions" (Augustine, *On the Profit of Believing* 1, *NPNF* 1 III, p. 347). "Heresy is a species of unbelief, belonging to those who profess the Christian faith, but corrupt its dogmas." In apostasy one who is baptized falls away from the faith totally, so as to "turn away from God altogether" (Tho. Aq., *ST* II–II, Q11–12, II, pp. 1225–29; John 6:65–67).

Whether Weak Faith Justifies.   Weak faith and strong faith share in all that Christ is, and hence equally justify. Yet faith may be more or less effective in bearing fruits and become more or less active in love. Though faith may increase, the efficacy of justifying faith is not proportional to its degree. For in justifying faith, all effectiveness is derived from that which calls faith forth, namely, grace.

There are indeed degrees of faith, yet justification is a no-holds-barred declaratory act of God that offers new birth. The justifying declaration is not itself something that grows and develops. It occurs once for all, eschatologically, and is received, like birth, in a moment, however long its period of gestation may have been. Classic exegetes concluded that weak or immature faith justifies (as in the case of the thief on the cross, Luke 23:43) as wonderfully as strong faith (Calvin, *Comm.* XVII, p. 311).

Weak faith may lack sufficient experience with the overcoming of temptation and sharing Christ's suffering to have grown in firm assurance of salvation. That may come with strength only through time and development, as with the exercise of a muscle. But the merit of Christ is equally effective whether faith is weak or strong. The strength of faith does not increase the merit of Christ. The weakness of faith does not diminish the merit of Christ (Luke 23:43; 17:5; 2 Cor. 10:15; 2 Thess. 1:3; Augustine, *Sermons on New Testament Lessons* XVII, *NPNF* 1 VI, pp. 310–13).

Whether Grace Justifies in Part or Whole. God's pardon is not partially addressed to some portion of one's behavior. The sinner united to Christ by faith is not declared in some aspect justified, or in proportion to his meager faith or hope or love. Rather this atoning declaration concerns the whole person and the whole of the person's activity. The full extent of Christ's righteousness is completely offered to the sinner (Luther, *Two Kinds of Righteousness, LW* 31, pp. 297–306).

No one can adequately enumerate all of one's sins. This does not prevent the penitent, however, from petitioning that all sins—even those unknown and unenumerated—be forgiven. Similarly, in pardon, it is not each sin separately that is isolated and forgiven independently, but rather all and together and once for all. As repentance is from the heart, so is pardon addressed to the heart, the unifying center of the emotive life. Just as one is not partially born, or born limb by limb or eye by eye, but rather all together, so is one pardoned—all together, for all one's motives, all acts, and all the dreadful consequences of all one's acts (Calvin, *Inst.* 3.4, 4.12).

John attested that "the blood of Jesus, his Son, purifies us from all sin" (1 John 1:7). There remain great differences in receptivity of grace among believers, some having followed the way far toward maturity, others having followed only briefly or with frequent stumbling. Yet both those who arrived at the vineyard early and those who arrived late are equally justified by the Lord's merit (Matt. 20:1–16; Augustine, *Sermons on New Testament Lessons,* XXXVII, *NPNF* 1 VI, pp. 373–78).

The great privilege of those born of God is to be free from guilt, free from condemnation, dead to sin (J. Wesley, *WJWB* I, sermon 19; *WJW* V, pp. 223–33). If it occurs subsequently that through infirmities we find the old syndromes reemerging, this reminds us that the carnal nature has not been wholly destroyed, but providentially is permitted to remain as a part of continued growth in faith, which grows only by being challenged. Though sin may *remain* in believers, it does not *reign* in those who have received justifying grace (J. Wesley, *WJWB* I, sermon 13; *WJW* V, pp. 144–46). Where pardon is reigning, sin cannot reign (Rom. 5:20–6:12).

This juridical teaching of plenary or full pardon is not inconsistent with the affirmation that pardon must be continually and daily renewed in practice. Insofar as one continues to sin, one continues to need pardon. Christians daily pray, "Forgive us our debts, as we also have forgiven our debtors, and lead us not into temptation" (Matt. 6:12, 13). Paradoxically those most keenly rooted in faith are those most likely to recognize their own sin most clearly.

Whether Justification Requires Time. Justification is an objective act of God, a declaration of acquittal. As such, it is addressed to humanity once for all in Jesus Christ, waiting to be received by faith. Sanctification, the Spirit's work to apply the work of Christ to the heart and life of the believer, is an experiential process beginning with a new birth (by justifying grace) and continuing with growth (through sanctifying grace) toward maturation (through completing grace). Sanctifying grace elicits gradual growth in believers, who may increase or decline in strength of faith. Justifying grace is always the same—simple and declarative, instantaneously addressed to all humanity in the cross, whether the faith receiving it is weak or strong (Pope, *Compend.* III, pp. 28–36; Hodge, *ST,* pp. 213–30).

To answer too quickly either that justification is instantaneous or that it is gradual may tend to mislead. If one says that justification is gradual, how can it be that a declaration is gradually made, for a declaration occurs in a moment. Yet if one says that justification is instantaneous, that may tend to be misunderstood as if justification were a particular or single or isolable emotive experience, thus subjectivizing the divine work of justification, as if it were mainly our experience rather than an act of grace (J. Wesley, *WJW* V, pp. 53 ff., VI, pp. 43 ff.).

It is better to answer that justification is a divine declaration for us that is received in a single, life-giving moment—for faith must begin at some moment in time, if at all—yet justification aims at being continually received and being developmentally appropriated in behavior. All this takes time. The Holy Spirit has time abundantly to lead persons toward the full consecration of their redeemed powers (Gregory of Nyssa, *The Life of Moses,* pp. 29–33, 133 ff.; *FGG;* Phoebe Palmer, *Entire Devotion to God*).

Pardon is a single act, perfect in itself, yet the realization of it in the heart by faith admits of many different types of human experiences through varied human cultures, and may so gradually emerge that its time of full acceptance is hardly specifiable or datable. In its earlier stages it may enjoy a fuller force of moral certainty than in its maturing stages, in which it brushes against doubt and perseveres through resistances (Calvin, *Inst.* 3.20–22, 4.1.20 ff., cf. 3.2.38–43).

Since justification is a declaration on our behalf, it changes our status before the law. That in itself does not require developing time, because it is addressed to all times. One may say that it has already occurred in Jesus Christ on the cross. Yet each one who lives in time requires some time to grow more fully aware of it (1 Pet. 2:2; 2 Pet. 3:18). Life in Christ does not come full grown, but grows as all life grows (2 Thess. 1:3). It is the work of the Spirit to enable this growth in the soul's own time.

Good Works

The active life of doing good works is the implied outcome of one's continuing to be accounted righteous (James 2:14–26). Where faith lapses entirely and its working in love dies, God does not continue to account our former faith to us for righteousness as if faith were still alive. The subjective continuity of our being accounted righteous is thus contingent upon faith that bears fruits worthy of repentance (Matt. 7:16–20; John Chrysostom, *Hom. on Matt.* XLII, *NPNF* 1 X, pp. 268–72). A total absence of good works would imply the lack of the justifying faith that works through love. Lacking any good works, the resulting life can hardly be called justified or faithful or accounted righteous (J. Wesley, *WJW* V, pp. 447–67).

Whether Good Works Are Rewarded.   Each of the beatitudes is accompanied by a promised reward. The merciful are promised to receive mercy. The pure in heart will see God. The meek will inherit the earth. They conclude, "Rejoice and be glad, because great is your reward in heaven" (Matt. 5:12; Calvin, *Inst.* 3.17, 18). In this way those good works enabled by grace and grounded in responsive faith will be brought to fruition in the heavenly reward merited solely by Christ's obedience (Rev. 2:10; James 1:12; cf. Augustine, *Letters, to Sixtus* 194.29· Ambrose, *Duties of the Clergy* I.15, 57).

The leading exponent of salvation by grace through faith, Paul, is also the preeminent teacher of heavenly reward for good works grounded in faith: "Each will be rewarded according to his own labor" (1 Cor. 3:8). "God 'will give to each person according to what he has done.' To those who by persistence in doing good seek glory, honor and immortality, he will give eternal life" (Rom. 2:6; quoting Ps. 62:12). From his final imprisonment he wrote to Timothy, "I have fought the good fight, I have finished the race, I have kept the faith. Now there is in store for me the crown of righteousness, which the Lord, the righteous Judge, will award to me on that day" (2 Tim. 4:7, 8). There can be no plausible doctrine of justification that altogether lacks a doctrine of heavenly reward in the sense of eternal life (Apology of the Augsburg Conf. IV, *BOC*, pp. 160–68).

But is it possible that such grace-enabled good works may also be the basis of temporal blessing (prosperity, health, living well)? Thomas answered that they can, but only so far as such temporal blessings conduce to eternal salvation (*ST* I–II Q114, I, pp. 1153–61). For the worldly, temporal successes and achievements may become a snare to further pride or envy (Clement of Alexandria, *Who Is the Rich Man That Can Be Saved? ANF* II, pp. 589 ff.). Timothy was taught realistically to expect that in this life "everyone who wants to live a godly life in Christ Jesus will be persecuted" (2 Tim. 3:12). Both Jesus and Paul repeatedly employed the metaphor of reward of future blessedness for faith working through love (Matt. 5:12; 6:1–6; 25:34–40; 1 Cor. 3:8; Col. 2:18). Good works engender in the faithful a character that corresponds with God's own holiness and love, making them more fit to receive God's gifts and share in God's kingdom as heirs of God's family (Hermas, *Mand.* 5.1.3; *Sim.* 10.3.2). Love is what brings us closer to God, since God is love. Those who love are children of God (1 John 4:16; 5:2; Augustine, *Hom. on Epist. of John* VIII, *NPNF* 1 VII, pp. 506–13).

The parable of the widow's mite makes it clear that the arithmetic quantity of good works is not the crucial criterion, but rather contextually doing all one can (Mark 12:42, 43; Calvin, *Comm.* XVII, pp. 113–14). Those who have limited ability or opportunity yet cooperate fully with the grace they are given are fully rewarded, whether weak or strong, mentally handicapped or geniuses. The criterion of heavenly reward is not a quantitative form of justice, but an equity that God is wise enough to render proportionally (Tho. Aq., *ST* suppl., Q96, III, pp. 2981–96). Trust him: "God is not unjust; he will not forget your work" (Heb. 6:10).

Whenever venturing to speak evangelically of the value of good works, it is well to remember that its entire premise is unmerited justification. The gracious ability of the justified to perform good works is grounded in God's own good work in Christ (Shepherd of Hermas, *Sim.* III.X, *ANF* II, pp. 54–55; Pohle, *DT* VII, p. 405; *Trent* VI.16, pp. 40–42).

Whether Works Merit Justification as with a Wage.   However good and commendable, good works are not meritorious in the sense of earning salvation. To earn is to produce a product or service worthy of a wage. No service can be proportionally rendered to God that makes God indebted to us, analogous to owing workers a wage (Matt. 20:1–16; Calvin, *Inst.* 3.14–16). "There is no proportion between the infinite worth of the salvation promised by God and the finite worth of man's works" (Fourteen Theses, Old Catholic Union Conference, *CC* II, p. 547).

There remains enormous disparity between our best temporal works and the eternal reward God promises to give us. Though death is viewed as the wage of sin (Rom. 6:23), it is not possible by analogy to view eternal life as the wage of good works, for though eternal life is indeed a reward, it is such only as a gift. "It is a reward because our works make us fit to receive it; but it is not wages, because it exceeds the intrinsic earning value of our works" (Hall, *DT* VIII, p. 274; cf. Tho. Aq., *ST* I–II, Q114.3).

Whether Justification Is Immoral.   Was it not Yahweh who declared, "I will not acquit the guilty" (Exod. 23:7)? Is justification then an immoral act, if the ungodly are acquitted?

Justification is made morally plausible by being always linked fittingly with the holiness and mercy of God on the cross and with the regenerating and sanctifying work of the Spirit. At the time the ungodly are acquitted, they are not yet fully transformed, yet God declares them just by virtue of their trusting relation to Christ. God does not justify sin, but declares sinners uncondemned insofar as they are united to Christ by faith. Christ is wholly just on their behalf, having fulfilled the law for them (John 3:17, 18; Rom. 8:1–4).

Whether the Absence of Good Works Invalidates Justification in the Death of Infants.   Jesus' welcoming embrace of children suggests that he had special affection for their innocence and promise (Matt. 18:1–5; 19:13–14). There is room for children in the kingdom of heaven. One must become like a child to enter there (Luther, *Concerning Rebaptism, LW* 40, pp. 242–43). Eternal bliss without children is unimaginable and lacking in plausibility.

The tradition of believers' baptism does not accept the premise that infants are capable of the responsive faith requisite to baptism. It insists that baptism is an act of faith requiring an age of discretion (Menno Simons, *Foundation of Christian Doctrine, CWMS,* pp. 130–42).

The remainder of the tradition, its majority though by no means unanimous voice, does accept this premise, but the issue remains much controverted. This tradition has often reasoned in this way: Those who die having been baptized in infancy appear to have little or no opportunity for any works whatever. As recipients of that history of sin common to all the children of Adam, they have nonetheless not exercised their freedom in any extensive way, and presumably not raised obstacles to the operation of the sanctifying grace given in baptism. Sin has not been given much if any opportunity to arise in them. Thus they are accounted righteous just as those who have been through a longer journey engaged in a lengthy combat with sin (African Code, canon CX, *NPNF* 2 XIV, pp. 496–97; Council of Florence, *SCD* 712, p. 229; Calvin, *Inst.* 4.14.21–16.23; French Confession of Faith, *COC* III, p. 366).

REGENERATION

Regeneration is the work of the Spirit by which new life in Christ is initially imparted to one dead in sin. It implies a change in the inward person by which a disposition to the holy life is originated, and in which that life begins. It is the act of God by which the governing disposition of the person begins to be responsive to the reconciling God (Formula of Concord III–VI, *COC* III, pp. 114–34).

The New Birth

Giving birth is awesome. In witnessing birth, one feels directly the unique value of human life. The pastor who visits a mother who has just given birth may on the same day visit a family that has lost a loved one in death. Nothing is more awe-inspiring than to be present in the midst of the coming or passing of life—birth or death. Christianity is intensely preoccupied with just such metaphors. The doctrine of regeneration is that part of the teaching of salvation that focuses upon the new birth of life that follows from faith. The Christian teaching of new birth seeks to establish its proper nature and definition, its agency, authorship, means, and effects.

Defining Regeneration. The term that systematically summarizes the teaching of the new birth is *regeneration.* The Greek word for regeneration, *palingenesia* (re-birth [Matt. 19:28; Titus 3:5] is a compound of again, *palin,* and birth, *genete*), means literally to "be generated again" or to be "born once more." Regeneration is that new beginning offered by the Spirit by which one is rescued from the dominion of sin and enabled with right affections to love God and keep God's commandments (Goodwin, *Works* VI, pp. 167–87; Wollebius, *CTC* 30–31, *RDB,* pp. 164–76; Wakefield, *CT* II, p. 425). It is a spiritual remaking, a *re*-creation by which the sinner becomes child of God.

New birth is not finally reducible to a psychological change or a moral turning or an external profession of religion or the mere observance of forms, rules, or duties of religion or a human remedy for human failures. New birth is the decisive work of God in the economy of salvation whereby spiritual life in Christ is imparted by the Holy Spirit (John Chrysostom, *Baptismal Instructions, ACW* 31, pp. 135–39). It is the birth of personal union with the living Christ. It amounts to a radical reversal of the direction of the will by which the selfless love of God begins to take the place of the godless love of self and of idolatrized creaturely goods (Augustine, Conf., IV, *NPNF* 1 I, pp. 69–78). At every phase it is the work of grace eliciting free human responsiveness.

The new birth has often been viewed as a definitive doctrine of *modern* evangelical Christians, who are identified as those "born again." Yet it is a basic teaching of *ancient* ecumenical Christianity. As such, it is a teaching shared by Christian believers of all times and places (Ussher, *Brief Declaration of the Universality of the Church, Whole Works of James Ussher*. 17 vols. Dublin: Hodges and Smith, 1848–1854, II, pp. 493–97).

Whether Multiple Rhetorical Expressions Point to Stages of the New Birth.   New life in Christ is described as a new birth (John 3:3–7; James 1:18; 1 Pet. 1:23) whereby a new nature is being given to the new creation in Christ (2 Cor. 5:17; 2 Pet. 1:4). A series of parallel terms describe this singular new birth:

> Born anew (John 3:7)
>
> Born of God (John 1:13)
>
> Born of the Spirit (John 3:5)
>
> Renewed by the Holy Spirit (Titus 3:5)
>
> Resurrection (Phil. 3:10)
>
> Passing from death to life (Eph. 1:1, 10)
>
> New creation (Gal. 6:15)
>
> New person (Eph. 4:24)
>
> Renovation of spirit (Eph. 4:23)
>
> Renewing of our minds (Rom. 12:2)
>
> Renewal in knowledge in the image of the Creator (Col. 3:10)
>
> Spiritual quickening of life where before there was not life (1 Pet. 3:18)

These terms do not point to differing stages of regeneration but to the single pivotal act of God's renewing of the human spirit in Christ, "as though He were creating us again" (*Letter of Barnabas* 6:11, *FC* 1, p. 200).

On Mixing Gold and Straw in the Foundation.   Few points of Christian doctrine are more crucial to evangelical preaching than new birth. A basic misjudgment about it will have a skewing effect upon all other teachings of salvation. Suppose one builds one's life upon personal experience of new birth in Christ yet intermittently adds other, weaker conceptual admixtures, thereby softening the good foundation. Much may go awry.

Paul likens the faulty building of the regenerate life to one who has oddly built a house by mixing gold and straw or by using both costly stones and hay. His metaphor is richly tragicomic: Assuming the foundation (personal union with Christ) is well laid, even if one later builds unwisely upon that foundation, in the final day, "it will be revealed with fire, and the fire will test the quality of each man's work." If the house of Christian teaching has been built with dubious and useless—even silly—admixtures (such as, in our time, a failed Marxism or an excessively hostile male chauvinism or a reactionary feminism determined by male chauvinism), the dweller may be saved if the personal-experiential foundation in Christ remains secure. The passage ends with a pathetic-comic twist: "If it is burned up, he will suffer loss; he himself will be saved, but only as one escaping through flames" (1 Cor. 3:12–15; cf. Calvin, *Inst.* 2.2; 3.20–24; Baxter, *PW* XX, pp. 388–90).

Whether New Birth Is Conceptually Distinguishable from Justification.   In justification a new relation with God is juridically declared. In regeneration, new life is given that bestows and embodies that new relationship. Justification refers to a change in one's standing before God; regeneration, to a new beginning of a life that manifests that new standing.

Justification is God's act, a declaratory act that comes to the sinner from without. Regeneration begins a new life in which that relationship is actually manifested within the believer's thoughts, words, and actions. Justification is what God the Son does for us, distinguished from what the Spirit begins to do in us through regeneration and continues through sanctification and union with Christ (J. Wesley, *WJWB* III, sermon 85; *WJW* V, pp. 506–13). Justification, new birth, adoption, and sanctification all mutually imply each other. Though distinguishable, they are inseparable teachings. The behavioral righteousness of the believer is evidence of new spiritual birth, for "everyone who does what is right has been born of him" (1 John 2:29). But behavioral righteousness is not a precondition of new birth, for no one is born due to meriting it (Calvin, *Inst.* 3.11; 4.15–16). Through regeneration the Spirit comes alive in us to begin to break the dominion of sin, to enable us to walk in the way of holiness (Goodwin, *Works* VI, pp. 151–78).

New birth is not a teaching detachable from justifying grace received through faith. Rather it is the act of the Spirit by which one is enabled to enter into this new life of grace-enabled justifying faith. It occurs the moment faith is given and received. What immediately follows upon the act of faith is variously described as pardon, new birth, and adoption into the family of God (Pope, *Compend.* III, pp. 5 ff.; Beyschlag, *NTT* II, pp. 453 ff.; C. Hodge, *The Way of Life,* pp. 286 ff.).

Justification pardons guilt; regeneration renews our broken spirit and fallen moral nature. A justification without a new birth would be like an act of pardon with nothing following it—no new life, no freedom, no responsiveness. To imagine one justified and not at the same time regenerated would be to imagine one whose past sins were pardoned but who is "left under the dominion of his sinful nature, and would necessarily continue to sin. Hence regeneration is represented as 'breaking the dominion of sin,' 'cleansing the moral nature,' 'being born again,' 'created anew'" (Tillett, *PS,* p. 136).

Justification functions out of forensic and juridical metaphors, whereas regeneration functions out of birth, creation, and resurrection metaphors. The agent of justification is the Son; of regeneration, the Spirit (Basil, *On the Spirit, NPNF* 2 VIII, pp. 5 ff.; Owen, *Works* 3, pp. 207 ff.; Strong, *ST,* pp. 471 ff.).

Justification "relates to that great work which God does for us, in forgiving our sins," while regeneration "relates to the great work which God does in us, in renewing our fallen nature." Justification is a change in the relation of God and humanity (hence a relational change), whereas new birth is the beginning of a behavioral (hence a palpable or "real" change) that actively manifests the change of relationship (J. Wesley, *WJW* V, pp. 212 ff.). These are not temporally separable. When justified, one is born of the Spirit. "In order of time, neither of these is before the other; in the moment we are justified by the grace of God, through the redemption that is in Jesus, we are also born of the Spirit; but in the order of thinking, as it is termed, justification precedes the new birth. We first conceive his wrath to be turned away, and then his Spirit to work in our hearts" (J. Wesley, *WJW* VI, p. 66; *WJWB,* sermon 45). "Logically (that is, in the order of thought), justification precedes regeneration; but chronologically (that is, in the order of time), justification and regeneration are contemporaneous" (Tillett, *PS,* p. 235).

Justification and adoption are characteristic teachings of Paul, shaped by courtroom and inheritance metaphors, whereas the new birth is a recurrent theme especially in John (but also found in Paul and in the general and Catholic epistles), shaped by the birth-growth metaphor. These two strands do not compete but complement. Those justified are sons and daughters of God, born of Spirit into the family of God. Justification and regeneration teachings are intrinsically related: "To those who believed in his name, he gave the right to become children of God" (John 1:12; Calvin, *Inst.* 3.3, 4.17.8).

Analogies of New Birth

This birth occurs through God's own initiative: "For you have been born again, not of perishable seed, but of imperishable, through the living and enduring word of God" (1 Pet. 1:23). As with the genesis of all creation, the new birth of persons occurs simply by God speaking a word to bring life out of nothingness.

The Analogy of Receiving Life. No one chooses to be born. One can only receive, not seize, life. No one can give birth to oneself. No one has ever claimed or demanded or even hoped to be born. Conception is a wholly receptive act of being quickened by another. So in the new birth do we wholly receive new life from God the Spirit (John 1:13; 3:1–8; 1 John 5:1–18).

One does not first seek to qualify for life and then ask to be born. One is first born, and only then are questions and hopes pertinent. Only after birth may one then begin to deal with the fact of life. As the living of life follows birth, so does the renewed life follow regenerating grace (1 John 3:9–10; Augustine, *Hom. on Epist. of John* V, *NPNF* 1 VII, pp. 487–93).

No one first becomes free and then is born. Rather one must first be born and only then can express freedom. So it is in the Christian life. Regeneration is absolutely prior to Christian freedom (Calvin, *Inst.* 3.19). As by physical birth one comes to life by entering into a wholly new environment, so by spiritual birth one is enabled to breathe in the new atmosphere of grace.

The Baptismal Analogy: Whether Birth of the New Life Requires Death of the Old. Without a rebirth of the affections from which actions spring, there is no reason to expect that anyone would manifest a life of faith or renounce idolatry or follow the way of holiness or accept salvation. Insofar as created goods are loved and idolized more than God, and persons remain bound to the sin that inordinately loves and idolizes creatures, no new life in the Spirit will emerge out of the history of sin (John 3:4–7; 1 Pet. 1:17–25).

The sacramental expression of new birth is baptism: "We were therefore buried with him through baptism into death" (Rom. 6:4). "Before beginning the second [regenerated life], it is necessary to put an end to the first" through repentance, which is "a kind of halt," so a pause intervenes before the movement in the opposite direction. "It seemed necessary for death to come as mediator between the [old and new life], ending all that goes before, and beginning all that comes after" (Basil, *On the Spirit* I.15, *NPNF* 2 VIII, p. 21). "You were taught, with regard to your former way of life, to put off your old self, which is being corrupted by its deceitful desires; to be made new in the attitude of your minds; and to put on the new self, created to be like God in true righteousness and holiness" (Eph. 4:23, 24; cf. 2 Cor. 5:17).

It is said that Ignatius Loyola once had dug for the novices of his order a grave, having them buried except for their heads, asking, "Are you dead?" To those who answered yes, he would reply, "Rise then, and begin to serve, for I want only dead men to serve me" (Strong, *ST*, p. 904).

The New Covenant Analogy: Circumcision of the Heart.   A related metaphor of new birth is circumcision—complicated but worth understanding. The promise was made to the covenant people that, when they take possession of the land of promise, "the Lord your God will circumcise your hearts and the hearts of your descendants, so that you may love him with all your heart and with all your soul, and life" (Deut. 30:6). The circumcised heart was set apart, consecrated wholly to God.

The theme recurs in the letter to the Colossians: "In him you were also circumcised, in the putting off of the sinful nature, not with a circumcision done by the hands of men but with the circumcision done by Christ, having been buried with him in baptism and raised with him through your faith in the power of God, who raised him from the dead" (Col. 2:11, 12; cf. Baxter, *PW* II, pp. 17, 18). The rites of circumcision in Israel and baptism in the New Israel (both rites of entry into the covenant community) were typologically correlated with a spiritual circumcision (a setting apart of life lived toward God) and a spiritual baptism (a life of penitence and faith that shares daily in Christ's death and resurrection; John Chrysostom, *Baptismal Instructions, ACW* 31, pp. 134–38).

Those who "put on Christ" (Gal. 3:27) do not merely clothe their fallenness with a deceptive outward cloak of righteousness. Rather the implication is that they are being inwardly cleansed of sin so as to become new creatures and children of God (Eph. 4:22 ff.; Col. 3:8 ff.; Pohle, *DT* VII, p. 317).

The Analogy of Creation Ex Nihilo: *New Creation.*   The spiritual breath or life of God is being imparted to one who lacks life just as abruptly and completely as the breath of natural life was imparted to Adam in the first creation. Grounded in this analogy, Paul taught, "Therefore, if anyone is in Christ, he is a new creation; the old has gone, the new has come! All this is from God" (2 Cor. 5:17, 18; cf. Gal. 6:15). "For we are God's workmanship [*poiema*], created [*ktisthentes*] in Christ Jesus to do good works" (Eph. 2:10). The evidence of this radical change is a life of love: "We know that we have passed from death to life, because we love" (1 John 3:14; Augustine, *Hom. on Epist. of John* V, *NPNF* 1 VII, pp. 487–93).

As the Father creates natural life out of nothing, so the Spirit, enabling the mission of the Son, quickens spiritual life *ex nihilo.* "For God, who said, 'Let light shine out of darkness,' made his light shine in our hearts" (2 Cor. 4:6; cf. Acts 26:18). "For you were once darkness, but now you are light in the Lord. Live as children of light" (Eph. 5:8).

No human willing can purchase this new life, as if grasped apart from grace. It comes purely as God's gift. God has "called you out of darkness into his wonderful light" (1 Pet. 2:9). The believer now belongs to a new creation that embraces all members of the body of which Christ is the head, all of whom, having been born anew, now live in Christ, having been "brought from death into life" (Rom. 6:13; cf. Eph. 2:5).

The Nativity Analogy: New Conception by the Spirit in Each Believing Soul. As Christ was preternaturally conceived by the Holy Spirit yet born in a natural way from the womb of a human mother, so each child of God must be begotten of the Holy Spirit in a birth that occurs precisely with and through a human body, a human soul, a human memory, intelligence, and will.

As birth begins a process that continues in growth, so does it occur that the new birth of justification continues in a process of sanctification (John 3:5, 6; Calvin, *Inst.* 3.1.4; 3.21.7; Schultze, *CD&ST*, pp. 138, 139).

One can only petition:

> Cast out our sin and enter in,
> Be born in us today.

> (Phillips Brooks, "O Little Town of Bethlehem," *MH* 100)

The Perichoresis *Analogy: New Union of Grace with Freedom.* As the Incarnate Lord did not appear without a human body and nature that became united personally to his divine nature, so in the work of grace in the new birth of sinners, divine and human agencies work together, with human willing cooperating responsively with divine willing. As the interpenetrating (*perichoresis*) relation of divinity and humanity in Christ remains a mystery, so does the birth of faith remain a mystery.

It is hardly plausible that one could be born without responding to it. As a baby is active in the birth canal, so is the whole person being reborn not just an inert lump, but intensely active amid rebirth, active in response to the work of the Spirit, repenting, grieving over sin, asking for pardon, trusting in Christ's righteousness, receiving the Spirit (Pope, *Compend.* III, pp. 3 ff.; A. Phelps, *The New Birth*, pp. 103–55). Though birth is a gift, this does not imply that one being born of God is completely lacking in responsiveness. For in receiving new life from God, one is by repentance and faith willingly consenting to have the Spirit work to change one's ruling disposition.

The human will is not a machine mechanistically driven by the Spirit, but rather a personal will that can receive a new spring of action. The efficacy of the Spirit's work is not contrary to but enabling of the activity of the human will. Regeneration is neither a divine work without human agency, nor human work apart from God, but a work of God performed under conditions of human willing (Augustine, *On Forgiveness of Sins and Baptism* II.8, *NPNF* 1 V, p. 47; Barth, *CD*, II/2, pp. 772 ff.; Ralston, *ED*, p. 349).

The Easter Analogy: New Life as Resurrection. The power at work in the renewal of life is that of the risen Lord, enlivened by "his incomparably great power for us who believe. That power is like the working of his mighty strength, which he exerted in Christ when he raised him from the dead" (Eph. 1:19, 20).

The faithful are called to live as if raised from the dead (Col. 2:12; 3:1–2), "to put on the new self, created to be like God in true righteousness and holiness" (Eph. 4:24). Those pardoned by justifying grace are "quickened together with

Him and raised into newness of life" (Col. 2:13, KJV). Those quickened are being raised into new life, having been dead to sin (Eph. 2:1–6). The moral quickening of believers occurs through participating in Christ's resurrection (Rom. 8:29, 30; Gal. 2:19, 20). The faithful are buried with him through baptism "in order that, just as Christ was raised from the dead through the glory of the Father, we too may live a new life" (Rom. 6:4; Athanasius, *Resurrection Letters* V, pp. 86–92).

New life born of God and resurrection are direct correlates. They point to the two pivotal events of the Christian year: Christmas and Easter—to the events of God's wonderful beginning and completing of his earthly ministry so as to inaugurate the new age—through incarnation and resurrection. As Christ was born and when crucified was resurrected, so the Christian who lives in Christ is born anew and in sharing Christ's death also shares Christ's resurrection, so as to live in Christ. "In his great mercy he has given us new birth into a living hope through the resurrection of Jesus Christ from the dead, and into an inheritance that can never perish, spoil or fade" (1 Pet. 1:3, 4; Goodwin, *Works* VI, pp. 151–64).

"As now a man who is physically dead cannot, of his own powers prepare or adapt himself to recover temporal life, so a man who is spiritually dead in sins cannot live" (Formula of Concord, 553, Jacobs, *SCF*, p. 231). "You were dead in your transgressions and sin." Now God has "made us alive with Christ even when we were dead in transgressions" (Eph. 2:1, 5). Therefore boasting is excluded. "What do you have that you did not receive? And if you did receive it, why do you boast?" (1 Cor. 4:7). "Apart from me you can do nothing" (John 15:5). "No one can come to me unless the Father who sent me draws him" (John 6:44). "Not that we are competent in ourselves to claim anything for ourselves, but our competence comes from God" (2 Cor. 3:5; Formula of Concord, I.1–2, *BOC*, pp. 466–72).

The Analogy of a New Heart.   If heaven is rightly described as a place of unmingled happiness where God's own life is enjoyed without reserve, then how could it be that boastful, lusty, proud sinners would be happy in such a place? For it is precisely characteristic of sinners to not love virtue, to take no pleasure in prayer or the praise of God. If future life with God is a sanctuary of everlasting Sabbath celebration, that would be the most burdensome thing imaginable to sinners (Dwight, *Theology* II, p. 408). To be readied for eternity with God, the sinner must have a new heart, a new disposition (Ezek. 18:31; 36:26; Wakefield, *CT* II, p. 429).

In new birth the stony heart is remade into a "heart of flesh," as promised by Ezekiel: "I will give them an undivided heart and put a new spirit in them; I will remove from them their heart of stone and give them a heart of flesh" (Ezek. 11:19; Jer. 31:31–34; Zech. 7:5; Rom. 2:5; J. Wesley, *NUOT*, p. 2209).

The End-Time Analogy: New Birth as the Here-and-Now Imparting of Eternal Life.   New birth answers the problem created by spiritual death through sin. It speaks to the basic human predicament of the absence of life—the death or total lack of spiritual responsiveness that results from the wretched history of sin (J. Wesley, *WJWB*, sermon 18, *WJW* V, pp. 212–23).

To those dead in sin, regenerating grace offers new life as if from above (John 3:1–8). Eternal life is life in the Spirit, received by faith. Precisely how eternal life is imparted is not subject to empirical investigation. God the Spirit is not an object.

No visible causality can be observed or tracked. But the experiential outcome can be tested and attested: new life in the Spirit, spiritual renewal, new creation (Fletcher, *Works,* IV, pp. 98 ff.).

Those born from above are continually receiving the very breath of life, life in the Spirit (John 3:16; 10:10; 14:6). "The Spirit is life" (Rom. 8:6). One born of God in faith "has crossed over from death to life" (John 5:24), for "the gift of God is eternal life" (Rom. 6:23). "So, then, the world had not eternal life, because it had not received the Spirit; for where the Spirit is, there is eternal life" (Ambrose, *Of the Holy Spirit* II.III.27, *NPNF* 2 X, p. 118). The time has now come when "the dead will hear the voice of the Son of God, and those who hear will live" (John 5:25).

The Slavery Analogy: New Birth as Liberation.   This new life is understood as liberation from bondage: "You have been set free from sin and have become slaves to righteousness" (Rom. 6:18). It is the truth incarnate that has "set you free" (John 8:32). "It is for freedom that Christ has set us free. Stand free, then, and do not let yourselves be burdened again by a yoke of slavery" (Gal. 5:1). "But now that you have been set free from sin and have become slaves to God, the benefit you reap leads to holiness" (Rom. 6:22; Henry, *CWB* 6, p. 406).

With bondage to sin now broken, one may exercise a new freedom to "pursue righteousness, godliness, faith, love, endurance and gentleness" (1 Tim. 6:11). "For sin shall not be your master, because you are not under law, but under grace" (Rom. 6:14).

The Holiness Analogy: New Birth as Setting One's Feet upon the Way of Holiness.   Regeneration is the beginning of a radical change in moral character from the inordinate love of creaturely goods to walking in the way of holiness (Calvin, *Inst.* 2.3.6). One who is being delivered from bondage to sin is being empowered by the Spirit to begin a new walk, a continuing life in Christ, both in inward disposition and outward action (J. Wesley, *NB;* Fletcher, *Works* IV, pp. 98–136; Watson, *TI* II, chap. 24; Pope, *Compend.* III, pp. 3–27; Miley, *ST* II, pp. 327–38; Burwash, *MCT* II, pp. 262 ff.; Wakefield, *CT,* pp. 424–45; Tillett, *PS,* pp. 227–50). In the regenerated life the Holy Spirit works economically, first to change the inner disposition of the soul, then to change the outward behavior.

One who persists in deliberately flouting known requirements of God cannot at the same time be one born of God (Baxter, *PW* VI, pp. 530–36). The deliberate ignoring of God's known requirement is incompatible with union with Christ, hence with regenerated life. The strong connection between new birth and sanctification is seen in key biblical texts that do not allow easy evasion: "No one who is born of God will continue to sin, because God's seed remains in him; he cannot go on sinning, because he has been born of God" (1 John 3:9). This does not imply that one having been born into the family of God cannot fall into sin, or act as if belonging to another family. For the same letter states that if, apart from grace, "we claim to be without sin, we deceive ourselves and the truth is not in us" (1 John 1:8). The struggle to keep oneself free from the entanglements of sin is aided constantly by grace: "We know that anyone born of God does not continue to sin; the one who was born of God keeps him safe, and the evil one cannot harm him" (1 John 5:18; Augustine, *Hom. on Epist. of John* V, *NPNF* 1 VII, pp. 487–93).

The Self-Offering Analogy.   Paul instructed those who shared new life through
Christ's resurrection, "Count yourselves dead to sin but alive to God in Christ
Jesus. Therefore do not let sin reign in your mortal body so that you obey its evil
desires" (Rom. 6:11, 12). You are to "offer yourselves to God, as those who have
been brought from death to life" (Rom. 6:13; cf. 12:1).

Regeneration does not imply an abrupt end to daily repentance or confession
or accountable love or obedience to the Word. For the new life is intended precisely to be continually lived, not to wither and die immediately after the birth has
occurred. The Spirit "who began a good work in you will carry it on to completion
until the day of Christ Jesus" (Phil. 1:6; Calvin, *Inst.* 3.18.1).

A concluding summary of these varied regeneration metaphors is offered in
Gregory Nazianzen's address to the newly baptized: Yesterday your soul was bent
by sin; today made straight by the Word. Yesterday you were being dried up by
hemorrhage; today you have "touched the hem of Christ and your issue has been
stayed." Yesterday paralyzed with no one to put you into the pool, today you have
help from "Him Who is in one Person Man and God." Yesterday you lay in the
tomb; today you have heard a loud voice, come forth, and were "loosed from the
bonds of your graveclothes." Yesterday full of leprosy, you have "received again
the Image whole." "Yesterday meanness and avarice were withering your hand;
today let liberality and kindness stretch it out." "If you were deaf and dumb, let
the Word sound in your ears"; if blind, "in God's Light see light, and in the Spirit
of God be enlightened by the Son, That Threefold and Undivided Light"
(Gregory Nazianzen, *Orat.* XL.34, *NPNF* 2 VII, p. 372).

Word and Spirit in Regeneration

Within the economy of the triune God, the work of calling, forming, preserving,
and superintending the kingdom of Christ is committed to the Holy Spirit. It is a
specific work of the Spirit to impart life—first in its original creation, and when
fallen into sin and death, to impart life anew (Owen, *Works* 3, pp. 105–52; Barth,
CD IV/1, pp. 733 ff.).

Agency in Spiritual Birth.   Quickening is throughout scripture a work of God's
Spirit (James 1:17–18). The acting power or agent in regeneration is God the
Spirit (John 3:3–7; Titus 3:5), the quintessential Bestower of life (*zōopoion,* Nicene
Creed, *COC* II, p. 57).

The Spirit attests Christ's work within the heart, enabling the grace necessary
for repentance, faith, and new birth (Augustine, *On the Grace of Christ* I.50–51;
NPNF 1 V, pp. 234–35; Hodge, *OOT,* pp. 445–64; 515–20; Clarke, *OCT,* p. 396;
Beyschlag, *NTT* I, p. 144). Through this work of the Spirit, the renewed individual is translated from one sphere of existence (realm, aeon, dominion, orientation)
to another: "For he has rescued us from the dominion of darkness and brought
us into the kingdom of the Son he loves, in whom we have redemption, the forgiveness of sins" (Col. 1:13).

"Regeneration is the work of the Holy Spirit; and the Spirit is the Author of that
new man." The benefit of regeneration "cannot remain when its Author is
shut out; the Author is not without the gift, nor the gift without the Author. If
you claim the grace, believe the power; if you reject the power, do not ask for the
grace. He who has denied the Spirit has at the same time denied the gift"

(Ambrose, *Of the Holy Spirit* II.VII.64–66, *NPNF* 2 X, pp. 122, 123; Goodwin, *Works* VI, pp. 47–52). "God sent the Spirit of his Son into our hearts, the Spirit who calls out 'Abba, Father'" (Gal. 4:6).

Faculties Transformed, Not Replaced.   This does not imply that in new birth the Spirit works wholly without the human will and affections, for the Spirit's distinct purpose is to begin to transform the will and affections. The Spirit works in and through the heart, affections, will, and behavior. Human faculties are not circumvented but given a new spring of action (Augustine, *The Spirit and the Letter* 5, 6, 52–54 *NPNF* 1 V, pp. 84–85, 106–7). Rebirth does not impart completely new human faculties, but reorders and enlivens those that already exist (Wakefield, *CT,* pp. 424–45; J. Watson, *The Doctrines of Grace*, pp. 61–76).

The Resistance Continues.   Due to the history of sin, humanity is in far worse shape than a stone or lump of clay, for sinners actively resist their salvation. The potter can mold the clay, but what if the "clay" has a determined will not to be molded? God does not force godliness or regenerating grace upon human beings, for if forced it could be neither truly godly nor truly just. God draws persons toward salvation by calling, illuminating, convicting, and enabling faith wherever there is an opening amid human resistances (John Climacus, *The Ladder of Divine Ascent*, step 4, sec. 121, p. 53). It is no simple work for the Spirit to create a pure heart and steadfast spirit, considering our recalcitrance (Ps. 51:10).

These resistances continue to war against the Spirit even after one is born of God. "For the sinful nature desires what is contrary to the Spirit" (Gal. 5:17). Even if "in my inner being I delight in God's law," nonetheless "I see another law at work in the members of my body, waging war against the law of my mind and making me a prisoner of the law of sin at work within my members" (Rom. 7:22, 23; Methodius, *On the Resurrection, ANF* VI, p. 372).

The Gospel Preached and Heard Through the Spirit.   New birth comes through hearing the gospel. "He chose to give us birth through the word of truth, that we might be a kind of firstfruits of all he created" (James 1:18; cf. Col. 3:10).

The Spirit works immediately in the heart and mediately through the word addressed in scripture and sacraments. The whole of Hebrew scripture—law and prophets—forms the backdrop for hearing the life-eliciting gospel, for "through the law we become conscious of sin" (Rom. 3:20).

Paul reminded the Corinthians that they had been personally born into the Christian community through his preaching, so much so that "in Christ Jesus I became your father through the gospel" (1 Cor. 4:15, KJV). Enabling the hearing of the word written and word preached, the Spirit draws persons toward union with Christ through the preached word, repentance, faith, conversion, and perseverance (Rom. 10:17; 1 Cor. 1:21; 1 Pet. 1:23; Formula of Concord, epitome, II, III, *BOC,* pp. 469–75). The word is "the sword of the Spirit" (Eph. 6:17) that cuts through human self-deceptions.

The Decisive Turn from Idolatry.   Those born anew worship not the idols of the old way of life but the true God revealed in the new man, Christ. The old Adamic aeon remains inveterately idolatrous, wishing both to have gods (creaturely values elevated to ultimacy) and to be god. Whether one has worshiped wealth, power, prestige, status, sex, or education, these passing gods are to be put away as gods, however valuable they may remain as creaturely goods. Postmoderns may be just as idolatrous as primitive pagans (Ezek. 6:1–10; Cyprian, *Treatises* VI, *ANF* V, pp. 465–68; Reinhold Niebuhr, *MMIS; NDM;* Oden, *SA*).

The human condition is such that it is bound to orient itself toward some center of value—that value that appears to someone to make other values valuable (Luther, *Large Catech., BOC*, p. 365; H. R. Niebuhr, *RMWC*). Before the history of sin, God was trusted as that center. Afterward, humanity became seduced by alternative claims to ultimacy. Eating of the forbidden fruit, they thought they would become as gods themselves (John Chrysostom, *Hom. on Genesis* 16, 17, *FC* 74, pp. 205–46).

Faith's joy in God can be celebrated even and precisely when creaturely values fail: "Though the fig tree does not bud, and there are no grapes on the vines, though the olive crop fails and the fields produce no food, though there are no sheep in the pen and no cattle in the stalls, yet I will rejoice in the Lord, I will be joyful in God my Savior" (Hab. 3:17, 18; Cyprian, *Treatises* V, *ANF* V, p. 463).

The Temple Rebuilt.   The very temple that had become ruined by sin is now being repaired and restored, the flame rekindled, the altar rebuilt (1 Pet. 2:4–8). There the beauty of the Lord is beheld and celebrated and inquired into night and day (Pss. 1:2; 29:2). The Spirit brings Christ as near to believers as if historically present (2 Cor. 3:16, 17; Kierkegaard, *PF, TC, CDisc.*).

Solomon remarked with astonishment at the dedication of the temple, "But will God really dwell on earth? The heavens, even the highest heaven, cannot contain you. How much less this temple I have built!" (1 Kings 8:27). No temple is fit for the indwelling of the Spirit except that set apart by God through the atoning work of the Son: the heart of the believer, humbled and contrite, yielded to the Spirit, which has become "the temple of the living God" (2 Cor. 6:16) where God rules and refashions the human spirit back into its original capacity to reflect the goodness of God (John Chrysostom, *Hom. on 2 Cor.* XIII, *NPNF* 1 XIII, pp. 342–45). There new life is being breathed into the dead (sinners enmeshed in the syndromes of sin), whose bodies by the Spirit become the temple of the Spirit (Eph. 2:21). The One whose name is Holy dwells with those who are contrite and lowly of heart (Isa. 57:15).

The Antecedent and Consequent State

It is unlikely that any will experience new birth without some hearing and understanding of the gospel, without conviction of sin, repentance, and the earnest desire to lead a new life in Christ. Those who assume they have power within themselves to repent and make themselves acceptable to God are least likely to experience spiritual birth from above (Luke 4:23; 5:31).

The Lost Condition, Prior to New Birth.   Spiritual birth is necessary because the human will has fallen into a condition of recalcitrant moral darkness and corruption. Under the conditions of the history of sin, the sinner is lacking moral compass, as in a fog. The wandering comes not merely from a lack of knowledge, but more profoundly from a weakened, broken, and self-deceiving will. "For what I do is not the good I want to do; no, the evil I do not want to do—this I keep on doing" (Rom. 7:19; Methodius, *On the Resurrection, ANF* VI, p. 371).

When the rudder of the soul is disabled, it leads persistently to "missing the mark." This lost condition, however, is more accurately described as being glad to miss the mark, to love darkness rather than light, to love the creature more than the Creator, intentionally to make one's permanent home in a relativistic moral fog (John 1:10; Rom. 1:18–32). The only light one may glimpse amid such a stormy sea is a lightning flash of judgment, not the healing light of day. There is no port for the storm, no compass for the vessel. Without a new pilot coming aboard to repair the rudder and redirect the ship to the port, disaster appears inevitable (1 Tim. 1:19; Hippolytus, *Christ and Antichrist* 59, *ANF* V, p. 216; Cantwell, *Personal Salvation,* pp. 151–57). Such is the "lost" moral state prior to regeneration.

Renovating Grace.   Regenerating grace illumines this vast moral darkness, renovates the moral will, empowers the will to do the good, takes away the love of sin and the despair over sin's seeming permanence. Trust in idols is displaced by trust in the mercy of God. The cacophony of idolatrous loves is refashioned into a symphony of creaturely values loved in relation to the love of God (Augustine, *Conf.* IV, X, *NPNF* 1 I, pp. 68–74, 142–45).

This basic reversal then gives better footing for one actually to begin removing and transmuting the state of corruption, reshaping it toward greater purity of heart and will. The regenerate life grows in attentiveness to God, maturing in the life now given, actually walking the way of holiness (Ambrose, *Of Christian Faith* I.1 ff., *NPNF* 2 X, pp. 201 ff.; Calvin, *Inst.* 3.3; Cantwell, *Personal Salvation,* pp. 160–64).

Cyprian's personal report of his own transformed experience is typical of early testimonies to new birth: "In my despair of better things I indulged my sins as if now proper and belonging to me. But afterwards, when the stain of my past life has been washed away by the aid of the water of regeneration, a light from above poured itself upon my chastened and pure heart; afterwards when I had drunk of the Spirit from heaven, a second birth restored me into a new man; immediately in a marvelous manner doubtful matters clarified themselves, the closed opened, the shadowy shone with light, what seemed impossible was able to be accomplished" (Cyprian, *To Donatus,* chap. 4, *FC* 36, pp. 9, 10; cf. Theodotus, *Excerpts, ANF* VIII, p. 44).

Positing the Beginning of a Fundamental Change of Disposition.   New life begins the moment the fundamental direction of one's disposition is toward Christ. There must be a time before and after that moment. The time before is described in the New Testament as death, darkness, and sin; the time after as life, light, and resurrection.

The essential direction of one's disposition is either for or against the saving work of grace. "He who is not with me is against me, and he who does not gather with me scatters" (Matt. 12:30). There is no state of neutrality to which one can finally retreat (Origen, *Comm. on Matt.* XVII.14, *AEG* II, p. 337; S. Kierkegaard, *Either/Or* II).

The New Birth Instantaneous, Enabling Gradual Growth. Whether new birth is instantaneous or gradual depends upon the point of view from which birth is seen. Viewed providentially, developmentally, and synoptically from the vantage point of the entire work of the Spirit in preparing, prevening, convicting, calling, enabling faith, and sanctifying, the whole process is seen as a *gradual* unfolding of the divine plan of salvation.

Viewed subjectively from the vantage point of one being born, there must be posited *some distinct beginning* of this life. In this sense new birth is by definition instantaneous. One must stretch the metaphor to think of a birth that occurs gradually over years of time. Pregnancy occurs over time, but birth occurs in a particular hour (J. Wesley, *WJW* VI, pp. 65 ff.; Kierkegaard, *PF,* pp. 68–138).

There may indeed be a gradual growth of the renewed soul, but in order to grow the soul must first be born. As life's ending at death is punctilial (ending at some *punctum,* point), so is life's beginning at birth. As "they die in an instant [*rega*]" (Job 34:20), so are they born.

When Jesus said to the thief on the cross, "Today you will be with me in paradise" (Luke 23:43), God's pardoning and regenerating action began occurring in the condemned man at that particular moment (Augustine, *Sermons on NT Lessons* XVII.7, *NPNF* 1 VI, p. 312). A single extraordinary biblical pericope, however, cannot become normative for all other descriptions of new birth, but must be by the analogy of faith set in context by proportional comparison with other references to new birth.

The Birth-Growth Metaphor. One reborn of God is not thereby immediately mature. Birth does not preempt but invites and enables the process of growth. One reborn of God is a neonate saint, awaiting a process of growth toward everfuller receptivity to the Spirit. Having been cleansed in new birth, one is drawn and called to express behavioral manifestations of the new life (Rev. 22:11; cf. Bellarmine, *De Iustificatio* I.1).

In new birth life is imparted yet not fully developed. "Growth follows life; but the growth is not in the process of regeneration. That process is complete when the life is imparted; but the life itself is not complete in the sense of development or maturity" (Merrill, *ACE,* p. 187). The new life in Christ is constantly being renewed. Do not lie, argued Paul, because "you have taken off your old self with its practices and have put on the new self, which is being renewed [*anakainoumenon*] in knowledge in the image of its Creator" (Col. 3:10; Calvin, *Comm.* XXI, pp. 211–12).

The Paradoxical Tension Between Regenerating and Sanctifying Grace. Regenerating grace enables life; sanctifying grace enables maturity and growth. Regeneration is sanctification at its earliest stage of being awakened, vitalized, readied to grow. Wherever persons are born from above, sanctifying grace has already begun to work. They are new creatures, born of God, washed, and already beginning to be sanctified in the Spirit (2 Cor. 5:17–21; Eph. 4:22–26). Regeneration is distinguishable from sanctification, standing as its beginning.

The attempt to set forth the relation between regeneration and sanctification may err in one of two directions: *Either* it may underestimate the power of grace to overcome sin in this life, which implies overestimation of the power of sin to resist grace. In doing so, it may despairingly assume that God is not capable or desirous of cleansing fully from all sin. *Or* it may unrealistically assume that the regenerate no longer has any ongoing battle with sin. But experience will soon show the believer that an extended struggle with sin continues after baptism and regeneration (Calvin, *Inst.* 3.3; Thirty-nine Articles, XVI, *CC*, p. 271).

The teaching of new birth, scripturally conceived, sustains this paradoxical tension. The change brought about by the Spirit is a radical one in which the dominion of sin is truly broken, though its consequences continue. Though remaining in believers, sin does not reign, and can no longer find a predominating foothold (Baxter, *PW* VII, pp. 20, 21; J. Wesley, *WJW* VI, pp. 65 ff.).

Whether the Mystery of the Spirit's Movement Is Analyzable. Why does the Spirit vivify some and not others? Move later rather than sooner? Inquiry into the antecedents of new birth raises perplexing questions of election, calling, God's foreknowing of our call, and foreordaining of the economy of salvation. It remains shrouded in the mystery of the Spirit's movement why some are brought to life and others resist. It is presumptuous to assume that human insight can identify precisely how, when, or why the Spirit works to bring life (Gregory Nazianzen, *Orat.* XXXI, *NPNF* 2 VII, pp. 318–28).

Scripture frequently enjoins the faithful not to inquire too anxiously into such enigmatic questions, but rather simply to trust God's design (James 1:18; Eph. 1:4–11; Rom. 8:28; Matt. 22:1–14). Classic exegetes delighted in the thought that Another is wiser than themselves. Faith is relieved that its own vast range of ignorance is complemented by the incomparable divine knowing (Dionysius the Areopagite, *Mystical Theology.* II, III, pp. 194–99).

God has reasons that human reason need not despair to fathom. They go deeper than the facile modern assumption that all ought equally to be saved, or that as many as possible ought to be saved whether they respond in faith or not, or that salvation can occur without facing the problem of sin (Augustine, *On Nature and Grace* 1–4, *NPNF* 1 V, pp. 121–23; Calvin, *Inst.* 3.11–24). "As you do not know the path of the wind, or how the body is formed in a mother's womb, so you cannot understand the work of God, the Maker of all things" (Eccles. 11:5). "The wind blows wherever it pleases. You hear its sound, but you cannot tell where it comes from or where it is going. So it is with everyone born of the Spirit" (John 3:7, 8; Ignatius, *Philadelphians* VII, *ANF* I, p. 83).

The work of the Spirit cannot be reduced to naturalistically observed causal chains or psychological descriptions. Psychology of religion seeks to understand the psychogenetic stages of development interfacing with the work of God, but always with weak eyes; meanwhile, the Spirit works invisibly (S. Kierkegaard, *The Concept of Anxiety;* W. James, *Varieties of Religious Experience*). Christian teaching need not become defensive in the presence of psychological analyses of conversion unless they pretend a complete or reductionistic explanation of being born of God (Outler, *Psychotherapy and the Christian Message*).

Necessity of the New Birth

Each particular life in Christ must have a beginning. Nothing grows without being given life to grow. By analogy, the individual Christian life must have a beginning: new birth. New life in Christ is the indispensable presupposition of growth in the Christian life (Goodwin, *Works,* VI, p. 73).

Must One Be Born Again? Is new birth necessary to the Christian life? Jesus said, "I tell you the truth, no one can see the kingdom of God unless he is born again" (John 3:3). "You must be born again," he told Nicodemus (John 3:7; John Chrysostom, *Tractates on John* XII, *FC* 79, pp. 32–36).

But this beginning is complicated by the history of sin. A history mired in sin cannot produce holiness. A new beginning must be made, but cannot be made out of a corrupted history. "Do people pick grapes from thornbushes, or figs from thistles? Likewise every good tree bears good fruit, but a bad tree bears bad fruit" (Matt. 7:17, 18). A new life in the Spirit must be imparted. We need new birth because we are "dead" (Eph. 2:1).

New Birth Is Necessary to Ready Sinners for Eternal Life with God. No one is prepared to come into God's presence whose transgressions have not been pardoned, or continue unabated having been pardoned. Grace calls and enables human behavior to refract God's own holiness. So long as sin remains in control of the will and nested in the human spirit, there can be no fitting approach to God. The inmost dispositions must be converted (Teresa of Avila, *Life*, *CWST* I, pp. 179 ff.). Idolatries must be cast out. "Therefore, get rid of all moral filth and the evil that is so prevalent and humbly accept the word planted in you, which can save you" (James 1:21).

Regeneration and the Means of Grace

It is not baptism of itself that saves, but God through grace who enables repentance and faith, of which baptism is a primary *mustērion, sacramentum*, sacramental act, sign, and evidence.

The Scriptural Correlation of Baptism and Regeneration. Baptism is introduced here because of its connection with rebirth, a connection that might be confusing if omitted. Salvation ordinarily comes by repentance, and justifying faith through grace accompanied by baptism, and regeneration through the work of the Spirit (Justin Martyr, *First Apology* I.61, 66; *Dialogue with Trypho* 29; Theophilus, *To Autolycus* 16, 61; note that in my previous studies, *Pastoral Theology* and *Ministry Through Word and Sacrament*, baptism as a means of grace and a public act attesting repentance is discussed in ways that need not be repeated here).

Baptism is closely associated with new birth in crucial scriptural texts. The apostolic preaching held repentance and baptism closely together: "Repent and be baptized, every one of you" (Acts 2:38). In instructing Nicodemus on the new birth, Jesus said, "No one can enter the kingdom of God unless he is born of water and the Spirit" (John 3:5; Augustine, *Comm. on John*, Tractate XI, XII, *NPNF* 1 VII, pp. 74–86).

Classic consensual exegesis held that regeneration is intimately tied with the grace of baptism, and not ordinarily received without baptism (John of Damascus, *OF* III.9, *NPNF* 2 IX, p. 78). Regeneration and baptism are viewed as two aspects of a single process of receiving new life: "My baptism was the beginning of life, and that day of regeneration the first of days" (Basil, *On the Spirit* I.10, *NPNF* 2 VIII, p. 17).

Those who receive the grace of baptism "go down into the water bewailing our sins and uncleanness, and come up from it having fruit in our hearts, having reverence and hope in Jesus in our spirits" (Barnabas 11.1), the heart thereafter being a dwelling of God the Spirit (8.15). Christ makes the church holy by "cleansing her by the washing with water through the word" (Eph. 5:26; Ambrose, *Of the Spirit* I.6, *NPNF* 2 X, p. 103).

The Pledge of a Good Conscience Toward God. The First Letter of Peter aptly compared those in Noah's ark who were "saved through water" to the water of baptism: "this water symbolizes baptism that now saves you also—not the removal of dirt from the body but the pledge of a good conscience toward God. It saves you by the resurrection of Jesus Christ" (1 Pet. 3:20, 21). The phrase "the pledge of a good conscience toward God" implies that it is not the intention of the author merely to speak of an outward rite of baptism as in itself efficacious, but of the grace of baptism that becomes inwardly confirmed by good conscience.

Baptism implies "destroying of the body of sin, that it may never bear fruit unto death . . . [while] living unto the Spirit and having the fruit of holiness; the water receiving the body as in a tomb figures death, while the Spirit pours in the quickening power, renewing our souls from the deadness of sin unto their original life. This is what it is to be born again of water and of the Spirit, the being made dead being effected in the water, while our life is wrought in us through the Spirit" in three immersions. "If there is any grace in the water, it is not of the nature of the water, but of the presence of the Spirit" (Basil, *On the Spirit* I.15, *NPNF* 2 VIII, p. 22).

Whether Baptism and Regeneration Are Distinguishable. An oversimplified identification of baptism and new birth, often called baptismal regeneration, seems to be placed in question by scriptural instances of persons being regenerated who seemingly were not baptized (the thief, Luke 23:42, 43; Cornelius, Acts 10:44, 48) and of persons who were baptized but apparently unregenerated (Simon Magus, Acts 8:13–23; Ananias and Sapphira, Acts 5:1–11). Hence, though not separable, baptism and regeneration are in some instances distinguishable.

Baptism is obligatory for all who would enter the new covenant community, just as circumcision was obligatory in Judaism. But baptism, especially when outwardly viewed and caricatured sociologically as a formal, expected, but eviscerated public rite, in itself is not represented as the instrument or direct cause of regeneration. The new person is not merely "born of water" but also of the Spirit (John 3:5). It remains a dismal, all too obvious observation that many appear to have been duly baptized with water and yet not sufficiently with the life-giving Spirit (J. Wesley, *WJWB* I, sermon 45, *WJW* VI, pp. 65–77; S. Kierkegaard, *Attack upon "Christendom"*).

The Washing of Rebirth: Conjoined Metaphors of Regeneration and Baptism. Despite the above disclaimers, rebirth is constantly understood in relation to the conjoined metaphors of washing and outpouring: "He saved us through *the washing of rebirth* and renewal by the Holy Spirit, whom he poured out on us generously through Jesus Christ our Savior, so that having been justified by his grace, we might become heirs having the hope of eternal life" (Titus 3:5–7, italics added). This "washing of regeneration" (KJV) occurs by the laver (basin or bath) of new birth (John Chrysostom, *Baptismal Instructions*, ACW 31, pp. 62–63, 135–38; J. Wesley, *WJWB* 2, pp. 211 ff.).

The laver was set at the entrance of Israel's tent of meeting as a visible sign of entrance into the life of the covenant community (Exod. 40:7, 11, 30; 38:8, 39; 1 Kings 7:30, 38). Aaronic priests ritually cleansed their hands and feet before entering the holy place. The washing referred to is a spiritual cleansing, not merely a physical occurrence. Without ceasing to be a physical act, it is a cleansing preparatory to entering into communion with God. Similarly, the "washing of rebirth" refers not to an external rite alone, but to the spiritual and moral turning and transformation to which baptism itself points (Acts 22:16; John 3:5; 1 Cor. 4:15; Hilary, *Trin.* IX.9, *NPNF* 2 IX, p. 158).

Why is baptism called not merely a laver of remission of sins or of cleansing but a laver of new birth (*loutrou palingenesias*, Titus 3:5)? "Because it does not simply take away our sins, nor simply cleanse us from our faults, but [does] so as if we were born again. For it creates and fashions us anew, not forming us again out of earth, but creating us out of another element, namely, of the nature of water," which constantly seeks the lowest plane, following the humbling love of the servant Messiah (John Chrysostom, *Instruction to Catechumens* I.3, *NPNF* 1 IX, p. 162).

When baptized, you "received white garments as a sign that you had put off the covering of sins, and had put on the chaste robes of innocence" (Ambrose, *The Mysteries*, 7.34, *FC* 44, p. 17). Baptism "pledged the recipient to a new life of faith and obedience; and, therefore, the whole transaction formed an era, a new departure, wherein the old life of sin was renounced and the new life of holiness was begun" (Merrill, *ACE*, p. 122).

The Grace of Baptism.   God covenants with the baptized to forgive sin, which begins "from that hour to renew thee, pours into thee his grace and Holy Spirit, who begins to crucify the nature and sin" (Luther, *WA* 2, pp. 728 ff.; Calvin, *Inst.* 4.15.1–3). The Holy Spirit through baptism offers, calls forth, and elicits regeneration in a spiritually blessed water in which the whole triune God is by grace effectively present. Once administered, it assures the believer of the continuing readiness of God to forgive sin (Gregory Nazianzen, *Orat.* XL, *NPNF* 2 VII, pp. 360–77; Luther, *EA* 16.69, 99; 46.266).

The spiritual birth that begins with baptism continues until death. It pronounces a sentence of death upon the sin of the fallen natural man (Augsburg Conf. IX, *CC*, p. 70). Though sin remains in the baptized, it is in principle shattered, and in this lies the consolation of baptism, that God has bound himself no longer to impute sin to the baptized faithful (Luther, *Sermon on the Holy Sacrament of Baptism*, 1519, *WA* 2.728–32; *SHD* II, p. 283). The Christian life is best described as daily renewal of one's baptism. The sinner may every day once again return to his baptism for comfort, for it has been given as a durable sign that God is gracious to sinners (Luther, *Large Catech.*, *BOC*, pp. 436–46; *EA* 16, pp. 103 ff.; *SHD* II, pp. 283–84; Calvin, *Inst.* 4.15.3–6).

Believers Baptist exegetes have held baptism to be not the cause but the sign of regeneration. Baptism accordingly would follow rather than precede regeneration, and by implication, only adult believers born of God would be baptized, in this view, whereby the inward change can be manifested outwardly through baptism (Menno Simons, *CWMS*, pp. 227 ff.; cf. Zwingli, *TFR, WZ* III, pp. 185–89). This brings up the next question.

Faith and Baptism. One is equally correct in saying that faith leads to baptism and that baptism leads to faith, for faith and baptism are interdependent teachings. Baptism is more than a sign that the believer has faith, as if faith were primary and the grace of baptism wholly secondary. Baptism is more than a public act of confession or a public testimony to one's faith (Thirty-nine Articles, XXVI, *CC*, pp. 275–76).

Conversely, baptism of itself is no substitute for active faith or faith becoming active in love (J. Wesley, *WJW* VI, pp. 65 ff.; S. Kierkegaard, *Attack upon "Christendom"*). As penitent, trusting acceptance of grace, faith is an assumed condition of baptism. (This is arguable even in the case of infant baptism on the premise that grace is being received proleptically through the faith of caring parents within the covenant community.) As sign of the inner and hidden grace of regeneration, and the offer, presentation, and guarantee of regenerating grace being offered to the believer, baptism is a visible accompaniment and consequence of faith (Luther, *Large Catech.* IV, *BOC*, pp. 436 ff.).

Baptism is thus both an event of the offering of grace and an event of the faithful reception of grace's self-offering. The grace that is offered and, one hopes, increasingly received in baptism is the forgiveness of sins, the gift of the Spirit. The sealing of that gift is the Spirit's assurance or pledge of eternal life (2 Cor. 1:22; Eph. 1:13). Yet this gift is not magic, or unilaterally coercive of the will. It can only be freely received.

As the people of God in the wilderness were figuratively "baptized into Moses" (1 Cor. 10:2) in the sea, yet later fell from faith into death, so must the new people of God be baptized into Christ. Even those who may "think they are standing firm" are cautioned to "be careful that you don't fall!" (1 Cor. 10:12; cf. Küng, *TC*, pp. 207–8).

Whether the Gift Is Indelibly Given. Once received, baptism can be denied or neglected but not deleted or erased. No one baptized ever became unbaptized. Those who, having been baptized, later become atheists and then later return to the faith of the church do not need to be rebaptized. One may forget or deface one's baptism, but one cannot erase its mark as God's own gift, blessed and ordered and embraced by God (Augustine, *Hom. on 2 Cor.* III, *NPNF* 1 XII, pp. 289–93; Innocent III, *SCD* 411, p. 160).

Baptism is the nursery of the *ekklēsia* (*seminarium ecclesiae*) by which persons enter the covenant community. This is why public confession of faith is so intrinsically connected with baptism, and why the creedal formulations and primitive theological efforts of the early church grew directly out of the rite of baptism, and why catechesis emerged in the context of baptism. "Baptized into union with him, you have all put on Christ as a garment" (Gal. 3:27, NEB; Calvin, *Inst.* 4.15–16).

To Whom Does God Offer the Grace of Baptism? The question of whether infants of faithful families are capable of an anticipatory form of faith that awaits their confirmation is a much-debated sore point. We are well advised not to set

premature limits upon what God the Spirit may or may not be able to do in bringing life to fallen human history.

Most agree that God the Spirit works within the lives of infants in a different
way than adults. Whether consciously in adults through justifying grace or
preliminarily in infants through prevenient grace, faith in itself can never become
a meritorious cause or ground, but only the ordered way of receiving grace. However the debates about infant baptism may proceed, the question of God's power
to work in infants hinges not on neonate capacity or activity but the divine determination to call and shape human life rightly from the beginning, hence prevenient grace. Faith whether in children or adults is essentially the readiness to
receive God's Spirit. Whatever anticipatory faith might be hypothesized in infants, it amounts essentially to a disposition toward God that is ready to hear more
and ready to believe God's promises, even as did Abraham when he "obeyed and
went, even though he did not know where he was going" (Gen. 11:8).

From scripture it is clear that God the Spirit may work in extraordinary ways
not only in the neonate but before birth. The word of the Lord came to Jeremiah,
saying, "Before I formed you in the womb I knew you, before you were born I set
you apart" (Jer. 1:5; cf. Gal. 1:15; Luke 1:41). When Jeremiah protested, "I do
not know how to speak; I am only a child," Yahweh replied, "Do not say, 'I am only
a child'" (Jer. 1:6, 7; Isa. 46:3; 49:1; Jer. 25:15–26). That infants can trust God
is clear from the Psalms: "You made me trust in you even at my mother's breast.
From birth I was cast upon you; from my mother's womb you have been my God"
(Ps. 22:9, 10; cf. Pss. 71:6; 139:13–16).

"There is no doubt that infants, members of the Church of Christ, do not have
such faith, i.e., so explicit, and, so to say, so perceptible to sense, as adults, in
whom the Holy Spirit is efficacious through the external hearing of the Gospel"
(Brentz, Apology of Wittenberg Confession, SCF, p. 236). "When we say that infants believe, it must not be imagined that they know or perceive the movements
of faith." Yet God the Spirit may work in them "so efficacious that they can receive
the grace of God and the forgiveness of sins" (Chemnitz, in Jacobs, SCF, p. 237).
Luther argued that God in some manner endows with faith infants brought for
baptism on account of the believing presentation of them and the prayer offered
on their behalf by their believing parents (Luther, WA 6.538; EA 28.416; cf.
Catech. 494; Augsburg Apology, IX, p. 178).

When Jesus "called a little child and had him stand among them," he delivered
one of his most memorable teachings: "Unless you change and become like little
children, you will never enter the kingdom of heaven. Therefore, whoever hum-
bles himself like this child is the greatest in the kingdom of heaven. And whoever
welcomes a little child like this in my name welcomes me. But if anyone causes one
of these little ones *who believe in me* to sin, it would be better for him to have a large
millstone hung around his neck and to be drowned in the depths of the sea" (Matt.
18:2–60, italics added). Even the little child here appears capable of proleptic
belief in God's coming. Such "little children" carried in the arms of their parents
were called to come to God the Son: "Let the little children come to me, and
do not hinder them, for the kingdom of God belongs to such as these" (Mark
10:13, 14).

Persons who have been in a preliminary way received into the church since
childhood, being born into families of earnest believers, are offered, even before
the age of accountability, "many privileges which others (not church-members)

have not: they are in covenant with God; have the seal thereof upon them, viz., Baptism; and so if not regenerate, yet are in a more hopeful way of attaining regenerating grace," standing under the care of the church and the believing family, and are thus subject to guidance and admonition as need shall require (Cambridge Platform XVI.7, *CC*, pp. 395, 396).

Prayer and Regenerating Grace. In addition to baptism and Eucharist, certain ordinary means of grace are provided to enable new spiritual birth and to sustain its continuing life. Among these are common worship and prayer.

In common worship we hear the Word read and preached. The scriptures are able to make us wise unto salvation (2 Tim. 3:15). "For you have been born again, not of perishable seed, but of imperishable, through the living and enduring word of God" (1 Pet. 1:23).

Those who seek new birth are specifically instructed to pray for it. The Spirit promises to help those who seek help. It hardly seems plausible that God would encourage us to pray, only to disappoint and reject us when we earnestly pray that his will be done in us. The psalmist's petition is prototypical: "Create in me a pure heart, O God, and renew a steadfast spirit within me. Do not cast me from your presence or take your Holy Spirit from me. Restore me to the joy of your salvation, and grant me a willing spirit, to sustain me" (Ps. 51:10–12; Augustine, *Comm. on Ps. LI*, *NPNF* 1 VIII, pp. 194–96).

It is hard enough to speak to one you have not personally met, harder with one estranged, hardest of all with one who is truly righteous with whom one has long been estranged. When headstrong sinners try to pray to One infinitely holy, these blocks to communication are powerfully felt.

But when God is understood as actively reconciling sinners who come to the cross, there is a new recognition of God's friendly entreaty to enter into open communication. Now prayers of the believer are offered freely, and welcomed by the Father. The praying soul finds rest (Augustine, *Conf.* I.1, *NPNF* 1 I, p. 45; Chafer, *ST* VI, p. 108).

> Thou know'st the way to bring me back,
>   My fallen spirit to restore;
> O for thy truth and mercy's sake,
>   Forgive, and bid me sin no more:
> The ruins of my soul repair,
>   And make my heart a house of prayer.
>
> (C. Wesley, "Weary of Wandering,"
> 1749, *HPEC*, p. 119; *CH* 186)

The New Affections of the Heart. New birth is followed by a life of reborn affections. Jeremiah prophesied, "I will give them a heart to know me, that I am the Lord. They will be my people, and I will be their God, for they will return to me with all their heart" (Jer. 24:7; cf. 31:33). The movement is from the center of the reclaimed self to the circumference of human society.

One who ascends the hill of the Lord must have "clean hands and a pure heart, who does not lift up his soul to an idol" (Ps. 24:4). Throughout scripture both sin and holiness are rooted in the heart as their center and source rather than primarily in external actions (Tho. Aq., *ST* II–II, Q2, III, pp. 1179–83). The center of Israel's lostness was that "their hearts were not loyal to him, they were not faithful to his covenant" (Ps. 78:37). "They are a people whose hearts go astray" (Ps. 95:10). The first commandment for the Christian life remains to love God "with all your heart" (Matt. 22:37; cf. Matt. 5:8; Rom. 10:10).

It is through a change of heart that the dispositional reversal occurs in the repentance and faith that enables love: "Love comes from God. Everyone who loves has been born of God, and knows God" (1 John 4:6, 7). One who is born anew is given a new heart with which to feel, a new life to live, a new hope to lay hold of, new desires to replace the outmoded syndromes of desire. "Everyone born of God overcomes the world" (1 John 5:4). Life is given to be redirected toward new purpose: God's own glory.

Hospitality to the stranger is grounded in God's hospitality to all of us strangers (Ambrose, *Duties, NPNF* 2 X, pp. 59–60). At Basil's hospital in Caesarea, his "care was for the sick and the relief of their wounds, and the imitation of Christ, by cleansing leprosy, not by a word, but in deed," where "disease is regarded in a religious light, and disaster is thought a blessing and sympathy is put to the test" (Gregory Nazianzen, *Orat.* 43.63, *CCC*, pp. 106–7).

The new life bears fruit: "the fruit of the Spirit is love, joy, peace, patience, kindness, goodness, faithfulness, gentleness and self-control" (Gal. 5:22). These fruits are possible because "Those who belong to Christ Jesus have crucified the sinful nature, with its passions and desires. Since we live by the Spirit, let us keep in step with the Spirit" (Gal. 5:24, 25).

Partaking of God's Own Nature.   By grace we may come to "participate in the divine nature and escape the corruption in the world caused by evil desires" (2 Pet. 1:4). "The end of the Gospel is to render us eventually conformable to God, and if we may so speak, deify us," wrote Calvin. God "made himself ours, so that all his things should in a manner become our things" (Calvin, *Comm.* XXII, p. 371). In being born anew we pass from death to life (John 5:24), becoming new creatures (2 Cor. 5:17), turning from darkness to light (1 Pet. 2:9), from hostility to love (Col. 1:21). In this way the image of God is being renewed in previously alienated humanity (Col. 3:10; Goodwin, *Works* VI, pp. 187–231).

These themes appear regularly in the definition of regeneration in the Protestant evangelical tradition as "a work of the triune God, which the Holy Ghost accomplishes in us by raising us up from the death of sin and making us *partakers of the Divine nature and life*" (*Catechism of the Evangelical Association*, Q 295, italics added). It is "a change of heart, wrought by the Holy Spirit, who quickeneth the dead in trespasses and sins, enlightening their minds spiritually and savingly to understand the Word of God, and renewing their whole nature, so that they love and practice holiness" (Baptist Abstract of Principles VII, *CC*, p. 341). By the new birth the faithful become "partakers of the divine nature and a holy disposition is given, leading to the love and practice of righteousness" (Southern Baptist Convention, 1925, *CC*, p. 347).

This partaking provides the basis for the companionship and communion of the faithful with God and with each other. Nothing is hidden. All motives and feelings are revealed and embraced in the embrace of the Father by the Son and through the Spirit. All fears, failures, doubts, and despairs are brought into this sphere of divine reconciliation and acceptance (Col. 1:12; 1 Cor. 10:17). "Mercy wishes thee to be merciful, righteousness to be righteous, that the Creator may be seen in His creature, and the image of God may be reflected in the mirror of the human heart" (Leo, *Sermons* XCV, *NPNF* 2 XII, p. 204).

The Spirit transforms broken human life: "He takes possession of a shepherd, makes him a Psalmist, subduing evil spirits by his song, and proclaims him King; if he possess a goatherd and scraper of sycamore fruit, He makes him a Prophet. . . . If He takes possession of Fishermen, He makes them catch the whole world in the nets of Christ, taking them up in the meshes of the Word. Look at Peter and Andrew and the Sons of Thunder, thundering the things of the Spirit. If of Publicans, He makes gain of them for discipleship, and makes them merchants of souls" (Gregory Nazianzen, *Orat.* XLI.14, *NPNF* 2 VII, p. 383).

5 Baptism of the Spirit

THE SPIRIT'S INDWELLING, BAPTISM, GIFTS, AND SEALING

Indwelling

The Spirit comes to abide in the faithful, to dwell (*oikeō*) in the community of those newly born of Spirit. This indwelling gift is given to all believers, not selectively to some (John 7:37; Acts 11:16–17), baptizing through the Spirit, distributing gifts, and sealing his promise to redeem to the uttermost (1 John 4:7–21; Ambrose, *On the Holy Spirit* III.11–14, *NPNF* 2 X, pp. 147–49).

The Holy Spirit Abides in All the Faithful. God gives the Spirit "to those who obey him" (Acts 5:32), who respond trustingly to the truth that Jesus is Lord. Characteristically, the Spirit is offered and given in and with personal trust in the Son, at the moment of believing response (Acts 10:44; 19:2; Eph. 1:13). When Paul asked, "Did you receive the Spirit by observing the law, or by believing what you heard?" (Gal. 3:2), the assumption is that the Spirit comes with and by responsive faith, the sole condition for this indwelling (Rom. 8:9; Owen, *Works* 3, pp. 207 ff.).

Justifying grace makes way for the personal indwelling of the Holy Spirit in the resurrected life of the responsive. "He who raised Christ from the dead will also give life to your mortal bodies through his Spirit, who lives in you" (Rom. 8:11; Tho. Aq., *ST* I–II, Q69, 70). This personal indwelling is a community-eliciting, unifying event: "For we were all baptized by one Spirit into one body—whether Jews or Greeks, slave or free—and we were all given the one Spirit to drink" (1 Cor. 12:13).

Whether Indwelling Is Identical with Regenerating Faith. It is not as though one first believes and later the Spirit comes to dwell. Rather, saving faith embraces the indwelling Spirit. Precisely in believing, the Spirit indwells. The only efficacious human response to saving grace is believing. Every believing, baptized Christian has by that fact received the Holy Spirit (*Longer Catech.*, Eastern Orthodox Church, 249, *COC* II, pp. 482, 483; Titus 3:4–6; Luke 11:13).

Though indwelling is not precisely the same as the baptism, sealing, and filling of the Spirit, none of these is detachable from new birth through the Spirit and baptism in the Spirit. "Whoever has been baptized anywhere in the name of Christ, at once obtains the grace of Christ" (fragment of a letter of Stephen, quoted by Firmilianus, letter 75, to Cyprian, *SCD* 47, p. 22; *CSEL* III 2, 815).

Grace is offered through belief-full baptism (Augsburg Conf. IX, *CC*, p. 70). As long as one continues in faith, the witness of the Spirit is continued (Clarke, *CT*, p. 152). "Just as when a sunbeam falls on bright and transparent bodies, they themselves become brilliant too, and shed forth a fresh brightness from themselves, so souls wherein the Spirit dwells, illuminated by the Spirit, themselves become spiritual and send forth their grace to others" (Basil, *On the Holy Spirit* 9:22, *NPNF* 2 VIII, p. 15).

Once Poured Out, the Spirit Remains to Dwell. The Spirit remains in those who have received the grace of baptism, who remain indelibly known of God. It is clearly promised that "the anointing you received from him remains in you" (1 John 2:27; cf. Ezek. 36:24–27; Augustine, *Hom. on Epist. of John* IV, *NPNF* 1 VII, pp. 482–85).

When we were baptized in faith, God the Spirit "anointed us, set his seal of ownership on us, and put his Spirit in our hearts as a deposit, guaranteeing what is to come" (2 Cor. 1:21, 22). Having given this seal, God does not later callously withhold or cancel it. "But you know him, for he lives with you and will be in you. I will not leave you as orphans" (John 14:17, 18; Augustine, *Comm. on John*, tractate XXV, *NPNF* 1 VII, p. 164).

Just as birth occurs once, followed by continued living, growing, walking, so does baptism. The Spirit empowers the Christian life with the ever-new daily filling and tabernacling of the Spirit (Rom. 8:9–11).

"Do not cast me from your presence or take your Holy Spirit from me," the psalmist prayed (Ps. 51:11). After Pentecost the prayer was answered: The Spirit came permanently to indwell the body of Christ. God as Helper-Advocate-Counselor has been given "to be with you forever" (John 14:16; John Chrysostom, *Hom. on John* LXXIII, LXXIV, *NPNF* 1 XVI, pp. 267–73).

Streams of Living Water from Within. The Spirit dwells in all who believe beginning at the regenerating moment when they believe. Jesus said, "'Whoever believes in me, as the Scripture has said, streams of living water will flow from within him.' By this he meant the Spirit" (John 7:38).

The love of God, having begun in faithful baptism, flows abundantly from the believer's heart, proceeding from the Spirit given to dwell within all who believe (Rom. 5:1–5; 8:9–11). The faithful are those who have received "not the spirit of the world, but the Spirit who is from God that we may understand what God has freely given us" (1 Cor. 2:12), who are "controlled not by the sinful nature but by the Spirit, if the Spirit of God lives in you" (Rom. 8:9a). The new life received by faith is precisely life in the Spirit.

The Spirit Continues to Abide in Struggling Believers.   The church at Corinth was a gross mixture of the carnal and spiritual, yet Paul says the Spirit was in all of them (1 Cor. 6:19). The Spirit continues to dwell even among believers who backslide and fall.

The New Testament does not warn that *if* you sin you will lose the Spirit, but rather enjoins: Live an upright life *because* the Spirit is dwelling within you. The Spirit is viewed constantly in the New Testament as an ever-offered gift, not a reward for having faith or good works. When obdurately resisted, the Spirit is grieved (Eph. 4:30).

The gift is given to all those who allow the Spirit to work in them so that faith becomes active in love (Gal. 5:6; Goodwin, *Works,* VI, pp. 52–60). That apostates have not freely received the Spirit is evident from their behavioral fruits (Jude 19). The absence of the Spirit indicates that one has not yet rightly or adequately received God's saving grace. "If anyone does not have the Spirit of Christ, he does not belong to Christ" (Rom. 8:9b).

Called by many names and received in many forms, the indwelling Spirit remains one single gift: "We call it the Gift, the Grace, Baptism, Unction, Illumination, the Clothing of Immortality, the Laver of Regeneration, the Seal, and everything that is honourable. We call it the Gift, because it is given to us in return for nothing on our part. Grace, because it is conferred even on debtors; Baptism, because sin is buried with it in the water; Unction, as Priestly and Royal, for such were they who were anointed; Illumination, because of its splendour; Clothing, because it hides our shame; the Laver, because it washes us; the Seal, because it preserves us, and is moreover the indication of Dominion" (Gregory Nazianzen, *Orat.* XL.4, *NPNF* 2 VII, p. 360).

You Are God's Temple.   Before the incarnation, the Spirit was attested as occasionally endowing persons for specific tasks (Judg. 14:6; 1 Chron. 12:18; 1 Sam. 10:10; 16:13). The language of the indwelling Spirit is found sporadically, as in Joseph (Gen. 41:38), Joshua (Num. 27:18), and Daniel (Dan. 4:8; 5:11–14; cf. Exod. 31:2).

After the resurrection the Spirit is now attested as dwelling continuously in the body of Christ. "Don't you know that you yourselves are God's temple and that God's Spirit lives in you?" (1 Cor. 3:16). "God's temple is sacred, and you are that temple" (1 Cor. 3:17; cf. 1 Cor. 6:19; 2 Tim. 1:14; Y. Congar, *The Mystery of the Temple,* pp. 21 ff.).

The indwelling Spirit intends to make the body of the believer a temple of God (1 Cor. 6:19). "Let us therefore do all things as those who have Him dwelling in us, that we may be His temples, and He may be in us as God" (Ignatius, *Eph.* 15.3, *ANF* I, p. 56; cf. *Philadelphians* 7.2; Ignatius, *Letter to the Magnesians* 14). "Blessed, then are ye who are God-bearers, spirit-bearers, temple-bearers, bearers of holiness" (Ignatius, *Eph.* 9.2, *ANF* I, p. 53).

Indwelling of the Spirit as Defining Characteristic of the Ekklēsia *in the Present Age.*   The indwelling of the Spirit may be viewed dispensationally as a time—not merely a chronological block of time, but a period of the divine *oikonomia* in which

the Spirit is being given to the believing community during the present age between ascension and Parousia. The Spirit could not have been given to indwell
with the new humanity before Christ had ascended (John 16:7).

When Paul contrasts having been "released from the law" with serving "in the
new way of the Spirit," he is contrasting two distinguishable divine economies or
dispensations—law and gospel. Rudolf Bultmann's project may be viewed as an
existential psychologization of traditional dispensationalism, in which the period
of time becomes collapsed into a moment of existential self-understanding. In the
New Testament the present age is viewed as a period of God's own saving time
(transcending both psychological-existential and chronological metaphors) in
which the Spirit indwells in the body of Christ. Hence Paul could write of "a new
covenant—not of the letter but of the Spirit; for the letter kills, but the Spirit gives
life" (2 Cor. 3:6), so "if you are led by the Spirit, you are not under law" (Gal.
5:18). In this new age, every believer is offered the continuing privilege of living
under the empowerment of the Spirit (Luke 24:49; Acts 10:38; Rom. 15:13, 19).

The faithful are exhorted to be *filled* with the Spirit (*plēroō*, Acts 4:8, 31; 13:9).
Indwelling as such is not the subject of moral exhortation, since indwelling is simply received as a gift. The imperative is to be fully receptive to the proffered indwelling of the Spirit (Eph. 5:18b–20).

Spirit Baptism

The Lucan account of Jesus' baptism holds closely together the baptism of Jesus
by John and the descent of the Holy Spirit accompanied by the heavenly confirmation of his eternal sonship (Luke 3:21, 22). "I baptize you with water for repentance," John told his followers, "but after me will come one who is more powerful
than I" who will "baptize you with the Holy Spirit and with fire" (Matt. 3:11;
Clement of Alexandria, *Stromata* 25, *AEG* I, p. 293). "God takes evil from us in two
ways—by Spirit and by fire" (Origen, *Hom. on Ezekiel* I.13, *AEG* III, p. 294).

The water and fire of baptism reshape the clay of humanity, as dramatically
summed up by John Chrysostom: "He took dust from the earth and made the
man; He formed him. The devil came, and perverted him. Then the Lord came,
took him again, and remolded, and recast him in baptism, and He suffered not
his body to be of clay, but made it of a harder ware. He subjected the soft clay to
the fire of the Holy Spirit. . . . He was baptized with water that he might be re-
modelled, with fire that he might be hardened" (John Chrysostom, *Eutropius*,
NPNF 1 IX, p. 259).

The Spirit's Ministry Is to Baptize. One of the ministries of God the Spirit is to
baptize those who believe into the body of Christ (Gregory of Nyssa, *The Great
Catech.* XXXII–XL, *NPNF* 2 IV, pp. 500–508). This ministry was prophesied by
John the Baptist (Matt. 3:11 and parallels) but was not instituted as indwelling
until after Christ's resurrection on the day of Pentecost (Acts 1:5), which Peter
called "the beginning" (*archē*, Acts 11:15; Barth, *CD* IV/4, pp. 44 ff.) of the life of
faith. The purpose of baptism is to join believers to the body of Christ through
the Spirit. "There can be no baptism without the Spirit" (Ambrose, *Of the Holy
Spirit* II.II.21, *NPNF* 2 X, p. 117).

From Watery Burial to Spiritual Resurrection. By this baptism, the Spirit joins each member to Christ's body, dying with his death and rising with his life (Rom. 6:1–10; Col. 1:12). "We are buried in the element of water that we may rise again renewed by the Spirit. For in the water is the representation of death, in the Spirit is the pledge of life, that the body of sin may die through the water, which encloses the body as it were in a kind of tomb. . . . The water, then, is a witness of burial, the blood is a witness of death, the Spirit is a witness of life" (Ambrose, *Of the Holy Spirit* I.VI.76, *NPNF* 2 X, p. 103).

Water is a fit figure of baptism by the Spirit because it is extremely permeable "on account of the subtility of its substance." Water is that lowly element of creation that best suggests the complete readiness of creation to receive the Spirit. Water humbly and readily cooperates with the Spirit to impart to creatures the power of grace. The waters of baptism in this way "imbibe the power of sanctifying" (Tertullian, *On Baptism* 4, *SHD* I, p. 133; *ANF* III, p. 671; cf. p. 676).

The grace of baptism persists unimpeded until we reject it by sinning. Then the grace of penitence is ever ready to enable us to reappropriate our baptism (Augustine, *Letters, FC* 18, p. 130).

Baptism Typified in Gideon's Fleece. Ambrose began his great treatise on the Holy Spirit with this curious analogy: As with Gideon, the drying of the fleece was a type of the dryness of the people of God, so the moistening of the threshing floor was a type of the Holy Spirit to be later poured out upon the Gentiles. The grace of God would come again and again like early dew upon the fleece. The scriptures promised this rain "upon the whole earth, to water the world with the dew of the Divine Spirit at the coming of the Saviour" (Ambrose, *Of the Holy Spirit,* prologue, *NPNF* 2 X, p. 94). This use of the metaphor of Gideon's fleece would continue in the centuries of exegesis following Ambrose as a type of Pentecost.

It was as if Gideon had already foreseen that the Spirit would in time be poured out upon all nations wherein all would be moistened with the dew of faith (Judg. 6:37, 38). Large numbers were not needed for the conquest, in the case of either Gideon or Pentecost. Only a few were disciplined by the rod of truth to lay aside superfluities. It is as if they were being gathered into a wine press, from which the wine would flow abundantly (Ambrose, *The Holy Spirit,* prologue, *FC* 44, pp. 35–39).

Ambrose began his discourse by praying that this water of the Spirit would come into his soul and rain upon the valleys of his mind that they might grow green, washing the steps of his mind and his heel to efface the curse. The fleece became a pictorial vision of the way God chooses to redeem "the whole world one by one" (Ambrose, *Of the Spirit,* prologue, 16, 17, *NPNF* 2 X, p. 95).

Baptism in, of, with, and by the Holy Spirit. Baptism is variously described as baptism *in* or *of,* or *with,* or *by* the Spirit. In Matthew 3:11, Mark 1:8, Luke 3:16, and John 1:33, the reference is to *Christ baptizing persons into the Spirit* (baptism in the Spirit). In Acts 1:5; 11:16, and 1 Corinthians 12:13, the reference is to *believers being baptized with or by the Spirit into the body of Christ* (Barth, *CD* IV/4, pp. 30–44, 73 ff.; Montague, *HS,* pp. 238 ff.).

It would be stretching exegesis, however, to suggest that this verbal distinction implies two separable baptisms, as if there were a preresurrection baptism *in* the Spirit and a postresurrection baptism *by* the Spirit. Rather, *baptizein en pneumati* was prophesied by John, first fulfilled at Pentecost, and administered and attested by the apostles as baptism *with or by* the Spirit. There is only one baptism (Eph. 4:5). Some modern readings of Spirit baptism tend inordinately to view it as glossolalia or under emotive or revivalist or sanctificationist metaphors. It remains a doubtful interpretation of Romans 6:1–4, Galatians 3:27, Ephesians 4:5, and Colossians 2:12 that the baptism of the Spirit is reserved for only some of the regenerated faithful after conversion (Walvoord, *HS*, pp. 138–46). Rather, the New Testament understands baptism of and by the Spirit as the privilege of all who have faith, all Christians, all who belong to the body of Christ. "You are all sons of God through faith in Christ Jesus, for all of you who were baptized have clothed yourselves with Christ" (Gal. 3:26, 27; John Chrysostom, *Comm. on Gal.* III, *NPNF* 1 XIII, pp. 29–30).

Whether Belief May Occur Without Baptism in the Spirit.   When Paul asked the disciples at Ephesus, "Did you receive the Holy Spirit *when you believed?*" (Acts 19:2, italics added), they answered, "No, we have not even heard that there is a Holy Spirit," having received only the baptism of John. This was not yet an adequate Christian faith and baptism. When Paul offered them Christian baptism, the "Holy Spirit came on them, and they spoke in tongues and prophesied" (Acts 19:6). This suggests that to be a disciple of John the Baptist was itself an incomplete act pointing toward completion in the work of the Son and the Spirit. If there remain in Christian communities those who have heard of Jesus Christ without having been endued with the power of the Holy Spirit, the Spirit continues to work to elicit a Spirit-filled faith (Acts 19:1–10; 1 Cor. 2:4, 5).

Unity in the Spirit Through Baptism.   The Spirit unites the body of Christ through the one baptism: "For we were all baptized by one Spirit into one body" (1 Cor. 12:13). This text assumes that baptism by the Spirit is coextensive with salvation and is universally given to all who believe. Paul was addressing a community of faith at Corinth troubled by various heresies and lack of discipline. Yet all were reminded of their being baptized by one Spirit into one body (Ambrose, *Duties* I.33, *NPNF* 2 X, p. 29).

The same idea appears in Ephesians: "There is one body and one Spirit—just as you were called to one hope when you were called—one Lord, one faith, one baptism" (Eph. 4:4, 5). Baptism by the Spirit is not subsequent to conversion or faith, but intrinsic to it. The unity of the gifts of the varied members of the body is assured by the Spirit. All believers are baptized by the Spirit into one body, fitly joined together (Eph. 4:16).

The faithful go with Christ to his cross, to his death, to his grave, and with him to his resurrection, all of which is once for all offered, received, enacted, and spoken nonverbally in baptism (Tertullian, *ANF*, pp. 256–80). Through baptism by the Spirit the faithful become identified with the body of Christ, living in union with Christ's risen body. They become one with Christ's righteousness, his dying and being raised, and his glory to come (John Cassian, *Conferences, NPNF* 2 XI, p. 186). The water used in baptism is the outward means of grace by which the outpouring of the Spirit is made visible, the inward grace outwardly signified as a type of death and resurrection (Hugh of St. Victor, *SCF*, pp. 282–304). Paul explained: "We were therefore buried with him through baptism into death in order that, just as Christ was raised from the dead through the glory of the Father, we too may live a new life" (Rom. 6:4). The baptized are "buried with him in baptism and raised with him through your faith in the power of God, who raised him from the dead" (Col. 2:12).

The narrative in Acts 8:14–17 shows the close correlation of the unity of apostolic faith and baptism of the Spirit into one community of faith. Though the Samaritans had been preemptively baptized in water, the gift of the Spirit was in an exceptional way withheld until the disciples came to lay their hands upon them, and in so doing made it clear that there would be no rivalry between the one called-out people in Samaria and Jerusalem.

The Sealing of the Spirit

Like baptism in the Spirit, the pledge of Spirit is proffered to all believers. The believer is sealed by the Spirit at the time of repentance and faith. Despite misdeeds, those who continue steadfast in faith remain sealed to the day of redemption (Eph. 4:30), assuming they "stand firm" (2 Cor. 1:21, 22). It is the very presence of the Spirit in the daily life of the believer that constitutes the seal—an identification peculiar to the economy of salvation (Ambrose, *Of the Holy Spirit* I.VI.79, *NPNF* 2 X, p. 103).

The Spirit as Seal of Ownership Confirming the Assurance of Salvation. Levitical priests who received lambs for sacrifice at the temple inspected them carefully for defects. Those approved were marked with the temple seal, indicating that they were fit for sacrificial offering. Grounded in this memory, John could say of Jesus that on the Lamb of God, "the Father has placed his seal of approval" (John 6:27).

Extending this received metaphor, Paul observed, "And you also were included in Christ when you heard the word of truth, the gospel of your salvation. Having believed, you were marked in him with a seal [*sphragizō*], the promised Holy Spirit, who is a deposit [*arrabon*] guaranteeing our inheritance until the redemption of those who are God's possession" (Eph. 1:13, 14; Montague, *HS*, pp. 221–26).

The Pledge of Inheritance. The sealing metaphor indicates a pledge or an earnest of an inheritance (*arrabon tes klēronomias,* Irenaeus, *Ag. Her.* V.8, *ANF* I, p. 533). Sealing conveys ownership, responsibility, security (John Chrysostom, *Eutropius, NPNF* 1 IX, p. 261; Calvin, *Inst.* 3.24). The seal promises that which will be brought to completion on a specified day—in this case, the last day. One seals one's agreements and promises with a stamp or wax seal that shows that the transaction (in this case, atoning grace received by faith) has been completed and confirmed. Once stamped or marked, it is not reversible. A seal implies an authorized securing and attesting of true ownership (Cyril of Jerusalem, *Catech. Lect.* XVII.35, *NPNF* 2 VII, p. 132). God places this stamp upon those who are fully committed to trust his Word. Think of the believer as enclosed in grace, as a document is enclosed in a sealed, wax-imprinted envelope. The Spirit is agent of this sealing (Ambrose, *On the Mysteries* 7, *NPNF* 2 X, p. 322).

The Spirit's work in the grace of baptism is like stamping a seal of ownership on the believer, pledging final uprighting. It is comparable to earnest money (pledge, deposit, *arrabōn*), which shows one's seriousness about ultimately fulfilling one's promise to make right (Cyprian, *The Unity of the Catholic Church*, ACW 25, pp. 48, 61).

In Sealing the Spirit Utters "Confirmed" to Belief. All of God's promises are yes in Christ, who "anointed us, set his seal of ownership on us [*sphragisamenos hēmas*], and put his Spirit in our hearts as a deposit [*arrabōna*], guaranteeing what is to come" (2 Cor. 1:21, 22). The faithful who receive the Holy Spirit in baptism are invited to count themselves as reconciled to God, whose signature is upon them awaiting the last day.

Sealing is closely tied with the teaching of the assurance of salvation. The believer is thereby made certain of God's promise and kept till the day of redemption. The Spirit pledges that all that has been promised will ultimately be fulfilled (Calvin, *Inst.* 3.2.12, 4.14.17–18). "God implants himself in the interior of that soul" in such a way that one need not "doubt that God has been in her and she has been in God" (Teresa of Avila, *Interior Castle*, mansion 5, chap. 1, p. 51; cf. Bermejo, *SL*, p. 220).

Chrism. Anointing with oil is a prefigurative type and external sign of the Spirit. The anointing-indwelling-sealing action of the Spirit is best viewed as a single multidimensional act. References to the anointing of the Spirit (Luke 4:18; Acts 4:27; 10:38; 2 Cor. 1:21; 1 John 2:20, 27) may be understood metaphorically as the indwelling and sealing of the Spirit (John Chrysostom, *Baptismal Instructions*, ACW 31, pp. 224–28; Cyprian, *Letters*, FC 51, p. 260). "The Spirit is the unction [ointment] and seal with which the Word anoints and seals all" that has been promised. The seal bears the image of Christ, "who seals, and those who are sealed partake of it, being conformed to it" (Athanasius, *LCHS* I.23, p. 124). "We are sealed by the Holy Spirit with the image and similitude of the Father's face, that is, of the Son" (Cyril of Alexandria, *Trin.* 5, MPG 75.945; cf. *Letters* 55.33–43, FC 77, pp. 30–36).

Chrism (from *chriō*, anoint), a mixture of olive oil and unguent or balsam, was used liturgically for the anointing or setting aside or sanctification of a person to a life task (Hugh of St. Victor, *SCF*, pp. 30 ff., 430 ff.). Confirmation became the sacrament of the chrism wherein those baptized liturgically received the Holy Spirit (John Chrysostom, *Baptismal Instructions*, ACW 31, p. 169). The richness of the oil and the fragrance of the balsam symbolized the fullness and beauty of the gift of the Spirit (Cyril of Jerusalem, *Catech. Lect.* XXI, NPNF 2 VII, pp. 149–50). After the font, the baptized were "anointed with a blessed unction—(a practice derived) from the old discipline, wherein on entering the priesthood, men were wont to be anointed with oil from a horn, ever since Aaron was anointed by Moses. Whence Aaron is [proleptically] called 'Christ [anointed],' from the 'chrism,' which is 'the unction'" (Tertullian, *On Baptism* 7, ANF III, p. 672). As Jesus was anointed (*chriō*) to preach (Luke 4:18), anointed "with the Holy Spirit and power" (Acts 10:38), so he anoints us, setting his seal of ownership on us (1 Cor. 1:21).

Baptism seeks confirmation in the continuing grace of the Spirit that follows the awakening of baptism: "For all the faithful ought to receive the Holy Spirit after baptism by imposition of the hand of the bishops, so that they may be found to be Christians fully" (Urban, *Epistle*, ANF VIII, p. 621).

Falling Away from One's Baptism.   As circumcision occurs only once, so does baptism. As circumcision brings persons initially into the covenant community, so does baptism. The circumcised Jew or the baptized Christian may later fall away from the original intention of the rite: inclusion in the covenant community (Proclus, *Hom.* 2, *MPG* 65, pp. 837–40). That does not invalidate the rite, but reveals its neglect (Luther, *Large Catech.* IV, *BOC*, pp. 436–46).

Confirmation (sometimes called chrism or unction, from 1 John 2:27) appears as a rite distinguishable from baptism as early as the time of Tertullian (*Of Baptism* 6) and Cyprian (*Epist.* 69, 70, *ANF* V, pp. 376–77). Reaffirmation or confirmation of one's baptism assumes that one intentionally is confirming the grace of the Spirit received in baptism. But even then one may still ever again fall away from one's intention in confirmation. Thus the sacrament of the Lord's Supper offers the grace of forgiveness to all penitents (Hugh of St. Victor, *SCF,* pp. 304 ff.; Luther, *Large Catech.* V, *BOC,* pp. 447 ff.).

Throughout this sequence, the baptism-anointing-sealing activity of the Holy Spirit is manifesting itself both punctially and gradually, beginning in time and continuing in time, analogous to incarnation and Pentecost. These varied metaphors of indwelling, pledging, sealing, setting apart mutually intermesh and reinforce each other. We were "baptized in the name of the Father and of the Son and of the Holy Ghost: first comes the confession [of the rule of faith], introducing us to salvation, and baptism follows, setting the seal upon our assent" (Basil, *On the Spirit* I.12, *NPNF* 2 VIII, p. 18).

Sealing Implies Moral Requirement.   There is an implicit moral requirement to walk in the way of holiness that accompanies the sealing of the Spirit: "And do not grieve the Holy Spirit of God, with whom you were sealed for the day of redemption. Get rid of all bitterness, rage and anger, brawling and slander, along with every form of malice. Be kind and compassionate to one another, forgiving each other, just as in Christ God forgave you" (Eph. 4:30–32; John Chrysostom, *Hom. on Eph.* XV, XVI, *NPNF* XIII, pp. 121–28).

"God's solid foundation stands firm, sealed with this inscription: 'The Lord knows those who are his' and 'Everyone who confesses the Lord must turn away from wickedness'" (2 Tim. 2:19). This means that those who confess him with their mouths but not with their lives are not among those whom the Lord knows are his, whom he has sealed unto the last day (Calvin, *Comm.* XXI, p. 227). Paul's assumption was that "my way of life in Christ Jesus" must agree "with what I teach everywhere" (1 Cor. 4:17).

The headband of the high priest that bore the inscription "Holiness to the Lord" (Exod. 39:30) looked anticipatively toward the personal coming of the Holy One: Christ "appeared so that he might take away our sins. And in him is no sin. No one who lives in him keeps on sinning" (1 John 3:6; Henry *CWB,* 1:442–43). Those who persist in sin thereby indicate their alienation from the body of Christ. Those who walk in the way of holiness refract the Spirit of holiness (Augustine, *Hom. on Epist. of John* IV, V, *NPNF* 1 VII, pp. 482–93).

Whether the Sealing of Grace Is Punctial as in Orders and Baptism.   The consensual exegetes noted this analogy between ordination and baptism: The moment of receiving holy orders brings the ordinand instantly into sacred ministry, even though the preparation for and actualizing of that ministry may require extended growth through time (John Chrysostom, *On the Priesthood*). Ordination does not take place over years of time, but on a particular day in time—punctially. Yet the ministry to which one is ordained can only take place gradually in unfolding time (Gregory Nazianzen, *Orat.* II, *NPNF* 2 VII, pp. 210–27; Gregory the Great, *Pastoral Care*, ACW 11, pp. 25 ff.).

Similarly with the sealing of the Spirit, sanctifying grace begins at a particular point to work toward habituated refractions of the holiness of God (Ambrose, *Duties, NPNF* 2 X, p. 41). As holy orders were considered indelible for those called to sacred ministry, so was the seal of baptism viewed as indelible to all called to faith, even if abused or neglected (Augustine, *Hom. on Epist. of John* IV, *NPNF* 1 VII, pp. 482–85; cf. *Hom. on 2 Cor.* III, *NPNF* 1 XII, pp. 289–93; Innocent III, *SCD* 411, p. 160).

The grace offered by the Spirit in baptism provides not only a momentary remission of sins but the continuing offer of sanctifying grace that grows with good works (Luther, *Large Catech.*, pp. 436–46; cf. *Trent* VII, Canons on Baptism, pp. 53–54). Luther concisely defined the gifts of the baptismal sealing: "It effects forgiveness of sins, delivers from death and the devil, and grants eternal salvation to all who believe" (*Small Catech.* IV.2, *CC*, p. 120; cf. *Letter of Barnabas* 11; Hermas, *Mand.* IV.3).

The Gifts of the Spirit

The Pauline teaching of spiritual gifts is concentrated primarily in Romans 12, and 1 Corinthians 12 and Ephesians 4 (compare these Pauline lists with 1 Pet. 4:10). *Charisma* is the gift of some God-given ability to render a service empowered by grace (Montague, *HS*, pp. 145–84).

Distributed for the Body.   These gifts (*charismata*) are given by the risen Lord to build up his body (Eph. 4:11) and administered by the Spirit, who presciently knows what gift best befits each believer for service (1 Cor. 12). A natural talent is a superior ability that emerges through genetic tendencies or environment or technical competencies. A spiritual *charisma* is a gift of divine grace that is evidenced by some ability that benefits the body of Christ (Rom. 12:6).

Spiritual gifts are not given to individuals as such, but to individuals on behalf of the whole body, the community of faith, not for self-congratulation but for upbuilding the body (*oikodomē*, Eph. 4:12, 16, 29; cf. Ryrie, *Basic Theology*, pp. 362–69). When a symphonic conductor selects violinists for a rigorous season of repertoire, he does not do so in order to advance their careers but to ensure that the music they create will be rightly balanced and harmonized. Similarly, when the Spirit distributes gifts to the body of Christ, it is not for personal self-aggrandizement, but rather for the health and upbuilding of the body (John Chrysostom, *Hom. on Eph.* X, XI, *NPNF* 1 XIII, pp. 99–108). As one does not light a fire to warm the stove but to warm the room, quipped Kuyper, so the Spirit does not distribute gifts to enhance individuals but the community on behalf of the world's redemption (*WHS*, p. 182).

Gifts of the Spirit are distributed not by human preference or private choice but as the sovereign act of God the Spirit (1 Cor. 12:12, 28). The responsibility of the recipient is to receive the gift proffered so as to develop and exercise it to the fullest (John Chrysostom, *Hom. on 1 Cor.* XXIX, XXX, *NPNF* 1 XII, pp. 168–80).

No lay member of the body is wholly lacking in gifts and tasks of ministry: "Each member is the church in the world, endowed by the Spirit with some gift of ministry and is responsible for the integrity of his witness in his own particular situation" (United Presbyterian Confession of 1967, *CC*, p. 700). The *charismata* of the primitive church were continued and bestowed upon the whole *laos*, some becoming adapted and reshaped into gifts peculiar to sacred ministry, particularly through the gifts of *presbuteros* and *episkopos*, which were commissioned to guard the apostolic teaching and given grace to interpret it (Irenaeus, *Ag. Her.* IV.26.5–7, *ANF* I, p. 498).

Whether the Whole Suffers with Each Dysfunctional Part.   God has organically joined the members of the body so that "its parts should have equal concern for each other. If one part suffers, every part suffers with it; if one part is honored, every part rejoices with it" (1 Cor. 12:25, 26). Hence members are to bear one another's burdens as if they were their own (Gal. 6:2).

"Brothers, if someone is caught in a sin, you who are spiritual should restore him gently" (Gal. 6:1), for in caring for the fallen brother, one cares for the whole body. Such mutual care is enabled by the Spirit. No part of the body can demean or disown other members without self-harm. "If I am a foot and wish the whole body to be a foot, I harm the whole body. God has arranged the parts in the body, every one of them, just as he wanted them to be. If they were all one part, where would the body be?" It would be a dead foot, not a living body. "As it is, there are many parts, but one body" (1 Cor. 12:18–20). "There are different kinds of working, but the same God works all of them in all" (1 Cor. 12:6; Calvin, *Comm.* XX, pp. 398–407).

The Distribution of Varied Gifts.   As no believer is lacking in all gifts (1 Cor. 12:7; 1 Pet. 4:10), so no one possesses all. Each depends upon the gifts of other members of the body to complete what is lacking in his or her own gift (John Chrysostom, *Hom. on 1 Cor.* XXIX, XXX, *NPNF* 1 XII, pp. 168–80).

Drab uniformity is not the characteristic style of the work of the Spirit, but rather variability, imaginative responsiveness, and exquisite diversity. At a given time, some of these gifts may be more urgently needed in the mission of the Son than others, but in due time all gifts are needed (1 Cor. 12:4–10). God's gifts continue to be given even to those unaware of them in ways providentially adapted to finite capacities. Among early typic apostolic recipients of the gifts of the Spirit were Philip, who is first found distributing relief to the poor (Acts 6:5) and later witnessing to the Samaritans (8:5), and Stephen, who engaged in acts of mercy and later became the first disciple to give his life for Christ (Acts 7).

All are asked to show mercy, but to some are given special gifts of benevolence. To the whole *laos* is given the task of witness and exhortation (Acts 1:8; Heb. 10:25), but some are given gifts and called more particularly to be evangelists and exhorters.

Though the command to serve one another is given to the whole church (Gal. 5:13), the gift of serving is given to some in greater measure. Whatever one's gift, it is to be developed, nurtured, and extended by one's cooperative effort responding to grace (*Doc. Vat. II*, pp. 29–30; H. Küng, "The Charismatic Structure of the Church," *Concilium* 4, pp. 41–61).

The economic principle of proportional adaptation was strikingly portrayed in Cyril's analogy: "By water all things subsist. . . . It comes down in one form, but works in many forms. For one fountain watereth the whole of Paradise, and one and the same rain comes down upon all the world, yet it becomes white in the lily, and red in the rose, and purple in the violets and hyacinths . . . the rain does not change itself and come down first as one thing, then as another, but *adapting itself to the constitution of each thing* which receives it, it becomes to each what is suitable" (Cyril of Jerusalem, *Catech. Lect.* XVI.12, *NPNF* 2 VII, p. 118, italics added).

Sexuality and the Diversity of Gifts.   Both marriage and singleness are viewed as spiritual gifts relating to sexuality, each one having "his own gift from God, one has this gift, another has that" (1 Cor. 7:7). The single person is given the gift of freedom from entangling commitments in order to have the opportunity to serve the Lord more freely (1 Cor. 7:32). The married person is given the gift of generativity and commitment to family to enable and nurture life (1 Cor. 7:29, 33). Though different gifts, each has its own challenges and requirements. Both are needed in the scheme of redemption to redeem the time (John Chrysostom, *Hom. on 1 Cor.* XIX, *NPNF* 1 XII, pp. 105–11; Calvin, *Comm.* XX, pp. 251–71).

The gracious complementarity of gifts of sexual difference was early recognized as "a great proof of providence." It was theologically significant that "males and females equally have teats, but only those of the female are filled with milk," and in the organs of generativity, the male "differs from the female only in that part of his body in which is the power of injecting seed" (Clementina, *Recognitions* VIII.32, *ANF* VIII, p. 174). The female, with no power to inject seed, complements the male, who has no power generatively to receive seed.

Complementarity of Spiritual Gifts.   Several varied lists of gifts of the Spirit are found in the New Testament. Among those frequently listed are *apostleship*, wherein one is sent on the mission of the Son by the Spirit (Eph. 4:11); *prophecy*, wherein one speaks the Word of the Lord (1 Cor. 14:1); *evangelization*, wherein one proclaims good news to all (Eph. 4:11; Acts 21:8); *pastoring* or shepherding the flock of God (Eph. 4:11); *teaching* the truth (Rom. 12:7); *confession* (1 John 4:2), and *exhortation* (Rom. 12:8); *healing* (1 Cor. 12:9, 28, 30) and *miracles* (1 Cor. 12:28); ecstatic utterance, speaking in other *languages*, and the interpretation of other tongues (Acts 2:4, 8; 1 Cor. 12:10); *discernment* (1 Cor. 12:10); *serving* (Rom. 12:7); and *administry* or governance (*kubernēsis*), which seeks to enable the work of ministry of others (1 Cor. 12:28; cf. Rom. 12:8; Theonas of Alexandria, *Epist. to Lucianus* IV, *ANF* VI, p. 159).

Also described among the spiritual gifts are *faith* (1 Cor. 12:9), *encouragement* (Rom. 12:8), the ability to *distinguish* true and false revelation (1 Cor. 12:10), the showing of *mercy* and generosity (Rom. 12:8), diligent leadership, wisdom, and knowledge (Rom. 12:8; 1 Cor. 12:28). Above all there is the summative gift of *love*, which shows forth God's own superabundant benevolence and mercy (Rom. 12:8).

The astonishing variety of gifts complement each other to build up the body. Apostolicity is a foundational gift, upon which other gifts are dependent, since no testimony is available to us except through the apostolate (1 Cor. 12:28; Eph.

4:11). Prophecy, in the sense both of proclamation and of discerning the will of God, is a gift given to both men and women (Acts 21:9; 11:27, 28; 1 Cor. 14; Joel 2). The gifts of miracle and healing (1 Cor. 12:9, 28, 30) were exercised on certain occasions by Paul, as at Ephesus (Acts 19:11, 12), yet not in the cases of Timothy or Trophimus or Epaphroditus (1 Tim. 5:23; 2 Tim. 4:20; Phil. 2:27) or in the case of Paul's own thorn in the flesh (2 Cor. 12:8, 9). One's calling to be an evangelist or pastor (Eph. 4:11) or servant or teacher (Rom. 12:7; 1 Cor. 12:28; Eph. 4:11, 12) is being authenticated and enabled by spiritual gifts commensurable with those tasks (John Chrysostom, *Hom. on Eph.* XI, *NPNF* 1 XIII, pp. 104–8; cf. R. Laurentin, *Catholic Pentecostalism;* Suenens, *A New Pentecost?* E. O'Connor, *The Pentecostal Movement in the Catholic Church*).

Lists of Charismata.   It is useful to visualize the varied lists of gifts of the Spirit in terms of three broad functions of the church: witness, community, and service.

GIFTS OF THE SPIRIT

	Marturia	**Koinonia**	**Diakonia**
Rom. 12:6–8	prophecy	exhortation	service
	teaching	liberality	giving aid
			acts of mercy
1 Cor. 12:4–11	wisdom	discernment	healing
	knowledge	interpretation	miracles
	faith	edification	
	prophecy		
	tongues		
1 Cor. 13	faith	hope	love
Eph. 4:11	apostles	pastors	
	prophets		
	evangelists		
	teachers		
1 Pet. 4:11	speaking		serving

Such New Testament lists were not seeking to exhaust all possible gifts, or present the gifts of the Spirit in systematic sequence. Rather, they are suggestive of the incalculable diversity of gifts that are bestowed upon the one body for the upbuilding of the whole as the Spirit sees fit (John Chrysostom, *Hom. on 1 Cor.* XIX, *NPNF* 1 XII, pp. 105–11).

Order and Proportionality in Distribution.   The gifts of the Spirit allow faith to be maintained through time in ways that cannot be assured by human means. The gifts of the Spirit awaken discipline in the will, which does not come merely through human initiative or rational planning. The gifts of the Spirit enable a new ordering of life, reordering the prevailing alienated ways of ordering priorities (2 Tim. 1:6; James 1:17; K. Rahner, *RR*, pp. 293–96).

In distributing gifts the foreknowing God "beholds the temper of each" and works proportionally in each recipient. The Spirit works both in those times and places we can see and those we cannot see; among those peoples for whom we have a name, and among those "for whom we have no names." To some are given the power of taming "hostile spirits," to others the gift of chastity, to others the gift of caring for the poor (Cyril of Jerusalem, *Catech. Lect.* XVI.22, *NPNF* 2 VII, p. 121). The Giver does not wastefully squander the *charismata*. The principle of parsimony is evident in the distribution of gifts of the Spirit.

Discerning and Testing the Gifts.   The discernment of the Spirit is itself a gift of the Spirit (1 Cor. 2:14; 1 Thess. 5:12; *Doc. Vat. II, Ch.*, sec. 13). "There is a diversity of Gifts, which stands in need of yet another Gift to discern" which is contextually most needed (Gregory Nazianzen, *Orat.* XLI.16, *NPNF* 2 VII, p. 384). Since gifts are constantly given anew, they may be at times hard to discern; the Spirit always works ahead of our discernment.

Paul warned, "Do not put out the Spirit's fire; do not treat prophecies with contempt. Test everything" (1 Thess. 5:19–21). The gifts of the Spirit are tested primarily by the criterion of whether they further the mission of the Son (1 Cor. 12:1–3).

Other Gifts.   Exegetes continue to debate whether the special gifts of faith healing, exorcism, and glossolalia are normative for all times or reserved for apostolic or very special times. Whereas all believers are baptized (1 Cor. 12:13), not all speak in tongues (1 Cor. 12:30).

Glossolalia, or speaking in tongues, and interpretation of tongues are gifts of the Spirit (1 Cor. 12:10) whose purpose was to communicate and authenticate truth from God. Like all gifts, these proved to be abusable. Early in the apostolic tradition we find constraints being placed upon the healthy practice of these special gifts: no one was to speak unless the message could be interpreted, and intelligible prophecy was to be preferred (1 Cor. 14). It was precisely while regulating, but not forbidding, speaking in tongues, that Paul states that "everything should be done in a fitting and orderly way" (1 Cor. 14:40). Fittingness (*euschēmosunē*) and order (*taxis*) are proper duties of self-governance. In the reordering shaped by grace, sufficient room must be left for Christian liberty, freedom of conscience, and the gifts of the Spirit.

Most would agree that the gifts of miracle and healing are more rare in the present than in the apostolic period, but not wholly absent (J. Wesley, *A Further Appeal to Men of Reason and Religion*, *WJWB* 11, pp. 141–53; cf. Irving, *CWEI*, V; Campbell, *NA*). We would be ill advised either to rule out the possibility of the Spirit's working today in miracle and healing, or to have no critical criteria to apply to alleged miracles and healings, which so often lead to fanaticism and manipulation.

Luke reported that "God did extraordinary miracles through Paul, so that even handkerchiefs and aprons that had touched him were taken to the sick and their illnesses were cured" (Acts 19:12). This is reminiscent of an earlier report that by touching the bones of Elisha a dead man was raised to life (1 Kings 13:21). Such ideas inevitably would lead to abuses, which would in due time force the Reformation to reject the teaching "that the souls of the dead have influence on the living," and the practice of "praying to the souls of the saints and the hope that power or holiness may come from the dead (from their graves, from their clothes, their bones, mementos, relics)" (Batak Confession, XVI, *CC*, p. 565; Calvin, *Inst.* 3.5.6, 7).

Whether the Apparent Inequalities of Gifts Are Unjust. The seeming inequalities of gifts only appear unjust when viewed rationalistically or individualistically from the viewpoint of human interests, self-expression, and pride. Seen in relation to the wholeness of the body of Christ, what at first might seem to be inequality displays a profound equity wherein all members are equitably needed within the whole body (Calvin, *Comm.* XX, pp. 251–71).

The ordered diversity of gifts does not mean that they are divided or fragmented, except in the sense that they are functionally distinguishable. They are offered within the context of the history of sin, which itself is shaped by social injustices against which the Spirit strives (Rom. 12; 1 Cor. 10:14–32).

The diversity of gifts does not mean that they are unequally valued by God, though one may function more urgently in a given moment. The working body needs teeth, but that does not imply that the teeth need to be biting all the time. That the body needs eyes does not imply that one must never close them. Each gift is needed, but not compulsively at all times (*Didache* 11, *ECW*, p. 233).

Wherever the Spirit is, the life of the church is being awakened (*ubi spiritus ibi ecclesia*). "For in Christ all the fullness of the Deity lives in bodily form, and you have been given fullness in Christ" (Col. 2:9). "As Christ is that fullness *bodily*, so the Holy Ghost is that fullness *spiritually*" (Pope, *Compend.* II, p. 331). "And in him you too are being built together to become a dwelling in which God lives by his Spirit" (Eph. 2:22).

Gifts, Fruits, and Virtues

Gifts of the Spirit in Isaiah 11:2, 3. In the primitive church, the laying on of hands followed baptism. Later, when baptism and confirmation became separable rites, confirmation became an important moment of ratification of baptismal vows preparatory to communion upon the age of accountability, ordinarily by laying on of hands of the *episkopos* (Anon., *Treatise on Rebaptism* 1–5, *ANF* V, pp. 667–69).

Sacramentally viewed, the sevenfold gifts of the Spirit were closely connected with confirmation or reaffirmation of baptismal vows, wherein by prayer and preparation one sought and sacramentally received the sevenfold gift of the Spirit, offering grace to walk the way of holiness (Augustine, *Comm. on Ps.* 150, *NPNF* 1 VIII, p. 681; Tho. Aq., *ST* I–II Q68, I, pp. 877–85; cf. Calvin, *Comm.* VII, pp. 374–75; Bermejo, *SL*, pp. 222–28).

Classic exegetes were intrigued by the thought that seven summative gifts of the confirming Spirit to the church had been anticipated by the prophet Isaiah:

wisdom, understanding, counsel, fortitude, knowledge, piety, and reverence for God. "The Spirit of the Lord will rest on him—the Spirit of wisdom and of understanding, the Spirit of counsel and of power, the Spirit of knowledge and of the fear of the Lord—and he will delight in the fear of the Lord" (Isa. 11:2, 3a; whether this enumerates six or seven gifts, the intent is to convey the fullness of the Spirit's gifts). Four are said to reclaim and perfect the intellect: *wisdom* and *understanding* pertain to the discernment of truth and its value (1 Cor. 1:24; Ps. 31:8); *counsel* (Isa. 9:6, LXX) and *knowledge* prudentially and rightly apply the truth to moral circumstances. The other three (variously translated) are said to reclaim and perfect the will: *power* or fortitude or courageous strength for spiritual struggle (1 Cor. 1:24), *godliness* or reverent piety or delight in truth (John 14:6), and *holy fear of God,* or the consecrated desire to please God (Ps. 110:10; *Decree of Damasus,* Roman Synod, A.D. 382, *SCD* 83, p. 33; Hall, *DT* VIII, p. 32).

By these gifts the Spirit imparts to the soul the readiness to respond to grace in all that pertains to salvation. Viewed from the new covenant, these gifts are offered through Word and Sacrament. The gifts of the Spirit make the faithful ready to discern and do the will of God, following the promptings of the Spirit whatever the context (1 Cor. 1:7; *Baltimore Catechism,* pp. 95–97). Grace awakens and enlivens quiescent spiritual capacities of sinners and helps them work out their salvation without displacing grace or exempting the will from disciplined effort (Ambrose, *Duties, NPNF* 2 X, p. 50).

Fruit of the Spirit.   The fruit of the Spirit is summarized by Paul: "But the fruit of the Spirit is love, joy, peace, patience [forbearance, long-suffering], kindness, goodness [benevolence], faithfulness [fidelity], gentleness [meekness, mildness], and self-control [modesty, continence]. Against such there is no law. Those who belong to Christ Jesus have crucified the sinful nature with its passions and desires. Since we live by the Spirit, let us keep in step with the Spirit" (Gal. 5:22–25). All these behavioral responses are made easy, light, and joyful by the power of the Spirit, from whom fruits spring (John Chrysostom, *Comm. on Gal.* V, *NPNF* 1 XIII, p. 42). The transformation enabled by the Spirit is organismically whole and all-embracing. As dead leaves fall from a tree in the winter, so the old fallen leaves (works of the flesh) gradually settle to the ground: adultery, fornication, hatred, strife, idolatry, envy, murder, drunkenness (Gal. 5:19–21). As new growth rises in the spring, there awakens the bud, then the fruits of Christian freedom, enabling faith to become active in works of love (Clement of Alexandria, *Stromata,* IV.8, *ANF* II, p. 420).

Cardinal Virtues of Sanctifying Grace: Faith, Hope, and Love.   Sanctifying grace confers and enables many forms of behavioral excellence (*arete*), or virtue. Faith, hope, and love are chief among them. They are offered and enabled by sanctifying grace and conferred by the means of grace (John Chrysostom, *Hom. on 1 Cor.* XXXIII, XXXIV, *NPNF* 1 XII, pp. 194–208; *Trent* VI.7). They begin to grow in the justified sinner in the new birth and gradually mature through the reception of sanctifying grace.

The character that emerges out of suffering produces hope, and "hope does not disappoint us, because God has poured out his love into our hearts by the Holy Spirit, whom he has given us" (Rom. 5:5). Paul summarized these gifts in a way that has subsequently imprinted all Christian moral teaching: "And now these three remain: faith, hope and love. But the greatest of these is love. Follow the way of love and eagerly desire spiritual gifts" (1 Cor. 13:12–14:1).

Thomas summed up centuries of consensual exegesis: "There are three theological virtues,—faith, by which we know God; hope, by which we trust to obtain Him; and charity, by which we love Him" (Tho. Aq., *Quaestiones Disputatae de Virtutibus in Communi,* art. 12; in Pohle, *DT* VI, p. 365). The grace offered in baptism is the beginning of faith, hope, and love in the Christian community. These virtues transmute natural moral virtues and enable them to grow in reference to final judgment and blessedness.

Cardinal Moral Virtues.   In advancing faith, hope, and love, sanctifying grace also confers and enables the growth of moral virtues, which though varied, have often been summarized as four cardinal types, following a Platonic-Aristotelian tradition long esteemed by Christian exegetes: prudence, justice, fortitude, and temperance (Tho. Aq., *ST* I–II, Q63.3). These are textually anticipated in Wisdom 8:7: "And if a man love justice: her labors have great virtues; for she teacheth temperance, and prudence, and justice, and fortitude."

Prudence seeks to perfect the intellect in forming judgments, justice shapes the will in guarding human rights, fortitude disposes the will under threat, and temperance inclines the appetites in the ordering of the passions. This language became implanted in the catechisms: "Prudence disposes us in all circumstances to form right judgments about what we must do or not do. Justice disposes us to give everyone what belongs to him. Fortitude disposes us to do what is good in spite of any difficulty. Temperance disposes us to control our desires and use rightly the things which please our senses" (*Baltimore Catech.,* p. 99).

These four excellent types of moral behavior are to some extent able to be nurtured by natural moral means, though always assisted by common and prevening grace. These are often distinguished from faith, hope, and love, which are most fully awakened not by natural but supernatural means—by the justifying and sanctifying grace offered in baptism and communion. They transform the natural moral virtues and place them in the context of eternal accountability (Tho. Aq., *ST* II–II, Q1 ff., I, pp. 1169 ff.).

Not only these excellent moral and theological habits but related virtues or excellent moral behaviors are commended in the effort to coalesce faith, social justice, and moral accountability: "Filial piety and patriotism, which dispose us to honor, love, and respect our parents and our country. Obedience, which disposes us to do the will of our superiors. Veracity, which disposes us to tell the truth. Liberality, which disposes us rightly to use worldly goods. Patience, which disposes us to bear up under trials and difficulties. Humility, which disposes us to acknowledge our limitations. Chastity, or purity, which disposes us to be pure in soul and body," and more generally religion, which is "the highest moral virtue since it disposes us to offer to God the worship that is due Him" (*Baltimore Catech.,* pp. 100, 101).

ADOPTION INTO THE FAMILY OF GOD

When the child of a stranger is received into an enduring bond in a family so as to convey to that child all the rights and benefits that belong to the natural children and heirs, that is called adoption. Christianly understood, adoption is that act of God by which we as strangers are received into God's family, conveying to us all the privileges of sonship and daughterhood (John Chrysostom, *Baptismal Instructions, ACW* 31, pp. 89, 90). Hence adoption is a more interpersonal and encompassing metaphor than forgiveness of debts, since it expresses the bonding of the stranger into a new relationship of covenant and undeserved inheritance (Gal. 4:4, 5; Eph. 2:12–19; Calvin, *Comm.* XXI, pp. 119–23).

Seeking explicit fairness in gender reference, we do better to refer to this teaching not alone as the doctrine of sonship (by which it is traditionally known), but of daughterhood-sonship, or adoption into the family of God. The intent of consensual teaching of sonship has been not to exclude but include daughterhood by generic reference within the notion of *huios* (descendant, offspring, son).

Adoption to Inheritance as Daughters and Sons

In the creation of humanity, God breathed into Adam and Eve his own life, after God's own likeness and image, making them children of God. This image of God, the original condition of sonship and daughterhood, lost by sin, is being restored in regeneration and adoption (Hilary, *Trin.* VI.18–25, *NPNF* 2 IX, pp. 104–7). To men and women who believe he gives the renewed right of heirship in the family: "the right to become children of God" (John 1:13). "If any one is formed in Christ, he is formed into a child of God" (Cyril of Alexandria, *Orat. on Isa.* II.4, Pohle, *DT* VII, p. 360).

The inheritance is not an immediate possession, but promised and received already in the form of hope. "An heir is born, not to immediate possession, but to hope, of wealth" (Beet, *New Life,* p. 245).

Justifying, Regenerating, and Adopting Grace Correlated.   By justification one is pardoned for offenses against the Father. By regeneration one is given new life in the Spirit. By adoption one is permitted to reenter the Father's family.

Justification removes obstacles between God and the sinner. Regeneration by giving new life breaks the dominion of sin and reorders the direction of the heart toward the love of God. Only on this basis may adoptive grace then make the new creature a son or daughter, a member of God's family, ready to receive the promised inheritance (Luther, *Comm. on Romans,* pp. 104–8).

Those justified become heirs (Titus 3:7). By adoption, they are "no longer foreigners and aliens, but fellow citizens with God's people and members of God's household" (Eph. 2:19). "*Justification* removes our *guilt,* which is a barrier in the way of our admission into God's family; *regeneration* changes our *hearts,* imparting a fitness for the family, and *adoption* actually *receives* us therein" (Weaver, *CT,* p. 176, italics added). "Justification consists in the pardon of the guilty, regeneration in the moral renovation of the unholy, and adoption in the gracious reception of those who are alienated from God and disinherited" (Wakefield, *CT* II, p. 434).

The New Testament conflates these powerful metaphors. One is born anew into a present resurrected life and an incomparable future family inheritance. "In his great mercy he has given us new birth into a living hope through the resurrection of Jesus Christ from the dead, and into an inheritance that can never perish, spoil or fade" (1 Pet. 1:3, 4). No one is justified without also being given new life in the Spirit and being adopted into the family of God (Calvin, *Inst.* 3.2, 3.20 ff.). Each implies the other. Adoption is not artificially separable from rebirth, but another way of viewing the same work of grace (Athanasius, *Ag. Arians, NPNF* 2 IV, pp. 440–45).

The only reason salvation teaching may be treated systematically is due to the orderly work of the Spirit, which is attested in scripture as ordinarily working in this sequence: Convicting grace reveals to the sinner the depths of the human predicament, leading to repentance. Justifying grace pardons sin and invites trusting faith in the forgiving God. Regenerating grace redirects our dominant affections from the godless love of self to the selfless love of God. Adopting grace welcomes us into the family of God (Westminster Conf. XII, *CC*, p. 208). Amid this transition, the Spirit witnesses within our spirits that we are children of God, assured of the undeserved inheritance of salvation (Calvin, *Reply to Sadolet, LCC* XXII, pp. 243–47; J. Wesley, *WJWB* I, sermons 9–11; *WJW* V, pp. 111–44). Accordingly, the order of salvation moves steadily from the teaching of repentance, faith, justification, regeneration, and the indwelling Spirit toward adoption, assurance, and union with Christ (R. Watson, *TI* II, chap. 24; Miner Raymond, *ST* II, pp. 361–72).

Adoption Defined.   Adoption (*huiothesia*) is that work of the Spirit by which we are received into the family of God and readied for eternal inheritance (Rom. 8:15–21; Athanasius, *Ag. Arians, NPNF* 2 IV, p. 381). Adoption suggests legal means by which a child not of the family can be taken into the family with full rights and privileges of that relationship. Such a person is ceremonially and legally born into a new life so as to enter fully into a new family. By adoption, the Father reinstates into his family as sons and daughters—hence heirs—those who, disinherited by sin, had become aliens and outcasts (Tho. Aq., *ST* II, pp. 2047, 2263). "Now if we are children, then we are heirs—heirs of God and co-heirs with Christ" (Rom. 8:17).

Seen by analogy to evangelical regeneration, evangelical adoption teaches that a fitting means has been provided by which a stranger alienated from the family of God may be brought into the family with full rights of communion with the Father (Gal. 4:5; Rom. 8:15; Eph.1:8).

The Westminster Confession carefully defined those who receive the "grace of adoption" as those who

> enjoy the liberties and privileges of the children of God;
> have his name put upon them;
> receive the Spirit of adoption;
> have access to the throne of grace with boldness;
> are enabled to cry, Abba, Father;
> are pitied, protected, provided for,
> are chastened by him as by a father;
> yet never cast off, but sealed to the day of redemption,
> and inherit the promises, as heirs of everlasting salvation.

> (XII, *CC*, p. 208, list format added)

Legal Adoption and Natural Generation: Heir by Grace, Not by Natural Right.   One may become a daughter or son in one of two ways: by birth or by legal adoption—by nature or by choice. Two metaphorical spheres are juxtaposed in these two ways: natural generation and legal adoption. Only by birth or adoption may one truly belong to a family (Summers, *ST* I, pp. 406–16). Those adopted are given the same full rights that natural sons and daughters enjoy in approaching a loving father with their needs and hopes.

This is not a two-tiered ordering of the family of God, with birth daughters being preferred over adopted daughters. Both civil and sacred adoption are gifts of the adopting parent, motivated by love and goodwill. The initiative comes strictly from the person adopting, and adoption may occur even without the knowledge of the adopted infant or child, for whom it has far-reaching consequences.

Both metaphors feed into the New Testament's description of a single theme: new life in Christ that permits full sharing in the family of God. By rebirth one is born anew into the family. By adoption one is claimed for the family. Both have the same effect so far as inheritance is concerned. Full sonship or daughterhood indicates the relation to the family, and adoption indicates the method of bringing the son or daughter into that relation (Pope, *Compend.* III, pp. 113–30; Miley, *ST* II, pp. 339–54).

In the same passage in which Paul declared that "in Christ" there is neither "male nor female" (Gal. 3:28), he elaborated, "But when the time had fully come, God sent his Son, born of a woman, born under law, to redeem those under law, that we might receive the full rights of sons [offspring, *huiothesian*]. Because you are sons, God sent the Spirit of his Son into our hearts, the Spirit who calls out, 'Abba, Father.' So you are no longer a slave, but a son; and since you are a son, God has made you also an heir" (Gal. 4:4–7).

The Legal Status of Those Adopted.   Thomas Aquinas defined adoption as "the gratuitous acceptance of a child of other parents to be the same as one's own child and heir" (*ST* IIIa, Q23.1). The legal metaphor assumes that the adopting father is not the paternal father; that the child is not heir by right but by choice and grace of the parent; that the adoption occurs by mutual consent, explicit or implied; and that upon adoption all affection and love due to one's own child would be due to this child (Gal. 4:7; Rom. 8:17; Calvin, *Inst.* 3.2).

In regenerative adoption, persons are born "not of natural descent" (not "from blood," KJV, or lineage or physical constituents of human life), nor from "a husband's will" ("the will of the flesh," KJV, from erotic or libidinal energies). Nor are they born due to "human decision" ("the will of man," KJV, the noblest power of human personhood—volition, free self-determination). All these are powerless to bring new life to the dead. Rather sinners must be reborn "from God" (John 1:13; Augustine, *Tractates on John* 2, FC 78, pp. 72–74). "We are not sons by creation, but by the 'new creation.' We become sons not by the natural birth, but by the Spiritual birth; not by generation, but by regeneration; not by being born, but by being born again—'born from above'—'born of the Spirit'—'born of God.' This is the adoption. It has redemption beneath it, and divine life in it" (Merrill, *ACE*, p. 148).

The Need for Adoption: Disinheritance, Loss of Title.   The pivotal premise of adoption is that sinners have lost all right to be viewed as children of God. The prodigals have run away to a far country. Their inheritance has already been irrecoverably forfeited. Even the image of God in humanity has become defaced and marred by sin (Calvin, *Inst.* 1.15). From the viewpoint of their original family rights, they are self-defined aliens, rebels, without title, having lost all rights of daughterhood and sonship. Even a king's son by rebelling against the king would lose the right of inheritance and be viewed as outlaw. Sonship implies moral responsibilities attached to being in the covenant relation of son (Calvin, *Inst.* 3.2.11, 3.15–17).

The delinquency of the son or daughter does not imply that the Father has ceased to love (Luke 15). The Father continues to seek the lost, awaiting their return, ready to forgive. Until the prodigal "comes to his senses" and turns back toward home, there is no way to proceed toward reconciliation. Even then, in Jesus' parable, the son humbly confesses, "I am no longer worthy to be called your son; make me like one of your hired men" (Luke 15:17, 19). The penitent prodigal is not left in doubt as to whether he is accepted by the Father, whose joy is communicated to him in the feast of the fatted calf (Antonius Melissa, *Fragment on Luke 15, ANF* II, pp. 582–83; *AEG*).

We are heirs only as joint heirs in union with the Son. "He who has the Son has life; he who does not have the Son of God does not have life" (1 John 5:12; Calvin, *Comm.* XXII, pp. 261–64).

The Right to Become Again a Child of God.   Apart from adoption, the slave of sin is blocked from the family of God. "Everyone who sins is a slave to sin. Now a slave has no permanent place in the family" (John 8:35). When Jesus' detractors, detesting the analogy, protested indignantly, "We are not illegitimate children," Jesus replied, "If God were your Father, you would love me, for I came from God and now am here." Testily he charged that they had decided to belong to a different family: "You belong to your father, the devil, and you want to carry out your father's desire" (John 8:41–44). The grace of adoption bridges the chasm between the history of sin and the holy God, making daughterhood-sonship once again plausible without demeaning the holiness of God.

To be a child of God is to be given grace to refract once again in time and space the holiness and goodness of the Father. That is the primary meaning of the phrase "created in the image of God"—able to mirror the goodness of God. Insofar as the sinner is unable to mirror the ground of goodness, a major spiritual renovation is required. Those dead in sins must be raised to new life. The dead do not raise themselves (Rom. 7:7–25).

The Son came to "his own, but his own did not receive him. Yet to all who received him, to those who believed in his name, he gave the right to become children of God" (John 1:11, 12). This is the legitimate title of those adopted: children of God. Whatever rights as children they might have had at the outset of human history have been long since collectively forfeited to the power of sin. They once again become daughters and sons of God by being born anew from above by faith (John 3:3; Gal. 3:26).

Discipline as Evidence of Inclusion into the Family.   In the new family under the governance of *Abba*, children have the distinct advantage of the caring discipline of a loving Parent. The purpose of discipline is correction and growth toward fuller responsible freedom, holy life, and happiness (Tertullian, *Of Patience* 11, *ANF* III, p. 714).

The key passage for this teaching is Hebrews 12, where we are reminded of "the exhortation that addresses you as children—'My child, do not regard lightly the discipline of the Lord, or lose heart when you are punished by him; for the Lord disciplines those whom he loves and chastises every child whom he accepts.' Endure trials for the sake of discipline. God is treating you as children; for what child is there whom a parent does not discipline? If you do not have that discipline in which all children share, then you are illegitimate and not his children. Moreover, we had human parents to discipline us, and we respected them. Should we not be even more willing to be subject to the Father of spirits and life? For they disciplined us for a short time as seemed best to them, but he disciplines us for our good, in order that we may share his holiness. Now, discipline always seems painful rather than pleasant at the time, but later it yields the peaceful fruit of righteousness to those who have been trained by it" (Heb. 12:5–11, NRSV; cf. Ps. 94:12; Prov. 3:11, 12).

The surest proof of inclusion in the family is the evidence of discipline. Those who are undisciplined have not yet entered the family. They cling to their own righteousness, resist the call to repent, and no longer benefit from the discipline always found in a loving, caring family. But under the disciplined life of faith, "How great is the love the Father has lavished on us, that we should be called children of God! And that is what we are!" (1 John 3:1). It is the disciplining Father who is preparing believers to "share in the inheritance" (Col. 1:12).

Adoption into the family does not imply a relaxation of all requirements or claims. Ironically the presence of spiritual struggle is itself evidence of adoption (Baxter, *PW* XXI, pp. 219–31). For after the Lord "takes possession of the heart," one "begins to hate what before he loved, and to love what he hated before. Thence comes that continual battle which is between flesh and the Spirit in God's children, while the flesh and the natural man, being corrupt, lust for things pleasant and delightful to themselves, and are envious in adversity and proud in prosperity, and every moment prone and ready to offend the majesty of God. But the Spirit of God who bears witness to our spirit that we are the sons of God, makes us resist filthy pleasures and groan in God's presence for deliverance from this bondage of corruption, and finally to triumph over sin so that it does not reign in our mortal bodies. Other men do not share this conflict since they do not have God's Spirit" (Scots Confession, XIII, *BOC* 3.13).

The Modern Dilution: Creation Imagined as Unlost Needs No Reconciliation. Modern secular piety claims on the simple grounds of creation a natural relation with God unimpeded by sin. All privileges and immunities of unhampered goodness are imagined to be equally distributed as if without reference to any actual history of sin.

This presumption tempts toward antinomianism. The secular imagination posits that if I am basically good and getting ever better, and my self-interested passions are reliable guides, if there might be a divine Giver or parent or source, such would not reject me for any conceivable reason. Such is the diluted modern version of the teaching of adoption by nature, not grace. A God who can't say no draws persons who never lack good intentions toward a Christ without a cross. Conscience amid modernity has become so seared that we imagine we are welcomed by God precisely while we are doing what God condemns (Reinhold Niebuhr, *NDM; Pious and Secular America*).

Christian teaching assumes the opposite: that the history we share with Eve and Adam has come to a disastrous end—our own sin, lacking spiritual vitality. The Father who loves all humanity compassionately does not approve all human folly. The Son who died for all did so precisely because prodigal humanity was resisting his goodness (Mark 10:33, 34).

God as caring *Abba,* a central teaching of classical Christianity, has been preempted by a thinner modern version of the "father[mother]hood of God and the brother[sister]hood of humanity" that denies the history of corrupted freedom and, in the interest of tolerance, romanticizes human innate goodness. This view promotes a distorted vision of the family of God, as if human creation had never actually fallen, so as to remove any need for rebirth from above. Though modernity clings desperately to the belief that we are by nature children of God, postmodern Christianity knows that we are "by nature children of wrath" (Eph. 2:3, KJV). It is only by the grace of adoption that we become children of God "through faith in Christ Jesus" (Gal. 3:26).

Total Divestment of Idolatries.   Adoption into the family of God implies turning completely away from reliance upon the corrupted world. Paul exhorted the Corinthians radically to turn from idolatries as sons and daughters in this family: "What agreement is there between the temple of God and idols?" (2 Cor. 6:16).

This requires saying a clear no to idolatrous loves within the world in order better to manifest the love of God for the world: "Therefore come out from them and be separate, says the Lord. Touch no unclean thing, and I will receive you. I will be a Father to you, and you will be my sons and daughters, says the Lord Almighty" (2 Cor. 6:17, 18; in reference to Isa. 52:11 and 2 Sam. 7:14; John Chrysostom, *Hom. on 2 Cor.* XIII, *NPNF* 1 XII, pp. 344–45). The walk of faith occurs in the world, but its guidance is not from the world. Finite goods are gratefully received and used, but not worshiped or served (1 Cor. 7:31; cf. 1 John 2:15–17; Calvin, *Inst.* 2.8).

Assurance of Salvation Through the Witness of the Spirit

One may actually own a vast treasure and be wholly unaware of it. The issue at stake in the teaching of assurance is how one comes to know one is included in the inheritance of the family of God. If it should be the case that one's regenerated life continued endlessly to be filled with doubtful conjectures as to the ground or truth claims of the new life, then the quality of the new life would be jeopardized and its vitality undermined by ambiguity. Grace provides whatever is needed to make the recognition of grace plausible (Ursinus, *Comm. Heid. Catech.,* pp. 323–24). The Spirit is working to find a way to overcome our resistances, even though this takes time, and though assurance may have to be discovered amid rigorous challenges (Calvin, *Inst.* 3.2, 3.8.8, 3.20; J. Wesley, *WJW* VI, pp. 77 ff.).

Assurance Defined.   Assurance is that part of Christian teaching that asks how personal salvation is made credible, plausible, knowable. Faith promises to bring to the faithful a blessed assurance of adoption into the family of God (Baxter, *PW* IX, pp. 53–59).

Scripture promises that this assurance is given by the direct witness of the Holy Spirit (Rom. 8:15, 16). Though the whole economy of salvation is the work of the triune God, assurance is a work of the Spirit. As the Father grants pardon, as the Son offers himself as a pardoning sacrifice, so the Spirit completes and consummates the mission of the Son by raising up new life, not only adopting the believer into the family of God, but also imparting to the believer the clear awareness of this reconciled relationship (Calvin, *Comm.* XIX, pp. 289–303). Wherever these testimonies and convictions are being clearly received and plausibly appropriated, there the grace of assurance is being awakened and applied by the Spirit (John Chrysostom, *Baptismal Instructions, ACW* 31, pp. 107–9).

The idea of assurance appears repeatedly in the New Testament: "Let us draw near to God with a sincere heart in full assurance [*plērophoria*] of faith" (Heb. 10:22). "We want each of you to show this same diligence to the very end, in order to make your hope sure" (Heb. 6:11).

God has not left assurance to conjecture. God attests it by his own Spirit. If one's acceptance is merely hypothetical and not experiential, then one's new life is placed under the cloud of doubt. "Hypothesis states that a thing may be so; experience alone proves the hypothesis to be true or false." Assurance of salvation "was known from scripture and experience to be the common lot of the people of God. It was not persons of a peculiar temperament who possessed it . . . during the forty years I have been in the ministry, I have met with at least forty thousand who have had a clear and full evidence that God, for Christ's sake, had forgiven their sins, the Spirit himself bearing witness with their spirit that they were the sons and daughters of God" (Clarke, *CT*, pp. 152–54).

Adoption and Assurance.   Adoption and assurance are so closely joined as to be virtually a single teaching: "Because you are sons, God sent the Spirit of his Son into our hearts, the Spirit who calls out, 'Abba, Father.' So you are no longer a slave, but a son; and since you are a son, God has made you also an heir" (Gal. 4:6, 7). By adoption we enter the family of God; by assurance we understand that this has indeed happened and is reliably knowable (Calvin, *Inst.* 1.17.7, 8; 3.24). The Spirit bears witness within, and assurance is what we feel as a result. It is by the power of the Spirit that we learn to say "Father" (Henry, *CWB* 6, pp. 664–65).

In ancient Rome, the adoption of a child was attested by a "witness to adoption." Similarly in our adoption into God's family, God's own Spirit witnesses jointly with our spirit that we are sons and daughters of God. Our cry, "Abba," is prompted by the Spirit's testimony within, so that we are assured that our filial confidence is no delusion (J. Wesley, *WJW* V, pp. 132–44; Shaw, *CT*, pp. 258, 259).

It is not accidental that grace offers assurance. Rather it is a property of grace itself to offer testimony of its own veracity. A property (*idion,* Lat. *proprium*) of grace is a quality that necessarily flows from grace, hence is found in all discrete expressions of grace. *Idion* is not the essence of a thing but that which always distinctively flows from something (contrasted by scholastic writers with accident, Heb. *miqreh,* Gk. *sumbebekos,* Lat. *accidens;* Pohle, *DT* VI, p. 378).

Conjoint Testimony of Scripture and Experience.   The witness of our own spirits corroborates the inner testimony of the Holy Spirit. It is testimony of a growing good conscience toward God. Even if it is not completely grown, one experiences good conscience as growing. This experiential testimony emerges directly out of reflection upon what we feel strengthening in our souls as a result of justifying grace. It is a conclusion drawn conjointly from scriptural testimony and a conscience void of offense (J. Wesley, *WJW* V, pp. 111–44).

Scripture teaches that everyone who has the fruit of the Spirit is a child of God. Wherever the fruits of the Spirit are being borne in experience, one is led naturally to conclude, Therefore I am a child of God (J. Wesley, *WJWB* I, sermons 10, 11; *WJW* V, pp. 111–34). "The testimony of the Spirit is an inward impression of the soul, whereby the Spirit of God directly witnesses to my spirit that I am a child of God; that Jesus Christ hath loved me, and given himself for me; and that all my sins are blotted out, and I, even I, am reconciled to God. . . . Thus 'the testimony of our own spirit' is, with the most intimate conviction, manifested to our hearts, in such a manner as, beyond all reasonable doubt, to evince the reality of our sonship" (J. Wesley, *WJWB* I, sermon 10, pp. 274, 276).

Conscience Bears Corroborating Witness. The believer's spirit bears testimony, responsive to and alongside that of the Holy Spirit, that one is adopted into the family of God. The function of conscience (*suneidēsis*) is to bear witness to God's requirement, "accusing or else excusing" actions (Rom. 2:15, KJV). If Paul was required to speak hard truth, he remained confident that his conscience was bearing witness to confirm truth even against our resistances (Rom. 9:1). To the Corinthians he wrote, "Our conscience testifies that we have conducted ourselves in the world, and especially in our relations with you, in holiness and sincerity that are from God. We have done so not according to worldly wisdom but according to God's grace" (2 Cor. 1:12, 13).

The same Spirit who convinces the sinner of sin convinces the faithful of pardon. The same One who pardons assures of pardon. At the point of conviction, one may be less aware of good conscience than of sin. Yet in due time the confirmation of good conscience comes to patient belief (1 Pet. 3:16–21).

Whether Temptations Continue Following Assurance. The teaching of adoption does not deny that the faithful ordinarily go through periods of temptation and doubt and may temporarily experience the eclipse of God. As Christ on the cross seems to express the experience of abandonment (Matt. 27:46), so do Christians at times feel intense doubt and inner division. Amid such trials, no prayer is more rightly conceived than "Lord, I believe; help thou mine unbelief" (Mark 9:24, KJV)—the experience of "faith, yet not full faith" (Augustine, *Sermons on New Testament Lessons* LXV, *NPNF* 1 VI, p. 454).

The Westminster Confession carefully formulated the assuring work of the Spirit through trials in this way: "True believers may have the assurance of their salvation [in] divers ways shaken, diminished, and intermitted; as, by negligence in preserving of it; by falling into some special sin, which woundeth the conscience, and grieveth the Spirit; by some sudden or vehement temptation; by God's withdrawing the light of his countenance, and suffering even such as fear him to walk in darkness and to have no light; yet are they never utterly destitute of that seed of God, and life of faith, that love of Christ and the brethren, that sincerity of heart and conscience of duty, out of which, by the operation of the Spirit, this assurance may in due time be revived, and by which, in the mean time, they are supported from utter despair" (Westminster Conf. XVIII, *CC*, p. 213).

Paul did not want the gospel to be drowned in ambiguities: "If you confess with your mouth, 'Jesus is Lord,' and believe in your heart that God raised him from the dead, you will be saved" (Rom. 10:9). No further evidence or stipulation or condition is needed or required. He wrote that "our Gospel came to you not simply with words, but also with power [*dunamei*], with the Holy Spirit and with deep conviction" (1 Thess. 1:5, *plērophoria*, full assurance).

Penitential self-examination focuses not upon the psychological dynamics of doubt and ambivalence, but upon the vitality of union with Christ: "Examine yourselves to see whether you are in the faith; test yourselves. Do you not realize that Christ Jesus is in you—unless, of course, you fail the test?" (2 Cor. 13:5).

God does not abandon the justified, unless irreversibly abandoned by them, but rather patiently offers grace to penitents and does not permit the faithful to be tempted more than they are able to bear (1 Cor. 10:13; *Trent* IV, *SCD* 804, 806, pp. 253–56; XXIV, *SCD* 980, p. 297). The divine requirement is not in principle impossible inasmuch as God does not deny sufficient grace to anyone, even those foreknown by God to reject grace (Councils of Orange II, *SCD* 200, p. 81; Quiersy, *SCD* 319, p. 121; *Trent* IV, *SCD* 827, 828).

Johannine Testimony to Assurance.   The teaching of assurance is written into the very purpose of the Johannine writings: "I write these things to you who believe in the name of the Son of God so that you may know that you have eternal life" (1 John 5:13).

A complex array of testimony points toward God's saving deed: "He did not come by water only, but by water and blood" (1 John 5:6). "The Spirit renews the mind, the water is serviceable for the laver [of cleansing], and the blood refers to the price. For the Spirit made us children by adoption, the water of the sacred Font washed us, the blood of the Lord redeemed us" (Ambrose, *Of the Holy Spirit* III.X.68, *NPNF* 2 X, p. 145; cf. 1 John 5:7, 8). "We accept man's testimony, but God's testimony is greater because it is the testimony of God which he has given about his Son" (1 John 5:9).

The inner witness of the Spirit of God validating the salvation event is available to all believers: "Anyone who believes in the Son of God has this testimony in his heart" (1 John 5:10; Baxter, *PW* XX, pp. 137–39). It seems implausible that with all this testimony, the earnestly seeking believer would still remain completely unillumined or unaware or unsure of its import. The teaching of assurance seeks to establish the reliable knowability of the saving event (Baxter, *PW* XX, pp. 151–54).

The receiving of assurance assumes a risk-laden choice to seek to do God's will. Only on this path will one "find out whether my teaching comes from God" (John 7:17). One does not first by reasoning "find out," conveniently reserving any decision to do God's will until later. Jesus taught, "By their fruit you will recognize them" (Matt. 7:16). "A bad tree cannot bear good fruit" (Matt. 7:18; Calvin, *Comm.* XVI, pp. 362–66).

Experiential Confirmation of Divine Testimony

A dramatic scriptural prototype of the experience of assurance is the man born blind whose sight Jesus restored, who did not pretend to explain how the change had occurred but was grasped by a single experiential fact: "Whether he is a sinner or not, I don't know. One thing I do know. I was blind but now I see!" (John 9:25).

By experience one may know as certainly as one knows that one is alive that one has been given new life in Christ. As an apricot is known experientially by its taste, so is assurance known by its inward testimony and adoption known experientially by its consequent new relationality. Paul did not hesitate to appeal to the experience of his hearers: "Have your great experiences been in vain?" (Gal. 3:4, NEB). "They had *experienced* the presence of God amidst their persecutions" (Calvin, *Comm.* XXI, p. 82, italics added).

Experiencing Faith, Hope, and Love.   The growing presence of faith, hope, and love confirm the Spirit's assuring work. Wherever *faith* is found trusting in God through human suffering, the Spirit's work is being confirmed experientially (Athanasius, *Resurrection Letters* 8, pp. 126 ff.). "I know whom I have believed, and am convinced that he is able to guard what I have entrusted to him for that day" (2 Tim. 1:12). "Anyone who believes in the Son of God has this testimony in his heart" (1 John 5:10).

Wherever *hope* is buoyant, the Spirit's work is being confirmed in time. "For in this hope we were saved" (Rom. 8:24), a hope that "does not disappoint" (Rom. 5:5; cf. Rom. 15:13; Titus 3:7; 1 John 3:3; Heb. 6:18, 19).

Wherever faith is becoming active in *love*, the Spirit's work is being confirmed interpersonally. A form of knowing emerges directly out of this active loving: "We know that we have passed from death to life, because we love our brothers" (1 John 3:14). "We know that we have come to know him *if we obey* his commands" (1 John 2:3, italics added). By this we know that saving grace is making possible this obedience (Calvin, *Inst.* 2.16.5–7).

Whether Poverty of Spirit May Attest Forgiveness.   Suppose one experiences faith, hope, and love, yet still feels doubtful of salvation. Suppose that serious self-examination reveals only poverty of spirit. An irony needs examination just at that point: "This then is how we know that we belong to the truth, and how we set our hearts at rest in his presence whenever our hearts condemn us. For God is greater than our hearts, and he knows everything" (1 John 3:19, 20; Kierkegaard, "Discourses at the Communion on Fridays," *CDisc.*, pp. 297–303).

In extremis, the very hungering and thirsting for righteousness itself is evidence of the emerging governance of the Spirit. The testimony of conscience against a misdeed is precisely evidence of the empowering work of the Spirit, hence may be trusted in and rested upon. For God is greater than our self-condemnation. One may know the depths of grief over sin, the hunger and thirst for righteousness, and the prayer of the sinner, and still behold confidently the convicting work of grace leading toward assurance (J. Wesley, *WJW* VI, pp. 77–97; Phoebe Palmer, *Faith and Its Effects*).

The Spirit works amid different personal temperaments. A person with a guilt-prone temperament may need the Spirit's help to move beyond self-condemnation. One who is ignorant of one's own guilt may need the Spirit's help to awaken and intensify the awareness of values negated (Gregory the Great, *Pastoral Care* III). It is best not to impose one person's experience normatively upon another, as if assurance must be the same for each. It is different in every individual precisely because each person is an individual (Gregory Nazianzen, *Orat.* II.28–33, *NPNF* 2 VII, pp. 210–11).

The Cry: Abba!   A confluence of supporting testimony flows toward this assurance: the Spirit speaking through scripture, preaching, and sacrament; the direct and efficacious presence of the Spirit witnessing in the heart; the indirect testimony of conscience not accusing of sin; and the fruits of faith. Each of these builds the sense of assurance of salvation. "We know that we live in him and he is in us, because he has given us of his Spirit. And we have seen and testify that the Father has sent his Son to be the Savior of the world" (1 John 4:13, 14).

When the cry "Abba, Father" emerges spontaneously from the depths, then one can be assured that grace is working from justification toward sanctification. It is ironic that the pivotal testimony assuring us of our restored relation to God is itself a simple *cry:* "Father"!

The key text that sets forth the Christian teaching of assurance is Romans 8: "Those who are led by the Spirit of God are sons of God. For you did not receive a spirit that makes you a slave again to fear, but you receive the Spirit of sonship. And by him we cry, 'Abba, Father.' The Spirit himself testifies with our spirit that we are God's children" (Rom. 8:15, 16). It is by two corroboratory witnesses that this confirmation is received: God's Spirit and our own spirit together bearing the same testimony (*summartureō*). Together they convince and assure.

> Exults our rising soul,
>   Disburdened of her load,
> And swells unutterably full
>   Of glory and of God. . . .
>
> His Spirit us he gave,
>   Who dwells in us, we know:
> The witness in ourselves we have,
>   And all its fruits we show. . . .
>
> Our nature's turned, our mind
>   Transformed in all its powers;
> And both the witnesses are joined,
>   The Spirit of God with ours.

(C. Wesley WHNS 96)

The Certitude of Hope.   Pastoral counsel wishes simultaneously to constrain excessive or undue self-confidence while confirming and encouraging a due sense of assurance. The caring pastor seeks to nurture a humble, modest certitude of hope (*certitudo spei*) but not an overconfident, boastful, or arrogant certitude that would lead persons to assume that they can never fall from a state of grace (Tho. Aq., *ST* II–II Q47–49, II, pp. 1398–1405; cf. Gregory I, *Book of Pastoral Rule;* Trent VI.9).

The faithful may be relieved of unnecessary anxiety about their salvation by asking whether they indeed are persevering in doing good, whether they love to pray, whether they are patient in suffering, and whether they attend upon the ordinances of God faithfully (Thomas à Kempis, *Imitation of Christ* III.54 ff.; Tho. Aq., *ST* II–II, Q112.5).

It may become a pressing pastoral issue as to whether grace, once received, is able to be lost. The consensual tradition on the whole has answered that the awareness of saving grace can be temporarily lost. When Paul wrote that he was disciplining his body "so that after I have preached to others, I myself will not be disqualified for the prize" (1 Cor. 9:27), he was assuming that such a disqualification is possible for one already in the race. When he admonished the Philippians to "work out your salvation with fear and trembling, for it is God who works in you to will and to act according to the good purpose" (Phil. 2:12, 13), he assumed not only that God is working but that our responsive coworking is required to bring our salvation into behavioral embodiment. "I worked harder than all of them—yet not I, but the grace of God that was with me" (1 Cor. 15:10).

The Grace of Proximate Incertitude.   When Gregory the Great was asked by an elderly woman whether she could be absolutely certain of her election, he replied, "You ask me something which is both useless and difficult; difficult, because I am unworthy to receive a revelation; useless, because it is better that you be uncertain with regard to your sins, lest in your last hour you should be unable to repent" (*Epist.* VII.25; this translation in Pohle, *DT* VII, p. 380; see *NPNF*).

John Chrysostom knew long before Freud the capacity in the heart for self-deception: for "many of our own works are hidden from us" (*Hom. on 1 Cor.* 2; cf. *Trent* VI.9, p. 35). It is of a moral certainty, not a metaphysical certainty, that Paul wrote when he said, "I am convinced [*pepeismai*] that neither death nor life, neither angels nor demons, neither the present nor the future, nor any powers, neither height nor depth, nor anything else in all creation, will be able to separate us from the love of God" (Rom. 8:38, 39).

If coarsely objectified as a flat object of empirical inquiry, the address of the Spirit becomes suddenly elusive, self-effacing, touching our lives only to conceal that touch in mystery. Though one may be grasped immediately by the indwelling Spirit, the forms of empirical certainty that are available to us remain those of finite creatures. It is a certainty of hope not sight, based upon faith, not manipulable possession (2 Cor. 5:7; Calvin, *Comm.* XX, pp. 221–22).

6 Union with Christ and Sanctification

The life of the believer is united with Christ's life. By faith, Christ's life and the believer's life become one (Hilary, *Trin.* IX.55, *NPNF* 2 IX, pp. 174–75).

UNION WITH CHRIST

Christ is in the believer no less than the believer is in Christ (John 14:20; Rom. 8:1, 9–10; Gal. 2:20). Christ is our inseparable life (*to adiakriton hēmon zen*, Ignatius, *Letter to the Ephesians* 3:2; *Letter to the Magnesians* 15; *SHD*, p. 65), our life forever, our true life (Ignatius, *Magnesians* 1.2; *Letter to the Smyrnaeans* 4.1; *Ephesians* 11.1).

By faith one becomes united with Christ, shares in his life, being justified by his merits. Sin does not have dominion in this new person, who is "not under law, but under grace" where sin no longer reigns unchecked (Rom. 6:14).

Christ's Life in Us

The sinner does not deserve life, but receives it through faith in Christ. Christ does not deserve death, but offers death through obedience on the cross for the sinner. In this way, Christ lives in the faithful, who are treated as if righteous, clothed in Christ's righteousness, adopted as children of the family of God (Phil. 1:21; Calvin, *TAAL*, pp. 134–35). In response to justifying grace, the sinner is restored to that communion with God which once characterized the original human condition. Human consciousness still possesses its own characteristic faculties, features, and individuality, yet is energized, informed, and penetrated by the life of Christ (Augustine, *On the Spirit and the Letter* 38, *NPNF* 1 V, pp. 98 ff.). The believer partakes of that new humanity of which Christ is the head, the body of Christ.

Paul stressed union with Christ's death and resurrection (Rom. 6). John stressed union with the Incarnate Son (John 6:53–57). The letters of Peter stressed sanctification as a partaking in God's nature (2 Pet. 1:4; cf. 1 Cor. 10:16–17; Rom. 8:17; K. F. A. Kahnis, *Die Lutherische Dogmatik* II, pp. 273 ff.). In each case the apostles were speaking of a singular unity that the believer experiences with God the Father through the Son: "Our fellowship is with the Father and with his son, Jesus Christ" (1 John 1:3).

In Christ.   In this intimate communion, Christ is said to be *in* the believer and the believer *in Christ*. "Therefore, there is now no condemnation for those who are *in* Christ Jesus" (Rom. 8:1, italics added). "Remain in me, and I will remain *in you*" (John 14:5, italics added). To be "in Christ" and to "have Christ in us" are interchangeable terms. "On that day you will realize that I am in my Father, and you are in me, and I am in you" (John 14:20).

In Galatians this union is most fully expressed. Being in Christ means that one participates in his death and resurrection: "I have been crucified with Christ and I no longer live, but Christ lives in me. The life I live in the body, I live by faith in the Son of God" (Gal. 2:20). This indwelling fellowship has moral consequences, implying a death to sin: "Those who belong to Christ Jesus have crucified the sinful nature with its passions and desires" (Gal. 5:24). It implies a dying to the world, a renunciation of all that keeps one turned away from God: "May I never boast except in the cross of our Lord Jesus Christ, through which the world has been crucified to me, and I to the world" (Gal. 6:14). "Therefore, if anyone is in Christ, he is a new creation; the old has gone, the new has come!" (2 Cor. 5:17; Calvin, *Inst.* 3.11.10; 4.15.6).

In this fellowship, the Spirit works so as to nurture a profound union of the soul with Christ (Calvin, *Inst.* 3.1). Union with Christ is offered to those in whom the Spirit dwells. It is a reciprocal indwelling mediated by the Spirit common to the Head and his members (Chemnitz, *TNC*, pp. 150–52; Pope, *Compend.*, II, p. 394). "He who unites himself with the Lord is one with him in spirit" (1 Cor. 6:20; Tatian, *Address to the Greeks*, XV, *ANF* II, p. 71). Paul's desire was simply to "be found in him" (Phil. 3:9).

The Indwelling Spirit of the Triune God.   Christ himself dwells in the justified soul born of God. The Son is present by the power of the Spirit, making known the love of the Father. The Spirit of the triune God is said to dwell in the believer (Augustine, *On Trin.* XV.18, 32). "We, apart from the Spirit, are alien and remote from God, and are united with the Godhead by participation in the Spirit" (Athanasius, *Ag. Arians* III.24, *ECF,* p. 297).

The Spirit indwells in the family of God. The Spirit carries on Christ's work, calling, gathering, transforming persons into likeness to Christ, communicating to them the benefits of redemption (Irenaeus, *Ag. Her.* V.8, *ANF* I, p. 533). Where the Spirit resides, Christ resides (Rom. 8:9–11).

Christian experience attests the peculiar, gracious presence of one God in three persons. "We know that we live in him and he in us, because he has given us of his Spirit. And we have seen and testify that the Father has sent his Son to be the Savior of the world. If anyone acknowledges that Jesus is the Son of God, God lives in him and he in God" (1 John 4:14, 15). The principal mark of the indwelling Spirit of God is responsive love: "If anyone loves me he will obey my teaching. My Father will love him, and *we* [Father and Son] will come to him and *make our home* [*monēn*] with him" (John 14:23, italics added). God is taking up abode in the faithful through the indwelling Spirit (Gregory Nazianzen, *Orat.* XXX, *NPNF* 2 VII, pp. 309 ff.). The faithful "ascend through the Spirit to the Son, and through the Son to the Father" (Irenaeus, *Ag. Her.* V.36.2, *ANF* I, p. 567).

"All the Trinitarian relations are reflected in the justification of the sinner. Thus regeneration corresponds to the generation of the Logos by the Father; adoptive sonship and the accompanying participation of the soul in the Divine Nature corresponds to our Lord's natural sonship and his consubstantiality with the Father; the indwelling of the Holy Ghost and His union with the soul, on the other hand, corresponds to the divine process of Spiration, inasmuch as it is preeminently a supernatural union of love" (Pohle, *DT* VII, p. 376; cf. John 14:23; 17:20 ff.).

To the Father through the Spirit, Paul prayed for the indwelling of Christ: "I pray that out of his glorious riches he may strengthen you with power through his Spirit in your inner being, so that Christ may dwell in your hearts through faith. And I pray that you, being rooted and established in love, may have power, together with all the saints, to grasp how wide and long and high and deep is the love of Christ, and to know this love that surpasses knowledge—that you may be filled to the measure of all the fullness of God" (Eph. 3:16–19).

Partaking of the Divine Nature

Life in union with Christ is like communion with the living Lord through the sacrament, partaking, eating, and drinking of him who was made known to the Emmaus disciples in the breaking of bread (Luke 24:35).

Participatio Christi.   As Christ partakes of the Father, so the believer partakes of Christ. This occurs prototypically in Eucharist: "Is not the cup of thanksgiving for which we give thanks a participation in the blood of Christ? And is not the bread that we break a participation in the body of Christ? Because there is one loaf, we, who are many, are one body, for we all partake of the one loaf" (1 Cor. 10:16, 17; Irenaeus, *Ag. Her.* V.2, *ANF* I, p. 528).

When Jesus' detractors asked, "How can this man give us his flesh to eat?" Jesus answered, "Whoever eats my flesh and drinks my blood remains in me, and I in him. Just as the living Father sent me and I live because of the Father, so the one who feeds on me will live because of me. This is the bread that came down from heaven" (John 6:56–58).

Believers live in Christ in all they do. They die with him, are raised with him, dwell with him eternally, and he with them. They share his righteousness, become sons through his sonship, heirs through his inheritance, pardoned through his sacrifice (Hippolytus, *Discourse on Holy Theophany* 8, *ANF* V, pp. 236–38; Calvin, *Inst.* 3.11, 4.17).

Theosis: *In What Sense Does Sanctifying Grace Enable the Soul to Partake of the Divine Nature?* Through Christ's glory and goodness, "he has given us his very great and precious promises, so that through them you may *participate in the divine nature*"—share the life of God in Christ through the Spirit—"and escape the corruption in the world" (2 Pet. 1:4, italics added; Tertullian, *Ag. Marcion* II.26–27, *ANF* III, pp. 317–19; Hippolytus, *Refutation of all Her.* X.29, *ANF* V, p. 151).

In new birth the regenerate shares in the nature of the spiritual progenitor. "No one who is born of God will continue to sin, because God's seed remains in him; he cannot go on sinning, because he has been born of God" (1 John 3:9). "So then, just as you received Christ Jesus as Lord, continue to live in him, rooted and built up in him" (Col. 2:7). Athanasius stated the principle in an influential formula: "He was made man that we might be made God [*theopoiēthōmen*]" (*Incarnation of the Word* 54, *NPNF* 2 IV, p. 65). "He was not, therefore, first man and then God, but first God and then man, in order that He might rather deify us" welcoming us into himself (Athanasius, *LCHS, To Serapion* 1.24, pp. 125–28; cf. *Defence of the Nicene Council* 14, *NPNF* 2 IV, p. 159; Irenaeus, *Ag. Her.* IV.38; Origen, *Ag. Celsus* III.28), bringing us into union with himself (Gregory of Nyssa, *Ag. Eunomius, NPNF* 2 V, pp. 172–81; Augustine, *Enchiridion* 37; sermon 144, 1; Pohle, *DT* VII, p. 342). "Being made like to God" is a consummating work of the Spirit (Basil, *On the Spirit* IX.23, *NPNF* 2 VIII, p. 16; cf. Ps. 82:6).

"The Holy Spirit works in us by himself, truly sanctifying us and joining us to himself; and by this coalescence and union of ourselves with him he makes us sharers in the divine nature . . . beautifying human nature with the splendour of the divinity" (Cyril of Alexandria, *Thesaurus* 34; *MPG* 75.958; cf. *Letters* 1, *FC* 77, pp. 13–33), whereby God "inserts his own sanctity into us" (Cyril of Alexandria, *Comm. on John* X, intro. *MPG* 74.293; Bermejo, *SL*, p. 110).

God offers himself to the creature in such an intimate way that the creature is raised up to and transfigured by divine grace (John of Damascus, *OF* II.12; cf. Pohle, *DT* VII, p. 344). Hence it may be celebrated that "now we are children of God, and what we will be has not yet been made known. But we know that when he appears, we shall be like him [*homoioi autō*]" (1 John 3:2). Hence the ancient exegetes spoke of a *henosis* or union of the Holy Spirit with the soul (Cyril of Alexandria, *Letters* 1, *FC* 77, pp. 13–33; cf. Pseudo-Dionysius [the Areopagite] *The Ecclesiastical Hierarchy* 1, sec. 3, *CWS*, p. 198).

Whether Divine Attributes May Become Proximately Communicated. At this point we are cautioned not to fall into an idolatrous or pantheistic merging of creature and Creator, as have some mystics (John XXII, *Propositions Ag. Eckhart*

10, *SCD* 510, p. 196) and quietists (Innocent XI, *Errors of Michael de Molinos, SCD* 1225, p. 331). The point is clarified by distinguishing incommunicable from communicable divine attributes.

Some attributes of God, such as aseity, are beyond being communicated to finite creatures, hence called incommunicable attributes, as when God is addressed as "infinite in being and perfection, a most pure spirit, invisible" (Westminster Conf., II, *CC,* p. 197). There is no possibility of the finite creature being made infinite, hence no *theosis* in that sense.

Other divine attributes can be refracted in human willing and action, for God is "most loving, gracious, merciful, long-suffering, abundant in goodness and truth" (Westminster Conf. II, *CC,* p. 197). God's mercy and love can be manifested in human mercy and love. Communicable attributes of the infinitely just and wise One may be communicated to the proximately just and wise finite recipient. This is why they are called communicable attributes. Restored human nature, like unfallen human nature, possesses a capacity for full and mature responsiveness to God unlike that of any other creature (Clement of Alexandria, *Stromata* VI.12, *ANF* II, pp. 502–4).

Whether the Perfect Love Enabled by Grace in Persons Is Distinguishable from That Predicated in God.   Though these divine attributes are communicable, they never are communicated to creatures in the fullness in which they exist in God, but only proportionally in relation to the limited capacities of creatures. Creatures are always changing, progressing and regressing in virtue, whereas God's excellence is such that God is always infinitely good and just, eternally merciful and wise. In this sense it is foolish to ascribe any absolute divine perfection, such as holiness, to the human condition. The excellence of which humans are made capable by grace is perfect and complete in its own way, but this way is far short of the distinctive way in which God alone is eternally perfect (Tho. Aq., *ST* II–II, Q24.7; Suarez, *De Gratia, OO* IX.6, 11).

Accordingly, Jerome posited two sorts of perfect responsiveness: that absolute perfection which "we must measure by the excellence of God; the second, which is within the range not only of men, but of every creature, and is not inconsistent with our frailty," as exemplified by "Job, and Zacharias, and Elizabeth, [who] were called righteous, in respect of that righteousness which might some day turn to unrighteousness, and not in respect of that which is incapable of change" (Jerome, *Ag. Pelagians, NPNF* 2 VI, p. 450). To be always without sin is a characteristic of the Divine power only (Jerome, *Ag. Pelagians, NPNF* 2 VI, p. 452).

Augustine showed that those reborn and adopted are both *like* God as having the firstfruits of the Spirit and receiving divine gifts, and *unlike* God in having the remnants of concupiscence lodged in the flesh (Augustine, *On Forgiveness of Sins and Baptism* 8–12, *NPNF* 1 V, pp. 47–49). We have been made sons and daughters of God, but "this is a grace of adopting, not the nature of the progenitor. The Son of God alone is God" (Augustine, *Comm. on Ps.* 50:2, Pohle, *DT* VII, p. 342; cf. *NPNF* 1 VIII, p. 178).

The Organic Cohesion of Life in Christ: A Vital, Spiritual, Indissoluble, Mystical Union

Whether the Union Is Organic.   Union with Christ is not adequately viewed as a union of comrades in shared moral endeavor or of business partners in a coalition of interests or as that between teacher and student. Nor does Christ dwell in us in the way that a parent influences a child or a therapist is close to a client. Rather, the union is conceived under organic analogies: cellular members of a living, functioning body, living branches of a living vine. As one "feeds and cares for" one's body, so "Christ does for the church—for we are members of his body" (Eph. 5:29, 30). Consequently, union with Christ is by definition a *living* union (Gal. 2:20; Col. 3:3, 4), not a conflation of separable objects. Mechanistic analogies would be adequate to inorganic things. Not so with life in Christ. "Behold," the Spirit says to the humanity cast out of the garden, "I plant thee in myself" (John Chrysostom, *Eutropius, NPNF* 1 IX, p. 259).

From a coordinate angle of vision, union with Christ is viewed as a form of dying, like seeds being planted. In *dying* to sin, the believer dies with Christ, entering daily into the full consecration that is willing to participate in God's suffering through service to the neighbor (Ignatius of Antioch, *Romans* 7–8, *AF,* p. 101). Union with Christ is therefore a participation in the resurrection. Through dying to sin, one is found to be *living anew, resurrected* in Christ (Calvin, *Inst.* 4.15–17). The life of faith is *hidden* in Christ, as if the body were buried. "For you died, and your life is now hidden with Christ in God. When Christ, who is your life, appears, then you also will appear with him in glory" (Col. 3:3, 4).

According to Leo, the Transfiguration taught the disciples to receive death without fear, its "foremost object" being "to remove the offence of the cross from the disciple's heart, and to prevent their faith being disturbed by the humiliation of His voluntary Passion, by revealing to them the excellence of His hidden dignity." Moses and Elijah appeared talking with the Lord, "in Whom is fulfilled both the promise of prophetic figures and the purpose of the legal ordinances: for He both teaches the truth of prophecy by His presence, and renders the commands possible through grace" (Leo, *Sermons,* LI, *NPNF* 2 XII, p. 163).

Whether the Union Is Spiritual.   Union with Christ is a *spiritual* union whose enlivening energy comes from God the Spirit. Christ in us and the Spirit's indwelling are used interchangeably by Paul. The Father who raised the Son "will also give life to your mortal bodies through his Spirit, who lives in you" (Rom. 8:11).

Christ's power is felt because Christ himself is present (Formula of Concord XI, *BOC,* pp. 624–32; *SCF,* p. 245). "If Christ is in you, your body is dead because of sin, yet your spirit is alive because of righteousness" (Rom. 8:10). As the Son has life by partaking of the Father, so the faithful have life by partaking of the Son (John 6:53–57; 1 Cor. 10:16, 17). Without loss of individuality, the spirit of the person is energized by the Spirit of Christ, so that "he who unites himself with the Lord is one with him in spirit" (1 Cor. 6:17).

This is not an empirically visible natural union or a rationalistic union of ideas or a moral union of ethical purpose, but an organic union by which we become "members of his body" (Eph. 5:29), whereby his life becomes our life (Col. 3:3, 4; John Chrysostom, *Hom. on Col.* VIII, *NPNF* 1 XIII, pp. 293–96).

Whether the Union Is a Mystery.   Union with Christ is a *mystical* unity of a body transcending empirical identity. The unifying mystery is "Christ in you, the hope of glory" (Col. 1:27; cf. Eph. 5:28–32). What Christ by his active and passive obedience secured from the Father becomes ours by virtue of our fellowship with him (Calvin, *Inst.* 3.1.1).

So interpenetrating is this union that Luther could "say with confidence: 'I am [one with] Christ,' i.e., Christ's righteousness, victory, life, etc., are mine; and Christ, in turn, says, 'I am that sinner,' i.e., his sins, death, etc., are mine, because he adheres to me, and I to him; for by faith we are joined into one body and one bone" in an "inherence, which is by faith, and whereby Christ and I are made as it were one body in spirit" (Luther, *Comm. on Gal.* p. 171; *SCF,* p. 246). The righteousness conveyed in this union is the believer's by grace through faith, but not by nature or achievement. They are made partakers of its benefits (Bunyan, *Works* I, pp. 302–12).

The Ennobling of the Soul in Friendship with God.   Grace has the effect of making the soul *beautiful,* as if the soul were a sculpture being shaped by the divine artisan (Ambrose, Pohle, *DT* VII, p. 349; Tho. Aq., *ST* II–II, Q145, I, pp. 1780–82; cf. *Comm. on Ps.* 25). The image of the triune God is being once again imprinted upon the soul, where Christ is being concretely formed (Gal. 4:19; Rom. 8:29; 1 Cor. 3:16).

Grace has the effect of drawing human persons into *friendship* with God, wherein the just "become the friends of God" (Wisdom 7:14; cf. Prov. 8:30, 31). "I have called you friends" (John 15:14). In love as friendship (*philia*) there is conscious mutual benevolence and affection between persons (Augustine, *Comm. on John,* tractate 85, *NPNF* 1 VII, pp. 351–52; cf. Aristotle, *Nichomachean Ethics* VIII; Tho. Aq., *Comm. on Four Books of Sentences* III.27, Q2.1.1). In giving to the friend, one feels that one is giving something to oneself and extending one's own interests (1 John 3:17). God honors with his friendship those who receive sanctifying grace.

The work of the Spirit is less paternal than collegial, friendly, participative, empathic, engaging, working supernaturally on and proportionally within human levels of understanding. "By the Holy Spirit we are established as friends of God," wherein that which is "specially proper to the friendship" is "to take delight in a friend's presence," for "one reveals his secrets to a friend by reason of their unity in affection, but the same unity requires that what he has, he has in common with the friend" (Tho. Aq., *SCG* IV.21, p. 123; cf. Augustine, *CG* XIX.8, *NPNF* 1 II, pp. 405–6; Fortman, *AHS,* p. 179). Marriage is the most intense and enduring form of friendship (Tertullian, *To His Wife, ACW* 13, p. 35; John Chrysostom, *Hom. on Eph.* XX, *NPNF* 1 XIII, pp. 144–47), hence a fit analogy of the union of Christ with the church.

In Union with Christ, All Believers Are United with Each Other.   The union each member shares with the head, unites each one to all members of the body (1 Cor. 12:12–30). The unity of Christ is already given in Christ, yet it is to be achieved as a task by the community of faith in diaspora around the world (*The Unity We Have and the Unity We Seek,* Lund Assembly, 1952, *CC,* pp. 577–78).

This distinction is pertinent for ecumenical hopes and struggles. In Christ we are one. Our task is to embody that oneness. Already we have unity in Christ. The indicative of radical unity becomes an imperative for our active embodiment. God's gift becomes our task. Union is fully and freely given to us in Christ, if only partially and inadequately received in faith (1 Cor. 2:12). Faith unites and transcends cultural diversity. Though souls are many, faith makes them one (Augustine, *The Creed* 2.4, *FC* 27, p. 293). In faith the "multitude of believers were of one heart and one soul" (Acts 4:32).

The Unity of Blessings. In Christ all benefits of salvation are united. Each evangelical privilege is referred to the same source. The many are one in him: God has "blessed us with every spiritual blessing in Christ" (Eph. 1:3). From Christ all spiritual blessings come, in Christ they cohere, and toward him they finally move. As the Spirit distributes and applies them to each one individually, they appear diverse but cohere as one blessing. Righteousness is from Christ—"God made him who had no sin to be sin for us, so that in him we might become the righteousness of God" (2 Cor. 5:21; John Chrysostom, *Hom. on Eph.* I, *NPNF* 1 XIII, pp. 50–51).

SANCTIFICATION

Jesus prayed for his disciples, "Sanctify them by the truth; your word is truth" (John 17:17). Paul called those who heard the gospel to "offer your bodies as living sacrifices, holy and pleasing to God—this is your spiritual act of worship" (Rom. 12:1; *Barnabas* 18–21).

Through sanctifying grace the moral disposition is being gradually transformed so that one spontaneously loves good and resists evil. God the Spirit is enabling the human self to will the proportionally greater good, so that the human will is being brought into greater conformity with the will of God (Augustine, *Enchiridion, NPNF* 1 II, pp. 240 ff.).

Sanctifying grace is the culminating phase of the Christian teaching of salvation. It is a key feature of the Christian moral life, integral to the life of prayer, familiar in liturgy and catechetical instruction (*Early Liturgies, ANF* VII, p. 547). The sanctification of all things by the Spirit is a theme that has not only personal and individual significance, but also political-cultural-eschatological import (Cyril of Jerusalem, *Catech. Lect.,* IV.16, *NPNF* 2 VII, p. 23). The vision of perfect love and sustained radical responsiveness to grace is not merely an individualistic vision but a life shared in a community. That embodiment occurs in a corporate body, a supportive community, a *communio sanctorum* (Calvin, *Inst.* 4.1, 4.10–12).

In order to be taught once again, it must be reformulated in the light of central attestations of scripture and consensual exegesis. When we study sanctifying grace as a church doctrine, we soon learn that it is a mystery pointing beyond itself to the wholeness of the Spirit's own quiet, inconspicuous action in our midst (Cyril of Jerusalem, *Catech. Lect.* XVI, *NPNF* 2 VII, pp. 115 ff.).

Modernity has secularized the Christian teaching of sanctification, naturalizing and reducing it to betterment of human life or moral improvement or political achievement or upward social mobility (C. Becker, *The Heavenly City of the Eighteenth Century Philosophers*). This has led hypermodern Christian accommodators to serious misjudgments about salvation and sanctification, resulting in the loss of vitality of these teachings. Biblical sanctification themes have been cut and squeezed into pop metaphors of psychological growth or stress reduction or creative management or realpolitik or social change or moral development.

Toward a Consensual Redefinition of Sanctification Teaching

Admitting that there have been sharp differences among theologians on sanctification (particularly in the last four centuries), it is our limited purpose to state those points on which Christians of widely different viewpoints generally concur. Long centuries of debate, however, have contributed to persistent exaggerations and distortions of sanctification teaching. Protestants have spoken too confidently of faith as if without works of love, pietists of emotive faith as if without intellect, and popular Catholicism of works of merit without justifying grace.

We will draw heavily from all these sources where pertinent in seeking a balanced, ancient-ecumenical view. We especially seek a reappraisal of sanctification teaching that could be received without serious offense to Baptists and Catholics, that could be examined without serious difficulties by Calvinists, Arminians, Lutherans, Social Liberals, and Pentecostals with a sense that their own teaching is being affirmed and the mind of the consenting, believing church accurately represented. Specifically, I am determined to allay the suspicions of Reformed critics who might assume that I might be pressing for an Eastern Orthodox or Wesleyan-Arminian view so as to ignore the profound views of sanctification in the Augustinian-Lutheran-Reformed tradition. Hence I am deliberately quoting frequently from Augustinian-Lutheran-Reformed sources on sanctification, which I believe to be very largely consistent with the line of argument that we have thus far developed from the ancient-ecumenical consensus.

Initially, several issues await being carefully worked through: whether justifying grace is distinguishable from sanctifying grace; whether these are chronologically sequenced; how sanctification relates to discipline and habituation; whether sacramental analogies apply; and whether the behavioral outcomes or effects of sanctifying grace are describable.

What Is Sanctifying Grace?   The *Westminster Catechism* provided a concise definition of sanctification as "the work of God's free grace, whereby we are renewed in the whole man after the image of God, and are enabled more and more to die unto sin and live unto righteousness." The standard American Calvinist interpreter, Charles Hodge (*ST* III, p. 213), stated the following points on justification and sanctification upon which Reformed teachings agree (and upon which, I believe, the ancient patristic consensus would concur):

Justification	Sanctification
What Christ has done for us	What the Spirit does in us
A completed, transient act	A progressive, continuing work
A forensic declaration	An effect of continuing grace
Enabling a changed relation	Enabling a change of character between sinner and the holy God
The same in all recipients	Varied in recipients

Sanctification "consists in the gradual triumph of the new nature implanted in regeneration over the evil that still remains after the heart is renewed" (Hodge, *ST* III, p. 224). During the entire time that sanctifying grace is continuing to work—throughout life—the believer is daily called upon to confess, repent, and pray for forgiveness.

The new birth begins a life that grows in responsiveness to grace and presses on in the way of holiness. The fullness of sanctifying grace is not ordinarily received immediately at the beginning of conversion but grows through an extended developmental process (Bonaventure, *The Soul's Journey into God, CWS*, pp. 59 ff.; R. Bellarmine, *The Soul's Ascension to God*).

The key Pauline text is Philippians 3: "Not that I have already obtained all this, or have already been made perfect, but I press on to take hold of [*katalabō*, capture, appropriate] that for which Christ Jesus took hold of me. Brothers, I do not consider myself yet to have taken hold of it. But one thing I do: Forgetting what is behind and straining toward what is ahead, I press on toward the goal to win the prize for which God has called me heavenward in Christ Jesus. All of us who are mature should take such a view of things. And if on some point you think differently, that too God will make clear to you. Only let us live up to what we have already attained" (Phil. 3:12–16).

It belongs to God's saving *oikonomia* that the faithful shall be made holy (consecrated, sanctified) by the indwelling Spirit, for "from the beginning God chose you to be saved through the sanctifying work of the Spirit and through belief in the truth" (2 Thess. 2:13). "It is God's will that you should be sanctified: that you should avoid sexual immorality, that each of you should learn to control his own body in a way that is holy and honorable" (1 Thess. 4:3, 4; John Chrysostom, *Hom. on Thess.* IV, *NPNF* 1 XIII, p. 390).

Setting Apart Under Law and Gospel. To sanctify something is to set it apart for holy use, to separate it out from the profane world for sacred employment. To sanctify (Heb. *qadesh,* Gk. *hagiazō,* set apart, separate) means to consecrate for holy purpose, to make holy in the proximate sense that finite creatures may maximally participate in God's holiness.

Under Levitical law, persons and things were set apart, separated, and offered to God for holy purpose. The temple, the tithe, the seventh day, the priesthood, and the vessels for holy use are Hebraic examples of such a setting apart (Gen. 2:3; Exod. 30). The furniture and utensils of the temple and priestly vestments were sanctified or set aside, consecrated wholly to that special service.

When the Levitical law was fulfilled in Christ, these forms of consecration were transmuted so as to point to the advance of the believer in progressive conformity of the whole person to the will and image of God (Gregory of Nyssa, *FGG,* pp. 81–84). "So, my brothers, you also died to the law through the body of Christ, that you might belong to another, to him who was raised from the dead, in order that we might bear fruit to God" (Rom. 7:4). Those in Christ still have to do with the law, but now the law is seen as enclosed in Christ. The law is not abrogated, but fulfilled in Christ. The believer is released from the law as a basis of divine acceptance, but not as a standard of obedience to God the Father made known in the Son through the Spirit (Gal. 3; Heb. 10:1–18). "But now, by dying to what once bound us, we have been released from the law so that we serve in the new way of the Spirit, and not in the old way of the written code" (Rom. 7:6). "For we maintain that a man is justified by faith apart from observing the law" (Rom. 3:28). "Do we, then, nullify the law by this faith? Not at all! Rather, we uphold the law" (Rom. 3:31; Tertullian, *On Modesty* 6, *ANF* IV, p. 79).

Whether Proximate Holiness Is a Radical Gift.   God's sanctifying work in us is not reducible to our work of moral exercises. No one is sanctified by his or her own power. Though sanctification elicits and requires discipline, it is not limited to acts of discipline. It is from beginning to end a work of free grace.

Dirty hands cannot clean themselves. The blind cannot by wishing see. The dead cannot voluntarily decide to rise. However much moral initiative I may apply, I cannot while spiritually dead raise myself up to new life. The soul that is spiritually dead is unable of itself to make the slightest move toward God. It is as if from the grave that the sinner hears the voice of redeeming grace, and is raised by its power (Luke 7:22; 1 Cor. 15).

As with justification, sanctification is God's own work, not our work apart from grace, not our merit added to Christ's merit. Just as no one can boast for being born, no one upon receiving sanctifying grace can make a claim of merit upon one's growth process (Gal. 6:14). In the presence of God's own holiness, our sin, like Isaiah's, reaches for a "live coal from the altar to sanctify our lips" (Kuyper, *WHS*, p. 441).

Whether Radical Effort Is Required in Response to Radical Grace.   Paul prayed for the church at Thessalonica, "May God himself, the God of peace, sanctify you through and through" (1 Thess. 5:23)—entirely, "wholly" (RSV). The church proclaims, admonishes, and teaches this energetically "so that we may present everyone perfect [*teleion,* mature] in Christ" (Col. 1:28). "For not on those who sleep, but on the diligent divine favors are conferred" (Ambrose, *Comm. on Luke* IV.49, *MPL* 15.1626).

Though sin remaining after baptism is encumbering, we are called to "make every effort to live in peace with all men and to be holy; without holiness no one will see the Lord. See to it that no one misses the grace of God and that no bitter root grows up to cause trouble" (Heb. 12:14). "Sanctification does not exclude all cooperation," but calls for "unremitting and strenuous exertion" (Hodge, *ST* III, p. 226).

The Necessity and Limits of Sanctification Teaching.   The believer after regeneration remains an active self-determining agent, hence ever prone to fall from grace. The necessity of sanctification is argued in the Reformed tradition on the basis of the holiness of God, whose temple the believer is. The holy God does not abide sin in his temple. "I am the Lord your God; consecrate yourselves and be holy, because I am holy" (Lev. 11:44). "But just as he who called you is holy, so be holy in all you do; for it is written: 'Be holy, because I am holy'" (1 Pet. 1:15, 16; Barth, *CD* IV/2, p. 515).

The holiness demanded is that we faithfully receive the gift of atoning grace day by day. Christ died to deliver sinners from not only the guilt but also the power of sin (J. Wesley, *WJW* V, pp. 223 ff.). The cross does not intend merely to address humanity juridically with a formal declaration of pardon, but to reshape each hearer actually and behaviorally toward the way of holiness. The work of grace would be incomplete if it did not make provision for the holiness of the believer (Winslow, *The Work of the Holy Spirit,* p. 108). "The highest righteousness of man is this—whatever virtue he may be able to acquire, not to think it is his own, but the gift of God. He then who is born of God does not sin, so long as the seed of

God remains in him, and he cannot sin because he is born of God. But seeing that, while the householder sleeps, an enemy sowed tares, 'The righteous man accuses himself when he begins to speak'" (Jerome, *Ag. Pelagians*, *NPNF* 2 VI, p. 454, referring to 1 John 4, 5, and Prov. 18:17).

We are not being asked to be wise above what is written, but to be made wise by what is openly and clearly written, leaving the more perfect knowledge of that which is seen as if through a glass darkly to that future illumination when we will "know fully, even as . . . fully known" (1 Cor. 13:12). The gracious purpose of God that is present in creation is gradually being revealed in the history of redemption, to be carried forward to a fitting consummation. God would not write a drama without a fitting ending, even if that ending is not yet grasped but only glimpsed (Winslow, *The Work of the Holy Spirit*, p. 110).

In response to the unanswerable question of why God has elected some and not others to be set apart for special tasks, the early church relished the Mosaic saying "The secret things belong to the Lord our God, but the things revealed belong to us and to our children forever, that we may follow all the words of this law" (Deut. 29:29).

The Surprising Breadth of the Consensus.   Just how far otherwise polarized evangelicals and Catholics agree on sanctification is clear from the major Reformed and Baptist confessions, which reflect much of this patristic consensus. The New Hampshire Confession defined sanctification as "the process by which, according to the will of God, we are made partakers of his holiness," and confessed "that it is a progressive work; that it is begun in regeneration; and that it is carried on in the hearts of believers by the presence and power of the Holy Spirit, the Sealer and Comforter, in the continual use of the appointed means, especially the Word of God, self-examination, self-denial, watchfulness and prayer" (*CC*, p. 337).

God does not command what is impossible (Hermas, *Mand.* XII.3). "This sanctification is progressive through the supply of Divine strength, which all saints seek to obtain, pressing after a heavenly life in cordial obedience to all Christ's commands" (Southern Baptist Seminary, *Abstract of Principles*, 1859, XII, *CC*, p. 342). "Sanctification is the process by which the regenerate gradually attain to moral and spiritual perfection through the presence and power of the Holy Spirit dwelling in their hearts. It continues throughout the earthly life, and is accomplished by the use of all the ordinary means of grace, and particularly by the Word of God" (Southern Baptist Convention, 1925, *CC*, p. 348).

The Lausanne Faith and Order Conference defined sanctification as "the work of God, whereby through the Holy Spirit He continually renews us and the whole Church, delivering us from the power of sin, giving us increase in holiness, and transforming us into the likeness of His Son through participation in His death and in His risen life" (*CC*, p. 570). These evangelical declarations on sanctification from the Reformed tradition are much closer to the patristic consensus than the polemics following Augsburg and Trent would lead one to believe.

Called to Holiness

Without Spot or Blemish.   Christ set himself aside sacrificially for our sakes, that we might be totally set apart for him: "For them I sanctify myself, that they too may be truly sanctified" (John 17:19). Christ "gave himself for us to redeem us from all wickedness and to purify for himself a people that are his very own, eager to do what is good" (1 Tim. 2:14).

Like an incomparably loving bridegroom, "Christ loved the church and gave himself up for her to make her holy, cleansing her by the washing with water through the word and to present her to himself as a radiant church, without stain or wrinkle or any other blemish, but holy and blameless" (Eph. 5:25–27; Methodius, *The Banquet* 8, *ANF* VI, pp. 319–20).

The covenant people of God are being enabled by grace to live the holy life, hence they are called to holiness. The Father chose us in the Son "before the creation of the world to be holy and blameless [*hagious kai amōmous*] in his sight. In love he predestined us to be adopted as his sons through Jesus Christ" (Eph. 1:4, 5). How could it be then said that sanctification might be considered an incidental or ancillary teaching?

Whether the Faithful Are Rightly Called Saints. The English word *saint* derives from the Latin *sanctus*—holy, consecrated. A saint (Gk. *hagios*) is one set apart whom God's grace is making holy, who in heaven will share fully in God's holiness, and in whose life is already recognizable some fruits of a holy, charitable, merciful, humble life (Eph. 1:18; 3:8, 18).

Note that the same term is applied to those who are justified and newly born in faith (1 Cor. 1:2), being separated from sin and consecrated to God's service. Some saints were "shut up in prison" (Acts 26:10). The saints at times required emergency relief (Rom. 12:13; 15:26). Their hearts were refreshed by acts of love (Philem. 7).

Every member of the body is called to be holy even as God is holy. In heaven, the praises of God are being sung and celebrated by all voices. There all are sharing maximally in God's holiness. So it can and should be on earth. But the earthly harp, intended to sound harmoniously with divine holiness, has broken strings (Pss. 49; 99; 137:2; Kuyper, *WHS*, p. 437).

Walking Worthy of One's Calling: Ephesians 4–6. Having been made a partaker of this body, the believer is invited and enjoined to remain trapped no longer in the premises of the old life, with its weary history of sin (Athanasius, *Resurrection Letters* 7, pp. 96–107). The Christian walk is distinguished from the former life, which has been characterized by futility and darkness and hardened hearts ignorant of God's own saving purpose (Eph. 4:17, 18). "Having lost all sensitivity, they have given themselves over to sensuality so as to indulge in every kind of impurity, with a continual lust for more" (Eph. 4:19).

The way of life to be put aside is that of the old self "corrupted by its deceitful desires" (Eph. 4:22), falsehood, stealing, seething anger, and unwholesome talk (4:25–29). "Get rid of all bitterness, rage, and anger, brawling and slander, along with every form of malice" (4:31), sexual immorality, greediness, obscenity, idolatry, deception (Eph. 5:3–6; John Chrysostom, *Hom. on Eph.* XIII, XIV, *NPNF* 1 XIII, pp. 112–21).

The walk of the new life is one of mercy, tranquillity, holiness, love, self-giving, righteousness (Eph. 4:20–5:2), being filled with the Spirit, giving thanks always (5:18–21). It is a life that reshapes all human interactions and relations—between husbands and wives, parents and children, and all those one meets daily in the

· domestic and economic orders (Eph. 5:22–6:9). The first half of the letter to
Ephesus set forth the calling or vocation of the called-out community. The conduct or walk of the community through redeemed time is the subject of the last
half (beginning "Therefore," Eph. 4:1, KJV), thus showing the intrinsic connection
between indicative and imperative, calling and community, teaching and practice.

To walk worthy of their calling, the faithful were to walk in unity shaped by
love: "Be completely humble and gentle; be patient, bearing with one another in
love. Make every effort to keep the unity of the Spirit through the bond of peace.
There is one body and one Spirit" (Eph. 4:2–4). The oneness of Christ's body is
animated by one Spirit, "one Lord, one faith, one baptism; one God and Father
of all" (Eph. 4:5, 6), yet within this unity there are diverse gifts of the Spirit (Eph.
4:7–16). The purpose of these gifts is "to prepare God's people for works of service, so that the body of Christ may be built up until we all reach unity in the faith
and in the knowledge of the Son of God and become mature, attaining the whole
measure of the fullness of Christ" (Eph. 4:12, 13).

A growing resemblance to the likeness of Christ occurs in the Christian life.
The faithful "will in all things grow up into him who is the Head, that is, Christ"
(Eph. 4:15; Gregory of Nyssa, FGG, pp. 211–13). By growing up in the mind of
Christ, one "may live a life worthy of the Lord and may please him in every way:
bearing fruit in every good work, growing in the knowledge of God, being
strengthened with all power" (Col. 1:10, 11). "For those God foreknew he also
predestined to be conformed to the likeness of his Son" (Rom. 8:27). "Nor must
we omit a more complete investiture of the Christian with the graces of the Spirit:
the *active* graces—faith, love, zeal, self-denial; the *passive* graces—meekness, long-
suffering, gentleness, peace" (Winslow, *The Work of the Holy Spirit*, p. 118).

Whether Justifying Grace Is Distinguishable from Sanctifying Grace.   There is
only one grace—God's. But God's grace works through both justification by the
Son and sanctification through the Spirit. Justifying grace works *for* the sinner;
sanctifying grace works *in* the penitent faithful. Whereas justifying grace erases
guilt through forgiveness, sanctifying grace seeks to uproot the behavioral causes
of guilt through the reshaping of human behavior. Whereas justifying grace offers the sinner a righteousness not his own, sanctifying grace seeks to enable a
freely willed righteousness that emerges cooperatively by grace-enabled freedom
responding to God the Spirit (Westminster Conf. XI–XIII, *CC*, pp. 207–9).

Justifying grace is juridically a *finished* work of the Son on the cross, while
sanctifying grace is actively a *continuing* and current work of the Spirit in our
hearts and social processes. In sanctifying grace, God's Spirit works precisely
within and around us, seeking and enabling our cooperative response, calling
upon all our redeemed powers to be applied to working out our salvation while
God is working in us to will and to do according to his good pleasure (Phil.
2:12, 13; Athanasius, *Ag. Arians, NPNF* 2 IV, pp. 333–36; J. Wesley, *WJW* VI,
pp. 506–13).

The terms *prevenient* and *justifying*, when used with grace, encompass both the
period of preparation that leads up to saving faith in the cross, and saving faith
itself. "Conversion" points to that decisive moment in which the sinner becomes
radically aware of atoning grace on the cross and receives it as applied to him- or
herself. At that point the sinner begins, by repentance and faith through God's
pardon, to be cleansed from sin. This opens the door and makes way for the sanc-

tifying grace that would make us holy. The grace of justification thus does not stand alone as a unilateral, monergistic (singly worked without willing cooperation) imputed decree, but is joined and imparted freely and coresponsibly in an extended interpersonal process by the grace of sanctification (Augustine, *On Man's Perfection in Righteousness, NPNF* 1 V, pp. 159–76).

Calvin rightly argued that justification and sanctification cannot be separated (*Inst.* 3.11.10). "Although we may distinguish them, Christ contains both of them inseparably in himself" (*Inst.* 3.16.1). Wesley similarly granted that the term *sanctified* was "continually applied by St. Paul to all that were justified," and that "by this term alone, he rarely, if ever, means saved from all sin," and that "it behooves us to speak in public almost continually of the state of justification," adding that we must also learn to speak "more rarely, in full and explicit terms, concerning entire sanctification" (*Larger Minutes, CC,* p. 382).

"A Christian is profoundly sanctified in the very core of his personality when he or she is incorporated through living faith and the waters of baptism into the glorified Christ. The Christian thereby becomes a new creature, acquires something he did not have before, drinks in the very paschal life of the risen Lord." As "the interior reception of the person of the Spirit within the Christian," sanctification is "an essentially trinitarian event, performed by the benevolence of the Father, through the death of Christ, in the person of the indwelling Spirit" (Bermejo, *SL,* pp. 1, 15, 16).

Lutheran and Reformed teaching tends to emphasize the sin remaining after baptism, while Catholic and Anglican teaching tends to stress the sin removed by baptism. Each view, however, embraces key affirmations of the other, even though differences remain. Catholic teaching does not sit easily with the thought that actual grace is powerless to undo actual sin. Protestant teaching does not sit easily with the distinction between venial and mortal sins, and prefers the premise that no unblemished state of grace is long sustainable in the flesh (cf. Council of Trent and the Augsburg Apology; Westminster Conf. and *Baltimore Catech.*).

Grace and Habit

Whether Sanctifying Grace Is Expressed as Good Habituation.   Grace can only become habituated in moral character if it has first become actually offered and received. Actual grace, the divine gift enabling persons to perform acts beyond their natural powers, is distinguished from the grace of habituation by which sporadic actions are brought into recurrent patterns of willing (William of St. Thierry, *The Golden Epistle* II.7, *Works* IV, Irish Univ. Press, 1970–, pp. 84–85).

The Christian life is a continuing habituation in the reception of justifying grace. The will may move increasingly toward a sustained, habituated condition of receiving grace. What may have been a transient awareness at the first moment of receiving justifying grace gradually may become a more enduring, habituated condition, a more permanent state of free consent sustained by sanctifying grace through Word and Sacrament. It is this habit-shaping grace that is sometimes called sanctifying grace (Tho. Aq., *ST* I–II, Q49–52, I, pp. 351–53).

Sanctifying grace is viewed by medieval Scholastics as working through habituation by forming behavior into stable patterns of responsiveness in the way of holiness so as to reflect the divine sonship (Tho. Aq., *ST* I–II, Q49–62, I, pp. 793–853; Hall, *DT* VIII, pp. 255–66). This habituation is enabled by the

Spirit through Word and Sacrament, and cannot be acquired simply or naturally by practice (Suarez, *De Gratia, OO* IV.2).

Though Lutheran and Reformed Protestants may brace at such language, fearing that it might subtly turn God's grace into a human performance, it is upon careful inspection much closer to deeper Protestant intentionality than often imagined. For scripture describes grace through metaphors such as seed abiding in the person (1 John 3:9), a new birth by which the Spirit comes to dwell in the soul (John 14:23), a treasure hidden in earthen vessels (2 Cor. 5:7), and a temple of the Holy Spirit (1 Cor. 3:16; Calvin, *Inst.* 1.13.15; Goodwin, *Works* VI, pp. 459–70; cf. Luther, *Treatise on Good Works, WML* I, pp. 189–90).

Consecration and Communion.   By a growing, ongoing process of *consecration* the believer becomes further set apart for service. By a growing *union* with Christ the behavioral disposition of the believer grows in grace, becoming increasingly cleansed from sin negatively and positively drawn to virtue and a steady disposition to do that which is pleasing to God (Hilary, *Trin.* VIII.7–12, *NPNF* 2 IX, pp. 139–41). In this way habituating grace elicits both a distancing from sin and a deepening union with God (Ambrose, *Duties, NPNF* 2 X, pp. 43 ff.; Kierkegaard, *Works of Love*).

Both aspects are called sanctification, or the reception of sanctifying grace. Sanctifying grace thus works negatively by purging idolatries and inordinate desires and positively by engendering virtues and dispositions that reflect God's own goodness and enable the soul to please and enjoy God (Juliana of Norwich, *RDL*, pp. 105–7).

The Sacramental Expression of the Dialectic in Baptism and Holy Communion. The sacramental prototype of *consecration* is the believer's reception of the grace of *baptism,* by which the believer is incorporated into the body of Christ, made a member of the family of God by adoption into sonship or daughterhood. The baptismal gift is ratified by the gift of the Holy Spirit in confirmation and the growth of Christian affections, whereby the believer is equipped with those gifts requisite to proceed on the journey toward the celestial city. The grace offered in baptism is confirmed, accepted, and ratified in confirmation. By this grace, the soul is indelibly imprinted with the seal of the Spirit. Those who are thus baptized and who have confirmed their baptism by being equipped with gifts of the Spirit are called in the New Testament the elect, or the saints (those set-apart) of God, implying not merely that they are called to the way of holiness, but that they are already in some measure walking in the way of holiness and growing in that way, being equipped and endowed with the gifts necessary to walk in that way (1 Cor. 6:11; 1 Thess. 5:23).

The sacramental prototype of growing *union* with Christ is Holy *Communion,* by which the believer is daily fed and nourished in life in Christ and sustained as a member of the family of God and heir of life eternal. The eucharistic gift feeds and sustains the believer on the hazardous way of holiness (Cyril of Jerusalem, *Catech. Lect.* XXII, *NPNF* 1 VII, pp. 151–53; cf. Bunyan, *Pilgrim's Progress;* Kierkegaard, "Discourses at the Communion on Fridays," *CDisc.*). By means of the grace of these sacraments and the living Word that they make visible, the believer is enabled to cooperate with grace in doing good works meet for repentance, each motive and step of which is enabled by faith through grace (Luther, *Treatise on Good Works, WML* I, I, pp. 187–94).

Growth in Grace

Wheat and tares grow together (Matt. 13:30). Frequently imperfections remain mixed with even the best qualities of the most faithful.

The Principle of Individuality: Why Sanctifying Grace Works in Each Person Differently. It is characteristic of the Holy Spirit to work personally and uniquely in each recipient to do what is proportionally and contextually required and salutary to draw that person closer to God. If this were not so, then there would be nothing to do after receiving God's pardon, no works of love in response to grace, only quiet receptive passivity that does not cooperate or cowork. Growth in grace does not occur through quiescent inactivism or simply doing nothing (James 2:26; Innocent XI, *Errors of Michael of Molinos, SCD* 1221–28, pp. 331–37; J. Wesley, *JWO*, pp. 353–76).

Each individual who has received justifying grace is not on precisely the same plane or point as others in the process of receiving sanctifying grace. Simplistic egalitarian criteria, whether bureaucratic, legal, or casuistic, are insufficient to grasp the contextuality of the work of grace. An imagined absolute equality of grace would undermine its contextuality and the historical concreteness of the Spirit's work in persons one by one. The Spirit wishes to save each person, the whole person, to the uttermost, to show a way through every trial, and to bring the faithful to final blessedness (Col. 3:1–17; Eph. 4:15–5:20; Augustine, *Conf.* VII, *NPNF* 1 I, pp. 102–15).

The Increase of Grace: Maturation in Grace Through Faith. It is in this subjective-receptive sense that the apostles did not hesitate to speak of grace increasing. Persons "grow in the grace and knowledge of our Lord" (2 Pet. 3:18). Paul promised that the Spirit who supplies grace will "increase your store of seed and will enlarge the harvest of your righteousness" (2 Cor. 9:10).

Growth in grace occurs by personal receptivity to the gifts of the Spirit. The gifts of the Spirit are given that "the body of Christ may be *built up* until we all reach unity in the faith and in the knowledge of the Son of God and *become mature* [*teleion*], attaining the whole measure of the fullness of Christ" (Eph. 4:12, 13, italics added). The whole body is promised this maturity in due time, though in some members it may await resurrection and final judgment. The apostle promised that "God is able to make all grace abound to you, so that in all things at all times, having all that you need, you will abound in every good work" (2 Cor. 9:8; John Chrysostom, *Hom. on 2 Cor.* XIX, *NPNF* 1 XII, p. 369).

The dialectic of maturing growth is expressed by Gregory the Theologian, presiding at the Second Ecumenical Council of Constantinople, A.D. 381, upon resigning his office, when he said of his beleaguered flock that "if it be not yet in perfection, it is advancing towards it by constant increase" (Gregory Nazianzen, *Orat.* XLII.6, *NPNF* 2 VII, p. 387). "The path of the righteous is like the first gleam of dawn, shining ever brighter till the full light of day" (Prov. 4:18). Samson remained "unconquered so long as he kept the grace of the Spirit" (Ambrose, *Of the Holy Spirit* I.intro.12, *NPNF* 2 X, p. 116).

By faith "we do now receive a certain portion of His Spirit, tending toward perfection, and preparing us for incorruption, being little by little accustomed to receive and bear God. . . . This however, does not take place by a casting away of the flesh, but by the impartation of the Spirit. . . . What shall the complete grace of the Spirit effect, which shall be given to men by God? It will render us like unto Him" (Irenaeus, *Ag. Her.* V.8.1, *ANF* I, p. 533).

The Neonate Analogy.   The newborn baby is perfectly complete as a human being from a potential point of view, yet incomplete and immature from a developmental point of view. The infant must grow and develop in body, soul, moral judgment, and spirit in order to become more fully matured as a human being.

The perfection of the seed is different from the perfection of the flower, yet both are capable of change, growth, maturation, and progress (Matt. 13:31; 1 Cor. 3:6). Immaturity, in this way, is far from being inconsistent with perfection, as the language is normally used, for "A child may be immature as to stage of growth, but at the same time be perfectly healthy. Growth of the body requires time and development, while health is an immediate state of the body which determines its present enjoyment and growth. Likewise in the spiritual realm, a newborn saint may have the fullness of the Spirit, while being nevertheless quite immature, and in contrast a mature saint may lack the fullness of the Spirit. . . . What physical health is to the growth of the physical body, the fullness of the Spirit is to spiritual growth" (Walvoord, *HS,* p. 191).

New Birth and Growth.   The finished work of Christ's earthly ministry occurred on the cross. The finishing work of the Spirit in the believer is currently at work in all seeking to live by faith (2 Pet. 3:18; Calvin, *Inst.* 3.19–20).

Though regeneration quickens life, it "does not effect the immediate and entire deliverance of the soul from all sin. A man raised from the dead may be and long continue to be, in a very feeble, diseased, and suffering state" (Hodge, *ST* III, p. 220). Regeneration is the beginning of a process that seeks to be completed in a maturing work of the Spirit (called sanctifying grace), evidences of which are seen in one who is walking steadily day by day in the way of holiness.

New believers are addressed not as "spiritual but as worldly—merely infants in Christ," to whom must be given "milk, not solid food" (1 Cor. 3:1–3). It was to the justified believers that Paul wrote, "Let us purify ourselves from everything that contaminates body and spirit, perfecting holiness out of reverence for God" (2 Cor. 7:1). For the "sinful natural desires" continue to oppose the Spirit even in believers (Gal. 5:17). Those who are "in the light" may not yet be entirely cleansed of sin (1 John 1:7, 8).

Since the sinner must be born anew before beginning to grow in holiness, the order of the Spirit is first justifying, then regenerating, then sanctifying grace— an order that if reversed creates mischief. "Sanctification has its commencement and its daily growth in a principle of *life* implanted in the soul by the eternal Spirit; and to look for holiness in an individual still *dead* in sins is to look for fruit where no seed was sown" (Winslow, *The Work of the Holy Spirit,* p. 105).

Whether Life May Grow in Vitality.   It seems, from one point of view, that life as such is not capable of being increased, for a person either experiences life or not. One who is dying either has some measure of life or at the point of death none.

The criterion of death is irreversible unresponsiveness. If so, then how can the metaphor of life be used as if it were increasing? The answer lies in the way we use images of vitalizing, as though life were diminishing and increasing according to its strength and energy, or vitality (Tho. Aq., *ST* I–II, Q112.4.3).

Life is given us proportionally as we are capable of receiving (Jerome, *Ag. Jovinianus* II.23, *NPNF* 2 IV, p. 405). All who live are alive, but some are more alive than others. One may still remain barely alive while hanging by a thread. Hence Cyprian reasoned, "It is a slight thing to have been able to attain anything; it is more to be able to keep what you have attained; even as faith itself and saving birth makes alive, not by being *received*, but by being *preserved*. Nor is it actually the attainment, but the perfecting, that keeps a man for God" (*Epistles* VI, *ANF* V, p. 284, italics added).

Growth in grace may come from intently hearing the Word and receiving the grace of the sacraments, and by increasing in works of love. It is a process of becoming proportionally and behaviorally more just (*iustiorem fieri*) by way of increase, rather than simply being made just or becoming just (*iustum fieri*) in a forensic or imputed sense (Pohle, *DT* VII, p. 388; Joyce, *CDG*, pp. 8 ff.; Suarez, *De Gratia, OO* IX.2; De Bellevue, *L'Oeuvre du S. Esprit ou la Sanctification des Ames*).

Whether Sanctifying Grace Is Received Gradually or in an Instant.   Grace works in time, like leaven (Matt. 13:33). It requires a continual dying to sin: "put to death, therefore, whatever belongs to your earthly nature: sexual immorality, impurity, lust, evil desires and greed, which is idolatry" (Col. 3:5).

Living faith is like a long-distance race not completed in an instant but only by continued running—more a marathon than a sprint. Growing, leavening, racing (hence mortification-vivification) does not occur juridically or once for all in an instant but continuously and actively (Acts 20:24; 2 Tim. 4:7; Heb. 6:1; 12:1).

Yet even though there is a process of growth required for every believer, there still may be moments when such grace for growing is incomparably given. It is rash to rule out the possibility that the Holy Spirit may flood the soul with sufficient grace that the trajectory of continued walking in the way of holiness is firmly set, even if not irreversibly determined (Bonaventure, *The Soul's Journey into God* VII, *CWS*, pp. 110–16; Fletcher, *Checks, Works* VII; P. Palmer, *PPSW*, pp. 185–208).

Justifying faith may be in principle victorious over sin yet not have rooted sin out altogether (Methodius, *Resurrection* I.1–65, *ANF* VI, pp. 361–62; *SHD* I 190). Some exegetes have pursued the view that at the moment of regeneration the believer is entirely sanctified, so that there is no distinction between the instantaneous grace of justification and the instantaneous grace of sanctification (Zinzendorf, *Sixteen Discourses;* cf. J. Wesley, *JWO*, pp. 367–76; *JJW* II, pp. 10–13, 487–98; Tillett, *PS*, p. 455). Without denying that there may be some remarkable instances in which no intervening growth process seemed to be required between the newly born reception of justifying grace and the fully matured reception of sanctifying grace, that does not seem to be the experience of most believers (John Cassian, *Conferences* XIV, *NPNF* 2 XI, pp. 435–45; J. Wesley, *WJW* VI, pp. 77–99).

Most who have experienced justifying grace find that the roots of pride and idolatry and anger have not been destroyed, but that they are being called upon to continue to struggle with the vestiges of sin, even though they have experienced complete pardon of their sins. A continuing work of grace is required, in the experience of most believers, following justification. For sin still remains or has remnants of vitality in the life of the believer even after receiving justifying grace (Augustine, *On Man's Perfection in Righteousness*, 19 ff., *NPNF* 1 V, pp. 164 ff.; Goodwin, *Works* VI, pp. 88–95; cf. J. Wesley, *WJWB* I, sermons 13, 14, *WJW* V, pp. 144–70).

Yielding and Filling: Mortification and Vivification

Faith requires an attitude of yieldedness or readiness to respond to the promptings of grace by the Spirit. By this daily yielding, one is enabled to become more conformed to God's will "that we may share in his holiness" (Heb. 12:10).

The Old Sin Nature Not Absolutely Dead in New Believers.   The new birth undermines but does not destroy the old nature, the flesh, the old Adam. The old orientation to the flesh comes under the influence of the Spirit, but has not been eliminated altogether (Rom. 7:21–23).

If all possibility of temptation or evil were eliminated, there would be no growth in grace, or confession, or prayer. But such is not the life in the Spirit. Flesh continues after justification to war against spirit. Previously the flesh had almost complete sway. Now the flesh is crucified with Christ, but this does not imply that the flesh has in every sense been utterly removed or the way of the flesh wholly circumvented. For flesh continues to lust against spirit (Gal. 5:17; John Chrysostom, *Baptismal Instructions, ACW* 31, pp. 141–42, 182–84).

The point is humorously put by Gregory: In baptismal faith the malignant spirit is "gone out of you, being chased by baptism. He will not submit to the expulsion. . . . If he finds in you a place, swept and garnished indeed, but empty and idle, equally ready to take in this or that which shall first occupy it, he makes a leap into it, he takes up his abode there with a larger train" (Gregory Nazianzen, *Orat.* XL.35, *NPNF* 2 VII, p. 373).

Self-denial.   Therefore *sarx* (the orientation to the flesh) must die daily (Rom. 8:1–11). Participation in Christ's death and resurrection is an event that must be chosen and rechosen day by day (Calvin, *Inst.* 3.3). Jesus assumed that the will is free to follow when he said, "If anyone would come after me, he must deny himself and take up his cross and follow me" (Luke 9:23).

Though the old life according to the flesh is not completely annihilated by the Spirit's regenerating activity, the new self is being called to live as if the old self were in fact truly dead (Col. 3:10; Eph. 4:24). You are to "count yourselves dead to sin and alive to God in Christ Jesus. Therefore do not let sin reign in your mortal body so that you obey its evil desires. Do not offer the parts of your body to sin, as instruments of wickedness, but rather offer yourselves to God, as those who have been brought from death to life" (Rom. 6:11–13).

One may grow in yieldedness to grace by daily surrender and obedience. "Therefore, brothers, we have an obligation—but it is not to the sinful nature, to live according to it. For if you live according to the sinful nature, you will die; but if by the Spirit you put to death the misdeeds of the body, you will live, because those who are led by the Spirit of God are sons of God" (Rom. 8:12–14).

Yieldedness: Total Surrender of Will. Under sin we once committed our bodies unreservedly to a kind of "slavery to impurity and every kind of wickedness." Now that grace has come in Jesus Christ we are free to commit our bodies totally "to righteousness leading to holiness" (Rom. 6:19).

The Christian life requires the simple surrender of the will to God. The will renewed through grace is empowered to yield that God's will "be done on earth as it is in heaven" (Matt. 6:10). In proportion as God's will is done in one's life, one is walking in the way of holiness. In proportion as one is able truly to say, "Nevertheless not my will but thine be done" (Luke 22:42), just in that degree is one receptively cooperating with sanctifying grace (John Cassian, *Conferences, NPNF* 2 XI, pp. 458–60).

The depth of the work of the Spirit within personal freedom is conditional upon the degree of yieldedness of the believer. The disciples at Pentecost were fully yielded, as was Peter before the Sanhedrin (Acts 2:4; 4:8), and the worshiping community after they had prayed (Acts 4:31). The martyr Stephen was fully yielded to the Spirit as he faced death (Acts 7:55), as were the apostles Paul (Acts 9:17) and Barnabas (Acts 11:25; cf. *The Martyrdom of Polycarp, AF,* pp. 139 ff.).

Subordination as the Way of the Servant. Consensual Christian teaching did not uniformly affirm only passive or restricted roles for women. It sought a theological language shaped by the reciprocity implicit in the creation of women and men (John Chrysostom, *Hom. on Eph., NPNF* 1 XIII, pp. 115–16, 123–24, 143–52; cf. David Ford, *Mysogynist or Advocate: Chrysostom on Women,* Drew dissertation, 1989). But this did not mean that all subordination metaphors must be abandoned, for it is none other than God the Son who has taken on the ultimate subordinate role and called men and women to follow this serving model in relating to each other as male (serving and caring for the woman) and female (serving and caring for the man).

Poverty is the way of the One who became poor for our sakes that we might become rich in spirit. So is subordination, humility, and yieldedness the way of the One who became lowly for our sakes that we might become exalted in spirit (John Chrysostom, *Hom. on Phil.* VII, *NPNF* 1 XIII, pp. 212–18; *Hom. on 1 Cor., NPNF* 1 XXI, pp. 153–57).

Becoming Filled with the Spirit. Numerous references are made, particularly in the Lucan tradition, to the condition of being fully yielded to or filled with the Spirit (*pimplemi,* Luke 1:15, 41, 67; Acts 4:8, 31; 13:9; *pleroo,* Acts 13:52). This refers to the calling to submit completely to the indwelling Spirit in order that God's own work may be accomplished (Calvin, *Comm.* XVIII, p. 561).

Immediately after his baptism Jesus was "full of the Holy Spirit, returned from the Jordan, and was led by the Spirit in the desert" (Luke 4:1). This filling was attested in the lives of the Baptist, Elizabeth, Zacharias, and the blessed Virgin (Luke 1). Similarly after the descent of the Spirit at Pentecost upon the disciples, "All of them were filled with the Holy Spirit" (Acts 2:4).

In Acts it is reported repeatedly that persons are filled with the Holy Spirit (*pimplemi pneumatos hagiou*). When Peter preached he was "filled with the Holy Spirit" (Acts 4:8). Chosen to be deacons were only those who were "known to be full of the Spirit and of wisdom" (Acts 6:3). Stephen was "full of faith and of the Holy Spirit" when he was chosen among the Seven (Acts 6:5).

Evidences of Filling.   The evidences of being filled with the Spirit are the works of faith active in love. Though the sealing and indwelling of the Spirit are given to all baptized believers, only those completely yielded to God and separated for responsive service are said to be filled with the Spirit (Phil. 1:11). They "make music" in their hearts to the Lord, "always giving thanks to God the Father for everything" (Eph. 5:20), ready always to "submit to one another out of reverence for Christ" (v. 21). The contrast is that between being drunkenly controlled by spiritous liquors and being fittingly empowered by the Spirit of God so that music pours out of one's heart in praise.

The faithful are exhorted to continue to "be filled with the Spirit" (Eph. 5:18) in the imperative tense, assuming that a receptive yieldedness remained their own responsibility, their own part in cooperating with the grace of the Spirit. Believers yielded to the Spirit will be empowered in their yieldedness, and fruits will be born from this empowerment. Believers can walk the way without committing known sin as long as they remain yielded to the Spirit. "Man is a vessel destined to receive God, a vessel which must be enlarged in proportion as it is filled and filled in proportion as it is enlarged" (F. L. Godet, *Commentary,* John, quoted by Gordon, *MS,* p. 91).

Though believers are viewed as the temple of the Spirit, they may remain resistant to the Spirit, and thereby miss the fullness of the varied ministries of the Spirit. This resistance is not irreversible, but may turn to yieldedness: When Ananias placed his hands upon Saul's blind eyes, he said, "'Jesus, who appeared to you on the road as you were coming here—has sent me so that you may see again and be filled with the Holy Spirit.' Immediately, something like scales fell from Saul's eyes, and he could see again. He got up and was baptized" (Acts 9:17, 18).

PERFECTING GRACE AND THE FULLNESS OF SALVATION

The Language of Perfecting Grace

The very Hebrew and Greek terms used in scripture to describe full salvation (*shalem, tamim, teleiosis, katartisis*) are, when appropriately nuanced, best designed to serve Christian teaching, and when rightly translated should not be avoided as if too controversial or dangerous.

The concepts of perfecting grace, holiness, sanctification, and perfect love are not merely sanctioned but specifically set forth, defined, and commended by scripture. To assume that the attempt at complete responsiveness to grace necessarily leads to pride and presumption is to misunderstand their scriptural intent. Although the language of full salvation in this life is not unambiguously or unanimously received ecumenically, it is arguably closer to consensual reception than its exegetic alternatives. Though what follows cannot be portrayed as unchallenged consensual teaching, it is a majority protoconsensual view awaiting fuller refinement.

A fine balance of tolerance and rigor is called for at this juncture. Where Catholic teaching tends to stress the sin removed by baptism, and Reformed teaching tends to emphasize the sin remaining after baptism, both views tend to need the corrective of each other.

The Perfect Sacrifice. The Lord by his "one sacrifice" has "made perfect [*teteleiok-en*] forever those who are being made holy [*hagiazomenous*]" (Heb. 10:14). This is a past act completed on the cross, but one in which believers now participate. The perfect work of Christ for the believer (positional perfection) is distinguishable from the maturing of those being made holy. "Jesus also suffered outside the city gate to make the people *holy* through his own blood. Let us, then, go to him outside the camp, bearing the disgrace he bore" (Heb. 13:12, 13, italics added). The completeness we already experience in union with Christ is distinguishable from but related to a growing process of maturing in the believer. "Perseverance must finish its work so that you may be mature and complete [*teleioi kai holoklēroi*], not lacking anything" (James 1:4).

Paul's "message of wisdom" to be spoken "among the mature [*teleiois*]" is "a wisdom that has been hidden and that God destined for our glory before time began" (1 Cor. 2:6, 7). What is "destined" is not our response but God's grace in the Son before time. Personally responsive maturation moves toward a goal that Paul assumed when he chided the Galatians: "Are you so foolish? After beginning with the Spirit, are you now trying to attain your goal by human effort?" (Gal. 3:3). He exhorted the faithful to "stop thinking like children," and "be adults" (1 Cor. 14:20), as those "of us who are mature [*teleioi*]" (Phil. 3:15). He urged even the irascible Corinthians to "aim for perfection [*katartizesthe*]" (2 Cor. 13:11).

Of "The Spirits of Righteous Men Made Perfect." Of the various Hebrew words sometimes translated "perfect," or "blameless" (*shalem, tamim*), it is usually contextually clear that the individuals referred to are not wholly without sin (Hezekiah, 2 Kings 20:3; David, Pss. 37:37; 101:2). When the Old Testament spoke of the upright man such as Noah or Job as "perfect" (Gen. 6:9; Job 1:1, 8), this did not imply moral sinlessness but complete sincerity of trust in God. They will be found in the heavenly city as "the spirits of righteous men made perfect" (Heb. 12:23; Calvin, *Comm.* XXII, p. 334).

Israel was commanded to be "blameless before the Lord your God" (Deut. 18:13). Yet the complete deliverance by the Spirit of every believer whose life is hid in Christ should not be simply equated with inherent moral perfection or the incapacity to sin (Calvin, *Inst.* 4.13; Chafer, *ST* VI, pp. 283, 284).

On Completing and Thoroughly Fitting: Teleioō *and* Katartizō. Of the thirteen Greek words sometimes translated "perfect," two in particular require analysis. The verb *katartizō* suggests completeness, or fittingness in all details, as if something is rightly adjusted and completely fitted to its purpose (2 Cor. 13:9; Eph. 4:12; 1 Thess. 3:10). The Spirit is giving gifts "for the perfecting [*katartismon*] of the saints" (Eph. 4:12, KJV), abundantly (not stingily) equipping and preparing God's people for works of service (John 10:10; Fletcher, *Checks Ag. Antinomianism, Works* VII; A. Clarke, *Christian Theology* XII, pp. 183–84).

The verb *teleioō* suggests completing, attaining, ending, perfecting, bringing something to its proper goal (1 Cor. 2:6; Eph. 4:13; Phil. 3:15; Col. 3:14; 4:12). *Teleioō* may mean to mature, to fulfill, to make full, or to come to a fitting conclusion. Such maturing is frequently sought and commended in this life by New Testament writers. The faithful are called to grow toward maturity through patience (James 1:4) and love (1 John 4:17, 18), in knowledge of the will of God (Col. 4:12) and in holiness (2 Cor. 7:1; Cyprian, *Treatise IX, ANF* V, pp. 484–90).

Those in Whom Grace Is Working Optimally.   Those in whom grace is working optimally are those presently answering the end for which God made them, who are cooperating maximally with sanctifying grace (Jerome, *Ag. Pelagians, NPNF* 2 VI, pp. 454–59; N. Burwash, *MCT* II, pp. 311–25). Those who are thoroughly cleansed from sin by faith and wholly consecrated to God have that mind in them that was also in Christ Jesus (Phil. 2:5). They are "filled with the fruit of righteousness that comes through Jesus Christ" (Phil. 1:11). They give thanks in all things (1 Thess. 5:16–18), praying without ceasing. They do not choose to set that which is wicked before their eyes (Ps. 101:3). Their passions and bodily appetites are put to the use for which they were intended (1 Cor. 9:24–27; Field, *HCT,* p. 227). God reigns without a rival in them.

The Augsburg Confession set forth this definition of Christian perfection: "For this is Christian perfection; honestly to fear God and at the same time to have great faith and to trust that for Christ's sake we have a gracious God; to ask of God, and assuredly to expect from him, help in all things which are to be borne in connection with our callings; meanwhile to be diligent in the performance of good works for others and to attend to our calling. True perfection and true service of God consist of these things" (Article 27, *Book of Concord,* p. 79; *CC,* p. 73).

Full Responsiveness Not Intrinsically Impossible.   There is no fated or absolute necessity that the regenerated life should remain arbitrarily bound by the power of sin, if God the Spirit is contextually offering grace sufficient to meet each and every successive temptation or challenge (John Cassian, *Conferences, NPNF* 2 XI, pp. 287–502). There is nothing intrinsically impossible about aiming toward "loving God with all our heart, mind, soul, and strength," wherein "all the thoughts, words, and actions are governed by pure love" (J. Wesley, *WJW* XI, pp. 366 ff.; VI, pp. 1–23, *WJWB,* sermon 76). That *teleiosis* which Paul enjoyed is not intrinsically beyond the reach of any (John Chrysostom, *Hom. on the Statues, NPNF* 1 IX, p. 373). It is not arbitrarily impossible to increase or grow in grace, to deepen and enrich the life of virtue in response to grace, or to improve in one's responsiveness to God's will (Council of Vienne, *SCD* 471, p. 188; *Trent* IV, *SCD* 802, p. 253).

Through many centuries the premise of perfecting grace has been often defended against skeptical detractors (Council of Constance, *SCD* 600–604, pp. 209–11; Alexander IV, *SCD* 458 f., p. 181; cf. Pius VI's response to the Synod of Pistoia, *SCD* 1580–90). There is nothing intrinsically to prevent one from becoming "ever more deeply, ever more existentially, seized by God's life. . . . It is simply the presence of God's love growing more intense, more radical and the transforming union becoming greater" (Rahner, *TI* 3, p. 143).

The Body Not of Itself an Arbitrary Limit.   Nowhere does scripture teach that the body is an absolute obstacle to the reception of sanctifying grace. Rather it teaches that the body, with all its passions, concupiscence, energies, libido, powers, and members, is to be taken captive to Christ and sanctified as a temple of the Spirit (Rom. 6:13; 1 Cor. 6:19, 20; 2 Cor. 4:10, 11; Heb. 10:22). There is no arbitrary limit to what the Spirit can do with a consecrated human life who cooperates steadily with grace (Palmer, *PPSW,* pp. 165–85). Every aspect of life is awaiting to be taken captive to Christ (Finney, *Sermons* IV.18; Mahan, *Christian Perfection*).

Sustained Radical Responsiveness to Grace Considered Juridically, Experientially, and Eschatologically

There is an implicit, operating distinction in the biblical teaching of sanctification between *positional* sanctification in Christ (1 Cor. 1:30) and *experimental* (or progressive or experiential) sanctification in relation to the believer's yieldedness to Christ (Eph. 5:26, 27; 1 Thess. 5:23; 1 Peter 3:18); and both of these are distinguishable from celestial or *final* sanctification in glory (1 John 3:2; Rom. 8:29). The Reformed tradition has wisely taught that "(1) all believers are *positionally* sanctified in Christ 'once for all' at the moment they are saved. This sanctification is as perfect as He is perfect. (2) All believers are *being* sanctified by the power of God through the Word, and this sanctification is as perfect as the believer is perfect. So, also, (3) all believers *will be* sanctified and perfected in glory into the very image of the Son of God" (Chafer, *ST* VI, p. 285).

Positional Completeness in Christ.   Paul addressed all believers at Corinth in the *positional* sense as saints, as "those sanctified in Christ Jesus and called to be holy" (1 Cor. 1:2, 30; 6:11). Yet the Corinthian letters were written to correct abuses of those who were still experimentally or *progressively maturing* in Christ by an extended process by which we "reflect the Lord's glory," being "transformed into his likeness with ever-increasing glory" (2 Cor. 3:18; cf. John 17:17; Eph. 5:26), which seeks to "grow in the grace and knowledge of our Lord and Savior" (2 Pet. 3:18). This process looks toward fitting future consummation, or *final* sanctification (1 Thess. 5:23).

Sanctification (*hagiasmos*) is used in the New Testament to point both to the continuing development of the Christian life and to its fulfillment. All believers, however imperfect, are referred to as "saints" or "sanctified" (Acts 9:13; Rom. 1:7; 2 Cor. 1:1; Eph. 1:1; Col. 1:2) in a way that appears to be synonymous with justification and regeneration; hence it is called in Reformed teaching *positional* sanctification. In this sense all who share life in Christ by faith, even weak faith, are being sanctified by the power of the Spirit (1 Cor. 1:2; Phil. 1:1). For faith requires and implies that one is dedicating, consecrating one's whole self to God and turning away from all that would detract from one's reconciliation with God.

Growth in Maturity in Christ.   Progressive sanctification is an ongoing process of daily rededication, reconsecration, mortification, and vivification of the whole person to God, living out one's baptism in time so as to allow new challenges and circumstances to draw one further on toward the fuller reception of grace and the deepening of purity of heart (1 Thess. 5:23; Heb. 12:14). This continuing, yielding consecration is not qualitatively different from the initial consecration, but rather it is growing and developing under conditions of temptation and contextual hearing of the Word. It is a continuing unfolding of what was implied in the initial act of consecration (Calvin, *Inst.* 3.3). Sanctification in this sense is "the continued transformation of moral and spiritual character so that the life of the believer actually comes to mirror the standing which he or she already has in God's sight" (Erickson, *CT* 3, p. 875).

Final Sanctification in Christ.   Finally, Paul prayed that God may "strengthen your hearts so that you will be blameless and holy in the presence of our God and

Father when our Lord Jesus comes" (1 Thess. 3:13). The sanctification *ultimately hoped for* is that by which the God of peace sanctifies "you through and through," by which "your whole spirit, soul and body be kept blameless at the coming of our Lord Jesus Christ" (1 Thess. 5:23). Exegetes differ as to whether this final sanctification may occur in this life or only at death or at the time of the general resurrection.

How the Maturity of Which Redeemed Humanity Is Made Capable by Grace Differs from Divine, Angelic, and Adamic Perfection

Antecedent and Consequent Power in God.   Is complete and unblemished responsiveness to grace possible within the history of sin? To answer we must first recall that the doctrine of sanctification is not primarily a teaching about the human capacity as such, but about the sufficiency of God the Spirit to transform all human capacities. It is less anthropology than pneumatology (Barth, *CD* IV/2, pp. 495 ff.; Outler, *TWS*, chap. 3).

To speak of the capacity of God, we must again distinguish between antecedent and consequent (or absolute and ordinary) power in God. Considered antecedently, nothing is beyond God's power, because it is God's. Absolute power can extend itself in any way without limitation. Unmitigated power can work without mitigation. Yet the primordial power of God has consequences, namely, the creation of proximate, temporal companionate wills that may in self-determination stand temporarily over against God's power (Origen, *De Principii* II.9, *ANF* IV, pp. 289–93; Oden, *LG*, pp. 67–82, 93–95).

As prevening, providential grace works through secondary causes, so does sanctifying grace work through and before and above and around and after other creaturely causes, and not merely unilaterally. It is a category mistake to assume that grace can be reduced to simple, unilateral divine causality, without positing other layers of cooperating causality. This is the oft-repeated error of monogerism, as bad a habit in hyper-Augustinianism as in certain expressions of Islam and prequantum scientific determinism. Though it is God who gives growth, it is Paul who plants and Apollos who waters (1 Cor. 3:4–6).

Whether the Maturing Love Enabled by Grace to Sinners Is Different from That Predicated in Angels.   The incorporeal angelic beings, who are assumed in scripture to be capable of serving God, exceed human capabilities enormously. For all human capabilities exist within a fallen history of sin and under conditions of corporeality. Of whatever level of maturity or radical responsiveness humans may be capable, it must be distinguished from angelic perfection, which does not labor under the bodily constraints of time and space with which human virtue must contend (Tho. Aq., *ST* I–I, Q50–74, I, pp. 259–355, cf. 521 ff.; II, pp. 1950–59).

Whether the Maturing Love Enabled by Grace to Sinners Is Different from That Predicated in Adam and Eve Before the Fall.   Whatever full responsiveness is now enabled by grace must be further distinguished from that originally enabled in Adam and Eve, for an intervening history of sin has drastically limited the choices available within fallen human history to choices between tainted values, goods, and eventualities, not untainted or unimpaired actions. The unimpeded love promised to sinners must function within the capacities given by grace to human beings within the contexts of fallen history (Reinhold Niebuhr, *MMIS*, *NDM* I, II).

Leibniz reasoned that "creatures receive their perfections from the influence of God," but "their imperfections are due to their own nature, which is incapable of being limitless" (*Monadology* 42, *TGS*, p. 209). "That God always acts in the most perfect and the most desirable way possible, is in my opinion the basis of the love which we owe to God above all things" (Leibniz, *Discourse on Metaphysics* 4, *TGS*, p. 206).

Refining and Qualifying the Teaching of Perfecting Grace

If one uncritically defines perfection as a simple state of freedom from sin attainable in earthly life without qualifying how freedom from sin differs from finitude or ignorance or error or infirmity, then the doctrine of radical responsiveness is a laughable straw man waiting to be knocked down. What qualifications are required in setting forth maturing or perfecting grace that will allow it to be taken seriously?

Human Infirmities Amplify the Perfections of Grace. The moral unlikelihood of extended impeccability is in part a function of human finitude and the very conditions of the human soul-body compositum. "The infirmity of human nature flows from four separate and distinct sources: (1) concupiscence (*fomes peccati*); (2) imperfection of the ethical judgment (*imperfectio iudicii*); (3) inconstancy of the will (*inconstantia voluntatis*); and (4) the weariness caused by continued resistance to temptation" (Pohle, *DT* VII, p. 120).

When all these forms of human infirmity conspire to limit human willing and acting, it seems plausible to speak in a virtual sense of a prevailing tendency to sin (*necessitas antecedens peccandi*), not as if the will were fated to fall, but in the awareness that it is highly unlikely that the will might continue interminably without special grace to resist an endless series of temptations (S. Kierkegaard, *The Concept of Anxiety*).

The tendency to sin does not destroy free will or the moral culpability of sin, nor does it imply that what God has commanded is formally impossible. Yet it does make free will vulnerable, and sin virtually inevitable. This is why a static form of perfection is virtually unattainable over a long period of time without the assistance of special grace (Tho. Aq., *ST* II–II, Q184, II, pp. 1950–60).

There is a thin but conceptually plausible line between the tendencies of human infirmity and voluntary transgression of known law (Clement of Alexandria, *Stromata*, II.14–16, *ANF* II, pp. 361–63). Hence Reinhold Niebuhr was right to insist that sin is "inevitable but not necessary" (*NDM* I, pp. 255 ff.). The theological equivalent of Murphy's law is "Whatever can fall, will fall," given time for the exercise of vulnerable freedom (Tho. Aq., *ST* I–II, Q109, I, pp. 1123–31).

Whatever sustained radical responsiveness is made possible by grace, it does not imply that all venial sin is overcome or that anyone becomes irreversibly impeccable (Council of Mileum II, *SCD* 107 f., p. 46; Council of Vienne, *SCD* 471, p. 188). "For if a man does not sin because he cannot sin, free will is destroyed, and goodness cannot possibly be due to his efforts, but must be part of a nature unreceptive of evil" (Jerome, *Ag. the Pelagians*, *NPNF* 2 VI, p. 454).

No one can decide how he is to be tempted, only how he is to respond to temptation. It is this variability that presents a continuing challenge to constant accountability to the sufficiency of grace. One may be able to resist successfully a thousand temptations in succession while a hidden one is taking over at a lower level of awareness. Hence Augustine was wise in warning, "Let no one say that he is without sin, but let us not for this reason love sin. Let us detest sin . . . [and] avoid grievous sins, and venial sins, too, as much as we can" (Augustine, *Letters* 181.8, *MPL* 33; cf. FC 30, pp. 121–27; 1 John 1:8).

Sustained Radical Responsiveness to Grace Does Not Imply Freedom from Error. Unimpeded responsiveness to grace does *not imply infallibility* or freedom from error or inerrant perception. As long as one remains in the body, one is liable to inaccurate perceptions that lead to errors of judgment, and deceptive appearances that tend toward erroneous conclusions. These conditions, being characteristic of human existence generally, remain characteristic of those walking the way of holiness even at their highest levels of accountability (Owen, *Works* 3, pp. 468–538).

Not only errors of judgment but "fears occasioned by surprise, unpleasant dreams, wandering thoughts in prayer, times when there is no joy, a sense of inefficiency in Christian labor, and strong temptations, are by no means inconsistent with perfect love" (Binney, *TCI*, p. 132).

Sustained Radical Responsiveness to Grace Does Not Imply Freedom from Finitude. One may be entirely consecrated to God and still remain subject to the infirmities and defects that inevitably accompany finite human existence. Even amid such defects of perception and limited attentiveness, these are not charged to conscience or accounted as sin if one's heart remains pure, one's will is yielded, and one's intention is shaped wholly by love of God and neighbor, inasmuch as "love is the fulfillment of the law" (Rom. 13:10; Clement of Alexandria, *Stromata* IV.6, *ANF* II, p. 414).

The saints may be misled by clouded memories or limited imaginations to form inaccurate impressions and hold distorted opinions. "This is a natural consequence of the soul's dwelling in flesh and blood. But a man may be filled with pure love, and yet be subject to ignorance and mistake" (Field, *HCT*, p. 228). Even where information is wrongly processed, the heart may remain pure, and every act spring from love. Such finitude is not properly viewed as sin if sin is willful disobedience to recognizable moral truth. The Manichaeanism that asserts that finitude is sin has long been consensually regarded as a heresy.

The holier the faithful become, the more they are likely to feel "their own ignorance, littleness of grace, coming short of the full mind that was in Christ" (Curtis, *CF,* pp. 377 ff.). Walking in the way of holiness does not imply that one may habitually love God without any admixture of egocentricity. Nor does it imply that one may know with certitude that one will persevere (*Trent* VI, *SCD* 802–6, pp. 252–55), or that God's own incomparable perfection has become reducible to that measure of holy love offered and enabled by grace within the limits of human finitude (Innocent XII, *SCD* 1327–46, pp. 343–44).

Sustained Radical Responsiveness to Grace Does Not Imply Static or "Sinless Perfection." The Council of Vienne, A.D. 1311–12, specifically rejected the doctrine of static sinless perfection, "that man in the present life can acquire so great and such a degree of perfection that he will be rendered inwardly sinless, and that he will not be able to advance farther in grace" (*SCD* 471, p. 188). The perfect love sought and attested is not a perfection that would pretend to eliminate unconscious sin or have nothing else to do, but rather a pure heart of faith active in love that is presently overcoming all habitual sin (Fletcher, *Last Check to Antinomianism* I, *Works* [1833], II, pp. 493, 494; Limborch, *Theologia Christiana* V.79, 2, 8, 14, pp. 658–61). No persevering believer remains in a static or fixed state, but rather is forever in motion, constantly toward or away from sanctifying grace (Jerome, *Letters, NPNF* 2 VI, pp. 273–75).

Sustained Radical Responsiveness to Grace Does Not Imply Antinomian License. Grace as radical gift does not at its best welcome into the tent the nose of the camel of antinomian license, which would tempt recipients to slacken their efforts to reflect the holiness of God in the name of Christian liberty (Luther, *Treatise on Good Works, WML* I, pp. 196–99). To reflect the holiness of God is a duty in which by grace believers are in some measure enabled despite residual sin after justification (Twenty-five Articles of Religion, X–XII, *CC*, pp. 336–37).

The cause of sanctification is not furthered by imagining that human beings in their sin are made quickly or without cost acceptable to God by some sort of instant holiness. Christianity seeks to show that the making holy of the human person is God's own work, yet accomplished in such a way as not to disavow human accountability and responsiveness (Augustine, *On Nature and Grace, NPNF* 1 V, pp. 121 ff.). The ever-pertinent caveat: God the Spirit offers sanctifying grace precisely *to sinners* trapped in ungodly living.

The way toward perfect love does not imply that one is no longer further required to keep the commandments (Council of Trent VI, *SCD* 804, p. 253), or no longer to seek virtue or love one's neighbor (Council of Vienne, *SCD* 476, p. 188). Such a supposed "perfection" tends toward antinomian license. Nor does sustained radical responsiveness to grace imply an immobile state, or death of the senses, or the deification of the flesh (John XXII, *SCD* 501 ff., p. 195; Innocent XI, *SCD* 1221 ff., pp. 331 ff.).

Some Reformed critics have argued that the notion of unimpeded responsiveness to grace operates with a "standard of righteousness that is much too low. . . . Their 'perfection' consists in being free from deliberate and objective acts of sin and does not take into account the subjective nature of sin as revealed by our Lord in Matthew 5:21–28" (Stevens, *Doctrine of the Christian Religion*, p. 275; cf. Hodge, *ST* III, pp. 245–59). That notion of perfect love which amounts to a diminution of moral requirement can only be a snare to the Christian life. In the direction of the opposite extreme, to set perfect responsiveness wholly out of reach is the most effective way of undercutting it. Rather, perfect responsiveness is "always wrought in the soul by faith, by a simple act of faith," which, due to sufficient grace, is not in any situation intrinsically impossible (Field, *HCT*, p. 240; P. Palmer, *Faith and Its Effects;* cf. Calvin, *Inst.* 3.17.15).

Sustained Radical Responsiveness to Grace Does Not Imply the Overcoming of Involuntary Transgressions. The life of perfect love commended in the New Testament is not a perfection according to an absolute moral law, but according to the remedial economy enabled by the cross, in which the heart, having been cleansed, fulfills the law by faith active in love (Rom. 4; 5; 13:8–10). The pivotal obstacle overcome by God's saving action is sin of every kind, not the infirmities of finitude imputed as guilt (Augustine, *On Grace and Free Will, NPNF* 1 V, pp. 443–68; Field, *HCT,* p. 241; J. Peck, *The Central Idea of Christianity;* R. S. Foster, *Christian Purity*).

The psalmist distinguished between willed sin and hidden sins not consciously willed: "Forgive my hidden faults. Keep your servant *also* from willful sins; may they not rule over me. Then will I be blameless" (Ps. 19:12, 13, italics added; cf. 119:133). One may be filled with the love of God and still remain liable to involuntary or unconscious or unavoidable transgressions (J. Wesley, *PACP,* p. 67). Classic exegetes are divided as to whether to call such sin, but united in the assumption of the sufficiency of grace to redeem all sin. No finite person can cease being finite. No *theosis* is posited by orthodoxy that ends finitude.

Sustained Radical Responsiveness Does Not Imply an Eradication of the Sin Nature.

John's letter specifically warned against the claim that sin is permanently eradicated upon belief in Christ (1 John 1:8). Yet in the next verse the letter enjoined believers to confess their sins that they may be purified "from all unrighteousness" (1 John 1:9).

This does not amount to a claim that the old sin nature is eradicated by faith, or that one is permanently made not able to sin. Rather, because of the work of the Son and the Spirit one is being given power step-by-step not to sin. One view wrongly pretends to end all future struggle with temptation and sin. The consensually received view rightly sees the struggle against temptation continuing but as being constantly addressed by sufficient grace (Augustine, *Ag. Two Letters of the Pelagians* IV. 24–31, *NPNF* 1 V, pp. 427–33; *CG, FC* 14, pp. 108 ff.).

If the complete eradication of all possibility of sin were God's way of dealing with our fallen nature, then there would be little point in talking further of the continuing work of the Spirit. Rather, both Paul and John teach that the sin nature continues after faith begins, yet the indwelling Spirit empowers the new person of faith sufficiently in each circumstance.

Sustained Radical Responsiveness to Grace Does Not Imply Freedom from Temptation.

The world, the flesh, and the adversary are not eradicated in this present age, though their power is being overthrown. The world continues, temptation continues, the flesh exerts its power, the devil rails, but amid all these challenging conditions, the Spirit works to enable fully adequate responses in each circumstance and growth toward an ever-larger pattern of full responsiveness (1 John 3:1–10; Chafer, *ST* VI, pp. 268–70).

Steady reception of sanctifying grace does not imply absolute freedom from temptation. Adam while innocent was tempted. Even Jesus who knew no sin was tempted in every way that characterizes human existence generally (*WL,* pp. 240–53). To be tempted is not to succumb. To be tempted is human and belongs to self-determining creaturely existence. To succumb is sin and belongs to fallen existence. Those whose feet are set on the path to full salvation do not become free from temptation, though they grow in their ability to overcome it (Pius V, *SCD* 1001–80, pp. 304–11). There is no point at which they can make no further progress in grace (Council of Vienne, *SCD* 471, p. 188).

Temptation is not merely external to the self but proceeds from within (Athanasius, *Life of Antony*, *NPNF* 2 IV, p. 207). With each new moral challenge to the will, there comes a new choice, which itself may strengthen or weaken the habits of holy accountability (Ignatius, *Tarsians* 8, *ANF* I, p. 108). Any choice may suddenly intensify the power of self-deception, or the power of the will to cooperate with grace so as to become at that moment victorious over sin.

Sustained Radical Responsiveness to Grace Offers No Grounds for Boasting.   No *tsaddiq* (just person, made upright, *dikaios*) will ever be heard boasting of his or her sanctification. No one who is struggling seriously against pride will be found referring to him- or herself as holy or completely matured in Christ (Jerome, *Ag. Pelagians*, *NPNF* 2 VI, p. 479). Yet paradoxically, the very one who does not claim maturity may be optimally gaining ever-greater maturation and fullness of growth in the Spirit.

The saints recognized that the closer they walked the way of Christ, the more were they aware of their own sinfulness and distance from the purity of Christ. As their vision became clearer, they could see their own imperfections more clearly (Calvin, *Inst.* 4.13; Teresa of Avila, *Life;* Thérèse of Lisieux, *Story of a Soul*). However far along the road one may be, it is always premature to "boast about tomorrow, for you do not know what a day may bring forth" (Prov. 27:1). For "our life here below has many turnings, and the body of our humiliation is ever rising, falling and changing" (Gregory Nazianzen, *Orat.* XVI.3, *NPNF* 2 VII, p. 248).

Exegetical and Systematic Issues of Sustained Responsiveness to Grace

Whether the Lord's Prayer Assumes That Sin Will Continue in Believers.   The Council of Carthage (A.D. 418) rejected the Pelagian view that the Lord's Prayer petition, "Forgive us our trespasses" (Matt. 6:12), does not pertain to the saints. Earlier the Second Council of Mileum (A.D. 416; *SCD* 108, p. 47) had rejected the view that the petition to forgive us our trespasses, when pronounced by saintly persons, was pronounced merely in token of humility, but not truthfully.

The full reception of sanctifying grace does not imply that one needs no longer to pray for forgiveness or ask the intercession of Christ (Council of Vienne, *SCD* 472, p. 188). For the Christian life is precisely the daily dying to sin and living to righteousness that constitutes the life of repentance and faith, continually reaffirmed and renewed. "Who can say, 'I have kept my heart pure; I am clean and without sin'?" (Prov. 20:10), especially as that might be uttered with respect to human infirmities, sins of surprise, errors of judgment, and moral misperceptions.

There are no liturgies of classical Christianity that fail to offer confession of sin. This does not place the way of holiness out of reach for believers, but puts believers constantly on the path of daily confession and renewal. Those justified still may have sin remaining in them, even if it is not reigning (Calvin, *Inst.* 3.3.11; J. Wesley, *WJW* V, pp. 156–71). Some therefore contend that in saying, "Forgive us our trespasses," the Lord's Prayer assumed that no believer can ever be completely free from sin; hence it is a tacit "acknowledgement that no Christian in this life is perfect" (Hodge, *ST* III, p. 247). But others point out that the same prayer earnestly petitions, "Thy will be done," and "Deliver us from evil." They note further that the prayer is in the plural, "our trespasses"; hence it could be prayed by one whose conscience is void of offense precisely while holding up before God the whole of humanity in its sin, asking for forgiveness. Thus they argue that the prayer for forgiveness does not assume that everyone must thereby remain inexorably or equally under the reigning power of sin (Watson, *TI* II.29, p. 545).

Whether One May Receive Perfecting Grace Proportionally in Certain Aspects While Remaining Imperfect in Others.   The reception of sanctifying grace remains imperfect or immature in whatever degree or proportion that it lacks the sustained development of fully embodied faith. The way of holiness is being perfected in that degree or proportion to which it is daily sustaining trust in God's righteousness. Consensual exegesis points in this direction: it is not common, though possible, for persons to respond continuously and fully to sanctifying grace in this life (Gregory of Ryssa, *Moses, CWS;* Benedict, *Rule;* Bonaventure, *The Soul's Journey into God, CWS,* pp. 110–16; cf. Symeon Metaphrastis, *Hom. of Makarios, Philok.* 3, pp. 322–36).

Can Completing Grace Be Lost?   The consummating grace that is received by faith can be lost by unfaith. "If a man, being regenerate and justified, relapses of his own will into an evil life, assuredly he cannot say: 'I have not received,' because of his own free choice of evil he has lost the grace of God that he has received" (Augustine, *On Admonition and Grace* VI.9, Pohle, *DT* VII, p. 394, cf. *NPNF* 1 V, p. 75). If the contrary were the case, it would be impossible to fall from a moment of perfecting grace. Then there would be no need for repentance of believers, hence no need for Eucharist, no need for preaching, and no need for discipline.

If one posits that a moment of completing grace is possible, that does not imply that it will be extended inevitably, for "if a righteous man turns from his righteousness and commits sin and does the same detestable things the wicked man does, will he live? None of the righteous things he has done will be remembered. Because of the unfaithfulness he is guilty of and because of the sins he has committed, he will die" lacking justifying faith (Ezek. 18:24). "So, if you think you are standing firm, be careful that you don't fall!" (1 Cor. 10:12; John Chrysostom, *Hom. on 1 Cor.* XXIII, *NPNF* 1 XII, pp. 131–38). Jerome argued that "you will remain sons of God so long as you refrain from sin" (*Ag. Jovinian* II.29, *NPNF* 2 IV, p. 410; cf. Bellarmine, *De Iustificatio* III.15).

Whether Redeemed Sinners Are Commanded to Be Perfect.   The divine command is to become mature and complete in the likeness of God—"Be perfect, therefore, as your heavenly Father is perfect" (Matt. 5:48). To this end Christ gave his life to redeem us and the Holy Spirit came to sanctify us. Perfect love is the end or goal toward which justifying grace points (Tertullian, *Ag. Marcion* I.24–29, *ANF* III, pp. 289–95).

"Be imitators of God, therefore, as dearly loved children and live a life of love, just as Christ loved us" (Eph. 5:1, 2; Polycarp, *Philippians* 8, *AF,* p. 133). "But among you there must not be even a hint of sexual immorality, or of any kind of impurity, or of greed, because these are improper for God's holy people" (Eph. 5:3; John Chrysostom, *Hom. on Eph.* XVII, *NPNF* 1 XIII, pp. 128–32). "For perfection of life the imitation of Christ is necessary, not only in the example of gentleness, lowliness, and long suffering set us in His life, but also of His actual death" (Basil, *On the Spirit* I.15, *NPNF* 2 VIII, p. 21), or readiness to die for the truth.

In What Way Justified Sinners May Refract God's Own Righteousness.   Christ's righteousness was indeed substituted for our unrighteousness, not so as to imply no further accountability or responsiveness on our part, but rather that we might refract God's own righteousness in our behavior by grace (Col. 3:10; Calvin, *Inst.* 4.17–19). The fulfillment of the law, impossible on the basis of the law alone, now becomes possible on the basis of grace, which works to elevate and transform human behavior (Luther, *Comm. on Gal., MLS*, pp. 134–45). Moral accountability and perfect love are progressively awakened by sanctifying grace working through Word and Sacrament (Gregory of Nyssa, *FGG*, pp. 81–84).

God asks us to be holy as God is holy in proportion as finite creatures may contextually refract God's own holiness (Matt. 5:48; Origen, *De Principii* IV.1.37, *ANF* IV, pp. 381–82). God's intent is that we not sin. But if anyone does sin, we have an advocate with the Father (1 John 2:1). God's saving plan intends that sin be displaced by righteousness of character among all who are to share God's own life eternally (Clare of Assisi, *Second Letter to the Blessed Agnes of Prague, CWS*, pp. 195–98).

Is There a Perfection That Admits of Continual Increase?   Can the fruits of the Spirit be augmented indefinitely under the conditions of human freedom? Is there some limit beyond which sanctifying grace cannot grow? Does growth in grace admit of continual increase?

However love may be perfectly enabled by grace at any moment, it is always capable of being further perfected by a love that may be enabled in a subsequent moment heretofore unimaginable. In this sense it is argued that there is no perfection that does not admit of continual increase (Eph. 4:15, 16; Phil. 3:13–17; Heb. 6:1; 1 Pet. 2:2–5; 2 Pet. 3:18; J. Wesley, *WJW* XI, pp. 366 ff.). "By a perfection of degrees is meant that highest perfection which consists in the highest exertion of human strength assisted by grace," a perfection "proportioned to the powers of each individual," consisting essentially of "a desire of making continual progress" (Hodge, *ST* III, p. 253, quoting Simon Episcopius). Even when the hearts of the faithful are "united and subjected unto the truth, so as not to obey any suggestion or temptation of the evil one, but to be free from actual sinning and transgressing of the law of God, and in that respect perfect," wrote the classic Quaker theologian Robert Barclay, "yet doth this perfection still admit of a growth; and there remaineth the possibility of sinning where the mind doth not most diligently and watchfully attend unto the Lord" (Barclay, *Theses Theologicae*, 1675, VIII, *CC*, p. 329).

Whether the Sufficiency of Grace Is a Sufficiency That Occurs at Every Stage of Development.   The athletic prowess of the child is not that of the young adult. To walk the way of holiness in full accountability is to walk each step with purity of heart unmixed by sullied motives, to love God without alloy. What that means at each step must be understood in relation to the capacity of the soul at that specific step (Gregory the Great, *Pastoral Care* III.1, *ACW* 11, pp. 90–92).

As misperceptions and defects are gradually overcome, as capacities increase, as the soul grows, as the mind becomes enriched with wisdom, so will moral requirements be sharpened and intensified. In childhood one might rightly expect a thinner experiential base than of someone older. In extreme old age one may rightly expect less mental acuity and physical mobility than at an earlier age. Yet at any age, sufficient grace is being offered for fully adequate responsiveness to whatever emerges within the finite limits of the situation (Gregory Nazianzen, *Orat.* II.28–33, *NPNF* 2 VII, pp. 210–11).

We have been given gifts "in accordance with the gradual progress of our education, while being brought to perfection in our training for godliness, we were first taught elementary and easier lessons suited to our intelligence, while the Dispenser of our lots was ever leading us up, by gradually accustoming us, like eyes brought up in the dark, to the great light of truth. For he spares our weakness" (Basil, *On the Spirit* I.14, *NPNF* 2 VIII, p. 21).

Christ "sanctified each stage of life" by making possible at that stage "a likeness to himself," which would in due course pass "through every stage of life. He was made an infant for infants, sanctifying infancy; a child among children, sanctifying childhood, and setting an example of filial affection, of righteousness and obedience; a young man among young men, becoming an example to them, and sanctifying them to the Lord. So also he was a grown man among the older men, that he might be a perfect teacher for all" (Irenaeus, *Ag. Her.* II.22.4, *ECF*, p. 80), "consummating in himself all things" and "joining man to Spirit and placing Spirit in man" (III.16.6, *ECF*, p. 81).

"The Lord has sent the Paraclete for this very purpose, that discipline might progressively be guided, ordered, and brought to perfection by his representative, the Holy Spirit. . . . The province of the Holy Spirit is just this; the guidance of discipline, the interpretation of Scripture, the reformation of the intellect, the advance toward better things. All things have their proper time and await their due season. . . . So righteousness was at first rudimentary, when nature feared God; then by means of the Law and the Prophets it progressed to infancy; thereafter through the Gospel it reached the fervour of adolescence; and now through the Paraclete it is being established in maturity" (Tertullian, *On the Veiling* 1, *ECF*, p. 132; cf. *ANF* IV, p. 27).

Flesh and Spirit

The Paradoxical Uprightness of the Saints.   Paradoxically, "We are then righteous when we confess that we are sinners" (Jerome, *Ag. Pelagians*, *NPNF* 2 VI, p. 454). "Even the holiest men, while in this life, have only a small beginning of this obedience; yet so that with earnest purpose they begin to live, not only according to *some*, but according to *all* the commandments of God" (*Heid. Catech.* Q114, *COC* III, p. 349; Kuyper, *WHS*, p. 469).

Leo the Great stated this point most profoundly for the ecumenical tradition: As our finite freedom "always has the possibility of falling back, so has it the possibility of advancing. And this is *the true justness of the perfect, that they should never assume themselves to be perfect* . . . because none of us, dearly beloved, is so perfect and holy as not to be able to be more perfect" (Leo, *Sermons* XL, *NPNF* 2 XII, p. 154, italics added). "Although Divine Grace gives daily victory to His saints, yet He does not remove the occasion for fighting," in order "that something should remain for our ever-changing nature to win, lest it should boast itself on the ending of the battle" (Leo, *Sermons* LXXVIII, *NPNF* 2 XII, p. 194). "Nothing is more effectual in prevailing with God than that a man should judge himself and never cease from asking pardon, knowing that he is never without fault. For human nature has this flaw in itself, not planted there by the Creator but contracted by the transgressor, and transmitted to his posterity. . . . And in this strife such perfect victory is not [so] easily obtained that even those habits which must be broken off do not still encumber us, and those vices which must be slain do not wound" (Leo, *Sermons* XC, *NPNF* 2 XII, p. 200).

No Trial, No Growth.   The faithful, whether young or mature in faith, are not exempt in this life from temptation or challenge or difficulty, but their hearts are being freed from bondage to sin (Jerome, *Letters, NPNF* 2 VI, pp. 24, 25). What remains of the power of sin after justification may spend its fury in temptation to pride, avarice, or idolatry. These temptations are one by one able to be resisted through the sufficient grace of Word and Sacrament (Calvin, *Inst.* 3.10).

The great Leo stated this point poignantly, "There are no works of power, dearly beloved, without the trials of temptations, there is no faith without proof, no contest without foe, no victory without conflict," even as "the Lord allowed Himself to be tempted by the tempter, that we might be taught by His example as well as fortified by His aid" (Leo, *Sermons* XXXIX, *NPNF* 2 XII, p. 153).

Daily Combat.   Meanwhile, the ancient adversary does not cease to "masquerade as an angel of light" and "his servants as servants of righteousness" (2 Cor. 11:14, 15). "He knows whom to ply with the zest of greed, whom to assail with the allurements of the belly, before whom to set the attractions of self-indulgence, in whom to instill the poison of jealousy; he knows whom to overwhelm with grief, whom to cheat with joy, whom to surprise with fear, whom to bewilder with wonderment; there is no one whose habits he does not sift, whose cares he does not winnow, whose affections he does not pry into" (Leo, *Sermons* XXVIII, *NPNF* 2 XII, p. 140). "The blasphemous fury of the despoiled foe frets, therefore, and seeks new gains because it has lost its ancient right. Unwearied and ever-wakeful, he snatches at any sheep he finds straying carelessly from the sacred folds, intent on leading them over the steeps of pleasure and down the slopes of luxury into the abodes of death. And so he inflames their wrath, feeds their hatreds, whets their desires, mocks at their continence, arouses their gluttony" (Leo, *Sermons* XL, *NPNF* 2 XII, p. 154; cf. C. S. Lewis, *Screwtape Letters*).

The way is not easy. "The path of virtue lies hid. . . . A great work and toil it is then to keep our wayward heart from all sin, and with the numberless allurements of pleasure to ensnare it on all sides. . . . Who 'toucheth pitch, and is not defiled thereby?' who is not weakened by the flesh? who is not begrimed by the dust? who, lastly, is of such purity as not to be polluted by those things without which one cannot live?" (Leo, *Sermons* XLIX, *NPNF* 2 XII, p. 160). "The vice of pride is a near neighbour to good deeds, and arrogance ever lies in wait hard by virtue" (Leo, *Sermons* XLII, *NPNF* 2 XII, p. 157). "Joy and sorrow are inseparable from a man: no part of him is free from the kindlings of wrath, the over-powerings of delight, the castings down of affliction" (Leo, *Sermons* XC, *NPNF* 2 XII, p. 200; cf. Goodwin, *Works* VI, pp. 464–89).

It is a deadly antinomianism that says that all one needs to do is once have faith in Christ and thereafter all subsequent moments are incorruptible bliss, leaving no sinful habituation to cut off, no further sin to mortify. One must not be ignorant of Satan's devices (2 Cor. 2:11), one of which is to nurture the illusion that the walk of faith is easy and broad, not narrow. "For the sinful nature desires what is contrary to the Spirit, and the Spirit what is contrary to the sinful nature. They are in conflict with each other, so that you do not do what you want. But if you are led by the Spirit, you are not under law" (Gal. 5:17, 18). This daily combat of the sinful nature with the Spirit begins with regeneration and continues until death (*An Ancient Homily by an Unknown Author* [*Second Clement*] 8–11, *AF*, pp. 63–66).

Whether Recognition of the Power of Sin Tends to Lead to Despair.   The Spirit works to help each believer to become realistically acquainted with the historical power of unredeemed sin, and of grace to overcome sin. Were the full depths of personal-social-political-economic sin to be prematurely revealed to the neonate believer, it might seem an irrecoverably heavy blow. "A *full* disclosure might have shut us up in hopeless despair" (Winslow, *WHS*, p. 121).

It is wiser that the Spirit works gradually to disclose the full range of sin. The self is not suddenly flooded and washed away by sin, but sin is revealed to the self gently and gradually as overcomable. Only by leading the faithful gradually into a deeper awareness of the power of sin is the desire for holiness more deeply engendered (Thérèse of Lisieux, *Autobiography of a Soul*). One need not despair over the discovery of the depths of evil in one's heart. For that discovery itself is powerful evidence that the Spirit is presently working (Winslow, *WHS*, p. 122). It is a gradual process by which one is more fully enabled to pray, "Search me, O God, and know my heart, test me and know my anxious thoughts. See if there is any offensive way in me, and lead me in the way everlasting" (Ps. 139:23, 24; Augustine, *Expos. on Ps.* CXXXIX, *NPNF* 1 VIII, p. 640).

Theodicy and Sanctification.   Any challenge may work toward one's salvation. Any affliction may increase the depth of the work of sanctifying grace (John Cassian, *Conferences*, *NPNF* 2 XI, pp. 351 ff.). "Before I was afflicted I went astray, but now I obey your word. You are good, and what you do is good" (Ps. 139:67–68).

Jeremiah was led by grace to "walk in darkness rather than light" that his prophetic vision might be sharpened: "He has walled me in so I cannot escape, he has weighed me down with chains," and "made my paths crooked" (Lam. 3:7, 9). In order to grow, God's people are "tested in the furnace of affliction" (Isa. 48:10). "God uses even evil for a good purpose, and in a wonderful way turns perversity to good account" (Abelard, *Christian Theology* I, *TGS*, p. 117), so that Joseph could say to his brothers, "You intended to harm me, but God intended it for good" (Gen. 50:20).

The Spirit's coming is "like a refiner's fire or a launderer's soap. He will sit as a refiner and purifier of silver, he will purify the Levites and refine them like gold and silver. Then the Lord will have men who will bring offerings in righteousness" (Mal. 3:3). This testing is required to burn away the chaff from the grain, to fire out the dross attached to the beautiful ore, without which they are less useful and beautiful. "Dear friends, do not be surprised at the painful trial you are suffering, as though something strange were happening to you. But rejoice that you participate in the sufferings of Christ, so that you may be overjoyed when his glory is revealed" (1 Pet. 4:12, 13). This Letter was not addressing those "whose voyage so far has been over a smooth and summer sea, whose heart's affections have never been sundered," but to the "experienced child of God" who knows what it means to share in Christ's suffering. "In what other school could these high attainments have been made but in the low valley of humiliation" (Winslow, *WHS*, p. 126).

Satan rages in defeat where the righteous continue faithful through adversity (John Chrysostom, *Hom. on the Statues, NPNF* 1 IX, pp. 366–71). Tertullian found telling evidence in the fact that the church grows precisely under persecution (*Apology* 50, *APT*, p. 105).

Countering Mystical-Perfectionist Exaggerations.   The exaggerations toward which some forms of private, community-detached mysticisms have been prone have been repeatedly addressed by consensual exegetes. They are the neglect of justification by faith so as to tend to make perfection an ascetic work, the expectation that one can rise above infirmities and errors of perception or judgment, and separation from the world (Luther, *Ag. the Heavenly Prophets, LW* 40, pp. 79 ff.; Calvin, *TAAAL;* Wesley, *Letters, To William Law; Appeals*).

The Spirit works patiently in the heart in ways beyond finding out. That must not invite an obscurantism that would appeal cheaply to mystery as if that would legitimately end the reflective process or constitute an adequate explanation (Peter Browne, *The Procedure, Extent, and Limits of Human Understanding*).

Whether Final Sanctification Takes Place Only in the Next Life.   Is one made perfect only at death? Must sanctification await death for its completion? Though it is possible for the Spirit to enable holiness as an instantaneous work of grace, it is more often a gradual work of grace that becomes fully matured only when, upon facing death, the faithful receive even death in the form of trust in God (Tertullian, *On the Soul* 50–58, *ANF* III, pp. 227–35). Though one dies only once, one may face death many times so as to require readiness for death. It is well to remember that it is not death as such that cleanses us from all sin, but the atoning work of Christ (1 John 1:7; Rev. 1:5).

Christians differ not so much on whether sanctification is possible, but whether it may occur before death. Some in the Reformed tradition have argued that death itself is a sanctifying transition for the elect, readying them for the holiness of God (Calvin, *Inst.* 3.3–11; Barth, *CD* III/2, pp. 590 ff.). Others argue, "We should expect to be saved from all sin before the article of death" (Wesley, *Larger Minutes, CC*, p. 382, June 17, 1746), and that it would be an offense to the sovereignty of God to assert that God the Spirit is impotent to save persons wholly from their sins while soul and body are united.

However these views may differ, there is relatively greater consensus on the point that holiness is fully commanded and required and sufficiently enabled in this life (Luke 1:74, 75; Titus 2:12; 1 John 4:17), but to what degree actualized under the conditions of sin remains debated.

Arguments Against Intrinsic Unattainability

Sustained radical responsiveness to grace is posited on the grounds that God would not command what is impossible, that God would not promise what is intrinsically unattainable, that it is duty to pray for holiness and the faithful are called to seek it, that there are attested examples in scripture of unreserved responsiveness to grace, and that texts that seem to argue unattainability are explainable on different grounds. Though each of these points is contested, they carry the weight of centrist exegesis.

Whether God Commands What Is Intrinsically Impossible.   There is little doubt that a mature, complete, continuing response to grace is enjoined repeatedly in scripture (Exod. 19:6; John 5:14; 2 Cor. 7:1; 13:1; Heb. 6:1; 12:14; 1 Pet. 1:15, 16). God would not *require* holiness in this life (Deut. 6:5; Luke 10:27; Rom. 6:11) if it were intrinsically impossible.

Abraham was commanded by Yahweh to "walk before me and be blameless" (Gen. 17:1). When Jesus called his disciples to "be perfect, therefore, as your heavenly Father is perfect" (Matt. 5:48), the meaning is, "'Be ye perfect in the perfection of grace as your heavenly Father is perfect in the perfection of nature'; in other words, each in his own way. For between Creator and creature no similarity can be expressed without including a greater dissimilarity" (*Fourth Lateran Council* 2, *TGS*, p. 124; cf. *SCD* 431, p. 171, *COD*, p. 208). Paul instructed the Corinthians, "Aim for perfection" (2 Cor. 13:11). "It is God's will that you should be sanctified" (1 Thess. 4:3). The letter to the Hebrews called persons to "go on to maturity" (Heb. 6:1).

If the way of holiness were intrinsically unattainable, how could it be meaningfully or reasonably commanded? Would it not make God out to be more foolish than we are to assume that God would command that which is impossible to be obeyed, or that God has placed a self-determining creature under requirement but incidentally given the creature no power or means to perform what is required? "God has given possible commands, for otherwise He would Himself be the author of injustice, were He to demand the doing of what cannot possibly be done" (Jerome, *Ag. Pelagians, NPNF* 2 VI, pp. 452, 459).

Whether God Promises What Is Intrinsically Unattainable.   God would not *promise* the fullness of salvation and unblemished holiness if intrinsically unattainable. This is a question distinguishable from whether the *command* is impossible.

A complete and mature life of loving holiness is clearly promised in scripture (Deut. 30:6; Ps. 119:1–3; Isa. 1:18; Jer. 33:8; Ezek. 36:25; Matt. 5:6; 1 Thess. 5:23, 24; Heb. 7:25; 1 John 1:7, 9). If intrinsically unattainable, must not one conclude that God's promise would be a sham, absurdly bound to fail? The very object of preaching is complete responsiveness to grace (Col. 1:28; Eph. 4:11–13). "You must receive the gift, not of a mere covering of your sins, but of a taking them clean away" (Gregory Nazianzen, *Orat.* XL.32, *NPNF* 2 VII, p. 372).

Repeatedly scripture points to the way of holiness and perfect love as the very object of covenant history and the practical end of Christ's work (Luke 1:68–75; 1 John 3:8; Eph. 5:25–27; Titus 2:14). Would it not then be contemptuous to assume its unattainability, so as to demean the cross of Christ by making it fruitless (Origen, *Hom. XXVI on Numbers, CWS*, pp. 251 ff.)? Rather, it is the Spirit who makes attainable our actual "return to the adoption of sons, our liberty to call God our Father, our being made partakers of the grace of Christ, our being called children of light, our sharing in eternal glory, and in a word, our being brought into a state of all 'fulness of blessing'" (Basil, *On the Spirit* I.15, *NPNF* 2 VIII, p. 22; cf. Rom. 15:29).

Whether One Should Pray for Holiness in This Life.   Consensual exegesis reasoned that the Spirit would not lead the Apostles to *pray* for holiness in this life if it were intrinsically unattainable. The apostles repeatedly prayed for the full and complete life of holiness and perfect love (John 17:20–23; 2 Cor. 13:9–11; Eph. 3:14–21; Col. 4:12; Heb. 13:20, 21; 1 Pet. 5:10). If intrinsically unattainable, the implication could be drawn that the apostles were deluded in this expectation, or misguided by the Spirit in prayer (Origen, *On Prayer, CWS*, pp. 132–37). The psalmist urged worshipers to meditate upon "the blameless" and "observe the upright" in contrast to the wicked who will be "cut off" (Ps. 37:37).

Whether There Are Examples of Saintliness in This Life.   Some skeptics of the efficiency of perfecting grace are willing to concede that believers are commanded to be holy as God is holy, and provided with the means of sufficient grace to become holy, and promised holiness ultimately in eternal blessedness, and called to pray for holiness, *yet* they do not see anywhere any examples of holiness. Agreeing that God promises to make the faithful holy, they argue that this occurs not in this life, but only at its end or after this life (Hodge, *ST* III, pp. 245, 246).

Yet even the Westminster Confession defined the purpose of the church as "the gathering and *perfecting of the saints in this life*" (XXV.3, *CC*, p. 222, italics added). Wesley, who argued for attainability, pointedly remarked that if he knew any who were perfected in love he would not name them because the skeptics, like Herod searching for the child, would instantly pounce upon them looking for something amiss (*WJW* XI, pp. 366 ff.; V, pp. 202–12; *WJWB*, sermon 17).

God would not have provided in scripture numerous *examples* of complete consecration and radical holiness in this life if it were for all others intrinsically unattainable. Among many examples of holy living in this life remembered in the sacred tradition are Enoch (Gen. 5:18–24; Heb. 11:5), Noah (Gen. 6:9; Ezek. 14:14, 20), Job (Job 1:8), Barnabas (Acts 11:24), and the apostles who labored among the Thessalonians (1 Thess. 2:10). In the *Stromata*, Clement of Alexandria set forth biblical examples of women of unfettered, mature faith, such as Judith, Esther, Susanna, and Sarah, and also a remarkable list of pagan women of ancient literature whom he thought had shown forth anticipatory elements of the life of perfect love—Lysidica, Leaena of Attica, Theano the Pythagorean, the daughters of Diodorus, Arete of Cyrene, and Aspasia of Miletus (IV.XIX, *ANF* II, pp. 431–32).

If even a single instance is found in scripture of one who is living "blameless" or "free from sin" or "perfect," its attainability is formally established. Others who appear to have walked in the way of holiness are found in Luke 1:6; 1 Corinthians 2:6; Philippians 3:15; Hebrews 12:23. There are other passages in which the teaching of full salvation is clearly implied in the text (Rom. 14:6–8; Gal. 2:20; Eph. 3:16–19; 4:12–16, 22–24; Col. 1:28; Titus 2:14; Heb. 12:14; 1 John 3:3, 9; 4:17; 5:18). Basil encouraged all who were intentionally "pressing onwards to perfection" (Basil, *On the Spirit* I.2, *NPNF* 2 VIII, p. 2).

Whether Certain Texts Argue for Unattainability.   Certain texts appear to support the argument that there is no full redemption from sin in this life and that it is impossible to live without sin: "There is not a righteous man on earth who does what is right and never sins" (Eccles. 7:20; cf. 1 Kings 8:46; 2 Chron. 6:36). "How then can a man be righteous before God?" (Job 25:4; Calvin, *Inst.* 2.7.5; 4.1.20).

Yet these passages make an empirical observation that so far as we have seen, no one who has been exercising freedom has not fallen into sin (Murphy's law). They do not specifically set forth the hypothesis that no one can under any or other circumstances ever live without falling into sin. They assert the virtual inevitability, but not the absolute necessity, of sin, a major difference. No one is exempt from temptation or not liable to sin or beyond the possibility of sinning in the ordinary exercise of human freedom (Jerome, *Dialogue Ag. the Pelagians, NPNF* 2 VI, pp. 448–52).

Another text that appears to argue for practical unattainability is 1 John 1:8–10: "If we claim to be without sin, we deceive ourselves, and the truth is not in us. . . . If we claim we have not sinned, we make him out to be a liar and his word has no place in our lives." Yet the context of these passages strongly requires the teaching of purification from all unrighteousness: "the blood of Jesus, the Son, *purifies us from all sin.*" The evident meaning is that Christ cleanses us from all sin, so that no one can now say, I have no need of Christ and no sin that needs to be cleansed. If we say that we have never sinned, hence do not need Christ's atoning work, we deceive ourselves. But "If we confess our sins, he is faithful and just and will forgive us our sins *and purify us from all unrighteousness*" (1 John 1:7–9, italics added). Twice this passage points the reader to the promise of complete purification from sin in Christ.

Luther argued that evangelical perfection is not to be thought of as a completed attainment so as to require no more repentance, but as a continual striving (*EA* 14.25). Yet who more than Luther spoke of the kingdom of God as the dominion Christ exercises in begetting faith and life through the word, and granting full forgiveness of sins (*EA* 14.181 f. 238 f; *SHD* II 277)? "The kingdom of God is nothing else than to be pious, orderly, pure, kind, gentle, benevolent and full of all virtue and graces; also, that God have his being within us and that he alone be, live, and reign in us. This we should first of all and most earnestly desire" (*WA* 2.98).

Paul's Teaching of Full Salvation

How Far Did Paul Attest His Own Blamelessness?   Paul called God as his witness that he had remained "holy, righteous and blameless" (1 Thess. 2:10). He did not hesitate to remind his hearers that he had not wavered in faith even amid suffering (2 Tim. 1:12), was fully ready for his eternal inheritance (Col. 1:12, 13), having "kept the faith" (2 Tim. 4:6–8), and was ready to submit to God's will "content whatever the circumstances" (Phil. 4:12), able to "do everything through him who gives me strength" (v. 13). Paul was attested by Luke as understanding himself to be fully willing to discharge the duties of his calling, whatever the hardship (Acts 20:20–26). If this is not walking blameless in the way of holiness, what could these attestations mean?

How then could Paul also consistently say, "There is no one righteous, not even one," "There is no one who does good, not even one"? The answer lies in the very point of this passage, which concluded, "Therefore no one will be declared righteous in his sight *by observing the law;* rather through the law we become conscious of sin" (Rom. 3:10b, 12b, 20). This point is then followed by the new alternative offered in Christ: "*But now* a righteousness from God, apart from law, *has been* made known" (Rom. 3:21, italics added).

It is sometimes argued that Paul did not regard his own life as fully matured in Christ, as suggested in his letter to Philippians: "Not that I have already obtained all this, or have already been made perfect, but I press on toward the goal to win the prize for which God has called me heavenward in Christ Jesus" (Phil. 3:12–14). Yet one must read further in the same passage to see that the same perfection that he had not attained in the heavenly sense was the final reward toward which he was already intently racing. He then called upon all who, like himself, were "perfect," in the sense of being cleansed from reigning sin, to be "like-minded" in pressing toward the goal (cf. 1 Cor. 2:6; John Chrysostom, *Hom. on Phil.* XI, XII, *NPNF* 1 XIII, pp. 234–42; Field, *HCT,* p. 231): "All of us who are mature [Gk. *teleioi;* KJV, perfect] should take such a view of things" (Phil. 3:15). When Paul stated he has not yet obtained the perfect prize in the heavenly sense, he appears to be saying: I am not among the babes in Christ. I have matured. But please do not think of me as having already been perfected in love as it will appear on the last day, for in that sense I have not attained, and seek that perfection above, and strive headlong to ready myself for it. Jerome argued that Paul was confessing that in this life "he had not yet apprehended, and was by no means perfect; but like an archer, aimed his arrows at the mark set up (more expressively called *skopos* in Greek), lest the shaft, turning to one side or the other, might show the unskillfulness of the archer . . . so that what to-day he thought perfect, while he was stretching forward to better things and things in front, to-morrow proves to have been imperfect. And thus at every step, never standing still, but always running, he shows that to be imperfect which we men thought perfect, and teaches that our only perfection is that which is measured by the excellence of God" (Jerome, *Ag. Pelagians, Letters, NPNF* 2 VI, p. 455).

Romans 7:14–25. That Paul is referring to himself in Romans 7 seems to be supported by the following points: He constantly uses the pronoun *I* to himself. "I" is used in the present tense. If so, this shows that even in the apostle there was no perfect love, but a continuing struggle between good and evil, spirit and flesh, that obscures every act seeking holiness. Yet it is common in scripture for writers to use the present tense *I* to describe the general human condition prior to faith or in some prior situation (Hos. 12:4; Ps. 66:6), and this is especially characteristic of Paul (Rom. 3:7; Gal. 2:18; 1 Thess. 4:17).

It remains under debate whether Paul was describing his own life as a struggling regenerate individual or life under the law. The latter view has stronger evidence. For in chapter 6 Paul had just urged the baptized faithful to "offer the parts of your body to him as instruments of righteousness" (Rom. 6:13). Yet the "I" described in chapter 7 is one who has remained in his "sinful nature a slave to the law of sin" (Rom. 7:25). The regenerate man does not continue in sin, does not sin that grace may abound (Rom. 6:1), has died to sin (6:2). The regenerate man is spiritual (Rom. 6:4), but the man of Romans 7 is carnal, unspiritual, sold as a slave to sin (7:14). Regenerate persons "have been set free from sin" so that "the benefit you reap leads to holiness" (Rom. 6:22). Paul seems to be showing what his own condition *had been* when he met Christ.

An impressive list of classic exegetes held that Paul in Romans 7 was not referring to his present bondage to sin but to his former "old" self now being transcended by grace. This was argued by Irenaeus, Origen, Tertullian, Basil, Theodoret, Chrysostom, Jerome, Ambrose, Cyril of Jerusalem, Macarius,

Theophylact, and at times though not always by Augustine (cf. Jeremy Taylor, *Sermon on Rom. 7:19, TPW;* Field, *HCT,* p. 238). Later Augustinians, Lutherans, and Calvinists have more often argued that Paul was describing his own continuing struggling self in Romans 7. Most classic exegetes of the East and many from the West view Romans 7 as a reference to one under the law, and Romans 6 as a reference to one under grace, but the point remains controverted.

Galatians 5:16–18.   Paul called the Galatians to "be free" and "not use your freedom to indulge the sinful nature" (Gal. 5:13). "So I say, live by the Spirit and you will not gratify the desires of the sinful nature. For the sinful nature desires what is contrary to the Spirit, and the Spirit what is contrary to the sinful nature. They are in conflict with each other" (v. 16, 17). Does this imply that there is no end to the conflict, that it necessarily must remain until death? That is to overread the text, for the very next verse is an appeal to life "led by the Spirit," wherein one is precisely "not under law" (Gal. 5:18; Calvin, *Comm.* XXI, pp. 163–64).

The Galatian audience was imperfectly formed, while growing in grace. The conflict between Spirit and flesh raged in them. They were neither wholly unjustified nor unsanctified, but believing recipients of justifying grace in whom sanctifying grace was beginning to work to bring them to full maturity in Christian freedom, wherein they might refract the image of God exquisitely (Luther, *Comm. on Gal., MLS,* pp. 153–65).

THE FULL CONSEQUENCES OF SALVATION: A REPRISE

In assessing the consequences in history of saving grace, salvation is being viewed from the vantage point of its effects, consequent ends, and results.

Salvation Viewed from the Vantage Point of Its Effects

Humanity dwells in that unique nexus of creation capable of being addressed by God with a redemptive word (Schmaus, *Dogma* 4, p. xi). Jesus is not a myth whose appropriation is achieved by an imaginative act of recollection, but a person contemporary with every human being. He invites each one he meets to receive the good news of God's own coming (Matt. 11:28; Kierkegaard, *PF,* pp. 22 ff.; *TC* II).

The Mediator represents God in the presence of humanity, and humanity in the presence of God, uniting in his person that which had become separated through the history of sin. No other human being has had this distinctive mediatorial and personal significance for all others. Jesus confronts each human being with a decision about whether this gift has saving significance or not (Mark 1:15, 8:34–38; van Oosterzee, *CD* II, p. 630).

Practical Effects of Sanctifying Grace.   The intended effect of sanctifying grace is the power to walk in the way of holiness. "You were taught" to "put off your old self," and to "be made new in the attitude of your minds; and to put on the new self, created to be like God in true righteousness and holiness" (Eph. 4:22–24). The practical effects of grace may be seen in the ways that grace illumines reason, enlarges the affections, draws the will toward the good, and enables the power of redeemed action.

Sanctification is not fundamentally a new series of actions, but a new heart, a new soul, a new life, out of which sinful actions are becoming less frequent and good actions more habituated. "I will give you a new heart and put a new spirit in you; I will remove from you your heart of stone and give you a heart of flesh. And I will put my Spirit in you and move you to follow my decrees (Ezek. 36:26–28).

Grace does not subvert human nature, but woos it, draws it delicately toward the good. "No one can come to me unless the Father who sent me draws him" (John 6:44; cf. 2 Cor. 3:5). If by sin the moral capacities died out, by grace one again becomes a living member of the vine, whereby life is brought to the soul (John 15:1–11; Gal. 2:20; 2 Cor. 7:4).

Some effects may lie for the time being deeply hidden in the wellsprings of human motivation, only later to make their way into behavior. Psychoanalysis has sought, layer by layer, to uncover unconscious motivations of neurotic behavior. Christian orthodoxy has sought through confession and pastoral counsel, layer by layer, to make clear the hidden outworkings of prevenient and cooperative grace working inconspicuously to redeem unconscious neurosis.

Traditional catechetical instruction summarized these effects of sanctifying grace: grace acts to make the *ekklēsia* holy and pleasing to God (Heb. 12:28; John 14:23), to adopt the faithful into the family of God (1 John 3:1), to make them each a temple of the Holy Spirit (1 Cor. 6:19, 20), and to show the way to eternal blessedness (Rom. 8:14–17; *Baltimore Catechism*, pp. 82–83).

Effects of Saving Grace: Redemption, Glorification, and Reconciliation. The consequences of salvation may be viewed from the perspective of its consequences for humanity, for God, and for the divine-human relation. For humanity, saving grace results in redemption. For God, saving grace is the final expression of divine glory that finally unites holiness with love in the only way possible. From the viewpoint of the divine-human relationship, salvation is the reconciliation of an estranged covenant relation.

Schematically viewed:

CONSEQUENCES OF SAVING GRACE

For Humanity	For God	For the Divine-Human Relation
Redemption	Glorification	Reconciliation
Humanity saved	God's glory revealed	God brought near

Through saving grace humanity is redeemed, the divine-human relation reconciled, and God glorified. These three angles of vision behold a single reality: God's saving work in the Son through the Spirit. They are often interfused in apostolic testimony.

Redemption speaks of how humanity has been saved by the death and resurrection of the Son. Glorification is what happens to God through salvation. Reconciliation speaks of the new divine-human relationship resulting from that redemption and glorification (Baxter, *PW* VIII, pp. 113–17; Pope, *Compend.* II, pp. 275, 276).

Redemption: The Effect of Salvation upon Humanity.   Redemption is what happens to humanity as a result of the atonement (Athanasius, *Ag. Arians, NPNF* 2 IV, pp. 330–36, 380–86). Redemption is the state of having been repurchased, or bought back (Chemnitz, *TNC,* pp. 211–25; Baxter, *PW* VIII, pp. 118–27). "You are not your own; you were bought at a price" (1 Cor. 6:19, 20). The price is the cross. This indicative requires an imperative: "Therefore honor God with your body" (v. 20). "You were bought at a price; do not become slaves of men" (1 Cor. 7:23). Through the cross, all human history becomes the beneficiary in principle of redemption.

The Son is the ransom freeing humanity from sin and death, setting the slave free, the price being the Son's own life blood (Gal. 3:13; 1 Tim. 2:6; Matt. 20:28). The purchase involves a change of ownership. The redeemed are God's own (Barth, *CD* I/1, pp. 116 ff.). The redemption is not by gold or silver, but by "the blood of Christ, a lamb without blemish" (1 Pet. 1:18). The Spirit works to enable the reception of this once-for-all gift.

Whether Liberation Is an Adequate Metaphor for Redemption.   Redemption (*lutrosis, apolutrosis*) is an overarching way of describing in a single word the liberation of a captive, release from slavery and death by payment of a ransom. The essential metaphor is that of "buying back" to free from imprisonment (Luke 1:68; 2:38; Rom. 3:24; 1 Cor. 1:30). A price (Greek: *time*) of ransom (*lutron*) is included in this purchase (*agorazein, agorazo, exagorazo,* to buy), which eventuates in a release (*luein*) of the prisoner. The whole sequence is viewed as a rescue (*ruesthai*).

Sin is like an oppressive slavery from which one cannot break free by one's own limited personal strength. In redemption there comes the help of another who pays the price of ransom that the slave cannot pay (Nicholas I, Roman Council of 860–863, *SCD* 328, p. 132; see *SCD* 355, 494, 550). By faith one is liberated to live as son or daughter of God, yet that cannot imply that one has been given license to fall again into the slavery of sin or to do whatever makes one feel good at the moment. Rather one is liberated now to be an accountable son or daughter in the family of God, to do the will of the Father, to become radically responsive to God.

Paul joined the three complex metaphors of justification, sacrifice, and redemption in the single notion that the faithful are "justified freely by his grace through the redemption that came by Christ Jesus. God presented him as a sacrifice of atonement, through faith in his blood" (Rom. 3:24, 25). The modern view that redemption simply means political or economic liberation, omitting the decisive element of substitutionary sacrifice for another under divine-human covenant, is a diluted interpretation of Paul's meaning.

The death of Christ renders God favorably disposed toward sinners so that when they have faith in Christ they can be freely justified by God's grace. Justification is explained by free grace; grace is understood as a premise of redemption; redemption is explained by the propitiatory death of Christ made personally available only by faith, which the Spirit calls forth, enables, confirms, and sustains (Athanasius, *Ag. Arians, NPNF* 2 IV, pp. 331–35; Curtis, *CF,* p. 302).

The work of the Son does not bring it to pass that the sins of the past vaporize as if they never occurred, for they did occur and they continue to have consequences; nor does the Son's death take away human responsibility for sin; nor does it imply that the sinner no longer deserves the penalty of law. Rather, "The death of Christ brings to pass a state of things under which it is possible for the administrator of justice to order the non-execution of the penalty, without any compromise of law, without any possible reflection upon the righteous character of the administrator, and without any sacrifice of the ends for which government is established and maintained." How? Through a substituted penalty that is equivalent to the just penalty, not an equivalent penalty "but the equivalent of a penalty" (Raymond, *ST* II, p. 261).

The Glory of God Manifested

By the Spirit the Triune Name Becomes Published Throughout the World. Through the work of the Son and the Spirit, the name, attributes, and governing ways of God are rightly and gloriously manifested. The triune name is published throughout the world; the holiness and love of God are at long last understood in their intimate interrelationship; and the divine ordering and governance of the world are fittingly vindicated, having been severely challenged and contested by sin.

It is fitting here to recall that the triune name could not be spoken until after the finished work of Christ and the outpouring of the Spirit. The triune work could be only vaguely glimpsed and intimated but not rightly grasped and named until the Son's resurrection and the Spirit's indwelling (Hilary, *Trin.* I.13–14, *NPNF* 2 IX, pp. 43 ff.).

The history of salvation had long awaited this moment: "Now is the Son of Man glorified and God is glorified in him. If God is glorified in him, God will glorify the Son in himself, and will glorify him at once" (John 13:31, 32). In the Son's resurrection and the Spirit's indwelling, the Son was glorified in the Father, and the Father was glorified in the Son, which could occur only when "the hour" had come (John 17:1; John Chrysostom, *Hom. on John* LXXX, *NPNF* 1 XIV, pp. 296–99). The disciples were immediately charged to "go and make disciples of all nations, baptizing them in the name of the Father and of the Son and of the Holy Spirit" (Matt. 28:19). If through God's energies God's essence was being made known, then through God's action God's name could now be rightly called and known and celebrated. On the day of Pentecost, the Spirit would empower the mission to make known the good news of the Father's sending of the Son through the power of the Spirit (Novatian, *Trin.*, *ANF* V, pp. 611 ff.).

Those newly born tend to think experientially from their experience of the Spirit backward through the Son to the Father: "When we receive gifts, the first that occurs to us is the distributor [Spirit], next we think of the sender [Son], and then we lift our thoughts to the fountain and cause of the boons [Father]." In due time the order of the baptismal formula is rightly grasped as "the original cause of all things that are made, the Father; of the creative cause, the Son; of the perfecting cause, the Spirit," so that "the first principle of existing things is One, creating through the Son and perfecting through the Spirit" (Basil, *On the Spirit* I.16, *NPNF* 2 VIII, p. 23).

The Gathering of a Community of Testimony.   Jesus died, bearing the penalty for human sin, thereby satisfying both the holiness and the love of God in a full disclosure of the divine intention toward humanity. Jesus rose from the dead, gathering to himself a new spiritual community, one body in Christ, sharing his death and life, a community organic in him. He rose from the dead with a glorified body that included this spiritual community of those who live in him, a body to be finally manifested in the final day, wherein all who believe in him shall take on not the body of human death but a spiritual body "conformed to the body of his glory" (Phil. 3:20, ASV; Tertullian, *On the Resurrection* 45–47, *ANF* III, pp. 578–81; cf. Curtis, *CF*, pp. 308–9). Those whose citizenship is in heaven now "eagerly await a Savior from there, the Lord Jesus Christ, who, by the power that enables him to bring everything under his control, will transform our lowly bodies, so that they will be like his glorious body" (Phil. 3:20, 21).

Whether Through the Son's Resurrection and the Spirit's Indwelling the Divine Perfections Are Made Known in Their Distinctive Complementarity.   Having discussed previously the divine attributes in some detail (*LG*, pp. 53–130), noting that they are best understood in relation to the ministry of the Son and the Spirit, it is useful now to see the divine attributes in close relation to resurrection and Pentecost. The deep interfusing of the two major moral attributes—holiness and love—are seen as an event in Christ's atoning death and the indwelling of the Spirit. Nowhere do we learn more about the attributes of God than at the cross.

Briefly stated: Holiness and love in God are uniquely understood as interrelated on the cross. The love of God was never fully grasped in nature as such or even in the history of providence, although God's just and intelligent ordering may indeed be glimpsed there. It was not until the finished work of the Son on the cross and the outpouring of the Spirit that the simple statement "God is love" (1 John 4:8) could be fully and rightly understood. "This is how God showed his love among us: He sent his one and only Son into the world that we might live through him. This is love: not that we loved God, but that he loved us and sent his Son as an atoning sacrifice for our sins" (1 John 4:9, 10).

Without God's holiness the cross was unnecessary. Without God's love the cross was impossible. The holiness of God opposes sin and requires punishment for sin. On the cross, "the mercy that provides and the justice that requires the Atonement are one in the recesses of the Divine nature" (Pope, *Compend.* II, p. 278). Love reconciles, unites, and reigns through the sacrifice of love in a way fitting to God's holiness.

It is not an exaggeration to say that we know nothing rightly or adequately or in a balanced way about God's attributes except as their coherence is discovered in a historical event—cross and resurrection. Christians preach no other God than the One nailed to the cross and raised from the dead (1 Cor. 1:23). There is no other God. The one God, Father, Son, and Spirit, is most fully beheld through the final deed of the Son illumined by the Spirit. God's revelation is complete in the work of the Father, Son, and Spirit, not needing a subsequent history to improve upon it (Gregory Nazianzen, *Orat.* XLI, *NPNF* 2 VII, pp. 378–84).

The Divine Economy Vindicated: The Death of Christ Is Declarative.   The purpose of redemption is to bring together the holiness and love of God as they cohere eternally in God. This harmonization could not have occurred by expressing either the holiness of God's requirement alone, or the love of God for sinners in a way inconsistent with God's holiness (Pope, *Compend.* II, pp. 402 ff.). The cross provided the way to understand both together. The Spirit now empowers the faithful to walk in that way. The holiness and love of God have been satisfied by this reconciliation. This is why it can be said that God was glorified on the cross (1 Cor. 2:8).

Through the Son's atonement, God is able to treat a sinner as if righteous without slackening the divine holiness. It is only through the atonement that God could be at the same time both "just and the one who justifies those who have faith in Jesus" (Rom. 3:26; cf. P. Stuhlmacher, "Zur neueren Exegese von Rom. 3:24–25," in *Jesus und Paulus,* ed. E. E. Ellis and E. Graesser, 1975, pp. 315–33).

The focus of the Son's atonement is upon the love of God overcoming the obstacles to divine-human reconciliation. God is love because the Father sent his beloved Son not as if on a riskless Sunday outing but nailed to a cross: "as an atoning sacrifice for our sins" (1 John 4:10).

By the death of Christ, the powers of darkness are defeated. "And having disarmed the powers and authorities, he made a public spectacle of them, triumphing over them by the cross" (Col. 2:15). In the presence of the cross it is clear that "the rulers of this age" are "coming to nothing" (1 Cor. 2:6). The final stage of this triumph is yet to come: "Then the end will come, when he hands over the kingdom to God the Father after he has destroyed all dominion, authority and power" (1 Cor. 15:24; John Chrysostom, *Hom. on 1 Cor.* VII, *NPNF* 1 XII, pp. 33–43).

The death of the Son is declarative, once for all declaring the righteousness of God. The cross is that event which makes clear that God is righteous without ceasing to love sinners. It vindicates the righteous governance of God by securing good ends both for God and humanity: for God the atonement vindicates the glory of God; for humanity the atonement provides a way for the holy God to forgive and save sinners (Anselm, *CDH;* Calvin, *Inst.* 2.6, 16).

The Spirit's Reconciling Ministry

The Effects of Saving Grace as Applied to the Divine-Human Relationship. Reconciliation (*katallage*) means that the favor of God has been restored to sinners who repent and trust in the efficacy of the death of Christ for humanity (Rom. 5:11; 11:15; 2 Cor. 5:18, 19). The enmity caused by sin has been removed with Christ's death. The indicative of the cross calls imperatively for a change in the human heart from enmity to friendship, from alienation to daughterhood and sonship. Reconciliation is the work of the Son through the Spirit, having restored fellowship and communication between God and humanity (Athanasius, *On the Incarnation of the Word, NPNF* 2 IV; Calvin, *Inst.* 3.2.2, 29; Barth, *CD* IV/2, 3 ff.).

The Welcoming God.   In this reconciliation, two sides of the relationship are significantly changed: God welcomes humanity, and humanity is called to accept God's welcome. God has mercifully set aside the long-standing quarrel with humanity due to sin. Human beings are invited to receive God's mercy and enter into a new relationship with the forgiving God (Luke 15:20).

The obedience of the Son on our behalf is complete. That leaves only the call to our obedience to respond to God's outreaching love. In the Son, God is reconciled to humanity. Now humanity is called to become reconciled to God, and to every neighbor met in the presence of God the Reconciler. "For God was pleased to have all his fullness dwell in him to reconcile to himself all things," a reconciliation that occurred "by making peace through his blood, shed on the cross" (Col. 1:19).

It is less exact to say that humanity is reconciling itself to God than that God is reconciling himself to humanity. For it is God who was doing the reconciling of "the world to himself in Christ" (2 Cor. 5:19). "All this is from God, who reconciled us to himself through Christ" (2 Cor. 5:18). In a subjective sense, we are not doing the reconciling. In an objective sense, however, we are being reconciled in an act that truly involves us.

The believer does not by dint of human courage navigate the stormy gulf of the divine-human controversy. God overcame that barrier in the cross. It is not that we have diminished our sins to a level of divine acceptability, but that God in Christ was "not counting men's sins against them" (2 Cor. 5:19; John Chrysostom, *Hom. on 2 Cor.* XI, *NPNF* 1 XII, pp. 331–35).

Whether God Is Both Reconciler and Reconciled. God is both reconciler and reconciled in the work of redemption. The Father has sent the Son who provides the sacrifice by which his favor toward humanity is restored. The Father is also the one reconciled through the satisfaction provided by Jesus' atoning death. The divine-human enmity has been overcome, and obstacles to communion removed by the indwelling Spirit (Heb. 2:17; Calvin, *Inst.* 2.6, 16).

The reception of this gift is ground for rejoicing: "For if, when we were God's enemies, we were reconciled to him through the death of his Son, how much more, having been reconciled, shall we be saved through his life! Not only is this so, but we also rejoice in God through our Lord Jesus Christ, through whom we have now received reconciliation" (Rom. 5:10, 11).

God first draws near to humanity in Christ, who invites humanity to respond by drawing near to God (1 John 4:19; James 4:8). God's action for us must be answered by an act on our side. God's freedom for us invites human freedom to respond. Grace does not disempower but enables self-determination. Salvation is not purchasable by human effort but received as purchased already by God, to be accepted by human gratitude (Col. 1:20–27).

The Spirit's Peacemaking Ministry as Gift and Task. If we are reconciled to God, we then have a ministry of reconciliation. God's peacemaking with humanity calls for human peacemaking in whatever sphere it is possible for human history to refract the divine peace.

The letter to Ephesus grasped the whole peacemaking event: "For he himself is our peace, who has made the two one and has destroyed the barrier, the dividing wall of hostility, by abolishing in his flesh the law with its commandments and regulations. His purpose was to create in himself one new man out of the two, thus making peace, and in this one body to reconcile both of them to God through the cross, by which he put to death their hostility" (Eph. 2:14–16). "Consequently, you are no longer foreigners and aliens, but fellow citizens with God's people and members of God's household" (Eph. 2:19; John Chrysostom, *Hom. on Eph.* V, VI, *NPNF* 1 XIII, pp. 70–79).

What Happened (indicative):	**Therefore (imperative):**
God reconciled us to himself.	God gave us the ministry of reconciliation.
Gift	Task
God has overcome the divine-human hostility. Christ is the Reconciler.	God has committed to us the message of reconciliation. Be reconciled to God.
Christ made peace with humanity.	We are Christ's ambassadors, as though God were making his appeal through us (2 Cor. 5:18–21)

Cosmic Reconciliation. God's reconciling work not only has relevance for human history, but its echoes are felt throughout the spheres of cosmic nature, the angelic hosts, and the entire eschatological audience to the drama of human history. For through Christ it pleased God to "reconcile to himself *all things* [*panta*], whether things on earth or things in heaven, by making peace through his blood, shed on the cross" (Col. 1:20).

The earthly history of sin has a cosmic audience, the incorporeal powers, whose destinies might have become forever corrupted if justice had not prevailed through this unique economy of salvation. "And what, we ask, would have been the effect upon, perhaps, millions of worlds, had the Almighty failed to require the penalty of the violated law? Would they not all have received license to sin with impunity? And would not the result probably have been fatal to the inhabitants of innumerable worlds?" (Ralston, *ED*, p. 231; cf. Wesley, *WJW* VI, pp. 241–53, 288 ff.).

The cross visually portrays God's arms stretched out in sacrificial suffering for the whole of nature and history, one arm embracing all past and the other embracing all future cosmic events, reaching once for all from the beginning to the end of time (Athanasius, *Incarn. of the Word* 24–25, *NPNF* 2 IV, pp. 49–50; Gregory of Nyssa, *Address of Religious Instruction* 32, *LCC* III, p. 311).

Among those who are baptized into the body of Christ, having become clothed in Christ, "There is neither Jew nor Greek, slave nor free, male nor female, for you are all one in Christ Jesus" (Gal. 3:28). "Here there is no Greek or Jew, circumcised or uncircumcised, barbarian, Scythian, slave or free, but Christ is all, and is in all" (Col. 3:11). In this community human peacemaking is concretely occurring, anticipative of the final day.

It is to this reconciling community that Jesus promised, "I tell you the truth, anyone who has faith in me will do what I have been doing. He will do even greater things than these, because I am going to the Father. And I will do whatever you ask in my name" (John 14:12, 13; Augustine, *Comm. on John*, tractates LXXI–LXXIII, *NPNF* 1 VII, pp. 328–33).

The Reconciling Invitation. The fountain of cleansing is open to all nations and peoples. All are invited to plunge in to be cleansed of sin and rise renewed (R. Robinson, "Come Thou Fount of Every Blessing," *WHNS*, 866).

The feast is set on the table, sufficient for all. The hungry are invited to eat and be filled. No one lacks for an invitation (C. Wesley, "Come Sinners to the Gospel Feast," *WHNS*, 2).

The prison doors are thrown open—the imprisoned are invited to live in freedom, not licentiously as they please, but free to live precisely as those whose lives had been bought with a price (I. Watts, "Come Thou Long Expected Jesus," *WHNS*, 688).

The bridge has been built between God and humanity over the gulf of sin. Pilgrims are invited to cross over to the city not made with hands (C. Wesley, "Come O Thou Traveller Unknown," *WHNS*, 140).

The Cohesion of Life in Christ

The central theme of this systematic theology is *life:* the living God, the Word of life, life in the Spirit. Divine life flows from union with Christ, who dwells in the faithful through the Spirit. Variable manifestations of grace are organically united in that relationship. "He who has the Son has life" (1 John 5:12). "I am come that they may have life, and have it to the full" (John 10:10). "The words I have spoken to you are spirit, and they are life" (John 6:63). If we have not beheld life, we have not begun to study systematic theology (Gregory Nazianzen, *Orat.* XVIII, *NPNF* 2 VII, pp. 254–69).

The objectifying study of life is hardly life itself. Finally the purpose of the study of salvation is not to dissect but to receive life. It is difficult for a dissecting, analyzing systematic theology to speak of living union with Christ through the Spirit without tending to destroy what it is trying to describe. For whatever is brought into the laboratory for dissection has already died, inasmuch as dissection can only take place of a dead thing. Dissection is necessary if we are to learn the anatomy of something physically inert, but paradoxically life itself cannot be dissected without first ending life. In the dissecting laboratory, one takes organs apart one at a time, detaches, examines, diagrams, describes them each singly and apart, but only if the organism is dead. No living organism can be alive while dissected. Dissection requires and presupposes death; hence there is an intrinsic tension between the objective analysis of salvation and the living of it.

The Unity of the Whole.   Life within an organism assumes the composite whole. Life resists the scalpel. Life in Christ requires the whole as united organically in the head. No part can be detached or rightly understood as detached. To dissect is to kill (1 Cor. 12; Eph. 4).

The teaching of salvation seeks to behold this whole, but at times sees only a part—repentance or faith or pardon or new birth or assurance. What appears to us as a pilgrim's journey is to God whole. Salvation is not many themes but one. Salvation implies a whole, spiritually enlivened person, growing in grace—not pieces of a puzzle, not parts of a machine (Eph. 2:1–8; 1 Tim. 1:15; 1 Pet. 1:1–10).

All loci of soteriology are brought together concretely in the active love of God and neighbor. "Repentance is but love abhorring sin and forsaking the world; faith is love embracing Christ; righteousness is love keeping the law; sonship is love doing the Father's will; assurance is love rejoicing in the light; holiness is love dwelling with God; charity is love thinking no evil" (Tillett, *PS*, pp. 296, 297).

The Celebration of Paradox Within That Unity.   The language of salvation teaching is drawn to paradox. In Christ God breaks the dominion of sin, yet remains to cleanse the remnants of sin. In Christ the faithful remain fully human, yet partake of the divine nature. In Christ one experiences eternal life, yet in the present already beginning. In Christ spiritual perfection is given, yet admits of continual increase. In Christ I live, yet Christ lives within me; I die, yet am raised. In Christ those who are walking the way of holiness are most keenly aware of their sins. In Christ conviction of sin characterizes the newborn believer imperfectly, and the mature believer perfectly. Each paradox of Christian salvation is celebrated when brought into a whole perspective and celebrated.

Because all grace comes from God, grace is one. Yet because the temporal condition that grace addresses is highly varied, the Spirit must work in different ways and paces at different times, places, and stages of human development. Hence in the economy of grace, Christian teaching has identified various levels at which grace shows evidence of operating.

"Being baptized, we are enlightened; being enlightened, we are adopted as sons; being adopted, we are made perfect"; hence a single work "has many names; gift of grace, enlightenment, perfection, washing" (Clement of Alexandria, *Paedagogus, The Teacher* I.VI.26, *ECF,* p. 180).

Metaphors of Evangelical Privilege: Incorruptible Court, Restored Family, Holy Temple.   God's mission to humanity is salvation. What is salvation? That grace in Christ in which one stands by faith, as empowered by the Holy Spirit. The circle of evangelical privileges that characterize this condition include three dimensions found in three metaphorical arenas:

Court	**Family**	**Temple**
Righteousness	Inheritance	Consecration

The evangelical privileges are: being accounted righteous before God, being given new life and spiritual birth into the family of God, and being fully consecrated to God. These privileges interfuse metaphors from three spheres that repeatedly meld in New Testament passages: court, family, and temple. The message of salvation draws together these three themes of grace corresponding with these three metaphorical spheres: forgiveness of sins, renewal of life, and being set apart for a holy life. The gospel announces a great reversal in human history, employing these three metaphors (Pope, *Compend.* II).

In the court, justification is the reversal of a sentence of death for sin. In the family, adoption to daughterhood-sonship is the reversal of an exclusion from inheritance, providing full rights as sons and daughters in the family of God. In the temple, the holy God can be approached by those whose lives are redeemed and set apart for holy love.

Various parts of the apostolic witness focus upon special aspects of this whole: Paul's gospel centers upon the righteousness of God, John's upon new birth into daughterhood-sonship in the family of God, and the letter to the Hebrews upon set-apartness through Christ's priestly ministry (Newman, *Ath.* II, pp. 130–35).

Each metaphor intends to speak of a single act of grace and not to separate its thematic focus from the others. Salvation is one gift of grace received by faith, not many gifts, not a series of stages or parts or pieces of doctrine. Each of the three themes describes varied benefits of a single divine act of saving grace. Each may occur instantaneously or gradually as the Spirit moves.

All three metaphors apply to persons the work of Christ by the power of the Spirit. The Spirit attests acquittal in the courtroom; resurrects life from the dead and entry into the new family of God; consecrates the new creature in the temple of God.

These metaphors constantly conflate and interfuse in New Testament texts. There is an implicit order in them that Christian teaching seeks to articulate. They are not synonymous, though intrinsically related and illuminative of each other: The old life has been judged and its sins forgiven at this court. New life is being offered in this family, where birthing, nurture, and recovered inheritance derive from generative, parental, and family metaphors. Full consecration to holiness is best understood in the setting of the temple in which dwells the incomparably holy God, made approachable through the once-for-all priesthood of the eternal Son (Heb. 8–10).

By Christ's righteousness, God does not judge our sin but supplies grace through which the righteousness of the law is fulfilled. Through Christ's sonship the believer is given new spiritual life and adopted into sonship-daughterhood. By Christ's priestly act the hindrances are removed so that the believer may approach God, cleansed from sin (1 John 2, 3).

However variously explained by means of different language spheres, salvation is one, celebrating one Lord, one faith, one baptism. If theology is conceptually prone to split salvation into various stages or doctrines, such is not the case with the apostolic testimony or the actual life it attests (Rom. 4, 5; Phil. 2; 1 Tim. 3:16).

No one has summarized the evangelical privileges more unitively than William Burt Pope: "The sinner absolved in the Court is by the same act received in the Family and consecrated in the Temple. The Judge, the Father, and the God are One. The Advocate, the Son, the High Priest are One. The penitent who stands at the bar, who is met as a prodigal at the door, who approaches the altar of consecration with only defilement in the soul which he comes to give back to God, is one and the same penitent" (*Compend.* II, p. 401).

Three Settings of the One Drama of Human History.   The human condition is grasped dramatically in these settings of righteousness, adoption, and sanctification. In the courtroom drama, God is Judge, the God-Man is Advocate-Mediator, and the accused is the sinner living out of a long social history of sin. An atonement is offered to satisfy justice whereby the Advocate-Mediator dies for the sinner. The sinner, previously condemned under the law, is now free to live. Repentance under this metaphor means confession and conviction. The expected sentence is remitted and pardon declared. The Spirit attests the pardon inwardly, whispering, You are free! There is no condemnation!

In the broken family drama, we learn scene by scene how the parent-child relation of trust became lost and how it is restored. The people of God are a family. The human predicament is portrayed as an inheritance squandered and the family disavowed. By regeneration a new life from above is offered. By adoption the new person, spiritually reborn, is given full rights of sonship and daughterhood, to share fully again in the inheritance of the family. The feast is spread in the family table: bread and wine. The banquet is for the returning prodigal. The Spirit witnesses quietly to the newly born family member, Call him Father! You are his own! Abba!

In the holy temple drama, the problem centers upon how one may be rightly admitted into the presence of the holy God in the holy temple. The person seeking admittance is filthy and corrupt. The saving deed occurs through the high priest himself who makes (and is) a once-for-all sacrifice. The Spirit witnesses inwardly to the supplicant, Go into the temple! You have been cleansed from all sin!

Salvation as the Narrative of the Work of Grace.   A single word summarizes the whole story: *salvation*. "For the grace of God that brings salvation has appeared" (Titus 2:11). Salvation is "the gift," "God's grace," "the gift that came by the grace of the one man, Jesus Christ," "the gift of God" (Rom. 5:15, 16). God's outpouring grace is its source, its means, and its result. Salvation is "about the grace that God has given" (2 Cor. 8:1). "By grace you have been saved" (Eph. 2:5). Through "his glorious grace" we have "redemption through his blood, the forgiveness of sins, in accordance with the riches of God's grace" (Eph. 1:7). This is the "gospel of God" (Rom. 1:1), "the power of God for the salvation of everyone who believes" (Rom. 1:16). God's mission is salvation. However varied the terms of description, they point to one salvation, one life in Christ.

The distinctive work of the Holy Spirit is to make accessible to hearers of the gospel this gift of salvation. The Spirit is the administrator of God's blessings, the agent through whom they are distributed, the witnessing One who attests their authenticity and meaning, who preserves the witnessing community through the hazards of time. Although salvation is summarily understandable as one act of grace, the benefits of salvation are not able to be received in a single moment, but rather require an unfolding personal and social history. They elicit growth in recipients through their gradual reception.

The Son promised that the Spirit would "guide you into all truth" (John 16:13), and would "take from what is mine and make it known to you" (v. 15). Paul prayed that "the fellowship of the Holy Spirit" would "be with you all" (2 Cor. 13:14). The Spirit's nurturing and guiding is highly contextual, not discernible abstractly or beforehand. When brought before authorities, the disciples were instructed not to worry in advance how to defend themselves, "for the Holy Spirit will teach you *at that time* what you should say" (Luke 12:12).

In the ancient world huge stones were moved by hoisting machines. Ignatius of Antioch (A.D. 35–110) must have been thinking of such a machine when he wrote to the Ephesians, "You consider yourselves stones of the Father's temple, prepared for the edifice of God the Father, to be taken aloft by the hoisting engine of Jesus Christ, that is, the Cross, while *the Holy Spirit serves you as a rope*, your faith is your spiritual windlass and your love the road which leads up to God" (*Ephesians* 9, *TGS*, p. 6, italics added).

PART III

The Church

That the church is an article of faith is made clear by its inclusion in the creed: "I believe in the holy, catholic church." If the church did not exist, then there would be no community in which to make this confession. The query, What is the church? whether skeptical or plaintive, always silently presupposes the existence of the church that asks the question.

7 The Community of Celebration

COMPLEMENTARY WAYS OF DEFINING THE CHURCH

Rudiments of Ecclesiology

The church's life is shaped by special attention and devotion to "the apostles' teaching and to the fellowship, to the breaking of bread and to prayer" (Acts 2:42). All essential elements of the church are embryonically present in this early fourfold description of the church: apostolic doctrine, community, sacrament, and common worship.

The Church Viewed as a Problem of Systematic Christian Teaching. Rufinus explained, "We do not say, 'We believe *in* the holy Church,' but 'We believe the holy Church,' not as God, but as the Church gathered together to God" (Rufinus, *Comm. on Apostles' Creed* 36, *NPNF* 2 III, p. 557). When the faithful confess, "I believe in the holy catholic church," the intent is not to displace faith in God with faith in the church. It means that they have faith that there indeed *is* one holy, apostolic, universal church that has its life in God (Hutter, *Loci* 521, in *SCF*, p. 375). To believe in the church is to live out of the conviction that grace abides in her, teaches and governs her common life, and flows from God to all the faithful (*Longer Catech,* Eastern Orthodox Church, 253, *COC* II, p. 483).

Complementary Ways of Looking at the Church: Coetus Electorum, Corpus Christi, Communio Sanctorum. Complementary classical definitions of the church stress varied perceptions of the church's essential center: the church as company of the elect or regenerate community (*coetus electorum*), or as body of Christ (*corpus Christi*), and as communion of saints (*communio sanctorum*).

These definitions stand together in close affinity analogous to triune reasoning: the One whose electing love calls the living community one by one into being is the Father; the One embodied in the church is the Son as head of the body; the One who brings together the community of life in the spirit is God the Spirit.

Whether Varied Perspectives Are Each Integral to the Whole. These three views of the church variously stress new life, reliable truth, and visible community. One tradition may have an astute grasp of the church as the place where new life is coming into being; another as the context in which authoritative teaching of reliable truth is being passed on. The third views the church essentially as a serving, reconciling visible community manifesting the love of God in the world. These three motifs belong together. When separated, they lose equilibrium and vitality and cease being mutually corrective.

Systematic reasoning on the church looks for wholeness in fitting these complementary themes together. When in certain periods of history one motif becomes so dominant that others tend to be misplaced, the vitality of the church is diminished.

Those who focus too exclusively on conversion tend to neglect nurture; those who focus too intently upon the sustaining of sacramentally mediated apostolic tradition may neglect serving ministries and conversion. Those who focus upon the serving nature of the community in response to the needs of the world may tend to forget the ground of their authority and apostolic identity. "Each of the three definitions of the Ekklesia shows us a special aspect of its basis: the transcendent (*electio*), the historical-objective (*corpus Christi*), and the spiritual-subjective (*sanctorum communio*). Each of them taken by itself would necessarily lead to a one-sided conception: either to an abstract spiritual intellectualism (the number of the predestined, *numerus praedestinatorum*), or to a sacramental hierarchism (the Body of Christ, *corpus Christi*), or to an emotional and pietistic individualism (the communion of the faithful, *communio fidelium*). Only in their unity do they reproduce the reality of the Ekklesia" (Brunner, *Dogm.* III., p. 27).

Strengths and Limits of Pietistic, Orthodox, and Activist Visions of the Church.
Classic consensual exegesis on themes concerning the church has sought to understand how the body of Christ though divided in history is one in Christ and one in the Spirit. The vitality of the church may be variously viewed from the viewpoint of personal conversion, or sacramental order, or base communities seeking structural change in the orders of social justice. These types have recurred in church history. Today we call them by terms familiar to contemporary church life. Evangelicals view things differently from Anglicans, Catholics, and Orthodox, who view things differently still from politically oriented social gospel and liberal visions of the church that focus upon social change and service. Yet the same Spirit of the triune God offers these variable gifts that need each other for completion.

Pietism stresses the mark of holiness. Orthodoxy stresses the church's apostolicity. Social activism stresses moral service to the world, and from a certain perspective, catholic inclusiveness. In this way the ancient question of the marks that define the church correlates with these three complementary histories.

Whether Varied Interpreters Inevitably Remember and Forget out of Their Own Special History.
Pietists sometimes forget that the church is an inclusive community. Liberals are prone to forget that the church is where new people are being radically born into life in the spirit from above. Those focused upon orthodoxy may tend to forget that the Holy Spirit is calling forth new forms of mission and distinctive forms of witness in ever-new cultural situations. It is not surprising that each one of us is prone to value and assess the church from the particular viewpoint of our own special (family-social-national-ethnic) history within it. We are prone to think xenophobically and egocentrically about alternative visions of the church that arise out of different social locations and histories. We judge others from our niche.

Those nurtured by the sacraments of orthodoxy find it easy to caricature the voluntary churchmanship of late-arriving Baptists as hokey individualism. Those spawned by charismatic preaching find it easy to dismiss the seemingly dense formality of Catholic sacramental life—all that smoke and hocus-pocus. Those who remain committed social activists look with despair toward the forms of Christian

institutionalization that seem only to affirm the political status quo—all that nationalistic chauvinism. How can these be brought together? That has been the
challenge to classic consensual exegesis from the outset.

A Typology of Recollections and Forgettings.   Schematically, this can be visualized
abstractly in the following rough typology, by which a gestalt of features clusters
around these three types of ecclesial reasoning. Each reader is likely to have
emerged out of one or another column, or combination of them, and thus may
tend toward forgetfulness or ignorance of the marvelous values in another arena:

MODEL

Coetus Electorum	**Corpus Christi**	**Communio Sanctorum**
TYPICAL HISTORICAL EXPRESSIONS		
Evangelical	Liturgical	Liberal
Revivalism	Eastern, Roman, Anglican traditions	"Mainline" Protestantism
Pietism	Catholic orthodoxy	Political theology
FOCUS OF COMMON LIFE		
Conversion	Sacramental life	Social action
Discipline of regenerate life	Unity of apostolic teaching	Relevant service in the world
Religion of the heart	Religion of the book	Religion of the people
KEY VALUES AND ACHIEVEMENTS		
Vitality	Authority	Solidarity
Inner life	Correct doctrine	Social change
TEACHING CONCENTRATION		
New birth	Authoritative doctrine and catechetics	Reconciling base communities
The individual	The eternal	The social
Personal Regeneration	Apostolic authority	Social action
CHURCH AND SOCIETY CORRELATION		
Christ against culture	Christ of or above culture	Christ transforming culture

HETERODOX TENDENCY

Gnosticism   Neoplatonic idealism   Pelagian pragmatism

FOCUS OF HUMAN PREDICAMENT

Sin   Heresy   Injustice

KEY MARK

Holiness   Apostolicity   Unity

These overlapping types offer a frame of reference for speaking of varied ways the Holy Spirit has worked for centuries in forming the church, a topic traditionally termed "offices of the Spirit in the Church." For evangelicals, the Spirit works in the church to inspire scripture, quicken the Word in our hearts, bear witness to our spirits that we are children of God (2 Tim. 3:10; Rom. 8:15–17). For catholic orthodoxy, the Spirit guides to all truth, assists in prayer, calls forth the sacramental life, intercedes with groanings that cannot be uttered (John 16:13; Rom. 8:26, 27). For social liberals, the Spirit works through the church to comfort those in trouble, bind up the brokenhearted, proclaim liberation for captives (Isa. 61:1; John 16:26; Rom. 8:22–25). Each needs the other. Each tradition at its best recognizes in the other something essential to its own ethos.

Tendencies and Temptations of Each.   Evangelical pietism tends to see the church as the arena where the Spirit is converting, sanctifying persons from sin, bearing the fruits of the spirit in individuals (Gal. 5:22, 23). Catholic orthodoxy sees the church as the sacramental arena in which the Spirit is equipping the body, and filling hearts with the perfect love of God and humanity (Eph. 4). Social liberals see the church as God's farm, bearing fruit for society, or hospital, caring for the wounded. Each of these three complementary views of the church needs admonition from its counterparts to more fully embody the work of the Spirit.

A justifying faith that neglects the upbuilding of a disciplined community of holy love is the perennial Protestant temptation. Holy mysteries of a church that misplaces justifying faith is the recurring Orthodox and Catholic temptation. A salvific individual regenerative experience that downplays church, sacrament, and ministry is the ongoing pietistic temptation. A social activism that forgets its enabling ground is the persistent temptation of the Protestant liberal vision of the church.

The Seminary as Playground of Defensive Reductionisms.   All theological disciplines deal with the church. From scripture we learn of its calling and founding. From church history and historical theology we learn of its development, and how scripture has been consensually and diversely interpreted in various periods. In Christian social ethics we inquire how the church is called to relate to its cultural, economic, and political environment. From liturgics, pastoral care, catechetics, homiletics, and administry, we learn how the life of the church is to be practiced and embodied. These varied approaches and disciplines flow into and out of the study of ecclesiology, which inquires into the origin, mission, nature, ordering, and destiny of the church.

The modern seminary is too often a place where the study of the church has become fragmented into quarreling disciplines, rather than united by common sharing in Christ by the Spirit. Modern guild biblical scholars view the church as a quaint obstacle to their special interests in free historical investigation. Church history and historical theology see the church as a product of historical forces to be investigated. Sociology of religion sees the church as an object of sociological investigation, as expressive of class stratification and gender and racial intransigencies. Psychology of religion and pastoral care view the church as a recalcitrant purveyor of parent tapes and superego constraints. Worst of all, systematic theology views the church as a laboratory for testing the theories, ideas, and hypotheses generated in despairing modernity. Each is a reductionism practiced by scholars defending some disciplinary territory. Insofar as the seminary has become dominated by these competing methodologies, it has failed to serve the apostolic tradition and offended against the rights of the laity to hear the unadorned word.

Amid this atmosphere, the intentional, systematic study of ecclesiology has tended to become lost. Ecclesiology has often been pragmatically reduced to the praxis of pastoral care, church administration, homiletics, education, and community organization. When administration is reduced to management, evangelism to technique, soul care to therapeutic strategy, and preaching to rhetoric, the doctrine of the church has been misplaced. The very accrediting agencies pledged to bring integration to the theological curriculum have reinforced these patterns of territorial privilege.

The Church: Toward a Preliminary Definition

The Word History of Ekklēsia (Qahal).   English words like *ecclesiology* are derived from the Greek words *ek* (out or from) and *kaleō*, to call out as by a herald. The *eccle* prefix has deeply embedded in it the Greek language idea of *calling out*.

This Greek word entered into the New Testament from the Septuagint, where it was used to translate the Hebrew *qahal*—assembly, congregation, those called out, gathered, congregated. *Ekklēsia* translated *qahal Yahweh* (called of the Lord) into Greek. The apostles used the word to refer to the act of assembling or the assemblage of persons brought together by God's own calling for the purpose of hearing the gospel and sitting at table with the living Lord. *Qahal* can refer to the whole congregation of Israel, whether or not in actual assembly, or to a local assembly called to stand in the presence of God. The assembly in intertestamental Judaism was called out of the world to make due sacrifices, select leaders, follow an ordered calendar of seasonal celebration, engage in ceremonies and ordinances, and teach the faithful of the history of revelation. All these functions continued, though in transmuted forms, under the New Testament *ekklēsia*.

There is one noteworthy difference that quickly emerged between *qahal* and *ekklēsia:* the *qahal* was, strictly speaking, a calling forth of men only, the circumcised, while the *ekklēsia* included women, children, and men, all those baptized. The Hebrew *'edah* (assembly, company, congregation, ceremonial community as a whole) is usually translated into Greek as *sunagōgē* (from *sun*, together; *ago*, to bring), a term occasionally applied to early Christian assemblies (James 2:2; 2 Thess. 2:1; Heb. 10:25). The gathered synagogue was largely intact and functional apart from the participation of women. The New Testament *ekklēsia* would from the outset have been considered quite incomplete without women. This is not an incidental sociological difference, but a far-reaching theological difference between early Judaism and early Christianity.

The Greek root word had the specific nuance of "an assembly of citizens called by the voice of a public crier, from the remaining crowd, as it were by name, and by the hundreds, for the purpose of hearing an oration" (Ursinus, *Comm. on the Hied. Catech.*, p. 286; cf. Doddridge, p. 338; Acts 19:32, 39, 41; *TDNT, GLNT,* q.v.). The church continues as *ekklēsia* because it is called forth, gathered by the call of God (Heb. 12:23; Deut. 4:10), assembling persons together before the Lord (Lev. 8:3). In the Romance languages the Greek idea of *ekklēsia* has been preserved in the Spanish *iglesia,* French *église,* Italian *chiesa,* and the Latin *ecclesia.* It is virtually impossible to think about Christianity at all without thinking about *ekklēsia* in the very language cognates of the first apostolic rememberers.

My Church: Jesus' Use of Ekklēsia *in Matthew 16:18.*   In Matthew's Gospel, Jesus did not hesitate to describe the *ekklēsia* as "my church" in a highly personal sense—my own assembly, my own called out people, and myself personally as their cohesion. Jesus said, "You are Peter, and on this rock I will build *my church* [*oikodomēsō mou tēn ekklēsian*], and the gates of Hades will not overcome it. I will give you the keys of the kingdom of heaven" (Matt. 16:18, italics added). Lutheran Orthodox theologian David Hollaz commented, "The meaning is, 'Thou art Peter, a man made of rock, standing upon thy confession just as upon a rock, or most firm *petra,* and upon this rock will I build my church, so that it may be made of rock, immovable and impregnable'" (*ETA,* p. 1295; Schmid, *DT,* p. 586; cf. Luther, *Ag. Rom. Papacy, LW* 41, pp. 326–32).

The personal phrase "my church" indicates that Jesus, according to Matthew, deliberately intended to form a continuing community of prayer, preaching, and discipline. He called and trained his disciples, and promised the coming of the Holy Spirit to guide them after his ascension. When Jesus said "my church," he was drawing near to his last days, as if to say, I am soon to leave; I will soon be at work to build my church, my continuing body present in the world of unfolding history until my return. It is from Jesus' own carefully and accurately remembered personal phrase, "my church"—spoken first in Aramaic and later in Greek—that the Greek term *ekklēsia* came to have preeminence thereafter over all other terms used to described the community of faith. The same word appears to have been widely shared by the varied tradition of Luke (Acts 5:11; 7:38), Paul (Rom. 16:5, 16; 1 Cor. 7:17; 11:16), Matthew (18:17), and all subsequent classic Christian exegetes.

Jesus viewed this assembly as a fitting context for the disciplining of the community. If an offender "refuses to listen" to those offering corroborated testimony of a misspent life or wrong teaching or disruption of the community, then "tell it to the church" (*ekklēsia,* Matt. 18:17) whose discipline has the power of binding and loosing on earth with eternal effect in heaven (v. 18). "My church," in Jesus' personal usage, is an indestructible communion of persons who are being upbuilt by their union with him, a communion of which Peter and the apostolic company were the first guardians, to whom were given the tasks of proclamation of the

Word, celebration of the sacraments, and disciplining of the faithful for eternal accountability (Cyprian, *Treatises* I, *ANF* V, pp. 421–29; Tho. Aq., *ST* suppl., Q18–23, III, pp. 2629–49).

The Spirit is building this community "on the foundation of the apostles and prophets, with Christ Jesus himself as the chief cornerstone" (Eph. 2:20). Jesus founded the church by personally calling and gathering the apostolate around himself, training, disciplining, and commissioning them to the ministry of proclamation and sacrament, expressly stating his irreversible intention to upbuild an ongoing community that would be commissioned with power and authorized to baptize, preach, discipline, and celebrate the paschal meal with the risen Lord. Jesus regarded this *ekklēsia* as sharing in the historical unfolding of the kingdom of God. It was to be a continuing community in which he himself would be a present participant (Matt. 26:26; 28:20; 1 Cor. 11:24, 24).

Continuity with the Ancient Covenant Community.   The new Israel stands steeped in continuity with the people of Israel, yet in it we behold all things being made new (2 Cor. 5:17; Barth, *CD* II/2, pp. 266 ff.). The new was born of the old. "Therefore every teacher of the law who has been instructed about the kingdom of heaven is like the owner of a house who brings out of his storeroom new treasures as well as old" (Matt. 13:52; Cyril of Jerusalem, *Catech. Lect.* XVIII.24, 25, *NPNF* 2 VII, p. 140).

At first the community of proclamation seemed to be like a sect within Judaism. There was no overt break with temple and synagogue. The gradual weaning of the church from its Jewish matrix would take many decades. It would await the fall of Jerusalem and the diaspora before the new Israel would come to full self-identity and separate existence. Only then would the elder serve the younger (Gen. 25:21–34; 48:14–21; *Barnabas* 13; 9.6; 10.9) and the new treasure heighten the beauty of the old.

In calling forth the *ekklēsia,* Jesus did not act against but within Judaic history It was not as if cleaning the slate of history, but as breathing new life into the ancient covenant community destined to redeem history, of which he himself was its essential remnant. He was deliberately reconstituting the people of God into an *ekklēsia* for all people, not for one particular land or cultural identity only (*Barnabas* 4.8). This people of faith he determined to make his own body. He sent the Spirit to nurture and discipline them for their eternal destiny, to guide the militant church to the holy city (Eph. 5:30; John 16:13).

The Renewed Israel.   The Jewish war of 66–70 ended in the destruction of the temple of Jerusalem, after which time temple taxes went to the Jupiter Capitolinus in Rome. The temple cultus ended. No more sacrifices were offered. With the destruction of Jerusalem, the center of gravity shifted in Judaism from Jerusalem to diaspora, and in Christianity from Jerusalem to Antioch, Alexandria, and Rome.

After A.D. 70 the history of Christianity was a history of the *ekklēsia* beyond Judaism. Under imperial Roman rule, "Jews and (circumcised) Jewish Christians were forbidden to enter the town and its environs, and circumcision was forbidden, under pain of death. Much later, from the third century, Jewish pilgrims were allowed to visit the west wall of the temple (the Wailing Wall) once a year" (Küng, *TC*, p. 113). Most efforts by Christians to convert Jews ceased, and by the second century the daily rabbinic prayer, *Schmone 'Esre,* included a curse upon "heretics and Nazarenes." The church viewed itself as the renewing of Israel, the new people of God (Rom. 9:6; 11:1, 2; Heb. 13:12; 1 Pet. 2:9, 10; Rev. 21:3). Christians recalled that "the sound form of our faith is from Abraham, and our repentance is from Nineveh and the house of Rahab, and ours are the expectations of the Prophets" (Ephraim Syrus, *Hymns, NPNF* 2 XIII, p. 299).

The Church and the Jews. Gentile hostility toward Jews anteceded Christianity. Similar attacks were made on Christians in the first three centuries. Jewish Christianity virtually disappeared shortly after the fall of Jerusalem. The Hebrew Bible was constantly studied by the early church, read consistently through the lens of its fulfillment in the resurrection (G. Dix, *Jew and Greek;* Barth, *CD* II/2, pp. 195 ff.; III/3, 210 ff.).

The roots of a false anti-Semitism are found in the twisted exegesis, which never gained catholic consent, that argued that all Jews were endlessly guilty of the crucifixion and the diaspora was an expression of that guilt. The diaspora, of course, had begun long before A.D. 70, for even "at the time of Jesus' birth only a fraction of Jews were living in Palestine" (Küng, *TC,* p. 135). Dialogue between Christians and Jews sporadically continued but too often was defensive, embittered, and polemical. The former Gentile hostility to Jews was taken over by the Constantinian imperial church, which soon forgot its own earlier days of persecution. Mixed marriages, office holding by Jews, and the building of synagogues were forbidden. Though some Christian leaders, like Gregory the Great, developed a more moderate policy toward the Jews, condemning enforced baptisms, the Justinian laws codified the oppression and set the conditions for ghetto existence. Jews lived outside the sacral empire both in Christianity and Islam, separated and denied equal privileges. The Islamic conquest of Spain was viewed by Jews as a liberation (B. Lewis, *The Jews of Islam*). The medieval and Reformation periods only worsened relations between Christians and Jews.

At length came the belated ecumenical repudiation of anti-Semitism: "The church repudiates all persecutions against any man. Moreover, mindful of her common patrimony with the Jews, and motivated by the gospel's spiritual love and by no political considerations, she deplores the hatred, persecutions and displays of anti-Semitism directed against the Jews at any time and from any source. . . . True, authorities of the Jews and those who followed their lead pressed for the death of Christ [cf. John 19:6]; still, what happened in His passion *cannot be blamed upon all the Jews then living, without distinction, nor upon the Jews of today.* Although the Church is the new people of God, the Jews should not be presented as *repudiated or cursed by God,* as if such views followed from the holy Scriptures" (*Doc. Vat. II, NR* 4, p. 666, italics added; cf. *Social Teachings of the World Council of Churches*).

The Covenant with Israel Continues—Judaism Not Invalidated by Christianity. The church had been prefigured in the Old Testament, from Abel's sacrifice onward. A new form of the covenant community was being brought into life through which all peoples would be blessed (Jer. 31:31–34; Acts 2:36; 13:32, 33; Eph. 3:6; Heb. 8:8). "In this context the community forming itself around Jesus, by dissociation from its former ethnic roots, achieves a universal significance," yet because

God's covenant is irrevocable, "the rejection of the Messiah by the Jews cannot make illusory the promises given to Abraham" (Schmaus, *Dogma* 4, p. 15; Rom. 9:6). God's faithfulness is never finally contingent upon the unfaithfulness of humanity (Rom. 3:3; 11:29; Luther, *CER*, pp. 119–28; cf. Calvin, *Comm.* XIX, pp. 411–12).

The new covenant community extended the call to the children of Abraham, and became Abraham's heir and seed (Rom. 4:12–16; 9:6–13; Gal. 4:20; 6:16). Jesus' mission was directed first to the renewal of the people of Israel. Only toward the end of his public ministry did he extend this call to a worldwide eschatological community that would stand in continuity with Israel, by offering the promise to all (Schmaus, *Dogma* 4, p. 20). Gentile Christians in this sense are sons and daughters of Israel, who call Abraham and Sarah their own father and mother, and who belong to the circumcision understood as circumcision of the heart by faith (Mark 12:26; J. Wesley, *WJWB*, sermon 17; *WJW* V, pp. 202–12).

This Gentile strain has been grafted onto the old olive tree, Israel. "The marriage of Moses to an Ethiopian woman whom he made a woman of Israel prefigured the grafting of the wild olive on to the true olive to share in its fruitfulness" so that the black "Ethiopian bride signifies the church of the Gentiles" (Irenaeus, *Ag. Her.* IV.20.12, *ECF*, p. 93, cf. *ANF* I, p. 492; Num. 12:1; Rom. 11:17; Origen, *Song of Songs* 2, *ACW* 26, p. 92). As Jacob, the younger brother with twelve sons, succeeded Isaac despite the claim of Esau, the church with twelve apostles would succeed the older brother (Irenaeus, *Ag. Her.* IV.21.3, *ANF* I, p. 493).

All the nations from north, south, east, and west will sit at table *with* Abraham, Isaac, and Jacob in the coming reign of God (Matt. 8:11, 12; Luke 13:28, 29). The distinction between Jew and Gentile, which before Christ was primarily a historical-racial-ethnic difference, now is transmuted into a distinction between responsiveness or nonresponsiveness to God's own personal coming (Acts 2:14–39). The distinction between circumcised and uncircumcised now becomes transmuted into a very different distinction between baptized and unbaptized (Gen. 17:12; Rom. 6; 1 Cor. 7:19).

This does not imply that the Jewish people are no longer heirs of the covenant. For Yahweh does not renege on promises (Rom. 11:29). Israel will finally be regathered and reformed prior to the final transmutations of history (Rom. 9–11; Isa. 1:9; 8:14; 10:22, 23), according to classical Christian exegesis.

As seed remains hidden in the ground while taking root, so the *ekklēsia* remained hidden in Israel until Christ's coming. Only at Pentecost was this already living, hidden organism brought to visible, historical birth and life. It is inexact to suggest, however, that the called out people came into being only at Pentecost, for that would imply a denial of the work of the Spirit in calling forth the people of Israel. It is the work of the Spirit to gather the elect, the called out people of God of all ages (Kuyper, *WHS*, p. 179). Thus *ekklēsia* may refer in recollection to the people of Israel in the old covenant (Acts 7:38), or forward in time to those being gathered in the heavenly Zion who are being made perfect, "the city of the living God" (Heb. 12:22, 23; Origen, *Ag. Celsus* III.30; VI.31), an assembly whose "citizenship is in heaven" (Phil. 3:20, 21).

The new Israel does not destroy but fulfills the promise of the old. The Jews remain forever God's own people. The church "draws sustenance from the root of that good olive tree onto which have been grafted the wild olive branches of the Gentiles [cf. Rom. 11:17–24]. Indeed the Church believes that by His cross, Christ, our Peace, reconciled Jew and Gentile, making them both one in Himself" (cf. Eph. 2:14–16; *Doc. Vat. II on Non-Christian Religions* 4, p. 664).

Israel has not been abandoned. It is the Gentile branch that has become grafted on to the good tree, Israel; it is not as if Judaism now must be regrafted upon Christianity. The election of the Gentiles, as of the Jews, is an act of divine mercy, not human merit, and a calling to service, not privilege. Gentiles, like Jews, may break covenant and forget the mercy of God. "If some of the branches have been broken off, and you, though a wild olive shoot, have been grafted in among the others and now share in the nourishing sap from the olive root, do not boast over those branches. If you do, consider this: You do not support the root, but the root supports you" (Rom. 11:17, 18). Even those branches that were cut off, assuming that they "do not persist in unbelief," "will be grafted in, for God is able to graft them in again" (Rom. 11:23). The intention of God has not been revoked that "all Israel will be saved" (Rom. 11:26). The Jews remain most dear to God, "for God's gifts and his call are irrevocable" (Rom. 11:29). Schalom Ben-Chorin could say that "the further I have gone along the road of life, the nearer I have come to the figure of Jesus" ("Judische Fragen um Jesus Christus," in *Juden-Christen-Deutsche*, p. 147; in Küng, *TC*, p. 148). Similarly, many Christians including I myself confess that the further along I go on the road to postmodern Christian orthodoxy, the nearer I feel myself moving toward the heart of rabbinic Judaism. They share faith and hope in the same God; the precise difference between Jews and Christians comes down to a single decisive point: "They believed in Christ which should come, we in Christ already come" (Irish Articles 82, *COC* III, p. 541).

The Called Community

Klēsis *and* Ekklēsia.   Those "called out" are "called together" by the Calling One. The community is not called forth by human initiative or voluntary agreement or a coalition of interests. It is God the Son who calls to discipleship. It is God the Spirit who draws the disciple toward the holy life.

If the church is by definition a gathering of those called, the notions of calling and church (*klēsis* and *ekklēsia*) are intimately intertwined. The *ekklēsia gathers* together those effectually *called* (Acts 2:39, 47). The church does not denote all humanity but those "called out" for life in the Spirit. *Ekklēsia* as the called together community depends entirely upon *klēsis* (calling). Those who share in this community are the *ek-klētoi*, those summoned together by the gospel, called out by the proclamation (*kerugma*). The terms used to describe this community are the church of God (*ekklēsia tou theou*), people of God (*laos tou theou*), and church of Christ (*ekklēsia tou Christou;* 1 Cor. 1:2; 11:22; Gal. 1:13; Heb. 11:25; Rom. 16:16).

Common worship expresses this calling and makes it concrete: "You are not to withdraw into yourselves and live in solitude, as though God had already pronounced you holy. Come and take your full share in the meetings, and in deliberating for the common good. Scripture says, 'Woe betide those who are wise in their own eyes'" (*Barnabas* 4.10, *ECW*, p. 197; Isa. 5:21).

Called as a Community.   Ekklēsia refers both to the active congregating of the community and to the community as a congregation. This community becomes *ekklēsia* by the repeated fact of its being summoned by the gospel, called to assemble to praise God. Congregation presupposes congregating. There is no noun without the verb. The church is precisely this coming together in response to God's own coming (Heidegger, *CT* XXVI.4–6). We do well not to abandon the community in which we received the regenerating word and power, the mother of faith (Tertullian, *To the Martyrs*, *FC* 40, p. 17), the bride of Christ, the "figure and copy of Jerusalem which is above" (Cyril of Jerusalem, *Catech. Lect.* XVIII.26, *NPNF* 2 VII, p. 140; Gal. 4:26; Calvin, *Inst.* 4.1.4).

The Word always meets us as preserved and recalled through a concrete historical community. There is no remembered apostolic teaching floating around abstractly or nonhistorically, apart from community (*Leiden Synopsis* XL.29, *RD*, p. 657). The communities of the New Testament appear to be never so large that they could not be informally called together on notice, so as to hear Paul's account of his missionary journey (Acts 14:27), for example, or to choose deacons (Acts 6:2–5).

The Called of God in the Lord's House.   Because even apostates and heretics would at times pretend to be the one, holy, catholic church, it became necessary even in New Testament times to distinguish the "congregations of the saints" (*ekklēsiais ton hagion*, 1 Cor. 14:33) from the apostate "synagogue of Satan" (*sunagōgē tou satana*, Rev. 2:9; 3:9, in reference to those who say they are what they are not). In order to distinguish the holy assembly of Christian believers from other assemblies, it was called the *ekklēsian tou theou* (the church of God; Acts 20:28; 1 Cor. 1:2; Gal. 1:13).

In time *ekklēsia* came to be applied to the place where these meetings were held. The Anglo-Saxon root word for *church* (Scots *Kirk*, German *Kirche*, Old Saxon *circe*, Swedish *Kyrke*, Slav *carkov*) stems from the Greek word *kuriakos*, belonging to the Lord, or the Lord's house.

The Company of Those Called.   The *ekklēsia* are those who are called, whose calling is being made effectual through the work of the Spirit. The *Heidelberg Catechism* stressed divine choosing and calling as the basis of *ekklēsia*, where "the Son of God, from the beginning to the end of the world, gathers, defends and preserves to himself, by his Spirit and word, out of the whole human race, a church, chosen to everlasting life, agreeing in true faith" (*Heid. Catech.* Q54; Ursinus, *Comm. Heid. Catech.*, p. 285). The Cambridge Platform defined the church as "the whole company of those that are elected, redeemed, and in time effectually called from the state of sin and death unto a state of Grace, and salvation in Jesus Christ" (*CC*, p. 387).

Coetus electorum (the company of the elect) has its origin in the eternal will of God, the primordial intent and decree of God to redeem sin and call forth a redeemed community. The church exists because God wills it to be so, not because persons first contractually or voluntarily agree that they desire to become a redemptive community. The fall of humanity was never willed by God, though it was permitted as an absurd expression of disobedience. To redeem humanity from the fall, the Father sent his Son to suffer for our sins. Those who respond to the good news of his coming are called out of the world on behalf of the world to attest this divine love (Calvin, *Inst.* 4.1 ff.). "You did not choose me, but I chose you and appointed you to go and bear fruit—fruit that will last" (John 15:16).

Defining the Church.   The Christian church is the community through whom the Holy Spirit administers redemption and distributes gifts, the means in and by which God makes his reconciling work in Christ present to humanity. The church is called from the world to celebrate God's own coming, and called to return to the world to proclaim the kingdom of God that is centered upon God's personal coming and expected return.

The prototype Protestant definition of the *ekklēsia* was fashioned at Augsburg: "The Church is the congregation of saints [*congregatio sanctorum*], in which the Gospel is rightly taught and the Sacraments are rightly administered" (Augsburg Conf., art. VII). Those in this community of the Spirit (*koinonia pneumatos*) or congregation of saints have fellowship with each other and with "the Holy Spirit who renews, sanctifies, and governs their hearts" (Augsburg Apology 163, *BOC*).

As head, Christ infuses his disposition, temper, and will into the community. The believer lives in spiritual association with those who believe in Christ and are sustained by him (Luther, *The Papacy in Rome* 1520, *MLS* I, pp. 197–251; *WA* 6.293–98). Luther argued (against medieval Scholasticism) that only word and sacrament are necessary to the existence of the church, and (against left-wing spiritualists) that without word and sacrament there can be no church (Luther, *Pagan Servitude of the Church*, *MLS*, pp. 249 ff.; *Concerning Rebaptism*, *LW* 40, pp. 225 ff.; cf. *WA* 8.163, 251–54).

Protestant evangelicals who stress new birth are more likely to define the church as "the whole company of regenerate persons in all times and again, in heaven and on earth . . . identical with the spiritual kingdom of God; both signify that redeemed humanity in which God in Christ exercises actual spiritual domin-ion" (Strong, *ST*, p. 887; John 3:3–5). The church is a spiritual people "regener-ated by the Holy Ghost" (Augsburg Apology 164, *BOC*), who "hear the voice of their Shepherd" and receive the promise of the Spirit (Schmalkald Articles, 335; cf. Luther, *Answer to the Hyper-Christian Book*, *LW* 39, pp. 218–22). "The Church of Christ is the whole company of those who accept Christ as their Lord and Sav-ior" (*Catechism of the Wesleyan Methodist Church*, p. 8), a "company of the faithful, called and gathered out of the world" who "by faith are partakers of all those good graces which are freely offered through Christ" (Second Helvetic Conf., *CC*, p. 141).

Pillar and Ground of the Truth.   The church is described by Paul as the pillar and ground of the truth (1 Tim. 3:15), God's own appointed means of upholding Christian truth in the world. Orthodoxy builds on this premise, defining the church as "that holy foundation made by the Incarnate Word of God for the sal-vation and sanctification of men, bearing His own authority and authentication, constituted of men having one faith and sharing in the same sacraments, who . . . trace their beginning through unbroken succession to the Apostles and through them to our Lord" (Androutsos, *Dogm.*, p. 262, cf. Merrill, *ACE*, p. 238). As such it is the extension of the work of the Incarnate Lord as prophet, priest, and king (Androutsos, *Dogm.*, pp. 264, 282).

As Christ is God personally with us, so is the church Christ personally with us, teaching his truth and transmitting his grace. "The Church of Christ is not an institution; she is a new life with Christ and in Christ, directed by the Holy Spirit. The light of the Resurrection of Christ shines on the Church, which is filled with the joy of the Resurrection, of triumph over death. The risen Lord lives with us, and our life in the Church is a life of mystery in Christ" (S. Bulgakov, *L'Orthodoxie*, p. 1; cf. Moss, *CF*, p. 245).

It is hard to improve upon the definition of the church provided by Ignatius: "Wherever Jesus Christ is, there is the Catholic Church" (*To Smyrna* 8, *ANF* I, p. 90). The church is the personal communion of those who have communion with the living Christ (Kaehler, *Wissenschaft der Chr. Lehre*, p. 385). The church is "at once the realization of God's gracious purposes in creation and redemption, and the continuous organ of God's grace in Christ by the Holy Spirit, who is its pervading life, and who is constantly hallowing all its parts" (Lausanne Faith and Order Conference, *CC*, p. 571).

The Community of Those Baptized.   The church consists sacramentally of all who have been baptized, who thereby have made a profession of faith in Christ and in the apostolic teaching—an audible, visible act in time and space. The church consists experientially of those who are united to Christ in living faith as members of the body to the head, who walk not after the flesh but after the Spirit (John Chrysostom, *Baptismal Instructions*, *ACW* 31, pp. 54–57, 100–101).

Sacramentally viewed, baptism remains the defining factor in the definition of the church: "The Church is the congregation of all baptized persons united in the same true faith, the same sacrifice, and the same sacraments" of which baptism is the gateway wherein one "becomes a member of the Church on receiving this sacrament. To remain a real member of the Church after baptism a person must profess the one true faith" (*Baltimore Catechism*, p. 102). All of the baptized faithful are actual, not merely potential, members of the body of Christ (Lambeth Conference of 1920).

The Love of Christ for His Church.   There is nothing more fundamental to the definition of the *ekklēsia* than that they are loved by the Son with a love willing to risk all for the beloved. "Christ loved the church and gave himself up for her to make her holy, cleansing her by the washing with water through the word, and to present her to himself as a radiant church, without stain or wrinkle or any other blemish, but holy and blameless" (Eph. 5:25–27).

The *ekklēsia* is unutterably loved, valued, prized by Christ, who offered his life for her. The bridegroom was willing to die for the bride, to ready her for the end-time wedding by cleansing her with baptism, washing away every hurt, so that she will be comforted, and without blemish, holy, completely ready for the final marriage feast celebrating the reconciliation of God and humanity (Rev. 19:7).

The intensely personal love of Christ for the church is richly celebrated by Chrysostom:

> He espoused her as a wife,
> He loves her as a daughter,
> He provides for her as a handmaid,
> He guards her as a virgin,
> He fences round her like a garden
> And cherishes her like a member:
> as a head He provides for her,
> as a root he causes her to grow,
> as a shepherd He feeds her,

as a bridegroom He weds her,
as a propitiation He pardons her,
as a sheep He is sacrificed. . . .
Many are the meanings in order that we may enjoy a part
if it be but a small part of the divine economy of grace.

(John Chrysostom, *Eutropius, NPNF* 1 IX, p. 262)

To penetrate further into the teaching of the church, the following sequence of questions must be unpacked: How was the church founded? What is its essential nature? What are its features and evidences? In what ways is it ordered to fulfill its mission? The doctrine of the church may be logically set forth in this sequence: the dominical establishment and foundation of the church by Christ; the essential character and nature of the church; and the constitution and organization of the church.

Bath and Meal

In acts of mercy to the homeless, the poor, and the alienated, the serving church offers simple acts of cleansing and feeding. Nothing is more prized to the hungry and homeless than a bath and a meal. Nothing is more characteristic of the church's essential identity and self-offering than bathing and feeding.

Jesus' Last Meal and the Founding of the Church.   Jesus' last meal can be called the founding assembly of the *ekklēsia,* a founding whose significance was fully grasped only later, after Pentecost.

Jesus' farewell meal was intentionally instituted to be repeatedly commemorated by his disciples until his return. It was to become the central event of the continuing life of the church, uniting all who believe in him (Liturgy of James, *ANF* VII, pp. 544 ff.).

On the night before he was betrayed, Jesus met with his disciples for the paschal meal that commemorated the exodus of the people of Israel from Egypt and the institution of the covenant at Sinai. Taking the cup, he said, "I will not drink again of the fruit of the vine until the kingdom of God comes." Taking the bread, he said, "This is my body given for you; do this in remembrance of me." He said, "This cup is the new covenant in my blood, which is poured out for you" (Luke 22:17–20).

Jesus knew that his death was bringing prophetic messianic expectation to a fulfillment and would constitute the institution of a new covenant. In offering food and drink to his disciples, he was offering himself unconditionally to them in a way that would become the incomparable event of the following day (Athanasius, *Resurrection Letters* 4, pp. 77–83). At this table they became one body with him, so that later Paul would write, "Because there is one loaf, we who are many, are one body, for we all partake of the one loaf" (1 Cor. 10:17).

Received from the Lord.   Paul explicitly stated that the tradition of the Supper came from the Lord himself, not from the fantasies of apostolic rememberers: "For I received from the Lord what I also passed on to you" (1 Cor. 11:23). The Semitic flavor of Mark suggests the Markan account of the Supper emerged out of its original Palestinian context. The differences between Pauline and Markan accounts make it unreasonable to posit a common Hellenistic source for both. The linguistic evidence indicates a common Aramaic source. The Qumran texts reveal a community of new covenant in which bread and wine were blessed at meals. These discoveries have tended to invalidate the speculative form-critical view that the Supper emerged out of a later Hellenistic tradition.

This meal has variously been called a *kuriakon deipnon* (supper of the Lord, 1 Cor. 11:20) or the "breaking of bread" (Acts 2:42, 46; 20:7, 11), or *eucharistia* (thanksgiving), or in the Western tradition *missa* (mass, sending, dismissal, blessing). The primitive sequence was, according to Paul: taking bread, breaking it, giving thanks, declaring, "This is my body, which is for you," eating the supper, and after the supper blessing the cup, saying, "This is the new covenant in my blood; do this, whenever you drink it, in remembrance of me" (1 Cor. 11:23–25).

The Paschal Meal Transmuted. What took place at that meal had epochal significance for salvation history. What had begun as a Jewish paschal meal commemorating the exodus from Egypt and the establishment of the covenant at Sinai ended by celebrating a new exodus from the Egypt of sin and the establishment of a new testament in the blood of God himself soon to be shed (Ignatius, *Philadelphians* 4, *ANF* I, p. 81).

As the people of Israel had been founded for this moment, so the new people of Israel were being formed in this moment. As the old covenant had been sealed with sacrificial blood, so was the new covenant to be sealed with Jesus' own blood (Justin Martyr, *First Apology* LXV–LXVI, *ANF* I, pp. 185–86, 527–28). As the paschal meal was a sign of departure from Egypt, so was the eucharistic meal a sign of a new departure, a spiritual exodus, liberation from bondage to sin, a "new migration of the People of God through the desert of tribulation and affliction" (Schmaus, *Dogma* 4, p. 23) toward the land of promise. "Israel according to the flesh, which wandered as an exile in the desert, was already called the Church of God" (*Doc. Vat. II, Ch.* 5; cf. 2 Esd. 13:1; cf. Num. 10:4; Deut. 23:1 ff.). The *ekklēsia* on earth continues to be a community called to journey toward a promised land, seeking that which is above. The "one Bread" is "the medicine of immortality" enabling life eternal (Ignatius, *Eph.* 20, *FC* 1, p. 95).

In offering broken bread, Jesus said, "This is my body, which is for you; do this in remembrance of me" (1 Cor. 11:24). The time frame of this remembrance was to be the indefinite stretch of time between ascension and Parousia. During this time the Lord would not be visibly present with his disciples but would remain spiritually present to them in a lively way through this sacrament of his self-giving, self-sacrificial atoning love (Mark 2:20; John Chrysostom, *Hom. on 1 Cor.* XXVII, *NPNF* 1 XII, pp. 157–63; Pannenberg, *The Church,* pp. 116–50).

This simple meal became the basis for the continuing memory of the *ekklēsia* of the Lord and the basis of apostolic expectation of Christ's return (*Liturgy of Mark, ANF* VII, p. 557). To continue its celebration until his return was one of the reasons for proclaiming the gospel to all. Thereafter the meeting of the disciples would be accompanied by the expectant hope echoing from the Aramaic tradition throughout the apostolic testimony: *"Marana tha"* ("Come, O Lord," 1 Cor. 16:22; Rev. 22:20).

The connected sequence was final meal, death, resurrection, ascension, indwelling of the Spirit, calling of the community of testimony. This community is

portrayed in early Christian art as being formed out of the wound in Jesus' side—
the blood of the Eucharist and the water of baptism. "From the side of Christ as
He slept the sleep of death upon the cross there came forth the wondrous sacrament which is the whole Church'" (*Doc. Vat. II, Lit.* 5, p. 140; cf. Augustine, *Comm.
Ps.* 138, *NPNF* 1 VIII, pp. 633–35; *Corpus Christianorum* XL, p. 1991).

Baptism as Instituted Rite of Initiation into the Body.   Admission into this one
body was from the outset administered by baptism: "The body is a unity, though
it is made up of many parts, and though all its parts are many, they form one
body. So it is with Christ. For we were all baptized by one Spirit into one body—
whether Jews or Greeks, slave or free—and we were all given the one Spirit to
drink" (1 Cor. 12:12, 13).

"I baptize you with water for repentance," John the Baptist preached. "But after
me will come one who is more powerful than I, whose sandals I am not fit to carry.
He will baptize you with the Holy Spirit and with fire" (Matt. 3:11). The Son did
indeed baptize the *ekklēsia* with the Spirit, bathed, cleansed, and immersed the
church in the life of the Spirit, at Pentecost, in a single baptism that once given
would continue to be given from Pentecost to Parousia for the whole body, for
whom there is "one, Lord, one faith, one baptism" (Eph. 4:5; Gordon, *MS*, p. 64).
Baptism with fire refers anticipatively to the final judgment in which the dross of
sin is being completely burned away from the good creation (Hippolytus, *Holy
Theophany, ANF* V, p. 235). The conditions of entrance into the community were
simple: repent, believe, be baptized, and you will receive the gift of the Holy Spirit
(Acts 2:38).

Baptism likewise reenacted Jesus' death and resurrection. Paul preached that
"all of us who were baptized into Christ Jesus were baptized into his death," and
that "we were therefore buried with him through baptism into death in order
that, just as Christ was raised from the dead through the glory of the Father, we
too may live a new life" (Rom. 6:3, 4). Just as in the physical body some cellular
tissue dies each day while new tissue is being created, so in the historic church
and the individual Christian life there is some dimension of dying daily, sharing
daily in Christ's passion and mission, willing to suffer for the sins of the world,
looking forward to sharing in final resurrection.

Exodus and Baptism.   The bathing and feeding images were foreshadowed by
the exodus, wherein "our forefathers were all under the cloud," and "they all
passed through the sea. They were all baptized into Moses in the cloud and in
the sea. They ate the same spiritual food and drank the same spiritual drink, for
they drank from the spiritual rock that accompanied them, and that rock was
Christ" (1 Cor. 10:1–4; John Chrysostom, *Hom. on 1 Cor.* XXIII, *NPNF* 1 XII,
pp. 133–38).

The fulfillment of this exodus prototype "appears in Christ our Lord, baptized
in water at the Jordan, and then baptized in the Holy Ghost, which 'descended
from heaven like a dove and abode upon him.' Then it recurred again in the waiting disciples who besides the baptism of water which had doubtless already been
received, now were baptized 'in the Holy Ghost and in fire'" (Gordon, *MS*, p. 65).
Subsequently they were called to live and walk and pray "in the Spirit," not according to the flesh (1 Pet. 4:6; Gal. 5:25; Eph. 6:18).

The whole body of Christ in all times and places was proleptically baptized into the Spirit once for all at Pentecost. As the cross was a once-for-all event, finished on Calvary, so was the personal coming of the Spirit a coming that occurred once at Pentecost and thereby was effectively given to the church for the whole period between Pentecost and Parousia. The continuing work of the Spirit is to vivify the body of Christ by maintaining its connection with the risen Head (Basil, *On the Spirit* I.12–15, pp. 18–22; Gordon, *MS*, p. 70). By being baptized in the triune name, and thus in the name of Jesus (Acts 2:38; 8:16; 10:48), one comes under the lordship and care of Jesus, one belongs to the crucified and risen Lord, sharing in his life, death, and resurrection (Gal. 3:26–4:7).

The Anointing of the Body. In this way the anointing of the head (the messiah) became the anointing of the body (the *ekklēsia*). This was symbolized in classic exegesis by the recollection that at Aaron's consecration the anointing oil poured on the head and beard also ran down profusely upon his body and his priestly robe. When the faithful live together in unity, "It is like precious oil poured on the head, running down on the beard, running down on Aaron's beard, down upon the collar of his robes" (Ps. 133:2), so that not only the head but the whole ongoing historical body dwells together in unity, profusely anointed by the Spirit (Augustine, *Comm. on Psalms*, Ps. 133, *NPNF* 1 VIII, p. 623).

When the Spirit once again in the house of Cornelius "came on them as he had come on us at the beginning," Peter "remembered what the Lord had said: 'John baptized with water, but you will be baptized with the Holy Spirit'" (Acts 11:16). The Spirit would soon open the door in Peter's mind to the possibility of the mission to the Gentiles.

Jesus and the Church

The Most Primitive Layers of Memory. Some critics argue that Jesus had no intention whatever of founding a continuing community, because he expected the end time soon and thought of himself as sent only to the lost ones of the house of Israel (Matt. 10:8). Classical exegetes appealed to apostolic witnesses to establish the fact that Jesus himself clearly intended to teach disciples, institute sacraments, and engage in a mission beyond the Jews to all nations.

Form-critics are prone to speculate on a complex hellenizing development before the distinct formation of the church. This tends to ignore just how early the Jerusalem church developed some of its most essential features: synagogue-like worship, eldership, preaching, service to the needy, baptism, and Eucharist. All were received from Judaism and transmitted in their basic form within the first two decades of Christianity, grounded in verbatim teaching specifically "remembering the words the Lord Jesus himself said" (Acts 20:35; B. Gerhardsson, *Memory and Manuscript;* M. Wilson, "The Jewish Concept of Learning," *Christian Scholars Review* 5:350–63).

In the most primitive layers of memory we can already identify the essential nucleus from which later formal definitions (episcopacy, triune teaching, two-nature Christology) developed. Like an embryo growing, the church did not come into existence without a historical struggle and gradual development, just as the body of the Lord did not form in the womb of the Virgin without gradual growth through stages. Nothing that happens in a religion shaped by the incarnation would or could happen nonhistorically, abstractly, arbitrarily, or lacking continuity with antecedents (Acts 20:17–38; Basil, *Letters* CCXLII-CCXLIV, *NPNF* 2 VIII, pp. 282–89; Hooker, *LEP*).

There is no good reason frantically to assume, as currently prevailing guild biblical academicians often do, that there can be no reliable ground of the truth of the church unless historians can find palpable evidence for it. The reality of the church does not hinge breathlessly on whether historians are able to define certainly the historical context in which the church arose. Nor is there reason to assume, as with some Reformed ecclesiology, that we must push every aspect of the arrangements of church polity and ministry back to the first four decades of the church's life. To approach matters of church governance too legalistically will end in failing to see the organic unity of the church's gradual growth through historical development (Vincent of Lérins, *Comm.* XXIII, *NPNF* 2 IX, pp. 147–49; *Longer Catechism of the Orthodox Church*, *COC* II, pp. 483–91; Newman, *The Development of Christian Doctrine*).

Whether Ecclesiology Follows Christology.   There can be no ecclesiology without Christology, because Christ is the life of the church. Without the head the body can do nothing (John 15:5). Likewise, there is no effective Christology without ecclesiology, for the word of the cross seeks a hearing among actually existing human communities. Christ affectionately offers and imparts to and provides for the church all that it needs to live and grow. The church affectionately offers to Christ its praise, worship, and thanksgiving. The church is impossible to understand or explain or account for without Jesus, without his initiative, his direct willing and enabling and sustaining of it (Eph. 1:22; Col. 1:18).

The ethic, liturgy, proclamation, and form of ministry of the *ekklēsia* are from above, divinely instituted, grace-enabled, responsive to the divine initiative, yet at the same time enmeshed in historical reality, which means the scandals of particularities of class structure, gender, race, nation, economic interest, and historical situation. The theandric premise undergirds every utterance of ecclesiology (Col. 1:24; John Chrysostom, *Hom. on Col.* IX, *NPNF* 1 XIII, pp. 276–79).

The Christian life does not consist in the merely legalistic following of the commands of Jesus, but in life in the Spirit that follows the way of the Lord in relation to ever-new circumstances. Nor is Christian ministry the simple legalistic following of first-century patterns of ministry, but rather allowing the *communio sanctorum* to be formed by Christ so as be enlivened and unified by him as head. Nor does the efficacy of the Lord's Supper hinge vulnerably upon historically authenticating the precise words of Jesus, but rather in participating in his life of atoning sacrifice. Nor is Christian proclamation and scriptural interpretation the precise repetition of the literal words of scripture texts, but rather a walking according to the way lit by the Word, a lively dialogue with holy writ as it impinges upon actual challenges today. Nor is hermeneutics the simple attempt to reconstitute historical conditions that prevailed in apostolic times, but to listen to how those patterns impinge upon our times and to allow our questions to be transformed by that dialogue.

The decisive reason for placing ecclesiology toward the end rather than the beginning of theology is not a sociological or psychological but a Christological argument: that the branches have life only in the Vine (John 15:1–8). Doctrinal reflection occurs only in an experiencing community, the church, where all who believe first meet the word and sacraments that condition and elicit belief. Every step of theological reasoning presupposes the living body of Christ, the church (Vincent of Lérins, *Comm. NPNF* 2 XI, pp. 133 ff.). It is by the watchfulness of the church that has scripture been preserved and transmitted. Since dogmatics begins with the proclaiming community, it is always church dogmatics. Yet the church did not precede the triune God who called it forth, nor did the Spirit's indwelling precede the Son's mission (Barth, *CD* I/1, pp. 3 ff., I/2, pp. 803 ff.).

The Birth of the Body of Christ. The postresurrection church, as Christ's continuing body in history, was effectively born at Pentecost (Acts 2). The Spirit had been repeatedly attested as present in human history prior to this moment, preparing, convicting, and saving the faithful by way of hope. But now a final calling and gathering of the people, an *ekklēsia*, was to occur, which was to constitute the mystical body of the risen Lord indwelt by God's own Spirit (2 Thess. 2:1–4).

It is as if Christ became once again born at Pentecost in a kind of second nativity, and the Pentecost recipients a neonate body indwelt by the Spirit, soon to grow and increase in wisdom, stature, and favor with God and humanity (Luke 5:52; Eph. 2:21). With Pentecost, "the Holy Ghost is given more perfectly, for he is no longer present by his operation as of old, but is present with us so to speak, and converses with us in a substantial manner. For it was fitting that, as the Son had conversed with us in the body, the Spirit should also come among us in a bodily manner" (Gregory Nazianzen, *Orat.* XXXI, *NPNF* 2 VII, pp. 318 ff.; cf. Gordon, *MS*, p. 60).

The Church's Adoration of the Son. Every act of worship in which the Son is fittingly adored points to the glorification of the Father by the Son through the Spirit (Phil. 2:10, 11; Rev. 5:13, 14). Petition is addressed to God the Father in the name of the Mediator by the power of the Spirit (2 Cor. 13:13; Jude 20, 21).

Reformed Scholastics warned that the undue adoration of the human nature of Christ might tend toward idolatry or ubiquitarianism. Yet it must be remembered that in the worship of Christ one is worshiping not the human nature of Christ as if it could be abstracted from the divine nature but rather the exalted Son in whom the divine nature is personally united with the human nature (van Oosterzee, *CD* II, p. 631). It is fitting that the *ekklēsia* render adoration and worship to the Son who is truly God (Luke 24:52; Acts 1:24; 7:59; Rom. 10:13; 2 Tim. 4:18; 2 Pet. 3:18).

Koinonia

Christianity has never been merely a matter of isolated individuals being converted and voluntarily joining together to constitute autonomous, voluntary organizations of believers. Rather the body of Christ is called out, by divine address, from the world from the outset as a corporate, social reality. There can be no absolute individualism in the body of Christ. The church is from the outset defined as a single living organism, an interdependent body with every member depending upon the community of faith made alive by the Son through the Spirit (1 John 1:1–7).

Church as Fellowship (Koinonia).   Christ called a living human community to proclaim and become the kingdom of God. He came to inaugurate the kingdom of God through a continuing transgenerational human community.

One reason the church was instituted was to meet the human need for *koinonia*—fellowship, mutuality, community. The church is a family set apart by God, belonging to a people set apart by God. Persons are social beings. Even God is not a lonely individual lacking sociality, being triune. God's plan includes and requires interpersonal testimony, interpersonal meeting, one-on-one passing on of the tradition of apostolic testimony. Persons are not saved in isolation but within a fellowship knit together by its common bond of union with Christ (Col. 2:2, 19; Calvin, *Inst.* 3.25, 4.16).

Whereas evangelical voices tend to emphasize the individual conversion that enlivens this community, catholic voices tend to emphasize the Head of the church who becomes embodied by taking form in the church. Catholics tend to say, Where the church is, there is Christ. Evangelicals tend to say, Where Christians are, there is the church. Each tradition needs the corrective of the other.

The Spirit Builds Communities, Not Merely Individuals.   Ecclesiology reflects upon the Spirit's work in bringing communities into being in response to grace. The corporate organism through which God the Spirit provides for the administration of the means of grace is the church. Pentecost was not an event in which the Spirit was poured out upon wholly separable or isolated individuals. Rather a community was created in which the embodiment of Christ's mission continued corporately after his ascension, as a household, a family, a community, *koinonia*, (Gore, *The Holy Spirit and the Church;* Pannenberg, *The Church*, pp. 9–23).

Ekklēsia becomes in time *koinonia*. Whether viewed locally or generally, the church is a fellowship, a shared social process involving primary engagement of persons in the family of God. This runs against the premise that the church is essentially an impersonal, imposed, hierarchical organization of offices and officers. It is a primary community of persons that meet, being called and summoned by the gospel. *Ekklēsia* is neither a mere juxtaposition of isolated individuals nor a coalition of independent groups that come together to form an agenda, but rather an organic community called by sovereign divine address (Phil. 2:1, 2).

The Nurture of Transgenerational Community.   Jesus must have known that the continuing body of witness and worship that would follow him would need some organization, leadership, polity, historical identity, and sociological structure. He did not, however, try to shape that structure in detail, but left much to his apostles to make judgments as the Spirit would lead them, taking times and circumstances into account. The earliest forms of Christian community and worship and proclamation shaped by the apostles are important guidelines even today. Yet they need not in their culture-specific details be regarded as woodenly binding on every period of the church's life (Thirty-nine Articles, XXXIV, *CC*, p. 277; Hooker, *LEP*).

As the new community created by Jesus was graciously adapted to the human condition, with all its social-historical specificity, so is the *ekklēsia* today called to be empathically adaptable to specific cultural differentia. Then as now the church is not an ideal beyond all reasonable possibility of actualization. It is not simply an expression of human hopes or cultural vitalities. It stands in rich, empathic continuity with each different human culture it meets, and only on this premise does it stand also in judgment of and in service to each distinctive human culture (Acts 10, 17:16–33; Pannenberg, *The Church,* pp. 36–44).

Following and transmuting familiar Jewish patterns of community nurture, Jesus himself continued to use external religious rites and institutions of worship and redemption as means of upbuilding community. The new institution reflected the new situation of the history of redemption that would prevail after his resurrection. The promised coming of the Holy Spirit would empower and make effective the embodiment of the new institution.

Community Intrinsic to Ekklēsia.   No one can simply become a Christian by oneself, or worship wholly by oneself, or be converted by oneself, or preach to oneself, or serve only oneself. That is not Christianity (D. Bonhoeffer, *Sanctorum Communio;* A. Dulles, *A Church to Believe In,* pp. 18 ff.). That would be like pretending that the pancreas gland could be taken out of the body and do a fine piece of work all by itself.

Christianity exists within a social organism, a corporate body. Christianity knows of no purely individualistic relation to Christ apart from the church (Leo XII, *The Unity of the Church, SCD* 1954–63; pp. 494–96). Yahweh meets the people of Israel as a people, not merely on an individualistic basis (Y. Congar, *The Mystery of the Church;* R. N. Flew, *The Nature of the Church;* H. de Lubac, *The Splendour of the Church;* H. U. von Balthasar, *Church and World;* H. Fries, *Aspects of the Church*).

Believers are not called out separately to live out a merely individuated relation to God but are called together and bound together as a people. "God did not elect individuals rent from each other but joined together" (Heidegger, *CT* XXVI, 1; *RD,* p. 657). The *ekklēsia* exists as an assembly, as "a company of Saints by calling, united into one body, by a holy covenant, for the public worship of God, and the mutual edification one of another, in the Fellowship of the Lord Jesus" (Cambridge Platform, *CC,* p. 388).

Against the Gnostic tendency to individualize *gnosis* apart from community, Irenaeus argued that "they have no share in this Spirit who do not join in the activity of the church (i.e. the catholic church, descending from the apostles). . . . For where the church is, there is the Spirit of God; and where the Spirit is, there is the church and every kind of grace" (Irenaeus, *Ag. Her.* III.24.1).

Cultural Particularity to Be Taken Seriously.   When Paul instructed the Corinthian church on such culture-specific matters as sexual difference, as illustrated by longer hair among women than men, he stated, "If anyone wants to be contentious about this, we have no other practice—nor do the churches of God" (1 Cor. 11:16). This seems to assume that common customs had already come to have authority in the churches, to which the churches had clearly assented, and that these customs, even if not revealed by God, still are best taken seriously (cf. 1 Cor. 7:17).

An ethos had emerged even by the church's third decade that had proximate authority. Each local ecclesial ethos was valued for what it was and assessed in relation to the mission of the perceived whole. "One person is incapable of being a church. . . . Ephesus is not Smyrna, and Pergamus Thyatira, but each one a distinct society of its self, having officers of their own which had not the charge of others: Virtues of their own, for which others are not praised: Corruptions of their own, for which others are not blamed" (Cambridge Platform, *CC*, pp. 390, 391).

Individual Decision Grounded in Community.   The sociality of Christianity does not override the fact that each person must decide for himself or herself whether God's Word is trustworthy. As no one can be born for another, so one cannot die for another, so one cannot be baptized for another. As every individual must die by himself, so an individual's faith must share in Christ's death as an intentional act of a single person (Rom. 6). Each individual believer is born anew from above, not en masse, but as an individual, yet this does not occur apart from a community of preaching and discipling and sacrament. Individual faith is unimaginable without a community of witness and support. When I say I believe, I do so within a community that says, "We believe" (*pisteuomen, COC* II, p. 57).

The Lord's Prayer begins not with "my" but "our" Father (Cyprian, *Treatise IV, ANF* V, p. 449). Paul longed to see the Christians at Rome "that you and I may be mutually encouraged by each other's faith" (Rom. 1:12). This mutuality and interdependent support is intrinsic to life in the Spirit.

Among Paul's most surprising statements concerned the sanctification of the unfaithful spouse: "For the unbelieving husband has been sanctified through his wife, and the unbelieving wife has been sanctified through her believing husband" (1 Cor. 7:14). Even when individual unbelief is recalcitrant, when seen within the social organism of family and sexual bonding, grace remains quietly at work seeking to redeem persons in and through durable covenants, not merely individualistically and alone (John Chrysostom, *Hom. on 1 Cor.* XIX, *NPNF* 1 XII, pp. 106–11).

Commending a community life for monastics, Basil observed that "in the solitary life both what we *have* becomes useless and what we *lack* becomes unprocurable, since God the Creator ordained that we need one another" (Basil, *The Longer Rules* VII, *CCC*, p. 109, italics added; 1 Cor. 12:12–26).

Whether the Church Is Local or Universal.   *Ekklēsia* denotes both the church as a whole and the local assembly of the whole church. A local or individual church is a company of those who are united in any given place in faith in Jesus Christ for worship, proclamation, and service in Christ. *Ekklēsia* could be applied to a gathering in a particular household, as was said of Priscilla and Aquila, greeting "the church that meets at their house" (Rom. 16:5) or in the home of Philemon and Apphia (Philem. 2; cf. Col. 4:15). The same word was used to refer to Christian assemblies in various cities such as the church of Antioch or Jerusalem or Caesarea (Acts 14:27; 15:30; 18:22; 1 Cor. 5:4; 1 Thess. 5:27) or the churches in a given area such as Asia (Rev. 1:4). Paul specifically praised the persecuted churches in Thessalonica for becoming "imitators of God's churches in Judea" (1 Thess. 2:14).

Ekklēsia may also refer to the whole company of believers of all places (1 Cor. 10:32; Col. 1:18). It was not deemed inconsistent to view the *ekklēsia* with a highly local focus as a congregation of the faithful united with the faithful everywhere, and then in the next moment to view it from within an eternal frame of reference as the *sanctorum communio* of all times and places who share the faith of each local congregation and embrace every distinct local expression of this unity and catholicity (1 Cor. 1:2; 4:17; 16:19; Col. 1:2, 24; Rahner, *RR,* pp. 296–99).

The Whole Is in the Part.   The local, visible *ekklēsia* is the whole (holy, catholic, apostolic) church expressed locally in a particular time and space. It is less analogous to a piece of territory in a land than a member of an organic body, wherein the whole body is intrinsically and interdependently related to that local community. The congregation does not merely belong to the church catholic, it *is* the church catholic celebrating the good news in some spot. The whole church is convened and called to being in that locale. The whole church is present locally, as in the case of "the church of God in Corinth" (1 Cor. 1:2), those of the whole company of the called out people who are meeting at Corinth. The church that gathers in one place represents the whole church in that place (Calvin, *Inst.* 4.1). One is baptized into the whole church, not a piece of it.

This is why the notion of an Asian church or a proletarian church or a black church or a white church is prone to be ethnocentrically misleading, implying that this is the segment of the church that belongs to white Americans or is staked out by some other racially or geographically defined sociological group. The church is by definition one (Eph. 2:11–21; 4:1–16; John Chrysostom, *Hom. on Eph.* V, *NPNF* 2 XIII, pp. 70–74).

The church is not made universal by adding up all the local churches and getting the sum, for the whole *communio sanctorum* is already there expressing itself locally by responding in faith to the call of the gospel. "For in their own locality these are the new people called (*vocatus*) by God, in the Holy Spirit and in much fullness" (*Doc. Vat. II, Ch.* 26, p. 50).

Holography is a lensless photographic method that uses laser light to elicit three-dimensional images by splitting the laser beam and recording on a photographic plate the interference patterns made by reflected light waves. In each discrete part of the holograph, the whole image is refracted, just as the whole DNA structure is embedded in each particular bodily cell. The whole church is related to the local church as the image photographed is related to the holograph. The local church may be said to be holosymmetrical in the sense that everything that is present in the church catholic is already implicitly or by analogy present anticipatively in that local community of celebration, a metaphor intuitively anticipated by Athanasius (*Defence of the Nicene Definition* V, *NPNF* 2 IV, pp. 161–66; *Four Discourses Ag. Arians* II. XVII, pp. 364–72).

Personally Lived Epistles.   Christianity is not merely a set of buildings or documents but living persons spanning nations, cultures, and vast epochs of history. The apostolic tradition is guarded not by an archival vault of written confessions but by persons in whom faith actually lives, who nurture communities who nurture faith. Each one is like a living document, letters of Christ to humanity (2 Cor. 3:2, 3).

Jesus did not leave behind him a set of formal written teachings signed "Jesus" so much as a living community that remembered him as having met them personally. In and through that community of persons he continues to work as a present partner with their work. To belong to that community means to live life in Christ, to belong to his body, to be énlivened by his life, to live in union with this one who lived his human life in incomparable union with God (Irenaeus, *Ag. Her.* V.13.4, *ANF* I, p. 540).

The Leitourgia *of the Church.*   The gathered community is called together to praise God for the salvation of humanity (Heb. 10:25). The work of the gathered people focuses on "the offering of gifts [*thusia*] and the conduct of public services" (*leitourgia*, work of the people, *laos* plus *ergia*, Clement of Rome, *Cor.* 40).

When the early Christian community gathered, they prayed (1 Cor. 14:14–16), sang psalms, hymns, and spiritual songs (Eph. 5:19; Col. 3:16), and heard readings from scripture (Rev. 1:2), including both the Old Testament canon and writings that were later to be New Testament canon (1 Thess. 5:27; Col. 4:16). They heard some duly recognized elder or leader who would exhort or prophesy or personally attest God's saving action (Acts 13:15).

The assumption of the gathering was that the risen Christ himself was present in their midst, attested by preaching (Matt. 28:20). "On the first day of the week we came together to break bread. Paul spoke to the people, and because he intended to leave the next day, kept on talking until midnight" (Acts 20:7). These discussions were intended to illuminate the understanding, not merely to intensify ecstatic utterance (1 Cor. 14:19–36).

Worship is not finally a matter of serving or satisfying human feelings, but of serving and rightly glorifying God through song, proclamation, teaching, and acts of mercy. Almsgiving was always regularly received in the church for the care of the poor: "On the first day of the week, each one of you should set aside a sum of money in keeping with his income" (1 Cor. 16:2). In the Eucharist one receives the grace of and remembers the meaning of the final meal Christ ate with his disciples, praying, "Remember, O Lord, your Church, save it from every evil, and perfect it in your love. Gather it together from the four winds and lead it sanctified into your kingdom you have prepared for it" (*Didache* 10:5).

Kingdom and Church

The Reign of God.   The reign of God is present wherever God's will is done. There God rules. The reign of God elicits and enables the church, which is an instrument of the kingdom. The kingdom is not simply synonymous with the church but creates the church, which stands as witness to and custodian of the kingdom (G. Ladd, *Jesus and the Kingdom,* pp. 259–72). Under the conditions of the Mosaic covenant, the reign of God was proximately expressed by the faithful people of Israel. Under the new covenant, the reign of God is proximately expressed by the faithful people of the church (Erickson, *CT* 3, p. 1042).

The church is an organic community for extending the kingdom that begins with Christ's ministry. Though subject to corruptions and abuses that stand as obstacles to the coming kingdom, the Spirit is given to cleanse these corruptions and guide the gathered community toward the truth (Acts 2:40; Titus 1:15; Hall, *DT* VIII, pp. 101–6; Stone, *OCD,* pp. 29–54; J. Denney, *Studies in Theology,* chap. 8). That the church is corruptible is evident from those described in the New Testament of Galatia, Corinth, and Pergamus, yet their temporary defection did not immediately dissolve their being as churches (Cambridge Platform, *CC,* p. 389).

The Son constantly "spoke about the kingdom of God" (Acts 1:3)—a summary phrase by which Luke summed up Christian teaching. Jesus taught his disciples to pray, "Thy kingdom come" (Matt. 6:10, KJV)—"a prayer that will end only when all prayer shall cease" (Pope, *Compend.* III, p. 260). The Lord appointed twelve to serve as the first overseers of the community by his own authority and commissioned them to pass the tradition along. He instituted means of grace by which the community would be strengthened and built up. In this proximate and anticipative sense, Augustine could say, "The church is even now the kingdom of Christ" (*CG* XX.9.1; sermons 213.7; 214.11) that awaits full expression in the heavenly city.

Not of This World. Against prevailing political messianisms, Jesus taught that the kingdom is not of this world (John 18:36; John Chrysostom, *Hom. on John* 84, *FC* 41, pp. 410–16). Its transmission is to be by testimony and persuasion rather than worldly methods of coercion (Luke 19:37, 38; Matt. 16:15–17; 28:18; Calvin, *Inst.* 4.10, 16–17).

Merely to adapt the church to the culture is not enough, for the church stands under the command "Do not conform any longer to the pattern of this world, but be transformed by the renewing of your mind" (Rom. 12:2). Nor can the church merely cling to archaisms or prefer human tradition to the divine address. Christ spoke also to us when he said, "You have a fine way of setting aside the commands of God in order to observe your own traditions" (Mark 7:9).

The Distinguishability of Church and Kingdom. The church is an expression of the governance of God, attesting God's already begun and coming reign. The kingdom is not reducible to the church. No classic consensual teacher ever taught simplistically that the church as it now appears is without qualification the kingdom of God. Some distinction between church and kingdom must be made, but it is difficult to make without falling into one or another error.

The church is distinguishable from the kingdom in these respects: The kingdom was incipiently present before Pentecost and before the founding of the Christian *ekklēsia*. The church seeks to be an actualization or proximate realization of the kingdom within the conditions of history. The kingdom is already the actualization of that for which the church hopes and works. The church seeks to extend the sphere of the kingdom in real-time human history (Acts 13:1–5; 20:28). The reign of God embraces, judges, and reconciles the whole of human history, including the circumcised and uncircumcised, the baptized and unbaptized (Matt. 8:11; 13:47–52).

Some in the church are said to be "not far" from the kingdom (Mark 12:32–34), while others remain far from it, and others live already within it and it within them (Matt. 21:28–46; Luke 17:20). Some who share in the kingdom do not share directly in the confession of the church. Some who are baptized and found outwardly in the church do not share deeply in the reality of the kingdom.

The citizenship of the faithful is finally "in that Kingdom which all man's sin is impotent to destroy, that realm of love and joy and peace which lies about all men, though unseen. It is to enter with Christ into the suffering and despair of men, sharing with them the great secret of that Kingdom which they do not expect" (*Evanston Assembly Message, World Council of Churches, CC*, p. 579).

The Kingdom of Heaven and the Present Reign of God.   The reign of God is not synonymous with heaven, for Jesus proclaimed the coming reign of God in terms that embraced and transcended the difference between heaven and earth. The kingdom of God is the kingdom of heaven, not for a future eternity alone, but also for the present. To reduce the governance of God to heaven is to forget that God's reign meets us in history. To reduce the reign of God to immortality is to miss the fact that the reign of God is being proclaimed as transcending the split between soul and body, and to neglect the gospel as the power to transform human existence. To reduce the reign of God to personal salvation is to neglect the social justice required by God's coming. The privatization and spiritualization of the reign of God can only proceed by neglecting the texts of the New Testament, written by apostles less trapped than modern individualists in privatized views of salvation, as if apart from the salvation of human history (Heb. 12:28–29; *Common Catech.*, pp. 90–91).

The *ekklēsia* does not make itself the object of its preaching but the One who called it forth by coming, the same One expected to come again (2 Cor. 4:5). The believer does not exist for the church, but the church lives to awaken and reawaken the believer to faith. The church itself is not the end of history but points to the end of history (2 Tim. 4:1, 2).

The Kingdom Being Made Visible.   Jesus prayed, "Thy Kingdom come, thy will be done on earth, as it is in heaven" (Matt. 6:10; Luke 11:2). The *ekklēsia* called forth by him is given the task of discipline of its members so as to actualize the kingdom. Faith and penitent baptism are its conditions of admission.

The visible church is the kingdom of God in the process of becoming embodied historically and proximately realized. The invisible church is a way of talking about the emerging eternal kingdom that is already remembering, celebrating, serving (Calvin, *Inst.* 3.20, 4.1).

The church is the historical means by which the reign of God is being taught and mediated to humanity. The coming kingdom is the theme that unifies the proclamation of the church (Acts 8:12). Yet "the kingdom of God does not come with your careful observation" or prompted by human manipulation (Luke 17:20). For "flesh and blood"—impenitent corrupted humanity, since it is unprepared—"cannot inherit the kingdom of God" (1 Cor. 15:50).

Spirit and Church.   There is no proper conception of the Father's sending of the Son without the Son's sending of the church by the power of the Spirit (John 20:21). In all of these tasks, the Spirit is found enabling, working, supplying, challenging (Rahner, "The Charismatic Element in the Church," *RR*, pp. 293–96).

Christ's body is indwelt by the Holy Spirit. The Spirit enables the responsiveness of each member or part of the organism, just as the life of the body enlivens every member and cell of the body. The Spirit awakens and effects in the church's life all that belongs to her unity, witness, and service (1 Cor. 2:4, 5; 4:19, 20). It is the Son by the Spirit who out of joy has come to serve and embrace the beloved bride (Rev. 21:2, 9, 22:17).

It is not demeaning to the church to say that the eternal Son gave himself up for her, his life for her life (Gal. 2:20; Titus 2:14). The *ekklēsia* is not less because addressed as "she," nor is the Son more because addressed as "he," nor is the Spirit less or more by being addressed conventionally in one language in the feminine and another in the neuter (Ps. 51:11; Mark 1:10; John 4:24; 16:13–15; Rom. 8:9).

THE CHURCH AS BODY OF CHRIST

The *ekklēsia* is the place where Christ is becoming embodied in history. As Christ's physical body was an instrument of redemption, so Christ's church continues to be employed as a means of the Spirit's redeeming work (Cyril of Alexandria, *Letters* 45, *FC* 76, pp. 191–95). "Now you are the body of Christ, and each one of you is a part of it" (12:27). The body of Christ (*soma Christou*) remains a more concise definition of the church than any other descriptive phrase. The body is an organism, and fits into a larger organic logic of Christian teaching.

The Organic Logic of Ecclesiology

The pivotal metaphors for the *ekklēsia* are biological (life), not intellectual (thought) or legal (law) or ethical (duty). Scripture speaks constantly of abundant *life* in Christ, not first of all about *correct ideas* about life, or *emotive feelings* or activities, or laws, or the *moral obligation* to preserve life, but rather to receive and live it. This is why the truest theologians are the saints. One cannot think of life or feel alive without first being alive. There can be no Christian duty or action apart from Christian life. Bringing the community of faith to life is the work of the Spirit (Rom. 8:1–11).

The Vine.   The body of Christ is not merely a clever turn of phrase or a rhetorical device but a vital relational reality.

Organic images abound in the apostolic testimony to the gathered community. The *ekklēsia* is likened to a farm to be cultivated, the tillage of God (1 Cor. 3:9) planted by the divine husbandman (Matt. 21:33–43). From the true vine, Christ, the branches are all abundantly supplied with nourishment and strength to bear fruit (John 15:1–11). Mechanical metaphors fall short. They lack only one thing: life (*nephesh, zōē, psuchē*).

The church is like a vine sending forth fresh shoots, pushing down roots, reaching for sunlight, hungering for righteousness, thirsting for refreshment, being fed from above. To share as a branch of this vine is to share in God's own life (John 15:5). The metaphor is simple, yet like any living organism, filled with complexity, growth, risk, and the mystery of the union of life with physical being (John Chrysostom, *Hom. on John*, *FC* 41, pp. 315–21; Hooker, *LEP* I.15.21).

The leaves of the vine are nourished by the vine itself, to which they are organically connected. Each branch is joined to the others in the one rooted vine (Ps. 80; Hos. 10:1; John 15:1–11; Col. 2:19). Every part of the organism is seen as related to the whole. The analogy is that of discrete members of an organism integrated into an organic whole (Jerome, *Ag. Pelagians* III.9, *NPNF* 2 VI, p. 477; Bermejo, *SL*, pp. 49–56). Where does the vine begin and the branch end? There is no way to draw a dissecting line, because the relationship is a living one. For "in him all things hold together, and he is the head of the body, the church" (Col. 1:18; Eph. 5:19, 20).

The Johannine vine metaphor corresponds remarkably with the intent of Paul's repeated exposition of the body of Christ. To the Romans, Paul wrote, "Just as each of us has one body with many members, and these members do not all have the same function, so in Christ we who are many form one body, and each member belongs to all the others. We have different gifts, according to the grace given to us" (Rom. 12:4–6).

An Organism, Not a Voluntary or Contractual Association.   The church is inadequately defined as a voluntary association of believers. This would be tantamount to saying that the members of my body individually elected to come together to create me. Rather, believers emerge only as members of the body, viewed as an organism, formed from within, Christ himself being the living center indwelt by the Spirit, whose members are expressions of his living body, each one being formed and imprinted by his person (John Chrysostom, *Instruction to Catechumens, NPNF* 1 IX, pp. 159–71; Gordon, *MS,* p. 61).

The relationship between believers, who are being sustained and presently exist in this organic union, is a far deeper and more profound relation than that which exists in a voluntary association based upon political or economic interests. As the body is not formed by the haphazard collection of parts but by organic growth of the coalescence of structurally united members, so does the church emerge in time (Pius XII, *Mystici Corporis* 16, p. 12).

The organic metaphor is entirely different from contractual metaphors. When a vine comes into being, the branches do not bargain for their separable interests or discuss with the roots and trunk whether they might join together in a vine, as if they had separate identity before their contract. Rather, they grow from the outset as an organism.

In a voluntary contractual society, persons come together and agree to form a society on some constituting premise, the unifying factor being their own initiative, interests, and agreement. Those who begin a voluntary society can also end it voluntarily.

The church is a different kind of society, more like a family than a debating society or business agreement. One does not enter into a family by one's own initiative or by mutual agreement or by contract but by being born into it and by growing in it. So one is born into the church by repentance, faith, baptism, and Eucharist (John 1:13; 3:1–8; 1 John 5:1–4).

Whether the Ekklēsia *Is Called into Being by Its Members.*   The members did not create the body, for they are the body. No body was ever created by its members. The members are formed only in the body. Even when a particular member fails or malfunctions or is cut off, the organism may continue (John 15:4–6). One cannot bring into being God's *ekklēsia* without God's own *klēsis* (a call by the unique One who calls) and the Spirit enabling the calling to be heard. The church is not of human devising. It does not belong to us. This family does not exist because people adopt each other but because they are adopted by God into the family of God (Rom. 8:23; Eph. 1:5).

The church is distinguishable from such organizations as the "Y," social action committees, political task forces, and relief efforts, insofar as these may function without Word and Sacraments. These functions may be expressive of the mission and interests of the church, but they are not the church itself. The church is not a humanitarian voluntary organization founded upon mutual interest or ethical zeal, but divinely instituted, given by God, tracing its descent not from Adam but from Christ (Mark 14:22; Scotch Conf. XVI, *COC* III, pp. 458–59).

The Unbreakable Relation of Member and Body.   One cannot dissolve one's family by mutual agreement. One will always remain a member of that family. So it is with the baptized in the family of God. What one becomes by baptism one never ceases to be, even when that baptism is to some degree forgotten or ignored (Ambrose, *On the Mysteries, NPNF* 2 X, pp. 317–25; Moss, *CF,* p. 244; Augustine, *On Baptism, NPNF* 1 IV, pp. 411–514).

The church is founded upon a covenant, but covenant is misunderstood if viewed as strictly analogous to bilateral transactions or agreements based on mutual benefit. Rather the covenant is that which God has initiated with humanity and fulfilled in Christ. The covenant, having not been initiated by humanity, cannot be unilaterally broken by humanity, for even when the covenant people forget the covenant, God remembers it and remains faithful to it (Hos. 11:8–11; Ambrose, *On Repentance* 1–5, *NPNF* 2 X, pp. 329–33; J. Wesley, *NUOT,* pp. 2487–93).

Headship of the Body.   Christ is the head of the body of which the faithful congregations and believers are members. God has appointed Christ "to be head over everything for the church, which is his body, the fullness of him who fills everything in a new way!" (Eph. 1:22, 23). Paul taught the *ekklēsia* at Colossae that they had "been given fullness in Christ, who is the head over every power and authority" (Col. 2:10). This does not imply that the church has legitimate governance over secular authority, but that Christ, whose Spirit dwells in the church, will in the end outlast all human powers and finally receive the promised kingdom of God (Second Helvetic Conf., *CC,* p. 143).

The whole body receives life from its relation to its Head, by whom it is governed and from whom it receives the cohesion necessary for growth (Boniface VIII, *The Unity and Power of the Church, SCD* 468, p. 186). "Just as the spirit of man through the medium of the head descends to vivify the members, so the Holy Spirit comes through Christ to Christians" (Hugh of St. Victor, *SCF,* p. 254).

The Primal Mystery of the Soul-Body Interpenetration in the Church.   The personal metaphor of the body of Christ is not adequately clarified by edifice metaphors such as temple, household, and building. The metaphor of a living organism is more subtle, unpredictable, and vulnerable, precisely because it is alive. The "life principle of this body is the Holy Spirit, though it can equally well be described as love, since the Holy Spirit is love personified" (Augustine, sermon 341; cf. sermons 276.4; 268.2, *MPL* 38).

The body analogy views the church as a living organism, a human body—not a primitive paramecium, but a highly developed organism—with lungs, circulatory system, synapses, life and breath, metabolism, all connected intricately together by a neural system and a brain that give the body direction, intentionality, will, self-determination (Lactantius, *The Workmanship of God, ANF* VII, pp. 281–95). The church is a living body, not a corpse, not a plaster statue, not a dead form lacking organic vitality. Hugh found "Nothing dead in the body, nothing alive outside the body" (Hugh of St. Victor, *SCF,* p. 254).

This is why the metaphor of the church as a building had to be stretched so as to become a "living building" with "living stones" (Eph. 2:19–22; 1 Pet. 2:4, 5; Hermas, *Vis.* 3; Bermejo, *SL*, pp. 56–61). The church is founded upon a rock, but that rock is the living Christ confessed by breathing, living, risking, trusting human beings addressed by grace (Tertullian, *On Monogamy* 8, *ANF* IV; *Modesty* 21, *ANF* IV; cf. *APT,* pp. 508–13). The foundation of the church is alive. This building has life within it. It is growing, and its parts are being knit together as a living organism (Aphrahat, *Demonstrations, On Faith, NPNF* 2 XIII, pp. 345–48).

This points to the *mystery* of the relation of Christ and his church, which is never finally reducible to empirical, sociological, or psychological analysis. When we apply to the church the same sort of empirical methods that we apply to the service club or the clinic, we glimpse only a small piece of the reality of the church (Luke 17:20).

The mystery of the church is seen by analogy to the mystery of the virgin conception, the holy nativity, the incarnation, and the resurrection. Terms borrowed from human experience (body, vine, branch, living building) describe as adequately as language can describe the profoundly organic relation of Christ to the church. Beyond this, theology can only point with joyful silence to the mystery of God's presence in Word and sacrament (Pius XII, *Mystici Corporis,* Boston: Daughters of St. Paul, pp. 7 ff.).

Whether Ekklēsia *Requires Organization.* The initiative for ecclesial order does not come first from the congregation itself autonomously, but organically from the grace of Christ forming the body (Gal. 4:19). This is spiritual formation. The local church can only come into being where Christ is being formed, hence where faith is being received, embodied, and practiced. Because the living church is related organically to the living Christ, it is indeed a visible society requiring organization. Its organization is an inevitable expression of its life (John 6:32–35; Rom. 6).

Suppose a huge oak tree loses a limb in a storm. It must reorganize its responses to make use of the new space available to light, so it reforms itself to reach up for the light that it needs for photosynthesis. Years later the botanist can detect how the tree had become adapted at a particular stage to new conditions. The tree has an organization, but it is merely an expression of its life (John 15:1–5). Its organization can be outwardly studied by botanists, but its life cannot be given to it by a botanist. All that horticulture can do is plant the acorn that has in it the DNA that will seek to fulfill itself concretely by becoming a living oak. Botanic analogies such as trees, however, are limited, because it is difficult to see how the tree has a head. We must think of human bodily life to pursue the analogy. The head directs the body, sends signals to the body as to how to respond, organizes response systems, directs the whole (Col. 1:18, 19; Augustine, *Comm. on John,* tractate LXXX, *NPNF* 1 VII, pp. 343–45).

Growing Interrelation of Members Within the Body. The individual growth of each Christian is seen in relation to the growth of the whole body in organic relation to Christ. Every baptized Christian is joined in one body. All are members one of another, all related to their Head and to each other organically (Eph. 4:25; Luther, *The Fourteen of Consolation, WML* I, pp. 166–67).

When the *corpus Christi* is functioning optimally, Christians are interdependently related to other Christians as one cell of the body is related to every other cell. All are guided by Christ as the body by its head, its mind (Eph. 2:19–3:6; 4:16). When bodily passions tyrannize over mind, when conscience is diminished by lust, the whole body malfunctions, losing intentionality. One who becomes puffed up with idle notions has "lost connection with the head, from whom the whole body, supported and held together by its ligaments and sinews, grows as God causes it to grow" (Col. 2:17). The aim of the Christian life is to speak "the truth in love," so that "we will in all things *grow up into Him* who is the head, that is, Christ" (Eph. 4:15, italics added).

Within this unified organism many complementary attributes are associated. Pope listed these "correlative qualities of the one Church of Christ" in paired opposites:

Unity	Diversity
Sanctity	Imperfection
Invisibility	Visibility
Catholicity	Localization
Apostolicity	Confessionalism
Indefectibility	Mutability
Glory	Meekness

Adopting "the method of connecting each attribute with its seeming counterpart," he demonstrated that "the true church of Christ is a body in which these opposite attributes unite" (*Compend.* III, p. 266).

The Incarnate Logic of Ecclesiology

The church is united without denying diversity, and diverse so as to express its unity—one without ceasing to be many, and many without ceasing to be one. For the church is the body of Christ, one body with two natures, divine and human, as in the incarnation there is one person with two natures. As Christ inhabits this temple, so he transcends it. The church as body of Christ has two natures, even as the Son is truly divine and truly human, eternal and temporal, in one body (Gregory Nazianzen, *Orat.* XXXVII.2, *NPNF* 2 VII, p. 338). This point requires a fuller exploration of the incarnate logic of ecclesiology.

Theandric Analogy. Although all analogies of the relation of Christ and the church are limited, being bathed in mystery, there is one analogy that best points to this union, the union between the two natures of Christ: God and humanity in theandric union. Christ is in the church giving it life in the same way that God is in the incarnate Lord, giving life to his human body (Phil. 2:6–8; John of Damascus, *OF* III.3, *FC* 37, p. 274). All this occurs by the enlivening power of the Spirit. As the human body of Christ grew in grace and favor with God, so the church is being called to grow in grace (Luke 5:52; Eph. 2:21). As Christ is one, so is his body (1 Cor. 12:12).

As God "willed to make use of our nature" in the incarnation, so did God will to impart grace to humanity "through a visible Church that would be formed by the union of men, and thus through that Church every man would perform a work of collaboration with Him in dispensing the graces of Redemption" (Pius XII, *Mystici Corporis* 13, p. 11). "As Christ is the Head of the Church, so is the Holy Spirit her soul" (Leo XIII, *Epist. Encyclical Divinum illud munus, DS* 3328, *AAS* 29, 1896, p. 650). By analogy the church is a mystical extension of the incarnation and the glorified body of Christ. The church *is* Christ continuing to live, continuing to reform its branches so that it can reach for the light. The life that flows through the church comes to expression in an organization, a structure of growth. The church has her very life in Christ, yet that life, like the messianic Servant's, is lived out in mission within the limitations of the world (Gregory Nazianzen, *Orat.* XXIX.20, *NPNF* 2 VII, p. 309).

Distinguishing Hypostatic Union from the Union of the Body of Christ. Two interrelated aspects of union may be distinguished: that union of divine and human natures which *belongs to Christ* is an absolute or unconditional union, as distinguished from the refracted forms of union with Christ that *the faithful actually experience* as a relative or conditional union—related to our condition and conditional upon the obedience of faith. This has pressed some Protestant orthodox exegetes to distinguish an *imputed or declaratory* union (juridically declared as being for us in justification and adoption) from an *imparted* union (actually given to us under the conditions of history). Others distinguish between a forensic union and a moral union, or between an ideal union (in which "no one who is born of God will continue in sin," 1 John 3:9) and a realized or actual union (in which "if we claim to be without sin, we deceive ourselves," 1 John 1:8).

"Christ is both in heaven and on earth; as he is called the Head of his church, he is in heaven; but in respect of his body which is called Christ, he is on earth" (Lancelot Andrewes, quoted in Gordon, *MS*, p. 62). This does not imply a direct hypostatic union between believer and Godhead, since only the Son is God present personally in the flesh, yet we by faith may participate in Christ's hypostatic union (Quicunque Creed, *SCD* 40, p. 16).

Spirit as Soul of the Church. Personalizing images abound: as Christ is head of this body, the Spirit indwells within the body, enlivening, leading, teaching, nurturing, and protecting the body, praying with the body (Rom. 8:22–27; Col. 1:18). Whereas the Son is the church's cohesion and organizing principle, the Spirit is its enlivening principle of empowerment.

Christ's life in the ecclesial body is compared with the life-giving function that the soul fulfills for the human body (Leo XIII, *Divinum illud munus*, Denzinger, *DS* 3328, *AAS* 29, 1896, p. 650). "What the soul is in our body, the Holy Spirit is in the body of Christ, which is the church" (Augustine, sermon 267.4.4, *MPL* 38, p. 1232; Androutsos, *Dogmatike,* pp. 268–73). Christ has shared with us his Spirit, who "gives life to, unifies, and moves through the whole body" (*Doc. Vat. II, Ch.* 7, p. 22). As soul is united to body in fleeting time, so is Spirit united with the church in developing history.

Since the Spirit personally enlivens the church, there is a sense of personal reality pervading the vitality of this community that is beheld through her actions, liturgy, seasons, and celebrations (Athanasius, *Resurrection Letters*). Without ceasing to be the activity of human beings, the church is enlivened by and is the activity of God. This relation is not rightly understood from pantheistic premises by which God would be regarded as identical with the body or social or natural process, but from the premise that the uncreated One is prior to all creation (Eph. 2:8–15).

The Incarnational Principle. The *ekklēsia* is in this qualified sense an extension and perpetuation of the incarnation. Analogous to Christ, the church is truly of God while not ceasing to be truly human (Col. 1:18; 2:9). "The Church is Christ manifest in the flesh, as Jesus of Nazareth was God manifest in the flesh" (W. Robinson, *BDC*, p. 101; cf. Origen, *Ag. Celsus* VI.48, *ANF* VII, p. 595).

The church lives and is sent, as the God-man lived and was sent into the time-space sphere of finitude (John 20:21). The word of the incarnate Lord is not dependent upon particular historical or cultural conditions, yet he comes precisely within the curious particularities of those conditions. Similarly the divinely instituted yet fleshly historical church does not depend for its mission and identity upon particular historical conditions, yet the body of Christ lives always here and now within particular historical conditions (Phil. 2:5–11).

As preexistent Word becomes fully human without ceasing to be God, so the *ekklēsia* in a particular time and place becomes fully historical, physical, and sociological without ceasing to be divinely empowered, instituted, and sent. In this way the Son incorporates human beings into his mission and allows human wills to become partakers of the divine nature through the Spirit (2 Pet. 1:4; Bermejo, *SL*, pp. 76–83).

God's Delight in and Unapologetic Use of the Body. As God has condescended to make use of the human body for the redemption of the world in the incarnation, so God makes use of human wills and bodies and institutions and intentions in the organic life of the church as body of Christ (Augustine, *Reply to Faustus* XXI.7–9, *NPNF* 1 VI, pp. 267–68). Human freedom is not ignored or circumvented in this embodiment but celebrated and transformed. The life of the body comes from the life-Giver, the Spirit, enabling life under the rule and governance of the Head (Col. 2:9–10). Those who demean the body demean its Giver (John Chrysostom, *Hom. on the Statues*, *NPNF* 1 IX, pp. 412–18).

God delights in the embodied church. Incarnational ecclesiology is not body-hating, but body-affirming. As the Son is embodied and cares for his body and is concerned when his body is endangered, so is the church whose life becomes embodied through the Spirit (Matt. 26:39–42; 1 Tim. 6:20). She cares for her body and is fittingly concerned when her body is endangered (Athanasius, *Defence of His Flight*, *NPNF* 2 IV, pp. 255–65; Cyril of Alexandria, *Letters* 45.7, *FC* 76, p. 193).

With characteristic brilliance, Nemesius showed how the body-soul union is grounded Christologically: "If the Logos, being God, could unite manhood to himself without yielding anything of his Godhead, there is no reason to doubt that soul can be in unconfused union with body" (Nemesius, *On the Nature of Man*, *LCC* IV, p. 304).

The Employment of Outward and Visible Means. Consistent with this pattern of the incarnation is the premise that the church actualizes her identity by outward and visible means—sacramentally. As God by becoming incarnate has not sullied the divine nature, so the church of God does not sully her character as holy by engaging in a mission within the world to draw humanity to God (John 12:32). Though earlier all humanity had been alienated, "now he has reconciled you by Christ's physical body through death, to present you holy in his sight" (Col. 1:22).

As in the incarnation, it is the Word who becomes flesh (John 1:14), not flesh that becomes Word. As in the theandric union, the priority always lies with the divine initiative, not with human responsiveness (John of Damascus, *OF* III.18, *FC* 37, pp. 319–20). The Son descends from heaven; he is not adopted by elevation from earth (*Eleventh Council of Toledo, CF,* p. 102). The prevenience of grace antecedes all human responsiveness. The human action in actualizing the mission of the church is responsive to the divine action in calling forth the church. The continued existence of the church is taken as historical confirmation of the divinity of Christ (Origen, *Ag. Celsus* III.30–37, *ANF* IV, pp. 476–79).

The church lives and works in the very sphere in which Christ lived and worked: human history, fleshly existence, finitude, suffering and death (John 1:14; 21:27). In Christ, God accommodates revelation to our human conditions (*ad modum recipientis);* similarly in the church the living God is being incarnated and embodied precisely amid the limitations of existence in time and space. This is the Way of the incarnate Lord—descent to finitude without ceasing to be Lord (Phil. 2). It therefore is the way of the church—engagement with the life of the world without ceasing to be God's own (Rom. 12).

Startling evidence for the naturalness of this analogy is found in Acts, where on the day of Pentecost three thousand souls were added and many more soon to be added—but added to whom? Not the visible community alone, but also "to the Lord" (Acts 11:24; 2:27; 5:14, KJV)! Believers were being effectively united to the Lord through the Spirit, incorporated into the body of the Head. Paul's continued suffering, analogous to Christ's suffering, was in his view "for the sake of his body, which is the church" (Col. 1:24).

The Spirit leads us "through things sensible to things spiritual." "Since it is not possible for the spirit in our state to pass through to that immaterial imitation and contemplation of the heavenly hierarchies unless it makes use of the material guidance to it, we regard the visible, beautiful things as reflections of the invisible loveliness, and the sensible odors as typifications of the spiritual largess, and the material lights as images of the immaterial glory" (Dionysius the Areopagite, *De coelesti hierarchia* I.3).

The Metaphorical Logic of Ecclesiology

The study of *ekklēsia* proceeds by inquiry into recurring metaphors and images used to speak of the church (Hooker, *LEP;* Minear, *ICNT*). The triune premise is deeply embedded in New Testament language about the church as bride, ship, household, people of God, flock, fellowship, building, body of Christ, temple of the Holy Spirit (A. Wainwright, *Trinity in the NT,* pp. 255–62; Erickson, *CT 3,* p. 1035).

Church as Beloved Bride. The relation of Christ and the church is prefigurative of the redeemed union of man and woman (2 Cor. 11; Eph. 5:21–33; Rev. 19:7–9). The metaphor had a long typological history, from Hosea (1–3), through Ezekiel (6, 23), Isaiah (54:4–8), Psalms (64), and the Song of Songs, before it was transmuted in the New Testament by Pauline and Johannine traditions.

The relation of God and people is viewed metaphorically in scripture as a marriage bond existing between a beloved husband and wife, often focused as an expected eschatological marriage celebration (Methodius, *The Banquet of the Ten Virgins* VIII, *ANF* VI, p. 319; Council of Vienne, *DS* 901). The readied church is as a bride adorned for her husband (Rev. 21:1–4; Second Helvetic Conf., *CC*, p. 143). The espousal of the bride begins at Pentecost. The wedding will be consummated at the final transmutation of history (Irenaeus, *Ag. Her.* V.25, *ANF* I, p. 566; *Doc. Vat. II, Ch.* 6).

When Isaac was to marry, the servant of Abraham was sent to search for the proper bride and bring her to Isaac. Classic exegesis delighted in this passage, viewed in the light of the triune premise, assuming that Rebekah was the type of the church, Abraham of the Father, and Isaac of the Son. The servant is the type of the questing, comforting Spirit who goes out on the mission to search for the bride, to persuade her to come joyfully to the wedding. Every step of the journey is a joyful one for the Spirit, a fragrant, pleasant journey and task. In this mission the Spirit is portrayed as telling the bride (the *ekklēsia*) the background story of the Son's (Isaac's, Christ's) miraculous birth, the willingness of the Father to sacrifice the Son on Mount Moriah, and the strength and grace of the Son (Gen. 24:1–67; Ambrose, *Isaac, or the Soul, FC* 65, pp. 9–69). The church is being sought out by the Spirit on behalf of the Son (Ephraim Syrus, *Hymns, NPNF* 2 XIII, p. 268).

Church as Flock. The *ekklēsia* is portrayed as the flock of Christ (Isa. 40:11; John 10:27, 28; Acts 20:28, 29; 1 Pet. 5:2). Of this flock Christ himself is caring shepherd (Isa. 40:11; Ezek. 34:11 f.), willing to give his life for the sheep (John 10:11–15; Clement of Rome, *Cor.* 16.1; *Doc. Vat. II, Ch.* 6). The church is a sheepfold whose door is Christ (John 10:1–10).

Church as Household of Faith. The family of God is compared to a household of God in the Spirit (Eph. 2:19), or household of faith (Gal. 4:10). In its early decades the *ekklēsia* had no buildings of its own. It met in homes (1 Cor. 16:19; Col. 4:15). The community sometimes gathered in the context of their secular responsibilities, such as those in "Caesar's household" (Phil. 4:22).

The *ekklēsia* is here being compared to a large household (*oikos*) with a complex economy and many interfacing relationships (Gal. 6:10; Eph. 2:19; 3:14, 15). Complementary gifts are required to make the economy work, distributed by a wisdom higher than our own. In this household, every member, every believer, has a calling, a niche, a place of service. No one does everything. The order required for a well-functioning economy or household is not an end in itself, but a means to peace, love, relative justice, and concord—values best attained when each member of the household is functioning optimally in behalf of the whole, not self-assertively in behalf of individual interest (Eph. 2:19–22).

Church as Building of God.   The church is "a spiritual house" (*oikos pneumatikos,*
1 Pet 2:5) of living stones resting on Christ the chief cornerstone. The church as
temple of God (1 Cor. 3:16, 17) is the building of God (1 Cor. 3:9) for the people
called of God (Rom. 1:6, 7). Jesus compared himself to the stone that the builders
rejected but that was being made into the chief cornerstone (Matt. 21:42; cf. Acts
4:11; 1 Pet. 2:7; Ps. 117:22). This edifice is called the house of God (1 Tim. 3:15),
in which the family of God dwells; the dwelling place of God with humanity (Rev.
21:3); the holy city, the new Jerusalem (Origen, *In Matt. 16:21, MPG* 13, 1443;
Tertullian, *Ag. Marcion* III.7, *MPL* 2, 357).

The church is represented organically as body of Christ and doxologically as
temple of God. As body the church acts as instrument of Christ's will, mission,
and work within the world. As temple the church is the place where the active
presence of God is celebrated, where all in its precincts consent to become the
sphere of Christ's habitation. "For we are the temple of the living God" (2 Cor.
6:16). "In him the whole building is joined together and rises to become a holy
temple in the Lord. And in him you too are being built together to become a
dwelling in which God lives by his Spirit" (Eph. 2:21, 22; *Epistle of Barnabas* XVI,
ANF I, p. 147).

Church as Ship.   The church is like a ship amid the oceanic hazards of history
(Apost. Const. II.7, *ANF* VII, p. 421). The called community is frequently compared to a ship under hazardous conditions of sail, requiring astute leadership,
with the risk of shipwreck always present (John 21:1–6; Acts 27; 1 Tim. 1:19).
Hippolytus compared the church to a ship in which Christ is the pilot, the rudder,
the two testaments of law and gospel; the anchor, the teachings of Christ; the
ladder, the ascent to heaven (*On Christ and Antichrist* 59, *ANF* V, p. 217). This
imagery leads to calling the part of the church where the people worship the nave
(*navis,* ship), picturing the basilica as ark of salvation and Christ as navigator.

Church as People of God.   Yahweh did not covenant with an already existing nation but created a people, brought them up virtually from nothing (1 Pet. 2:9).
He first called Abraham, then the seed of Abraham—Isaac, and Jacob and all the
sons and daughters of Israel. The original covenant people of God foreshadowed
and prepared the way for the renewed covenant people of God (Irenaeus, *Ag. Her.*
IV.36; IV.2, 15; III.9.1; Justin Martyr, *Dialogue with Trypho* 123.6; Pastor of Hermas, Vis. 2.2.6).

In the New Testament the people of God came to refer not only to the seed of
Abraham but more so to a postresurrection community whose proclamation
would address all nations, all cultures (1 Pet. 2:10; Clement of Rome, *Cor.* 30.1;
59.4). The people of God prior to the incarnation were a special people, the people of Israel, the seed of Abraham (Calvin, *Inst.* 1.11.7, 2.10.10). The renewed
people of God after the resurrection were not a specific race or tribe or ethnic
identity, but a missionally reconstituted people who would be found reaching out
for all peoples, all nations, the Gentiles (Tertullian, *Ag. Marcion* 1.21, *ANF* III,
p. 286; *Apology* 21, *ANF* III, pp. 34–36; Clementina, *Recognitions, ANF* VIII,
pp. 145–46).

First to be invited into the new people were the people of the old covenant (cf.
Luke 14:16–23) and only later the nations generally. The church has become the
promised seed (Gal. 3:16–29), a peculiar people (Titus 2:14; 1 Pet. 2:9; Eph.

1:14; Second Helvetic Conf., *CC*, p. 143). Both Gospels (cf. Matt. 3:9; 5:13–15; 11:16–24; 22:8, 9) and epistles (Gal. 3; 4; 1 Cor. 10:18; 2 Cor. 6:16; Rom. 4:1– 25; 9:11; Phil. 3:2–4; cf. Schmaus, *Dogma* 4, pp. 45–47) develop the theme of the renewed spiritual people of God. "Only by seeing the Church as the people of God can we understand the idea of the Church as the body of Christ" (Küng, *TC*, p. 225).

The *temple* of the former covenant became the *people* of the new, the body of Christ (Origen, *Ag. Celsus* VIII.19, *ANF* VII, p. 646). In exhorting the Corinthians to the way of holiness, Paul asked, "What does a believer have in common with an unbeliever? What agreement is there between the temple of God and idols? For *we are the temple* of the living God (1 Cor. 6:15, italics added; cf. Lev. 26:12; Jer. 32:38).

8 Marks of *Ekklēsia*

BY WHAT EVIDENCES IS THE CHURCH RECOGNIZABLE?

The *ekklēsia* is *one* because it shares in a single body, *corpus Christi*, the risen Lord. It is being made *holy* by participating by faith in the perfect holiness of the Son through the power of the Spirit. It is universal or *catholic* because it offers the whole counsel of God to the whole world. It is *apostolic* because it is sent into the world even as the Son was sent. These are reliable marks of the church (Nicene-Constantinopolitan Creed, *COC* II, p. 58).

The unity of the church is not a voluntary act of uniting by the members of Christ's body, but rather the unity of the one body that is enabled by the Spirit. The holiness of the church is not found in the moral purity of her members, but in the One Holy Spirit who calls the *ekklēsia* and sets it apart for service. The catholicity of the church does not hinge on whether this testimony is actually extensive throughout every square foot of territory on earth but rather hinges on the universality of the Spirit's mission and the wholeness of the Word's counsel. The apostolicity of the church is not self-sending but being shaped by the Spirit's own sending (Matt. 10:16; John 20:21). To say the church is one, holy, catholic, and apostolic is to confess the Holy Spirit as the one who unites, cleanses, and sends the church to the whole world.

Through her catholicity the *ekklēsia* reaches out to all the world with the whole truth of the Word. From her apostolicity the *ekklēsia* grounds herself in the recollection of the events of God's own coming. By her holiness the *ekklēsia* refracts the holiness of God amid the fallen world. By her unity the *ekklēsia* proximately expresses in time the oneness of Christ's body so as to unite anticipatively all humanity to God's reconciling activity (Amsterdam Assembly, Message, *Man's Disorder and God's Design*).

The fundamental requisite of the church is the presence of Christ. "For no one can lay any foundation other than the one already laid, which is Jesus Christ"

(1 Cor. 3:11). It was only when Peter confessed, "You are the Christ," that Christ said, "On this rock I will build my church" (Matt. 16:15, 18). The cornerstone of the church is faith's confession that Jesus is the Christ. Whether Christ is or is not present is the question of whether the church exists or does not exist (Barth, *CD* I/2, pp. 215 ff.).

The Question of Attributes and Criteria of the Church

Whether There Are Marks of the Church.   Whatever is necessary to the church's existence is an essential attribute or criterion of it. What are these essential features?

Not every group or assembly that calls itself Christian has a legitimate right to the name. The right to the name is conditioned upon fulfilling criteria that belong to the church (Luther, *On the Councils, LW* 41, pp. 150–54, 164–67).

Are there some signs (*sēmeion, signa, criteria*) or marks (*stigma*), or characteristics (*proprietates*), or notes (*notae*) or predicates that signal clearly where the *ekklēsia* is to be found? Are certain attributes of communities able to be tested to distinguish between authentic and counterfeit claims, between orthodoxy and heterodoxy, truth and falsity? If not, we are left with no way to identify the *ekklēsia* even if it should be there.

The classic, consensual answer is that the church is recognizable by means of distinguishing marks that differentiate it from other social processes (Council of Constantinople II, *SCD* 213–27, pp. 85–90; Fourth Lateran Council, *SCD* 430–31, pp. 169–71; Calvin, *Inst.* 4.1.9; 4.2).

Because Christ is one, the church seeks to embody that oneness. Because Christ is holy, the church seeks to reflect that holiness. Because Christ's love is whole and addressed to all, the church's address is whole and for all. Because Christ was sent, the church is sent to share in his redemptive apostolate (John of Ragusa, *Tractatus de Ecclesia* 1431).

Variable Lists of Essential Features of a True Church.   Attempts to account for essential features of the church vary in different traditions, though often in complementary ways. Some focus relatively more upon apostolic succession of the historic episcopacy, while others focus upon some particular form of church governance (congregational, presbyterial, or episcopal) as essential and necessary to a true church; others hold that a particular liturgy or confession marks the difference between true and false bodies of worship and confession.

Among scholastics of the Reformed tradition the attributes of unity, holiness, indefectibility, universality, imperishability (Heppe, *RD*, p. 662) are considered reliable marks of the church. Various other attributes and criteria have been applied at various times as descriptive criteria of the true church, among them antiquity, efficaciousness of teaching, union of members under one visible head, holiness of the lives of members, validated miracles, prophetic vision, the unhappy end of the church's enemies.

"Gravina found six, Pazmany seven, Suárez eight, Bellarmine fifteen, Bozi a hundred" marks of the church (Küng, *TC*, p. 266; cf. Jacobs, *SCF*, p. 386; Barth, *CD* IV/1; Brunner, *Dogm.* III, 117 ff.; Schmaus, *Dogma* 4, pp. 81 ff.). The seven signs of the church listed by Luther were preaching, baptism, Supper, the power of the keys, ordination, prayer, and suffering under persecution (*On the Councils and Church* III, *WML* IV, pp. 335–70; cf. Küng, *TC*, p. 267).

Word, Sacrament, and Discipline

The Centrist Ecumenical Tradition.   The most widely received, traditional, consensual Protestant definition (Second Helvetic Conf., *CC*, p. 146; Calvin, *Inst.* 4.1.7–12; 4.12–14) is:

Word
Sacrament
Discipline

Prior to this Protestant definition, from the fourth century on, four attributes have been most often designated as necessary and sufficient marks of the church:

Unity
Holiness
Catholicity
Apostolicity

These are found prototypically in the Nicene-Constantinopolitan Creed (*SCD* 86, p. 36; cf. Eastern Form of the Apostolic Creed, *SCD* 9, p. 9; and the Creed of Epiphanius, *SCD* 14, p. 10; *COC* II, p. 34; cf. John of Ragusa, *Tractatus de Ecclesia*, 1431; Juan de Torquemada, *Summa de Ecclesia*, 1486; Hosius, *Confessio catholicae fidei*, 1531; Trent, *Catechism*). In Protestant, Catholic, and Orthodox teaching, the discussion of the reality, identity, and mission of the church has usually been organized around these points. We will begin by defining Word, Sacrament, and holy discipline as primary premises of any attempt to distinguish truth from falsity in the nature of the church, and then proceed to discuss the one, holy, catholic, and apostolic nature of the church. The consolidating thesis: *That ekklēsia in which the Word is rightly preached and sacraments rightly administered and discipline rightly ordered will be one, holy, catholic, and apostolic* (Ursinus, *Comm. on Heid. Catech.*, pp. 288–91). Thus the variable lists are complementary, not contradictory.

Word, Sacrament, and Holy Discipline as Premises of the Attributes of the Called People.   Classic Protestant teaching commonly cites three attributes or notes or outward signs by which one may discern whether a community of faith is truly a church. These three cohere: "The true and essential and visible marks of this pure Church are the pure preaching and reception of the word, sealed through the lawful use of the sacraments and maintained by the use of the keys or ecclesiastical discipline, according to Christ's institution" (*Leiden Synopsis* XL, 45, in *RD*, p. 670; cf. Luther, *EA* 22.113; 31.315; Batak Conf. VIII, *CC*, p. 561).

The First Premise: Preaching of the Word.   The most crucial sign of the church in the Protestant tradition is the pure preaching of God's Word, a right "profession of the true, pure, and rightly understood doctrine of the law and the gospel" (Ursinus, 289). "God's people cannot be without God's Word, nor can God's Word be without a people" (Luther, in Jacob, *SCF*, p. 384). The surest mark of the true church is that in it one hears the pure gospel proclaimed (Luther, *On the Councils and Church* III, *WML* V, pp. 340–43; cf. *EA* 31.366). In his farewell to the Ephesian elders, Paul said, "I have not hesitated to proclaim to you the whole will of God" (Acts 20:27).

The church speaks truly in proportion as its proclamation is in harmony with apostolic teaching (Clement of Alexandria, *Stromata* VII.17, *ANF* II, pp. 554–55). Where the old, true doctrine of the gospel is preached and the Apostles' Creed confessed, there is the *communio sanctorum* (Luther, *WLS* I, pp. 256 ff.; *EA* 12.245–50). The creed contains all the essential articles of baptismal faith (Luther, *Sermons on the Catechism, SML,* pp. 207 ff.; *EA* 28.413, 414; 9.29 ff.). By their own acknowledgment, the ancient councils are not on their own autonomous authority true, but true because they rehearse the prior truth given by the Spirit to the apostles (Luther, *On the Councils and the Churches, WML* V, pp. 131 ff.; *Appeal, MLS,* pp. 415 ff.; *EA* 25.251–68). The Spirit engenders in the believing community confidence in the truthfulness of the teaching of the Apostles' Creed (Luther, *EA* 23.249).

Yahweh promised Isaiah, My word will "not return to me empty, but will accomplish what I desire and achieve the purpose for which I sent it" (Isa. 55:11; Calvin, *Comm.* VII, p. 172). Though many seeds may be lost in rocky soil, some come to fruition (Matt. 13; Mark 4; Luke 8). Wherever the church is, these seeds of the gospel are being planted. "The Word is the appointed means by which God's grace is made known to men, calling them to repentance, assuring them of forgiveness, drawing them to obedience and building them up in the fellowship of faith and love" (Lausanne Conference on Faith and Order, *CC,* p. 571).

"When the word of God, through the ministry of those who preach, falls upon the ears of the flesh, the action of divine power is mixed with the sound of a human voice, and He that inspires the preacher's office strengthens also the hearer's heart" (Prosper of Aquitaine, *The Call of All Nations* I.7, *FEF* III, 2042, p. 195). This criterion is offended if there is a substantial failure to hold duly ordained representative teachers accountable to the doctrinal standard of canonical scripture, or if those authorized to teach Christian doctrine publicly cherish heterodox opinion so as to lead astray the laity, who have a right to hear the gospel (Hollaz, *ETA* 1306–12; Schmid, *DT,* pp. 589–99; Jacobs, *SCF,* p. 383; Oden, *AMW*).

Second Premise: Due Administration of Sacraments.   A second attribute or note or visible sign by which one may discern whether a community of faith is truly a church, is that the church is present where the use of the sacraments is in accordance with their dominical institution. "The right and proper use of the sacraments" (Ursinus, *Comm. Heid. Catech.,* p. 288) is a sign of authenticity in the church.

Jesus himself commanded his disciples to "do this in remembrance of me" (Luke 22:19). Christ gave himself up for the church "to make her holy, cleansing her by the washing with water through the word" (Eph. 5:26). Because intentionally instituted by the Lord, there can be no church without a fitting sacramental life. From the outset, those who have confessed Jesus as the Christ and "who accepted his message *were baptized"* and were immediately found devoting themselves to "the apostles' teaching and to the fellowship, *the breaking of bread* and to prayer" (Acts 2:41, 42, italics added). Where no one is baptized, there is no church (Cyprian, *Epistles* 72, *ANF* V, p. 382). Where the farewell meal is uncelebrated, one has no right to expect the true church.

Word is logically and theologically prior to sacrament in the Reformed tradition, for the essential efficacy of the sacraments is the Word that enlivens. Yet we
are rightly reminded by liturgical traditions that it is always the community to
which the sacraments are entrusted that proclaims the preached word and that
the bath and meal were firmly established before Pentecost.

(Those who might understandably expect here a thoroughgoing discussion of
the sacraments are apprised that a future study is projected in liturgical theology
to complement these three volumes in systematic theology. A fuller exegetical and
constructive inquiry into liturgical issues is planned that could not be managed
within the stretched boundaries of this project.)

Third Premise: Disciplined Christian Life.   The active practice of disciplined
Christian life is a sign of the true church. Where no Christian behavior is beheld,
there can be no *ekklēsia*. Where no attention is being given to daily walking the
way of holiness, we have no right to expect the true church. Where the church is,
there it is being authorized to order the life of discipleship and exercise discipline
(by the use of the keys or ecclesiastical discipline), according to Jesus' teaching in
Matthew 18:18.

"The exercise of church discipline to combat sin" remains today a "sign of the
true church," which includes "the pastoral care of the members of the Church;
the preserving of the pure doctrine through the exercise of spiritual discipline
and the opposing of false doctrines; the doing of works of mercy (*diakonia*)" (Batak Conf. IX, *CC*, p. 562).

This criterion is variously defined as the life of obedience, or good order, or
prudent exercise of ecclesiastical discipline, or zeal for good works, or pastoral
guidance under the ministry of the Word (Calvin, *Inst.* 4.12; Melanchthon *CR*
XII.599–602; Ursinus, *Comm. on Heid. Catech.*, pp. 288–89). It requires "obedience to the divine commands as to sincere religious worship of God alone and as
to holiness of life" (Petrus van Mastricht, *Theoretico-practica Theologia* VII.1.20;
Heppe, *RD*, p. 670). There remains some debate as to whether the third is an
essential sign, or whether it simply follows from the first two. Traditions stemming
from Genevan reform tend to hold it as essential, whereas Lutheran teaching is
prone to treat it as ancillary to Word and Sacrament (Luther, *The Papacy*, *WML* I,
p. 361; Calvin, *Inst.* 4.10, 11).

It is consistent with the plan of salvation that a visible community should arise
as a result of God's saving work, a community of persons who acknowledge Christ
as Lord and Head, who are united by their union with Christ through the Spirit.
Where word, sacrament, and discipline are found, the true church is certainly
present (Calvin, *Inst.* 4.1.7–9).

On Weighing Evidences

*Whether, When Proximate Corruptions Arise, Such Evidences Can Be Hon-
ored.*   Even where errors are perpetrated by the church as manifested in one
locale, still if word, sacrament, and discipline are upheld, the true foundation, Jesus Christ, has been preserved. Despite blemishes and temporary de-
partures from accountability to scripture, a church may remain fundamentally
grounded confessionally and liturgically in Jesus Christ, living in Christ, and

embodying his own life (Matt. 16:18; 1 Pet. 1:24, 25; Conf. of Dositheus 10–12, *CC*, pp. 491–97).

Where corruptions have not become profoundly subversive of the very foundations of the faith, it may be said that the purity of preaching has been proximately retained. These criteria can only be applied under the ambiguous conditions of history: "The more purely the Word of God is preached in a Church, and the nearer the preaching and doctrine comes to the norm of Holy Scripture, the purer will be the Church; the further it recedes from the rule of the Word, the more impure and corrupt will be the Church. Nevertheless it does not cease to be a Church because of some corruption, since God always begets and preserves for Himself a holy seed and spiritual sons, even when the public ministry of the visible Church has been corrupted" (Gerhard, in Jacobs, *SCF*, p. 384). "The more or less sincerely, according to Christ's institution, the Word of God is taught, the Sacraments are administered, and the authority of the Keys is used, the more or less pure are such Churches to be accounted" (*COC* III, Irish Articles 69, p. 538).

Though many errors pervaded the Corinthian and Galatian churches (1 Cor. 15:12; Gal. 4:21), they remained churches because they had not been utterly corrupted but only sporadically or selectively so, and had not obstinately defended these errors. Hope remained that whatever deficits were appearing, they could be restored. The oneness of the church leaves room for different opinions as to how the articles of faith are to be interpreted, provided the canon of apostolic teaching is duly affirmed as criterion of the church (Thirty-nine Articles, VI, XXXIV, *CC*, pp. 267–67, 277–78).

Admonition Against Ecclesial Trivialism.   The believer need not dissociate from a communion because it appears to lack some particular ancillary teaching or departs from received liturgical practice in some incidental way. Where there is a good faith effort to maintain purity of preaching, lawful sacramental life, and discipline in earnest, one may conscientiously embrace a church even if blemished (Calvin, *Inst.* IV.1.12).

Absolute purity is not required in a church that has both wheat and tares. Donatist and puritanical demands for ecclesial perfection may themselves be evidence of a harsh and partisan spirit inconsistent with the unity of the church. We are called to embrace the visible church that reasonably expresses these signs. To turn our backs on such a church just because it is offending temporarily is hazardous to the faith that must look to the body of Christ to be nurtured. For the community, not the autonomous individual, is *mater fidelium* (Calvin, *Inst.* 4.1.4), birthing and nurturing faith, inasmuch as "we are not children of the slave woman, but of the free woman" (Gal. 4:31). In this mothering community, "we are both born and brought up right to the end of our lives" (Olevian, p. 222, in Heppe, *RD*, p. 671). We do well not to impose upon the church a compulsive perfectionism (Calvin, *Inst.* 4.20.2, 5, 7).

Melanchthon sharply remarked, "Let us not praise those tramps who wander around and unite with no church, because they nowhere find their ideals realized [because] something is always lacking" (*Loci*, 3d ed., Jacobs, *SCF*, p. 415; cf. *LCC* XIX, pp. 133–47). The physician cannot abandon the busy hospital for a quiet health resort where only sound applicants are admitted. The pastor cannot withdraw from an inattentive congregation to find a tidier circle of select saints. The Christian teacher cannot withdraw from his or her students to work only with specialized scholars (John Chrysostom, *On the Priesthood* III, *NPNF* 1 IX, pp. 45– 60; Jacobs, *SCF,* p. 414).

Summarizing Marks of the Church: Organization of the Diverse Loci of Ecclesiology. The church is one, finding its oneness in Christ. The church is holy, set apart from the world to mediate life to the world and bring forth the fruits of the Spirit amid the life of the world. The church is catholic in that it is whole, for all, and embracing all times and places. The church is apostolic in that it is grounded in the testimony of the first witnesses to Jesus' life and resurrection, and depends upon and continues their ministry.

These marks of the church are traditionally ordered and defined in this fourfold pattern by the Nicene Creed, here listed in English, Greek, and Latin:

Marks of the Church

One	*mian*	*unam*
Holy	*hagian*	*sanctam*
Catholic	*katholiken*	*catholicam*
Apostolic	*apostoliken*	*apostolicam*

This formulation has stood as the framework upon which classic exegetes have summarily described what is essential to the church. The Roman Symbol (Apostles' Creed) confessed simply, "I believe in the holy catholic Church." The Nicene-Constantinopolitan Creed confessed four specific notes of the church: oneness, holiness, catholicity, and apostolicity (*COC* II, p. 59; *Longer Catech.*, Eastern Orthodox Church, 67, *COC* II, p. 456). "By the marks of the Church we mean certain clear signs by which all men can recognize it as the true Church founded by Jesus Christ" (*Baltimore Catechism* 12.3154, p. 116).

The unity of the church cannot be empirically observed except by sharing empathically in the life of proclaimed word, the enacted sacrament, and the lived-out discipline. So it is with holiness, apostolicity, and catholicity, which may be easily bypassed by the objectivizing observation of scientific inquiry. Not subject to wooden empirical verification, these marks are only spiritually discerned. If any should become permanently obscured, however, that is an indication that the church needs to be reformed—which means once again formed by Christ's own life (Calvin, *Inst.* 4.1).

To learn whether or not a body is the body of Christ, one may then ask whether its life is being expressed as one, holy, universal, and apostolic (Barmen Declaration, *CC*, p. 519). It is implausible to imagine a true church apart from the unity of Christ's body, the holiness of Christ's sacrifice, the universality of the Spirit's mission, and the apostolicity of the remembering community (Hilary, *Trin.* VII.4– 8, *NPNF* 2 IX, pp. 119–21).

UNITY

The First Mark: *Mian Ekklēsian*

An early eucharistic prayer glimpsed the vision of unity: "Even as this broken *bread* was scattered over the hills, and was gathered together and became one, so let Thy Church be gathered together from the ends of the earth into Thy king-dom" (*Teaching of the Twelve Apostles* IX, *ANF* VII, p. 380; cf. Cyprian, *On the Unity of the Church*, *ANF* V, pp. 421–29; *Epistles* 62.13, *ANF* V, p. 362).

The claim of oneness instantly generates a maze of problems: If divided in time, how is the church one in Christ? Is the unity of the church based upon common doctrine? A shared liturgy? Loyalty to a certain affiliation or type of governance? A particular way of reasoning about a particular confessional teaching such as baptism or ministry or justification?

Unity Defined.   Christ founded only one church (John 10:16; 21:15; Heb. 3:6; 10:21; Eph. 5:27; Rom. 12:4, 5). In ascribing unity to the church, we mean that all the members of the church constitute one body, having one head, one origin, one faith, one baptism. They are united by their bond to the one living Lord (Eph. 4:2–15; 1 Cor. 1:10; Gal. 1:6–8; Irenaeus, *Ag. Her.* I.10.2).

The church is said to be one in the precise sense that "it is gathered by one Lord, through one Baptism, into one mystical body, under one Head, governed by one Spirit, bound together in the unity of a common faith, hope, and love" (Gerhard, *LT* XI, 35, Schmid, *DT* p. 588). "The church is one because it is one body with one spirit and one head" (*Eastern Orthodox Catechism* 189, p. 46). "All the regenerate children of God have an inner union and communion with one another through their common faith in Christ" (Jacobs, *SCF,* p. 374). "This unity does not consist in the agreement of our minds or the consent of our wills. It is founded in Jesus Christ Himself" (Lausanne Conference on Faith and Order, *CC,* p. 573).

Correlating the Unity of Trinity, the Church's Unity, and Human Unity.   As the soul of a person has only one body, so the Spirit dwells cohesively in the body of Christ. As the head can have only one body, so the church must be one. As the husband (Christ) has only one spouse (the church), so must all who are united with Christ be one with him. Two bodies, two or more spouses, would confuse and alienate, and lose the purity of love (*Doc. Vat. II, Decree on Ecumenism* 8, pp. 22–23; *Ec.* I.2, pp. 343–45).

The church is "a people made one with the unity of the Father, the Son and the Holy Spirit" (Cyprian, *Treatises* IX.23, *ANF* V, p. 454, *MPL* 4, 553; cf. Augustine, sermons 71, 20, 33, *MPL* 38, 463; *Doc. Vat. II, Dogmatic Constitution on the Church* 4). The unity of the church "finds its highest exemplar and source in the unity of the Persons of the Trinity" (*Doc. Vat. II, Decree on Ecumenism* 2). The unity of the triune God signals and anticipates the unity of the *ekklēsia*. The unity of the church presages the unity of humanity. Though it does not actually include all humanity, and at times appears to be a negligibly small flock, the *ekklēsia* is "an instrument for the redemption of all, and is sent forth into the whole world as the light of the world and the salt of the earth" (*Doc. Vat. II, Ch* 9; Matt. 5:13–16).

"God is one, and Christ is one, and His Church is one, and the faith is one, and the people is joined into substantial unity of body by the cement of concord. Unity cannot be severed; nor can one body be separated by a division of its structure, nor torn into pieces, with its entrails wrenched asunder by laceration. Whatever has proceeded from the womb cannot live and breathe in its detached condition, but loses the substance of health" (Cyprian, *Treatises, Unity of the Church*, *ANF* V, p. 429).

The Premise of Unity Already Established Within Judaism. In the religion of Israel prior to the Babylonian captivity, there was only one temple. The unity of the people was symbolized by this oneness. The high priest was the visible symbol of unity of the covenant community under the one Lord.

After the captivity the synagogues were built, and there were many local places of worship, yet the temple remained in Jerusalem. Thereafter the unity of the people was sustained genealogically, and by a unified canon that received general consent. It was not until the destruction of the temple in A.D. 70 that a crisis arose in the unity of the Jewish people in diaspora. Yet even then, Jerusalem remained the symbolic center of unity, even if not a political reality (*Liturgy of James, ANF* VII, pp. 537–50).

New Testament Assumptions Concerning the Unity of Ekklēsia. Christ intended that the church be one, since he prayed explicitly for its oneness and spoke of it always as one in him. "Holy Father, protect them by the power of your name—the name you gave me—so that they may be one as we are one" (John 17:11).

Jesus prayed "that all of them may be one, Father, just as you are in me and I am in you. May they also be in us so that the world may believe that you have sent me. I have given them the glory that you gave me, that they may be one as we are one: I in them and you in me. May they be brought to complete unity to let the world know that you sent me and love them even as you have loved me" (John 17:21–23). Insofar as the oneness of the church is recognizable by beholding its Lord, the faithful are able to discern where the true church exists (Hilary, *Trin.* VI.38–41, *NPNF* 2 IX, pp. 112–13).

The principle texts on unity of the church are from Paul: "Make every effort to keep the unity of the Spirit through the bond of peace. There is one body and one Spirit—just as you were called to one hope when you were called—one Lord, one faith, one baptism; one God and Father of all" (Eph. 4:3, 4). "From him the whole body, joined and held together by every supporting ligament, grows and builds itself up in love, as each part does its work" (Eph. 4:16). "Because there is one loaf, we, who are many, are one body, for we all partake of the one loaf" (1 Cor. 10:17; Ignatius, *To Philadelphians* 3). Paul was not merely engaged in individualistic, one-on-one conversions but in building up the whole church everywhere, viewing each local church as intrinsically united with the mother church in Jerusalem (Rom. 15:31; 1 Cor. 16:1–3).

The unity of the scattered congregations is created by the one living Lord. They experience their kinship whether in Africa or Asia, with the earliest churches at Jerusalem, Antioch, Alexandria, and Rome. This affinity was evidenced by their organic connection with each other, marked by intercommunion and mutual recognition of *episkopoi*. For "in Christ we who are many form one body, and each member belongs to all the others" (Rom. 12:5; Justin Martyr, *Dialogue with Trypho* 63). Jesus said, "I have other sheep, that are not of this fold; I must bring them also, and they will heed my voice. So there shall be one flock, one shepherd" (John 10:16, RSV).

One Flock in Many Localities. Though the New Testament does not hesitate to speak of the churches in the plural form (1 Cor. 16:19; Gal. 1:2; 1 Thess. 2:14; Rev. 1:11), all local churches are extensions and expressions of the one body unified in its head Jesus Christ and enlivened by the indwelling Spirit. The one church as such is more than the many churches added up (John Chrysostom, *Hom. on Eph.* XI; Clement of Rome, *Corinth* 37, *ANF* I, p. 15). All the faithful are citizens of one commonwealth, "living under one Lord, under the same laws," as "fellow citizens with the saints" (Second Helvetic Conf., *CC*, p. 141; 1 Tim. 2:4, 5). "Whether I say 'husband and wife' or 'head and body,' you must understand me to mean a unity. Thus the same Apostle heard the voice saying, 'Saul, Saul, why are you persecuting *me?*'" (Augustine, sermon 341.12, *LCF*, p. 240; Acts 9:4). The "me" Paul was persecuting was not merely isolated believers but the Lord who made them all one.

The Unity of the Church in Combat and in Victory: Militant and Triumphant. Because God preserves the gathered people through time, and because persons live and die, some who belong to the church are alive, others dead, and others yet unborn. It is from this structural condition of the church's temporal existence that it becomes necessary and useful to distinguish between the present and promised church, or church militant and triumphant (Pastor of Hermas, *Sim.* IX, *ANF* II, p. 43).

The regenerate remain in constant conflict with the world, the flesh, and the adversary (Rom. 7:23; Gal. 5:17; 1 John 5:4). They struggle daily against the powers of evil (Eph. 6:10; 1 Pet. 5:8, 9). This ceaseless combat has caused the church while in the world to be called the church in combat or church *militant,* assuming not a military but a spiritual struggle (John Chrysostom, *Baptismal Instructions, ACW* 31, pp. 58–60; Calvin, *Inst.* 3.3–2; Barth, *CD* I/2, p. 841).

The church of the celestial city is composed of victors in this worldly battle who have passed beyond all earthly conflicts, who having been faithful here have been given a crown of life (Rev. 2:10). It includes persons of all nations, tribes, peoples, tongues who live now in ceaseless praise of God (Rev. 7:9). Hence it is called the church *triumphant* (Calvin, *Inst.* 2.16.16). The error of "triumphalism" is prone to transfer the eschatological victory into some form of present political triumph. The church embraces not only a sociological structure now visible in the world, but also those who have died in Christ and those yet to believe and be united in him (Barth, *CD* I/2, p. 661).

There is a skeptical tendency in accommodative, secularized Christianity to distrust any talk of a church triumphant. Given the premise of absolute relativism, triumphalism has become a term of scandal and embarrassment. Any hint that the promised church is already being realized is disavowed. There is an accompanying Protestant tendency to view the visible church as practically nonexistent, since the church appears virtually nowhere as absolutely pure, perfected, united, holy, or catholic (Brunner, *The Misunderstanding of the Church;* cf. Küng, *TC;* L. Boff, *Church: Charism and Power;* E. de Schmedt, *Acta synodalia, Doc. Vat. II,* II.4, pp. 142–44).

The same single body that struggles against the principalities and powers, and that expects even more severe difficulties in the future, is at the same time already victorious by virtue of its being presently united with its head in the heavenly city, anticipating that completed joy in the Lord wherein all the faithful shall praise God together at the end of days (1 Cor. 15:54–57; Pope, *Compend.* III, p. 286). The distinction between the church in combat and the church in victory is a theological distinction pertaining to the unity of the church and her union with her Lord, more than a sociological description (1 John 5:4–5).

The Destiny of the Church.   The community of faith that within history struggles in combat with the remaining outrages of the history of sin has an exalted future of promise: to share in Christ's righteousness, to enter into fellowship with the Father by union with the Son by the power of the Spirit (1 Tim. 6:12).

Grace works to transform sinners entirely. Grace seeks so to infuse sinners with God's own redeeming power that they are being here and now readied for sharing in God's own life eternally. The community of faith is portrayed as already being presented as a bride to Christ, loved by him, arrayed in fine linen (Rev. 19:7, 8), without spot or wrinkle or blemish (Eph. 5:27), joint heir of his suffering and glory (Rom. 8:17; 1 Cor. 6:2, 3).

Johannes Wessel, one of the forerunners of the Reformation (died 1489) wrote, "All saints have fellowship in true, essential unity: as many as cling to Christ with one faith, one love; under whatsoever prelates they live; however the latter may ambitiously contend or dissent or err, even though they be heretics; in whatever localities in space; separated by whatever intervals of years; and this is the *communio,* of which we speak in the Creed" (*De Communio Sanctorum,* Opera, Groningen, 1614, p. 809; cf. *De Potest. Ecclesiastica,* p. 752; *SHD* II 212). From this union, no declaration of priest or prelate or council may separate one who shares in the *congregatio omnum predestinatorum* (Wyclif, *LCC* XIV). On this assumption it became possible for believers to approach the abuses of the church critically.

Unity and Diversity

The Historical Trajectory of Unity and Disunity.   During most of its first millennium, the church was one church—proximately one in teaching, worship, polity, and disciplinary practice. This does not deny that there were varied cultures and assertive parties within the ecumenical whole, but the consent was very general to the ecumenical conciliar definitions from the third century to 1054, when East and West split apart, a split that has remained for almost a thousand years. A half millennium later Protestantism would fragment the church into many parts.

If the first millennium ended with the church split in two, the second millennium is ending with the church split into thousands of pieces, autonomously governed, even competing, fighting like siblings. The third millennium faces the task of once again practically embodying the unity that we already have juridically in Christ (*The Unity We Have and the Unity We Seek,* Third World Conference on Faith and Order [Lund, Geneva: *WCC,* 1952], pp. 33–34).

Unity in Diversity.   In its outward forms in specific times and places, living in particular cultures, the church always appears sociologically as diverse, yet remains one in its essential unity (*unitas essentialis*) when viewed theologically— united in Christ its head, unified by one spirit (Eph. 4:4), in the unity of one faith (Eph. 4:5), which expresses itself in the unity of love (Basil, *Letters* 92, *NPNF* 2 VIII, p. 178).

The idolatrous overvaluation of unity results in uniformity, a tyrannizing excess of superficially imposed unity. The undervaluation or neglect of unity is divisiveness and egocentricity, imagining that one's own individualistic opinion is more important or more clearly ordained of God than the received consensual tradition (1 Cor. 1:10–17).

The Spirit sustains the unity of the church by enjoying and enabling centered variety, not uniformity, and by seeking and praying for reconciliation whenever centrifugal forces become intense (Eph. 2:14; Cornelius I, *The Monarchical Constitution of the Church, SCD* 44, p. 21). "All true portions of Christ's Church necessarily possess its faith, its apostolic ministry, its sacraments, its manner of worship, its fundamental precepts, and its typical *ethos* or spiritual atmosphere" (Hall, *DT,* p. 175).

The eschatological song the elders sing in the presence of the lamb in the end-time revelation celebrates variety in unity of the one who with his blood "purchased men for God from every tribe and language and people and nation" (Rev. 5:9), all of whom are joined in unity by the lamb. Since the church is called to dwell patiently in all cultures and generations of time, it must have one eternal Head to animate the body and make it one (Eph. 4:4–6; 1 Cor. 3:10, 11; *Longer Catech.*, Eastern Orthodox Church, 259, *COC* II, p. 485).

The Church Already Has Dominical Unity in Christ.   How is the inclusive church to be considered at the same time united, if it is inclusive of apparent contradictories: both living and dead, combatants of both sides of warring nations, of distant generations of the faithful, of infinitely varied political opinions and parties and cultures? The consensual answer is clear: the called community is united in the One appointed "to be head over everything for the church, which is his body, the fullness of him who fills everything in every way" (Eph. 1:22, 23). The unity we already have, we have in Christ, not as a human achievement but as a gift manifested in Christ's presence at table unifying the diversity of the churches (1 Cor. 10:16, 17).

The church's unity is not merely a unity of the presently existing church but more so a unity in Christ of the company of believers of all times and places, a large and diverse family of sinners who are being made holy by faith in Christ (J. Wessel, *De Poenitentia*, pp. 778–81, in *SHD* II, p. 212; Brunner, *Dogm.* III, p. 127; Rahner, *RR*, pp. 300–305).

"Since the Church has received this preaching and this faith, as we have said, although she is scattered through the whole world, she preserves it carefully, as one household: and the whole Church alike believes in these things, as having one soul and heart, and in unison preaching these beliefs, and teaches and hands them on as having one mouth. For though there are many different languages in the world, still the meaning of the tradition is one and the same. And there are not different beliefs or traditions in the churches established in Germany, or in Spain, or among the Celts, or in the East, or in Egypt or Libya" (Irenaeus, *Ag. Her.* I.10.1–2, *ECF*, p. 92).

How Far Is Unity Scandalized by Divided Christendom?   Unity is a crucial mark of the church because insofar as there is visible catholic consent, it enriches the plausibility of the church's one testimony to the divided world. Insofar as there is a spirit of divisiveness standing as a distraction to universal consent, the church's mission is hampered. The disciples are known by their love for one another (John 13:34, 35; 1 John 3:11–20). When the divided church approaches the world with ambivalence, uncertainty, and identity diffusion, it elicits despair within the church and confusion externally.

Confession of human brokenness is a central dimension of the teaching of the unity of the church: "We humbly acknowledge that our divisions are contrary to the will of Christ, and we pray God in His mercy to shorten the days of our separation and to guide us by His Spirit into fulness of unity" (Lausanne Conference on Faith and Order, *CC*, p. 573). "Our separation has prevented us from receiving correction from one another in Christ" (Amsterdam Assembly, *WCC, CC*, p. 575). The unity of the church is frustrated and chagrined, but not brought to nought, by divided Christendom (Deitrich of Niem, *Ways of Uniting and Reforming the Church* 1410, *LCC* XIV, pp. 149 ff.).

Whether Institutional Divisions Destroy the Unity of the Church in Its Head. The present divisions of the church are to some degree rightly regarded as divisions within, rather than complete or irreversible separations from, the church. The Augsburg Apology reasoned analogically, "Just as dissimilar spaces of day and night do not injure the unity of the Church, so we believe that the true unity of the Church is not injured by dissimilar rites instituted by men" (169; Jacobs, *SCF*, p. 398).

Present divisions do not utterly destroy the apostolicity or holiness of the church, but they place a cloud over premature claims of catholicity and unity. Meanwhile each confessional body is united with other confessional bodies by their common participation in Christ, but this does indeed tend to make divided Christendom a scandal to the world, almost incomprehensible to those we seek to serve and to whom we attest unity in Christ.

Whether Denominations Should Repent of Their Uniqueness. God the Spirit works with human flesh to persuade, consecrate, and sanctify, just as God the Son works through human flesh to justify. Given the recalcitrance of the history of sin, it is not surprising that the Spirit would work in very different ways amid different cultures and subcultures. The varied ways of the Spirit seem to sociological eyes to be entirely lacking in unity and plagued with chaotic cultural diversity and moral contradiction, unless the sociologist has learned to behold sin and grace from the vantage point of the incarnation, hypostatic union, and *perichoresis* (J. Ellul, *The Humiliation of the Word;* cf. P. Berger, *Rumor of Angels, The Sacred Canopy*).

Amid these conditions, little is gained by focusing simply on calling upon the denominations to repent of their uniqueness. Precisely through their diversity, varied cultural settings are being served, sustained, and nurtured. It has often happened that a vital denominationalism has been replaced by a pallid and ineffective ecumenism.

Sadly, not all claims and attempts at manifesting the unity of the church do indeed rightly express that unity in Christ. Too many pretentious pseudoecumenical efforts have been themselves divisive, intolerant, ultrapolitical, misconceived, utopian, abusive, nationalistic, and culturally imperialistic. All this has occurred under the banner of modern bulldozer ecumenism.

Hence modern ecumenical movements are themselves called to repentance on behalf of the unity of the church. Without true repentance, it is doubtful that the varied houses of Protestantism can speak confidently of the one body of Christ. Those of us who have lived our lives as Christians in churches associated with the World Council of Churches have seen enough to be wary of any proposed union that would tend to obstruct or diminish the vitality of the church's mission or exchange it for a mess of political pottage. Church membership becomes relatively meaningless to the degree that secular humanistic moral teachings are baptized as Christian teaching and moral standards of church membership lowered to the lowest common denominator in the interest of high-sounding cross-cultural inclusiveness, often spurred on by the rhetoric of cheap grace.

The disunity of the church remains an embarrassment and cause of repentance for all of divided Christendom. Yet the existence of Protestant denominational structures is not in itself something to be lamented altogether or regarded as outside the bounds of providence or incapable of redemption. For the denominations emerged in order better to manifest the marks of the church, especially holiness and apostolic accountability. There always remains some possibility of reform of semi-apostate churches. It is often better to seek reform within than simply abandon those church bodies to rampant secularization.

The Ecumenical Spirit

Fairly Applying the Tests of the Church.   We do well to avoid inflammatory stereotypes and prejudicial statements that do not fairly represent the condition of other Christians and make further dialogue even more difficult than it has already been made by the history of division (Augustin Bea, *The Unity of Christians*). Yet within the ecumenical spirit there remains a danger of a false irenicism or indifferentism (J. Wesley, *WJWB* sermon 39, *WJW* V, pp. 492–504; *Doc. Vat. II, Ec.* 4, *Dir. Ec.* 2; *CMM,* pp. 105, 106).

Meanwhile it remains fitting that Christians join in prayer with other Christians separated from them by institutional divisions, to petition for the grace of unity, and to express the ties that bind each one to Christ. "For where two or three come together in my name, there am I with them" (Matt. 18:20).

The tests of the church should not be applied to particular churches so as to rationalize one's own church tradition or discredit other traditions of Christian experience. One stereotypic pattern that should be avoided is that of limiting the true church criteria to old-line or established churches so as to preemptively exclude as schismatic the smaller and less auspicious church bodies. Another more subtle, more modern stereotypic pattern that should be avoided is that of limiting "true church criteria" to particularist features (of polity or idiosyncratic doctrine) so as to denounce as corrupt virtually all ancient traditions of Christian experience. This is the bitter result of modern chauvinism, radical feminism, and compulsive avant-garde progressivism. The hope that sustains my argument here: by recovery of ancient ecumenical consensus, the areas of agreement in modern ecumenical conversation may deepen and expand.

It remains dubious to attempt to fashion a "union whose only aim is to promote an external unity" (Dorner, *SCDoc.* IV, p. 371). Given the deteriorating state of official, bureaucratic ecumenism today, some are tempted to launch a direct attack on the pretenses of modern ecumenical politicism. It is all too easy to blast it for its ideological narrowness, lack of catholicity, hyperliberal partisanship, neglect of evangelicals and Catholics, its chronic unorthodoxy, lack of empathy for the laity, its worship of organization and centralization, its pretension that only through it will God work, its neglect of broadcast media, its knowledge elites, with their resulting class-oriented biases, and on and on. But such a polemic would only serve to disparage good intentions gone awry.

Unity Celebrates Difference.   Genuine unity in the whole body of Christ is not merely a matter of improved organizational management. It is a unity enabled by the Spirit that awakens legitimate diversity without imposing premature uniformity. Real differences existed within the early church that were often related to differences in the immensely varied cultural contexts to which the gospel was being addressed. Christians rooted in synagogue worship were more reluctant to give up Jewish ceremonies such as circumcision. Hellenizing Christians spoke a different language than that familiar in the Jerusalem church. A distinction emerged early between the churches of Macedonia and the churches of Asia, from the time of Paul's second missionary journey. There were distinctions between the wealthy of port cities and the poor of Jerusalem that the one church sought to overcome.

Even in the New Testament there were divisions in the church (1 Cor. 11:19, 19; Gal. 1:6–9; 1 John 2:18, 19), which the apostles deplored (1 Cor. 1:11 ff.; 11:22). But this spirit of divisiveness has accelerated in history so that millions of communicants of one branch of the vine cannot communicate at Table with millions of another.

No one need despair of an imagined disunity that is actually only a beautiful expression of human variety and that may also be seen from another viewpoint as an expression of the true humanity and catholicity of the body of Christ. Nor do we need despairingly to turn life in the Spirit into a lockstep hunger for uniformity or organizational centralism that loses touch with the grass roots or that would tend to efface the legitimate variety of church traditions. Their emergence is in part due to sin (Gal. 5:19–21) but also to the resplendent varieties of human cultures, symbol systems, and historical differences. Had the church failed to address these cultural heterogeneities, its worldwide mission would have been to that degree defaulted. The church expresses its oneness precisely through variety and flexibility.

The Spirit-led church is capable of facing and ameliorating conflict within itself. The apostolic church was never without differences. Paul admonished Peter (Gal. 2:11), and Barnabas had serious differences with Paul (Acts 15:39). The church at Antioch, though preaching the same Christ, had different viewpoints about circumcision. Such differences were used creatively by the Spirit for the perfection of the church: "For thus it pleases God to use the dissensions that arise in the church, to the glory of his name, to the setting forth of the truth" (Second Helvetic Conf., *CC*, p. 145; 1 Cor. 11:19).

Ecumenic Hospitality.   The one church has become expressed in innumerable varieties that could not have been expressed under the rigorous conditions of medieval ecclesiomonism or post-Tridentine uniformism. He who warned against pouring old wine into new wineskins (Mark 2:22) did not hesitate himself to set in motion new institutional structures and social constructs. Out of his mission have come a profusion of orders, movements, missions, and labors. By means of these varieties, spiritual formation has been deepened, missionary activity extended, and attention given to aspects of apostolic testimony previously neglected.

This variety may be celebrated without tending to idealize the divisive spirit. A sectarianism that cuts itself off from communion with other Christian traditions and asserts a partial or one-sided aspect of the apostolic witness must be the subject of earnest intercession with the hope of restoration, even if this takes centuries to accomplish.

The task of irenic theology is to assess the nearness and distance of varied traditions from each other, not to gloss over these distances or clothe them with false assurances of unity or promises that can only end in disappointment and resentment (*Uppsala Report, CC*, pp. 590–95; Bermejo, *SL*, pp. 19–37). A kind of ecumenical hospitality is required to welcome guests from other church traditions that they may teach us what they can out of their particular historical experience. "As we learn more of each other, we shall more clearly discern this common heritage and express it more fully" (New Delhi, *WCC, Message, CC*, p. 588). Being united in Christ, all who call him Lord are called to care for each others' welfare, use good judgment in consulting, and seek to manifest their unity in Christ in whatever ways the Spirit makes contextually possible (Ignatius, *Eph.* 10, *Trallians*, 8).

The modern ecumenical movement was born on that day in 1910 when an Asian delegate to the World Missionary Conference at Edinburgh said something like the following (no one knows precisely who made this remark, but the gist of it is as follows): "You have sent us your missionaries, who have introduced us to Jesus Christ, and for that we are grateful. But you have also brought us your distinctions and divisions; some preach Methodism, others Lutheranism, Congregationalism, or Episcopalianism. We ask you to preach the Gospel to us and to let Jesus Christ himself raise from among our peoples, by the action of his Holy Spirit, a Church conforming to his requirements. . . . This Church will be the Church of Christ in Japan, the Church of Christ in China, the Church of Christ in India; it will free us from all the *isms* with which you colour the preaching of the Gospel among us" (M. Villain, *Unity: A History*, pp. 29, 30).

In Nonessentials, Liberty.   The faithful are instructed to keep the bond of peace with all who love the Lord, however different they may be from our own perceptions and preferences. The motto remains valid: *In necessariis unitas, in non necessariis libertas, in utrisque caritas* (In essentials unity, in nonessentials liberty, in all things charity).

More bricks are added to the walls of partition that separate Christians when they exclude those who seem to be culturally different from themselves. Better to pray with and for them the prayer of our Lord "that all of them may be one, Father, just as you are in me and I am in you. May they also be in us so that the world may believe" (John 17:20, 21).

Resisting Sectarianism and Syncretism.   A poignant picture of the divided church was sketched by Basil in A.D. 374. The present state of the churches is like "some naval battle which has arisen out of time old quarrels, and is fought by men who cherish a deadly hate against one another, of long experience in naval warfare, and eager for the fight." As the rival fleets rush together, "watchwords are indistinguishable," and "all distinction between friend and foe is lost" in an "unmeaning roar" where "not a word from admiral or pilot can be heard." This is precisely what Basil thought had occurred in his own time with the Pneumatomachi and Macedonian disputes in which "every landmark of the Fathers has been moved; every foundation . . . shaken." "No sooner have the enemy gone by than we find enemies in one another," under conditions where "scripture is powerless to mediate." "We have become more brutish than the brutes" (Basil, *On the Spirit* III.30, *NPNF* 2 VIII, p. 48, 49). Yet by means of the Second Ecumenical Council only seven years later, these heresies were virtually silenced.

Sectarianism places undue stress upon distinctive features of a given church tradition, so as to lead to pride and self-congratulation. Syncretism, on the other pole, that is willing to do almost anything to gain an external unity, is susceptible to mating with any ideological partner around, usually at the cost of loss of centered orthodoxy.

The church of one generation can become prisoner to the historical-cultural forms of either its own or a preceding generation and thereby deny the catholicity of the church that moves through and beyond all generations. The modernist-relevancy illusion is trapped in the present. The archaist-traditionalist illusion is trapped in the past. Neither the mind-set of faddist, discontinuous ever-changeability nor that of immutable *immobilismo* can adequately express the body of Christ in history. "The real Church not only has a history, it exists by having a history" (Küng, *TC*, p. 13).

Varied images of the church appear already in the New Testament, since the New Testament was written under a variety of different missional conditions. But that does not imply that there were unresolvable tensions within the New Testament views of the church. The New Testament does not offer a systematic ecclesiology but a moving series of glimpses of the living church in differing situations. The centeredness of its witness must have been grasped through the diversity of its witnesses. Amid the many words the one Word was forming the one body, and the one Tradition forming itself through many traditions.

The church attested in the New Testament is already the whole church, bearing and guarding the full deposit of faith. It is not as if that church required some subsequent generation(s) of Christian testimony to complete what was incomplete in it. The task today is not simply to copy those apostolic models woodenly but to pray for the same Spirit to form the church today who formed those models of *ekklēsia* in apostolic times (D. Bonhoeffer, *The Cost of Discipleship*).

The Truth of the Conflicting Confessional Traditions

To some it may seem disingenuous that systematic ecclesiology seeks to affirm and discover proximate truth even in traditions of church teaching that appear to conflict with each other. Here as everywhere ecumenic theology is seeking the ground of general lay consent wherever it can be honestly identified. This is not accomplished by ignoring or disavowing particular church traditions, but rather by affirming their richness and vitality.

Godly persons are to be found in all church traditions, even those that have noticeable elements of heretical teaching (*BOC*, pp. 3 ff.). It is not surprising that a variegated Christendom over two millennia would develop varied (and even at times conflicting) confessions, creeds, catechisms, and symbols of faith that seek to express the leading truths of those various traditions, national churches, cultures of Christian faith, and confessional bodies. Though the variety of these symbols of faith sometimes attest the disunity, hence the sin, of the church, it also is the case that this variety is indirectly and ironically a cultural-historical expression of the catholicity of the church. What Christians of varied centuries hold in common (such as the written canon, Apostles' Creed, baptism, and Eucharist) are much more crucial and decisive than the points upon which they differ. In the bread to be consecrated many grains go to form one loaf (*Didache* IX.4).

The Valid Functions of Confessional and Doctrinal Standards.   Confessions or standards of doctrine serve several purposes. They guide church members in attesting the central truth of scripture. They serve as an authoritative standard to which appeal is made during times of controversy. They may serve not only as a functional constitution for the community but also as a kind of banner or flag or symbolic declaration to the world of the ecclesial community's identity. They regulate those responsible for the teaching office of the church, especially those whose ordination calls them to accountability in preaching and instructing confirmands. They unite a diverse church body in a common doctrinal purpose, distinguishing it from the world and from all counterfeits. They defend against abuses such as the misuse of church property by those who do not share the views of the traditioning body. For all these reasons, the confessions of varied church bodies continue to fulfill certain meaningful roles, and should not be considered always as counterecumenical or alien to the ecumenical spirit.

The Proximate Truth of Particular Church Bodies.   Christians of one family of churches are ill-advised to fixate upon the wrongs or evils or misjudgments or bad faith of another family or branch of Christianity, or to ignore the defects of their own church tradition. Differing church bodies are one insofar as the Word is preached purely and the sacraments rightly administered so as to elicit a disciplined community of faith. They are apostolic insofar as they hold the same apostolic teaching that has united Christians to Christ from all times and places. They are proximately catholic insofar as they seek to make their contribution to the whole body of Christ without maliciously impugning the character of other confessional bodies. "All particular churches have a claim to be regarded as Christian so long as they have not lost, but still exercise, the essential characteristics or signs of the Church—Word and Sacrament" (Dorner, *SCDoc.* IV, p. 371).

Every particular expression of genuine faith in Christ participates in the one, holy, catholic church, the communion of saints. No particular expression of the church can rightly claim to be exhaustively identical with the whole. There is finally one shepherd and one fold. Wherever Christ is believed and followed and worshiped, the *ekklēsia* exists. Yet this cannot imply that it remains a matter of indifference which church one belongs to (Jacobs, *SCF,* pp. 399–401). Lacking grave objections or emergent apostasies, the presumption remains in favor of staying within the church tradition in which one was born, or reborn in faith, weaned, and fed, so as to be nurtured to maturity.

Rectifying Schism and Heresy.   Schism is a rupture of the unity of the church destroying the peace of the church and vexing the love that rightly should prevail in the body of Christ (Cyprian, *Treatises* X, *ANF* V, pp. 491–96). Schism means dissension, division, partisanship (John 7:43; 9:16; 10:19; 1 Cor. 1:10; 11:18;

12:25). Schism (*schisma*) implies the partisan following of a special interest or party. The schismatic spirit may attach itself either to a defensive establishment mentality or to a chronically dissenting mentality. "Schism may be the sin of the community left as well as of the community leaving" (Pope, *Compend.* III, p. 274).

"In the creeds of some churches the foundation, while affected by errors inseparable from the foundation, has not been overthrown; in other churches again, the errors overshadow the saving truth of the Gospel in a most deplorable manner, so that it is hard to discover even some remnants of the One Holy Church" (*Doc. Vat. II*, p. 182). Vatican II concluded, "In some real way" the separated brothers and sisters remain "joined with us in the Holy Spirit, for to them also he gives his gifts and graces and is thereby operative among them with his sanctifying power," even when they "do not profess the faith in its entirety" (*Doc. Vat. II, Ch.* 15, p. 34). "One cannot impute the sin of separation to those who at present are born into these Communities and are instilled therein with Christ's faith. The Catholic Church embraces them as brothers, with respect and affection" (*Doc. Vat. II, Ec.* 3). Yet these divisions contradict the will of Christ, cause the world to be offended by the divided church, and damage the cause of preaching the gospel.

In schism and heresy the unity of the church seems to be temporarily split asunder. "A schismatic is one who while preserving faith's foundation departs from some rite of the Church or from a received doctrine or, for some other reason, from the Church. A heretic is one, who convulsing the foundations of faith either directly or by inevitable inference gives persistent battle on behalf of his heresy" (Alsted, *TSD*, p. 689, in Heppe, *RD*, 669). Meanwhile the deeper unity of the church is never lost and never can be insofar as it already exists in the one Head, but individuals and groups can choose to separate themselves from this unity.

Hairesis means a self-chosen view, as distinct from the traditionally received apostolic teaching (Tertullian, *Prescription Ag. Her.* I–XXX, *ANF* III, pp. 243–58). Heresy is a self-willed choice of individual interpretation as opposed to consensually received scriptural teaching (1 Cor. 1:10). Heresy is the "obstinate advocacy and propagation of error directly attacking the foundations of the faith"—etymologically the term indicates "an arbitrary or self-determined choice separating one from the unity of the Church" (Jacobs, *SCF*, p. 411). Within the context of Judaism the *hairesis* (Heb. *min*) referred to a sect or party, and was applied by varied audiences to Pharisees, Sadducees, Nazarenes, and to the early church (Acts 5:17; 15:5; 24:5, 14; 26:5; 28:22). Those who presume to retain the name *Christian* yet reject the ancient ecumenical faith can hardly be vital parts of the living Vine. Both *schisma* and *hairesis* require continuing intelligent resistance and patient efforts at reconciliation (Cyprian, *On the Unity of the Catholic Church*, *ACW* 25, pp. 52 ff., 74 ff.).

HOLINESS

The most complete disclosure of holiness is that personal form which becomes incarnate within the history of sin to die on the cross. God does not evidence holiness by utterly separating from the history of sin, but by engaging and transforming it.

The Second Mark: *Hagian Ekklēsian*

It is an article of faith found in the most ancient forms of the baptismal creed that confesses: "I believe in the *hagian ekklēsian*" (holy church, Marcellus of Ancyra, *COC* II, p. 48; cf. *SCD* 1, 2, p. 3). *Credo in sanctam ecclesiam* implies that I believe that the church is made capable of reflecting the divine holiness, not that the church as such possesses holiness independently. The primitive African and Gallican Baptismal Creeds avoided any misunderstanding by confessing *credo per sanctam ecclesiam*—"I believe *through* the holy church" (F. Loofs, *Symbolik*, 1902, *In sancto spiritu als Formulierung des gallischen Taufsymbols,* pp. 12, 13, italics added; Brunner, *Dogm.* III, p. 130).

The Sanctity and Imperfection of the Church.   As body of Christ, the church is necessarily holy, yet its holiness is enmeshed in continuing human imperfection and finitude until the end of history. The church is holy while not ceasing to be subject to the infirmities of the flesh that accompany all historical existence (John Chrysostom, *Hom. on Eph.* XX, *NPNF* 1 XIII, pp. 144–45). Christ "loved the church and gave himself up for her to make her holy, cleansing her by the washing with water through the word, and to present her to himself as a radiant church, without stain or wrinkle or any other blemish, but holy and blameless" (Eph. 5:25, 26). This cleansing is still taking place, still in the process of being fashioned and elicited (Calvin, *Inst.* 4.1.17–22).

The holiness of the church is best expressed in the imperfect or unfinished tense—that God is now sanctifying the church, now calling forth a *communio sanctorum.* "You also, like living stones, *are being built* [*oikodomeisthe*] into a spiritual house to be a holy priesthood" (1 Pet. 2:4, italics added), destined to be "a holy nation, a people belonging to God" (1 Pet. 2:9). The church is being made holy, having been called forth by the Son, and is now being sanctified by the Spirit (*Eastern Orthodox Catechism* 192, p. 46; cf. Roman Council, *SCD* 288, p. 112).

What Makes the Church Holy?   The church is holy because her Lord is holy (1 Cor. 1:30), and her task is to fashion her members after her Lord (Ignatius, *To Smyrna, FC* 1, pp. 118–24; Irenaeus, *Ag. Her.* III.24, *ANF* I, p. 458; Cyprian, *On the Unity of the Church* 6, *ANF* V, pp. 412–19; Augustine, sermon 214, *FC* 38, pp. 130–42). The church is holy because she is sanctified by Christ through his passion, teaching, prayer, and sacraments (*Longer Catech.,* Eastern Orthodox Church, 267, *COC* II, p. 487). The church is holy because she "teaches, according to the will of Christ, holy doctrines, and provides the means of leading a holy life, thereby giving holy members to every age" (*Baltimore Catechism,* p. 119).

Seventeenth-century Lutheran John Gerhard reasoned textually about the church's holiness in this way: "The Church is said to be holy, from 1 Cor. 14:33; Rev. 11:2; because Christ its Head is holy, Heb. 7:26, who makes the Church partaker of His holiness, John 17:19; because it is called by a holy calling and separated from the world, 2 Tim. 1:9; because the Word of God, committed to it, is holy, Rom. 3:2; because the Holy Ghost in this assembly sanctifies believers by applying to them, through faith, Christ's holiness . . . awakening in them the desire of perfect holiness" (Gerhard, *LT* XI.36; cf. Batak Conf. VIII, *CC,* p. 560). Similarly, Ursinus said the church "is called holy because it is sanctified of God by the blood and Spirit of Christ, that it may be conformable to him, not in perfection, but by the imputation of Christ's righteousness, or obedience; and by having the principle of holiness; because the Holy Spirit renews and delivers the church from the dregs of sins by degrees, in order that all who belong to it may commence and practice all the parts of obedience" (*Comm. Heid. Catech.*, p. 289; cf. Luther, *WA* 8.163).

The Sanctity Peculiar to the Believing Community. Hagios (Heb. *qadosh*, Lat. *sancta*), holy, is applied to the church as a body and to believers whose lives, set apart for service in the world, are unreservedly consecrated to God for the salvation of the world. In this new creation of the Spirit those who are called (*kletoi*) from the unregenerate world are gathered into the church (*ekklēsia*) to be regenerated for service in and witness to the world (Athanasius, *Resurrection Letters* 7, pp. 111–23). Jesus called his disciples "out of the world" (John 17:6) precisely while viewing them as "still in the world" (v. 11) but not "of the world" (v. 14). He specifically prayed that the Father might not "take them out of the world" but "protect them from the evil one" (v. 15), for "I have sent them into the world" (v. 18).

The purpose of the church is to gather out of the world a people of God whose lives are hid in Christ, who "gave himself for us to redeem us from all wickedness and to purify for himself a people that are his very own, eager to do what is good" (Titus 2:14). The missional implication is that the church is intended to be consecrated wholly to God on behalf of the world. The ascetic implication is that the *ekklēsia*, being "called out," is required to be separate and distinct from whatever is alien to God, precisely while working to save it. The notion of holiness includes both these implications: consecrated to God and set apart from the world while reaching out for the world in its alienation (Barth, *CD* IV/1, pp. 685 ff.).

Positional-Juridical Sanctity in Christ. As "holiness unto the Lord" was stamped on the bells of the horses and cooking pots in ancient Israel (Zech. 14:20), so this holiness is stamped on every button or sandal, every discrete action and aspect of the church (Athanasius, *Resurrection Letters* 11, pp. 72–79). A kind of sanctity is imputed to the church by the atoning deed of the Son on the cross.

The whole church is already in some sense sanctified merely by having received the Word, for, "You are *already clean because of the word* I have spoken to you" (John 14:3, italics added). This imputed holiness is not overcome by the aroma of corruption that pervades the context to which the *ekklēsia* is addressing itself, and in which, due to its explicit hands-on mission, it must to some degree partake (Acts 13:34).

Paul addressed his first letter to Corinth "to those sanctified in Christ Jesus and *called to be holy [kletoi hagioi]*, together with *all those everywhere who call* on the name of our Lord" (1 Cor. 1:2, italics added). Those who having been made holy positionally in Christ are now called practically to walk in the way of holiness, along with others everywhere who pray and hear the Word, however imperfectly. Called by the holy God to holiness, the church calls upon the holy God for the grace that enables a proximate reflection of God's holiness under the conditions of sin (Rom. 12:1; 1 Pet. 1:13–24; Luther, *On the Councils*, *LW* 41, pp. 143–57).

Imputed Holiness and the Embodied Sanctity of the Church. This juridical, positional holiness in the body of Christ is constantly seeking to manifest itself in a practicing, living community of word and sacrament (1 Pet. 2:1–3). There is no fooling the Lord, for "the Lord knows those who are his," yet this makes it ever more imperative that "everyone who confesses the name of the Lord must run away from wickedness" (2 Tim. 2:19). This is the twofold watchword that Paul left with Timothy in his last letter, as if carved in indelible letters on the foundation stone of the church. The New Testament writings generally were written to the saints, among whom were many whose unholiness was being admonished, resisted, forgiven, and transformed. John's Revelation warned the *ekklēsia* at Ephesus to "remember the height from which you have fallen!" Lacking repentance, the Lord will come "and remove your lamp stand from its place" (Rev. 2:5). Yet the continuing misdeeds, latent apostasies, and proximate fallenness of the Ephesian and Corinthian churches did not imply that they had lost entirely all aspects of the holiness that inheres in the body of Christ.

How the Bride Is Being Made Beautiful.   Christ loves the church not because of her beauty, but despite her lack of it, eliciting beauty from her eyes. No one stated this point more delicately than John Chrysostom: "For he who loves does not investigate character: love does not regard uncomeliness: on this account indeed is it called love because it oftentimes hath affection for an uncomely person. Thus also did Christ. He saw one who was uncomely (for comely I could not call her) and He loved her, and He makes her young" (Eutropius, *NPNF* 1 IX, p. 262; cf. S. Kierkegaard, whose *Works of Love*, pp. 153–71, seems to depend at this point upon Chrysostom).

Signs of Emergent Holiness.   Signs of an imperfectly emergent holiness may appear in one who is as yet still noticeably corrupt. The church on behalf of its holiness does not say to this person, Please come back when you are fully holy and then you will be baptized and invited to the Lord's table. Rather, the church on behalf of its holiness must draw as near to this person as possible so as to bring Christ's goodness to sinners and sinners to Christ's goodness at each step along the way. This is seen in Jesus' own receiving-confronting attitude toward notorious but penitent sinners, whom he held to be closer to the kingdom than those who feign righteousness (Matt. 21:31, 32; Hall, *DT* VIII, p. 188).

Gregory the Great recognized how difficult it is to honor the church's imputed sanctity without unnecessarily driving out those who are truly seeking to embody it while doing so imperfectly (Gregory the Great, *Pastoral Care* II.7–10, *ACW* 11, pp. 68–86). At the same time one is being made holy by penitent baptism and faith in justifying grace, one may remain tempted by disbelief or lack of charity. Through the ministry of word and sacrament it is hoped that one will be nurtured toward the way of holiness.

The Incarnational Paradox of the Church's Sanctity.   The deeper irony is that the signs of sin that attach to the church are indirect evidences of its holiness. It could not be a holy church if it had clean hands, as if separated from its mission and task of saving sinners. The very purpose of the church is the transformation of sinners; hence the paradoxical proximity of sin to the church (Conf. of Dositheus XI, *CC*, p. 495).

The distinctive function of the church is to bring sinners to the way of holiness. This requires that the church should love at close quarters the sinners it is called to save, to draw near precisely to the sinners it is called to redeem and sanctify. The church appearing to have no sin within its precincts is likely to be a church that has forsaken its mission (Augustine, *On Continence* 25, *NPNF* 1 III, p. 390; Hall, *DT* VIII, p. 193). Since the Christian community remains salt, light, and leaven within the world, it cannot remove itself wholly from the world without removing itself from its arena of apostolic mission. It purifies and cleanses its life only by a constant rhythm of distance and closeness to the world, gathering for worship and scattering for vocation (Matt. 5:13–16; John 16:17–33).

The church cannot arbitrarily limit its ministries to those who are most likely candidates for sainthood. As in triage, those most desperately fallen are most urgently sought and cared for, as in the parable of the lost sheep. The church has repeatedly found in the most notorious sinners its most brilliant and winning advocates (from Mary Magdalene and Paul to Saint Francis and John Newton). The skid row missions have nurtured many saints, who would not have been blessed had the church abandoned the skid rows (Mark 2:17; Palmer, *PPSW*, pp. 222–30).

The incarnational paradox is that the Mediator without sin came to expiate sin (Heb. 2:17; 7:26; 2 Cor. 5:21). Likewise the church, while "embracing in its bosom sinners," remains *"at the same time holy and always in need of being purified,"* hence it is always seeking "the way of penance and renewal" (*Doc. Vat. II, Ch.* 8; *CMM*, p. 118, italics added). This does not diminish but intensifies the call of the church to holiness and mature embodiment of the life of love.

Ironic Evidences of the Church's Holiness. The chief proof of the church's holiness, ironically, is that it is found among sinners, redeeming, reaching out, healing, and sanctifying. It is "as the cockle and darnel and chaff are found among the wheat, and as wens and swellings are in a perfect body, when they are rather diseases and deformities than true members of the body. And therefore the Church is very well compared to a drag-net which draws up fishes of all sorts; and to a field, wherein is found both darnel and good corn" (Second Helvetic Conf., *CC*, p. 149; Matt. 13:26).

Distasteful fish are inevitably caught in the dragnet of general proclamation and mass evangelization, which catches all kinds (Matt. 13:47–50). The final sorting out will occur only on the last day (Matt. 3:12). Till then, let God judge. If the church's task is to stimulate holiness at close quarters, it cannot militate against her character as holy that she has hypocrites and false members in her midst. Insofar as the church retains unworthy members, it prays for their amendment (Merrill, *ACE*, p. 245).

That sinners can become saints is proof of the effectiveness of the means of grace provided the church. Tares remain among the grains of wheat until the end of time. "Let both grow together until the harvest" (Matt. 13:30; Origen, *Hom. on Josh.* XXI.1, p. 447; *AEG* III, p. 16). It is hazardous to the wheat when the farmer tries absolutely to remove every tare, once rooted. "The tares are to be tolerated either when they cannot be distinguished or cannot be removed without injury to the wheat," as any gardener knows (Banks, *MCD*, p. 287). Like the ark, the church contains all kinds of creatures in its precincts, clean and unclean (Gen. 6:19; Tertullian, *On Idolatry* 24, *ANF* III, p. 75; cf. Gregory I, *Hom. on Ezek.* II.4.16, 17). That sinners especially resort to the church in crisis times is an empirical evidence of her proximate holiness (John Chrysostom, *Hom. on the Statues*, *NPNF* 1 IX, pp. 364–66, 406). It is an ironic turn of logic that the very "efforts of others to prove that the Church is not holy show that they acknowledge holiness as a mark of truth" (*Baltimore Catechism*, p. 120)!

The Welcoming of Penitents.   Callistus of Rome (217–222) set forth a penitential rule of great significance to the subsequent practice of repentance (*SCD* 42, p. 21). It concluded that because the Lord takes "no pleasure in the death of the wicked, but rather that they turn from their ways and live" (Ezek. 33:11), and because it is not for us to judge others (Rom. 14:4), contrite penitents like the prodigal are to be readmitted to the Lord's Table. The blood of Christ cleanses from all sins (1 John 1:7; cf. Tertullian, *On Modesty* 13–21, *ANF* IV, pp. 86–99; Hippolytus, *Refutation of All Her.* IX, *ANF* V, pp. 128–34).

After Callistus, the church was no less a community of set-apart people, but more clearly the community of the forgiven and forgiving people of God. The more generous policy of Callistus had become general practice by the middle of the third century, even to the controversial point of receiving penitent apostates who had lapsed during persecution (Cyprian, *Treatises* III, *ANF* V, pp. 437–46; *Epist. 55, ANF* V, pp. 347–50).

About A.D. 251 a schism arose between two papal candidates: one, Cornelius, maintained the Callistian position on the lapsed, and the other, Novatian, wished to return to the practice of restricting the penitence of apostates. Otherwise orthodox in doctrine, Novatian sought to build a church of the pure (*katharoi*), a congregation limited to actually holy individuals (Eusebius, *CH* VI.43, *NPNF* 2 I, pp. 286–90; VII.8, p. 296; cf. Socrates, *Ecclesiastical History* I.10, *NPNF* 2 II, p. 17; Athanasius, *To Serapion, Epist.* IV.13). Novatian was consensually rejected on this point, and his purist views never thereafter gained the consent of the laity. By the time of Cyprian the continuity of the holiness of the church was viewed as personified in the historical succession of overseers to the apostles, acting as a collegium on behalf of the whole *laos* to embody representatively the unity and holiness of the church (Cyprian, *Epist. 33, ANF* V, pp. 312–14).

Three complementary positions thus emerged early in the primitive teaching of the church's holiness vis à vis penitential practice, all of which would reappear within Protestantism: Novatian argued that the locus of holiness is in the individual believer; Cyprian argued that the church's holiness focuses upon the linear historic succession of *episkopoi;* the tradition of Rome focused upon the penitence of the whole community especially as beheld at the Lord's Table (*SHD* I 175).

The Modern Neglect of the Holiness of the Church.   Few theologians in the twentieth century have given serious attention to the holiness of the church—among the happy exceptions are some neoevangelicals (especially Wesleyan evangelicals), some ecumenists (especially those influenced by Bonhoeffer), and a sprinkling of Anglican, Roman, and Eastern Orthodox writers.

The most prominent modern theologians have grossly neglected the holiness of the church. Process theology has not developed a cohesive ecclesiology at all, much less a teaching of *sanctorum communio.* Moreover, a fatal weakness of neoorthodoxy was the absence of any clear reflection upon the holiness of the church. Brunner argued the church into invisibility, Moltmann into ideology. Reinhold Niebuhr was so fixated upon the sin of the church that he could not glimpse even the slightest edge of its holiness. Tillich was generally bored by the visible church.

Wherever Bultmann spoke of the church as an empirical community, it appeared to be a deterioration of the kerygma. Insofar as liberation and ecological theologies have approached the theme of ecclesial holiness, they have focused mainly upon blaming the visible church for war, ecological disaster, racism, poverty, and nationalism. After decades of neglect, the ancient ecumenical celebration of the holiness of the church begs to be recovered.

Whether the Church Is Being Made Holy

Thesis: Through its calling, destiny, patience, and repentance, the church is being made holy.

The Church Is Being Made Holy Through Its Calling.   The church is holy because its calling is holy. Only on this premise could Paul view the baptized as saints or the elect as positionally justified in Christ precisely while rebuking, instructing, and admonishing them ethically.

Each baptized member shares juridically in the holiness of the body of Christ by faith, even if in particular ways remaining proximately immature, unfinished, unholy. The holiness of the Lord shines and radiates precisely through the sins of believers (Hall, *DT* VIII, pp. 189–92). It is precisely through our human weakness that God's strength is made perfect (1 Cor. 1:25–27; 2 Cor. 12:7–10; J. B. Lightfoot, *Philippians,* p. 81).

The justification of sinners does not imply the justification of sin. Faith in the holiness of the church does not imply that the church can rest easy in its proximate unholiness (J. Wesley, *Earnest Appeal, WJWB* II, pp. 37–95, *WJW* VIII, pp. 1–45; Moltmann, *CPHS,* p. 22). The church is called to sanctity, and is being made holy through this calling. Every Christian is called to aim by clear and distinct resolve at daily walking in the way of holiness (W. Law, *Serious Call to the Devout and Holy Life*). The call to holiness is addressed to each believer. No one has rightly heard the call to active faith who has not at the same time heard the call to holy living (Calvin, *Inst.* 3.16–21; Hall, *DT* VIII, p. 197).

The Church Is Being Made Holy Through Its Expected Consummation and Destiny.   Despite historic uncertainties, the future glory of the church is made certain by the will of God from eternity. God intends and decrees to have an unblemished celebrant assembly in eternity. Against this *ekklēsia* the gates of hell shall not prevail (Matt. 16:18). Eschatologically viewed, she is a "Holy City, the new Jerusalem, coming down out of heaven from God, prepared as a bride beautifully dressed for her husband" (Rev. 21:2; Ambrose, *On the Mysteries* 7, *NPNF* 2 X, pp. 321–22).

The church is not being made holy through its own imaginative political activity: "We repudiate the false teaching that the church, in human self-esteem, can put the word and work of the Lord in the service of some wishes, purposes and plans or other, chosen according to desire" (Barmen Declaration, *CC,* p. 522).

The Church Is Being Made Holy Through Patience and Repentance.   The church is being made holy by waiting upon God's holiness to elicit proximate human holiness, waiting upon God's timing to allow the seeds of holiness to grow in time. This is why a key evidence of the holiness of the church is patience (*hupomomē*, Rom. 5:3, 4; 15:4, 5). The *ekklēsia* is called to let patience have her perfect work (James 1:4), to run with patience the race that is set (Heb. 12:1), and in patience to possess her soul (Luke 21:19).

The church is being made holy through repentance, which paradoxically emerges precisely in the process of recognizing her own unholiness. The repentance leading to faith in the Word is a recurring, defining act of this community. A principal characteristic of this set-apart community when it is most truly being itself is its readiness to recognize the sin of her members. Among human organizations the church is the only one that takes sinners into her membership primarily because they are sinners (Matt. 9:13; Origen, *Ag. Celsus* III.59, *AEG,* pp. 161–62; Guthrie, *CD,* p. 359). No time is exempt from being the "time for judgment to begin with the family of God" (1 Pet. 4:17).

No special skills of sociological observation are needed to see that there are few sins in the world that are not also found among the baptized. No church has yet become purified from lust, nationalism, envy, pride, or racism, and the list could go on. The Bible does not characteristically try to dissemble the sins of the people of God, either publicly or before God. Rather the *qahal* (assembly) is precisely the place where they are to be brought to the specific awareness of the depths of their own sin in order to receive convicting and forgiving grace (Amos 5:21–27; Jer. 7; Isa. 1; 1 Cor. 1:10–13; Gal. 2:11–14; Phil. 1:15–17). The temple is no place for the pretense of righteousness.

Perplexities of the Holiness of the Church

Among the host of issues that remain are whether sinners are embraced by inclusive ascription in references to the holiness of the church; whether good people exist outside the church; whether the sacraments are invalidated by the ministry of unholy leaders; whether excommunication is a meaningful expression of the holiness of the church; and whether obstinate sinners are to be found in the church triumphant.

Whether Believers Only Are in the Church.   Is the church restricted to only those born anew from above? Or only those who are fully responding to sanctifying grace? Or does it include all sinners who seek repentance and faith? On what terms does it invite and draw near unbelievers?

Unbelievers are mixed with believers in this fellowship of Word and sacrament (Augsburg Apology VI, VII, *BOC,* pp. 168–78; Westminster Conf. XXV, *CC,* p. 222). They do not yet organically and truly belong to the church insofar as they lack faith, but they are outwardly attached to it as dead leaves to a living vine or a parasite to an animal (Gerhard, *LT* XI, 50; Schmid, *DT,* pp. 596–99; Jacobs, *SCF,* p. 373).

The church in a broad sense (*large dictu*) includes all those baptized. The church in the narrower sense (*stricte dictu*) consists in the faithful and obedient respondents to the grace of baptism. "Since Gerhard, the Lutheran dogmaticians have preferred to use the terms: *die Kirche im eigentlichen und uneigentlichen Sinne*" (the church properly speaking, and the church in a wider or improper, diffuse sense; Neve, *Luth. Sym.,* p. 187).

The church in its narrow definition is composed of those who truly believe, whose faith is active in love. Implanted within and clinging to this community are catechumens who are learning, those whose baptism is as yet unconfirmed, and others who share to some degree in the intention of the church and receive its sacraments and hear its Word, but whose faith is in varied ways immature or defective, needing further growth (Calvin, *Inst.* 4.2).

Even within the much loved *ekklēsia* at Philippi Paul acknowledged "with tears" that "many live as enemies of the cross of Christ" (Phil. 3:18), as distinguished from those whose "citizenship is in heaven" (3:20). The account of Ananias and Sapphira suggests from the outset that the corrupted have been mixed with believers (Acts 5:1–11). Despite all efforts, there have remained among baptized members in all generations some unresponsive to grace (Ambrose, *De virginitate*, chap. VIII, n. 48, *MPL* 16, 278; *CMM*, p. 118).

Whether by Synecdoche Sinners Are Included Ascriptively in the Church's Holiness. May it be meaningfully said that sinners belong to God's holy church? In what sense are sinners rightly included in ascriptions of the holiness of the church?

Classic exegesis freely employed synecdoche in its reasoning (from Gk. *sunekdochē*, by inclusive ascription), a figure of speech by which the whole of a thing is spoken of as a part, or a part for the whole, such as bread for food, or the army for a soldier (John Cassian, *Ag. Nestorius*, *NPNF* 2 XI, pp. 602–3). You are now reading a book, even though in reality you are now only reading one sentence of a book, yet in reading this one sentence you are indeed reading this book. Similarly we speak of the church as holy, yet by generic ascription including sinners. The church is made up of the faithful who are born anew of the Spirit, which by inclusive ascription embraces those who are planted and growing together with them in a visible body (Matt. 13:26–40; Irenaeus, *Ag. Her.* IV.66.1–2, *AEG* III, p. 14; IV 40.2–3, *ANF* I, p. 524; Calvin, *Inst.* 4.1).

Some outwardly have all the appearances of belonging to the church, being baptized, professing Christianity, frequently using the means of grace, yet may not be in the presence of God true believers whose hearts are being regenerated by grace. But they are by synecdoche called *hagian ekklēsian*, the holy church, wherein there is ascribed to the entire assembly that which belongs properly to a part of it and characteristically to the whole of it. Those lacking regeneration and the fruits of holiness may be members by association or outward profession or baptism, even while they lack the evidences of faith (Augsburg Apology, *BOC*, pp. 126–27, 168 ff.; Schmid, *DT*, p. 591).

Corpus Mixtum. Hence it is crucial in ecclesiology that we be prepared to distinguish whether we are using the term *ekklēsia* in its broader or stricter definition. Fallen members of the *corpus mixtum* cannot be said in the strict sense, but only by synecdoche, to be one, holy, catholic, and apostolic. It is sadly possible that apostasy may predominate in some parts of the church that is otherwise called holy. What remains undefiled about the true church is its pure Word and Sacraments duly administered (Ursinus, *Comm. Heid. Catech.*, pp. 288–89).

The church in this world is always engaged in a struggle between flesh and spirit, always in transit from sin to grace, from division to unity, always expressing its holiness as a community of sinners being redeemed, and its catholicity as a particular community in time and place pointing beyond itself to the one, whole *communio sanctorum* (Gal. 5; Matt. 13:24–43).

Whether Truth and Falsity Are Distinguishable Only at the End of History.   The Shepherd of Hermas was among the earliest to think seriously about the disjunction between the holy formation and the unholy appearance of the church. Only by the constant offering of repentance is this disjunctiveness proximately overcome (*Sim.* 9.7.2; 9.18.3, 4; 10.4.4). In winter, living and dead trees appear to be alike. So in the church in time, the distinction remains unclear between just and unjust, to be revealed at the end of time (*Sim.* 3.2, 3). Only in the future judgment, when the unjust are cast out, will the difference be revealed (*Sim.* 4.2). The church therefore both is and is not a true communion of saints on earth. The church consists of those who are on the way toward being made holy by grace. The church as we behold it in history is until the harvest of history a *corpus mixtum* composed of all that are called and baptized, including hypocrites and unbelievers mingled with believers. Yet it is the believers that most truly and properly constitute the church (Belgic Conf. 27–30, *COC* III, pp. 417–22).

Not all who fold hands in worship are "lively and true members of the Church. For there are many hypocrites, who outwardly do hear the word of God, and publicly receive the sacraments, and do seem to pray unto God alone through Christ," yet remain "altogether destitute of the inward illumination of the Spirit of God, of faith and sincerity of heart." Their true character only will be "at length laid open" (Second Helvetic Conf., *CC*, p. 148). The struggling historical church (militant, in combat with the world, the flesh, and the adversary) is on its way toward the perfect love and praise of the celestial church triumphant.

The difference between wheat and tares is not finally seen until both lie on the threshing floor. Meanwhile there is a difference between those who belong to the family and those who temporarily inhabit the house (Augustine, *On Baptism* V.21, *NPNF* 1 IV, p. 471).

False Remedies to the Unholiness of the Church.   It is folly to withdraw from the church because it lacks the full evidence of holiness in particular places or persons or situations, for to withdraw from the preaching of the Word and the means of grace in common prayer and sacrament is to cut oneself off from the very vine from which nourishment comes (John 15:1–8). It is equally futile to attempt to exclude all sinners from the church. This typically results in a false legalism or pride or self-righteousness pretending to be grace. Legalistic culture-bound standards of conduct and biases may parade as faultless measures of holiness. These legalisms in time mock true faith and may elicit defiant reactions against excessive puritanism (Augsburg Apology IV, *BOC*, pp. 107 ff.).

Rather than banishing sinners from the church, the Lord's Table calls all to repentance. In approaching that table, the eucharistic community will be aided by time-tested historical models of pastoral care and confession. "The true Catholic Church is that in which there is confession and repentance" (Lactantius, *DI* IV.30, *ANF* VI, p. 134).

Gregory the Great stated this irony deftly, "Good things are so to be preached that ill things be not assisted sideways. The highest good is so to be praised that the lowest be not despaired of" (*Book of Pastoral Rule, NPNF* 2 XII, p. 69).

Whether Obstinate Sinners Remain in the Church Triumphant.   Obstinate sinners who remain within the outward body will ultimately be cut off, due to their own obstinacy (*Longer Catech.*, Eastern Orthodox Church, 269, *COC* II, p. 488).

Not all who are now nominally found to be associated with the visible church on earth will enter the holy city. Not everyone who says, Lord, Lord, will enter the kingdom (Matt. 7:21; 12:50; 13:36—43). "If anyone does not remain in me, he is like a branch that is thrown away and withers" (John 15:6; John Chrysostom, *Hom. on John* LXXVI, *NPNF* 1 IV, pp. 278—81).

The case is starkly stated in Hebrews, "It is impossible for those who have once been enlightened, who have tasted the heavenly gifts, who have shared in the Holy Spirit, who have tasted the goodness of the word of God and the powers of the coming age, *if they fall away*, to be brought back to repentance, because to their loss they are crucifying the Son of God all over again" (Heb. 6:4—6, italics added). The falling away refers to an untimely falling away near death, so that no further opportunity is offered for repentance (cf. Matt. 13:24—30, 41—42; 1 Cor. 9:27; Phil. 2:12).

Whether It Is a Scandal to Faith That Civic Virtues Exist Outside the Church. God has not reserved all human virtues exclusively for those who have faith in his coming. Some tell the truth who would not go near a church. Some who think of the church as hypocritical have high integrity themselves. Some repulsed by formal religion are deeply attentive to the poor, at times more vitally than pious church members. They do not share in God's family, but they themselves raise good families, remain faithful marriage partners, live tranquil and benign lives, do little harm.

The *ekklēsia* does not despise or envy or demean these people, but praises God for the presence of the Spirit in their lives, going before them with prevenient grace and supplying them with sufficient, actual grace, eliciting in them their co-operation with God's requirements for the good life (Augustine, sermon 214.11, *FC* 38, p. 141). The church rejoices at the presence of God in the human community generally in all history and nature, as we celebrate in the teachings of general providence, conscience, reason, law, civic and moral virtue.

Whether the Holy Sacraments Are Invalidated by the Ministry of Unholy Leaders. Since the sacraments are God's gift, the tarnished moral character of the person administering them cannot detract from the value of the gift offered, for "he gives not what is his own, but God's" (Augustine, *Answer to Letters of Petilian* II.30.69, *NPNF* 1 IV, p. 547). At length the Donatist notion that the unregenerate cannot communicate the means of grace had to be disavowed. The Augsburg Confession declared it "lawful to use the Sacraments which are administered by evil men" (art. VIII, *COC* III, p. 19; cf. *CC*, p. 70; Anglican Thirty-nine Articles, XXVII, *CC*, p. 223).

The means of grace do not cease being efficacious just because they are at times administered by neurotic characters. Jesus commended obedience to the teaching office of the very teachers of the law whom he opposed: "The teachers of the law and the Pharisees sit in Moses' seat. So you must obey them and do everything they tell you, but do not follow their example" (Matt. 23:2, 3, *TCNT*; cf. Calvin, *Inst.* 4.10.26).

The church is holy not because of the presumed holiness of its clergy, but because its laity receives the Word and Sacrament, the triune teaching, the apostolic faith. The tares cannot be cast out before the end time, as Novatians and purists wish. Scriptures that speak of the unmixed holiness of the church refer to its end in the heavenly city (Augustine, *SHD* I, p. 317). Now holy by virtue of its holy word and sacraments, then the church will be holy in all its members. Word and sacraments are made effective by the presence of Christ and are "effectual to the godly, although they be administered by ungodly ministers" (Second Helvetic Conf., *CC*, p. 160). "For if the rays of that visible sun are not stained by contact with any pollution when they pass over the foulest places, much less is the virtue of him who made that visible [sun] fettered by any unworthiness in the minister" (Anastasius II, *Epist.* 1.7, *SCD* 169, p. 72).

Even when baptism is administered by an unfaithful minister, the intent embedded in baptism, Augustine argued, was to become incorporated in the one church. Hence even an unauthorized baptism in the triune name would mark one indelibly with the brand of Christ. Such baptism, while valid and not requiring later rebaptism, would remain inertly inefficacious until it became effectively activated by admission to the one, holy, catholic, apostolic church (Augustine, *On Baptism*, *NPNF* 1 IV, pp. 411 ff.). He also taught that heretical baptism, while latently and technically valid, "worked death" in those who outwardly received it while obdurately resisting it (*On Baptism* III.13.18, *NPNF* 1 IV, p. 441, cf. IV.10.15; 40.78).

Who Is Rightly Prepared to Commune at the Lord's Table?   The celebration of the Lord's farewell meal is intended for those who, having been baptized into the community of faith, are thus deliberately seeking the regenerate life and seeking sanctifying grace. Only the penitent are ready for the Lord's Table. Only the baptized faithful, who having fallen, have again received the grace of contrition, are ready to share in the Eucharist. This classic teaching does not imply absolute moral perfection as requisite to the Lord's Table (Formula of Concord, art. VII, *COC* III, pp. 135–46).

If the intent of the eucharistic invitation is to be fulfilled, there must be some Spirit-enabled self-examination and discernment of the Lord's body and blood. "The man without the Spirit does not accept the things that come from the Spirit of God, for they are foolishness to him, and he cannot understand them, because they are spiritually discerned" (1 Cor. 2:14).

Those who have a disorderly walk are to be admonished (2 Thess. 3:6–15). One "ought to examine himself before he eats of the bread and drinks of the cup. For anyone who eats and drinks without recognizing the body of the Lord eats and drinks judgment on himself" (1 Cor. 11:28, 29). Paul specifically instructed the Corinthians that they were not to eat with "anyone who calls himself a brother but is sexually immoral or greedy, an idolater or a slanderer, a drunkard or a swindler" (1 Cor. 5:11). No one is ready for the unifying sacrament of the one body who is sowing seeds of discontent and creating division among the body (Rom. 16:17). Divisive persons should be twice admonished, and, "After that have nothing to do with him" (Titus 3:10).

The Ephesian church was commended in its rigorous view that it would not knowingly "tolerate wicked men," having "tested those who claim to be apostles but are not" (Rev. 2:2; cf. Matt. 18:17; 1 Cor. 5:5). "The wisest and most faithful application of the best tests will never secure an absolutely pure Church, but that is no argument against the use of tests. Rather it is an argument in their favor. If strictness often fails, laxity must be still worse" (Banks, *MCD*, p. 289).

Avoiding Excess.   No church body or confessional tradition is wholly without its special history of dissent. Dissent is healthy for the constant critique of the church. Repeated patterns of excess recur in the two millennia of Christian traditions.

Among paired types of recurring excesses: a formal religion that loses charisma, or charismatic gifts that misplace decency and order; intellectualism at the cost of passion, or enthusiasm to the neglect of reflection; idealism at the cost of realistic prudence, or prudential realism at the cost of the loss of vision; individual, privatized religion at the cost of community, or social religion at the cost of individual accountability.

In each case the best guide to the recovery of equilibrium is found in the incarnate Lord, as truly God and truly human, wherein the finite becomes the vehicle of the infinite and the earthly vessel bearer of the heavenly treasure (1 Cor. 4:7).

Whether Saving Grace Is Received Outside the Church

There is finally no salvation apart from faithful response to God's coming, which is declared through preaching or anticipatively received in the form of hope among those without opportunity to hear (Rom. 10:10–15; Heb. 11:4–10).

Whether "Outside the Church There Is No Salvation."   In this sense the classic tradition of consensual exegesis confirmed Cyprian's dictum "There is no salvation outside the church" (*extra ecclesiam nulla salus, Letters* 73:21, *FC* 51, p. 282; *ACW* 25, pp. 49–51, 63–65; cf. Augustine, *Letters* 141.5; Luther, *EA* 10.162, 444; 48.218 f.; Calvin, *Inst.* 4.1.4, *Geneva Catechism,* Q104–5). The hoping and believing community is wide enough to embrace both Noah and the thief. It is overreading Cyprian to conclude that all are damned who remain unbaptized, for that would damn Abraham into whose bosom the faithful are drawn (Luke 16:22–23).

It was not a superfluous act when Christ instituted the church as the way to salvation, or a mere footnote when Christ provided the church with means of scripture and sacrament by which subsequent humanity might be saved from sin and death. As true Vine he says to the branches, "If a man remains in me and I in him, he will bear much fruit; apart from me you can do nothing. If anyone does not remain in me, he is like a branch that is thrown away and withers" (John 14:5, 6).

As no child is born without a mother, it is difficult to imagine how faith could be given birth apart from the matrix of a hoping, believing, attesting community. For who can hear without a preacher (Rom. 10:14)? The petitions of the faithful are best offered "where two or three come together in my name" (Matt. 18:20), not in defensive isolation.

To separate from the church is to separate from the head of the church. To leave the ark of Noah during the flood is to court disaster. To be without the plank of the church amid the stormy history of sin is hazardous to the soul (Second Helvetic Conf., *CC,* p. 147).

The Possibility of Salvation Outside the Church.   The possibility of salvation outside the church rests on four arguable grounds:

1. The honoring of one's parents, which itself is a divine command (Exod. 20:12), may make it more understandable that a believer of another religion

should earnestly follow parental guidance, assuming that the truth of God's own coming has not been plausibly set forth.

2. Those who have had no opportunity to hear or approach the revealed truth cannot be made responsible for fully responding to the truth, though they must respond to whatever truth they know.

3. When the truth is ineffectively presented, it may be that the reason and conscience of the hearer sincerely and rightly resist the apparent inconsistencies or seeming injustices that accompany the presentation of the truth. Here reason and conscience must be respected by faith, which must itself undertake clearer proclamation.

4. God is not bound to the means of grace appointed to the Christian community. It is rash to assume that there cannot be other extraordinary acts of grace or any other means by which the Spirit can address the conscience and the heart. When it is stated that outside the church there is no salvation, the assumption prevails that we are speaking of the whole *qahal*, the called people of God, which includes those who have a sincere anticipatory intent to trust God's promises (as in the case of Abel and Abraham), who would have trusted further had they had sufficient opportunity. "All just men from the time of Adam, 'from Abel, the just one, to the last of the elect,' will be gathered" (*Doc. Vat. II, Ch.* 2, p. 16).

On these premises it is reasoned, "No Orthodox can maintain that all outside the Church are damned. As a personal problem, the answer of the question must be left in the hands of Him 'who desireth not the death of a sinner' but wills 'that all men be saved'" (Merrill, *ACE*, p. 240; 1 Tim. 2:4). "For we know that God had some friends in the world that were not of the commonwealth of Israel" (Second Helvetic Conf., *CC*, p. 147). The Westminster Confession cautiously stated that there is no *ordinary* possibility of salvation outside the church (XXV.2), leaving extraordinary means to God.

The Proximate Desire of the Unbaptized. Following Hebrews 11, classic exegetes have specifically allowed for a mode of sharing in the saving faith of the church by "desire," as distinguished from "actually" (Tho. Aq., *ST* I–II, Q4, I, pp. 602–8). Those who remain outside the pale of baptism can nonetheless be saved by making use of the graces God gives them preveniently: "Those who are outside the Church through no fault of their own are not culpable in the sight of God because of their invincible ignorance. Persons who make use of the graces God gives them, even though they are not members of the true Church, actually have the desire to become members inasmuch as they wish to use all the means ordained by God for their salvation" (*Baltimore Catechism*, pp. 130–31).

This teaching of an implicit intent toward baptism makes it possible to hypothesize that one may be saved without formally joining the church, provided that one is ignorant of the necessity of doing so, and would have done so had one understood its necessity. Accordingly, the minimum possible content of the desire or *votum* that might conceivably enable salvation apart from the church would be a yearning toward the divine, or toward truth and goodness (Schmaus, *Dogma* 4, p. 89; cf. *Mediator Dei* and *Mystici Corporis*).

Christ said, "I have other sheep that are not of this fold; I must bring them also, and they will heed my voice" (John 10:16, RSV). Is this a reference to the Gentiles generally, or only to Gentiles who would believe? Or more broadly to those who have some implicit desire or intent to believe? Rahner has argued that God may have included the unbaptized and unchurched in the divine economy in ways insufficiently grasped by the church (Rahner, *RR*, pp. 211–24, 270–77).

The blessed martyrs who died without opportunity for baptism were viewed *de jure* as having been baptized, as are those who have a declared intention to be baptized even though the event has not yet occurred (the former is sometimes called the baptism of blood, and the latter baptism of desire).

A Caution Against Indifferentism. Remembering the above qualifiers, the church remains the bodily instrument and context in which Christ's saving work is remembered, celebrated, interpreted, and applied to human life. Though the Spirit is not bound by the confines of the *ekklēsia,* the Spirit chooses to work through Word and Sacrament to call the community to the Lord (Augsburg Apology, *BOC,* pp. 168 ff.).

The indifferentist principle must be resisted which assumes that all ways to God are equally well intended and that it makes no difference what one believes as long as one hopes to lead a good life, and that even if one wishes only narcissistic self-gratification, social determinants may be blamed. The oxymoron of absolute relativism errs by *attaching the same value to the teaching of falsehood as to the teaching the truth.* The sad irony of egalitarian ideology is that the virtue of equality has led to indifferentism, as if the essential truth of democracy might be supposed to be a new dogmatism advocating absolute indifference to the truth (Neuhaus, *The Naked Public Square*).

All who desire saving grace must avail themselves insofar as is possible of the means of grace, which ordinarily means placing themselves within the orbit of the believing community. In this sense it remains a sociological axiom that "no one comes to the Father except through" the Son (John 14:6). "Salvation is found in no one else, for there is no other name under heaven given to men by which we must be saved" (Acts 4:12). There are not a dozen theandric messiahs but *monogenēs* (John 3:16, only begotten)—the one and only Son.

It is undermining to the church's mission to reduce the church to a voluntary organization of persons debating and searching for an improved philosophy of life. The church is of God, not merely "a sort of university in which scholarly methods and the results of individual inquiry are determinative," despite "the undoubted place which scholarly inquiry has in fortifying the Church's teaching" (Hall, *DT* VIII, p. 158).

The Visibility of the Church

Some have concluded that the nature of the church is something like Plato's vision of an ideal moral community that, though as yet unrealized, is known in our minds as a powerful, moving idea. Classical Christian exegetes repeatedly have disclaimed this understanding of the church, due to its docetic lack of visibility, presentness, and historical palpability (Council of Constantinople II, *SCD* 216, p. 86; Chemnitz, *TNC,* pp. 280–82). Here idealism becomes a snare. Moltmann tilted toward docetic exaggeration in arguing that "the church never existed" in "a form in which faith and experience coincided" (*CPHS,* p. 21).

It is clear that the body of Christ of which Paul speaks is a visible community, not an ethereal, nonhistorical, utopian "no-place," to be found only in the imagination. We are not "dreaming about some Platonic republic" or state lacking reality or an imaginary community to be found nowhere actually in history, because "we teach that this church actually exists" (Augsburg Apology, *BOC*, p. 171). It is into a visible body that men, women, and children visibly enter by a visible rite of baptism and taste and chew an actual loaf.

Whether the Church Is Visible.   As the incarnate Lord came visibly amid human society, so does the body and bride of Christ express herself visibly amid human societies, ministering with tangible signs of grace and ordered in a visible fellowship that stands in succession to the apostles. As Christ has two natures, divine and human, so does the church offer divine gifts with human hands and speak the divine Word through human sentences (Leo, *Symbol of Faith, SCD* 344, p. 141).

The company of the redeemed is "invisible, in respect of their relation wherein they stand to Christ," and "visible in respect of the profession of their faith, in their persons, and in particular churches" (Cambridge Platform, 1648, *CC*, p. 387; cf. Calvin, *Inst.* 4.1). The church is "called *visible*, not only because the men as men are visible, but because outwardly they profess Gospel truth and celebrate the sacraments according to the lawful use for which they were instituted by God. It ought to be called *invisible* because of the Spirit and true faith, which reside in the mind alone, which no man can see, which God alone knows" (Braun, *DF* II.IV.24, 22, 7; *RD*, p. 668, italics added; Barth, *CD* IV/1, p. 654). The church "*must* be visible because it is composed of human beings and exists for human beings. By being visible the Church is being true, not false, to its essential nature" (Küng, *TC*, p. 35).

The Case Against Hypervisibility and Hyperinvisibility.   The dated polemics of Catholics against the Protestant teaching of invisibility and of Protestants against the Catholic teaching of visibility, now dysfunctional, must be reconceived. Wyclif, Hus, and Luther were correct to oppose the reduction of the church to a visible, culture-entwined, medieval institution. In stressing the invisible nature of the church, their intent was to reform the visible church, not abandon or idealize it.

The intent of Catholic teaching was correct to stress the visible corporateness, order, historicity, social palpability, and cross-cultural engagement of the *ekklēsia*. The intent of Protestant teaching was correct to stress the invisible dimensions of election, grace, and faith: "It is called invisible, not that the men who are in it are invisible, but because the faith and piety of those who belong to it can neither be seen, nor known, except by those who possess it" (Ursinus, *Comm. Heid. Catech.*, p. 287; cf. Küng, *TC*, p. 37).

The Visibility of Baptism and Eucharist.   The visibility of the church is made clear in the visible rite of baptism with water. Life in Christ is sustained by the visible bread and wine of the Eucharist and in the verbal preaching of the Word heard by living persons in a hearable service of worship. The community's discipline can only occur within a visible sphere (Heb. 12:1–12). Its ministry and laity are actual persons (1 Tim. 3). Even the glorified, resurrected, spiritual body is visible, or capable of being made visible (John 20:27).

The recalcitrant ungodly may be members of the church considered outwardly insofar as they too enunciate her prayers and say her confession and eat her bread. Meanwhile their own recalcitrance tends to stain the very ethos in which they are outwardly beheld. Anyone can pretend to worship. Verbally mouthing the Creed does not necessarily imply that one is affirming it from the heart. Theologically and ethically considered, such word-sayers are not in the fullest sense members, though they may be viewed outwardly as members through their baptism.

Catholic, Orthodox, and most classic Protestant teachers stress the visible act of baptism as primary indicator of membership. Some subsequent Protestant teachings place greater stress upon effectual calling, faith, regeneration, piety, and holy living as evidences of membership (Riisen, *FTCT* XVI.8.1; *RD*, pp. 665–66). This makes for an ever-incipient dilemma: In seeking to cleanse and purify the church by means of discipline, any act of exclusion may become excessive. Conversely, in opening the church to recalcitrant sinners, any act of inclusion risks becoming excessive (J. Wesley, *Appeals, WJWB* 2; *WJW* VIII, pp. 1 ff.). The church characteristically invites sinners to the Lord's Table provided they are truly penitent. If worship is not to become an elitist act, then the earthly church visible will inevitably be to some extent a *corpus mixtum*, rather than a pure body (Augsburg Apology, *BOC*, pp. 168–78).

The Body Not Limited to Its Visible Form.   Though visible, the church is not exhaustively described as an object or circumscribed by a particular space or limited to visible, observable facts or data that can be empirically investigated. For the Christian life is hid in Christ. Our poor eyes cannot adequately see the line that divides true and false believers holding the same communion cup, eating the same loaf. What the empirical sociologist has eyes to see is only the visible. What only God has eyes to see adequately is the invisible (2 Tim. 2:19; Wollebius, *CTC*, 111; *RD*, p. 667). What angels and saints see imperfectly, God sees perfectly.

The kingdom is not of this world (John 18:36) and does not come with observation (Luke 17:20). The life of faith remains hidden in Christ (Col. 3:3). Its sphere is neither empirical nor measurable nor political nor economic nor physical as such, but embodied spirit, glorified body, enfleshed word. "The Spirit will not give to the visible Church new and promising secular methods of political, diplomatic, economic and sociological organization, which would assure it of greater independence, a more important voice in affairs, or stronger positions of power" (von Balthasar, *Sponsa Verbi,* p. 13).

The unity of the church prevents us from speaking of two churches, one visible and the other invisible, for the church is still one, even when it remains invisible "in respect of inward communion with Christ" and visible "in respect of outward profession" and association (B. Pictet, *TC* XIII.1.7; Heppe, *RD,* p. 665).

Organization as an Expression of the Church's Visibility.   Even within the earliest Christian congregations, there were extensive evidences of considerable organization: elections, stated leaders, defined leadership roles, lines of authority, stated times of meeting, disciplinary measures for recalcitrants (1 Cor. 5:13; 1 Tim. 1:20), funding and support systems, letters of recommendation, procedural norms and rules (1 Cor. 7:17; Acts 15:28), rites and ceremonies, a known membership (1 Cor. 5:12), and qualifications for membership (Acts 1:23–26; 2:41, 42, 47; 18:27; Rom. 15:26; 1 Cor. 5:4–13; 16:1, 2; 2 Cor. 3:1; 11:16; Phil. 1:1; 2:30; Col. 2:5).

All this appears to have developed within the period of Paul's and Luke's ministry, before the destruction of Jerusalem, and the rudiments of it were already in place in the Jerusalem church before Paul's conversion. For Paul did not enter the church without being baptized (Acts 9:18). It was a definable organization that Paul was persecuting (Acts 9:2). Simple individual conversion was not sufficient. Cornelius and his companions had received the Holy Spirit but were required to be baptized into the community of faith (Acts 10:48).

Before Pentecost Jesus' followers were generally called disciples. After Pentecost they are more characteristically called "the assembly of God," "the fellowship of saints," "the brethren," or "the churches," indicating a palpable organization and emerging structure. They gathered on the first day of the week to break bread and hear scripture expounded (Acts 20:7); widows were enrolled (1 Tim. 5:9); all things were to be done decently and in order (1 Cor. 14:40); collections were gathered for the saints of Jerusalem (Rom. 15:26); members were cautioned against irregular attendance (Heb. 10:25).

This evidence resists theories of a purely spiritual or invisible church, as if lacking governance or formal organization. It resists individualistic theories of Christianity as primarily individual piety dissociated from community. The modern fantasy that autonomous individuals on their own initiative formed themselves into churches as voluntary organizations runs directly counter to the historical witness of the church to its identity as formed by Christ as his living body (Eph. 4; Minear, *ICNT;* Montague, *HS;* Heron, *HS*).

Iconoclasm Rejected: The Struggle Against Excessive Invisibility. The extended debate over icons (from *ikon,* figure, representation, likeness) became a test case of the visibility of the church. The assault on pictorial expressions of Christian teaching was launched at the Synod of Elvira, A.D. 306, which held that "there ought not to be pictures in the church, nor should that which is worshiped and adored be painted upon the walls." When in 726 the emperor proscribed the use of images in worship, his action elicited opposition that would rage until settled at the Seventh Ecumenical Council, A.D. 787, which held that visible images of Christ, the cross, and events of holy memory may be fittingly depicted on stone, walls, vessels, or vestments. By them the beholder is "more readily . . . lifted up to the memory of their prototypes, and to a longing after them" (Council of Nicaea II, 787, *CC,* p. 35). It is worth noting that it was a woman (Irene, wife of Leo IV) who led the struggle of the church against state-led iconoclasts (destroyers of images) in this crucial victory for the visibility of the church (*SCD* 302 ff., pp. 121 ff.). "He who shows reverence to the image, shows reverence to the substance of Him depicted in it" (Nicaea II, 787, *SCD* 303, p. 121). "For the honor of the image passes to the original" (Basil, *On the Holy Spirit* 18.45).

John of Damascus set forth the classic defense against incipient Manichaeanism: the whole of creation is a picture of God (*Images* I.11); the spiritual is revealed only through matter (*Images* I.16; II.19); through matter one moves from bodily vision to spiritual vision (*Images* III.12, 25). But the image as such is to be revered "not as divine, but as filled with divine energy and grace" (*Images* II.14).

Docetic Fantasies of Invisibility. Any view of the church that tends to fixate upon invisibility risks becoming as unhistorical and nonincarnational as Docetism. Wherever monergistic divine omnicausality is overstated, there is a corresponding tendency to understress the visible church and the moral responsibilities of the

Christian life. If the election of the faithful is wholly pretemporal, absolute, un-conditional, and unknown to the visibly seeing eye, it is easy to slip toward the premature conclusion that there is little need for the visible church.

The church is not an abstract idea, but living people enlivened and touched by Christ, persons having particular parents, a particular walk, a distinctive culture and time, and who die a particular death. This community is not an intriguing dialectical notion, but flesh and blood.

Lacking visibility the church could not have founded schools, hospitals, or-phanages, hospices. Nor could it hallow marriages, hold common worship, or administer sacraments. The faithful cannot look with indifference upon the insti-tutional, visible body that has delivered them the message of the gospel, baptized, instructed, and supplied them every means of grace (Augsburg Apology, *BOC,* pp. 171–77; Schultze, *CD&ST,* p. 187). The living Lord may not be visibly present where two are three are gathered together in his name, but he is nonetheless with them, and the fellowship they have in him has visible evidences (Matt. 18:20; 1 Cor. 5:4).

The Disputed Tradition of Thinking About the Invisible Church.   The rejection of Wyclif and Hus by Rome hinged principally on their view that the church was finally invisible (Council of Constance, *SCD* 1109; 1164; 1180; 1187, 1191, 1194). In the post-Constantinian period Augustine had drawn an influential distinction between the *ecclesia invisibilis* and the Theodosian church (following the Emperor Theodosius). This distinction (between the elect known to God and the visible church as an institution recognizable by everyone) was later to become greatly expanded by Zwingli and Calvin (Brunner, *Dogm.* III, p. 131). Zwingli took special delight in defining the church as invisible (*Exposition of the Faith*). Calvin at times stressed so heavily God's secret election of the predestined that the church ap-peared to be discernible only to God (*Inst.* 4.1).

After the corruptions of the medieval period, when attempts at reform fell short, a more rigorous doctrine of the church understandably seemed needed. It then became an intense preoccupation of Reformed ecclesiology that the true church is not finally that familiar visible body at all, with all its follies and prob-lems, but rather an invisible community of those hiddenly elected by God from eternity, whose names are known only to God (Bucer, *de Regno Christi, LCC* XIX).

The church is not simply the name we give to atomized, separated, scattered, elect individuals who love the Lord, for as such they are not an organic, living community or body, as assumed in the New Testament. A community known only to God and lacking the elements of an organized society could hardly be the church to which Paul wrote (1 Cor. 12:12; Cyprian, *Treatises* I, *On the Unity of the Church, ANF* V, pp. 412–29; Moss, *CF,* p. 225). The church in which the Word is heard and Sacraments administered is visible as a local assembly gathered in a particular locale and as a worldwide community scattered amid the nations, bear-ing testimony and exercising various gifts (Ursinus, *Comm. on Heid. Catech.,* p. 287; *Leiden Synopsis* XL.33; *RD,* p. 666).

"The New Testament teaches neither that all the elect are necessarily to be glori-fied, nor that any individual is absolutely and unconditionally predestined to glory. Election in the New Testament has for its reference baptismal life, and while future glory is the destiny which Baptism brings within human reach, the baptized, that is the elect, still have to make their calling and election sure. Their glorification is contingent, and not absolutely predetermined in each case. Only the Church corporate is absolutely predestined to glory" (Hall, *DT* VIII, p. 85).

The Roman magisterium, while not denying the invisibility of God the Spirit, stresses the church's visibility through sacrament. Reformed Protestantism, while not denying the church's visibility, tends more to stress the church's ultimate invisibility through its emphasis upon election by grace. The scholastic Roman temptation is to treat the church too bureaucratically and hierarchically, as if the church is impossible to identify without the hierarchically ordered ministry and sacraments. The scholastic Reformed temptation is to treat the church too invisibly and individualistically, as if the true church is virtually impossible to identify as an actual community within history. Each needs the corrective critique of the other.

The Sign of Contradiction

The Christian life is lived in but not of the world (John 17:14–19). It is not conformed to the world but is being transformed within it by the renewing of minds in Christ (Rom. 12:1, 2). The Christian is already a citizen of a celestial city precisely while living amid earthly history. That God is holy does not imply that God is unrelated to the world, but related to the world by judging and redeeming it.

The church exists as a sign of contradiction within the world (Matt. 18:7; 1 Pet. 2:8). The premises of the kingdom of God contradict and oppose the kingdoms of this world. Those who follow the holy One of God (Mark 1:24; John 6:69) are prepared to suffer with their Lord and if necessary be sacrificed as he was (Cyprian, *Treatises* XI, *ANF* V, pp. 496–501; Athanasius, *Resurrection Letters* 10, pp. 162–69). They expect to bear the cross daily in their own time and place, deny themselves, and follow the crucified, risen Lord (Calvin, *Inst.* 3.7).

In the World for the World.   However contrasted with the world, the church seeks to be for the world in a deeper way than the world can imagine being for itself. The mission, like the Lord's, is not "to condemn the world, but to save the world through him" (John 3:17). However acquainted the church is with the world in its own time, the church remains "like a stranger in a foreign land," as it "presses forward amid the persecutions of the world and the consolations of God" (Augustine, *CG* XVIII.51, 2; *Doc. Vat. II, Ch.* 8; G. Tavard, *The Pilgrim Church*).

Only by speaking the language of its own period can the church declare the perennial gospel addressed to all times and places. The church is called to discern the signs of its own times, attentive to whatever is occurring in its own special period of history, viewed from within the context of the anticipated meaning of universal history. The Barmen Declaration makes clear that the gospel is not a matter of looking to the signs of the times to determine the Christian proclamation. "We repudiate the false teaching that the church can turn over the form of her message and ordinances at will or according to some dominant ideological and political convictions" (Barmen Declaration, *CC*, p. 521).

The *ekklēsia* is called to become fully humbled so as to take on earthly form, adapt itself to the temporal sphere, in order that it may fulfill its mission within and for the world, while yet not becoming indebted to the world. Insofar as the church is enmeshed in a history of sin, seeking to attest God's love within that history, it cannot keep its hands clean from the ambiguous loves of that history. It cannot avoid all critics and detractors if it is to enter empathically into conflicting cultures. Hence the church does not inordinately expect that it will always suitably embody the body of Christ or invariably attest the pure Word or unerringly walk in the way of holiness as long as it is engaged in this earthly struggle. But it does hope for a final plenary cleansing at the end of history to ready it for eternal presence with the Lord who calls it even now to be holy and without blemish (Eph. 5:27).

Gathering and Scattering.   The sent church does not forever turn inward as a gathered community, but also faces outward in scattering to penetrate the vocational spheres. Its members earn honest bread in the world through fitting means. The neighbor is duly served amid the varied vocations. God is duly served through service to the neighbor. The poor are the church's only possessions (Ambrose, *Letters, NPNF* 2 X, pp. 419, 436).

Where brokenness is found in the world, the church mends, where hunger, it feeds, where suffering, it assuages. Some sins are economically intertwined, politically complicated, and cannot be simply mended by individual acts of mercy. They may require the magistracy or official persons or complex organizations to be attentive to their vocation and find better ways to act justly and love mercy. The people of God are called to do whatever is at hand to do, act with all their might, and hear the neighbor's cry and answer it, loving the ones they see (Eccles. 9:10; Luke 10:33–35; S. Kierkegaard, *Works of Love*).

The Missionary Structure of the Church.   The missionary structure of the church is intrinsically related to its unity, holiness, apostolicity, and catholicity—as *one* body, *set apart, sent* to all. The missionary activity of the church springs from the church's very nature and identity and unity with Christ. "It perfects her Catholic unity by this expansion. It is sustained by her apostolicity. It exercises the collegial spirit of her hierarchy. It bears witness to her sanctity while spreading and promoting it" (*Doc. Vat. II, Mis.* 1; *CMM,* p. 152).

Missions are undertakings by which "the heralds of the Gospel, sent out by the Church and going forth into the whole world, carry out the task of preaching the Gospel and planting the Church among peoples or groups who do not yet believe in Christ" (*Doc. Vat. II, Mis.* 6; *CMM,* p. 154; Tho. Aq., *ST* I Q43.7, I, pp. 224–25; I–II Q106.4, I, p. 1107; *Comm. on the Sentences,* book I, dist. 16, Q1, 2; Uppsala Assembly, *Renewal in Mission, CC,* pp. 671–82). The missionary task seeks to engender indigenous Christianity within various cultures, so that native churches will be sufficiently established that they may become endowed with their own maturity and vitality and make their own unique contribution to the whole church and the world (Titus 1:5–2:10; *CMM,* pp. 156–59).

The Body-Soul Unity of Organismic Ecclesiology.   The church is less like a soul without body than an enfleshed soul. "As the assumed nature inseparably united to Him serves the divine Word as a living organ of salvation, so, in a similar way, does the visible social structure of the Church serve the Spirit of Christ who vivifies it" (*Doc. Vat. II, Ch.* 8; *CMM,* p. 94; Eph. 4:16). As Christ's living body in history, the church enlivened by the Spirit is visible in time and space.

As body and soul do not constitute two persons but one, so do visible and invisible aspects of the church constitute the one true church. As the Redeemer is truly human and truly divine, yet not two persons, so the church is truly visible and invisible, yet not two churches. "The line of demarcation that distinguishes the true brotherhood from a sham brotherhood is invisible, but the brotherhood itself is just as visible as was the bodily existence of Jesus Christ" (Brunner, *Dogm.*, p. 22; cf. Barth, *CD* IV/2, pp. 618 ff.).

Hence one is not misguided in speaking of the church as the visible community of the baptized, with all her faults, incipient apostasies, potential and actual corruptions, and rooted tares among the wheat. The alternative theory is frightening, for a strictly invisible church could not be a body in history. It is merely an ideal, and a dangerous plaything of naive idealists (Hooker, *LEP;* Oden, *Beyond Revolution,* "The Strange Case of the Invisible Church").

The visibility proper to the church is not different from the visibility proper to human actions generally. As my soul takes visible form in my body, so does the Spirit take visible form in the church, yet to say that is merely to point to a mystery, for in both cases the visible body points beyond itself to its hidden spring in the will, and beyond that to its hidden soul, its very life, its activating, enlivening principle (Gregory Nazianzen, *Orat.* XXX, *NPNF* 2 VII, pp. 313–17). As with the incarnation Word became flesh in the Son, so after Pentecost the Spirit becomes enfleshed in the called out people of God. Yet in both cases those who behold the Son or the church with reductionistic eyes, and not the eyes of faith, may see little but the decaying skeleton of sociological organization, while the enlivening soul remains enigmatic. The holy God does not offer himself as a visual object of inspection to be trampled underfoot or diminished by empirical analysis, so as to make of the truth a lie (Quicunque Creed, *SCD* 40, p. 16).

Ecclesiology from Below or from Above?   The church embraces "the gift of love from above and the answer of love from below" (Schmaus, *Dogma* 4, p. 65). In *The Word of Life* we explored the argument that Christology neither begins exclusively from below nor from above but always from the unified theandric person, divine and human in one person. Now it is pertinent to make the analogous point with respect to ecclesiology: The study of the church does not begin with sociology or psychology or philosophy, which then looks around desperately to see if it can find some basis for hypothesizing God on empirical grounds. Nor does ecclesiology assert the initiative of the Son and Spirit in such a way as to circumvent human cooperation and community. Rather from the outset the church is an interfacing, dynamic divine-human *psuche-soma, corpus Christi.* As in Christology we cannot separate the two natures (divine and human) without offense to the one theandric person, so in ecclesiology we cannot artificially separate the hidden grace of word and sacraments from the visible structures of preaching, eating, drinking, exegesis, and religious communities that mediate that grace. The church is not exempt from conditions that prevail in voluntary organizations: the expression of interest, the dynamics of power, the routinization of charisma. For because the church exists in human history, it is not dismissed from the very sociological and moral conditions that prevail in history. The church is not finally explainable as a hereditary succession based on race or genetics or family tradition, but this does not deny that through families and primary social relations, persons are brought into the covenant community. The church is the community of those who by grace believe in Christ, without ceasing to be a visible organization, community, and social process through which salvation is being offered under the conditions of history.

CATHOLICITY

The church is constituted *kath' olou*—according to its wholeness—or as we say in English, *catholic*. The church is called catholic because she is not bound to a particular place or time. The one church that lives in Christ has the characteristic of being one throughout the whole earth. "That which concerns the whole" is the root meaning of catholic.

That church is catholic which professes the whole faith that the whole body of Christian believers has in all its times and places professed (Vincent of Lérins, *Comm.* 2.6, *FC* 7, p., 270). The underlying conviction is that wherever belief in the triune God emerges throughout the known world among the various nations, races, languages, nationalities, classes, and cultures, in all sorts of political systems, economic orders, and social situations, there is the one body of Christ. The church by definition is *kath' olou* in this sense (*Martyrdom of Polycarp, ANF* I, pp. 39–42; Irenaeus, *Ag. Her.* III.4, *ANF* I, p. 417; Androutsos, *Dogm.*, p. 280).

The Third Mark: *Katholikēn Ekklēsian*, Defined with Respect to Fullness of Consent, Wholeness of Doctrine, Embracing All Cultures, Places, Particularities, and Times

The term *church catholic* (*katholikēn ekklēsian*) appears early in Christian testimony, as in the writings of Ignatius about A.D. 110: wherever Christ is, there is the *katholikēn ekklēsian* (*Smyrna* 8.2; cf. *Martyrdom of Polycarp* 8.1), the church universal, which has Christ as its center and the apostles as its teaching elders (Ignatius, *Philadelphians* 5.1).

In the rule of faith, as typified by the Apostles' and Nicene-Constantinopolitan Creeds, catholicity is confessed as a defining mark of the church (Pearson, *EC* 145–50; Journet, *CWI*, pp. 526 ff.; Darwell Stone, *EVO*, pp. 135–39; Hall, *DT* VIII, p. 199). This is a reliable test: if the church should bar from its doors some particular nation or race or gender or culture, one would then know instantly that it is not constituted *kath' olou.*

The rule by which catholicity has been most commonly judged since the fifth century is the Vincentian canon: That is catholic which has been believed by all Christian believers in varied cultures, places and times from the outset of apostolic testimony. "Every care must be taken that we may hold fast to that which has been believed everywhere, always, and by all. For this is, then, truly and properly Catholic. . . . This general rule will be correctly applied if we pursue universality, antiquity, and agreement" (Vincent of Lérins, *Comm.* II.1, *FEF* III, 2168, p. 263). By the criterion of universality, we confess that faith to be true which is confessed by the whole church throughout the whole world. By the criterion of antiquity, we follow the ancient definitions of the apostles as faithfully delivered by their successors through consensually received interpreters (Tertullian, *Ag. Marcion* IV.3–5, *ANF* III, pp. 348–50; Nicetas of Remesiana, *Explanation of the Creed, FC*

7, p. 50). By the criterion of consensual agreement, we adopt the definitions received by general lay consent in ecumenical council.

Classic writers spoke of the wholeness and universality of the church in several interrelated ways: "It is called Catholic then because it extends over all the world . . . teaches universally and completely one and all the doctrines which ought to come to men's knowledge . . . brings into subjection to godliness the whole [of humanity] . . . and because it universally treats and heals the whole class of sins which are committed by soul or body, and possesses in itself every form of virtue which is named, both in deeds and words, and every kind of spiritual gifts" (Cyril of Jerusalem, *Catech. Lect.* XVIII.23, *NPNF* 2 VII, p. 140).

Fullness of Consent to the Whole of Apostolic Teaching. The church is celebrated as universal [katholikē] with respect to the fullness of consent given to the whole of catholic truth (Tertullian, *Prescription Ag. Her.* 20–28, *ANF* III, pp. 252–56). Wherever there is consent to apostolic teaching, there the whole church is becoming embodied. To say, "I believe in the holy *catholic* church," means that one believes in the same teaching of the same *ekklēsia* that true believers have received since apostolic times and in all the places where that faith has been truly received (Tertullian, *Ag. Marcion* IV.3–5, *ANF* III, pp. 348–50). "That which was from the beginning, which we have heard, which we have seen with our eyes, which we have looked at and our hands have touched—this we proclaim" (1 John 1).

Whether That Teaching Is Catholic Which Does Not Embrace All That Is Necessary for Salvation. As the churches of the late second century faced heretical challenges, the term *catholic* increasingly took on the added nuance of "wholeness of received doctrine." The church is celebrated as universal with respect not only to the completeness of its consensual reception but to the wholeness of its doctrine. By this mark the believer today can be assured that the church in our time endeavors to teach the same fully adequate doctrine that the apostles received from Christ and seeks to do so in relation to emergent or changing cultural contexts. *The church is catholic because its teaching is comprehensive, embracing all that is necessary for salvation.*

Teachers of Catholic doctrine are distinguished from schismatic word manipulators who teach only some broken piece of the truth of the whole. The church is catholic because consent to this whole truth has been given from ancient times by all those everywhere who share life in Christ. The church does not commend one favorite doctrine in one locale and a different doctrine in another according to local preference or partisanship but the whole counsel of God everywhere (Tertullian, *Prescription Ag. Her.* 20–28, *ANF* III, pp. 252–56).

Whether Catholicity Requires Mission to All Cultures. The church is celebrated as universal with respect to human cultures, for she is not tied or finally indebted to any one condition of humanity, being "gathered from all classes" and "of every nation" (Ursinus, *Comm. Heid. Catech.*, p. 289). *The church is catholic because her mission is universally addressed to all cultures.*

Peter's primitive world vision pervades the cross-cultural Christian imagination: "I now realize how true it is that God does not show favoritism" but accepts those from every nation who "fear him and do what is right" (Acts 10:34, 35).

Current attempts to embody an "inclusive community" faintly echo the ancient call to catholicity.

The people of the old covenant were born as progeny of Abraham. It was very difficult for one not born of a Jewish mother to become a Jew. Yet the Hebrew prophets looked for a time in which the covenant would be extended to all the nations, the Gentiles. Catholicity is that characteristic of the church that makes Yahweh's good news available to all and requires the church to seek universal proclamation and diffusion (Augustine, *Letters, FC* 18, pp. 92 ff.).

This affirmation does not imply that the church's Eucharist is indiscriminately offered to all, including those who have not consented to her teaching or not undergone her discipline. To offer baptism or Holy Communion to the impenitent would be to ignore discipline as essential to the nature and task of the church. Rather, catholicity means "that no other barrier to full communion will be erected than that which is made necessary by human wilfulness and by the maintenance of catholic principles and discipline" (Hall, *DT* VIII, p. 201).

Those who enter the church by baptism do not thereby pretend to cease having a particular ethnic identity or race or culture or social class, though baptism brings one into a renewed, transmuted relation to all other races, ethnic identities, cultures, and classes. One does not have to first become baptized as a European to be a Christian. Christian baptism and community existed for half a dozen centuries before the cultural-national formation began of what we know today as Europe.

"The Church is free to ground itself firmly in the culture and life style of every people to whom it is sent. Otherwise it would die like a potted plant with no roots in the local soil, rather than find life as a seed which dies to bear fruit. There is no single culture peculiarly congenial to the Christian message; each culture is to be both shaped and transcended by that message" (Nairobi Assembly, *WCC, Message, CC,* p. 603).

Whether Catholicity Requires Mission to All Places.   The church is celebrated as universal with respect to place. *The church is catholic because it is not confined to a local identity but dispersed over the entire globe,* as distinguished from the people of the old covenant, who received the inheritance of a particular land. The church is a fellowship that transcends all national and regional identities (Augustine, *Answer to Letters of Petilian* II.33–75, *NPNF* 1 IV, pp. 552–68). For this reason Paul is said to have preached to the "utmost bounds of the west" (Clement of Rome, *Corinth* 5, *FC* 1, p. 14).

The apostles were commissioned to make disciples of all nations, to baptize, and to teach all that Christ has commanded, with the promise that Christ would himself attend these ministries. "And this gospel of the kingdom will be preached in the whole world as a testimony to all nations" (Matt. 24:14). The risen Lord empowered the church by the sending of the Spirit and commanded recipients to "be my witnesses in Jerusalem, and in all Judea and Samaria, and to the ends of the earth" (Acts 1:8). It would be a mark of a false church if it failed to proclaim the word everywhere to all who would hear, just as much as if it failed to baptize in the triune name or teach the whole counsel of God. By that failure one could easily tell that the church was not acting "according to the whole" (*kath' olou*). The church that is uncommitted to taking the whole message everywhere cannot be *kath' olou*. Paul understood that "faith comes from hearing the message, and the message is heard through the word of Christ" (Rom. 10:17). This is why "their voice has gone out into all the earth, their words to the ends of the world" (Rom. 10:18, quoting Ps. 19:4).

This need not be taken woodenly to mean that the church must be physically present in every square inch of the world. For that would result in making the church coterminous with the world, with no distinction between them. Nor does it imply that the church must be simultaneously meeting every Sunday in every village in the world. The meaning is rather that the church's message is intended for the whole world, seeking to walk wherever human beings walk (Matt. 24:14; John 3:17; *COC* III, pp. 914–25).

There is an intimate connection between the catholicity of the church and its worldwide missional effort. "The 'Catholic' nature of the church was always the strongest missionary motive" (Brunner, *Dogm.* III, p. 124). The church is catholic because it is apostolic (Augustine, *On the Unity of the Church* 6.11–13; *Hom. on John*, tractate XXXII.6, *NPNF* 1 VII, p. 195). Lacking a mission to the whole, it is not the whole church (Pannenberg, *The Church*, pp. 44–69). Augustine challenged the Donatists by asking them to explain why Christ "should suddenly be found surviving only in the Africans, and not in all of them? The Catholic Church exists indeed in Africa, since God willed and ordained that it should exist throughout the whole world. Whereas your party, which is called the party of Donatus, does not exist in all those places in which the writings of the apostles, their discourse, and their actions, have been current" (Augustine, *Epistles* 49.3, *LCF*, p. 240).

Whether the Church Becomes Less Catholic in Becoming More Local.   The church is celebrated as universal precisely with respect to its variable locality and the particularity of its coming into being. Since it is universal, the church is constantly coming into being in highly particular historical situations. *The church is rightly called catholic insofar as it does not cease to be universal as it becomes intensely local.* The universal church expresses itself as a particular congregation when only some (never all of all times) bodily assemble to share the good news, hear the word of scripture interpreted, and share in fellowship with the living Lord. Even a church in a house (*kath oikon*, Rom. 16:5) is an expression of the church universal.

The local church may, while holding to catholic teaching, adapt to local conditions without losing its catholicity (Leo IX, *Symbol of Faith*, *SCD* 343–50, pp. 140–42). Catholicity affirms particular churches as members of the one, whole body of Christ becoming embodied in a particular place. Hence the church at Corinth shares in the whole church and expresses the church universal in that particular place (Augustine, *Letters*, *FC* 12, pp. 242 ff.).

Whether Catholicity Embraces Past, Present, and Future Faithful.   *The church is catholic in that it embraces believers of all ages of history, past, present, and future.* To the church catholic belong all who have ever believed and all who ever will believe in the saving work of the triune God. The church is celebrated as universal with respect to time.

The church existed in the form of anticipatory belief before Abraham: "Hence there were besides, and before Abraham, other worshippers of the true God, whose priest Melchizedek was," all of whom belonged to the "one true Church of all times" (Ursinus, *Comm. Heid. Catech.*, p. 290). "And surely I am with you always, to the very end of the age" (Matt. 29:20). "My Spirit, who is on you, and my words that I have put in your mouth will not depart from your mouth, or from the mouths of your children, or from the mouths of their descendants from this time on and forever" (Isa. 59:21).

The church is celebrated as universal with respect to its durability, transcending all specific, fleeting historical events and cultures, "because it will endure throughout every period of the world" (Ursinus, *Comm. Heid. Catech.*, p. 290). The church is "catholic or universal because, destined to last for all time, it never fails to fulfill the divine commandment to teach all nations all the truths revealed by God" (*Baltimore Catechism*, p. 121).

Whether Catholicity Has Ever Occurred. Has an actual "catholic ethos" ever emerged to express the ideally envisioned catholicity of the whole church? Only proximately, never completely. Yet never since Pentecost has the church been wholly lacking in catholic ethos. The responsiveness of particular communities of faith to the wholeness of the Holy Spirit varies widely from time to time. The eighteenth-century Moravian village of Bethlehem, Pennsylvania, may have been as catholic in spirit as medieval ultramontanism.

Complementary Nuances of Catholicity

Due to the cross-cultural conditions intrinsic to Christian mission, the notion of catholicity was from the outset destined to have complementary layers of meanings. It is always reaching out for ever-new audiences in an ever-expanding mission.

Three nuances of the adjective *catholic* are recurrently interwoven in the history of *ekklēsia:* cross-cultural adaptability, the temperament of patient tolerance, and centered orthodoxy.

Cross-cultural Adaptability. The adjective *catholic* has fittingly taken on the meaning of inclusive, *cross-cultural adaptability.* Since orthodoxy is called and sent into every cultural context, it has at its best become exceptionally adept at movement from one language to another, one political sphere to another, one economic system to another, without feeling a compulsive need to subvert each and every culture it enters (Eusebius, *HCCC* II, III, pp. 71–154).

Admittedly such cultural adaptivity is not uniformly characteristic of all forms of orthodoxy and certainly not of all local members of the church, but it does characterize the most catholic elements of orthodoxy and seeks to pervade its leadership and much of its laity. It is an unhistorical Enlightenment caricature of orthodoxy to imagine that it has no cross-cultural adaptability, for we indeed find such adaptability in Eastern Orthodox and Roman Catholic traditions, and in the classic Protestant tradition, both in establishment and in dissenting forms:

> Moravian hymn and Roman chant
>   In one devotion blend,
> To speak the soul's eternal want
>   Of Him, the inmost friend.

One prayer soars cleansed with martyrs' fire,
  One choked with sinners' tears.
In Heaven both meet in one desire,
  And God one music hears.

                                        (J. Lowell, "Godminster Chimes")

The Temperament of Patient Tolerance.   Out of this history of adaptability, the
adjective *catholic* has recurrently taken on the meaning of *a temperament of patient
tolerance.* Since the church is called and sent into every cultural context, it has
engendered tolerance toward cultural varieties wherever it has remained most
true to its catholic mission. Admittedly the church at times has been intolerant
and unfair toward some, but just to that extent has it lacked the characteristic of
catholicity that remains a mark of the true church (Phil. 4:5; Eph. 4:2).

Meanwhile outspoken advocates of hypertolerance and the rhetoric of absolute
relativism have exhibited demeaning forms of intolerance, chauvinism, and cultural ethnocentrism, often in the name of toleration. The deeper source of the
church's tolerance, however, is not Enlightenment optimism about human nature
or Stoic assumptions about the universality of reason or simplistic egalitarianism
or the abstract visions of utopian idealism. Rather catholic tolerance is grounded
directly in the gospel of God's love for all. It is gentle and patient because it seeks
to reflect God's own gentleness and patience (Gal. 5:23; Eph. 4:32; Col. 3:12;
1 Tim. 6:11).

Centered Orthodoxy.   Precisely amid this history of adaptability and caring tolerance, the adjective *catholic* has steadily borne the meaning of *centered orthodoxy.*
The catholicity of the church does not move from culture to culture simply by
cheap accommodation, but by being itself, by sustaining its own distinctive identity and norms while entering empathically even into what might otherwise seem
to be alien cultural situations. The history of orthodoxy is not characterized by
cultural rigidity, but astonishing flexibility and openness to cultural variety (Matt.
28:19; John 4; Acts 1:8).

The moral strength of the Christian apologists has been their attempt energetically to communicate with cultured despisers of Christianity, not withdraw from
them. If in reaching out they tended to select those features of Christianity that
were more easily accessible to the cultivated pagan philosophical mind of the day
(the unity of God, the Logos, moral virtue, immortality, and political tolerance),
that tendency later had to be corrected. A skillful and subtle effort has been made
since the second century to show the coincidence of Christian teaching with the
best of heathen philosophy (Justin Martyr, *First Apology* 20–22, *FC* 6, pp. 55–58;
Athenagoras, *Plea* 3–12; *ANF* II, pp. 130–34; Clement of Alexandria, *Exhortation
to the Heathen, ANF* II, pp. 163 ff.; Theophilus, *To Autolycus, ANF* II, pp. 94–121;
Aristides, *Apology,* in Eusebius, *CH* IV.3.3; Minucius Felix, *Octavius, ANF* IV,
pp. 173 ff.). Like Tillich and Bultmann of our time, they sometimes carefully selected Christian teachings that could be more conveniently assimilated into their
cultural situation. The danger is that the substantive content of the rule of faith
easily becomes lost in the translation. In Tillich and Bultmann we see a distinct
neglect of full-orbed catholicity of teaching, even amid the good intention of
reaching out for a particular audience.

Whether the Idea of Catholicity Is Prone to Be Abused by Apparent Proponents of Catholicity.   The concept of catholicity has on occasion become vulnerable to becoming captive to certain misuses precisely by those who seem to be defending catholicity (Augustine, *Answer to Letters of Petilian* II.33–75, *NPNF* 1 IV, pp. 552–68; Hall, *DT* VIII, pp. 212 ff.).

Catholic is not rightly to be used as a synonym for such expansiveness that it implies vagueness or repudiation of its guardianship of its own sacred deposit of truth (Council of Lyons II, *SCD* 461–66, pp. 183–86; Vincent of Lérins, Commonitory, 21–25, *NPNF* 2 XI, pp. 146–50). Nor does catholicity mean simply all those who call themselves Christian regardless of their lack of other tests of the church such as holiness and apostolicity. It is a mistake to yield the term *catholic* to a particular group or tradition or political party or denomination, as if it is an idea that evangelicals or low-church Protestants might get along without. As *evangelical* is a term that deserves to be reclaimed by liturgical traditions, so *catholic* is a term that deserves to be reclaimed by evangelical traditions (Baxter, *The True Catholick*).

It is not uncommon for those who reject consensual Christian teaching to desire nevertheless to use the church instrumentally to legitimize their own idiosyncratic biases. When the *ekklēsia* allows itself to be used in this fashion, it is not being truly catholic and is not contending for the catholic faith.

Those who assert personal opinions as if they were consensual catholic teaching abuse catholicity. Subjective experiences or individual opinions can never be the criteria of catholicity unless informed by consensual teachings that meet canonical tests. It is a deceptive use of *catholic* that takes advantage of the goodwill of a proximately tolerant and adaptable church to superimpose upon that idea teachings that are inimical to the church.

Interlude: Whether the Mark of Catholicity May Be Found in a Separate Church Body

This personal interlude is written especially for readers who may have difficulty imagining how or why I could remain committed to my own received church tradition, given the other views I have expressed.

The deeper question may be put to any Protestant: Is it possible that a particular church body or denomination could display the essential mark of catholicity? Though I am seeking to represent the ancient ecumenical tradition within the postmodern situation, it would be foolish to deny that I view this situation from within the experience of a particular church tradition. I wish here to make a modest comment on my own particular church tradition, which I identify somewhat complexly with the highly qualified hyphenated phrase Ancient Ecumenical-Vincentian-Anglican-Wesleyan (or more straightforwardly "Anglican evangelical"), without any pretense that it is normative for other traditions.

Despite some of the myopias of ancient conciliarism and of the Anglican evangelical tradition (like excessive optimism, doctrinal latitudinarianism, compulsive pragmatism, class insensitivities, and recurrent softheadedness) it has one feature that I particularly admire: its strength is its irenic conserving realism. Wherever revolutionary fanaticism approaches, it finds itself nurtured by a deeply ingrained conservative instinct that tem-

pers the wildness of revolutionary fantasies. It seeks change moderately
and incrementally rather than abruptly or coercively. The broad scope of
English political history may be described as a series of compromises and
halfway measures that moderated problems gradually but did not resolve
them completely, that made modest adjustments but resisted absolute, abstract, rationalistic and radical visions of total change (Edmund Burke, *Reflections on the Revolution in France;* J. H. Blunt, *Reformation of the Church of
England*). Continuity and free consent and diversity have been highly valued in this tradition (F. W. Puller, *Continuity of the English Church; Our Place
in Christendom;* F. Hall, *Historical Position of the Episcopal Church*). The
Anglican wing of the Reformation resisted the anarchic-revolutionary-
idealistic-rationalistic syndrome better than the Dissenting wing. This kept
the English Reformation relatively more in touch with its patristic, catholic, and medieval roots than was the Reformed dissent.

There remained within the Anglican *eirēnikon* many parties, all held together by a common tradition of prayer (*BCP;* J. Wand, ed., *The Anglican
Communion;* More and Cross, eds. *Angl.;* S. Niell, *Anglicanism*). The assumption was that theological differences that did not require a break with
the language of the liturgy would run their own course and find fitting
resolution, and the rule of prayer would fittingly circumscribe and correspond with the rule of faith (*lex orandi, lex credendi*). There remained much
room for varied opinions, and on the whole a spirit of comparative toleration was engendered. Excessive elasticity (latitudinarianism tending toward
indifferentism) was always the peril of the English Church spirit. But the
unity of the great diversity was premised on the assumption that the Holy
Spirit has remained at work to preserve and unite the church and overrule
exaggerated loyalties and providentially hedge the ways of sin. The Vincentian appeal to antiquity and catholicity became the shaping principle of
the Anglican reformation (Hall, *DT* VIII, p. 230). This spirit was consistent with a longer irenic history of the English church in which it sought to
mediate the union of Anglo-Saxon kingdoms into a single nation. There is
a profound sense in which the unity of the British people was an achievement of the church. *Ecclesia Anglicana* had to struggle for its identity
against both pope and crown. Both Magna Carta and Elizabethan Settlement are expressions of that centeredness (S. Neill, *Anglicanism;* Hall, *DT*
VIII, p. 228).

If this tradition has been strong on unity, antiquity, freedom, diversity,
and toleration, it has at times become less robust in rigorous exegesis and
systematic teaching of Christian doctrine. It has simultaneously fostered
both the growth of the modern ecumenical spirit and the gradual deterioration of systematic theology. This tradition welcomed and encouraged
historical biblical criticism and scientific inquiry early on, but itself fell as a
fairly easy victim to modern chauvinism and cheap accommodations to
modernity. Although the Anglican ethos has intermittently sought to walk
the way of holiness and taught Christian perfection and the assurance of
the Spirit, it has seldom shown the sort of strength in systematic theology
that has been so characteristic of the Reformed tradition of dissenting
Protestantism. My own Wesleyan evangelical branch of the Anglican tradition, despite many failures, still forms a useful bridge between Protestants

and Catholics, while maintaining deep theological and disciplinary affinities with the Eastern Church tradition. The Anglican evangelical tradition remains quietly very Catholic and anciently ecumenical in teaching and discipline, holding to the teaching of scripture, the primitive church, the rule of faith summed up in the creeds and affirmed by the undisputed Ecumenical Councils (J. Wesley, *Letter to C. Middleton, WJW* X, pp. 1–79; cf. Lambeth Conference, 1867; R. T. Davidson, ed., *The Lambeth Conferences*), and to the Reformation teaching of justification by grace through faith. Its modest claim to share in the church catholic is nothing other than that Word and Sacrament have not been abandoned, nor have ancient conciliar formulations. Its method has remained intuitively Vincentian even when Vincent had been largely forgotten, stressing consensual themes of the faith of ancient conciliar Christianity, tending until recently to regard special fads and specializations and doctrinal systems as passing developments lacking official standing or absolute authority. Like Anglicans, the Wesleyan family of evangelicals have never been quite willing to sanction a single party, whether liberal or conservative, socialist or fundamentalist, latitudinarian or pietistic, left or right, yet have continued to affirm the Apostles' Creed and celebrate a predominantly Cranmerian (which is largely an ancient catholic) liturgy and a hymnody that much of Christendom continues to sing.

When I despair over modern Protestant quasi-apostasies and dilutions, I have imagined myself walking the road toward Canterbury or Rome or even Antioch, but in saner moments I feel deeply grateful to have been nurtured by my own church tradition, which effectively bequeathed to me some of the essential marks of catholicity even while bearing many scars and warts of pietistic individualism and denominationalism. I hope this low-keyed, critical celebration of my own church tradition does not annoy Lutherans or Baptists or Roman Catholics or charismatics who may have their own reasons for feeling uneasy about particulars of this tradition. My purpose remains that of articulating an ecclesiology wherein each of these valued partners in dialogue might feel that their own tradition is rooted in reasonably undistorted form in the ancient ecumenical tradition.

Perpetuity, Imperishability, Indefectibility

The one, holy, universal church is promised imperishable continuance, even if particular churches or local bodies or denominations may fail or atrophy. Her future finally is not left to human willing or chance, but to grace.

Whether the Church Will Continue.   Many branches of the seasonally changing vine may drop off or become dysfunctional and atrophy, but the church itself will be preserved till the end of the age (Heidegger, *Med.* XXVI.11, *RD*, p. 664). The destiny of the church is eternally secure. Though individuals may fall, and even whole communities lose their bearings during particular periods, the church will be preserved (John 16:6, 13). God will not be left without witnesses in the world (Acts 14:17). "One holy Christian church will be and remain forever" (Augsburg Conf., art. VII, *CC*, p. 70).

Meanwhile the church continues to be vulnerable to those hazards that accompany historical existence generally. The Holy Spirit does not abandon the church amid these earthly struggles but supplies that grace of perseverance by which the church is enabled to remain Christ's living body even while being challenged by forgetfulness, heresy, apostasy, persecution, and schism. The church will be preserved to "proclaim the Lord's death until he comes" (1 Cor. 11:26).

Whether the Church Is Indefectible. Against the church "the gates of hell shall not prevail" (Matt. 16:18, KJV; cf. Luke 1:33; 1 Tim. 3:15). This means that the church will *never decline into total forgetfulness,* because guided by the Spirit, who is promised always to accompany the church (John 14:16; Matt. 23:20), even when the church fails to listen. The church insofar as she is guided by the Spirit does not fall entirely away from the fundamental truth or into irretrievable error. She is preserved by grace, not by human craft or design (Matt. 7:25).

Despite temporary apostasies, it is unthinkable that God would allow the church finally to become absolutely and continuously apostate or to lose all touch with the righteousness that Christ has once for all bestowed upon her. "For you have been born again, not of perishable seed, but of imperishable, through the living and enduring word of God. For 'All men are like grass,'" but "'the word of the Lord stands forever.' And this is the word that was preached to you" (1 Pet. 1:24, 25; Calvin, *Comm.* XXII, pp. 57–60).

Scholastic teachers distinguished between different levels of erring. Errors are said to be either fundamental, so as to overthrow the very foundation of the faith, or nonfundamental, so as to leave undisturbed its essential foundation (Gerhard, *LT,* XI.143; Schmid, *DT,* p. 590). The promise of indefectibility is not toward a particular congregation or denomination or generation or family of churches or passing period of history, but rather the whole church to preserve her from fundamental error in the long course of history—to the end (Matt. 28:20; *Longer Catech.,* Eastern Orthodox Church, 271, *COC* II, p. 488). Even in the worst imaginable calamities of future history there will still be a church, even if only a remnant.

Whether the Church May in Any Sense Be Said to Be "Without Fault." It is promised to the called out people of God that they shall endure until the end of time. Insofar as the faithful are sustained by pure Word and Sacrament, adhering to the "faith once delivered," their sacrifice is received by God as faultless (Ambrose, *Six Days of Creation* IV.2, 7, *FC* 42, p. 131; John Chrysostom, *Two Homilies on Eutropius NPNF* 1 IX, pp. 245–65, *MPG* 52, p. 402; *Confession of Dositheus* 10–12, *CC,* pp. 491–97).

The church "does not err, so long as it relies upon the rock Christ, and upon the foundation of the prophets and apostles" (Second Helvetic Conf., *CC,* p. 143). Insofar as "she lets herself be taught by the Holy Spirit through the Word of God," Calvin argued that "the church cannot err in things necessary for salvation" (*Inst.* 4.8.13). Though particular assemblies may lapse, relapse, or collapse, because of the Spirit's guidance, the elect people of God "cannot wholly wander away or fall from salvation" (F. Burmann, *Synopsis Theologiae* VII.1.25), for all those called will not be allowed to err at the same time. Though grace does not coerce, neither does it ever bat zero in any given season.

Catholic and Protestant Teaching on Indefectibility. Catholic teaching holds that infallibility and indefectibility are attributes of the church, "qualities perfecting the nature of the Church" (*Baltimore Catechism*, p. 124). Yet Catholic teaching does not interpret this strictly as impeccability, or freedom from all sin: "The Church has never held that the Pope cannot sin" (*Baltimore Catechism*, p. 127). According to the first Vatican Council, the pontiff is not infallible merely because he is pope, but when and insofar as he speaks *ex cathedra* as teacher of all faithful Catholics: "The exercise by the Bishop of Rome of his teaching authority is, under carefully defined conditions, infallible or without error" (Vat. I, *SCD* 1832–40, pp. 455–57; cf. *Common Catech.*, p. 646).

Classical Protestantism affirms that "the church does not err" in the sense that the whole church does not at any given time err, and it does not err in the foundation, even if in temporary and nonfundamental ways it may (Ursinus, *Comm. Heid. Catech.*, p. 291). It seems hard to believe that God would create the church at great cost only to let it fall finally into permanent or irremediable error. Indefectibility is more a teaching of the power of the Holy Spirit than of the self-sufficiency or wisdom of the church as such (Calvin, *Inst.* 4.1). The Holy Spirit is promised to "teach you all things and will remind you of everything I have said to you" (John 14:26).

Though Protestants may concede that the church is ultimately sure or certain or indefectible (*asphalēs*) insofar as it clings to the revealed word (Zwingli, 1828 *Ausgabe* III.129), still amid the history of sin the church is ever prone to forgetfulness and fallibility. That community which is being called by the Holy Spirit will not be found falling irretrievably into apostasy, so as to make it impossible for all subsequent generations to hear the good news, yet this does not imply that the church is secure from making mistakes or errors of judgment. The relative fallibility of the church in time is itself a Protestant dogma.

Always some seed of faith remains buried in the ashes even of the most divided and corrupt church. Sometimes such seeds may seem to survive marginally as endangered species, as *sparsi per totum orbem*, as remnants of former vitalities of covenant communities. Yet wherever Word and Sacrament are being transmitted and delivered, they are never without some effect, for "my word" shall "not return to me empty, but will accomplish what I desire" (Isa. 55:11), says the Lord. Although the church in some cultures or times appears extinct, becoming "so obscured and defaced that the Church seems almost quite razed out," "yet, in the meantime, the Lord has in this world, even in this darkness, his true worshippers" (Second Helvetic Conf., *CC*, p. 148; 1 Kings 19:18; Rev. 7:4, 9), where the foundation is standing sure and the Lord knows who are his (2 Tim. 2:9), as we have recently rediscovered in the church in China during the Cultural Revolution, and Russia after the failed coup of 1991.

Fallibility Within the Historic Church. Abuses arise among those associated with the church not only because of human infirmities and finitude, but because the church is seeking steadily to redeem recalcitrant sinners. That redemption does not occur instantaneously. It occurs through a process in which sinners are brought into a sphere in which long-habituated sins can be gradually rehabituated, restored, reconciled, and transformed (Luke 5:31).

Since fallible and sinful persons are the recipients of God's saving grace (for the healthy do not need a physician, Mark 2:17), as long as the church exists within the conditions of the history of sin, the church will be prone to being distorted and will be vulnerable to those who wish to use it for their own purposes. Until the consummation of salvation history, when the incurably wicked will be cut off from the living vine, the called out people will be distortable (Ps. 37).

To flee from the scene of human corruption would be to flee from the church's own mission and servant ministry. But insofar as it is truly the body of Christ living in faith, hope, and love under the life-giving power of the Spirit, the church can never become absolutely or finally or fatally corrupted (Matt. 16:18).

Among diseases of the history of sin that continue to challenge, tempt, and plague the church and resist its full growth are the partisan spirit that would divide it, the heretical spirit that would lead it to distort or forget apostolic teaching, the antinomian spirit that turns Christian liberty into libertinism, the legalistic spirit that would turn grace into law, the naturalistic spirit that would treat grace as a determinant of nature. Despite these infirmities and challenges permitted by a kind providence to strengthen the church and enable it to grow stronger, the body lives on, the vine sends forth new shoots, the Spirit enlivens and heals, the Head continues to guide and order the whole organism (John 15:1–5; Col. 1:18).

The continuing renewal of ecclesial life never comes by avoiding or excluding sinners, for their redemption is the reason the church exists. Clean-hands purists of all periods tend to flee the task of serving sinners, unlike Jesus who mixed with them, ate and drank with those most despicable and rejected, and profoundly identified with all sinners on the cross. The body of Christ continues to struggle against tendencies toward a Montanism that would exclude sinners based on their lack of Spirit, a Donatism that would exclude sinners based upon inauthentic ministry or regionalism, and a purist Novatian rigorism that would exclude sinners based upon their moral deficiencies (Council of Arelas I, SCD 53, p. 25; Siricius, To Himerius, SCD 88, p. 37).

Caucus-oriented special interest politics, which so harmfully characterizes the modern church, tends to undermine the spirit of catholicity in the church. While the caucus is fixated upon particular special interests, catholicity is struggling to embody the whole and ensure the health of the commonweal. The caucus mentality has gained ground precisely amid an ethos in which catholicity was being outwardly praised but practically neglected, often in the name of liberal ecumenism.

Intergenerational, Conciliar Indefectibility. The ecumenical councils and major consensual teachers attest ultimate indefectibility of the church as a gift of grace (Council of Nicaea I, SCD 54, p. 26; Athanasius et al., To the Bishops of Africa 1–6, NPNF 2 IV, pp. 489–92; Basil, Letters 114, FC 13, pp. 241–42; Gregory Nazianzen, On the Great Athanasius, Orat. XXI, NPNF 2 VII, pp. 269–80; Cyril, Letters 39 FC, 76, pp. 147–52). The patristic exegetes assented to the councils as evidence of the assent of the whole church. It is this universal consent that is said to be reliable, and finally indefectible.

Though the Holy Spirit is the actuating principle of this indefectibility, the consent of the whole *laos* is given as an evidence and external criterion of ecumenicity. The Holy Spirit does not introduce new or postapostolic doctrine through the conciliar process, but rather acts to illuminate and guard from error the apostolic witness. This effort is not mechanically actuated by the Spirit, but works in a normal human manner through debate, inquiry, parliamentary deliberation, voting, and the apparatus of policy formation (Merrill, *ACE*, p. 249).

What Accounts for the Perennial Vitality of the Church?   The history of the church is not one of uninterrupted progress or ekstasis, without challenge or chastisement. Pascal pictured Christianity as a thousand times having appeared to be "on the point of universal destruction, and every time that it has been in this condition, God has raised it up by some extraordinary stroke of his power" (Pensées, in Jacobs, *SCF*, p. 377). Each seeming defeat readies the community for a deeper level of understanding. Each apparent victory readies the community for a deeper level of conflict.

The residual vitality of the church, even in periods in which it seems to have been totally undone, is an amazing story recounted in actual human history, with startling recoveries after long periods of malaise and apparent death. The worst periods of martyrdom are characteristically accompanied by the profoundest movements of the Spirit. The deepest sloughs of demoralization and libertinism are accompanied by such correctives as those of Benedict of Nursia, Bernard of Clairvaux, Francis of Assisi, Luther, Calvin, Teresa of Avila, Edwards, Wesley, and Thérèse of Lisieux. To now, the promise has held, even against great odds, that the gates of hell have not prevailed against the *ekklēsia*.

Today, amid the failures of modern bureaucratic ecumenism, the moral catastrophes of broadcast ministries, the growing secularization of the church—all embarrassing, persistent facts—it would seem that the *ekklēsia* is once again profoundly imperiled. But just in the midst of these facts, the Spirit continues to work powerfully to restore the church to its intrinsic oneness, holiness, universality, and apostolicity.

APOSTOLICITY

Defining the Fourth Mark: *Apostolikēn Ekklēsian*

The church is not a group of people groping for a philosophy of life appropriate to modern conditions, but a living body already being shaped by apostolic teaching. Holding steady to that teaching is a principal mark of the authenticity of the *ekklēsia*.

Apostolicity is intrinsically interwoven with the other marks of the church: Only that church that is one can be catholic. Only that church that is united in the one mission of the one Lord can be apostolic. Lacking that holiness which is fitting to the obedience of faith, one finds neither apostolicity nor catholicity. Only that church that is formed by the apostolic memory can be united in one body with the Lord.

The Sent Ones.   The church is apostolic insofar as it retains, guards, and faithfully transmits its apostolic mission. Those sent by the Son are the apostolate. As Christ was sent by the Father, the apostles were sent, empowered by the Spirit, and the continuing apostolate is still being sent (John 20:21; Cyprian, *Treatises* I, *ANF* V, pp. 421–29; Lactantius, *Of the Manner in Which the Persecutors Died* I, II, *ANF* VII, p. 301).

The apostolate is sent on the authority of the Son, to whom "all authority in heaven and on earth has been given" (Matt. 28:18), to engage in the mission of the Son by the power of the Spirit. "As the Father has sent me, I am sending you" (John 20:21). "When the time had fully come, God sent his son" (Gal. 4:4). Jesus is the model of the *apostle,* the one sent. "Therefore, holy brothers, who share in the heavenly calling, fix your thoughts on Jesus, the apostle" (Heb. 3:1). Jesus is apostle in the sense of being commissioned and authorized by God the Father and sent into the world (Luther, *Lectures on Heb., LW* 29, p. 144).

The time of the apostolate begins with the ascension and ends only with the Parousia. The commission is to make disciples, baptizing and teaching "to the very end of the age," knowing that the Son is "with you always" by the power of the Spirit (Matt. 28:19, 20), who will "guide you into all truth" (John 16:13) and empower the apostolic mission (Acts 1:8).

The church does not merely *have* but *is* a mission, the historical embodiment of the mission of the Son through the Spirit (Barth, *CD* IV/4, 50 ff.). The church does not elicit mission, but rather mission elicits, awakens, and empowers the church. *Missio dei* embraces all that the church is and does in its life in the world. This called out community has a key role to play in the history of the emerging reign of God (Matt. 13; 2 Tim. 1:1–14; Heb. 12:22–28).

The Calling and Sending of the Twelve.   After praying to the Father, the Son called to himself those whom he wished to assist him in his work. He sent them to preach the good news of the kingdom (Mark 3:13–19; Matt. 10:1–42), first to Israel, and then to all nations (Rom. 1:16), that they might make disciples everywhere. The Spirit was promised to supply them with gifts of ministry (Matt. 28:16–20; Mark 16:15; John 20:21–23; Eph. 4). They were confirmed in their mission on the day of Pentecost (Acts 2:1–26), in accord with Christ's promise that they would receive power when the Spirit came to be his witness to the ends of the earth (Acts 1:8; *Teaching of the Apostles, ANF* VIII, pp. 667–72).

Jesus' call to discipleship is best viewed in relation to the farewell meal that would constitute a new covenant, a new exodus, a new People of God. The narratives of Jesus' call to discipleship (Mark 1:16–20; Matt. 4:18–22) were formed in the pattern of Yahweh's call of persons to special mission under the old covenant (Abraham, Moses, David, leaders and prophets; Gen. 22:15; Exod. 19:3; 2 Kings 3:10–13; Joel 2:32).

The calling of the Twelve took place before the resurrection. Their calling was sealed and confirmed by the resurrection. Only after the earthly ministry was completed could the apostles be duly authorized and commissioned to attest Christ's work, especially his resurrection (Matt. 28:18–20; Acts 1:8; Pannenberg, *The Church,* pp. 44–69). The term *apostle* was applied not exclusively to the Twelve but also to Barnabas (1 Cor. 9:5, 6), Junias and Andronicus (Rom. 16:7), Apollos (1 Cor. 4:6, 9), and others, yet it was typically exemplified by the Twelve.

The Gathered and Scattered Ekklēsia.   The very purpose of the coming together of the community is in order that they may be sent. They come together to receive grace, and scatter to declare grace. They gather to hear the Word of God's reconciling love for the fallen world, and scatter to embody that love within that world. *Ekklēsia* exists for the purpose of the apostolate. The faithful now scattered in the world are to be finally gathered in the world to come (Ezek. 34:11–16; Matt. 26:31; John 16:17–33; *Didache* 9–10, *ECF,* pp. 231–32).

The church gathers to praise God, proclaim his Word, baptize, break bread, pray for the world, and enjoy life in communion with the Son. Having gathered, the church "disperses to serve God wherever its members are, at work or play, in private or in the life of society. . . . Their daily action in the world is the church in mission to the world. The quality of their relation with other persons is the measure of the church's fidelity" (United Presbyterian Confession of 1967, *CC,* p. 699).

Apostolic Authorization.   The institution of apostolic emissaries reported by Luke (6:13; 9:10–12; 22:3, 14, 47; Acts 6:2) had its roots in the Old Testament (2 Chron. 17:7–9). The *sheluchim* had the duty of carrying out a mission precisely, as emissaries on behalf of another. The Greek verb *apostello* translates the Hebrew *shalach* (to send). A *shaliach* is the directly authorized agent of another, assigned to a specific task, authorized to engage in a special service or mission (Mark 3:14; 6:7; 11:11; Matt. 10:1–5; 11:1).

Jesus did not passively wait for a miscellany of disciples to choose him. He actively called and selected them. The relation he established with them was not characteristically focused upon his interpretation of Torah as such (as was typical of the relation of rabbi and disciple) but upon his person. He formed the disciples into a unique community of persons in communion with his distinctive theandric personhood (Irenaeus, *Ag. Her.* III.preface, 1, *ANF* I, p. 414; *WL,* pp. 164 ff.). He then transferred his authority to the apostles in amazingly direct terms: "He who listens to you listens to me; he who rejects you rejects me; but he who rejects me rejects him who sent me" (Luke 10:16; cf. John 15:20; Schmaus, *Dogma* 4, p. 27).

Why Twelve?   The Twelve were chosen by Jesus, prepared by him, and accompanied him throughout his journeys in order to be able to attest his earthly ministry during its entire course of development. They were initiated by him into the mysteries of the coming kingdom (Mark 3:34). Some accompanied him to the Mount of Transfiguration. Only the Twelve were present at the farewell paschal meal.

The number twelve had special significance analogous to the twelve tribes descending from the twelve patriarchs (Matt. 19:28; Acts 26:7) whose restoration was expected in the messianic time. The twelve patriarchs prefigured the new community of faith, the new covenant, the restoration of Israel. When Judas, one of the original Twelve, became apostate, he was quickly replaced so that the number of first-generation apostles would again be complete (Acts 1:12–26). The Twelve were sent out to proclaim the coming kingdom, heal, cleanse lepers, drive out demons (Mark 6:7–13; Matt. 10:5–8; Schmaus, *Dogma* 4, pp. 24–26).

Apostolicity as Defining Mark of the Church.   Apostolicity remains a defining mark of the church of each generation (Roman Council of A.D. 680, *SCD* 288, p. 112; Leo IX, *Symbol of Faith, SCD* 347, p. 141; Council of Lyons II, *SCD* 464–68, pp. 184–85). It is an evidence by which one tests whether the attestors bear true or false witness—by asking whether their testimony is apostolic, whether it teaches what the apostles taught (Gal. 1:8, 9; Journet, *CWI,* pp. 526 ff.). It is inadequate, however, to test the apostolicity of a community merely by its language, for its language may sound apostolic without bearing the fruits of apostolicity (Jerome, *Letters* 84, *NPNF* 2 VI, pp. 175–81).

The church that forgets Hebrew scripture and the apostolic interpretation of it cannot be the apostolic church. Those who purport to be Christian teachers but bear testimony contrary to apostolic teaching fail to display a distinctive mark that defines the church. An alleged *ekklēsia* that lacks the mark of apostolicity might continue to live parasitically off of the vital residual wisdoms of the apostolic tradition while ignoring that tradition practically (Irenaeus, *Ag. Her.* III.1–4, *LCC* I, pp. 370–77).

The church is described by Paul as the pillar and ground of the truth (1 Tim. 3:15), God's own appointed means of upholding Christian truth in the world. Christ entrusted the keys of discipline to the apostles and their successors, authorized the great commission, and sent the Spirit to empower their mission (Matt. 16:19; Tertullian, *Prescription Ag. Her.* 20, 32, *APT*, pp. 469, 481). The church is "apostolic because it has been transmitted to us by the Apostles and their duly consecrated successors" (*Eastern Orthodox Catechism* 194, p. 47).

Accurate Recollection

Accurate recollection of apostolic testimony was understood to be undergirded and ensured by the guidance of the Holy Spirit. Subsequent generations of attestors are perennially pledged and bound to recall accurately and noninvasively the salvation event as received (1 Cor. 9:1, 2; Gal. 1:19, 20; 1 Thess. 2:7).

None were chosen in the first generation of the apostolate without having accompanied Jesus personally during his entire earthly journey (Acts 1:21, 22), and without having met the risen Lord, and without being personally commissioned by him to testify to him (Luke 24:48; Acts 13:31; 2:32; 3:15; 10:39–43). These elements were considered constitutive of the first generation of the apostolate, whose recollection subsequent generations of the apostolate would transmit.

Eyewitness Testimony Required Faithful, Accurate Transmission. Though a direct eyewitness to an unrepeatable event cannot be cloned or reduplicated, a subsequent reporter may trustably attest to the truthfulness of a previous eyewitness. All Christian testimony and experience stands in this sort of succession (Origen, *First Principles,* preface, *ANF* IV, p. 239). The disciples at second hand (noneyewitnesses) do not receive a new, separable, improved, or different revelation but attest to the original revelation centered on the events of cross and resurrection and upon personal meeting with the theandric mediator (Kierkegaard, *PF; CUP*).

The task of the apostolic successor is not to improve upon the message or embellish it or add to it one's own spin or personal tilt or idiosyncratic twist, but rather simply to remember and attest it accurately, credibly, intelligibly, contextually. To assist in correct remembering, the Holy Spirit has enabled the apostolic testimony to be written down in a canonically received body of writings consensually received as normative apostolic teaching. Amid each cultural variation, subsequent apostolic witnesses are solemnly pledged and bound to the apostolic canon as norm of Christian teaching. Paul made a distinction between his own opinions, which were to be duly considered, and those received from the apostles, which were to be obeyed (1 Cor. 1:1; 4:1–7; 7:12, 40).

Antiquity and Apostolicity. Antiquity and apostolicity are closely intertwined criteria (Vincent of Lérins, *Comm.* 27–33, *FC* 7, pp. 320–32). For how could the apostolic message be adequate if it only reached back a decade or a century? Or if it only reached back to the ninth decade of the first century, lacking earlier roots? To be apostolic, the apostolic tradition must date back to the earliest eyewitnessing attestors of God's own coming.

This is why the appeal to apostolicity is by definition an appeal to antiquity in the Christian tradition (Luther, *Ag. Hanswurst, LW* 39, pp. 197–213). The appeal to novelty is viewed as *hairesis*, an alternative choice different from the prevailing apostolic tradition (Tertullian, *Prescription Ag. Her.* 4–6, *ANF* III, pp. 244–46; Vincent of Lérins, *Comm.* 4–10, *NPNF* 2 XI, pp. 133–38). If "what issues from the Apostles is from the beginning," reasoned Tertullian, then "what is earlier is truer" (*Ag. Marcion* IV.5, *ECF,* p. 139; *ANF* III, p. 349).

Paul's Special Apostolate to the Nations. Paul did not understand his own apostolate to be separable from the pre-Pauline tradition, as is evident from this admonition: "But even if we, or an angel from heaven, should preach to you a gospel contrary to that which we preached to you, let him be accursed" (Gal. 1:8, RSV).

Paul did not invent a new gospel, but merely carried it to a new audience. Paul's gospel was an explication of pre-Pauline teaching of the Jerusalem church, which he viewed as the binding norm for his own mission and proclamation (Gal. 1:13–20; 2:2; 1 Cor. 11:23–29; 15:5). Though Paul did not accompany Jesus throughout his earthly ministry, he did meet him personally on the road to Damascus. Paul understood himself to be an apostle directly called by the risen Lord (Gal. 1:1).

Paul's apostolate was specifically directed to the Gentiles, whereas the pre-Pauline apostolate had been originally addressed to the Jews (Acts 15). The apostles affirmed Paul's commission to the Gentiles (Gal. 2:7). Paul demonstrated his loyalty to the Jerusalem church by collecting for its poor (1 Cor. 16:1–3; 2 Cor. 8; Rom. 15:26–28) and by returning there, especially for major feast days (Acts 18:21; 20:16). In describing the gospel the Corinthians had received, he made it clear that he had only delivered to them the tradition he had received from the pre-Pauline apostolate, that Christ died for our sin, was buried, was raised, and appeared "to all the apostles." "Last of all, as to one untimely born, he appeared also to me. For I am the least of the apostles, unfit to be called an apostle, because I persecuted the church of God" (1 Cor. 15:7–9).

Adaptability Without Dilution. The apostolate guards the original testimony without ceasing to apply it meaningfully to the context of local and prevailing conditions. The preaching must occur in a particular language using culture-specific symbol systems in a definite economic and political order, yet without ceasing to affirm the original apostolic teaching (2 Cor. 4).

As with catholicity, apostolicity does not imply a rigid lack of adaptability to varied culture formations. The glory of the apostolic tradition is precisely its ability to meet, flexibly confront, and dialogue with different cultures, to become all things to all men and women on behalf of Christ. Apostolicity is not incapable of responsiveness, but attests a living body of Christ that lives with each new form of cultural life emergent in human history (Eph. 2:19–3:1). Because histories change people, and because the apostolic testimony must be attested in ever-new historical situations, it is a necessary feature of the apostolic tradition that it both guard the original testimony and make it understandable in these new cultural settings. Failing either is to default on the apostolic tradition. Far from implying immobility, apostolicity requires constant adaptation of the ancient apostolic testimony to new historical situations and languages, yet without changing or modifying or diluting the primitive witness (Irenaeus, *Ag. Her.* III.3, *ANF* I, pp. 415–16).

Some complain that if the church focuses attention on its own apostolicity it will tend to forget its mission to the world, as if caring for its own identity would stand as a threat to expressing its identity in mission. Any notion of apostolicity that fails to engage in mission is a misconceived apostolicity. The subtler danger is the failure to get one's own identity straight as one moves toward the ever-evolving world in mission. To transform the world, the sent church must first understand what it means to be the church, else it simply becomes a pale reflection of the world.

The idea of apostolicity has elicited a controversial set of issues, the details of which still divide Catholic, Protestant, and Orthodox traditions. Irenic theology seeks to articulate a common view that all parties of the controversy can find acceptable.

Apostolicity and Succession

Intrinsically connected with the idea of apostolicity is that of succession, though it has been since the sixteenth century intensely debated whether this necessarily implied a literal, linear, tactile, historical succession. The basic affirmation of the apostolicity of the church does not specifically require or supply a particular theory of how that apostolicity is transmitted intergenerationally. Regardless of how the succession is viewed, whether symbolic or actual, the line of succession between the apostles and present apostolic witness is conceived as a continuous line of testimony sustained by the Spirit (*Didache* 11.1, 2; 13.2; 15.1).

From the day of Pentecost onward the disciples "continued steadfastly in the apostles' doctrine and fellowship" (Acts 2:42 KJV). The implication is that the continuing church holds the same doctrines that the apostles taught, as witnesses chosen, claimed, and addressed personally by the Lord (2 Tim. 1:12–14).

This apostolic teaching is sufficient for salvation, and remains pertinent to each successive historical period without addition, modification, or imagined improvement. The church is apostolic insofar as it stands in historic continuity with this primitive *ekklēsia* (Eph. 2:20; Rev. 21:14; Matt. 16:18; Jerome, *Ag. Jovian* I.26, *NPNF* 2 VI, pp. 365–66; Augustine, *Exposition on Psalms*, Ps. 86, *NPNF* 1 VIII, pp. 409–19; Gregory the Great, *Moralia on Job* XXVIII.5, *MPL* 76, pp. 455–56).

Succession and Canon.   Christianity adopted from Judaism the practice of designating a canon—a list of sacred writings consensually received by the worshiping community as authorized teaching and reliable recollections of the history of revelation (Irenaeus, *Ag. Her.* III.2.2–4, *ANF* I, pp. 414–17; Tertullian, *Prescription Ag. Her.* 19, *ANF* III, p. 251; Eusebius, *CH* V.20.6, *NPNF* 2 I, p. 268; *HCCC*, p. 424; Synod of Laodicea).

Problems of interpretation emerged when alternative interpreters used the same words of scripture but with different, nonconsensual meanings. This necessitated a conciliar process that sorted out consensual meanings from arbitrary interpretations (Athanasius, *Defence of the Nicene Council, NPNF* 2 IV, pp. 149 ff.; cf. *NPNF* 2 XIV passim). A criterion had to be found for the right interpretation of scriptures that would make clear that the heretics had no legitimate right to distort the scriptures (Tertullian, *Prescription Ag. Her.* 15–19, *ANF* III, pp. 250–51; cf. Irenaeus, *Ag. Her.* I.8–10, *ANF* I, pp. 326–32), though each of their distortions proved providential in clarifying the mind of the believing church. The core criterion was liturgical: the baptismal formula as summarily explicated in the rule of faith and further interpreted by ecumenical conciliar consent, all of which were finally accountable to the written word of apostolic testimony.

The church hears the testimony to the resurrection only through the apostolic tradition. There is no other pathway back to the risen Lord that might bypass the apostles and their successors (Jude 17). There is no apostolic witness without the *ekklēsia*'s canon and transmission of apostolic writings. Church traditions emerge only as applications and interpretations of the apostolic witness. "Apostolic succession is therefore a question of a continual and living confrontation of the Church and all its members with this apostolic witness; apostolic succession is fulfilled when this witness is heard, respected, believed, confessed and followed" (Küng, *TC*, p. 356).

It is primarily the whole church, and not merely discrete individuals, that succeeds the apostles and embodies apostolicity. It is the whole church catholic and not merely a fragment of it that is the temple of the Spirit, built on the foundation of the apostles (Eph. 2:20).

Whether Succession Is a Correlate of Baptismal Confession. The ancient Christian exegetes consensually taught that the most condensed expression of apostolic teaching was the ancient baptismal confession that could be traced directly to Christ himself (Matt. 28:19–20; Irenaeus, *Ag. Her.* III.preface, *ANF* I, p. 414, cf. 526; Tertullian, *Prescription Ag. Her.* 20, 21, *ANF* III, p. 252). This became the core of the rule of faith that later became the received text of the Apostles' Creed.

In order to support the authenticity of this core, it was thought necessary to clarify the unbroken succession of overseers in the "mother churches," especially in Rome, where believers from all places had gathered early under Pauline and Petrine leadership (Hegisippus, in Eusebius *CH* IV.22.1–3; Irenaeus, *Ag. Her.* III.3; V.20.1).

Tertullian challenged the heretics to produce their own lists of direct succession of *episkopoi* in such a way as to make it clear that their predecessors were in direct succession to the apostles who accurately reported the events of God's saving work in the Son. The principle: "Whatever is the first is true, and whatever is later is adulterated" (*Ag. Praxeas* 2, 20). "It is because of this that these churches are reckoned as apostolic, as being the offspring of apostolic churches. Every kind of thing must needs be classed with its origin. And so the churches, many and great as they are, are identical with that one primitive Church issuing from the Apostles, for thence they are all derived. So all are primitive and all apostolic, while all are one. And their unity is proved by the peace they share" (*Prescription Ag. Her.* 20, *ECF,* p. 138; cf. *ANF* III, p. 252). This concern for direct historic succession was intensified by the challenge of Gnosticism in the second century, which threatened to rob the church of her distinctive language (Apostolic Constitutions VII.IV.4, *ANF* VII, p. 478).

The Need for a Succession of Apostolic Teachers: Whether There Is a Linear Link of Episkopoi.   The apostles passed this ministry to the next generation, and that generation passed it to the next, and so on, to fulfill this ministry in each succeeding historical situation in perpetuity and without interruption until the Lord's return. The necessity of some sort of succession to the apostles grows out of the continuing temporal nature of the apostolic commission, which would extend "to the very end of the age" (Matt. 28:20; Origen, *Ag. Celsus* V.12, *ANF* IV, p. 548). It assumes the finitude and physical death of all particular personal witnesses.

It might seem that the authentication of the ministry of any succeeding generation would depend entirely upon the faithfulness and accountability and accurate testimony of generations bridging from the original Twelve. This leads to the anxiety that each generation of Christian memory might be only one generation from extinction. But this anxiety tends to forget the promise of the Spirit and to remember only human forgetfulness. Rather, the continuity depends upon the continuing calling and awakening work of the Spirit (Barth, *CD* II/2, pp. 430 ff., IV/3, 208 ff.; Rahner, *RR*, pp. 289–96).

The apostolate does not seize this testimony as if a matter to be remolded in human hands, but only speaks in response to God's own speech, learning obedience by suffering as did the Son (Heb. 5:8; Phil. 2; Barth, *CD* IV/2, pp. 304 ff.). "No one takes this honor upon himself; he must be called by God, just as Aaron was. So Christ also did not take upon himself the glory of becoming a high priest. But God said to him, 'You are my Son,'" who "although he was a son, he learned obedience from what he suffered" (Heb. 5:4, 5, 8; Calvin, *Comm.* XXII, pp. 116–19).

Episkopos *and Historic Succession.*   One crucial way by which this succession has in fact been visibly and plausibly transmitted through its long history is by means of an historical succession of overseers, or *episkopoi.* But the linear act of historical succession as such does not of itself suffice to guarantee authentic testimony, otherwise every minister ordained in the historical succession of the apostles would have been faithful to the apostolic witness, and this is not the case (Augustine, *Correction of the Donatists, NPNF* 1 IV, pp. 633–51).

Rather, to the historical succession must be added the grace of accurate recollection and obedience to the original apostolic testimony, and the grace-enabled determination to guard and transmit it without novel accretions or substitutions. An ambassador duly authorized and sent on behalf of an official authority who changes the message en route, who revises, innovates, or substitutes or supposedly improves upon the meaning of the original message so that it means something else, is not a faithful ambassador (Gal. 1:1–10; 2 Cor. 5:20).

What the apostolate is to the universal church, the eldership is to the regional and local church, typically assuming the *episkopos* as a type or paradigm of the shepherding Christ (John 10:1–16; 1 Tim. 3:2; 1 Pet. 2:25; Ignatius, *Trallians* 2.1; 3.1; *Magnesians* 2; 6.1; *Smyrnaeans* 8.1). Every genuine local expression of the Christian community is a refraction that mirrors the whole body of Christ in time and eternity. The attentive but unseen overseer of the community, Christ, is visibly present through the attentiveness of the overseeing *episkopos* (Ignatius, *Magnesians* 3.2; Rom. 9.1).

Whether Apostolicity Depends upon the Absolute Indefectibility of Any Individual Minister.   The mark of apostolicity requires not only the tactile laying on of hands in due order, but the due transmission of apostolic teaching. The act of ordination points beyond itself to the task of transmitting the sacred deposit of faith to succeeding generations (2 Tim. 1:14; Irenaeus, *Ag. Her.* III.4, *ANF* I, pp. 416–17). This guarding and transmitting activity is entrusted prototypically to the *episkopoi* (Ignatius of Antioch, *Eph.* 6, *ANF* I, pp. 51–52; Hooker, *LEP* VII.4). The *presbuteroi* (elders) have specific responsibilities in implementing this activity locally. It is finally to the whole lay apostolate that the transmitting action is committed. If it should happen that on a remote island no pastor or bishop in the apostolic tradition remained alive, then the guarding of the apostolic tradition would devolve directly upon the laity (Luther, *WLS* 111–18, III, pp. 40–42), as it in fact did in Japan under the shogunate, in the Stalinist Ukraine, and during the Chinese Cultural Revolution.

Although grace is offered in ordination, the bare event of ordination in historical succession to the apostles does not of itself ensure that the apostolic testimony will be rightly guarded or effectively transmitted. As parents may give birth to a genetically defective child, so may the church ordain defective *episkopoi* or *presbuteroi*. If it happens that the word is not preached adequately or the sacraments duly offered to the people, the apostolic ministry has thereby been temporarily but never irreversibly defaulted. Whether a particular order and organization is necessary to the being (*esse*, essence) of the church (Ignatius) or the well-being of the church (*bene esse*, Cambridge Platform, *CC*, p. 392) remains a debated point.

If the apostolicity of the church becomes at some particular time temporarily defective, the Spirit can be supplicated and counted upon to revive the church in apostolic teaching in due time. Here John the Baptist's maxim pertains: "And do not think you can say to yourselves, 'We have Abraham as our father.' I tell you that out of these stones God can raise up children for Abraham" (Matt. 3:9; John Chrysostom, *Hom. on Matt.* XI, *NPNF* 1 X, pp. 69–71).

Protestant Reservations Concerning Historic Succession.   Apostolicity is viewed by Protestants as an indispensable mark of the church in the sense of the pure preaching of the word. Yet many reject the historic episcopate as an indispensable mark of apostolicity on the grounds that the New Testament probably knew nothing of a diocesan episcopacy and regarded elders and bishops as the same office (Acts 20:17, 28; Titus 1:5, 7; 1 Tim. 3:1, 8; 1 Pet. 5:1; *Didache* 15, *ECW*, p. 235). Timothy was ordained by presbyters (1 Tim. 4:14).

As late as Jerome, the patriarch of Alexandria was consecrated by presbyters: "For even at Alexandria from the time of Mark the Evangelist until the episcopates of Heraclas and Dionysius the presbyters always named as bishop one of their own number chosen by themselves and set in a more exalted position. . . . For what function, excepting ordination, belongs to a bishop that does not also belong to a presbyter?" (Jerome, *Epist.* 146.1, *NPNF* 2 VI, p. 288; cf. D. Stone, *EVO*, pp. 46, 47; Gore, *C&M*, pp. 115–30).

Paul admonished the elders of Ephesus, "Keep watch over yourselves and all the flock of which the Holy Spirit has made you overseers. Be shepherds of the church of God, which he bought with his own blood" (Acts 20:28). "And the things you have heard me say in the presence of many witnesses entrust to reliable men who will also be qualified to teach others" (2 Tim. 2:2). Paul instructed Timothy that the *episkopos* must be "able to teach," able to "take care of God's church," "not be a recent convert," and must guard the deposit of faith and pass it on by appointing elders to maintain and proclaim it (1 Tim. 3:2–7; 2 Tim. 1:14; Titus

1:5−9). What is commended here is clearly a succession of teaching, but it remains controverted as to whether it is a linear, tactile, historic succession. Reformed interpreters view apostolic succession more in terms of contemporary obedience than linear historic succession: "The church maintains continuity with the apostles and with Israel by faithful obedience to his [Christ's] call" (United Presbyterian Church Confession of 1967, *BOConf.* II, a, 1).

Whether Linear Succession Can Be Established Historically.   Against these objections, there remains a steady tradition that holds (as stated by the *Confession of Dositheus*) that it was the Lord himself who appointed James, and "after James another succeeded, and then another, until our own times. And, therefore, Tertullian in his Epistle to Papianus called all Bishops the Apostles' successors," and in this he was preceded by Clement of Rome and Ignatius of Antioch. In the same way "Andrew seated Stachys on the Throne of Constantinople, in his own stead," and Mark became bishop of Alexandria, and Evodius of Antioch by apostolic order. Without this apostolic ordering, "all the priests in the world could not exercise the pastorate" (Dositheus X, *CC*, p. 493; cf. Ignatius, *Magnesians* 2, 6, 13; *Philadelphians* 4, 7, 10; Eusebius, *CH* I.1, III.4, *NPNF* 2 I, pp. 81−82, 136−38).

Apostolic succession is viewed by Eastern Orthodox teaching as "the unbroken connection of a hierarchy with Christ and the Apostles through the Sacrament of holy Ordination" (*Eastern Orthodox Catechism* 197, p. 47). In the Roman tradition, ordained ministers are successors of the apostles "because they have received their power of orders by valid consecration through an unbroken line of successors of the apostles, and have received their power of jurisdiction through their union" with the successors of the apostles (*Baltimore Catechism,* p. 113).

The church, as conceived in Catholic and Orthodox and Anglican traditions, consists in churches shepherded by bishops whose consecration goes back in linear succession to the apostles and whose task is the transmission of apostolic testimony. Hence "historic episcopate" is viewed as a mark of the church, implying that only those ministers who have been ordained in that succession are aptly and fittingly sent as *presbuteroi*. Ministries that have emerged, often for legitimate reasons, apart from this formal succession and at times in protest against it, are not to be regarded *prima facie* as false but as ambiguously manifesting one of the marks of the church, according to this view.

Ignatius of Antioch is the predominant early witness to historic episcopal succession as essential to the church (yet debates remain as to whether the text of Ignatius has been tampered with). Ignatius established the principle that the one episcopate was the bond of unity of the diverse, multicultural *ekklēsia*. The chief minister was to be the guarantor and guardian of order and true doctrine against false teachers and divisiveness. He viewed the ministry of *episkopoi* as belonging to the essence of the church and as based upon dominical and apostolic authority (*Trallians* 2, 3; *Eph.* 5, 6) and the validity of Eucharist as dependent upon the authenticity and continuity of episcopal oversight (*Smyrnaeans* 8; cf. Cyprian, *On the Unity of the Church, ANF* V, pp. 421−29). He concluded that *episkopos* is so intrinsic to *ekklēsia*, and *ekklēsia* to *episkopos*, that if anyone should disjoin from apostolic oversight, he or she thereby would elect to disavow the *ekklēsia* (Ignatius, *Letters, ANF* I, pp. 50−96).

Eusebius specifically sought to trace the lines of apostolic succession, but found or left some matters doubtful (Eusebius, *CH* I.1, III.4, *NPNF* 2 I, pp. 81−82, 136−

38; cf. Kirk, *The Apostolic Ministry;* Gore, *The Ministry of the Christian Church).* The accounts given by Eusebius are probably reliable generally, and correspond with what we know of the developing organization of the community at the time of Paul (Rom. 12:6–8; 1 Cor. 12:29–30; 1 and 2 Timothy, Titus).

"We are in a position to enumerate those who were by the apostles instituted bishop in the churches, and the successions of these men to our own times. . . . The blessed apostles, then, having founded and built up the church [at Rome], committed into the hands of Linus the office of the episcopate. Of this Linus, Paul makes mention in the Epistles to Timothy. To him succeeded Anacletus; and after him, in the third place from the apostles Clement was allotted the bishopric, who had seen the blessed apostles, and had associated with them, and had the preaching of the apostles still echoing in his ears, and their tradition before his eyes. . . . To this Clement there succeeded Evarestus. Alexander followed Evarestus; then sixth from the apostles, Sixtus was appointed. . . . And this is most abundant proof that there is one and the same vivifying faith which has been preserved in the church from the apostles until now" (Irenaeus, *Ag. Her.* III.3.2, 3, *NE*, pp. 118–19). Irenaeus, upon whom this argument has so often depended, attested that he himself had seen and met Polycarp, who lived to be very old, who departed this life in martyrdom "having always taught the things which he had learned from the apostles, and which the Church has handed down" (Irenaeus, *Ag. Her.* III.3.4, *ANF* I, p. 416).

Of the perennial vitality of the apostolic tradition, Hall wrote, "Nowhere in human history can we find any parallel to the uninterrupted maintenance in many lands, through twelve or thirteen centuries, of a working polity so complex and delicately adjusted, and yet so well determined and coherent, as this one is. And at the end of four additional centuries its sway is still as complete as ever in three-fourths of Christendom" (*DT* VIII, p. 153).

Those who challenge historic episcopal succession point to "the heresy of popes like Liberius and Honorius, which was condemned by the Council of Constantinople in 680, and to the infamies of popes like John IX, XIII, XXII, and Alexander VI" (Banks, *MCD*, p. 294). Some Protestants are tempted to imagine that they can spring, as with seven-league boots, from the twentieth to the first century and back again without any contamination by any other century. Some advocates of linear succession are tempted to imagine that all they need is the historic succession itself to guarantee the grace of ordination. Each needs the other. Extreme advocates of both positions will find needed correctives among the wiser advocates within their own traditions.

Laying On of Hands, Apostolicity, and Episcopacy. The received means of passing on or devolution of intergenerational ministry is by the laying on of hands with prayer by the power of the Spirit. The *episkopoi,* by which the grace of this succession is ordinarily maintained, ordered, directed, and symbolized, is not independent of or external to the body of Christ, but an expression of the body of Christ (Ignatius, *Smyrnaeans* 8–9).

The *episkopoi* do not *de novo* call forth or give birth to the body, but the body needs, calls forth, and requires these supervising functions. The episcopacy often appears in early Christian literature as the ordinary expression of the organic and historical nature of the church. Yet even this ordinary expression admits of extraordinary and legitimate exceptions—Clare of Assisi, Dame Juliana of Norwich,

Cranmer, Roger Williams, Phoebe Palmer, and Martin Luther King, Jr., are examples. If an unbroken linear historic succession is required to validate ordination, many Protestant pastors lack valid ordination. Viewed from the vantage point of historic succession, the validity of Anglican orders depends on how one answers the question of whether Archbishop Matthew Parker's consecration of 1559 was valid (Cooke, *Historic Episcopate;* cf. Kirk, *The Apostolic Ministry); just as* the validity of Methodist orders depends upon how one answers the question of whether the line from the Anglican succession to Wesley to Coke and Asbury was arguable as a special case contingent upon the continued absence of ordered Anglican sacraments in the post-Revolutionary American situation (J. Wesley, *Letters,* "To 'Our Brethren in America,'" *JWO,* p. 83; cf. Lord Peter King, *An Enquiry into the Constitution, Discipline, Unity and Worship of the Primitive Church;* cf. E. Stillingfleet, *Irenicum).* Different communities of recollection answer these questions very differently.

Although subject to abuse and corruption, the principle of historic succession has proven to be enormously valuable in the history of the church, especially in times of persecution and social upheaval. Those who especially remember its abuses do well also to remember its times of courage and capacity for *marturia.* Those who best celebrate its normative character also recognize its corruptibility.

Apostolicity as a Principle of Criticism.   Apostolicity itself is a critical principle that brings its own acid "hermeneutic of suspicion" to modern ideological critics. What is apostolic we let the apostles tell us; we do not tell the apostles. If the record of their testimony is fundamentally defective, there is no way that the church can begin to learn the truth, for the truth about Christ is attested only by original eyewitnesses and their trustworthy attestors, and these are called the apostolate. Surely the Spirit would not leave such an important matter up to the jaded imagination of form-critics (Maier, *The End of the Historical Critical Method;* Wink, *BHT*).

Contemporary witnesses are called to assess every subsequent testimony by its correspondence with the original testimony of the apostles. The working premise is that the Holy Spirit would not allow a truly debilitating or defective testimony to be transmitted to the church. Like music, the words of the apostles are savored and enjoyed by the remembering *ekklēsia* (John Chrysostom, *Hom. on the Statues, NPNF* 1 IX, p. 331).

When criticism is working speculatively, as if historians could be the judges and arbiters of the documents of testimony rather than the text being the judge and constrainer of the interpreter, then there is danger that pretentious criticism may set itself between the apostolic testimony and contemporary hearers, as if to say, "Sorry, you can meet the real apostles only if we historians introduce you to them." This premise has led to the temporary expanding employment of a knowledge elite, but hardly to improved historical inquiry. Good textual inquiry does not lord it over the texts but is called to listen to them.

Does modern historical criticism represent a devastating challenge to the principle of apostolicity? Briefly answered, no. When criticism is working well, so that an orthodox skepticism places in question the speculations of the historical critics, there is nothing to fear from historical inquiry into the tradition of transmission of apostolic testimony. There is only the task of improving it and bringing it closer to the facts of the Incarnate, risen Lord and his body the Church.

Questions of Petrine and Roman Leadership

The charge given to the whole apostolate was culminated and focused particularly upon Peter ("the rock"), who from the outset seems to have been principal spokesman for the Twelve (Mark 8:29; Matt. 18:21; Luke 9:5; 12:41; John 6:67, 68). Regularly listed first among the apostles (Mark 3:16–19; Matt. 10:1–4; Luke 6:12–16; Acts 1:13), Peter was chief among witnesses to the resurrection (1 Cor. 15:5). In crucial references, Peter appears to be called to a special role of leadership in the apostolate (Matt. 16:13–19, Luke 22:29–32; John 21:15–17). That Peter was leader of the Twelve seems clear from Paul's references to him and from many other New Testament references. Paul carried out the mission to the Gentiles that Peter led and interpreted (Acts 10–15).

Exegesis of Matthew 16:13–19. This passage is found in all ancient manuscripts. That the text has Palestinian provenance seems implied in the Aramaic tone of its language (Simon bar Jonah, and the metaphors of binding and loosing). Simon was doubtless first called by the Aramaic form Kepha, and only later by the Greek form Cephas, which was Paul's usual designation of him (Gal. 1:18; 2:7–14; 1 Cor. 1:12; 3:22).

The "rock" to which Jesus referred in giving Simon the surname Peter was the revelation that he acknowledged when he confessed, "You are the Christ, the Son of the living God" (Matt. 16:16). Jesus observed that "flesh and blood has not revealed this to you, but my Father who is in heaven" (Matt. 16:17, RSV). "Now this name of Peter was given him by the Lord, and that in a figure, that he should signify the Church. For seeing that Christ is the rock (Petra), Peter is the Christian people. For the rock (Petra) is the original name. Therefore Peter is so called from the rock; not the rock from Peter; as Christ is not called Christ from the Christian, but the Christian from Christ," as if to say "'upon this Rock' which thou has confessed ... 'will I build my Church.' I will build thee upon Myself, not Myself upon thee" (Augustine, *Sermons on NT Lessons* XXVI, *NPNF* 1 VI, p. 340; Matt. 16:17–19).

In being given a new name by Jesus, Simon Peter was given a new apostolic role as "rock," as chief confessor of God's singular revelation. Receiving a new name in biblical reference implied receiving a new life, a new identity, a new calling, a new responsibility (cf. Gen. 3:20; 4:1; 5:29; Isa. 17:14; 62:2; Hos. 2:16–18).

During the entire period between incarnation and final judgment the *ekklēsia* is being built, analogous to the gradual construction of a building (John 2:19; Mark 14:58; 15:29). To have stability in space and durability in time it must be built upon a confessional rock. That rock is the revelation Peter attested. Even the gates of hell will not prevail against this testimony to this revelation, Jesus promised. The *ekklēsia* is thus protected by the Spirit not from mutability but from absolute defection. Christ himself is finally the foundation, the rock, upon which the church is built.

Why Peter, and not another? The answer can only lie in the mystery of God's own choosing. The same question can be asked of Israel or Moses or Abraham or Jeremiah—why these and not others? The Hebraic answer is simply that Yahweh chose them. The *why* remains a gracious mystery.

It was specifically to Peter that Jesus said, "Simon, Simon, Satan has asked to sift you as wheat. But I have prayed for you, Simon, that your faith may not fail.

And when you have turned back, strengthen your brothers" (Luke 22:32; Henry, *CWB* V, pp. 812–13). Having been tested, in due course Peter did strengthen the faith of the other apostles. Before this occurred, the divine economy permitted the trial of Jesus to become a temptation to shake the faith of all the disciples. In Jesus' prayer that Peter's faith not fail, the narrative seems to suggest that the future of the whole apostolate in some sense hinged upon the steadiness of Peter. Whether his faith proved to be firm (as a "rock") was decisive as to whether the faith of the others would survive rigorous testing. Peter was kept by the Son's intercession from falling permanently.

Peter's Leadership of the Apostles. In John 21:15–19, Jesus summoned Peter three times to "feed my lambs." Peter's threefold commission served to invert and transpose his previous threefold denial of Christ. The threefold repetition of the question and answer was a formula of installation by which authority was transferred in a legal and juridical manner. The analogy is of the owner of the flock turning over complete responsibility for the feeding and protection of the flock to one shepherd who would ensure proper order for other shepherds to continue the task (John Chrysostom, *Hom. on John* LXXXVIII, *NPNF* 1 XVI, pp. 331–33). The passing of shepherding authority is traditionally symbolized by the passing of the staff.

Peter indeed is recalled in the New Testament as leading the apostles in the preaching of the gospel, in courage to face persecution, in the disciplining of erroneous faith and practice, and in the mission beyond Palestine (Acts 1:15–26; 2:14–40; 5:1–11; 8:14–25; 9:32–42). No leadership decision of Peter's was more far-reaching than his baptism of the family of Cornelius, the Gentile centurion in Caesarea (Acts 10:1–48), wherein the mission of the church to Gentiles was first established as a precedent.

Peter played the leading role at the Apostolic Council in Jerusalem presided over by James (Acts 15), where the decision was made not to impose circumcision on Gentile Christians. Even in the conflict between Peter and Paul in Antioch, where Paul says he "opposed him to his face, because he was clearly in the wrong" (Gal. 2:11; cf. Gal. 2:11–21), still it was not Barnabas whom Paul rebuked but Peter, thereby once again indicating his role as leader of the apostolate (Schmaus, *Dogma* 4, pp. 33–40).

The Historical Importance of Rome. Rome was the crossroads of the known world. It was understandable that the diverse communities of faith spread out among many nations would look to the leadership in Rome for normative patterns accountable to the apostolic tradition. There can be little doubt that from the days of Peter and Paul, the church at Rome was exercising wide influence on the church in other locations (Irenaeus, *Ag. Her.* III.3, *ANF* I, p. 415). Both Peter and Paul had led and instructed the Roman church, and according to tradition both were martyred in Rome. Rome was the only apostolically founded church in the western Mediterranean, and the one that maintained an unsullied apostolic tradition, in some ways, longer than some Eastern sees.

It is not surprising that the Roman bishop would be looked to for guidance of the whole church in a manner parallel to the way each bishop guided a diocesan church. Ecclesial disputes were referred to Rome for settlement just as legal questions of empire were referred to civil authorities of Rome. Matthew 16:18 was viewed as granting authority to the successors of Peter. In time Eastern Orthodoxy would view the Roman See as schismatic.

Augustine was responsible for firming up many teachings of the doctrine of the church that had more loosely anteceded him: church as *corpus mixtum* of tares and wheat, the church as necessary for salvation, sacraments as conveying grace to the elect, hierarchical organization, and especially the primacy of Rome. Augustine's influence would continue not only through the medieval period but into Protestantism.

In the medieval period hierarchical authority became more elaborately institutionalized as ecclesiastical feudalism developed. Bishops gained secular jurisdictions from state powers, and these coercive powers were grossly abused. Hildebrand (Gregory VII, 1020–85) claimed that the pope had power to depose other bishops, and extraordinary theocratic temporal powers, such as the power to influence and unmake kings. The correction of these abuses would lead in due time to the Protestant Reformation, which was as much an ecclesiological as a soteriological reversal.

The Reformation Critique.   The Reformers held the church accountable to the written word of apostolic testimony. The power of the keys was assumed to be the pardon announced in the preaching of the gospel. The universal priesthood of Christ was understood to be shared by all believers, whose representatives are ordained ministers. Where the gospel is rightly preached and the Sacrament duly administered there is the one true church (Augsburg Confession; Thirty-nine Articles).

Protestants ask why if Rome was the center of Christianity Constantine moved the capital from Rome to Constantinople in 330? And why canon 28 of Chalcedon granted "equal privileges" to Constantinople (*NPNF* 2 XIV, p. 287)? And why a collegial rather than a monarchical episcopacy was evident as late as canon 6 of Nicaea (*NPNF* 2 XIV, p. 15).

Presbyterial governance sought to affirm apostolic succession, but located the succession in correct belief rather than episcopal office. It emphasized faithfulness to apostolic tradition rather than literal historical succession (Calvin, *Inst.* 4.2.2–3). Congregationalists viewed the congregation as the basis for the authority of ministry to be ordained by the *laos* in a particular locality. "The visible Church came to be identified by many with a congeries of denominational Churches, which were apt to be regarded one and all as volunteer human organizations, and were often governed on puritan lines, as rightly excluding those who fail fully to conform to current ideals of Christian conduct" (Hall, *DT* VII, p. 50).

Meanwhile the Anglican Reformation continued to hold that there is no true church apart from the historical succession of bishops; that Eucharist administered by priests in this succession imparts grace to the church; and that the ecumenical councils of the undivided church taught reliable orthodox Christian teaching (Thirty-nine Articles, *CC*, pp. 273–78; Lambeth Quadrilateral, *COC* III, pp. 947–54).

Unity and Succession as a Recurrent Tension.   In ancient Israel there was only one temple. Under such conditions, there could be no schism. The high priest represented the unity of the covenant people of God. After the Babylonian captivity, worship in the synagogues became more diffused and localized. The struggle between the synagogues' diversity and the primitive unity of the covenant people was destined to be played out again in Christianity.

Novatian was a presbyter at Rome who laid claim to being the valid Roman bishop. The resulting disruption intensified the necessity of making sure that rival bishops not compete in the same jurisdiction. Conciliar decisions gradually came to express legitimate authority to coordinate the policies of metropolitan sees, patriarchates, and exarchies under varying conditions (*NPNF* 2 IV).

Cyprian (c. 200–258), bishop of Carthage, established the view that each bishop within his own jurisdiction has full authority of episcopal leadership, yet all bishops are to maintain a coordinated, cooperative, mutually respectful collegial relationship whose unity had dominical grounding in the Lord's calling of Peter (*Treatises* I.4, *ANF* V, p. 422). He saw the diversity of the church as brought into unity by a unified episcopate. He viewed Rome as the center of unity while resisting absolute Roman jurisdiction (Cyprian, *Letters* 55.24, *FC* 51, p. 149; *Letters* 51.24, *ANF* V, pp. 331–35; cf. *Letters* 39, *ANF* V, p. 318).

Challenges to Apostolicity

As long as the apostles were alive they held the church together by their unified witness. Although they spread in all directions, their testimony was thought to be the same, and they themselves constituted the center of authority for teaching and community.

As the apostles gradually died, the need for a clear, cohesive teaching authority was increasingly felt. More attention had to be given to the transgenerational guardianship of the sacred testimony to Jesus' life, death, and resurrection.

Heresy as Novelty. The need for firm governance was increased by the emergence of early divisive heresies, notably those of Docetism, Gnosticism, and Montanism. Heresies were considered to be of recent formation, unable to trace their origin to the apostles (Irenaeus, *Ag. Her.* III.4, *ANF* I, p. 417). A heretical view will "proclaim by its diversity and contrariety that it originates neither from an Apostle nor from an apostolic man; for the Apostles would not have diverged from one another in doctrine; no more would the apostolic man have put out teaching at variance with that of the Apostles. . . . This test will be applied to those churches of a later date, which are daily being founded" (Tertullian, *Prescription Ag. Her.* 32, 36, *ECF,* p. 139; cf. *ANF* III, pp. 258–60).

Heresy is any self-willing choice that departs from apostolic teaching. Wherever a heresy has led to a breach of unity of the body, it is called schism, meaning either strife within the community or more particularly separation from it. Irenaeus made it clear that the proliferation of heresies made it necessary to stress that bishops were official guardians and interpreters of the apostolic tradition (*Ag. Her.* III.3.1, *ANF* I, p. 415; cf. IV.26.2, 23.8; Tertullian, *Prescription Ag. Her.* 32, *ANF* III, p. 258).

The Challenge of Gnosticism to Apostolicity. Gnosticism had its chief influence in the middle of the second century, claiming to pass on the secret knowledge of salvation through mystical knowers who viewed themselves as guardians of secret traditions of sayings of Jesus. The consensual church answered the Gnostics that all authentic memories and traditions concerning Jesus were known to the *episkopoi* and were not secretly passed on by erratic or idiosyncratic prophets or charismatics. The bishops were able to trace their succession in each seat of ecclesiastical authority back to the apostles, often within the living memory of the rememberers, or through a series of successions over several generations. The reliable memory of the events surrounding Jesus was thought to be adequately known and remembered by the bishops, not by secretive groups like the Gnostics.

In response to Gnostic secrecy and flight from the world, Irenaeus argued that the church had from its beginnings publicly set forth a historically demonstrable succession of overseers in a given locale as a means of ensuring correct teaching. The teaching of historic succession hinges upon the basic assumption that God came into history. Christianity does not speak of a redemption taking place apart from history in an esoteric circle of initiates who seek purity by separation from the world. The linear historical succession of Christian leaders was, for Irenaeus, an implication of historical revelation and the scandal of particularity, stressing the public, visible transmission of teaching through intergenerational succession (Irenaeus, *Ag. Her.* II.3, *ANF* I, pp. 415–16; *Common Catech.,* p. 633). In response to heretical challenges, the church gradually developed a defense characterized by the monarchical episcopate, the rule of faith, and the canon.

The Written Word as Defense Against Heresy.   In baptism the rule of faith was learned by heart and confessed. The prototypes of the Apostles' Creed were memorized baptismal formulae and hymns and summarizing confessional statements (*COC* II, pp. 3–57; *CC*, pp. 12–26). These had received generally accepted form by the middle of the second century. Meanwhile the lists of received apostolic writings began to circulate, and by the fourth century were consensually defined (*SCD* 1–40, pp. 1–19; Council of Rome, *SCD* 84, p. 33; Eusebius, *HCCC*, p. 424).

These became the bulwark of the church's defense against heresy. Those who did not accept the rule of faith and the canon of sacred apostolic teachings, and who were not under the discipline of bishops in an established succession, were not to be considered reliable teachers of ecumenical Christian teaching. By the time of Irenaeus and Tertullian we have a reasonably settled rule of faith, a body of documents widely received as apostolic testimony, and authorized lists of succession of bishops.

PART IV

Human Destiny

The future is not a minor category or ancillary addendum to Christian teaching, but intrinsic to all its other aspects (Irenaeus, *Ag. Her.* V, *ANF* I, pp. 526–67). Its final position among the articles of the creed does not imply a diminution of its importance, but a firm stress upon its finality.

In this entire series there have been numerous references to issues of eschatology. Now, following the sequence of the Apostles' Creed and virtually all other complementary early statements of the rule of faith (Profession of the Presbyters of Smyrna, c. 180, Irenaeus, c. 190, Interrogatory Creed of Hippolytus, c. 215, Nicaea, 325, Constantinople, A.D. 381, *CC*, pp. 16–31), we consider more deliberately "life everlasting."

All things in Christian teaching point to a coming consummation. All the vital energies of the prophets, apostles, and martyrs focus on events yet to come that will illumine all present life.

Human life attains its final end not in this life but in a future as yet unpossessed. The truest, fullest blessedness does not appear in temporal life, but in eternal life to come (Titus 1:2; 3:7; Baxter, *The Saints' Eternal Rest*). The drama of human rebellion in history comes to recognition only in its last scene. The symphony is not played out until its last note.

9 Last Things: Death and Personal Survival

Human beings are not asked whether they wish to be born. They are asked only to live accountably between birth and death, after which there is no further opportunity to choose. Having been made without our choice, we come to a final accounting only as a result of our actual choices (Heb. 10:26–31). We do not reach our final destination without some choice on our part (Tertullian, *On the Soul* 42, 51–53, *FC* 10, pp. 274–75, 290–96). Whether mercifully or abruptly or ambivalently, death ends the choosing process enmeshed in time.

Now "we share in his sufferings in order that we may also share in his glory" (Rom. 8:17). Yet even now the faithful "with unveiled faces all reflect the Lord's glory" and "are being transformed into his likeness with ever-increasing glory" (2 Cor. 3:18)

LAST THINGS

God's design is not yet consummated, though its consummation has been anticipatively revealed. The study of its consummation is the last, the crowning, topic of classic consensual exegesis. The inquiry into that consummation as a cohesive Christian teaching is called eschatology. The location of issues of death, personal survival, resurrection, and final judgment at the *end* of the sequence of theological topics does not imply that these matters are relegated to the level of an appendix or afterthought. Rather, this traditional order highlights the final hope that frames and radically contextualizes all other temporal affirmations.

Eschatology is the critical discipline that considers all things that pertain to the life to come insofar as they are revealed by scriptural testimony as commonly beheld through the eyes of generations of consensual interpreters. A notoriously difficult and enigmatic subject, it is not only the capstone of systematic theology, but may rightly be regarded as its foundation stone, the final premise that informs all other questions of theological reasoning (Benedict XII, Benedictus Deus, *SCD* 530–31, pp. 197–98; Belgic Conf. XXXVII, *COC* III, pp. 433–36).

Framing the Final Issues

Eschatological reasoning inquires into how creatures who, having their beginning in God, and having fallen and received redemption in God, have their final destiny and end in God. Eschatology builds upon all anteceding theological inquiries, seeking to face all those opaque issues that have to do with what shall be. It asks on the basis of scripture, What yet lies ahead, for both person and cosmos? A major portion of classic Christian teaching concerns the future in which God's

369

consummating promises are yet to be fulfilled and vindicated (1 Cor. 3:22; Gal. 5:5).

The Range and Import of the Subject.   A presumed account of Christianity that did not mention its future-tense hope would be grossly truncated. The expected End says something decisive about God—that God will vindicate justice beyond this present sphere—and about the world—that all human motives will come under fair, omniscient divine judgment (Ps. 35:24–27; 1 Pet. 4:17).

Deliverance from sin has begun but still awaits final consummation. The glory of God's kingdom is already present, awaiting ultimately to be made completely present. "I consider that our present sufferings are not worth comparing with the glory that will be revealed in us," for which "the creation waits in eager expectation" (Rom. 8:18, 19). Meanwhile, amid human folly God makes even "human wrath" to praise the divine majesty (Ps. 76:10, NRSV). If providence awaits consummation, it is foolish to speak of theodicy or social justice without reference to the future of God's mercy and justice. No small amount of Christian ethical teaching is directly tied to the promise of the justice of God in the end of history. There is enduring moral relevance for the here and now in the inquiry into the future life.

Living Between the Times of Christ's Coming and Coming Again.   What lies between now and the end is the subject of a vast constellation of theological issues sometimes called the last things (*ta eschata*) or *consummatione saeculi, sunteleia aionos,* or eschatology. These terms point to scriptural references to "the last days" (Isa. 2:2; Mic. 4:1), or "the last time" (*eschatos ton chronon,* 1 Pet. 1:20), or "the last hour" (*eschate hora,* 1 John 2:18). The "last days," according to Old Testament prophecy, are the days immediately preceding the final messianic coming and the end of world history as presently known (Mic. 4:1; cf. Acts 2:17; John 6:39–54).

The New Testament writers, having witnessed the messianic coming in Jesus Christ, and the end of history anticipatively recognized and fulfilled, continued to expect the "last days" (*eschatai hemerai*) as those that would consummate in the coming again of the Lord in the end time (2 Tim. 3:1; 1 Pet. 1:5). A distinction is made between "this age" (*olam hazzeh,* Gk. *aion houtos*) and "the coming age" (*olam habba,* Gk. *aion mellō, aiōnis tois eperchomenois,* Eph. 2:7): Those who finally reject the work of the Holy Spirit will find no *shalom,* "either in this age or in the age to come" (Matt. 12:32; cf. Luke 18:30; Gal. 1:4; Col. 1:26).

The New Testament understands the salvation event to be both occurring in the present by faith and awaiting future consummation. Life is now being lived in between the time of the Savior's incarnate life and the Savior's return (2 Thess. 2; Rev. 1:1–8).

The New Testament teaching of the future is set in an apocalyptic framework that looks toward a revelation (*apokalupsis,* manifestation, appearing), a coming yet to be revealed (Luke 12:2; 17:30; Rom. 16:25; 1 Pet. 5:1; Gal. 3:23; John Chrysostom, *Comm. on Gal.* III, *NPNF* 1 XIII, p. 29). Much of the apocalyptic literature anteceding the New Testament looked toward a messianic era of earthly fulfillment whose center would be a New Jerusalem (Dan. 9; Joel 3; Zech. 14; Heb. 12:22; Rev. 21:2). The messianic age would be a preparation for the consummation of all things. The time from now to the end was called the present age. That which would dawn after the consummation of all things was called the age to come.

There is no uniform description of the sequence or character of these events. The most central feature of Jewish apocalyptic expectation prior to the New Testament was the general resurrection accompanied by judgment and separation of just and unjust (Dan. 12:2; Matt. 25:46; Acts 24:15; 2 Pet. 2:9). Some taught the resurrection of the just and the unjust, some of Israel only, some of the righteous only (Matt. 25:46; Mark 12:18; Acts 23:8; 24:15; 1 Cor. 15).

The faithful already live anticipatively in the new age by faith in the resurrected Lord (Rom. 6). Eternal life is viewed as already present (1 Tim. 6:12; 1 John 5). Believers are already presently sharing in the coming reign of God. Nonetheless, amid continuing history there still remains this period "between the times" in which the reign of God has been inaugurated yet not consummated as expected in the last days. In commending both physical training and godliness to Timothy, Paul instructed him to be simultaneously accountable for the "promise for both the present life and the life to come" (1 Tim. 4:8).

Life Everlasting: An Article of the Creed.   The Apostles' Creed confesses baptismal belief in "the communion of saints, the resurrection of the dead, and the life everlasting." The Nicene-Constantinopolitan Creed concludes, "We look for the resurrection of the dead and the life of the world to come" (*CC*, pp. 24–25, 33). Only from this final vantage point may the structure of the rule of faith be fully reviewed. Thomas Aquinas set forth the unity of the fourteen articles of the creed in two phases: The first speaks of the unity of the triune God. "Three articles are reserved for the three divine persons. Three other articles are formulated about the effects produced by God: creation, which pertains to nature; justification, which pertains to grace; reward, which pertains to glory. Thus seven articles altogether are devoted to the divinity. Concerning the humanity of Christ seven more are proposed. The first is on the incarnation and conception of Christ. The second deals with the nativity. . . . The third article is on the death, passion, and burial; the fourth on the descent into hell; the fifth on the resurrection; the sixth on the ascension; and the seventh treats of Christ's coming for the judgment" (Tho. Aq., *Compend. of Theology*, chap. 246, pp. 308–9). It is from this simple structure of the primitive baptismal formula that we get the structure of systematic theology. Far from inventing this structure, Thomas merely expressed what had been consensually received for centuries before him.

Individual and Cosmic Destiny.   Eschatology deals with the end and meaning of the whole of human history. In this framework it deals with the end and meaning of the future of every discrete human person and of the natural history of the cosmos (Rom. 8:18–27). The subject is not exhausted by asking what happens to an individual person beyond the grave, or even to human history generally. It also encompasses the cosmos, incorporeal spiritual creatures (angelic and demonic powers), and nonrational creatures (Gregory of Nyssa, *The Great Catechism* V, VI, *NPNF* 2 V, pp. 478–80).

To handle such varied questions, the subject of eschatology is sometimes divided into two parts: general eschatology, which deals with the future of history and cosmos, and individual eschatology, which deals with the future life of the individual believer. Thus one may distinguish the final end of the person as an individual from the final end of humanity within the context of the cosmos.

The Trajectory of Topics.   Protestant scholasticism summed up "the four Last Things: death, the resurrection of the dead, the final judgment, and the end of the world" (Quenstedt, *TDP* IV, p. 534, Schmid, *DT*, p. 625; cf. Ecclus. 7:40). A similar organization of loci is found in Catholic scholastic theology, that "the four last things of man are Death, Judgment, Heaven (Purgatory), and Hell" (Pohle, *DT* XII, p. 2). These topics are ordered around a chronological premise systematically conceived: death and the abode of the dead, the general resurrection, Christ's coming again, final judgment, the end of the world, and eternal life.

A more extensive list includes the following loci, the sweeping trajectory of the concluding part of systematic theology: the correlation of sin and death; the death of the just and unjust; life after death, personal survival; the intermediate state of the just and unjust; the general resurrection; the glorified, spiritual body; the future return of Christ; signs of his coming; the Lawless One; millennialism; the norm, process, and time of last judgment; the Judge, the judged, and the sentence; the separation; consummation; the new city of God; new heaven, new earth; the eternal destiny of the wicked; hell as separation from God; theories of afterlife probation, universalism, and annihilationism; the destiny of those who heard no good news; the communion of saints; eternal life; the dwelling of the righteous; the vision of God; the praise of the triune God.

Reserve in Eschatological Reasoning

Before plunging headlong into these subjects, it is well to remind ourselves that time-bound human reasoning is ill equipped to speak of what is not yet. Present reasoning proceeds on the basis of assumptions about time and space that cannot be transferred or applied to eternity. We have developed set habits of time-bound reasoning that are humbled and challenged by the unknowability of the future.

Eschatological Modesty.   No human eye can penetrate the future. Reason can only make conjectures. Passion and imagination may dream or imagine a future condition (Geo. Bull, *Harmonia Apostolica,* dissertation II, chap. X, sec. 13 f., *LACT*, p. 127, *Angl.,* p. 320). Jesus' own self-constrained modesty about the time of his return stands as an example to the faithful of eschatological modesty (Matt. 24:36; Mark 13:23; Acts 1:6, 7; Gregory the Great, *Letters, To Eulogius, SCD* 248, p. 97).

In this future arena, empirical reasoning is far more impotent than in present matters. From philosophy, psychology, medicine, and perhaps parapsychology we can gain small scraps, but hardly enough to count on. Aware of the stubborn limitations of finite reasoning, Christian orthodoxy can do no better than listen carefully to scripture attesting God's promises, through the ancient traditions of exegesis that have sought consensually to read scripture by the analogy of faith.

Calvin thought it "rash to inquire into matters unknown more deeply than God allows us to know" (*Psychopannychia, RD,* p. 695; *Tracts and Treatises* II, pp. 291 ff.). Irenaeus wrote of the cryptic number 666, "It is therefore more certain, and less hazardous, to await the fulfillment of the prophecy, than to be making surmises" (*Ag. Her.* V.30.3, *ANF* I, p. 559).

Some have ceased to have confidence in Christian teaching about the future because it appears to say either too little or too much. Indeed eschatology may be taught falsely so as to detract from the importance of this life or trivialize historical existence or foster the illusion of escape from human responsibility. But rightly conceived, the teaching of the end of history is a teaching about the meaning of history. The promise of the future is rightly taught as impinging upon the present (1 Cor. 15:58; *ACC*, p. 95). By contrast, eschatology may be falsely taught so as to pretend that it has detailed keys to contemporary events. These temptations call for eschatological modesty, but not to the extent of catatonic immobility. The poverty of human language does not detract from the experiential vitality of the Christian hope.   ·

The subject remains of extraordinary importance, whatever its intrinsic limitations. Every other act of prayer, every article of catechesis points toward some dilemma that has only a future conclusion or resolution. Every other sentence of worship and theology remains incomplete without eschatology.

Scripture as Guide.   The scripture's witness remains binding even while it speaks in metaphors of what our minds do not fully fathom. Paul quoted Isaiah 64:4, "'No eye has seen, no ear has heard, no mind has conceived what God has prepared for those who love him,' but God has revealed it to us by his Spirit" (1 Cor. 2:9). Biblical revelation concerning the future employs metaphors from time and space reality to point to that which lies beyond time and space.

The purpose of scriptural testimony to the future life is not to describe in detail what will happen as if with scientific certainty, but to console, encourage, and engender hope in what God has provided in the future, and faithfulness in this world (2 Pet. 3:11; Gregory Nazianzen, *Orat.* 7, 18, *NPNF* 2 VII, pp. 229 ff., 254 ff.). "The Bible uses the earthly, human categories of time and space not primarily to describe literally *where* we will be and *how* we will exist 'after time,' but to describe symbolically *who* we will be. It is not primarily interested in the 'furniture of heaven' or the 'temperature of hell,' but in *people* and whether they will be together with or separated from God" (Guthrie, *CD*, p. 386).

The analogy of faith is a key principle of biblical eschatology. We learn about the future divine-human relation by thinking analogically about what God has done in the past and is doing in the present divine-human relation. Hope is attached to the One whom we have come to know personally in the history of revelation. Faith hopes for completion of what remains unfulfilled but anticipated in the history of redemption, for clarity in what remains stubbornly ambiguous, for victory over what still remains disputed, for reliable vision of what remains in time uncertain. The future is read in the light of God's self-disclosure in the past (John Chrysostom, *Hom. on 1 Cor.* XXXIV, *NPNF* 1 XII, pp. 201–9; Barth, *CD* IV/3, 777 ff.; IV/4, 74 ff.).   ·

Why So Little Is Known of the Future.   Why does God's revelation leave us so much in the dark on such an important subject? Would not it seem more consistent with the new age of Jesus Christ that prophecy now would come to a new level of explicit insight, and that believers would not only hope but know the future?

There is a providential reason why finite reasoning is left walking by faith rather than by sight: "It is the glory of God to conceal a matter" (Prov. 25:2). The study of the future remains, according to God's wisdom, a matter of the meekness of faith, not the pretense of elaborate knowledge. The study of the end time can only proceed within some particular time and place. It is a probationary study in which the limits of all human knowing are on trial.

The prototypical sin of humanity was the attempt to penetrate forbidden knowledge (Gen. 2:17). Knowledge of the future seems to remain under this prohibition insofar as human consciousness remains implacably enmeshed in the categories of time. In daily Christian life, "time is strangely blended with eternity, though it is still time" (Pope, *Compend.* 3, p. 367). The future remains impenetrable except in the form of promise through the revealed Word.

When the disciples met the risen Lord, they asked him, "Lord, are you at this time going to restore the kingdom to Israel?" He answered in his last words to them on earth as reported by Luke, "It is not for you to know the times or dates the Father has set by his own authority" (Acts 1:6, 7). Following this instruction by Jesus, eschatology proceeds modestly as the least pretentious of all topics of Christian teaching.

Faith is called to live by hope, content to live with what we cannot know by sight, searching the scripture for what has been graciously revealed. With all its limitations, the study of the promise of last things remains a source of humble wonder and consolation for Christian believers. The study of the future holds extraordinary blessing: "Blessed is the one who reads the words of this prophecy, and blessed are those who hear it and take to heart what is written in it" (Rev. 1:3). The blessing does not consist in the fact that one might certainly know what will happen, but in the living hope that amid not knowing, one may learn to trust the consummator. "Dear friends, now we are children of God, and what we will be has not yet been made known. But we know that when he appears, we shall be like him" (1 John 3:2).

The key: The faithful reason about the future out of personal meeting with the risen Lord. Little can be said about the future apart from having been personally met by the resurrected Lord in the grace of baptism and at the Lord's Table. The vision of eternal life is an expression of sharing in Christ's own life, death, resurrection, and exaltation.

Consensus on Some Eschatological Points Is Still Forming.   Eschatology, despite its importance, remains less consensually matured than other articles of the creed. Though most other subjects of theology have been explored with reasonably full adequacy in their twenty centuries of development, there has not yet formed a definitive ecumenical eschatology on many details that can claim to stand consensually as the mind of the believing church. Many theories remain and compete. Wide differences remain on eschatology between adventists and amillennialists, social activists and pietists, evangelicals and liberals.

The aim of irenic theology is to state as well as possible the mind of the believing church. We will attempt to do so here as much as elsewhere. Yet we find a greater challenge here, and warn the reader that the consensus is not at points so firm as elsewhere. Where necessary, we will set forth complementary positions as the best judgment of irenic consensual reasoning, hoping not to rule out any major contributor to the intended vision of the whole.

Whether Consensual Definition Is Incomplete in Eschatology.   The task of irenic eschatology as an issue of systematic theology is not to rehearse a history of the development of ideas of the future or to delve extensively into comparative religion concerning competing ideas of the future life. Rather it is to look for the consensually interpreted texts of scripture that may rightly be said proximately to convey the mind of the believing church, despite persistent ambiguities.

In this arena, formal theological definition has often been preceded and decisively influenced by liturgical practice and experimentation, as in the case of prayers for the dead. As early as the second- and third-century Roman catacombs, there are ample evidences of rites and prayers for the faithful dead. Such prayers and practices clearly assumed life after death, and perhaps the embryonic idea of a probationary period after death and before final judgment. Exegetical reasoning about these practices would develop much later.

The apostolic writers generally assumed or affirmed personal survival beyond death, the return of Christ, the general resurrection, and general judgment. Though Trinitarian and Christological doctrines received detailed conciliar attention, common points of eschatological teaching were broadly affirmed but not explicitly developed. They appear regularly as points of exegesis and preaching and liturgy, but not as precisely worked out conciliar formulae.

It took considerable time for varied theories to form on some questions of eschatology: whether there is or is not an intermediate state, whether the coming of Christ is before or after the millennium, whether death ends all possibility of coming to faith. Among early controverted themes were Origen's theories of universalism and eternality of the soul, which would later be consensually rejected; Augustine's amillennial vision of the church as City of God; Gregory the Great's legitimation of purgatory; the medieval sacraments of penance and unction. The Reformation provided a new exegetical basis for doctrines of the future life, but much of the substance of the earlier tradition remained. Pietism focused upon heart religion and conversion as the basis for entry into heavenly bliss; rationalism retained the idea of personal survival yet based on rational argument rather than revelation; and millennial reflection in due time worked out various systems of prophetic interpretation that would compete for consensual acceptance.

Whether the Gospel Transcends Eschatological Despair. Why should we not expect the continuation of a history that has become heavily laden with the consequences of sin? Why not spend our limited energies on political change or economic development? Too often, in despair, the modern ethos has reduced eschatology to politics or economics or city planning or law enforcement or ecological despair. Each of these has their own competing plans and hopes for social transformation, justice, and peace.

Even supposing a wonderful future society might emerge from coordinated political effort, what could guarantee its permanence? Suppose that such a utopian society, if now impossible, is even achieved in a third or fifth millennium—what would it have to offer those who lived in previous millennia? If the payoff of future hope is a this-worldly society yet to come for others, how does this hope impinge morally upon our present suffering and sacrifice to help it come about?

It is frightening to feel the deep despair over the possibility that human history could self-destruct. Christianity remains realistic about the capacity of humanity for gross sin such as might destroy the planet, but hopeful that God's purpose will be fulfilled even under the worst scenarios of human folly. The worst modern fantasies are hardly more horrible than those of ancient apocalyptic imagination.

Christian eschatology does not have to do merely with human wish projections, philosophical speculations, rational arguments, nativistic optimism, or humanistic hopes for social transformation. Rather it speaks of a future that has already met us in Jesus Christ. "Christ realized what is still a hope for us" (Augustine, in Kasper, *CCF,* p. 328).

It was an expectation planted long before New Testament times that God the Spirit was acting in present history so as to reveal how God's promises were in coming times to be fulfilled: "Concerning this salvation, the prophets, who spoke of the grace that was to come to you, searched intently and with greatest care, trying to find out the time and circumstances to which the Spirit of Christ in them was pointing when he predicted the sufferings of Christ and the glories that would follow. It was revealed to them that they were not serving themselves but you, when they spoke of the things that have now been told you by those who have preached the gospel to you by the Holy Spirit sent from heaven" (1 Pet. 1:10–12). As early Christian preachers searched scripture to discern the grounds of their hope in the fulfillment of God's promises, so do believers today, who look forward to God's justice and holy love becoming clear in future history and finally at the end of history.

Elementary Eschato-logic

Whether Eschatology Is a Special Locus of Pneumatology.   God the Spirit works to remake the whole of creation into the new creation begun in the Son. This is why eschatology is often viewed systematically from within the frame of reference of the work of the Holy Spirit. This way of sequencing does not imply that eschatological reasoning is reserved exclusively for the work of the Spirit, for we have already seen how decisive it is for Christology. Christology looks backward toward the Son's coming and forward to the Son's coming again. Pneumatology looks backward in time to the once-for-all self-offering of the Son on the cross and forward in time to the full application of God's promise in the Parousia.

Meanwhile, the Spirit's converting and sanctifying work is still in process. Faith looks expectantly to its full consummation. The believer united with Christ by faith looks ahead to a fuller union with Christ in eternity. The history of sin cannot be the last word about humanity. Humanity has been met by the cross and in gross terms has either believed or disbelieved. Human beings continue generation after generation to hear and respond to God's good news. The unfolding story of human history is not yet over. The Spirit still has work to do to complete the Son's mission. This does not mean that the cross is incomplete, for the cross is a finished work, but one that welcomes the Spirit's work in order that it be appropriated by subject selves. All these points demand that we say something more about the future, positing an end of history, even though frail language trembles at the task.

Whether Questions of Eschatology Arise Inevitably out of Finite Human Existence.   Reflection on the future is not unique to Jews and Christians, but found generally in human consciousness. Wherever human life is being lived, it is drawn toward those most persistent human questions: whence and whither?

Is there an end toward which nature and history are moving? It seems absurd to conscious beings that life could be so full of value and meaning and then end suddenly, abruptly, and absolutely with death. What remains? Why are we here?

Can we reliably know anything about the future? Are our hopes merely projections of our human needs and fleeting passions? Do future hopes distort present responsibilities?

The Hope of Personal Survival in the History of Religion and Science. Animism is saturated with the imagination of spiritual survival after death. Hinduism and Buddhism speak of an endless cycle of transmigration of souls. Islam's faith is strongly focused upon the expectation of heaven.

No one lives without hope. The history of religions is filled with texts expressing hope beyond death. To pretend to be a religion without any teaching of the future life is oxymoronic. There abides in human consciousness "an indestructible instinct of the resurrection" even among those who deny it with their lips (Cyril of Jerusalem, *Catech. Lect.* XVIII.5, *NPNF* 2 VII, p. 135).

In the last hundred years, the premise of human survival beyond death has become a scientific hypothesis in the study of paranormal phenomena, the attempt to account for widespread reportage of near-death experiences or allegedly after-death experiences, supposed communications with the departed, déjà vu awareness, extrasensory perception, parakinesis, telepathy, and so on. None of these inquiries provide sufficient evidence for drawing rational conclusions, but they do suggest that the preoccupation with the future remains a prevailing tendency of modern and postmodern consciousness, and not something that accidentally appears only within the particular ethos of Judaism and Christianity.

Whether a Consensus Gentium *Can Be Identified.* Some have argued that the belief in personal survival is so nearly universal that it is difficult to find any culture, ancient or modern, where is it not found. Even where brutally suppressed by a police state, the expectation of final judgment does not disappear, but tends to emerge ever more strongly (Solzhenitsyn, *The Gulag Archipelago*).

This has led to the argument from popular consent (*consensus gentium*)—that the recurrence and universality and persistent vitality of belief in survival after death suggests that it is so knitted into human consciousness that it cannot be repressed without denying our fundamental humanity. Gregory of Nyssa argued that the persistence of eschatological questions in human life points to the plausibility of personal survival (Gregory of Nyssa, *The Great Catechism* V, *NPNF* 2 IV, p. 479).

Modestly stated, the argument from popular consent asserts that although disbelief in personal survival may be occasionally found in human cultures, the belief in personal survival beyond death is found in virtually all nations of all historical periods and all stages of civilization. It is thus hypothesized as a premise of human consciousness by virtue of its universality and persistence in human history. Any view that possesses such general reasonable assent must be received attentively as a plausible premise until disproved. Arguably any view so recurrent is likely to emerge out of the very constitution of human nature.

DEATH AND PERSONAL SURVIVAL

A bit of me dies when I lose a friend. The loss of anything significant may serve as a herald of death. To lose something inestimably precious is a little like dying, reminding me of the vulnerability of all creatures including myself. Life is incipiently threatened each day by potential sickness and accident, against which we try to insure ourselves. One's earthly life is the swift interval between birth and death (Donne, *Meditations;* Shakespeare, *Sonnets*).

Death

In one sense death is not a subject that belongs to the study of the last things, but is with us from the beginning, potentially if not actually. "In the midst of life we are encompassed by death," said an eleventh-century hymn (*media vita in morte sumus*, Notker, Duffield, *LH,* p. 140; cf. Jacobs, *SCF,* p. 490). Luther inverted this maxim: "If you hear the Law, it will say in the language of the ancient chant: 'In the midst of life, we are in death.' But the Gospel and faith invert this, and sing, 'In the midst of death, we are in life'" (Luther, *On Genesis* VI, 206, *SCF,* p. 491).

Whether Death Accompanies All Life.   We are born. We grow. We work. We die. All die: parents die, children die, the children of children will die.

No one has expressed the pathos of this more ironically than Chrysostom: "Nothing is weaker than human affairs. Whatever term therefore one may employ to express their insignificance it will fall short of the reality; whether he calls them smoke, or grass, or a dream or spring flowers, or by any other name; so perishable are they, and more naught than nonentities" (John Chrysostom, *Eutropius, NPNF* 1 IX, p. 250).

Facing death is the universal human condition. "When the time drew near for David to die," he said to Solomon, "I am about to go the way of all the earth" (1 Kings 2:2). "Death passed upon all" (Rom. 5:12, KJV).

Death may come sooner or later. It may occur with or without pain. But nothing is more certain in life than that it will come to an end (Aphrahat, *Demonstrations, Of Death, NPNF* 2 XIII, pp. 402–9). Each one's last act is already foreknown: to die. "It is appointed for mortals to die once" (Heb. 9:27, NRSV). The universality of death of human beings is interpreted Christologically "as a consequence of their federal relation to the first Adam, that they may rise again with the second Adam" (Harries, *TM,* p. 279; cf. Rom. 5:12–17).

Whether Awareness of Death Deepens Life's Significance.   Precisely because life is strictly limited, it becomes by that measure more important. As the sick man's prognosis is shortened, the value of his remaining days tends to be heightened. Now is our only time to act, to decide. Hence it becomes important to "be very careful, then how you live—not as unwise but as wise, making the most of every opportunity" (Eph. 5:15; cf. Col. 4:5).

Time flows. Each moment is a potentially delicious gift. None can be replaced or retracted, once gone. No moment lasts. One's loving, believing, and one's very being as a person is chosen ever anew with each moment (S. Kierkegaard, *Either/Or* II).

Suppose every moral decision were forever subject to endless revision. Would not all moral seriousness thereby be infinitely postponable? If there were no death, it seems difficult to conclude that there could be much significance to historical life, since life's significance as decision hinges on its limitation in time. If so, oddly enough, death is what makes life meaningful, for this life is morally serious only if it ends (Ambrose, *On Belief in the Resurrection* II. 124, *NPNF* 2 X, p. 195; V. Frankl, *The Doctor and the Soul*). The equation is precise: Those who take life seriously take death seriously. Those who take death seriously take life seriously. Where death is avoided, life is avoided. Only one who has accepted the reality of death is prepared to accept life (John 12:24; 2 Cor. 5:14, 15; John Chrysostom, *Hom. on the Statues, NPNF* 1 IX, pp. 373–76).

Whether Death Ends the Period of Probation of the Will.   God gives us only this fleeting time upon earth to make decisions, to shape our own responsive existence, to hear and respond to the divine address, to live for or against the good in each moment (Josh. 24:15). When we die, the time for deciding is past (Gen. 27:2–10). The burden of freedom is lifted; the wealth of freedom spent.

Nature does not permit life without death. Only if a kernel of wheat falls to the ground and dies does it produce many seeds (John 12:24).

Death ends the condition of pilgrimage through the world and inaugurates the consummation, excluding further temporal choices. "Night is coming, when no one can work" (John 9:4; cf. Matt. 26:42; 25:13). Human life is in this way analogous to the falling of a tree: "in the place where it falls, there will it lie" (Eccles. 11:3). Death means unequivocal limitation. No one can "obtain after death that which he has neglected to secure here" (Augustine, *Enchiridion* 110, *NPNF* 1 III, p. 272; cf. Cyprian, *Letter to Demetrius* 25, Pohle, *DT* XII 14). The view is generally rejected that those who, having wavered between belief and unbelief, die in sin will be allowed to make or reverse a final decision after death.

The Test.   Life puts every person to the test. Life itself is the examination (S. Kierkegaard, *Gospel of Suffering*, pp. 60–61). Finally life absolutely requires one to face one's finitude. From beginning to end we are called to acknowledge our lives as creatures under limitation. It is a test that lasts not an hour but a lifetime. Death is the last event in the probation that constitutes life.

We try to avoid death. At funeral parlors the cosmetics lie thick. We apply euphemisms to every aspect of the finality of death. In modernity, "death has replaced sex as the subject too obscene for polite society" (Guthrie, *CD*, p. 377).

Whether Life Is Separable from the Body.   Through time and accident, the body becomes worn, ravaged, diseased, dysfunctional, and damaged to the point where the soul (i.e., life) no longer can continue to be expressed through it. At the point where the last evidence of aliveness irreversibly leaves the body, we say that a person is dead. Death, traditionally defined, is the cessation of finite, natural, bodily life caused by the separation of the soul from the body (Augustine, *CG* XIII, 6, *NPNF* 1 II, p. 247; cf. Brochmann, *UTS* 354, Schmid, *DT*, p. 624). "When death severs soul from body, the body lies completely still and passive, just like a workman's tools after he has gone away and left them lying" (Nemesius, *On the Nature of Man, LCC* IV, p. 226).

Soul (*nephesh*) is the life principle of the unified person. Soul is not a part of the body, but intrinsic to the life of the body. The language of modernity prefers to speak reflexively of "self" rather than "soul" as the unifying center of personal life. Classically viewed, the soul is not a separable part of the person alongside the body, but the very aliveness of the living person in dialogue with God, oneself, and other selves. This is what "separation of the soul and body means: the cessation or rupture of the previous relation to the environment and the community" (Kasper, *CCF*, p. 336). Irreversible unrelatedness is the basic primitive meaning of *sheol*. By way of contrast, the faithful dead are being united with their Lord in a communion of saints.

Death is more fittingly described under the metaphor of severance than annihilation. In death life is separated from the body, and the sinner from God (Tho. Aq., *ST* supp., Q70.1, III, p. 2837). The soul-body interface that in its original creation was intended to continue without end, now, due to sin, must face death (Lactantius, *DI, FC* 49, pp. 189 f., 211–17).

The Living Soul.   It belongs to the soul to live. The very definition of the *nephesh* is "that which is alive," that by which one becomes a "living being" (Gen. 2:7). In death the soul does not cease with the cessation of the body (Athanasius, *Contra Gentes, NPNF* 2 IV, pp. 20, 21). The soul continues to live by virtue of the powers that belong to its nature.

The life of a plant is that which makes it possible for the plant to take in food, receive energy from nutrients, grow, adapt to surroundings, and reproduce. Life is precisely that which distinguishes the living plant from the shell of a plant that does not have those capacities, hence is a dead organism. Life is not only the time one is alive, but the manner of one's living. One participates in life to the degree that one has vigor, soundness, ebullience, and vivacity consonant with one's creaturely potentialities (Isa. 38).

Why Life Is Not Synonymous with Existence.   As life, according to scripture, is more than mere existence, so is death more than the mere cessation of existence. "If life does not include the gift of existence, then death does not include the loss of it" (Banks, *MCD*, p. 268). One may exist and not be very much alive. One may be profoundly alive and have only a thread of existence.

What Christ came to bestow is not bare existence but abundant life, "life to the full" (*zōēn perisson,* John 10:10). Death is not the direct antonym for existence. It is not bare corporeal existence that is forfeited by sin in death, but more fundamentally breathing, pulsating, personal life. Through disobedience humanity is finally sentenced to experience the separation of the soul or life from the body. Death is seen as a type of separation from God, first in sin, then in the cessation of physical life, and finally in the last judgment if unredeemed. Separation of the soul from God is the only death that finally may come to the soul.

What Makes the Body Alive?   The Genesis account of creation made a fundamental distinction between the body as such and that which makes the body alive: First, "the Lord God formed the man from the dust of the ground," and only then "breathed into his nostrils the breath of *life,* and the man became a living being [*nephesh*]" (Gen. 2:7, italics added). The difference between dust and life is the breath of God. To be formed of dust into plastic existence is not yet the same as becoming a living being by being breathed upon by God. This very dust created as body "returns to the ground it came from" awaiting resurrection, while in death "the spirit returns to God who gave it" (Eccles. 12:7; Lactantius, *DI* II.13, *ANF* VII, pp. 62–63).

The attributes of that which animates a creature are different from the body of the creature. The body has mass, magnitude, density, weight, solidity, and physical form. That which animates the body (the breathing Spirit of God enabling *nephesh, psuchē*) has none of these. For life itself has no mass. Life weighs nothing. Life cannot be measured. Life cannot be touched or moved like an object from one place to another (Ps. 39:4–6).

The living person possesses attributes that cannot be reduced to measurable material formulae: consciousness, imagination, reason, desire. No computer can track them adequately, and the computer itself is their creature and artifact. The functions of the self-transcending soul (willing, reasoning, imagining, thinking) are distinguishable from though related to bodily functions (nutrition, respiration, blood circulation, muscular motion, reproduction). These are not reducible to physical properties or empirical descriptions. The soul does not have physical dimension in the same sense as the body, and to look for it is to misunderstand one's eyes (Nemesius, *On the Nature of Man*, LCC IV, pp. 224 ff.; Calvin, *Inst.* 3.25.6).

Yielding the Spirit.   Biblical metaphors of death are departure (Phil. 1:23; 2 Tim. 4:6), dissolution, decease, demise, release, return to dust (Gen. 3:19), the "outcome" (Heb. 13:7), "the end" (Matt. 10:22). Death is described in both Testaments as a giving up of the ghost or spirit (Job 14:10). When the psalmist wrote, "Into your hands I commit my spirit [*ruach*]" (Ps. 31:5), and when Jesus on the cross used the same phrase in addressing the Father (Luke 23:46; cf. Matt. 27:50; John 19:30), what was it that was being committed and received? Surely not the body only, for that was soon to die. Nor was it merely his breath in a literal sense, for what difference could that last portion of air make? Rather it was the living spirit (*pneuma*) as distinct from the body that was being committed to God in death (Luke 23:46). James assumed that "the body without the spirit is dead" (James 2:26).

Facing martyrdom, Stephen prayed, "Lord Jesus, receive my spirit" (Acts 7:59). Stephen's spirit was received in the divine presence even while his body was dying. One cannot speak in this way without implying some sort of personal survival after the death of the body. Similarly, Paul assumed that this side of death one continues "to remain in the body," whereas to die is "to depart and be with Christ" (Phil. 1:20–23).

Physical, Spiritual, and Eternal Death Distinguished.   Death is understood in scripture in three distinguishable forms: physical, spiritual, and eternal. *Physical (temporal) death* consists in the permanent cessation of bodily life caused by the separation of the soul from the body (Augustine, *CG* XIII, 6; Clement of Alexandria, *Stromata* 7). It is the condition in which all vital functions cease permanently until the resurrection. To die is to cease to live, to lose vital power, to expire, to perish. The physical body is resolved into its constituent elements by death.

In addition to this usage, there are in scripture typological or figurative usages of the term death: *Spiritual death* is the fall from grace caused by sin. *Eternal death* is the final state of separation from God, sometimes called "the second death" (Rev. 2:11; 20:6; 21:8), "everlasting destruction," being "shut out from the presence of the Lord" (2 Thess. 1:9), or "destruction" (Gal. 6:8; Phil. 3:19). In the cross, God forgave sinners, enabling them to escape the second death, eternal separation. Grace through faith is victorious over spiritual death even in this life by means of the new birth, so that even while temporal death is occurring, it is being transformed into a spiritual blessing (John Chrysostom, *Hom. on the Statues*, *NPNF* 1 IX, p. 374). Meanwhile, this side of final resurrection, physical death remains as an effect of the history of sin that God has required and wisely allowed within the moral order of the cosmos.

The picture of the dust of creation returning to the dust of death is poignantly portrayed at the close of Ecclesiastes, where the faithful are called to "remember your Creator in the days of your youth, before the days of trouble come," when "the grass-hopper drags himself along and desire no longer is stirred. Then man goes to his eternal home and mourners go about the streets. Remember him—before the silver cord is severed, or the golden bowl is broken; before the pitcher is shattered at the spring, or the wheel broken at the well, and the dust returns to the ground it came from, and the spirit returns to God who gave it" (Eccles. 12:1, 5–7).

By death the tabernacle of the soul's earthly home is dissolved. The tents are stricken, and the soul leaves the body. Once the blood congeals and *rigor mortis* sets in, it is clear that the animating *psuchē* has left the body. The living soul does not end with death, though the soul suffers the loss of the body. The continuity of personal life is clearly taught in Luke 23:43; 16:19–31, and Revelation 14:13.

At death the body returns to the earth to await the resurrection. The still living soul does not have to proceed to some particular place to be judged but stands already in the presence of the omnipresent God (Luke 16:20–25; Heb. 9:27; Sulpitius Severus, *Life of St. Martin, FC* 7, p. 113). At the moment of death, the time of deliberating and willing is over, the time of preparation and trial complete.

By Sin Comes Death

Whether It Is Fitting That Human Beings Should Die. It is fitting that those who have participated in a history of sin and contributed to it their own twisted actions and their consequences should be subject to the moral requirement that accompanied all human life: those who sin "surely die" (Gen. 2:17). The correlation is precise. "Then, after desire has conceived, it gives birth to sin; and sin, when it is full-grown, gives birth to death" (James 1:15).

Whether Human Life Would Have Continued Had Humanity Not Fallen into Sin. Other corporeal creatures are destined by nature to die, but humanity, made in the image of God, was originally created to remain alive to forever reflect God's goodness. Prior to the fall, soul and body were created to be forever united.

To some it seems an odd point of Christian teaching that God does not will death in humans. The sacred texts lead us to conclude that without sin humanity made in God's image would have risen above the general law of natural death (Gen. 2; 3). The tree of life points to sinless eternal continuity in fellowship with God. This moot point is something like the question of whether the Son would have become incarnate had humanity not sinned. There is no clear answer in scripture. What we know is that sin did occur and with sin death. After genera-tions of experience with death, human death still appears to reason to be some-how contrary to the appropriate ordering of creation (Leibniz, *Theodicy;* Kant, *Fundamental Principles of the Metaphysics of Morals*).

Whether Death Is a Consequence of Sin. Traditionally stated, our first parents were endowed with bodily immortality (Council of Mileum, canon 1, *SCD* 101,

p. 44), but lost this through sin (Council of Orange, II, canon 1, *SCD* 174, p. 75; Trent, session V, canon 2). "For the wages of sin is death" (Rom. 6:23; cf. 1 Cor. 15:21, 22). The intrinsic connection between sin and death was recognized by all ancient Christian writers, following the firmly established Hebraic tradition (Job 14:1, 2; 16:22; Pss. 89:48; 90:10; Eccles. 7:2; 8:8).

Death is not morally natural to humanity. The inevitability of death is an inexorable consequence of Adam's fall. Physical death is not the natural result of the original or intended human condition, but the result of spiritual death through sin (Rom. 4:25).

Whether Man and Woman Together Chose the Way of Death.   The history of sin began when man and woman sought to play God, to reach for the tree of life on their own by arrogant grasping, against the divine prohibition. Together male and female, humanity freely chose death. Equally man and woman broke the order of creation. If woman was first in yielding to temptation, man was first in following (Gen. 3:6; John Chrysostom, *Hom. on Genesis* 16, *FC* 74, pp. 207–21).

Hence it is said that the cause of death is sin. Paul explained that "sin entered the world through one man, and death through sin, and in this way death came to all men, because all sinned" (Rom. 5:12). The fall is a federal act, involving all humanity. It was "through the disobedience of the one man the many were made sinners" (Rom. 5:19). For "by the trespass of the one man, death reigned through that one man" (Rom. 5:17; cf. 1 Cor. 15:21).

Whether Death Is Punishment for Sin.   Death came by sin as divine judgment of sin. The primordial command was unequivocally clear, with no ambiguities: "You are free to eat from any tree in the garden, but you must not eat from the tree of the knowledge of good and evil, for when you eat of it you will surely die" (Gen. 2:17). The resulting judgment and its basis are also clear: "To dust you will return," because you "ate from the tree about which I commanded you, 'You must not eat of it.'" (Gen. 3:19). Death is the ordered and fitting expression of the holiness of God confronting human sin (Ps. 90:7, 11; Calvin, *Inst.* 2.8.59). Death is described as a curse (Gal. 3:13), a judgment upon sin (Rom. 1:32), "the last enemy to be destroyed" (1 Cor. 15:26). Death is not the primordial will of God, but only consequent to sin; hence one cannot say that human death was made by God (Wisd. of Sol. 1:13).

Why Time Is Allowed for Repentance.   If God had been attentive only to justice, lacking mercy, God would have imposed the sentence of death immediately upon the heels of the first sin. Mercifully God has determined to restrain sin to allow time for repentance (Rom. 5:17; 1 Cor. 15:45; 2 Tim. 1:10; Heb. 2:14). Had God executed punishment in Eden immediately, there would have been no human history. Because mercy restrained justice, the history of humanity, in its glory and wretchedness, has proceeded.

The Death of Believers

Readiness to Die.   Death is certain, time is short, "for we were born only yesterday and know nothing, and our days on earth are but a shadow" (Job 8:9; cf. 9:25). The time of death is unknown. "Moreover, no man knows when his hour will come" (Eccles. 9:12). Death ends each and every capacity to exercise freedom within the conditions of time.

Moreover, the end of history is as yet unknown except in the form of hope. The prudent person is always prepared for death (Eccles. 9:10; Rev. 22:1; Ps. 90:12). "So you must be ready" (Matt. 24:44). "Be dressed ready for service and keep your lamps burning, like men waiting for their master to return from a wedding banquet, so that when he comes and knocks they can immediately open the door for him" (Luke 12:35, 36). Those who live well have no fear to die (Clem. II, 5). Believers do not fear death but sin (John Chrysostom, *Hom. on the Statues, NPNF* 1 IX, pp. 371 ff.).

The grace of God teaches us to live "godly lives in this present age, while we wait for the blessed hope—the glorious appearing of our great God and Savior, Jesus Christ" (Titus 2:12, 13; cf. Rom. 12:11–14; 2 Pet. 3:11). We are instructed by scripture to remember our vulnerability to death—*memento mori*—to ready ourselves for death and live life in awareness of radical finitude (Ps. 90). For death, when life is lived in Christ, is no longer the final word (Rahner, *RR*, pp. 352–56).

The Death of Believers. Those united with Christ by faith understand that his death is the pattern for their death (Athanasius, *On the Incarnation, NPNF* 2 IV, pp. 47–52). Though he resisted the prospect of death like any ordinary human being, in dying, Jesus freely yielded his spirit into his Father's hands (Luke 23:46). Not seeking death, he trusted God the Father to raise him to new life. Though we may rightly follow our natural instinct by resisting death, we are being given the opportunity each day to offer up our lives to God, ready to die for the truth, confident that we shall live as Christ lives (Calvin, *Inst.* 2.10.14; 3.24, 25).

For those who die in Christ, life is not taken captive by death, but rather buried and raised anew to glory (Cyprian, *Letters, FC* 51, pp. 17–19). Death when naturally viewed appears as our "last enemy." Viewed under grace it has lost its sting (1 Cor. 15:26). The believer has "crossed over from death to life" (John 5:24). In death the life of faith changes from glory to glory (2 Cor. 3:18). The terror of death is overcome by grace through faith active in love. Though death is a penalty for sin (Council of Mileum II, SCD 101, p. 44; Council of Orange II, SCD 175, p. 75), death for Christian believers is transformed into a penalty whose sting is dissipated (1 Cor. 15:56). "If we die with him, we will also live with him" (2 Tim. 2:11).

Death brings its own form of comfort to those who have suffered much. For death ends all temporal suffering, all complicity in sin, and all future burdens of decision making (2 Cor. 4:16, 17; Rev. 14:13).

The Westminster Confession recapitulated the classic Christian teaching of death succinctly: "The bodies of men, after death, return to dust, and see corruption; but their souls (which neither die nor sleep), having an immortal subsistence, immediately return to God who gave them. The souls of the righteous, being then made perfect in holiness, are received into the highest heavens, where they behold the face of God in light and glory, waiting for the full redemption of their bodies" (XXII.1, *CC,* p. 228).

Dying and Sanctifying Grace. Every day the faithful are called to choose anew the way of dying to the world and living to God. Each day offers the opportunity to hand ourselves over in the complete consecration of all our redeemed powers to God's care (Cyprian, *Treatise VII, ANF* V, pp. 469–75). In physically dying, the baptized are doing once for all what symbolically and proleptically they have been doing each day since their baptism. "I die every day—I mean that" (1 Cor. 15:31). Said Ignatius of Antioch, "I am truly in earnest about dying for God. . . . I am his wheat, ground fine by the lions' teeth to be made purest bread" (Romans 4, *ECW*, p. 104). Without a glimmer of morbidity or necrophilia, when faced with death by totalitarian power, Ignatius was ready to say to his persecutors, "Allow me to receive the pure light. When I reach it, I shall be fully a man" (Ignatius, *Romans* 6.2, *SHD* I, p. 66; cf. *FC* 1, p. 111).

Physical death remains a genuine natural evil for the faithful, who know from the sacred text that death is not finally meant for those made in God's image. Nonetheless death in believers is made subservient to their sanctification, so that even death serves the interests of the coming reign of God. The recollection that life ends in death has the beneficial effect of drawing the faithful away from idolatries and toward trust in God. In this way death is taken up even into the economy and quiet ordering of grace (Cyprian, *Treatises* I, *ANF* V, p. 548). Death itself is viewed as a final passage to the presence of the living God.

Death brings to consummation the sanctification of believers, so that in death they may become "the spirits of the righteous made perfect" (Heb. 12:23, NRSV). "If, then, when death takes possession of a man, it drives life away from him, and proves him to be dead, much more does life, when it has obtained power over the man, drive out death, and restore him as living unto God" (Irenaeus, *Ag. Her.* V.12, *ANF* I, p. 537).

That the faithful are glorified in death means, in the language of Protestant scholasticism "(1) full and accomplished sanctification, the body of sin and death having been laid aside; (2) transportation by the angels to heaven; (3) immunity from the miseries of this life; (4) the fruition of heavenly joy and glory; (5) the praising and lauding of God and Christ; (6) the longing for and expectation of full glorification, both by the restoration of its own body, and by God's final deliverance of the Church" (J. Altingius, *Methodus Theologiae didacticae,* p. 119, *RD,* p. 695).

Instead of remaining simply an unwelcome final enemy, even death has come to be employed and sanctified in the divine economy so as to bring the faithful under discipline from glory to glory (Gregory of Nyssa, *FGG,* pp. 129–37). "Blessed are the dead who die in the Lord" (Rev. 14:13). Death serves the constructive purpose of making dust of the old body in order that the resurrected body may rise uncorrupted (Lactantius, *DI, FC* 49, pp. 499–502). As history moves toward its final term, death is being abolished (1 Cor. 15:54–56).

Metaphors of Faithful Death.   Death is something like a *departure* from this life to another. In his last communication with Timothy Paul expected an immediate end to his life: "For I am already being poured out like a drink offering, and the time has come for my departure [*analuseos,* unmooring, unloosing]. . . . Now there is in store for me the crown of righteousness, which the Lord, the righteous Judge, will award to me on that day" (2 Tim. 4:6, 8).

Death for believers is transformed into a *rest* from labor (Rev. 14:13) and a *relief* to the afflicted (2 Thess. 1:7). It is said to be a sleep in Jesus (1 Thess. 4:14), in the sense that in Christ death is no more permanent than sleep that is followed by an awakening.

As the *tent* of this body is put aside (2 Pet. 1:14), the spirit returns to God (Luke 23:46; Acts 7:59). "For while we are in this tent, we groan and are burdened, because we do not wish to be unclothed but to be clothed with our heavenly dwelling so that what is mortal may be swallowed up by life" (2 Cor. 5:1–4). In the resurrection the perishable is "clothed with the imperishable" (1 Cor. 15:53).

Meanwhile this side of death, at the Lord's Table the believer is being fed regularly so the spiritual body born in baptism may be nourished toward eternal life, finally to be raised up on the day of his coming (John Chrysostom, *Baptismal Instructions, ACW* 31, pp. 150–52). Each service of Word and Sacrament, of meeting with the risen Lord, is an occasion for preparation of the final meeting with the Lord in death and the ensuing life eternal. Christians facing terminal illness receive the grace of Eucharist, aware that Christ himself will be their companion on the way to the next life. That is the meaning of the last Eucharist, called Viaticum (on the way).

The Death of Nonbelievers.   Death is especially viewed with sadness for those who, knowing of God's mercy, refuse to receive it and are determined to live without it. The death of the impenitent means that no further opportunity is given for eternal life. In dying, one's capacity for rebellious willing ceases, and thus death makes one's isolation from the font of goodness intractable. This condition of departure or separation from God is what is meant by hell, a subject to be discussed in due order after the general judgment.

Immortality

Job's question remains a perennial human query: "If a man dies, will he live again?" (14:14). Our limited purpose remains to state the classic Orthodox-Catholic-Reformed consensus on this point, even if that consensus has been challenged by historical critics. The unfeigned, accurate, straightforward delineation of the internal reasoning of the classic position will go far in answering many legitimate questions of critics.

Only God Has Absolute Immortality.   Orthodox teaching shrinks from the excessive claim that a creature could be essentially or necessarily eternal. Eternity is an attribute of God, not the creature. Christian hope is not fixed upon the indestructibility of the natural soul of individual human beings, but God's redemptive power (Lactantius, *DI, FC* 49, pp. 191–94, 492–98).

In the absolute sense, God "alone is immortal [*athanasian*]" (1 Tim. 6:16). This does not imply that human creatures cannot be given a share in immortality. It merely affirms that God is the only one who has immortality as a necessary attribute (Calvin, *Inst.* 3.25). God alone necessarily exists. All other beings have a borrowed or derived or dependent existence. Such is as true of the created human soul as of the body. To affirm personal survival after death is not to imply that the survivors were uncreated.

Life Survives Death.   With this qualification, Christianity affirms that creaturely human life survives bodily death. The human body is mortal, but the vital center of human selfhood is still destined for life with God when all the cells of the body have long decayed (Cyprian, *Treatise VII, ANF* V, pp. 469–75).

Eternal life with God is not claimed by Christians as a right but as a part of the divine economy of salvation that by grace allows unimpeded and unending communion with God (Lactantius, *DI* III.13, *ANF* VII, pp. 80–81). "To those who by persistence in doing good seek glory, honor and immortality [*aphtharsian*], he will give eternal life" (Rom. 2:7). "The immortality or continued conscious existence of man's spirit is everywhere assumed in Scripture and nowhere proved" (Pope, *Compend.* III, p. 372).

Life beyond death is not an intrinsic human possession such that sinners might boast that they have something that even God cannot destroy. Rather the life that God gives, God continues to sustain. This sustenance occurs not by natural durability or merit but by grace. Humanity in God's image is endowed with the gift of immortality from God's hand, not as an autonomous natural quality (Gen. 1:26, 27; Ambrose, *Belief in the Resurrection* II.22 ff., *NPNF* 2 X, pp. 177–80).

Nor does the Christian teaching of the soul claim that its immortality results from the soul's immateriality. The term *immortality* has a place in Christian vocabulary only if qualified to mean that the living soul created in the image of God does not die with physical death and awaits the resurrection for its glorious reembodiment. Even at that it does not express with full adequacy the Christian understanding of the future life, which centers more on God's resurrecting mercy than on the bare notion of autonomous individual survival.

Human Purpose Does Not End in Death.   Radical materialism and reductive naturalism posit no plan or engendering purpose or ultimate goal in human existence. Christianity posits a meaningful plan and a divine intention for humanity (Lactantius, *Epitome of the Divine Inst.* LXVII, *ANF* VII, p. 251) that extends beyond nature and historical time.

Among Protestant voices, Luther's rings clearest on this point: "It cannot be God's intention to permit Christians thus to suffer continually while they live, to die because of it and remain dead. It would be incompatible with his eternal, divine truth and honor manifest in his Word. . . . Necessarily, then, he has planned a future state for Christians and for non-Christians, in either instance unlike what they know on earth. Possibly one of the chief reasons why God permits Christians to suffer on earth is to make plain the distinction between their reward and that of the ungodly" (Luther, *SML* VIII, pp. 381–82). "If, now, it were not true that there is a future life, no greater deception would ever have appeared on earth." "If there is a God, we shall live not only here but also there, where He Himself lives" (Luther, *Letters, WA* 5:418, *WLS* 2, p. 780).

Israel's Hope of Immortality.   Against the view that there is no Old Testament hope for personal survival or immortality, classic Christian exegetes have been attentive to numerous allusions that assume continuing life after death. "Multitudes who sleep in the dust of the earth will awake: some to everlasting life, others to shame and everlasting contempt" (Dan. 12:2). Job expressed a confident expectation of a future vision of God: "And after my skin has been destroyed, yet in my flesh I will see God" (Job 19:26). The translation of Enoch (Gen. 5:24) and Elijah (2 Kings 2:11) point to some life beyond the grave. The people of God are being gathered to a place that is to the spirit what the grave is to the body (Pope, *Compend.* III, p. 376), "the place appointed for all the living" (Job 30:23). When

Abraham "breathed his last," he was "gathered to his people" (Gen. 25:8; cf. Gen. 25:17; Num. 20:24).

The heart of Israel's hope of personal survival hinged on its faith in the steadfast covenant love of God, who would never abandon the faithful, even in the grave: "My body will also rest secure, because you will not abandon me to the grave, nor will you let your Holy One see decay" (Ps. 16:10). Even the grave cannot rob life from the one whose shelter is the Lord (Pss. 17, 46, 91). Some psalms exude confidence in the expectation of communion with God after death, when flesh fails (Ps. 73:23–28), when one awakens after death, where "in righteousness I will see your face" (Ps. 17:15). "God will redeem my life from the grave; he will surely take me to himself" (Ps. 49:15). Who can read the psalms plausibly with the assumption that the writers knew nothing of a future life?

There were stern warnings in the Old Testament against consulting the dead or "familiar spirits," or persons thought to be able to summon the dead and speak with them (Lev. 19:31; Deut. 18:11; Isa. 8:19). These warnings, far from denying the impossibility of such communications, warn against their potentiality for idolatry, and mark Israel off from idolatrous nations.

By the intertestamental period the late Judaic hope of personal survival had achieved more explicit definition: "But the souls of the righteous are in the hand of God, and no torment will ever touch them," for "their hope is full of immortality" (Wisd. of Sol. 3:1, 4; cf. 3:15, 16; 15:3, 4).

The Doctrine of Immortality Through Resurrection in the New Testament.   It is common in the history of revelation for certain teachings to be revealed gradually through historical experience. The Davidic, prophetic, and Wisdom teachings of immortality could only be adequately made clear after the resurrection of Jesus Christ, who having "destroyed death" has "brought life and immortality [*aphtharsia*] to light through the gospel" (2 Tim. 1:10). "For the perishable must clothe itself with the imperishable, and the mortal with immortality [*athanasia*]" (1 Cor. 15:53; Ambrose, *On Belief in the Resurrection* II.53–75, *NPNF* 2 X, pp. 182–86). That souls of believers survive death is apparent in such passages as Matthew 10:28 and Luke 23:43. Jesus is "the resurrection and the life. He who believes in me will live, even though he dies, and whoever lives and believes in me will never die" (John 11:25; Augustine, Comm. John, *NPNF* 1 VII, pp. 270–78).

Those who welcome God's own coming in faith have already passed from death to life (John 5:24; 2 Cor. 5:1). Jesus taught that "even Moses showed that the dead rise, for he calls the Lord the God of Abraham, the God of Isaac, and the God of Jacob. He is not the God of the dead, but of the living, for to him all are alive" (Luke 20: 37, 38). Jesus thereby understood that Abraham was yet living, and he repeated this point in his parable of the Rich Man and Lazarus (Sister Macrina, *On the Soul and the Resurrection, NPNF* 2 IV, pp. 447–48). When the beggar of Jesus' parable died, "the angels carried him to Abraham's side. The rich man also died and was buried. In hell, where he was in torment, he looked up and saw Abraham far away, with Lazarus by his side" (Luke 16:22, 23), and spoke to him. "Abraham's bosom" was another term for the resting place of the pious dead. The parable suggests that the souls of the righteous enter immediately after death into a state of happiness, and the souls of the unjust are by their behavior separated from the divine presence. That souls of unbelievers survive death is taught in Matthew 11:21–24; Romans 2:5–11; 2 Corinthians 5:10.

Whether Christian Eschatology Can Employ Arguments from Natural Theology

A subsection of speculative philosophy is devoted to the questions of the human future and destiny. Christian eschatology differs from philosophical eschatology in that it is relatively more free to hear the address of scripture.

Arguments for Immortality in Natural Theology. That the soul survives the body has often been argued on the basis of four premises: from the extraordinary powers of the soul itself, from the desire for life embedded in the soul, from the unequal distribution of good and evil in this present life, and from the general consent of humanity (see above, p. 377).

The *metaphysical* argument is based on the assumption that the soul is not composed of parts, and being incapable of division, is incapable of dissolution. Though the body decomposes because it is made up of varied elements, the soul does not decompose because it is simple and indivisible. The argument proceeds from the simplicity and immateriality of the soul to its necessary existence (Plato, *Phaedo*). The soul is not a spatial compound, hence cannot decompose. There is no adequate analogy between the destiny of the body and the destiny of the soul. Hence Plato argued that wherever life has emerged, it is indestructible.

The *teleological* argument states that God would not have planted in our hearts such aspirations and desires only to bring them to an abrupt end in death.

The *moral* argument states that because virtue does not receive adequate reward in this life, there must be a future life if the Orderer of time is just. It is evident that the demands of justice are not fulfilled in this life; hence one must hypothesize a future life in which present inequities will be righted. "Righteousness cannot gain full fruition except by the triumphant satisfaction of love's requirements, never obtained in this life. Unless future continuance affords time and proper conditions for such satisfaction, righteousness must fail of fruition—a conclusion which our moral reason rejects" (Hall, *DT* X, p. 17). The very success of evil in this life is proof that future judgment is a necessary moral hypothesis (Clementina, *Recognitions* III.38–40, *ANF* VIII, p. 124).

Rejecting other arguments for immortality, Kant proposed a version of the Christian moral argument for immortality as a postulate of practical reason, that this world's injustices require the premise of a future world of justice where history's wrongs are righted—not original with Kant but received from the patristic tradition and neatly laundered for the language currency of the Enlightenment (Kant, *Critique of Practical Reason; Fundamental Principles of the Metaphysics of Morals*).

Whether Philosophical Arguments May Be Correlated with Christian Eschatology. These philosophical arguments are not properly proofs, but efforts to account for the persistent conviction that human beings survive death. Like all other arguments of natural theology, they exist as hypotheses awaiting fuller disclosure in the history of revelation. Their value is cumulative rather than demonstrative.

Though scripture is not in tension with these arguments, there is little in scripture that would place weighty importance upon a bare fact of survival or simple continued existence of the soul, a colorless immortality independent of the divine economy of grace and judgment. Rather, the biblical focus remains upon the blessedness or lack of it in the life lived after death. This quality of future life is determined by one's overall lived-out relation to God in this life. There are moral conditions that attach to the inheritance of eternal life, whose fulfillment depends crucially upon one's faith in response to grace (Matt. 25:45, 46; 1 John 5:12).

"That the soul survives is as incapable of scientific disproof as of scientific proof" (Jessop, *ICD*, p. 103). "I cannot imagine how my physical nature will remain in union with the spiritual after my death, but I see that as a weakness of my imagination, not as determining what is really possible" (Strange, *Catholic Faith*, p. 160).

Whereas parapsychology and spiritualism (or spiritism) look for quasi-scientific proof, Christianity has shown minimal interest in these inquiries. The Christian teaching of the future life is largely a doxological meditation based upon the Spirit's speaking in scripture to experience, not a rational or scientific demonstration. It is difficult to adapt these philosophical arguments for the soul's survival into Christian theology without considerable readjusting, especially to the teaching of resurrection (Methodius, *On the Resurrection, ANF* VI, pp. 364–77; Arnobius, *Ag. Heathen* 33–54, *ANF* VI, pp. 446–54; Lactantius, *DI* VII.9–13, *ANF* VII, pp. 205–11).

"In contrast to the dualistic conception of immortality expressed in the Greek body-soul schema, the biblical formula of immortality through awakening is trying to impart a collective and dialogic conception of immortality; the essential part of man, the person, remains; that which has ripened in the course of this earthly existence of corporeal spirituality and spiritualized corporeality goes on existing in a different fashion. It goes on existing because it lives in God's memory. . . . The distinguishing mark of man, seen from above, is his being addressed by God. . . . What we call in substantialist language 'having a soul' will be described in a more historical, actual language as 'being God's partner in a dialogue'" (Ratzinger, *IC*, pp. 273–75).

ISSUES OF THE INTERMEDIATE STATE

It is difficult to apply categories of time to the intermediate period between death and resurrection. "God sees not time lengthwise but obliquely . . . before God it is all in one heap" (Luther, *Comm. Peter and Jude*, pp. 312 f., in *LC*, p. 238). Calvin thought it "neither lawful nor expedient to inquire too curiously concerning our souls' intermediate state. Many torment themselves overmuch with disputing as to what place the souls occupy" (*Inst.* 3.25.6).

Between Individual Death and the General Resurrection

That condition in which the soul exists between death and the resurrection is called the intermediate state. It is distinguished from the present state of life, on the one hand, and the final resurrected state, on the other.

Pastoral Importance.   What becomes of the soul after death? Is the soul conscious? However intriguing, these questions hardly admit of precise consensually received conclusions, but they remain important to those who face death, hence are a recurrent concern of pastoral care, particularly care of the bereaved.

There is some difference of opinion as to whether the souls of the righteous pass into an intermediate state between death and final judgment, or stand immediately in the presence of the Lord. Principal alternatives may be envisioned as follows:

AGREED	CONTROVERTED	AGREED
The Present State	**An Intermediate State**	**The Final State**
Ending in death of believer and unbeliever	Sleeping or awaiting or **No Intermediate State** Directly to bliss Immediate translation	Heaven/Hell

Christians differ in the way they interpret the pertinent texts, but most affirm that we may rest content that after death the believer is in the hands of God awaiting resurrection. The prevailing interpretation: *The souls of the just are conscious of their joy in the presence of Christ after death and before resurrection. The souls of the unjust are conscious of their absence from the glory of the Lord after death and before resurrection.* Both enter immediately after death into an intermediate state of awaiting final judgment.

Whether the Will of a Particular Individual Is Changeable After Death. With death ends the capacity to will in an earthly sense to influence causality in history. "Whatever your hand finds to do, do it with all your might, for in the grave, where you are going, there is neither working nor planning nor knowledge nor wisdom" (Eccles. 9:10).

The dividing line is fixed at death, and not subject to further pleadings or reviews. Between the rich man and Lazarus, "a great chasm has been fixed, so that those who want to go from here to you cannot, nor can anyone cross over from there to us" (Luke 16:26). "Souls immediately after their separation from the body become unchangeable in will, with the result that the will of man cannot further be changed, neither from good to evil, nor from evil to good" (Tho. Aq., SCG IV, chap. 92, pp. 338, 339).

As long as the direction of the soul can be changed by choice, one remains in a state of struggle or combat with incipient temptation. Immediately upon death, that condition ends. One then comes into a condition of awaiting to receive or to be deprived eternally of the benefits of a life rightly lived. "When it [the soul] shall, then, be separated from the body it will not be in a state of motion toward the end, but in a state of rest in the end acquired. The soul's will, therefore, will be immovable regarding a desire for the ultimate end" (Tho. Aq., SCG IV, chap. 94, p. 344). "What we are in the process of becoming when we die we shall surely be when we come to the final judgment" (Hall, *DT* X, p. 178).

Distinguishing Particular and General Judgment. The judgment of the individual soul is traditionally called particular judgment, posited as occurring immediately after death, as distinct from general judgment at the end of this-worldly history (Tho. Aq., *ST* supp. Q69.2, III, p. 2831). Thomas Aquinas (*SCG* IV, chap. 96, p. 345) argued that immediately after death the soul receives a just retribution for what it has done in this life by becoming immediately aware of its destiny await-ing resurrection day (cf. Council of Lyons II, *SCD* 464, p. 184; Benedict XII, *SCD* 530, p. 197). The end-time judgment awaits the event in which the resurrected body is rejoined to the soul. The posited time between them is called the inter-mediate state.

PARTICULAR JUDGMENT	GENERAL JUDGMENT
Immediately upon death	The last judgment
Soul	Resurrected body
Singly	Together
Separately	Common

Every person shall "appear before the judgment seat of Christ, that each one may receive what is due him for the things done while in the body, whether good or bad" (2 Cor. 5:10; cf. Rom. 2:6; Rev. 20:12–13; 22:12). Immediately after death, accord-ing to much classic exegesis, there is a particular judgment, wherein the soul becomes aware of its final destiny (Augustine, *Homilies, John* XLIX.10, *NPNF* 1 VII, p. 274). God illumines the soul inwardly so the condition is self-recognized.

Scriptures that refer to the saints coming immediately into the presence of the Lord after death are commonly considered under the topic of particular judg-ment, as distinguished from those events of divine general judgment that occur at the end of the world. The destiny of each individual soul is therefore known im-mediately after death, but the final sentence upon the unjust is not executed until the last day (Augustine, *The Soul and Its Origin* II.4, *NPNF* 1 V, p. 334).

Ursinus summarized the distinction, "There are two degrees in the consum-mation of eternal life. The one is when the souls of the righteous, being freed from the body, are *immediately* carried into heaven; for in death they obtain a de-liverance from all the evils of this life. The other is that greater, and more glorious degree to which we shall attain in the *resurrection* of our bodies, when we shall as-cend into heaven perfectly redeemed and glorified, and see God as he is" (Ursinus, *Comm. Heid. Catech,* p. 323, italics added).

The theandric mediator, Jesus Christ, is the judge at both the particular and the general judgment. General judgment, later to be discussed, is final and plenary. Particular judgment is usually thought to be anticipatory of final judgment and individually administered. All are "destined to die once, and after that to face judgment" (Heb. 9:27).

The Intermediate State of the Just and Unjust

The Intermediate State of the Righteous. The spirits of believers at death are with God. They are the "spirits of the righteous made perfect" whose names are "enrolled in heaven" (Heb. 12:22, 23, NRSV). Alive and conscious (Matt. 22:32; Luke 16:11; 1 Thess. 5:10), they enjoy a state of rest and blessedness (Rev. 6:9–

11). "The spirit returns to God who gave it" (Eccles. 12:7). The souls of the righteous dead appear to enter upon this state immediately, according to Luke 16:22 and Revelation 14:13 (see also Phil. 1:23; 1 Thess. 4:17; Council of Lyon, *SCD* 457, 464, pp. 180, 184; Benedict XII, *Benedictus Deus SCD* 530, p. 198; *Trent* VI, *SCD* 800, 809, pp. 250, 256).

Protestant formularies teach that the souls of faithful, forgiven, and undefiled believers (saints) immediately after death are with Christ. The soul "after this life, shall be immediately taken up to Christ its head." It is also taught that "this my body, raised by the power of Christ, shall again be united with my soul, and made like the glorious body of Christ" (*Heid. Catech.*, Q 57). "We believe that the faithful, after bodily death, go directly unto Christ" (Second Helvetic Conf., XXVI). Believers, having responded to justifying and sanctifying grace, are destined to reawaken in Christ either immediately after death or at least by the time of the resurrection to enter "a building from God, an eternal house in heaven, not built by human hands" (2 Cor. 5:1–8).

That the righteous after death have not yet received glorified resurrection bodies is suggested in 1 Thessalonians 4:16 and in 1 Corinthians 15:52, where an interval is assumed between Paul's time and the time of the Lord's return with the rising of the dead in Christ (John Chrysostom, *Hom. on 1 Thess.* VII, *NPNF* 1 XIII, pp. 352–55; Luther, *Comm. on 1 Cor.* 15, *LW* 28, pp. 191–213; cf. Strong, *ST*, p. 998). Paul regarded it as an error to teach that the general resurrection "has already taken place" (2 Tim. 2:18; cf. 1 Thess. 2:2).

Whether the Intermediate State Is Distinguishable from Heaven. Some caution that "we are never so to regard the doctrine of the intermediate state that it even suggests *heaven*" (Curtis, *ChrF*, p. 398). The point in dispute has to do with when heavenly bliss begins—immediately upon death, or awaiting final judgment?

In the parable of the rich man and Lazarus, the blessedness of believers apparently begins immediately after their death. Lazarus is pictured in Abraham's bosom, while the rich man is in Hades. In this parable the intermediate state seems to be subdivided into two spheres: the place to which the just beggar Lazarus had gone, Abraham's bosom; and the place of torment to which the unjust rich man had gone (Luke 16:23–31). "The fact that there still remain in the soul some tokens of our composite nature, even after its dissolution, is attested by the dialogue in Hades. For although the bodies had been committed to the tomb, some physical means of identification still attached to the souls, by which Lazarus was recognized, and the rich man was known" (Gregory of Nyssa, *On the Making of Man* 27, *LCF*, p. 164; cf. *NPNF* 2 V, pp. 418–19).

That believers at death enter paradise immediately seems implied in the words spoken to the thief on the cross. Jesus promised the thief that "today you will be with me in paradise" (Luke 23:43). Paradise is the garden of return, the resting place of the pious dead. The text seems incompatible with any notion that consciousness ends in death or that the soul is destroyed in death (Calvin, *Inst.* 3.25.6). Yet both Luke 16:23–31 and Luke 23:43 are interpretable as future references.

Justin Martyr taught that souls after death enjoy bliss in the interval between death and general resurrection (*Dialogue with Trypho* 80, *ANF* I, p. 234; cf. Irenaeus, *Ag. Her.* V.31, p. 560). Tertullian thought that martyrs entered heaven immediately upon death to behold the beatific vision (*On the Soul* 55, *ANF* III,

p. 231; Ambrose, *On Belief in the Resurrection* 20–44, *NPNF* 2 X, pp. 177–80; similarly Novatian, Origen, Eusebius, Gregory Nazianzen). Hall cautiously concluded, "That perfected saints see God before their full beatification at the last day seems probable" (Hall, *DT* X, p. 92).

The medieval tradition taught that "The souls of the [perfectly] just are received immediately into heaven" (Second Council of Lyons, A.D. 1274, in Pohle, *DT* XII, p. 24). Benedict XII declared in 1336 that the souls of the saints enter heaven immediately after death and behold God face to face, while souls needing purification enter heaven after purification (*SCD* 530, pp. 197 ff.; cf. *DS* 1000, *NR* 901–2, *DS* 857, 1305; *NR* 926; *LG* 49; *CCF*, p. 335).

In due course medieval scholastic teaching would distinguish five spheres of afterlife: heaven for the just; hell for the unjust (Hades is alternatively construed by some to have two divisions, one for the just—paradise, Abraham's bosom—and the other for the unjust); *limbus infantum* for unbaptized infants (who miss the beatific vision due to their implication in unransomed hereditary sin, though they remain unpunished for actual sin, and capable of a natural beatification); *limbus patrum*, where the Old Testament fathers and believing ancients await resurrection; and afterlife purgation, where the imperfect faithful are cleansed and fitted for heaven (Fourth Lateran Council, *SCD* 429, p. 168; Council of Lyons I, *SCD* 457, p. 180; Benedict XII, *SCD* 531, 535, pp. 197–99; Tho. Aq., *ST* supp, Q69.4–6, III, pp. 2833–35). Most of the definitions in this subsection remain to some degree controverted, hence can hardly be called ecumenically received teachings.

The Foretaste of Eternal Happiness. In the Eastern church tradition it is confessed that at death souls "depart immediately either to joy, or to sorrow and lamentation; though confessedly neither their enjoyment, nor condemnation are complete. For, after the common resurrection when the soul shall be united with the body, with which it had behaved itself well or ill, each shall receive the completion of either enjoyment or of condemnation" (Conf. of Dositheus, XVIII, *CC*, p. 506).

Having died, but awaiting general resurrection, "The souls of the righteous are in light and rest, with a foretaste of eternal happiness; but the souls of the wicked are in a state the reverse of this." The fullness of happiness is not posited as being experienced immediately upon death, because "the perfect retribution according to works shall be received by the perfect man after the resurrection of the body and God's last judgment" (*Longer Catech.*, Eastern Orthodox Church, 372, *COC* II, p. 503; 2 Tim. 4:8; 2 Cor. 5:10).

Whether the Believer Is Separated from Christ in Death. At death, the believer is not separated from Christ, but from the body. Paul drew this distinction (2 Cor. 5:6–8; cf. Phil. 1:19, 20):

At home in the body	Away from the body
Away from the Lord	At home with the Lord

"Away from the body" suggests separation of the soul from the body in death. The consensual reading of these texts has drawn the conclusion that the souls of the pious dead are with the Lord. To be absent from the body is to be present to the Lord.

Similarly: "I desire to *depart and be with Christ,* which is better by far; but it is more necessary for you that I remain in the body" (Phil. 1:23, italics added). Even though Paul wished to be immediately with Christ upon his death, he believed it to be for the church's good that he "remain in the body." This could hardly have been said without the expectation of an immediate joy in the presence of the Lord at death (Calvin, *Inst.* 3.25.6). Nothing, exclaimed Paul, shall separate us from the love of Christ—"neither death nor life," "neither the present nor the future" (Rom. 8:38).

Whether Paradise Is a Particular Sphere of Heaven.   Paradise is a garden metaphor alluding to the restoration of conditions that prevailed in the garden of Eden (Gen. 2:8 ff.). Paradise appears to be at times used as a synonym for heaven or an allusion to a type of heaven (Luke 23:43; 2 Cor. 12:2–4; Rev. 2:7; Lactantius, *DI* II.14, *ANF* VII, p. 63). Paradise is called heaven in a different sense than final bliss (Tertullian, *Apology* 48, *APT,* p. 98, cf. 118n).

Like the metaphor "Abraham's bosom" (Luke 16:22), paradise sometimes refers to the intermediate state of the righteous between death and resurrection. Paul described himself as once—fourteen years ago—"caught up to the third heaven" (2 Cor. 12:2), whether in the body or out of the body he did not know (v. 3). This "third heaven" Paul also called "paradise" (2 Cor. 12:4). It remains debated as to whether the fullness of afterlife blessing begins upon entry into paradise or becomes heavenly bliss only in heaven, and whether paradise and heaven are distinguishable or whether one is inclusive of the other.

Sheol and Resurrection in the Old Testament.   Already in the Old Testament there was posited a differentiation between the future condition of the just and unjust. The general resurrection of the just and unjust will end whatever intermediate state is posited. Though the just hoped for deliverance from Sheol, no such hope would be thought possible for the unjust.

Though Sheol is usually translated "hell," it did not have reference to eternal punishment in its earlier development. Sheol is variously portrayed as a place of darkness or silence (Job 10:21, 22; Ps. 94:17) or forgetfulness (Ps. 88:12), separated from God's presence (Ps. 6:5), lacking awareness of earthly memories (Eccles. 9:5, 6, 10). In Job's gloomiest picture he expected to "go to the place of no return, to the land of gloom and deep shadow, to the land of deepest night, of deep shadow and disorder, where even the light is like darkness" (Job 10:21, 22; cf. Isa. 14:15–20). As the light of revelation increased, the expectation of the future life was set in greater readiness for the proleptic disclosure of the final things in the ministry of Jesus Christ, which is even yet awaiting final confirmation at the end of history.

The Intermediate State of the Unjust.   Those who have died in disbelief await final judgment under conditions of separation from God or alienation (Tertullian, *On the Soul* 56, *ANF* III, pp. 232–33). Those who "do not obey the gospel" will be "shut out from the presence of the Lord" (2 Thess. 1:8, 9). The souls of the wicked are pictured in a state of alienation resulting from their guilt as they await the resurrection and general judgment when they will be finally separated from God's holiness through their own recalcitrant decision (Benedict XII, *Benedictus Deus SCD* 530–31, p. 197). Insofar as they have consciousness, it is portrayed as loss of joy for not being allowed to enter into the presence of God (Luke 13:28; 16:28). They are portrayed as in prison, under guard, being held for the day of judgment (2 Pet. 2:9; Hippolytus, *Ag. Plato* I, *ANF* V, p. 221).

To further complicate the picture, in the New Testament, Hades sometimes means the abode of the dead in general, and at other times it refers to one of its spheres—either Paradise (Luke 23:43; 2 Cor. 12:4; Rev. 2:7) or Gehenna (Matt. 5:22–30; 10:28; 18:9; 23:13–15; Mark 9:43–47; Luke 12:5; James 3:6), which originally referred to the Valley of Hinnom, a place that became the scene of sacrifices to Moloch ànd later served as a garbage dump, smoldering endlessly. At times the term Hadès is used in the Old Testament sense of Sheol as the place of all departed souls; elsewhere it refers to the place of desolation (Matt. 11:23), or as that which cannot prevail against the gathered people of God (Matt. 16:18).

Whether Consciousness May Be Posited of the Soul After Death. Scripture portrays believers as engaged in a conscious life in dialogue, in communion with God immediately after death (2 Cor. 5:8; Phil. 1:23; Rev. 6:9; 20:4). The soul after death has "a purely spiritual life accompanied by full consciousness, and determined as to happiness or unhappiness by the result of the particular judgment held immediately after death" (Pohle, *DT* XII, p. 7). The premise of a conscious intermediate state is found in the transfiguration narrative (Luke 9:28–36; Proclus, *Orat.* 8, *MPG* 65, pp. 763–72), the words of Christ to the dying thief (Luke 23:39–43), and the notion of the communion of saints (2 Cor. 13:14; Rev. 8:3, 4).

Whether the Soul Sleeps in Death. The soul after death is not characteristically viewed in the New Testament as remaining in a totally unconscious or unresponsive state or lack of sapient capacity, though it is not incorrect to view it metaphorically as a sleeping state or soul-sleep. Note that sleep does not necessarily imply unconsciousness. One can use the metaphor of sleep and still view the intermediate state as one of consciousness.

The saints united with the Lord are described as those who sleep in Jesus: "so we believe that God will bring with Jesus those who have fallen asleep in him" (1 Thess. 4:14). He is their cemetery (*koimeterion*). Luther regarded the condition of faithful souls after death as "a deep strong, sweet sleep," considering "the coffin as nothing other than our Lord Jesus' bosom or Paradise, the grave as nothing other than a soft couch of ease or rest" (Luther, *Christian Songs, Latin and German, for Use at Funerals, WML* VI, pp. 287 f.). This is why the early Christians called their places of interment "not places of burial or graveyards, but *coemeteria*, sleeping chambers, *dormitoria*, houses of sleep" (Luther, *Gospel Sermon, Twenty-fourth Sunday After Trinity, SML* VIII, pp. 372–74).

The dead are spoken of metaphorically as sleeping (Dan. 12:2; Matt. 9:24; John 11:1; 1 Cor. 11:30; 15:51; 1 Thess. 4:14), but here the language of analogy is not intended to be applied literally (John Chrysostom, *Baptismal Instructions, ACW* 31, p. 176). Only when one takes the metaphor of sleep as a literal description do such passages become bewildering.

The sleeping metaphor remains a controversial hypothesis (Tertullian, *On the Soul* 58, *ANF* III, p. 235; cf. 43, *FC* 10, 278). Whereas Luther was attracted to the idea of the soul sleep, Calvin wrote against it (Calvin, *Psychopannychia, CR* V.171 f., *Tracts* III, p. 415; *Inst.* 3.25.6; cf. *Catholic Encyclopedia,* s.v. "John XXII"). The Forty-two Articles of 1553 rejected the view "that the souls of such as depart hence do sleep," in the sense of "being without all sense, feeling or perceiving until the Day of Judgment" (Hall, *DT* X, p. 73).

10 The End of Human History

EXPECTED EVENTS OF THE END TIME: RESURRECTION, RETURN, MILLENNIUM, AND JUDGMENT

Having set forth key teachings concerning the resurrection of Jesus in the second volume of this series, *The Word of Life,* I find a broad range of topics remain to be discussed on the future of human history. Key subjects include the general resurrection, the final coming, millennial questions, final judgment, the final destinies of the just and unjust.

The General Resurrection of the Dead

The Greek tradition held that the soul existed before and after earthly life, hence one's true life is the life of one's soul, the body being ancillary to the human person. The Hebraic tradition viewed the human person as a single composite reality of inspirited mud, grounded in the earth yet capable of transcendence, in an interface so closely woven that it was unthinkable that one could be a person without a body of some sort. The New Testament makes frequent reference to the "resurrection of [all] *the dead*" (Matt. 22:31; Luke 20:35; Acts 4:2, italics added), so as to underscore the expected event as corporate experience as well as corporeal.

The Resurrection of the Body. It is an article of the creed to "believe in the resurrection of the body" (*SCD* 6, p. 7). "We look forward to the resurrection of the dead and the life of the world to come" (Creed of the 150 Fathers, *CC,* p. 33). The point recurs in virtually every form of the rule of faith. The Faith of Damasus confessed more explicitly, "We believe that cleansed in his death and in his blood we are to be raised up by him on the last day in this body with which we now live" (*SCD* 15, p. 11; cf. Creed of the Council of Toledo, *SCD* 20, p. 13).

On his return, the Lord is expected to call the dead from the grave to be raised up by the power of God. "I tell you the truth, a time is coming and has now come when the dead will hear the voice of the Son of God and those who hear will live" (John 5:25; Tertullian, *On Resurrection, ANF* III, p. 572).

Defining Resurrection.   Early preaching consisted in "proclaiming in Jesus the resurrection of the dead" (Acts 4:2). What Paul preached could be summarized simply as "Jesus and the resurrection" (Acts 17:18). To deny the resurrection is, according to Jesus, to have no knowledge of scripture (Matt. 22:29). It was the defining error of the Sadducees against which Jesus actively taught (Mark 12:18–23; Luke 20:27–33; Acts 23:6–8).

Resurrection (*anastasis*, a standing or rising up again, *egersis*, being raised up) is defined in the Eastern Orthodox *Longer Catechism* as that "act of the almighty power of God, by which all bodies of dead men, being reunited to their souls, shall return to life, and shall thenceforth be spiritual and immortal" (366, *COC* II, p. 502). "For if they define death as the separation of soul and body, resurrection surely is the re-union of soul and body" (John of Damascus, *OF* IV.27, *NPNF* 2 IX, p. 99). "All men shall rise again with their own bodies, which they now have, to receive according to their deeds" (Fourth Lateran Council). Resurrection means the reuniting of body and soul at the end of days. Resurrection is the action of God by which the bodies of all times and places, just and unjust alike, though reduced to dust, shall be restored to the souls from which they were separated by death, to be united for eternity in either nearness or distance from God (Pearson, *Creed*, art. XI; Wesleyan Church Articles of Religion, *DSWT*, p. 160; Liddon, *Easter in St. Paul's* XXIII).

Whether the Resurrection Is of the Just and the Unjust.   The key text is from John—"a time is coming when all who are in their graves will hear his voice and come out—those who have done good will rise to live, and those who have done evil will rise to be condemned" (5:28, 29).

Some passages of scripture appear to speak only of a resurrection of the just (Isa. 26:19; Luke 14:14). Yet Daniel expected the multitudes now dead to "awake: some to everlasting life, others to shame" (Dan. 12:2).

The reason why scripture more often sets forth resurrection teaching as if only about the just is, according to Calvin, "for Christ came properly not for the destruction of the world but for its salvation. Hence in the creed also there is mention solely of the blessed life" (*Inst.* 3.25.7).

In Paul's defense before the earthly governor Felix, he did not hesitate to point out that all finally must be accountable to the heavenly judge, for there will be "a resurrection of both the righteous and the wicked" (Acts 24:15). This is unambiguously affirmed in the Athanasian Creed (Quiquncue): "whence he will come to judge all living and dead: at whose coming all men will rise again with their bodies, and will render an account of their deeds; and those who have behaved well will go to eternal life, those who have behaved badly to eternal fire" (*CC*, p. 706).

Inclusiveness of the Final Event. When this call comes, all will hear, though dead (Gregory of Nyssa, *The Great Catechism* XVI, *NPNF* 2 IV, p. 489). "Do not be amazed at this, for a time is coming when all who are in their graves will hear his voice and come out—those who have done good will rise to live, and those who have done evil will rise to be condemned" (John 5:28, 29).

All nations are included (Matt. 25:32); "great and small" (Rev. 20:12) will stand before the final judge (Heidegger, *Med.* XXVIII, 37; *RD*, p. 701). The intention of the phrase in the psalm "the wicked will not stand in the judgment" (Ps. 1:5) is that those who are wicked will appear but will be unable to stand in the final judgment (Aphrahat, *Demonstrations, Of Death, NPNF* 2 XIII, p. 406).

"I Am the Resurrection." Jesus not only taught but was the resurrection. From his resurrection the disciples learned what to expect of the end of history. The coming resurrection is already being proleptically experienced in the present by those whose lives are hid in Christ. "I am the resurrection and the life. He who believes in me will live, even though he dies; and whoever lives and believes in me will never die" (John 11:25, 26). The resurrection event embraces not only Jesus' resurrection but ours, both "the 'first resurrection' from the death of sin to the life of righteousness, and the 'second resurrection' or call back from physical death to life. 'Blessed and holy is he who shares in the first resurrection!'" (Wollebius, *RDB*, p. 181, quoting Rev. 20:6).

The resurrection of the believer is a sharing in Christ's resurrection. "But Christ has indeed been raised from the dead, the first fruits of those who have fallen asleep" (1 Cor. 15:5). "And if the Spirit of him who raised Jesus from the dead is living in you, he who raised Christ from the dead will also give life to your mortal bodies through his Spirit, who lives in you" (Rom. 8:11).

Old Testament Prototypes Anticipatory of Anastasis. Though *anastasis* is a New Testament teaching, it is anticipated in many Old Testament types showing the power of God to renew life and restore lost possibilities, according to ancient Christian exegesis. Joseph was raised from the pit. Isaac was raised up from virtual death and given life by God's providence, just as Abraham was poised to follow the command to sacrifice him. The return from Babylon (Ezek. 37), the taking of Enoch (Gen. 5:24), Elijah and the son of the woman of Zarephath (1 Kings 17:21), Elisha and the Shunammite's son (2 Kings 4:34) were all regarded by ancient Christian exegetes as anticipatory types of the coming resurrection of the Son, and ultimately of all (Methodius, *Of the Resurrection, ANF* VI, pp. 373–76; cf. Ambrose, *FC* 44). Events like the salvation from the great flood and the exodus were viewed, in the light of Jesus' resurrection, as a kind of baptism, a resurrection. These ancient narratives formed the background of interpretation of New Testament accounts of the daughter of Jairus (Mark 5:41), the widow of Nain (Luke 7:15), Lazarus (John 11), and those who arose at the burial of Jesus (Matt. 27:52).

The Distinctive Christian Teaching of the Resurrection of the Body. "That Christ died, pagans and enemies believe; but that Christ rose is the peculiar faith of

Christians" (Leiden Synopsis, LI.3, cf. Heppe, *RD*, pp. 695–701). The expectation of the general resurrection of the body is a carefully nuanced teaching that arguably marks off Judaism and Christianity as distinct among major world religions. Resisting dualisms, it honors the body as integral to human nature. It views death not as mere natural process but as enemy. Death is not merely an event of nature but the consequence of sin.

The resurrection *locus classicus* of Hebrew scripture is enunciated amid the patient suffering of Job: "I know that my Redeemer lives, and that in the end he will stand upon the earth. And after my skin has been destroyed, yet in my flesh I will see God. I myself will see him with my own eyes—I, and not another" (Job 19:25–27; Jerome, *To Pammachius* 30, *NPNF* 2 VI, p. 439).

Whether Resurrection Posits Immortality.   In the resurrection the dead will rise "again at the end of the world and become immortal" (*Eastern Orthodox Catechism*, p. 92). There is a close association of the two ideas of resurrection and immortality in Christian teaching.

Thomas Aquinas provided a classic mode of reasoning why, upon rising, there will be no dying again. Resurrection is required to accomplish God's purpose for humanity because "man's ultimate perfection demands the reunion of soul and body," for the human person without body is missing something essential, hence "a natural desire rises within the soul for union with the body; its will cannot be utterly stilled until it be reunited with the body, in other words, until man rises from the dead." "Since it is immortal, we infer that the soul will be again joined to body" (Tho. Aq., *Compend. of Theology*, chap. 151, *TATT*, pp. 406, 407).

Thomas argued the congruity of resurrection with reason in this way: "It is against the nature of the soul to be without the body. But nothing that is against nature can be lasting. Therefore the soul will not be forever without the body. Thus the immortality of the soul seems to require the resurrection of the body" (Tho. Aq., *SCG* IV, chap. 79, in Pohle, *DT* XII, p. 136; cf. *TATT*, p. 406). Those who rise by Christ's merit will suffer death no more, because by his passion he has "repaired the deficiencies of nature which sin had brought upon nature" in death. "But the resurrection is not ordered to the perpetuity of the species, for this could be safeguarded by generation. It must, then, be ordered to the perpetuity of the individual: but not in the soul alone, for the soul already had perpetuity before the resurrection; therefore, in the composite: Man rising, therefore, will live forever" (*SCG* IV, chap. 82.1–7, pp. 308, 309). "We ought to be judged, and if need be punished, in the composite human nature in which we have done good or ill" (Hall, *DT* X, p. 150).

The life that one receives in creation was found to be mortal through the consequences of sin. The person is deprived of life in time by bodily death. The body in this life is given as a temporary housing for the person through creation (2 Cor. 5:1–5). Congruently, the life that one receives by resurrection is found to be immortal through the consequences of grace. The person is given life anew through the new correspondence of body with soul in the resurrection of the dead. The body is given a glorified form through the resurrection (Tho. Aq., *SCG* IV, chap. 82.7, p. 310). Whereas in the first generation soul was created after body, following the generation of the body, adapting itself to the body, in the resurrection the process is reversed: the body becomes adapted to the already existing soul, following after the soul.

Celebration of the Body

There is in Jewish and Christian hope of the resurrection of the dead no contempt for the body, nor is there an idealization of the disembodied soul.

Precisely What Is Raised in the Resurrection?   The body is greatly honored in
Christianity (Rom. 6:19; 12:1; 1 Cor. 6:19, 20; 9:27), not only in the incarnation,
which is the coming of God in the flesh, but the resurrection as well, which is the
reuniting of the human body-soul composite for an eternal destiny near to or
separated from God (Justin Martyr, *On the Resurrection* VII, *ANF* I, p. 297).

The Christian hope risks distortion if stated as if it were essentially a hope for
the soul's escape from the prison of the body into a purely spiritual realm. Christianity hopes for the renewal of the whole person, where I will again be myself,
will live again in my glorified body (Ignatius, *Smyrna* 2–9, *AF*, pp. 111–13).

What is dead is the body, not the animated liveliness of the body that is the
psuchē. Precisely speaking, the *psuchē* does not need to be raised but rejoined to
the body.

It is the body revivified that rises in the resurrection. "It is precisely the substance of this our flesh but without sin, which will rise again" (Formula of Concord, 548, in Jacobs, *SCF*, p. 494). *"This corruptible* and *this mortal* is our present
body, and this is the thing which rises again. To deny this, and to affirm a purely
spiritual resurrection is against the Christian faith" (Tho. Aq., *SCG* III, chap. 79,
TATT, p. 405, italics added).

The Body Revivified.   Manichaean rejection of matter as evil is itself rejected by
resurrection teaching. Calvin regarded it as a Manichaean error to think that the
flesh, being unclean, cannot rise again, as if to imagine that what is infected with
the taint of sin could not be divinely cleansed (Calvin, *Inst.* 3.25). The body is the
temple of the Holy Spirit. Though the seat of unruly affections, pride, and vanity,
the body rightly understood is a divine gift that may in turn be completely
consecrated.

The body as such is not treated as an encumbrance but as necessary when
viewed within the economy of salvation. "It is not the body, but the corruptibility
of the body, which is a burden to the soul" (Augustine, *CG* XIII.16; cf. 1 Cor.
6:19; Rom. 8:20–23; Gal. 5:17). "Man is so constituted by nature that every line
of the spirit's receptivity and expression is conditioned and accomplished by the
use of matter; and no evidence exists that the supernatural elevation of human
nature hereafter will bring this law to an end" (Hall, *DT* X, p. 162).

The resurrection is of the body, but not simply this natural body of flesh, as if
it could be spiritlessly restored, for "flesh and blood cannot inherit the kingdom
of God, nor does the perishable inherit the imperishable" (1 Cor. 15:50). Rather
God is preparing a body suitable to the conditions of eternity in the divine presence (Rufinus, *Comm. on Apostles' Creed* 40, *NPNF* 2 III, pp. 561–63). "If there
is a natural body, there is also a spiritual body" (1 Cor. 15:44). Spiritual body
does not mean body made out of spirit but body completely enlivened by spirit,
just as the present psychical body is indwelt and empowered by the soul (1 Cor.
15:44–46).

"Paul teaches not the resurrection of physical bodies but the resurrection of
persons, and this is not in the return of the 'fleshly body,' that is, the biological

structure, an idea which he expressly describes as impossible ('the perishable can-not become imperishable'), but in the different form of the life of the resurrection" (Ratzinger, *IC*, p. 277).

For the Body.   That the Lord is for the body is evident in the incarnation, where he assumed not only a human soul but a body. The body of Christ has extraordinary importance in Christianity. His body was offered as a sacrifice on the cross. The Supper is a participation in his body (John 6:35–40). Ultimately our very bodies are to be redeemed. "Offer your bodies as living sacrifices" (Rom. 12:2). "Do you not know that your bodies are members of Christ himself?" (1 Cor. 6:15).

The whole body is understood metaphorically as set apart for service, as a temple. The Spirit is at work to renew and sanctify the hands (Eph. 4:28), the mouth (Eph. 4:29), the tongue (1 Pet. 3:15), the eyes (Ps. 119:37), the ears (James 1:19), and all the "parts of your body" as "instruments of righteousness" (Rom. 6:13).

Some at Corinth were saying that food was meant for the stomach and the stomach for food, as the genitals were meant for sexual activity and sexual activity was ordered for the genitals. Paul countered with a far-reaching principle: that the body is meant "for the Lord, and the Lord for the body" (1 Cor. 6:13).

The Same Person.   Since it is the whole person that God loved and redeemed, the restored whole person is promised as a future hope in Jewish and Christian teaching (Tertullian, *Apology* 48–50, *APT*, pp. 98–100).

Resurrection is the complete and final restoration of the whole person. Only on the premise of this restoration is one able to complete one's eternal destiny of closeness to or distance from God (Origen, *OFP* III.6, pp. 245 ff.).

"Resurrection is the restoration of the same human body to life in the same substance, less mortality" (Bucanus, *IT* XXXVII.2, Heppe, *RD*, p. 701). If the notion of "same body" is not assumed in the definition, it risks being diluted into the notion of the resurrection of a different body (Irenaeus, *Ag. Her.* V.32, *ANF* I, p. 561). "If the soul did not resume the same body, there would be no resurrection, but rather the assumption of a new body" (Tho. Aq., *ST* supp., Q79.1; in Pohle, *DT* XII, p. 139).

The glorified body is not a different body, but a different form of the same body. "We shall arise, clothed not in air or some other flesh, but in the self-same [now-glorified flesh] in which we live, exist, and move" (Eleventh Council of Toledo, *DS* 347). Final judgment would make little sense if "new bodies were to be brought before the judgment seat" (*Inst.* 3.25.7, cf. Augustine, *Ag. Adimantus* XII.5 *Sermons* XII.10.10; *Unfinished Treatise Ag. Julian* I.95). The glorified body is distinguished from the earthly body, yet in continuity with it (Athenagoras, *Resurr. of the Dead,* chap. II ff.). "For He did not raise the soul without the body but the body along with the soul; and not another body but the very one that was corrupt" (John of Damascus, *OF* IV.27, *NPNF* 2 IX, p. 100). "The whole body, whether it withers away to dust, or dissolves into moisture, or crumbles away to ashes or passes off in vapor, is removed from our eyes, but it still exists for God" (Minucius Felix, *To Octavius* 34, *FC* 10, p. 393).

Whether the Atomistic Dissolution of the Body Confounds the Resurrection.   Does this imply that precisely the same cells and molecules that once constituted our body will be regathered and recomposed? No. For even in earthly existence, there is no such continuity. The body is constantly changing materially, and has been doing so since infancy (Gregory of Nyssa, *On the Making of Man* XXVII–XXX, *NPNF* 2 IV, pp. 418–27). Yet its basic features have continuity, due to their genetic coding. The DNA molecules provide a unique, specific code for every individual that stamps each one as distinctive. There is no precise molecular identity between the grain of wheat buried in the ground and the harvest gathered the next summer, but there is clearly continuity of the organism (Sister Macrina, *On the Soul and the Resurrection, NPNF* 2 IV, p. 466). God will find fit means to guarantee the sameness of the body without construing this as precisely the same cellular identity. The identity of the person will remain, as one person may survive several physical bodies metabolically during a given lifetime. "The human beings that rise again are the identical human beings who lived before, though their vital processes are performed in a different way" (Tho. Aq., *Compend. of Theology* 155, *TATT*, p. 408). Metabolically, "the human body changes its material composition every seven years or so. Hence there can be no absolute bodily identity even in this life" (Pohle, *DT* XII, p. 141). The Pauline teaching of the "same body" does not require a restoration even more fixed and absolute than ordinary metabolic changes require.

The parent's life may be dissolved in death while the child's body lives on with a genetic structure in continuity with the parents'. Similarly, even while the physical body is being dissolved in time and death, the glorified body will live on, having been given life in baptism, fed by the Eucharist, and clothed in glory at the last day (Cyril of Jerusalem, *Catech. Lect.* XVIII.7, *NPNF* 2 VII, p. 135; cf. Hall, *DT* X, p. 156).

"For just as, not existing before I was born, I knew not who I was, and only existed in the potentiality of fleshly matter, but being born, after a former state of nothingness, I have obtained through my birth a certainty of my existence; in the same way, having been born, and through death existing no longer, and seen no longer, I shall exist again just as before I was not, but was afterwards born. Even though fire destroy all traces of my flesh, the world receives the vaporized matter, and though dispersed through rivers and seas, or torn in pieces by wild beasts, I am laid up in the storehouses of a wealthy Lord" (Tatian, *Orat. Ag. the Greeks* 6, *ANF* II, p. 67).

Whether, Lacking Resurrection, There Is Moral Absurdity. If one posits a history full of injustice without a resurrection, the power of evil would be greater than the power of God, and a major defect would persist in the economy of salvation (Tertullian, *The Resurrection of the Flesh* 41–49; *ANF* III, pp. 575–82). "If there is no resurrection, neither is there any God nor Providence, but all things are driven and borne along of themselves" (John of Damascus, *OF* IV.27, *NPNF* 2 IX, p. 99).

Resurrection is a necessary link in the moral chain of divine promises. There are many obstacles to the complete fulfillment of the covenant in this life. The covenant promises perfect happiness uncharacteristic of this life. Resurrection must be morally posited to actualize the full happiness promised by God.

"Why do the wicked live on, growing old and increasing in power?" (Job 21:7). There is a moral embarrassment in providence if this question is not dealt with finally (Gregory of Nyssa, *On the Making of Man* XXI, *NPNF* 2 IV, pp. 410, 411). At some point the serious moral consciousness must posit a future life in which justice is better done than in history (Tho. Aq., *SCG* IV, chap. 79, *TATT*, p. 407).

"You must charge God with lack of justice, if there be not judgement and recompense after this world." How could God be righteous if murderers go forever unpunished? No one who presides over the games crowns the athlete while he is striving, but "waits till he has seen how every competitor finishes" (Cyril of Jerusalem, *Catech. Lect.* XVIII.4, *LCC* 4, p. 180; cf. *NPNF* 2 VII, p. 135).

Whether to Come Alive the Seed Must Be Buried.   The body that dies becomes subject to the decomposition of its constituent parts, abandoned to the general laws of matter. Can an identity be preserved amid this disintegration? Paul answered with a metaphor: "But someone may ask, 'How are the dead raised? With what kind of body will they come?' How foolish! What you sow does not come to life unless it dies. When you sow, you do not plant the body that will be, but just a seed, perhaps of wheat or of something else. But *God gives it a body* as he has determined, and to each kind of seed he gives its own body" (1 Cor. 15:35–38, italics added).

The seed must be buried to come alive. It must pass into a certain sort of decay and dissolution in order that the seed may then disengage from its old form and begin to sprout. Similarly our bodies die, that by dying they may enter at length into a new life.

The Living Organism from the Dying Seed.   The body of the seed dies but the principle of life in the seed remains ready to come alive once buried. The new plant is a new body, distinguishable from the seed, but it has grown out of the seed (*Longer Catech.*, Eastern Orthodox Church, 367, *COC* II, p. 503; Minucius Felix, *Octavius* 34).

Though there is a vast change, the former identity is not destroyed. The changed form does not imply a breach of organic continuity or a transubstantiation of matter into spirit or the transmigration of souls from one body to another, for it is the same *soma* that is "delivered from its present subjection to the animal *psuchē,* and is subjected to the higher *pneuma*" (Hall, *DT* X, p. 151). The flesh that cannot inherit incorruption has reference strictly to the native power and limitations of the present physical *soma*. Though the body cannot of itself inherit incorruption, it can put on incorruption in the form of being clothed with the imperishable when raised by the power of God (1 Cor. 15:50–54).

Sister Macrina was Gregory of Nyssa's teacher on the resurrection. From the creation narrative we learn that first the earth brought forth the plant, then the seed grew when buried in the ground, and from this the same form of the original growth sprang up anew. This is what happens in the resurrection: *"the return of human nature to its primal condition."* So it is with humanity, "Originally we also were, in a sense, a full ear, but we were withered by the torrid heat of sin; and then on our dissolution by death the earth received us. But in the spring of the resurrection the earth will again display this naked grain of our body as an ear, tall, luxuriant, and upright" (Sister Macrina, *On the Soul and the Resurrection,* as told to Gregory of Nyssa, *LCF,* p. 165, italics added; cf. *NPNF* 2 V, pp. 466–67).

We Shall Be Like Him

In raising the dead, the Lord will give the bodies of the faithful a new spiritual form (Calvin, *Inst.* 3.25). Although it is not revealed exactly how they are to appear, Paul was confident that the risen faithful would be like the risen Lord, our risen bodies like his risen body, no longer subject to illness and death (1 Cor. 15:50–58).

The Risen, Glorified Body. If the new body is more glorious than the old, it is unreasonable to grieve inordinately over the loss of the old body. "So will it be with the resurrection of the dead. The body that is sown is perishable, it is raised imperishable; it is sown in dishonor, it is raised in glory; it is sown in weakness, it is raised in power; it is sown a natural body, it is raised a spiritual body" (1 Cor. 15:42, 43).

That the risen body is spiritual does not imply that it has become so etherealized as to be no longer a body. It will be distinguishable from what it now is, yet still remain a body with the power of movement, yet without the digestive-reproductive functions of the animal economy. The notion of a spiritual body remains a mystery. From scripture we are taught as much as we need to know. The "need to know" principle applies in this special assignment: life. We are being equipped by grace with what we need to know, trusting in One who was resurrected from the dead (Hugh of St. Victor, *SCF*, pp. 456–61).

The Nature of the Resurrection Body. It remains a mystery of faith that the risen body of Christ was the same body as he had in earthly life, yet with changed attributes. "With what kind of body will they come?" (1 Cor. 15:35). What are the properties of the resurrection body? Our Lord's risen body reveals the pattern of the resurrection body, for "our citizenship is in heaven. And we eagerly await a Savior from there, the Lord Jesus Christ, who, by the power that enables him to bring everything under his control, will transform our lowly bodies so that they will be *like his* glorious body" (Phil. 3:20, 21, italics added).

Jesus offered his risen body to the test of the senses: "Touch me and see; a ghost does not have flesh and bones, as you see I have" (Luke 24:39). Yet his glorified body had astonishing features: incorruptibility, agility, and radiance. His risen body was the same identity, for he was recognizable; yet a change of form had taken place. The body changes from a decomposing earthly body to a glorified body without impairing its original identity (Origen, *Ag. Celsus* V.16–19, *ANF* IV, pp. 550–51). The Alexandrian tradition stressed the change in the spiritual body (Origen, *Principles* II.10, *ANF* IV, pp. 293–96; Clement of Alexandria, *Stromata*), while the Latin tradition stressed the continuity in identity of the body (Tertullian, Lactantius, Augustine, Jerome). "Their bodies remain truly human, though they are invested with an immortality coming from a divine strength which enables the soul so to dominate the body that corruption cannot enter" (Tho. Aq., *Compend. of Theology* 155, *TATT*, p. 409).

Events in Jesus' Ministry as Anticipative of the Resurrection. The transfiguration was a type of the glorified body, where Jesus' "face shone like the sun, and his clothes became as white as the light," and "there appeared before them Moses and Elijah, talking with Jesus" (Matt. 17:2; cf. Luke 9:29; Proclus, *Orat.* 8, *MPG* 5, pp. 763–72). Jesus there and elsewhere anticipated his resurrection, showing "some of the endowments of a glorified body; of light-footedness, when he walked on the waves; of delicacy, when he broke not open the Virgin's womb; of invulnerability, when he escaped unhurt" (Tho. Aq., *ST* IIIA, Q45.1.3, *TATT*, p. 410; Cyril of Jerusalem, *Catech. Lect.* X.7, *NPNF* 2 VII, p. 59).

Endowments of the Glorified Body. The risen (glorified-spiritual) body is being endowed with all that is requisite for life in the presence of the holy God. The vision of God is finally beheld only through the eyes of the resurrected body (1 John 3:2; 1 Cor. 13:12).

God is able to change the body so as to make it a fit temple for the glorified spirit. "These are then the four conditions of the glorified body: fineness [subtility], radiance [brightness, *claritas*], impassibility, and agility" (Tho. Aq., *Compend. of Theology* 168, *TATT*, p. 409). The risen body will enjoy a bliss and perfection and beauty that reflects its joyful participation in the completeness and beauty of God (Tho. Aq., *ST* supp., III, Q83–85, pp. 2911–27).

The risen bodies "will be perfectly purged of all earthly lees and dregs, all senses rendered purer, all movements and actions more perfect, and because they will be removed from the necessities of this animal life, sleep, rest, food, drink, medicines, clothes, etc., and because they will be perfectly subject to the Holy Spirit, and their souls regenerated by It and so they will have leisure for spiritual actions only" (Riisen, *FTCT* XVIII.24, Heppe, *RD*, p. 708).

The risen body will not die, because it is "raised imperishable" (1 Cor. 15:42). "There will be no more death or mourning or crying or pain, for the old order of things has passed away" (Rev. 21:4). The risen body will be capable of reflecting the glory of God, because it is "raised in glory" (1 Cor. 15:43). The same body is "raised in power," so as to be engaged without interruption in the praise of God, knowing no weariness or fainting.

In its glorified state, the soul will be given as much or greater excellence than existed in humanity before the fall. There will be understanding without error, light without shadow, wisdom without ignorance, reason without obscurity, memory without forgetfulness, volition without depravity, joy without sorrow, and pleasure without pain. If in the state of innocence Adam and Eve were able not to sin, in the state of glory the renewed humanity will not be able to sin (Wollebius, *RDB*, p. 189; cf. J. Wesley, *WJWB* II, sermon 60, *WJW* VI, pp. 241–52).

These inferences are drawn from scripture texts about the resurrection body of the faithful, and inferences from the narratives of the risen Lord, but there is less to go on with respect to the risen bodies of the unjust. They will also live on, but lacking these qualities of glory, brilliance, perfection of powers, agility, and spirituality. More than this the wisdom of God has not revealed (John of Damascus, *OF* 37, *NPNF* 2 IX, pp. 99–101).

Nothing Is Too Hard for the Lord. What Abraham said of Yahweh is pertinent to resurrection hope: nothing is too hard for the Lord (Gen. 18:14; cf., Jer. 32:17, 27). God is as able to restore the unity of the person as to create the person in the first place. "God created us out of nothing; why should He not be able to re-awaken that which is destroyed?" (Cyril of Jerusalem, *Catech. Lect.* XVIII.6, *NPNF* 2 VII, p. 135). What would appear more incredible to a thoughtful person than "that from a small drop of human seed," or semen, "bones and sinews and flesh be formed into a shape such as we see? . . . But as at first you would not have believed it possible . . . yet now see them . . . so also judge that it is not impossible that the bodies of men, after they have been dissolved, and like seeds resolved into earth, should in God's appointed time rise again and put on incorruption" (Justin Martyr, *First Apology* 18, *ANF* I, p. 169).

What otherwise appears impossible is possible with God (Tertullian, *Ag. Praxeas* 10, *ANF* III, p. 605). "We expect to receive again our own bodies, though they be dead and cast into the earth, for we maintain that with God nothing is impossible" (Justin Martyr, *First Apology* 18, *ANF* I, p. 169).

Whether Resurrection Presents More Difficulties for Belief Than Creation. Though above reason, resurrection is not contrary to reason, any more than is creation contrary to reason. Resurrection is simply a new creation.

If one can believe that the world has been created and exists in all its complexity, one can believe that the resurrection can occur in all its complexity. "Why should any of you consider it incredible that God raises the dead?" (Acts 26:8) if God is able to create *ex nihilo*? Is it more unreasonable to resist evidences of God's overcoming love merely because they come in an unaccustomed form? Minucius Felix thought that creation was just as full of wonder as resurrection, for "it is more difficult to give a beginning to what does not exist than to recall into existence what has once existed" (*To Octavius* 34, *FC* 10, p. 393). Cyril reasoned that we ourselves are already a resurrection, simply by virtue of being alive. For are not our bodies made "from weak and shapeless and simple elements," from which we are gathered together so as to become a "shipwright, builder, architect, craftsman, or legislator? Cannot God, who has made us out of imperfect materials, raise us up when we have fallen into decay? He who thus frames a body out of what is vile cannot He raise the fallen body again?" (Cyril of Jerusalem, *Catech. Lect.* XVIII.9, *NPNF* 2 VII, p. 136). "Impute then not weakness to God from a comparison of thy feebleness" (*Catech. Lect.* XVIII.3, *NPNF* 2 VII, p. 134).

On Resurrection Reasoning.   Resurrection is viewed as a "pure article of faith" that cannot be known except by revelation, which transmutes natural reasoning. When Paul preached the resurrection in Athens, Luke's account notes that "some of them sneered" (Acts 17:32). When he proclaimed it before the Roman governor, he was thought to be insane (Acts. 26:8). Even the disciples had great difficulty conceiving of the possibility of their Lord's resurrection. Upon its first report "they did not believe the women, because their words seemed to them like nonsense" (Luke 24:11; cf. John 20:25; Matt. 28:17).

"Although the resurrection of the dead is beyond [the power of] nature, and [understanding it] is beyond [the capacity of] corrupt reason, it is not contrary to nature, or right reason. Right reason indeed teaches both that the dead can be raised, and that they must be. The former is learned from God's omnipotence and the latter from his justice" (Wollebius, *RDB,* p. 182). Resurrection is necessary for God's penal justice as much as for salvation.

"Christ rising again is the univocal cause of our resurrection" (Tho. Aq., *ST* supp., Q76.2, III, p. 2880). Such an effect cannot be "the result of any natural cause, but solely by the divine power" (*Leiden Synopsis,* LI.22, in Heppe, *RD,* pp. 698 ff.). The final cause or purpose of the resurrection is "the revelation of the justice and mercy of God; justice in the raising of the wicked for condemnation; and mercy in the raising of the righteous for eternal life" (Wollebius, *RDB,* pp. 182, 183; cf. Tho. Aq., *ST* supp., Q79, III, pp. 2889–2901).

Whether the Body Will Have a Particular Age at the Resurrection. Sister
Macrina, defining resurrection as "the restoration of man to his original state,"
held that there is neither age nor infancy in the resurrected body (Sister Macrina,
On the Soul and the Resurrection, NPNF 2 IV, pp. 462–68). Augustine argued that
all in heaven would be young in age, in the prime of life, for that is the period of
peak perfection of bodily competencies (*CG* XXII.19, 20, *NPNF* 1 II, p. 498).
Those who were blind, lame, maimed, or paralyzed shall rise again with "an entire
and perfect body" (*Enchiridion* 85–91, *NPNF* 1 III, pp. 264–65; Tertullian, *On
the Resurrection* 57, 58, *ANF* III, p. 590). Gerhard argued that all will rise at the
age and stature they had at death, remembering the phrase that both "great and
small" will be present in the kingdom (Rev. 11:18).

Peter Lombard argued that believers will conform to the stature of Christ, for
Paul hoped that the believers might all "become mature, attaining to the whole
measure of the fullness of Christ" (Eph. 4:13), who predestined the faithful "to
be conformed to the likeness of his Son" (Rom. 8:29). Similarly Thomas: "But all
must rise in the age of Christ, which is that of youth, by reason of the perfection
of nature which is found in that age alone. For the age of boyhood has not yet
achieved the perfection of nature through increase; and by decrease old age has
already withdrawn from that perfection" (Tho. Aq., *SCG* IV, chap. 88, p. 329).

Whether Food or Sex Will Be Fitting for the Resurrected Body. Every soul will be
reunited with its own body. There will remain a distinction of sexes, yet without
the exercise of sexual function (Matt. 22:30; Augustine, *CG* XXII.17; *Leiden Synopsis* LI.37; in Heppe, *RD*, p. 701). One's sexual identity in the resurrection remains intrinsically an aspect of one's personal identity. The notion that women
will be changed into men was consistently refuted, for the One "who created both
sexes will restore both" (Augustine, *CG* XXII.17, *NPNF* 1 II, p. 496). Thomas
specifically opposed the view that "the feminine sex will be absent" in the resurrection (*SCG* IV.88, p. 328).

Thomas wrote an entire chapter of *Summa Contra Gentiles* on why there is no
requirement for food or sex in the glorified body. The gist of the argument: We
need food and drink to nurture the earthly body, to prevent it from deteriorating
and allow it to grow. In the risen life there is nothing to cause the glorified body
to deteriorate or tend toward corruption (*SCG* IV, chap. 83, pp. 311 ff.; cf. Sister
Macrina, *On the Soul and the Resurrection, NPNF* 2 IV, pp. 462–64).

Similarly sex is ordered primarily toward "that generation by which what cannot be perpetually preserved in the individual is preserved in the species" (Tho.
Aq., *SCG* IV, chap. 83.2, p. 312). Because there is no degeneration of risen bodies,
there is no need for generation. But suppose sex and food were "simply for the
pleasure," there still results an awkward dilemma. Nature ordered food and sex
for this reason: "lest the animals, in view of the labor, desist from those acts necessary to nature, which is what would happen if they were not stimulated by pleasure. Therefore the order is reversed and inharmonious if those operations are
carried out merely for pleasure" (Tho. Aq., *SCG* IV, chap. 83.10, pp. 314, 315; cf.
Luke 20:34–38).

In any event, the Lord seems to have settled the question for Christian teaching
by saying, "When the dead rise, they will neither marry nor be given in marriage;
they will be like the angels in heaven" (Mark 12:25), unless someone is foolish
enough to argue that "the beatitude of angels is imperfect because the angels lack

the pleasures of the brutes—which is completely absurd." Thomas gave the name "spiritual chiliasts" to the error that "in the resurrection men will have use of food and sexual pleasure as they do now" for "a thousand years" in "an earthly kingdom" (Tho. Aq., *SCG* IV, chap. 83.13, 14, p. 316). When Christ ate and drank after his resurrection, he did so "not out of necessity, but to establish the truth of His resurrection" (Tho. Aq., *SCG* IV, chap. 82.19, p. 318).

PAROUSIA

At the end of history, the Son is expected to return to earth. The biblical texts suggest that Christ will return in a glorious, public, sudden, and visible manner. It is an article of faith that Christ, having ascended into heaven, "is coming to judge the living and the dead" (Roman Symbol, *SCD* 2, p. 5).

The Return of Christ

In the era in which Jesus lived, the present age was sharply contrasted with an expected coming age (*olam habba*). The point of transition would be the day of the Lord. With Jesus' resurrection the question arose as to whether this coming age had arrived. A new era had been inaugurated, yet he was expected to come again to complete his saving work. There is good reason despite form-critical skepticism to conclude that Jesus himself expected and taught of his return (*parousia*, Calvin, *Inst.* 2.16.17; O. Cullmann, *The Early Church*, pp. 143–65; G. R. Beasley-Murray, *Jesus and the Future*).

Until He Comes.   All New Testament writers looked forward to the consummation of the kingdom of God that was inaugurated in the ministry of Jesus. At the Last Supper he said, "I will not drink again of the fruit of the vine until that day when I drink it anew in the kingdom of God" (Mark 14:25). Paul wrote to Corinth, "Whenever you eat this bread and drink this cup, you proclaim the Lord's death until he comes" (1 Cor. 11:26). The faithful are to "eagerly wait for our Lord Jesus Christ to be revealed" (1 Cor. 1:7; cf. *2 Clement* 9.1–6).

The expectation of his return impressed itself deeply upon the minds of Jesus' followers. His return is not an incidental matter in New Testament documents, but a recurrent subject of searching discourse by both Jesus and the apostles. The Fourth Gospel recalls that in his last gathering with his disciples he said directly, "if I go and prepare a place for you, I will come back and take you to be with me" (John 14:3; John Chrysostom, *Hom. on John* 73, *FC* 41, pp. 281–91).

In the Same Personal Way.   Just before his farewell meal, he had reminded the disciples that they would "see the Son of Man coming on the clouds of the sky, with power and great glory." Having come first in weakness and humility, he would come again in power. His personal coming would be visible as an event in history that "all the nations" would be able to behold (Matt. 24:30), not an imaginary or fantastic or invisible event. "We do not know what is coming to us. But we know Who is coming" (*Evanston Assembly Message, WCC, CC,* p. 581).

Immediately after his ascension two heavenly messengers announced, "He will come back *in the same way* you have seen him go into heaven" (Acts 1:11, italics added). This suggests that his future coming will be, like the incarnation and ascension, personal and visible (Rev. 1:7; 19:11–16; F. F. Bruce, *The Book of Acts*, pp. 40–44). His personal resurrection and ascension is to be completed by his personal return to judge. This return will signify a final victory over the powers of evil yet remaining in history, a victory he promises to share with his called out body, the *ekklēsia*. The victory marks the consummation of history, and of the history of revelation.

From Above.   "Let no one, therefore, look for the Lord to come from earth, but out of Heaven" (John of Damascus, *OF* IV.26, *NPNF* 2 IX, p. 99). The descent will be *from* "the clouds" just as the ascension was *into* them.

Clouds suggest both the serenity of divine holiness and the severity of divine judgment. They also suggest a great multitude of heavenly witnesses (Heb. 12:1). God's glory is often said to appear in a cloud or the clouds (Exod. 16:10; 19:9; Num. 12:5; 2 Chron. 5:13). At his transfiguration a cloud overshadowed him (Matt. 17:5), at his ascension a cloud received him (Acts 1:9); so his final return will be from clouds of divine majesty and glory in a way that can be beheld by all. "Look, he is coming with the clouds, and every eye will see him" who is called "the Alpha and the Omega" (Rev. 1:7, 8).

Parousia Defined.   Several complementary terms were used to point to this event. First and foremost, his return is called the Parousia, literally, presence (1 Cor. 15:23; 1 Thess. 2:19; 2 Pet. 1:16), inadequately translated as "second coming," which suggests repetition of an event that has already occurred once. Rather it is the consummation of what was begun in the incarnation.

This coming or presence is also called his *epiphaneia,* appearance (2 Thess. 2:8; 1 Tim. 6:14; 2 Tim. 4:1, 8), and his *phanerōsis,* manifestation: "For you died, and your life is now hidden with Christ in God. When Christ, who is your life, appears [*phanerōthē*], then you also will appear with him in glory" (Col. 3:3, 4). This coming will constitute a final *apokalupsis* or unveiling, the removal of all that now obstructs our temporal beholding of Christ (2 Thess. 1:7; 1 Cor. 1:7; 1 Pet. 1:7). The last day will finally disclose that the meaning of all history has from the outset been hidden in Jesus Christ, the Alpha and Omega of history (Rev. 1:8; 22:13; Calvin, *Inst.* 2.15–16; 4.18.20).

In this final appearance, the servant (*doulos*) form of the body of Christ will be glorified. As his coming as incarnate Lord ended in his sacrificial action of atonement, so his final return will not be to deal with sin, but to save from final destruction those who await him. "Now at His first coming when Christ came to be judged, He appeared in the form of weakness. Therefore at the second coming, when He will come to judge, He will appear in the form of glory" (Tho. Aq., *ST* supp., Q90.2, III, p. 2947).

The Tenses of His Appearing Summarized in Hebrews 9:24–28.   In the past tense, *Christ appeared in his earthly ministry that ended on the cross.* The appearance of the incarnate Lord came to a climactic end in his sacrificial death and resurrection: "But now he *has appeared* [*pephanerōtai*] once for all *at the end of the ages* to do away with sin by the sacrifice of himself" (Heb. 9:26, italics added). Paradoxically, the *end* of the ages is here referred to in the *past* tense as having already occurred anticipatively on the cross and in the resurrection of Jesus.

In the present tense, in the period between ascension and Parousia, Christ is *currently appearing in heavenly intercession* for humanity: "For Christ did not enter a man-made sanctuary that was only a copy of the true one; he entered heaven itself, *now to appear [nun emphanisthenai]* for us in God's presence. Nor did he enter heaven to offer himself again and again, the way the high priest enters the Most Holy Place every year with blood that is not his own. Then Christ would have to suffer many times since the creation of the world" (Heb. 9:24–26, italics added).

In the future tense, Christ *"will appear a second time, not to bear sin, but to bring salvation to those who are waiting for him"* (Heb. 9:28b). The same person who suffered on the cross will come again at the end of history. The whole sequence is summarized: when Christ "offered for all time one sacrifice for sins," through his atoning work on the cross, "he sat down at the right hand of God" (Heb. 10:12) in heavenly intercession; "so Christ was sacrificed once to take away the sins of many people, and he will appear a second time" (Heb. 9:28a).

The Time of His Coming

The Purposeful Uncertainty of the Hour of Judgment.   The ironic parallelism of death and judgment is deftly captured by Gerhard: "Just as death is certain, but the hour of death is uncertain, so it is certain that the final judgment will at some time follow, but the hour of judgment is uncertain" (Gerhard, *LT* XIX, p. 274; cf. Schmid, *DT*, p. 648; Wollebius, *RDB*, p. 178)!

Why purposefully uncertain? "As Christ would have us to be certainly persuaded that there shall be a day of judgment, both to deter all men from sin, and for the greater consolation of the godly in their adversity: so will he have that day unknown to men, that they may shake off all carnal security, and be always watchful, because they know not at what hour the Lord is coming" (Westminster Conf. XXXIII.3, *CC*, p. 229; Ambrose, *On Christian Faith* IV.17, *NPNF* 2 X, p. 311).

It is uncertain how many generations will continue until the end, even as in old age, the last age of bodily life, there is no known fixed time (Augustine, *Eighty-three Questions*, Q58). "For what He refused to tell the apostles, He will not reveal to others" (Tho. Aq., *ST* supp., Q77.3, III, pp. 2883–84). "He scatters the fingers of all calculators and bids them be still" (Augustine, *CG* XVIII.53, cf. *NPNF* 1 II, p. 394).

Whether the Parousia Is Impending, Soon, or to Be Delayed.   Paul in his early letters expected an early return of the Lord (1 Thess. 4:13–5:10; 2 Thess. 1:7–10; 2:1–12), but by the time of his later letters this sense of imminence seems to recede, and return is envisaged as a fuller cosmic event (Col. 1:12–20; Eph. 1:10) that might be delayed. He gradually focused more upon the certainty of the consummation than the time, calling hearers to work and not merely to wait. In Crete and Ephesus he urged Timothy and Titus to work toward establishing the *ekklēsia* on the assumption that it must be prepared to have an extended intergenerational future before the consummation.

The transition was precisely described by Francis Hall: "It is a striking evidence of the primitive certainty as to the main point in our Lord's apocalyptic teaching that He would come again at the last day, that the shock of disillusionment concerning the time of His coming, caused by its unexpected delay, did not in the least weaken the confidence with which the doctrine of His second advent was handed on and carefully retained by the postapostolic Church. Instead of discovering a mistake as to the time on our Lord's part, and of thus losing confidence in the main purport of His prediction, Christian writers initiated the task, continued ever since, of interpreting the relevant parts of His apocalypse in harmony with the fact of delay" (Hall, *DT* X, p. 132).

Whether the Apostles Mistook the Shortness of Time to the End.   Did Jesus mistakenly teach that his final coming was immediately at hand, presumably shortly after his ascension? If so, the two thousand intervening years would stand as a damaging testimony against his good judgment. Instead, those passages that speak of his coming as near or impending may refer to his resurrection or his coming in spiritual power on the day of Pentecost or to the coming of judgment in the destruction of Jerusalem, not to his final coming. They may refer to "the coming of Christ in ceaselessly visiting His Church. So that, perhaps, if we consider them carefully, we shall find that none of them refers to the coming advent," but rather "these signs that are mentioned in the gospels, such as wars, fears, and so forth have been from the beginning of the human race: unless perhaps we say that at that time they will be more prevalent" (Tho. Aq., *ST* supp., Q73.1, III, p. 2863).

There are embedded textual evidences that Jesus specifically tried to indicate to his disciples that the time of his reappearing might be long delayed. In the parable of the ten virgins he pointedly noted, "The bridegroom was *a long time in coming*" (Matt. 25:5, italics added). Again, in the parable of the talents, the Lord would come to "settle accounts" only *"after a long time"* (Matt. 25:19, italics added). Such parables may have intended to counter the immediatist idea "that the kingdom of God was going to appear at once" (Luke 19:11). Jesus expressly taught that a series of events would occur before his final coming (Matt. 24:5–14, 21–31; cf. 2 Thess. 2:2–4). Against a completely realized eschatology, the notion that the day of the Lord has already happened is specifically repudiated by Paul (2 Thess. 2:2).

The Rhetoric of Foreshortening.   The return is imminent, but not necessarily immediate, a distinction that has spawned much mischief. That is imminent which hangs over, threatens, projects over (*imminens*), appears as if it could happen at any time. The root word does not mean it is certain to come soon, but that its coming could be at any time. The radicality of final judgment is rhetorically reinforced by the idea of immediacy, but this does not necessarily mean simple temporal nearness.

However soon or late, it appears to be quite intentional on the part of Jesus to impress upon the minds of his hearers the expectation of his imminent return. With this purpose in mind, he employed the prophetic rhetorical device of foreshortening the future so as to view it from the standpoint of eternity, as if a thousand years were but a day. Jesus employed the prophetic rhetoric of an imminent end, yet made it clear that the specific time of the end was known only to the Father (Mark 13:32).

Jesus impressed this expectation upon his hearers, who then tended rhetorically to put these imminent terms into an immediatist time frame (Acts 1:6, 7). In the decades in which the New Testament was being written and redacted (A.D. 40–90), we can already see a gradual accommodation to the delay of Christ's coming. "Concerning the coming of our Lord Jesus Christ and our being gathered to him, we ask you, brothers, not to become easily unsettled or alarmed by some prophecy, report or letter supposed to have come from us, saying that the day of the Lord has already come" (2 Thess. 2:1, 2). Even in his last letters Paul still expected the return soon, though he was aware that he might not live to experience it.

By the time of the writing of 2 Peter there was some greater awareness of a lengthening delay. The people were being urged "to live holy and godly lives as you look forward to the day of God and speed its coming" (2 Pet. 3:12). This suggests that the church may have played some part in delaying the Parousia. The burden is on God's people to "work to hasten it on" (*speudō*, v. 12, NEB).

There remains a tension in John's Gospel between the proclamation that the judgment of this world is now (12:31), and future judgment (5:28, 29; 6:39–54; 14:3; for various views, see Bultmann, *John*, p. 261; Guthrie, *NTT*, p. 800). The "last day" language radicalizes judgment, and reinforces the finality of the events set in motion by the incarnation and resurrection (Origen, *John*, fragment 90, *AEG* V, p. 105; J. A. T. Robinson, *In the End, God*, p. 59). The Augsburg Confession was composed in 1530 in a time that its proponents interpreted as "these last times of which the Scriptures prophesy," in which "the world is growing worse and men are becoming weaker and more infirm" (Augsburg Conf., *CC*, p. 82).

Concerning Those Who Too Eagerly Ask When. Those disciples were reproved who asked too specifically, *When?* They were taught rather to be ready at any time. The day is known only to God. "It is not for you to know the times or dates the Father has set by his own authority" (Acts 1:7). "No one knows about that day or hour" (Mark 13:32). The faithful are called to leave to God the time and manner of "the day of the Lord" (1 Cor. 5:5; Phil. 1:6).

This did not imply that there would be no signs indicating the end time, but that short of that time "the Lord wished the time of the future judgment to remain hidden, that men might watch with care so as not to be found unprepared" (Tho. Aq., *Compend. of Theology*, chap. 242, p. 301). With the Turk nearing Vienna, the papacy falling away, and the world "cracking on all sides," Luther confessed his intuition "that the world will not endure a hundred years" (*Conversations with Luther* [*Table Talk*], pp. 250 f.; cf. *Correspondence* II, no. 869, p. 516). Yet four hundred years later, we know that these events, as portentous as they seemed, were yet to bear fruits of the Spirit that would themselves become a part of the larger, more patient economy of providence.

There is something demonic in those who cynically, almost eagerly, wait for God to destroy the first creation, as if there were something virtuous in beholding destruction. It is not intended that a preoccupation with his return will lead the faithful to undervalue his first coming or the first creation, or to fixate on the details of his return so as to neglect the significance of his incarnate life and atoning death or mission to the fallen world. Such fixations are politically hazardous. To "compute the times" is "to wish to know what He himself said that no one can know" (Hugh of St. Victor, *SCF*, p. 452).

Testing False Attestations of the End. Since prophecy is only fully grasped in its fulfillment (1 Pet. 1:11), these consummating events may not be clearly recognizable until they are already in the process of happening. Meanwhile we are instructed to "not believe every spirit, but test the spirits to see whether they are from God, because many false prophets have gone out into the world" (1 John 4:1). The crucial test is the simple confession of Jesus Christ as incarnate Lord. "The spirit of the anti-christ, which you have heard is coming and even now is already in the world" is precisely characterized by the failure to acknowledge Jesus as God's own coming (1 John 4:2, 3).

Signs of His Coming

Though uncertain as to time, the approach of the day of his coming will be accompanied by signs. Even if the signs may take an extended period for their fulfillment, the coming itself will be sudden (Mark 13:36; Luke 21:34, 35; Matt. 24:42–44).

Signs of the Times to Precede the General Judgment.   The descriptions of the signs of the end usually include a series of tribulations—wars, famines, earthquakes, persecutions, and apostasy, and the emergence of counter-Christs (*Longer Catech.*, Eastern Orthodox Church, 234, *COC* II, p. 481). It seems clear from history generally, however, that these signs are reasonably frequent in ordinary history, hence belong to the structure of this dying world—ascension to Parousia. There have always been natural disasters and outrages against oppressed peoples. These signs exhort us to be aware of our finitude and sin and to be constantly awake to the hope of God's own coming.

The signs that appear as portents of vast disruption in history will recur with greater frequency and intensity as the end approaches (*Barnabas* 4.4; Schmid, *DT*, p. 647; Jacobs, *SCF*, p. 507). Several key passages portray these signs, especially Matthew 24, Mark 13, and Luke 21 (G. R. Beasley-Murray, *Jesus and the Future*), as well as Paul's letter to the Thessalonians and the Book of Revelation. Exegetes differ as to whether these are to be literally or metaphorically interpreted. Virtually all the signs that appear in Mark 13 and Matthew 24 recur among the woes of the Apocalypse (G. R. Beasley-Murray, *Revelation*, p. 130; cf. Rev. 6). It remains debatable among classic exegetes whether or how they may fit together as an overall pattern.

Distinguishing the Historical Destruction of Jerusalem from the End of the World.   It is sometimes difficult to sort out the extent to which these texts were speaking of the actual historic event of the destruction of Jerusalem or the end of all historical events. When Jesus wept over Jerusalem he felt the pain of those who had not known what would bring them peace (Luke 19:42). Only the end will bring final *shalom* to Jerusalem.

The actually beheld event of the destruction of Jerusalem became a prevailing archetype for interpreting the general denouement of all things (Dan. 12:1; Matt. 24:21, 22; 2 Pet. 3:9). The desolating sacrilege of Daniel was employed to interpret the destruction of Jerusalem, which was seen as a foreshadowing of all end events (Irenaeus, *Ag. Her.* V.25, *ANF* I, pp. 553, 554; Eusebius, *CH* III.5–10, *NPNF* 2 I, pp. 138–46; Guthrie, *NTT*, pp. 794, 795). "Such were those which Christ predicted concerning the destruction of Jerusalem, as type and at the same time agency of his coming" (Wollebius, *RDB*, p. 179).

The Universal Preaching of the Gospel: The Calling of the Gentiles. Among other signs of the end were the complementary signs of the calling of the Gentiles and the gathering of the people of Israel. A worldwide dissemination of the gospel is expected among all nations (Mark 13:10; Rom. 11:25). "And this gospel of the kingdom will be preached in the whole world as a testimony to all nations, and then the end will come" (Matt. 24:14); "and you will be my witnesses in Jerusalem, and in all Judea, and Samaria, and to the ends of the earth" (Acts 1:8). All the nations will be given an opportunity to enter the kingdom (Acts 15:14; Rom. 9:24–26; Eph. 2:11–20) before the final judgment. God will not allow the historical process to end until all societies have an opportunity to respond to the news of God's mercy (Origen, *Ag. Celsus* II.13, *AEG* V, p. 128).

This does not imply that the end must await the literal conversion of every single living person, but that the gospel must be preached, the testimony given, the offer of forgiveness extended to all before the end, and that there will be believers in all nations (John of Damascus, *OF* IV.26, *NPNF* 2 IX, p. 98; cf. John Chrysostom, *Hom. on Matt.* 76, *NPNF* 1 X, pp. 456–62; A. L. Moore, *The Parousia in the New Testament*). The end will not come before that time, according to Augustine: "How long after that time it will come, we do not know. The only thing we know for certain is that it will not come sooner" (*Letters* 199.4, 48).

The Gathering of Israel. Both Testaments attest a future return or restoration or conversion of Israel (Zech. 12:10; 13:1; 2 Cor. 3:15, 16). The gathering of Israel had been elaborately promised by the Old Testament prophets (Isa. 1:24–27; 60:15–22; Jer. 3:12–18; Ezek. 20:40–42; Amos 9:11–15; Mic. 7:18–20; Zeph. 3:19, 20; Zech. 8:1–9; Hollaz, *ETA*, 1263 ff.).

The prototype is found in the Deuteronomic covenant, that "when you and your children return to the Lord your God and obey him with all your heart and with all your soul according to everything I command you today, then the Lord your God will restore your fortunes and have compassion on you and gather you again from all the nations where he scattered you. Even if you have been banished to the most distant land under the heavens, from there the Lord your God will gather you and bring you back. He will bring you to the land that belonged to your fathers, and you will take possession of it" (Deut. 30:2–5). Christian exegesis viewed this as a firm promise to Israel to be fulfilled before the end of history (John of Damascus, *OF* IV.26, *NPNF* 2 IX, p. 99).

During the dispensation of the gospel God will continue gathering his people until the fullness (*pleroma,* the full number of the elect) of the Gentiles has come into the kingdom, and so the *pleroma* of Israel (inclusive of the faithful among Jews and Gentiles) will be saved. The sequence was rehearsed by Jerome: "When the multitude of nations will come in, then this fig-tree [Israel], too, will bear fruit, and all Israel will be saved" (Jerome, *Comm. on Habakkuk* III.17, in Pohle, *DT* XII, p. 106).

In the final accounting, the absurd alienation between Jews and Christians will cease. "The eschatological hope common to Jews and Christians is that all, including Israel, will recognize the one common Messiah at a gathering of the peoples in universal peace (*shalom*). According to Christian conviction, he has already appeared in Jesus Christ" (*CCF,* p. 343).

Commenting on Ezekiel 1:16, Ambrose wrote, "The wheel, then, within the wheel is life under the Law, life under grace; inasmuch as Jews are within the

Church, *the Law is included in grace.* For . . . circumcision of the heart is a sacrament with the Church" (Ambrose, *Of the Holy Spirit* III.XXI.162, *NPNF* 2 X, p. 157, italics added)!

All Israel Will Be Saved.   Meanwhile God has not rejected his beloved people of covenant (Rom. 11:1). A remnant of Israel has been chosen by grace (11:6) through whom "salvation has come to the Gentiles" (11:11). Out of Israel has come "riches for the world" (11:12). Even though the hearts of some were hardened to the good news (11:7), Israel continues to be loved by God (11:28), "for God's gifts and his call are irrevocable" (11:29). God is using Israel's hardening of heart as the precise instrument to catapult the gospel beyond Jerusalem to the ends of the earth.

The hardening of Israel is always only partial, not absolute. "Israel has experienced a hardening in part until the full number of the Gentiles has come in. And so *all Israel [pas Israēl] will be saved*" (Rom. 11:25, 26, italics added; Irenaeus, *Ag. Her.* IV.2.7, *ANF* I, p. 465; C. K. Barrett, *Romans*, p. 223; F. J. Leenhardt, *Romans*, p. 293; J. Murray, *Romans* II, p. 98). "If the part of the dough offered as firstfruits is holy, then the whole batch is holy; if the root is holy, so are the branches. If some of the branches have been broken off, and you, though a wild olive shoot, have been grafted in among the others, and now share in the nourishing sap from the olive root, do not boast" (Rom. 11:16–18; Wollebius, *RDB*, pp. 180, 181).

Extreme Depravity and the Pretense of Security.   Paul's last known communication to Timothy declared, "There will be terrible times in the last days. People will be lovers of themselves, lovers of money, boastful, proud, abusive, disobedient to their parents, ungrateful, unholy, without love, unforgiving, slanderous, without self-control, brutal, not lovers of the good, treacherous, rash, conceited, lovers of pleasure rather than lovers of God—having the form of godliness but denying its power" (2 Tim. 3:1–5).

The world will be inundated with defiant wickedness (Matt. 24:12, 37–39; Luke 17:28–30). The air will be poisoned by deceit. Under these conditions the perishing live under a "powerful delusion" that will cause them to "believe the lie" (2 Thess. 2:11). This depravity is to be accompanied by a pretense of extreme security, as in the days of Noah, and of Lot (Luke 17:26, 28). "While people are saying, 'Peace and safety,' destruction will come on them suddenly" (1 Thess. 5:3; Origen, *Comm. on Matt.* 56, *AEG* V, pp. 164–67; Wollebius, *RDB*, p. 179).

The Decline and Oppression of the Church Through the Multiplication of Heresies.
Jesus taught that at the end "many false prophets will appear and deceive many people. Because of the increase of wickedness, the love of most will grow cold, but he who stands firm to the end will be saved" (Matt. 24:11, 12). "Watch out that no one deceives you. For many will come in my name, claiming, 'I am the Christ,' and will deceive many" (Matt. 24:5).

False teachers will not only promote error but attempt to make error the standard teaching of the *ekklēsia*. Attempts of the faithful to correct this error will call forth ridicule, contempt, and persecution. This, of course, is a recurring phenomenon in the history of Christianity. Every heresy has sought to make itself official teaching. In the end these efforts are expected to reach their most intense form in a "great apostasy" that will precede the Parousia.

Persecutions of the godly are to be expected (Mark 13:9; Rev. 11:7; 12:4; 13:7; 17:6; 18:24; 20:4). "Then you will be handed over to be persecuted and put to death, and you will be hated by all nations because of me. At that time many will turn away from the faith, and will betray and hate each other" (Matt. 24:9, 10).

Skeptics will doubt that history will ever be brought to a fair or appropriate consummation: "First you must understand that in the last days scoffers will come, scoffing and following their own evil desires. They will say, 'Where is this "coming" he promised? Ever since our fathers died everything goes on as it has since the beginning of creation.' But they deliberately forget that long ago by God's word the heavens existed and the earth was formed out of water and by water" (2 Pet. 3:3–5). The argument against Christ's return was hard to counter under the conditions of vast social sin. So will the *ekklēsia* be tested.

The Lawless One. The lawless one will appear just before the final judgment. "And then the lawless one [*anomos*] will be revealed, whom the Lord Jesus will overthrow" (2 Thess. 2:8). "The coming of the lawless one will be in accordance with the work of Satan displayed in all kinds of counterfeit miracles, signs and wonders, and in every sort of evil that deceives those who are perishing" (2 Thess. 9, 10). The lawless one is the son of perdition who will devise a rebellion so oppressive as to be distinguished as *the* rebellion (*he apostasia*, 2 Thess. 2:3), where he will seek to be viewed as the equivalent of God, demanding worship of himself in the temple. "Don't let anyone deceive you in any way, for that day will not come until the rebellion occurs and the man of lawlessness is revealed, the man doomed to destruction. He will oppose and will exalt himself over everything that is called God or is worshiped, so that he sets himself up in God's temple, proclaiming himself to be God" (2 Thess. 2:3, 4).

All that restrains this lawlessness is the patient mercy of the triune God. "And now you know what is holding him back, so that he may be revealed at the proper time. For the secret power of lawlessness is already at work; but the one who now holds it back will continue to do so till he is taken out of the way" (2 Thess. 2:6, 7). Chrysostom and Jerome regarded the Roman Empire as a form of this restraining influence (John Chrysostom, *Hom. on Thess.* IV, *NPNF* 1 XIII, pp. 388–92; cf. Ladd, *TNT*, p. 530).

The Overthrow of the Antichrist. What Paul referred to as the man of sin and lawless one is likely the same one whom John called the *antichristos* or pseudo-Christ (1 John 2:18, 22; 4:3), the archenemy of humanity who in the last days will be inspired by Satan to deceive the nations and persecute the saints (2 Thess. 2:3–12; 2 John 4; Matt. 24:5, 24; Hippolytus, *Treatise on Christ and Antichrist*, *ANF* V, pp. 204–19; Tertullian, *APT*, p. 122).

The time of apostasy reaches its culmination in the Antichrist, who is portrayed in Revelation 13 as a blasphemous beast. Many false teachers were called "anti-Christs"—those who embodied a spirit in opposition to Christ (1 John 2:18, 22; 2 John 7; Athanasius, *LCHS* II.9) at loose already in the world (1 John 4:3). These are a collective designation for apostates and schismatics who may at some point gather under a single head, a prototypical Antichrist (Dan. 7:25; *Barnabas* 4.4–13, *ACW*, pp. 196–97).

Apostasy and persecution are always latent in church history, but at times they appear ultimately menacing to the destiny of the church. From the outset the early church was persecuted first by the Jews, then the Greeks, then the Romans, then the barbarian hordes. In the modern period Christians of various traditions have continued to be persecuted, Armenian Christians by the Turks, Orthodox Christians by the Stalinists, evangelicals by Castro, Catholics by the Pol Pot genocide, and both Jews and Christians by the Nazis. Unfortunately the list goes on, and seems to continue endlessly among Christian minorities in Ethiopia, Mozambique, South Africa, North Korea, Iran, Nepal, and Burma.

Prototypical apostates have in various periods been identified by various interpreters as the singular Antichrist: Nero and Valerian particularly in the Roman period, Genseric in the Vandal period, Mohammed in the early Middle Ages, the Cathari and Albigenses in the Middle Ages, the corrupted papacy by Reformation writers, and in the modern period notably Hitler, Stalin, and Mao (Commodianus, *Instructions* XLI, *ANF* IV, p. 210; Lactantius, *DI* VI.17; Athanasius, *Hist. Arians* 77, *CCC,* p. 42; cf. Jerome, *Comm. on Dan.* VII.8; Calvin, *Inst.* 4.1.12; 4.7; Newman, "The Patristic Idea of Antichrist," *Discussions and Arguments on Various Subjects,* pp. 44–108). The formal denial of Jesus as the Christ is the key characteristic of the Antichrist (1 John 2:22; 4:3; 2 John 7; Hippolytus, *Fragments of Commentaries, Daniel, ANF* V, pp. 177–90). The Antichrist concentrates in himself the whole history of apostasy (Cyprian, *Letters, FC* 51, pp. 190–98, 261–66). Though a mystical number (666) is attached to his name, Irenaeus warned that the number is capable of being fitted to many names so it is unwise to draw rash conclusions from the number (Irenaeus, *Ag. Her.* V.28–30, *ANF* I, 556–59). "The Abomination of Desolation is the image of the emperor which he set up in Jerusalem; so will it be in the days of Antichrist, who will set up his image in all the churches of the world" (Hippolytus, *Comm. on Matt., AEG* V, p. 130; cf. Eusebius, *Demonstration of the Gospel* VIII.2; *CH* III.7).

Extraordinary Events and Disturbances in Nature and History.   The apocalyptic prophecies of Mark 13 (cf. Matt. 24 and Luke 21) are taken by ancient exegetes to refer to the end events. They are expected to include famines and earthquakes as "the beginning of birth pains" (Matt. 24:7, 8), the obscuring of sun and moon by the brightness of his glory, the falling of stars from heaven, with the powers of heaven being shaken (Matt. 24:27–29), eclipses, changes in the heavens, and other extraordinary natural disturbances (Origen, *Comm. on Matt.* 39–56, *AEG* V, pp. 112–69; Tertullian, *Ag. Marcion* III.3, IV.39).

Unrestrained sedition, famine, and pestilence are signs of the end. "You will hear of wars and rumors of wars, but see to it that you are not alarmed. Such things must happen, but the end is still to come. Nation will rise against nation, and kingdom against kingdom" (Matt. 24:6, 7; Luke 21:9–11; Hippolytus, *Daniel* IV.17, *AEG* V, pp. 124–25). "When these things begin to take place, stand up and lift up your heads, because your redemption is drawing near" (Luke 21:28).

The Presence of the Spirit Until the Return of the Son.   However ambiguous may be the struggle between the kingdom of God and the kingdoms of the world within history, at the end of history God's glory and judgment will be manifest. Meanwhile "we wait for the blessed hope—the glorious appearing of our great God and Savior, Jesus Christ" (Titus 2:13). Paul felt deep affinity with "all who have longed for his appearing" (2 Tim. 4:8).

Jesus had warned his disciples of wrenching, difficult times ahead, and assured them of his presence through the Spirit until his personal return (Matt. 24:21–27). It required an implicit triune premise to assert that God the Son was already present in the Spirit, to be fully disclosed at the end of the new age. Far from an inner contradiction, both affirmations were required by triune logic.

Alpha and Omega

The end time will reveal that the Word spoken in Jesus' life and death was the Word spoken from the beginning of history, and will be the same Word spoken at the end of history (John 1:1–3; Rev. 22:13). With this consummation what was already a completed work on the cross in justification will become a completed work in the continuing body of Christ in sanctification. All other historical powers will be judged in the light of the last power.

The first and last letters of the Greek alphabet (alpha and omega) were used to symbolize the beginning and end. Christ is the Alpha and Omega of all things (Rev. 22:13), the one "who is, and who was, and who is to come, the Almighty" (Rev. 1:8). The consummation brings to final fulfillment what was begun in creation and having fallen was renewed in the incarnation.

Countering Immanental Historical Optimism.   However debatable may be the references to the final abomination, Antichrist, and lawlessness, they sharply resist the illusion of an ever-increasing, progressive, immanentally developing justice in history (John of Damascus, *OF* IV.26, *NPNF* 2 IX, p. 98). There seems little room in this view of history for the optimistic premise of evolutionary historical progress. Such naïveté about history contradicts too much historical experience. The New Testament rather is braced for a period of tribulation at the end when the faithful will be under unprecedented attack (Mark 13:3–23; 2 Thess. 2:1–3; Rev. 12:13–18; Hugh of St. Victor, *SCF,* pp. 452 ff.).

Fallen human nature does not change within the premises of the history of sin, even though history itself is full of change. Even the most impressive technological "advances" (nuclear energy, microchips, television, space exploration, multinational enterprise) can be distorted by the self-assertive will, no matter how well intended. Far from decreasing evil, technology may tend to increase and complicate the power of evil. It is folly to imagine that greater scientific knowledge will eliminate sin.

Instead of moving toward a benign utopia, world history is moving toward a cataclysmic struggle out of which will come a cosmic transformation—a new heaven and a new earth. Only after this ordeal can it be announced that "the kingdom of the world has become the kingdom of our Lord and of his Christ" (Rev. 11:15).

The Faithful Colony.   The present church is viewed by analogy as a colony of citizens in a faraway land whose loyalties and affections remain closely attached to their home country, for "our citizenship is in heaven. And we eagerly await a Savior from there," who "will transform our lowly bodies so that they will be like his glorious body" (Phil. 3:20).

In this alienated world the full life of the church is not yet completely realized. Her essential unity is fragmented. Her holiness is stained by apostasy. Her apostolicity is racked by heresies. Her catholicity is blocked from complete diffusion in all the world. These conditions may last until "the end of the age" (Matt. 13:40), while in the interim wheat and tares will grow tangled together (Matt. 13:30). But on that day the Lord will come to complete the struggling church. The church is actively awaiting that day, able to survive its darkest hours because of that hope. The faithful community desires his coming, fervently expects it, rejoices that God has promised to complete his purpose in history and make his victory finally known throughout the world.

Ethical Imperatives Embedded in the Parousia Expectation. All exhortations concerning the end are intended to have a practical, ethical meaning: calling persons to current responsibility. Whatever we do now will stand under the judgment of God at the end. All injustices that occur in ongoing history are in the process of being finally brought to correction in the presence of the holy God at the last day (2 Pet. 3:10–12; 1 John 3).

We are therefore to be prudent and watchful, for we know not on what day the Lord comes (Matt. 24:42). He will come unexpectedly, as a thief in the night (Matt. 24:43; 1 Thess. 5:1, 2), with the suddenness and unexpectedness of a flash of lightning (Matt. 24:27, 39, 44). The prayer of the early Christian communities, "Come O Lord" (1 Cor. 16:22; Rev. 22:20; *Didache* 10:6), was a prayer for justice.

Each hearer is called to live life *as if* the final day were overhanging: "Now learn this lesson from the fig tree: As soon as its twigs get tender and its leaves come out, you know that summer is near. Even so, when you see all these things, you know that it is near, right at the door. I tell you the truth, this generation [*genea autē*] will certainly not pass away until all these things have happened" (Matt. 24:32–34, cf. Mark 13:30; Luke 21:32; Origen, *Comm. on Matt.* 48–50, *AEG* V, pp. 149–55; cf. G. R. Beasley-Murray, *A Commentary on Mark Thirteen*). Since the Greek for "this generation" can also mean race or family, the implication may be that the people of God and the family of God are being preserved through the changing seasons of history until the last day, when God's justice will be done.

The Outcome of the Return Is the Gathering of the Beloved Community. The coming again of God the Son is promised primarily to the *ekklēsia* as a community, not to isolated individuals. He shall come "to present her to himself as a radiant church, without stain or wrinkle or any other blemish, but holy and blameless" (Eph. 5:27). This glorification is to the believing community what bodily resurrection is to the individual believer (Jacobs, *SCF*, p. 504).

After gathering the faithful from the world over (Mark 13:27), he will lead them to the throne of the Father in heaven. The church will be presented in her perfected form after the removal of unworthy members. Angelic agents "will weed out of his kingdom everything that causes sin and all who do evil" (Matt. 13:41, 42). If debates about the holiness of the church have persisted throughout history, they will be resolved at the end of history.

Creation Awaits Parousia. All creation is viewed as awaiting this consummation. "The creation waits in eager expectation for the sons of God to be revealed," when "the creation itself will be liberated from its bondage to decay and brought into the glorious freedom of the children of God" (Rom. 8:19–21). There is a correspondence between the groaning of creation and the groaning of the faithful, for "we ourselves, who have the first-fruits of the Spirit, groan inwardly as we wait eagerly for our adoption as sons, the redemption of our bodies" (Rom. 8:23).

THE MILLENNIUM

The expectation of a messianic earthly reign of a thousand years is present before the time of Jesus in the literature of late Judaic apocalypticism. It held a strong conviction that the world as we know it is being readied for the consummation of God's purpose (*1 Enoch* 91, 93; *Pss. of Solomon* 17–18; *2 Esdras* 7:28 ff.; 12:34; *Apocalypse of Baruch* 29:1–8). Though Jesus did not condone the idea of a coercive political kingdom, he did lead his disciples to expect a spiritual kingdom sharply distinguishable from the kingdoms of this world. The New Testament actively employed vibrant images from the Jewish apocalyptic tradition to interpret its own messianic history. Crucial among these was the metaphor of a thousand-year reign in which Satan would be bound.

The millennium (a thousand years) is the time when the Messianic Deliverer is expected to reign on earth (Isa. 2:3; Dan. 7:14; Zech. 14:9). In this time it is expected that Satan will be restrained (Rev. 20:2), that righteousness and peace will come to the whole world (Isa. 11:3–5; 2:4), and that the fruitfulness of the earth will increase abundantly (Isa. 35:1, 2).

Revelation 20 occurs in a highly symbolic context, and since the millennial teaching is found preeminently (some say exclusively) in this passage, it should be conceded that it is hazardous to make a symbolic passage the principle of interpretation for all other relatively nonsymbolic passages. The main questions of millennialism hinge on whether the texts point literally or symbolically to an earthly reign of Christ, and whether that will occur before or after his glorious return. There remains a lack of consensus on interpretation of key millennial passages. Three positions continue to compete as normative interpretations:

Realized millennialism holds that the millennium has already occurred or is occurring. *Postmillennialism* holds that the return will occur after the millennium. *Premillennialism* holds that the return will occur before the millennium.

Realized Millennialism

Realized or Symbolic Millennialism.   Realized millennialists contend that the millennium is either an already present or an emerging reality. The millennium is now being fulfilled on earth. There is to be no future literal-political earthly kingdom besides the fruits that are already beginning to be borne. Rather the kingdom of God and the kingdoms of this world will continue in a mixed fashion until the Lord's return.

In this view, the presently ongoing millennial age will conclude with Christ's return and judgment. There is in this view resistance to detailed speculative explanations of present history as the fulfillment of specific prophecies.

Augustine and Other Key Representatives.   Augustine discussed Revelation 20:1–10 in some detail in the *City of God* (XX.7–14, *NPNF* 1 II, pp. 426–34), reasoning by analogy of faith with other passages of scripture that the millennial kingdom is best viewed as the present Christian era wherein the powers of evil are already being restrained and the church being given time to proclaim the gospel. The strongman Satan is being bound up by Christ on the cross and in the descent into the netherworld (Luke 11:21–23; Mark 3:27; Augustine, Sermon 259.2). Ultimately, "to the strong, even the devil is weak" (Ambrose, *Of the Holy Spirit* I.intro.11, *NPNF* 2 X, p. 116), though penultimately he may be permitted to rage before his final collapse.

During this postresurrection period the gospel is being preached with the hope that Christ will increasingly reign in human hearts. The millennium is not to be awaited but has already begun. The church constitutes the proximate firstfruits of the kingdom of God on earth (Augustine, *Enchiridion* 111, *NPNF* 1 III, p. 273).

Augustine's view became prototypical for much Western Christianity, both Catholic and Protestant. When the glorious return did not occur in the year A.D. 1000, the idea of millennium increasingly became viewed symbolically as a long though unspecified period of time. One prevailing interpretation by the Reformers was that the fury of Satan was loosed on the early church during the first three centuries of persecution, after which came the period of Constantine when a relative peace (*pax Romana*) was given, which prevailed for a thousand years, roughly until about A.D. 1300, when the Ottoman Turkish empire emerged to end that peace (Gerhard, *LT* XX, 124 ff.; Schmid, *DT,* pp. 651, 652) and the papacy became vastly corrupted.

Among different types of realized millennial views were those of Clement of Alexandria, Origen, Dionysius, Tyconius, Augustine, Thomas Aquinas, and much classic Reformation and Counter-Reformation teaching. Consensual Lutheran teaching was well attested by Quenstedt: "Since the second advent of Christ, the general resurrection, the final judgment, and the end of the world are immediately united, and one follows the other without an interval of time, it is manifest that, before the completion of the judgment, no earthly kingdom, and life abounding in all spiritual and bodily pleasure, as the Chiliasts or Millenarians dream, is to be expected" (Quenstedt, *TDP* IV, 649; Schmid, *DT,* p. 650).

The term *chiliasm* (from the Greek word for thousand, *chilioi*) was used by the consensual tradition to refer to a false teaching that focused inordinately upon sensual indulgence in an earthly kingdom of a thousand years. Eusebius attributed this idea to Cerinthus, a Gnostic of the first century (*CH* III.28). Among those rejected by the Augsburg Confession for this interpretation were "Papias, Joachim (Abbot of Fiora), the Fanatics and Anabaptists, Casper von Schwenkfeld, and others" (Augsburg Conf. XVII, 4). Papias allegedly believed the saints would enjoy morally licit earthly pleasures for a thousand years, wherein the kingdom of Christ will be with unparalleled fertility "established bodily [in material form] upon this very earth" (Eusebius, *CH* III.39.12, *SHD,* p. 70; cf. *NPNF* 2 I, p. 172).

One Thousand—a Sacred Number.   Thomas Aquinas thought that the "thousand years" of Revelation 20:2 referred to "the whole time of the Church in which the martyrs as well as other saints reign with Christ, both in the present Church which is called the kingdom of God, and also—as far as souls are concerned—in the heavenly country; for 'the thousand' means perfection, since it is the cube whose root is ten, which also usually signifies perfection" (*SCG* IV, p. 329; cf. Augustine, *CG* XX.6–8).

Though Protestants generally reject the uncritical identification of the church with the kingdom of God, the same point is made by Protestants such as B. B. Warfield, who held that the millennium was symbolic of the condition of the bliss of the redeemed in heaven, hence not to be interpreted literally as an earthly-historical reign. "The sacred number seven in combination with the equally sacred number three forms the number of holy perfection ten, and when this ten is cubed into a thousand the seer has said all he could say to convey to our minds the idea of absolute completeness" (B. B. Warfield, "The Millennium and the Apocalypse," *Biblical Doctrines,* p. 654).

The Realized-Millennial Critique of Premillennialism. This position is most commonly called amillennialism, suggesting the absence of or lack of interest in the millennium, but the term is a misnomer. This position does not argue against a millennium but that there is to be expected no future literal, earthly-historical millennium that is not already present in some form. Both pre- and postmillennial positions reject realized millennialism for failing to view the millennium sufficiently seriously as a biblical promise to be literally fulfilled in history.

According to the realized view, the millennium of Revelation 20 is not to be read as a literal thousand years but an indefinite symbolic period of the church age. These exegetes note that the thousand-year reign is not mentioned apart from the most symbolic of all books of the New Testament, the Revelation (Henry, *CWB* 6, pp. 1179–81; W. Hendricksen, *More Than Conquerors,* pp. 11–64). "The Apocalypse is a prophetic book, full of most abstruse visions, as well as allegorical and quasi-enigmatical forms of speech, difficult to be understood, and therefore to be expounded according to the analogy of the faith, based upon clear and perspicuous Scripture passages" (Hollaz, *ETA,* p. 1259; Schmid, *DT,* p. 653).

"Sound exegesis requires that the obscure passages of Scripture be read in the light of the clearer ones, and not *vice versa*" (Berkhof, *ST,* p. 715). "It is not proper to construct a dogma alone from a book concerning whose canonicity there has been such extended dissent, and to make it the standard whereby to interpret the plain language of books whose authority is more thoroughly established" (Jacobs, *SCF,* p. 516). According to this view, premillenarianism depends too much "on the literal interpretation of a highly symbolic passage (Rev. 20:1–6), which has no real support elsewhere in the New Testament" (M. Hughes, *CF,* p. 233). "The binding [of Satan] cannot be literal since a literal chain could not hold a powerful spiritual being" (Guthrie, *NTT,* p. 870). The New Testament does not hope for a literal reestablishment of theocracy.

Among other leading Protestant spokespersons for realized millennialism are A. Kuyper, H. Bavinck, G. Vos (see also A. Hoekema, *The Bible and the Future,* and Jay Adams, *The Time Is at Hand*). These views are not to be confused with that realized eschatology which argues that Jesus did not expect a future Parousia (C. H. Dodd, *The Parables of the Kingdom;* J. A. T. Robinson, *Jesus and His Coming*).

Postmillennialism

Postmillennialists tend to appear as historical optimists who believe in the triumph of the gospel in human society (S. J. Case, *The Millennial Hope;* H. F. Rall, *Modern Premillennialism and the Christian Hope*). Many have a gradualist and progressive view of the coming kingdom, wherein Christ, though physically absent, is gradually coming more and more to reign upon the earth and will come when that process has come to completion. Postmillennialists expect history to get better, not worse.

Defined.   Postmillennialism means that Christ will return after the gospel has been preached to all and has taken full effect among the nations. The glorious return will occur after the millennial kingdom has been established.

The postmillennial sequence is conceived as follows:

World mission	Kingdom on earth	Christ's return	Resurrection/ Judgment	Eternity

The petition "Thy will be done on earth as it is in heaven" is expected as a growing world-historical condition. It is expected that the will of God will be done on earth either literally for a thousand years or figuratively for a long period of time. The "thousand years" is sometimes (as in realized millennialism) taken symbolically. This position is much like realized millennialism except that the latter does not expect a future earthly reign of Christ distinguishable from the present church age. Among varied representatives of postmillennialism are Joachim of Fiora, Daniel Whitby, Cocceius, Witsius, and Rauschenbusch (Rauschenbusch, *Theology for the Social Gospel;* see also Hodge, *ST* III, pp. 861–68; Strong, *ST* III, pp. 1010 f.; I. Murray, *The Puritan Hope*).

Objections to Postmillennialism.   Instead of portraying history as progressively improving, opponents argue that the New Testament tends rather to see the time immediately before the end as one characterized by apostasy, persecution, and suffering (Matt. 24:6–14; 2 Thess. 2:3–12; 2 Tim. 3:1–6; Rev. 13). In the light of human self-assertiveness, it has seemed excessively optimistic to many readers of scripture to assert that an earthly messianic kingdom would directly emerge out of the shambles of the history of sin, or that peace would reign under the present conditions of finite history, and all nations would turn to Christ for a thousand years.

To argue that the gospel will permeate society in the present age runs against the grain of those parables of the kingdom that do not look for universal acceptance of Christ in this age (Guthrie, *NTT*, p. 872). The Augsburg Confession rejected the view that "before the resurrection of the dead, saints and godly men will possess a worldly kingdom, and annihilate all the godless" (art. XVII, *CC*, p. 73).

Suppose we pin our hopes on the next thousand years of scientific, technological, and social change (or even more optimistically upon the next century). Who does not hope that humanity will improve on its present folly? But is there any evidence that would reasonably lead one to conclude that in the year 3000 people will be morally better than in 2000? Is there any insurance against the ever-incipient moral decline of humanity, however great the achievements of one or more generations? Will not human beings find ways in the next millennium to use innocent people to further their own vested interests, to treat people as things and things as God, and to deceive themselves in the process? The Christian hope is not an end of realism. Its hopes lie not in a gradual improvement of human nature but in divine grace amid human self-assertiveness.

Premillennialism

The following more complicated sequence is fairly typically envisioned by premillennial teachers (with some variation among interpreters):

Before the Millennium:
  Evangelization of the world
    Apostasy and tribulation
      Antichrist
        Armageddon
          Parousia (before the millennium, hence premillennial)
            First resurrection of dead saints
              Transfiguration of living saints
                Translation to meet the coming Lord
When the Millennial Kingdom Is Established:
                  Antichrist slain or restrained
                    Restoration of Israel
                      The nations turn to God
                        Millennial peace
After a Thousand Years:
Satan unrestrained
                      Satan's final revolt fails
                        Second resurrection: unjust raised
                          Last judgment
                            New heaven and earth
                              Eternity

What Is Premillennialism?   Most premillennialists expect a literal fulfillment of the unconditional promises made to Abraham and David. Most current dispensational premillennialists expect Christ to return bodily for an earthly reign of a thousand years or its equivalent. They expect Christ to return before the millennium to institute the kingdom promised to David. "At the close of this age premillennialists believe that Christ will return for his church meeting her in the air (this is not the Second Coming of Christ), to establish his kingdom on earth for a thousand years, during which time the promises to Israel will be fulfilled" (C. Ryrie, *The Basis of the Premillennial Faith,* p. 12).

Scriptural Grounds for Positing a First and a Second Resurrection: Revelation 20. Most references (excepting Rev. 20) assume only one resurrection—that of the just and the unjust (Matt. 25:46; Acts 24:15; cf. Luke 14:14).

The key text positing two resurrections is found in John's vision of the saints who "came to life and reigned with Christ a thousand years. (The rest of the dead did not come to life until the thousand years were ended.) This is the first resurrection. Blessed and holy are those who have power over them, but they will be priests of God and of Christ and will reign with him for a thousand years" (Rev. 20:5, 6).

On this ground, premillennialists posit two future resurrections with a thousand years between them (Erickson, *ST* III, pp. 1214 ff.). At the conclusion of the millennium, Satan, having been restrained for a thousand years, will be loosed to make a final assault on the kingdom of God, only to fail: "When the thousand years are over, Satan will be released from his prison and will go out to deceive the nations in the four corners of the earth" (Rev. 20:7, 8).

Realized millennialists interpret this text differently, viewing the "first resurrection" as repentance, faith, baptism, and spiritual regeneration, and the second as the general resurrection. "All the just who live during this time have a first resurrection by Baptism and reign with Christ so long as they are in the state of grace; and they have a second resurrection at the end of the world. Paralleling this is the first death by sin, and the second death in hell" (Trese, *The Creed—Summary of the Faith;* cf. Augustine, *CG* 20.6–7, *NPNF* 1 II, pp. 425–28).

National Israel. Israel is expected to have a key role in the last days. Some hold that the nation of Israel has been given an unconditional covenant promise to be restored, so when the church's mission is complete, God will then turn to fulfill the hopes of national Israel (Justin Martyr, *Dialogue with Trypho* 81 ff.; *First Apology* I.11). Others hold that Israel's role will be found within the church, and must be interpreted as a spiritual kingdom.

Irenaeus on the Sabbath of Creation. Irenaeus expressed a premillennial view characteristic of the first three centuries: The present world would endure six thousand years (analogous to the six days of creation), after which there would be a period of suffering and apostasy that would accelerate until the coming of the Antichrist, seated in the temple of God. The entire apostate throng is headed up by the Antichrist, "recapitulating in himself the diabolic apostasy . . . he will tyrannically attempt to prove himself God" (Irenaeus, *Ag. Her.* V.25.1), whereupon Christ will appear, the saints will be resurrected, and the kingdom will be established on earth for another thousand years, the seventh millennium (*Ag. Her.* V.28.3; 33.2).

This seventh millennium corresponds to the seventh day of creation, when God re-creates the world and the righteous, thus hallowing the last day of the world's week as a millennium of rest and peace. For one day with God is as a thousand years (Ps. 90:4). A new city of God, a new Jerusalem, would then become the center of a new period of peace and righteousness (Matt. 26:29; Irenaeus, *Ag. Her.* V.33.3, 4). At the end of this thousand-year reign, the final judgment will occur, a new creation will make way for eternity (*Ag. Her.* V.36.1). The dawning of the eighth day was for the *Letter of Barnabas* analogous to the Christian's Lord's

Day, the day on which Christ rose from the dead and ascended into heaven (15.5–9, *AF*, pp. 294–95).

Early Advocates of Premillennialism.   Premillennialism was the dominant position among the ante-Nicene Fathers (see G. Peters, *The Theocratic Kingdom*): Justin Martyr (*Dialogue with Trypho* 80.1), the Pastor of Hermas, the *Letter of Barnabas,* Irenaeus (*Against Heresies*), Methodius (*On the Resurrection*), Commodianus (*Instructions* XLIV, *ANF* IV, p. 212), and Tertullian (*Ag. Marcion* III.24).

By the time of the Decree of Gelasius, A.D. 493 (*SCD* 161–66, pp. 66–70), several of the ante-Nicene teachers with premillennialist assumptions were being regarded as inadequate in various ways: Lactantius, Nepos, Commodianus, and Victorinus of Pettau. Among those who earlier had resisted certain aspects of premillennial exegesis were Clement of Alexandria, Dionysius of Alexandria, and Athanasius (Pohle, *DT* XII, p. 159). Premillennialism was more fundamentally challenged by Origen, Augustine, and the Greek Fathers, who argued that the millennial kingdom had begun with the incarnation. Among Protestant advocates of premillennialism are Bengel, Irving, van Oosterzee, Ellicott, Darby, the Adventists, Christadelphians, Plymouth Brethren, and a host of modern interpreters.

Parousia and Rapture in Dispensationalism.   Recent premillennialism has increasingly become wedded to dispensationalism in many circles (as seen in Darby, Scofield, and Gaebelein, but with exceptions such as R. H. Gundry and G. E. Ladd). Dispensationalists typically divide the return of Christ into two events that occur in different spheres: his coming *for* the saints (the rapture—in the air) and his coming *with* the saints (the day of the Lord—on the earth).

The first of these is the Parousia, his coming *for* the saints (1 Thess. 4:15, 16), that coming which results in the rapture of the saints, when Christ does not come to the earth but remains in the upper air, when both those who have died in the Lord and living saints are caught up to meet the Lord in the air. "For the Lord himself will come down from heaven, with a loud command, with the voice of the archangel and with the trumpet call of God, and the dead in Christ will rise first. After that, we who are still alive and are left will be caught up [*harpagesometha,* seized, snatched] together with them in the clouds to meet the Lord in the air" (1 Thess. 4:16, 17). By this means the faithful will be united with the coming Lord and transformed into the same resurrected state as the heavenly *communio sanctorum.* Paul elsewhere spoke of the mystery of an instantaneous transformation of living believers (1 Cor. 15:51, 52) and of believers being promised glorious bodies like Christ's own body (Phil. 3:20, 21). A sudden removal of the faithful connected with the Lord's coming is suggested in Matthew 24:40–41 (=Luke 17:34, 35), where of two men in the field, one shall be taken and the other left, and of two women grinding, one is taken and the other left.

This coming is followed, according to dispensationalists, by a seven-year period in which the signs of the end occur (the gathering of Israel, the great tribulation, and the Antichrist). After this interval is another coming of the Lord *with* the saints in which he returns to earth.

Objectors argue that it is doubtful that the texts intend to refer to two distinct comings, because Parousia and "day of the Lord" are used interchangeably (2 Thess. 2:1, 2, 8; 2 Pet. 3), and because the coming of the Lord at which the elect are gathered is represented as following the tribulation (Matt. 24:29–31;

Berkhof, *ST*, p. 696); hence it is argued that the second coming is a single event. There is much debate as to when the period of tribulation might come—the time of Jacob's trouble, a time of unprecedented judgment (Jer. 30:7; Isa. 22:5; Zeph. 1:14–18).

Pretribulation Premillenarianism.   A debatable subquestion concerns whether Christ will take away (or rapture) the church from the world *before* the great tribulation (pretribulationism) or *after* (posttribulationism).

Pretribulationists believe that the church will be saved (raptured in the air) before the seven-year tribulation. This sequence assumes that Israel and the church are under separate covenants:

Apostasy increases in the church

    Resurrection of the dead in Christ
    Translation of living saints

        Rapture of saints to heaven
        Christ comes to take the church away *to* himself before the tribulation

            The seven-year tribulation
            Armageddon, end of tribulation

            Regathering of Israel

                The final coming of Christ *with* the saints

                The final judgment
                Separation of sheep and goats
                Satan is bound for a thousand years

                    The earthly kingdom of one thousand years of visible, terrestrial restoration of Davidic kingship

                    Saints reign with Christ
                    New Jerusalem

                        End, millennial kingdom
                        Satan loosed briefly
                        Satan defeated, cast in bottomless pit

                        New heaven
                        New earth

                        Eternity

Mid- and Posttribulation Premillenarianism.   According to posttribulation exegesis, the church will not be taken before the tribulation but will go through it and be taken after it. The order is the same, yet with the rapture and second coming of Christ following the tribulation. The hope is not that believers will be taken away from the earth before the tribulation, but that they will be kept by the Lord through whatever occurs (G. Ladd, *The Blessed Hope*, p. 122; R. Gundry, *The Church and the Tribulation*, pp. 12–24; A. Reese, *The Approaching Advent of Christ;* M. Erickson, *Contemporary Options in Eschatology*, pp. 163–81, *CT* 3, p. 1224; J. B. Payne, *The Imminent Appearing of Christ*).

Because the church participates in the suffering of her Lord, and is familiar with suffering, it should not be surprising that she also will face a final tribulation: "In this world you will have trouble. But take heart! I have overcome the world" (John 16:33; cf. Acts 14:22; Rom. 5:3; 2 John 7). "My prayer is not that you take them out of the world but that you protect them from the evil one" (John 17:15).

To further complicate the picture, a "midtribulation dispensationalism" holds a mediating position that the church will participate in the first half of the seven-year tribulation, but not the more severe last half (Buswell, *STCR*).

Ideological Tendencies in Pre-, Post-, and Realized Millennialism.   There are often ethical-political-ideological tendencies and implications in each of these alternative definitions (see Troeltsch, *STCC*).

Postmillennialism, as typified by Arminian-Wesleyan-Holiness exegesis, has taken a more transformationist view of the civil and political order, tending to see the church as actively engaged in the responsibility to change society in conformity with the divine claim. The political tendency is toward active transformation of society from injustice to justice as an act of eschatological accountability.

Premillennialism, as typified by much recent Reformed dispensational exegesis, tends toward a more realistic ordering of politics toward the restraint of evil that is not likely to diminish until the Lord's return. The political tendency is toward conservatism, an emphasis on law and order, and historical pessimism.

Realized millennialism, as typified by Augustinian exegesis, has tended to identify the millennial kingdom with the church herself, and her sacramental life as the extended incarnation of Christ in history. The political tendency is toward a close linkage of an established church with state protection, the idealization of the state, and at worst, ultramontanism.

Postmillennialism blends more easily with Arminian synergism, while premillennialism blends more easily with Calvinism's stress on the divine decrees. Postmillennialism held sway during the period of nineteenth-century optimism, and tended to recede with the disillusionment of utopian idealism after World War I. Postmillennialism has flourished in periods in which the church seemed to be succeeding in its worldwide mission, and receded in periods in which that mission seems to be faltering. The social gospel is more closely associated with a- or post- than premillennial views. Premillennialism has often rigorously argued that the promises of God to national Israel will be literally and explicitly fulfilled in the millennium.

Premillennialists oppose historical optimists who believe in the triumph of the gospel in human society. Against the historical optimism of postmillennial gradualists (who expect history to get better), the relative historical pessimism of premillennialism holds that the millennium will begin with a sudden cataclysmic event only after history has seriously deteriorated. They have an abrupt notion of the coming kingdom, where Christ will come only when things get maximally worst. Premillennialists expect history to get worse before it gets any better. Only after Christ personally comes will there be millennial peace, universal harmony in nature and history.

Which position is correct? There is no ecumenical consensus. The Vincentian method probably points more toward realized millennialism than its alternatives, but not with much confidence (for other views, see G. Ladd, *The Blessed Hope;*

M. Erickson, *Contemporary Options in Eschatology;* L. E. Froom, *The Conditionalist Faith of Our Fathers*). The "already/not yet" tension in the texts accounts for much of the potential for diverse interpretation (Phil. 3:12; 2 Thess. 2:7; 1 John 3:2; Rev. 2:25).

GENERAL JUDGMENT

At his "coming all men shall rise again with their bodies, and shall give account for their own works" (Quicunque Creed). This is the concluding event of history. What happens "after" final judgment is not history, but eternity beyond history. By this event the remedial dispensation is ended. History is at an end. There is no more time for action, only for final accountability.

The Final *Krisis*

The teachings that comprise the doctrine of the last judgment are familiar to those who sing the hymns of the church, join in its supplications, read its poetry, and hear its scripture. The topics ahead: the last assize, the mediatorial judge, the universality of judgment, the charge, inquiry, sentence, and execution of sentence.

Krisis (judgment) implies a discrimination or separation or crossroads, a parting of the ways (John 12:31; Heb. 9:27). It is to such a juncture that every person comes on the last day (Augustine, *CG* XX.27–30, *NPNF* 1 II, pp. 447–51; Sulpitius Severus, *Life of St. Martin, NPNF* XI, p. 14).

The Creedal Article.   In the Apostles' Creed the *ekklēsia* confesses that Christ "shall come to judge the quick and the dead." The Nicene-Constantinopolitan Creed affirms, "He shall come again with glory to judge both the quick and the dead" (Creed of the 150 Fathers). The Eastern Form of the Apostles' Creed confesses the one who, having ascended, "comes in glory to judge the living and the dead, of whose kingdom there will be no end" (Cyril of Jerusalem, *Catecheses, SCD* 9, p. 8). The Creed of Epiphanius looks toward "the just judgment of souls and bodies" (*SCD* 14, p. 10).

Last Judgment Defined.   "The last judgment is the judicial act by which on the last day, immediately upon the resurrection of the dead, Christ in great majesty and glory will pronounce sentence on all men, will separate the elect from the reprobate, and adjudge the former to life eternal, the latter to unquenchable fire" (Bucanus, *IT* XXVIII, 4; Heppe, *RD,* p. 703). God will "judge the peoples with equity." For "he comes, he comes to judge the earth. He will judge the world in righteousness and the peoples in his truth" (Ps. 96:13).

The last judgment is the consummation of a continuing judicial activity that has been proceeding in history. Christ is the final judge under whom all moral acts come to judgment (John Chrysostom, *Baptismal Instructions, ACW* 31, p. 183). On the last day will be revealed the character and destiny of each free moral agent, followed by a final separation of the just and unjust (Pearson, *EC,* art. VII). It is difficult to imagine any Christian teaching more universally received than this. It is rejected chiefly by those who, having abandoned scripture, cherish the delusions of modern optimism. In this final court, sin is understood in its essence simply as unresponsiveness to God's saving activity.

Coming, Sitting, Gathering, Separating. Four active verbs characterize the judging work of the Son as portrayed in the parable of the last judgment. "When the Son of Man *comes* in his glory, and all the angels with him, he will *sit* on his throne in heavenly glory. All the nations will be *gathered* before him, and he will *separate* the people one from another as a shepherd separates the sheep from the goats" (Matt. 25:31, 32, italics added). The structure of eschatological reasoning follows generally along this order: Parousia, the Judgment Seat, the Gathering for Judgment, and the Judgment itself.

The essential event of final judgment is a discriminating separation of those who are to be with God eternally from those who are to be sent away from God's presence (Irenaeus, *Ag. Her.* V.27, *ANF* I, p. 556; Strong, *ST,* pp. 1023–29). As at the Son's nativity, temptation, passion, resurrection, and ascension, good angels will attend and assist in final judgment—assembling, separating, monitoring, and conducting (Matt. 13:41, 42, 49; 24:31; 25:31; 1 Thess. 4:16, 17; 2 Thess. 1:7; Jude 14; Tho. Aq., *ST* supp., Q76.3, III, p. 2881; Wollebius, *RDB,* p. 183).

The Time and Place of the Judgment. After resurrection follows judgment. The dead are raised in order to be judged. "Therefore judge nothing before the appointed time; wait till the Lord comes. He will bring to light what is hidden in darkness and will expose the motives of men's hearts. At that time each will receive his praise from God" (1 Cor. 4:5, 6).

The synoptic Gospels tend to place the emphasis upon final judgment at the end of the age (Matt. 13:39), whereas John's Gospel stresses present judgment. The final judgment in effect records the judgment that persons "already" pass upon themselves by their present relation to Christ. "Whoever does not believe stands condemned already" (John 3:18). The tender conscience races to judgment: "The sins of some men are obvious, reaching the place of judgment ahead of them; the sins of others trail behind them" (1 Tim. 5:24).

Judgment is portrayed not merely as a rational idea but an event expected to occur on a particular "day of judgment" (John 5:28, 29; 2 Pet. 3:7), "that day" (Matt. 7:22; 2 Tim. 4:8), "the day of God's wrath, when his righteous judgment will be revealed" (Rom. 2:5). "For he has set a day when he will judge the world with justice by the man he has appointed" (Acts 17:31).

Lactantius thought the "day" would last a thousand years (*DI* VII.24). Thomas Aquinas thought that "the divine power will bring it about that in an instant everyone will be apprised of all the good or evil he has ever done" (*Compend. of Theology,* chap. 244, p. 305).

What matters is not the speculative details of time and place, but the certainty of judgment (Lactantius, *The Wrath of God, FC* 54, pp. 96 ff.). "For God will bring every deed into judgment, including every hidden thing, whether it is good or evil" (Eccles. 12:14). "Our God comes, and will not be silent; a fire devours before him, and around him a tempest rages. He summons the heavens above, and the earth, that he may judge his people" (Ps. 50:3, 4).

Judgment Entrusted to the One Who Was Judged. The court is overseen by the triune God (Heb. 12:23; Rom. 2:5; Ps. 98:9)—whose judgment is sometimes ascribed to the Father (John 8:50; Acts 17:31; 1 Pet. 2:23) or to the Spirit (John 16:8), but most often portrayed as being personally consummated and administered by the God-man, Christ himself (Matt. 25:31, 32; Acts 10:42; Phil. 2:10), who knows our infirmities (Heb. 2:18).

The Father "has entrusted all judgment to the Son" (John 5:22). The Father does not judge apart from the Son, but only in and through the Son (Hilary, *Trin.* VII.20, *NPNF* 2 IX, p. 126). Mercifully, it is by true man (the Son of man who has fully shared the human condition, being tempted in every way) that humanity is judged. The theandric mediator is "the one whom God appointed as judge of the living and the dead" (Acts 10:42), to whom the Father has given "authority to judge because he is the Son of Man" (John 5:27).

There is an ironic correspondence between the two articles: "suffered under Pontius Pilate," and "he shall come to judge." The judge bears in his own body the marks of his passion for the adjudged. The judge is the man on the cross who has already been condemned for the sins of the world. It is morally fitting that the same God-man who came to save humanity from sin should be the judge of sin. The work of redemption is to be fittingly ended by the one who began it. We are judged by one who can empathize with our human condition and can understand the obstacles that make our lives so imperfect, yet who remained sinless through the pain and struggle of resisting temptation.

No Appeal.   From this extraordinary court "there will be no appeal, because by his death he acquired for himself the right of Lordship over all men" (Riisen, *FTCT* XVIII, 9; Heppe, *RD,* p. 703), as "Lord of both the dead and the living" (Rom. 14:9). "Furthermore, the office of judge is a suitable recompense by way of exaltation, corresponding to the humiliation of Christ, who was willing to be humiliated to the point of being unjustly judged by a human judge" (Tho. Aq., *Compend.* 241, p. 297).

The judgment will be final and unchangeable, with no appeal. The judgment to come will be the last or eternal judgment (Heb. 6:2). Eternal destiny is fixed by conduct in earthly life. Until then: "Long as the lamp holds out to burn, the vilest sinner may return" (Harries, *TM,* p. 289).

The Mercy and Justice of the Judge.   The mercy of the final judge is wholly just, and the justice of the judge incomparably merciful. Lacking either infinite mercy or justice, it could not be God's judgment. These attributes are not contradictory but complementary, and best recognized as complementary on the cross. They are to be eternally united by insurmountable wisdom on the last day (John Chrysostom, *To the Fallen Theodore, NPNF* 1 IX, pp. 97–102).

The radiance of mercy is precisely that it is just. The glory of justice is that it is merciful. A justice exercised unmercifully would fail to express the love of God. A mercy exercised unjustly would undermine the moral order. "Indeed the unrighteous cannot endure the contact with God which is the central joy of eternal life" (Hall, *DT* X, pp. 167–72; C. S. Lewis, *The Great Divorce*). "Without holiness no one will see the Lord" (Heb. 12:14).

This judge is the searcher of all hearts, who "holds in his hand your life and all your ways" (Dan. 5:23), who knows intimately "everyone's heart" (Acts 1:24). "The most profound secrets of the Saviour's gracious will to His people can never be known till then" (Pope, *Compend.* III, p. 413).

Comfort and Dread in the Presence of the Judge.   The faithful do not dread the final judgment, for "we are not to come before any other Judge than he who is our Advocate and who has taken our cause in hand" (Calvin, *Geneva Catechism,* Q87; cf. *Revelation of Esdras, ANF* VIII, pp. 571–74). The comfort of final judgment is "that in all affliction and persecution I may await with head held high the very Judge from heaven who has already submitted himself to the judgment of God for men and has removed all curse from me" (*Heid. Catech.,* Q 52). Paul was confident that there was in store for him "a crown of righteousness, which the Lord, the righteous Judge, will award to me on that day" (2 Tim. 4:8).

The Echo of Righteous Judgment by the Upright.   The saints and martyrs and, indeed, all believers will in some sense sit and judge empathically with Christ by concurrence (Matt. 19:28; 1 Cor. 6:2, 3; Rev. 20:4; Tho. Aq., *ST* supp., Q89.1, III, p. 2939; Wollebius, *RDB,* p. 185). "Those will judge with Him—sitting with the judge, as it were—who adhered to Him more than others"—the apostles— and "those who follow in the footprints of the Apostles" (Tho. Aq., *SCG* IV, chap. 96, p. 346). "And some will judge by giving their approval to the sentence; in this way all the just shall judge" (Tho. Aq., *Compend.* 245, p. 306; cf. Wisd. of Sol. 3:7 f.).

The Moral Meaning of Final Judgment

Any judgment short of final judgment would risk being incomplete, hence unjust.

Why Final Judgment?   After one dies, one's influence continues. The deceased lives on in memory, reputation, progeny, and in the "projects on which he had set his heart." For "no action can be fully assessed before it is finished and its results are evident." "A full and public verdict cannot be pronounced and sentence passed while time rolls on its course" (Tho. Aq., *ST* IIIa, Q59.5, *TATT,* pp. 401, 402).

This is why there must be a judgment at the end of history, and not merely at some point within history. The effects of one's life are not known at the time of death. The evil done by Hitler and Stalin continues to plague the world long after they are gone, and in generations yet unborn. It is therefore reasonable that the final judgment be rendered only after all accounts of all historical agents are in, namely, at the end time. Works "continue to extend their influence throughout all time as a stone thrown into the water creates successive and ever widening circles" (Jacobs, *SCF,* p. 530), which influence is only known by God's omniscience, hence only revealed at the final judgment.

Whether the Justice of God Requires Final Judgment.   The incomparable justice of God requires a final judgment, for in this life many if not most evils remain unjudged or crudely judged (Pss. 103:10; 92:7; Luke 6:24, 25; Rom. 9:22). If justice is inadequately exercised in this present life, surely another life, another sphere, another city is required to perfect it. Only at the end of history is it the proper time for judgment, for "judgment belongs to the term" where all things are "brought to their end" (Tho. Aq., *ST* supp., Q88.1, III, p. 2935).

Within history the poor suffer the violence of the ungodly, good remains unrewarded, evil unrequited. The righteous have repeatedly "faced jeers and flogging, while still others were chained and put in prison. They were stoned; they were sawed in two; they were put to death by the sword. They went about in sheepskins and goatskins, destitute, persecuted and mistreated—the world was not worthy of them. They wandered in deserts and mountains, and in caves and holes in the ground. These were all commended for their faith, yet none of them received what had been promised. God had planned something better for us so that only together with us would they be made perfect" (Heb. 11: 36–40).

Such injustices have been commonplace in the history of sin, while the wicked prosper. If God is just, we cannot be satisfied that justice is fully adequate in this historical sphere. We hypothesize, from conscience, that an exact and impartial justice must somehow follow, even if we cannot now behold it. According to Malachi, we weary the Lord by constantly and anxiously asking here and now, "Where is the God of justice?" (Mal. 2:17). Scripture rather points us toward a final judgment beyond history wherein God will answer all human queries about divine justice (John Chrysostom, *Hom. on the Statues, NPNF* 1 IX, p. 339).

Only the divine character can be the guarantor of the goodness and justice of the final judgment. Abraham appealed to God on behalf of the righteous of Sodom: "Far be it from you to do such a thing—to kill the righteous with the wicked, treating the righteous and the wicked alike. Far be it from you! Will not the Judge of all the earth do right?" (Gen. 18:25).

Whether God Acted Justly by Leaving Time for Repentance.   Suppose God had provided no time for repentance, and no time for grieving over the consequences of sin—would the world be a better place? There must be some lag time between sin and judgment if God is to provide time for repentance, and time for the consequences of sin to be experienced and grieved over (2 Pet. 3:9). Sometimes it takes a very long time for the consequences of sin to be realized and corrected.

Suppose the contrary, that God might have created a world in which no time whatever was provided between sin and its punishment. That would have reduced sin drastically, but would have given less opportunity for the play of responsible freedom and conscience. God apparently opted for the conditions of freedom that now prevail in human creation—human self-determination that is prone to sin that has repercussions in succeeding generations. Without positing the very freedom that risks falling into sin, human existence would be reduced to pure determinism. The person would hardly be distinguishable from a billiard ball, lacking the capacity for self-determination and divine-human companionship that God permits and apparently desires.

These conditions make it necessary to conclude that the full and adequate judgment of sin cannot rightly occur before death, and that final judgment cannot occur before the end of history. The forms of judgment of sin that do occur before death are often roughly conceived and prejudicially framed. Hence this-worldly justice, however important, cannot be finally or irreversibly decisive for the destiny of the person in the presence of God.

Kant thought that some future judgment was rationally required by the disparity between conscience and historical injustice (*Prolegomena to the Metaphysics of Morals, LLA; Critique of Pure Judgment*). He argued that ethics is "not really the doctrine of how to make ourselves happy but of how we are to be *worthy* of happiness" (*Critique of Practical Judgment* II.2.5, *TGS,* p. 249).

Much modern consciousness, however, following Hegel, Schelling, and Freud, has tended to view moral judgment as entirely immanental within historical processes. The classical Christian consensus viewed final judgment as distinguishable from the continuing judging activity of God in and through history and from immanental human judgment. God is at work within history as Judge, but that work in itself must be completed beyond history if the apparent absurdities of history are to become meaningful.

Conscience Anticipates and Awaits Final Judgment. Conscience awaits final judgment (Acts 24:25). Our own moral self-awareness compels us constantly to pass judgment on our own actions to assess their rightness or culpability.

The correspondence between conscience and final judgment is set forth in this powerful testimony from John's epistle: "This then is how we know that we belong to the truth, and how we set our hearts at rest in his presence whenever our hearts condemn us. For God is greater than our hearts, and he knows everything. Dear friends, if our hearts do not condemn us, we have confidence before God" (1 John 3:19–21). We may be either too harsh on ourselves or too lenient, but the all-merciful One who judges us finally in the end will judge according to God's own justice, which is finally already knowable on the cross.

The Moral Meaning of Freedom Finally Vindicated Only at the End. Each person is responsible to God for his or her personal moral conduct. The present state of the probation of freedom is followed by a future judgment of lives lived in free self-determination. There is no meaningful freedom in a moral universe without positing some sort of final accountability and judgment.

The thought of final judgment impinges powerfully upon current moral behavior, and upon conscience. It may cause extreme discomfort, as it did in the case of Felix when Paul "discoursed on righteousness, self-control and the judgment to come" (Acts 24:25). The maneuvers of avoidance implicitly attest the moral meaning of freedom.

The Dramatic Structure of Moral Decision. The conclusion of the drama of a personal history remains unknown until after this life is closed. What could be more dramatic? "Man knoweth not his own end" (Eccles. 9:12).

No further appeal can be made after history's last act. There is no time for another scene. Heaven and earth will pass away, but the final word on that day will not pass away. The audience of the drama is finally all who have ever lived in history, gathered together on the final day (Nicene Creed, *SCD* 54, p. 26; Lateran Council, *SCD* 255, p. 102; Council of Toledo XI, *SCD* 287, p. 111; Trent, Profession of Faith, *SCD* 994, p. 302). The scene of final judgment, ironically, is the only time biblically envisioned when all humanity will be beheld together as a single human community.

The Universality and Individuality of Judgment

Universality and individuality remain in creative tension in this final scene: judgment is for all with all assembled, yet each is judged individually.

The Redeemer Judges as a Negative Expression of His Redemptive Work. The work of judging is best viewed in relation to the primary mediatorial work of the Redeemer. By analogy, "the punishment and expulsion of unruly scholars [is] not the main duty of a schoolmaster" (Jacobs, *SCF,* p. 519). "A physician says to a sick man: 'I want you to get well, I cannot save your life; but I want to help to do it.' But if the sufferer will not allow this or accept his services as doctor, the latter says: 'Now I will not talk to you as your doctor, but, because you compel me, I must be your judge and say: You are going to die'" (Luther, *EA* 48, pp. 294 ff.).

That Christ "did not come to judge the world, but to save it" (John 12:47) does not imply that Christ has no judging functions, as is evident from the next verse: "There is a judge for the one who rejects me and does not accept my words; that very word which I spoke will condemn him at the last day" (v. 48). Though God desires the salvation of all, God does not coerce the will of the unjust to accept divine mercy. "This is the verdict: Light has come into the world, but men loved darkness instead of light because their deeds were evil" (John 3:19). "For judgment I have come into this world" (John 9:39), yet judgment as such is never the primary purpose of his coming but the consequence of the negation of his saving activity (John 3:17; Mark 4:12; Isa. 6:9).

The Universality of Judgment. All rational creatures must become finally accountable to the Creator. Because all rational creatures are moral creatures, and because God is the moral orderer of creation, those standing under judgment must be all humanity—every generation collectively and every person individually (Matt. 12:36, 37; Rom. 14:10; 2 Cor. 5:10), all having any degree of rational self-determination. All are accountable for the moral use of whatever capacities are given them, not merely to themselves, but to their Giver (Tho. Aq., *ST* III supp., Q89; Pearson, *EC,* pp. 300–304).

"Small and great" will come before him, even infants and innocents, even "those who did not sin by breaking a command, as did Adam" (Rom. 5:14). In a judgment transcending all social class and caste divisions, "the great will be without their ensigns of dignity, and the poor without their marks of abasement; for then moral distinctions alone will be regarded. The oppressor and the oppressed will be there; the former that his violence may be returned upon his own head, and the latter that his wrongs may be redressed" (Wakefield, *CT* 2, p. 625).

The Individuality of Judgment: Each One According to Deeds. No one can serve as conscience for another. Finally each conscience is called to account, one by one. Conscience is in this life anticipatory of the judgment to come.

The universality of judgment does not deny but confirms the individuality of judgment, whereby "each of us will give an account of himself to God" (Rom. 14:10, 12). This need not imply an extended, formal judicial procedure for each one; this divine judge is capable of instantly grasping the truth about the course of one's life, because that truth is already fully present to God's memory. Basil thought it "likely that by an inexpressible power, every deed we have done will be made manifest to us in a single moment, as if it were engraved on a tablet" (Basil, *Comm. on John* I.18, *MPG* 31; cf. Pohle, *DT* XII, p. 154). It will then be clear to all whether one is prepared to live in the presence of God or not.

Whether God Remembers Forgiven Sin in the Final Judgment. What has been already forgiven will not be called to account on the last day (Turretin, *ITE* XX.vi.17; Heppe, *RD,* p. 705). "For it is the part of an advocate not to publish, but to cover" (Jacobs, *SCF,* p. 525). In him there is no condemnation (Rom. 8:1). Whoever "hears my word and believes him who sent me has eternal life and will not be condemned" (John 5:24). In this sense those who believe will escape judgment in the sense of condemnation.

Those whose lives are hid in Christ will stand in this judgment without spot or wrinkle (Eph. 5:27). The father receives the prodigal without making a long list of wayward behaviors (Luke 15:20). If the godly recall their own sin, it will be to praise God's mercy. "The righteous and the unrighteous shall be judged differently. The former shall be judged but not condemned, but the latter shall be both judged and condemned. In this sense, Scripture says that the righteous shall not be judged" (Wollebius, *RDB,* p. 184). Those who die in faith have already discovered that their sins are blotted out, cast into the depths of the sea, remembered no more by God (Isa. 43:25; Jer. 31:34; Ezek. 18:22).

Whether the Final Inquiry Reveals the Secrets of the Heart. Final judgment is not portrayed as a secret proceeding, for its purpose is to expose the secrets of sinners (Matt. 6:4, 6; 12:36 ff.; 1 Cor. 4:5; 1 Tim. 5:24, 25). It is described as that day when "God through Jesus Christ will judge the secret thoughts of all" (Rom. 2:16, NRSV). This does not imply that all the already repented sins of the redeemed will be once again dragged out and publicly made known, even though once forgiven. For they have already been removed as far as is east from west (Ps. 103:12). The purpose is the final publication of all unrepented sins "that all may know from what a depth of sin and misery the grace of God had delivered them" (Wakefield, *CT* 2, p. 627).

As it is a principle of law that one should face one's accuser, so it is fitting that "every eye shall see him" (Rev. 1:7). "Those who are to be judged ought to see the judge" (Tho. Aq., *Compend. of Theology,* chap. 241, p. 296). The sight of his coming will be a joy "to all who have longed for his appearing" (2 Tim. 4:8), who have longed to "see the king in his beauty" (Isa. 33:17), and a terror to the unjust.

That the judgment of all unrepented sin will be visible and will appear to all is taught for these reasons: for the glory of God, that the justice and mercy of God may be manifested; that the promises of God may be fulfilled; that the godly may be exalted and Christ glorified; and that all things may be fitly judged before the conclusion of history (Gerhard, *LT* XVIII, 35; Schmid, *DT,* pp. 644, 645; Leiden Synopsis LI, 55; Heppe, *RD,* p. 708).

"Sharper than any double-edged sword" is the divine Word. "It penetrates even to dividing soul and spirit, joints and marrow; it judges the thoughts and attitudes of the heart. Nothing in all creation is hidden from God's sight. Everything is uncovered and laid bare before the eyes of him to whom we must give account" (Heb. 4:13).

The Full Disclosure of Mixed Motives. Thomas astutely reasoned, "A judicial investigation is not necessary unless good and evil actions are intermingled. When good is present without admixture of evil, or evil without admixture of good, discussion is out of place" (Tho. Aq., *Compend. of Theology,* chap. 243, p. 303);

hence both the perfectly good and perfectly wicked are judged without further inquiry. But if some have faith but lack charity, or in cases where faith and charity are diluted by excessive attachments, a thorough examination of such complex circumstances is required by divine justice (Tho. Aq., *Compend. of Theology*, chap. 243, pp. 303, 304).

Because feelings and motives affect conduct, especially when formed into reinforced habits and cherished dispositions, these are fit matters to be subjected to judgment (1 Cor. 4:5; *Longer Catech.*, Eastern Orthodox Church, 231, *COC* II, p. 480). The purpose of examination is not that the judge may receive new information, for all things are already known by God (Sister Macrina, *On the Soul and the Resurrection, FC* 58, p. 267). Rather the investigative judgment clearly makes known to each person why each is judged as a whole faithful or unfaithful, the former rejoicing in God's mercy and the latter acceding to God's justice.

"In the day when God shall judge each one's conscience will bear witness to him, and his thoughts will accuse and defend him"; all merits and demerits will be seen at a single glance (Tho. Aq., *ST* supp., Q87, III, pp. 2932–34; Job 8:22). "A kind of divine energy will come to our aid, so that we shall recall all of our sins to mind" (Augustine, *CG* XX, *NPNF* 1 II, pp. 420 ff.).

The Judgment of Deeds and Words Both Omitted and Committed.   Not only deeds are judged but words, which have such powerful effects in human relationships. Wordy folk must deal with the final Word. Sentence makers do not escape the final sentence. Those who write or speak words (including the many of this book) will "give account on the day of judgment for every careless word they have spoken" (Matt. 12:36; cf. James 3:2).

Both what we do and what we neglect doing are subject to final judgment. For the habits we willfully neglect to amend, we remain responsible. For our negligence by which others are harmed, we are responsible.

The entire range of conduct and character of every human being is to be divinely assessed—every word, thought, and deed (Matt. 12:36, 37). "I am he who searches hearts and minds" (Rev. 2:23).

On the last day, love will cover a multitude of sins (1 Pet. 4:8), for love is the pivotal feature of the Redeemer and the redeemed character. Acts of mercy to the defenseless will then be recognized by the Just One, even if unrecognized by those who engaged in them as a matter of course.

The Judicial Process

Due judicial process consists in being fairly brought into a just court for the purpose of being charged, having one's cause fairly examined, being judged, receiving sentence, and having the sentence executed. All these elements are embedded in the narratives of the last judgment.

The Anticipative Internal Expression of Judgment: Conscience.   Conscience is the inward bar of judgment. All rational persons are already "a law for themselves, even though they do not have the law, since they show the requirements of the law are written on their hearts, their consciences also bearing witness, and their thoughts now accusing, now even defending them" (Rom. 2:15, 16). What happens penultimately in conscience happens ultimately in final judgment: "For we must all appear before the judgment seat of Christ, that each one may receive what is due him for the things done while in the body, whether good or bad" (2 Cor. 5:10).

The Norm of Judgment: According to One's Deeds in the Body.   The standard by which judgment proceeds is the holy will of God, equitably administered "according to what they had done, as recorded in the books" (Rev. 20:12). The metaphor of accurate records in detailed books is employed in scripture to portray the final accounting of those being judged (Rev. 20:12; cf. Ps. 50:21; Wollebius, *RDB*, p. 184).

Some have greater responsibility, having received greater gifts; others less (Matt. 11:21–24; Rom. 2:12–16). The measure of light and truth granted will impinge upon final judgment. Those who have Moses and the prophets are to be judged by a different standard than those without them (Matt. 11:24; Luke 12:48; 16:29). Those who have not heard the gospel will be judged by the law of their own nature, their conscience guided by their reason, and the law written in their hearts (Rom. 2:14, 15). Jews will be judged by the law and prophets: for "all who sinned under the law will be judged by the law" (Rom. 2:12). Those who have heard the Gospel will be judged "according to the Gospel," the good news of God's own righteousness in which they may share by faith (Hollaz, *ETA*, p. 1246; Schmid, *DT*, p. 644). Final judgment focuses upon whether one has been responsive or not to the actually offered gifts of God (Hugh of St. Victor, *SCF*, p. 464).

All that is judged negatively finally comes down to whether one has or has not responded trustingly to God's prevening and cooperating grace. "Whoever believes in him is not condemned, but whoever does not believe stands condemned already because he has not believed in the name of God's one and only Son" (John 3:18). The righteousness that saves is not "a righteousness of my own that comes from the law, but that which is through faith in Christ—the righteousness that comes from God and is by faith" (Phil. 3:9).

Judged According to, Not on Account of, Deeds.   This does not imply that good works are finally of no importance to God. The Pauline formula is that all will be judged *according to their works as they are fruits of faith, not on account of their works apart from faith* (Wollebius, *RDB*, p. 184; Jacobs, *SCF*, p. 523). "This explains in part the truth of the seemingly opposed propositions that our works cannot save us, and that we are to be judged and finally rewarded according to them. We are to be judged *according to* rather than *on account of* deeds" (*non propter, sed secundum opera*, Hall, *DT* X, p. 179). The pivotal issue is always, Did faith become active in love? Did faith express itself in deeds of mercy? Were the poor relieved, was charity shown toward all, were enemies forgiven? Faith is the engendering source and works the expression of the Christian life, assuming that your work is "produced by faith, your labor prompted by love, and your endurance inspired by hope" (1 Thess. 1:3). The faithful are justified "by faith without the merit of works, and with the evidence of works" (Pope, *Compend.* 3, p. 417).

Reaping One's Own Sowing.   Those who depart do so not merely by divine predetermination, but because of their own recalcitrant will. "A man reaps what he sows. The one who sows to please his sinful nature, from that nature will reap destruction; the one who sows to please the Spirit, from the Spirit will reap eternal life" (Gal. 6:7, 8).

The sinner is understood as the author of his own character, reaping the fruit of his own choices. Character molds destiny. That human freedom is divinely aided does not diminish its quality as freedom, for all self-determining beings are given grace adequate for salvation if they cooperate with it. It is the ultimate directionality of the character that makes the judgment irreversible, a crystallization due to moral choice, not coercion (Origen, *Principles* II.10, *ANF* IV, pp. 293–96). This does not deny social or genetic or biological or cultural determinants, but focuses upon one's own free response to all conceivable determinants.

The Blessed and the Cursed.   The sentence is described by Christ himself: the judge will separate the sheep from the goats (Matt. 25; cf. 2 Cor. 5:10). Despite variable rewards according to deeds, the fundamental decision in a court is finally described simply: guilty as charged, or not guilty. Only two classes of response finally are provided for in the parable: left or right, blessed or cursed. The sentence is either, "Come, you who are blessed by my Father, take your inheritance," or "Depart from me, you who are cursed" (Matt. 25:34, 41). The just are taken up into Christ's presence, while the unjust depart from Christ's presence. The sequence moves from judgment in determining the sentence, and condemnation in pronouncing it, to execution in administering it (Pope, *Compend.* 3, p. 420). The decree of the just judge has to do with the overall weight of innocence or guilt of those judged (Hippolytus, *Ag. Plato* I, *ANF* V, p. 221).

Whether Judgment Is Event or Symbol.   The picture of the great assize, by analogy with earthly courts, is a metaphor attempting to communicate the essence of a process that cannot be pictured. The trumpet sounding, the bodily change occurring in the twinkling of an eye, the judge and the judgment, the separation of sheep and goats, the new Jerusalem—these are the "sound words" by which our inadequate perceptions are rightly oriented, despite their limitations.

Though symbolic language is constantly utilized by scripture to point to the final judgment, it would be a vast miscalculation to view final judgment as a non-event or to reduce it to merely metaphorical status (Irenaeus, *Ag. Her.* V.35, *ANF* I, p. 565). Nor is it wise to view final judgment as a continuing, immanental-historical process, as distinguished from an event effectively ending history. Final judgment is an event that only God can enact. It is not reducible to our judgment of ourselves, hence not to be psychologized, politicized, or subjectivized. "Too late do they believe in eternal punishment who were unwilling to believe in eternal life" (Cyprian, *To Demetrian* 24, *FC* 38, 189).

On the other hand, the courtroom scene is not to be taken so woodenly or literally that its figurative elements cannot be proportionally interpreted. The books to be opened on the last day are not literal books made with paper and ink; rather, the book of life is Christ in whom the faithful are hid (Phil. 4:3; Rev. 5:1–9; 13:8). "To say, 'We don't like figures and metaphors; we prefer the literal,' is, to say the least, not very thoughtful talk" (Banks, *MCD*, p. 370), for in scripture physical references can point metaphorically to spiritual realities (Augustine, *CG* XX; *NPNF* 1 II, pp. 421 ff.; Tho. Aq., *ST* supp., Q88.2, III, p. 2936).

The Fulfillment of the Work of Salvation.   The judgment complete, the Lord will lead his own into glory, where they will reign with him forever (Council of Toledo XI, *SCD* 287, p. 111). With the final judgment, the history of salvation comes full circle in the mode of eternal fulfillment (Lactantius, *DI, FC* 49, pp. 522 ff.). The work of the Holy Spirit in sanctifying what was begun in creation has come to completion. What was begun for the believer on the day of baptism, and what was begun for the church on the day of Pentecost, will have come to full consummation, the kingdom established (Matt. 25:34–40), the power of evil bound (Rev. 20:1–3).

Three events of transformation exceed our understanding: creation, redemption, and consummation. The mode of each ending or beginning transformation remains a mystery of the triune God.

How may one prepare for final judgment? Each time one receives the Eucharist, the memory of Christ's death is being kept until he comes. The faithful have Christ's own word that he will raise them up on the last day if they share in his body and blood by faith.

Consummation: The End of the World

History is not like Penelope's tapestry, constantly being rewoven and constantly undone, in eternal recurrence. Nor is it like the myth of Sisyphus, who rolled the stone uphill only to have it roll forever down again. Rather Jews and Christians understand that history is characterized by the revelation of meaning through events in a linear trajectory that leads toward a final consummation, not the absurdity of eternal repetition.

End of the Age (Consummatio Saeculi).   "The things concerning Me have an end" (Luke 22:37, kjv). The final moment is a vanishing point in which all the rays of creation converge, only to become a new beginning point.

After judgment comes the end of this world (*sunteleia tou aiōnos toutou*), according to Jewish and Christian expectation, and the beginning of the future age. The present state is to be destroyed by fire, not to end the world as such, but to make a new world out of the old, a new heaven and new earth that will not pass away (Isa. 65:17). "For this world in its present form is passing away" (1 Cor. 7:31).

The entire visible creation, implicated in the history of sin, is hastening toward a *krisis* in which it shall be dissolved and renewed. One who confesses the beginning of the world's existence must necessarily agree as to its end (Gregory of Nyssa, *On the Making of Man* XXIII, *NPNF* 2 IV, p. 413). In the consummation God will be "all in all" (1 Cor. 15:28). The expectation is that "creation itself will be liberated from its bondage to decay" (Rom. 8:21). All things will be reconciled in him (Col. 1:20). God has promised to reestablish or gather up all things (literally re-head, sum up all things, *anakephalaiōsasthai ta panta*) in Christ (Eph. 1:10).

"Heaven and earth will pass away, but my words will never pass away" (Matt. 24:35). The earth and heavens "will perish, but you remain; they will all wear out like a garment, like clothing you will change them and they will be discarded. But you remain the same, and your years will never end" (Ps. 102:26, 27). "The heavens have now their working-day clothes on; but then they will put on their Sunday robes" (Luther, quoted in Jacobs, *SCF*, p. 534). "All the stars of the heavens will be dissolved and the sky rolled up like a scroll; all the starry host will fall like withered leaves·from the vine, like shriveled figs from the fig tree" (Isa. 34:4). "Amen flames on the nations" (Commodianus, *Instructions* XLIII, *ANF* IV, p. 211; Rev. 3:14). The visible heavens are like the shell of an egg from which a newborn creation, a new chick, may issue (Clementina, *Recognitions* III.28, *ANF* VIII, p. 121).

The Renewed Destiny of the Cosmos.   The purpose of God in redemption is not merely to prolong creation quantitatively, but to redeem and perfect it qualitatively. This consummation has begun irreversibly in Jesus Christ. The consummation does not come by human action, political strategy, revolutionary planning, or evolution, but by God's own completing activity. This does not mean that God's kingdom lacks political consequences, or that there is therefore no need for peacemakers or the struggle for justice in history. Rather it means that however imperfect is our own struggle for peace and justice, it will be perfected by God's own peace and justice finally beyond history. By the same Word of God spoken in creation "the present heavens and earth are reserved for fire" (2 Pet. 3:7–11). By "present heavens" is meant the upper regions of the present cosmos, not the eternal dwelling place of God. "Since the world was, in a way, made for man's sake, it follows that, when man shall be glorified in the body, the other bodies of the world shall also be changed to a better state" (Tho. Aq., *ST* supp., Q74.1, III, p. 2865). On the assumption that the "dwelling should befit the dweller," Thomas argued that the world was made to be humanity's dwelling, so that when humanity is renewed, "the world will be likewise" (Tho. Aq., *ST* supp., Q91.1, III, p. 2949).

If the blessed are to enjoy God forever and the unjust to depart eternally from God's presence, one must posit a surviving condition in which this is to occur. "This corruptible world shall come to an end, and shall be transformed into another, incorruptible" (*Longer Catech.*, Eastern Orthodox Church, 370, *COC* II, p. 503). "The entire bodily creation will be changed—and suitably—to be in harmony with the state of [those] who then will be. And because [they] will then be incorruptible, the state of generation and corruption will then be taken away from the whole bodily creation. . . . Therefore, just as nature in generation does not have as end the reduction of matter from potency to act, but something consequent on this reduction—namely, that perpetuity in things by which they approach a divine likeness—so the end of heavenly motion is not the being reduced from potency to act, but something consequent on this reduction: namely, to be made like to God in the act of causing" (Tho. Aq., *SCG* IV, chap. 97, pp. 346, 347).

The regeneration of the human person takes place within the cosmic-historical context in which God's plan is to "restore everything" to its original unfallen condition. This final renovation is described in Paul's letter to Romans, chapters 4–8, and in the apostolic preaching of Acts, where Christ is expected to "remain in heaven until the time comes for God to *restore everything*" (Acts 3:17–21, italics added), as promised long ago. Sister Macrina defined the resurrection as nothing other than "the re-constitution of our nature in its original form" (*On the Soul and the Resurrection, NPNF* 2 IV, p. 467).

The Age's Ending as New Beginning.   Some contend that as the earth was not destroyed in substance by the flood, neither will the earth be destroyed in substance in the consummation. Rather "this world in its present form is passing away" (1 Cor. 7:31) to make way for a cleansing and a new setting-in-order (Rom. 8:19–22; Rev. 21:1; Pope, *Compend.* III, p. 424). Other texts appear to argue for an utter destruction of substance, not merely a transformation of qualities (Ps. 102:26, 27; Isa. 51:6; Matt. 24:35; 2 Pet. 3:7, 10, 12). The metaphors here are "vanish like smoke," "be dissolved," "melt," "burn," "pass away," and "be no more" (Wollebius, *RDB*, p. 188; Schmid, *DT*, p. 655). Though both these metaphorical sets seem stark and absolute, they express something fundamental: the created world is not itself eternal, but the radical gift of the Creator.

Is there something ecologically dangerous in the idea that the world is transitory? The answer is yes, if one systematically forgets that the transitory is also profoundly valuable, and the gift of God the Creator, given for human stewardship. But that forgetfulness would be a gross distortion of the intention of the Christian doctrine of creation.

Augustine held the balance correctly: "The form passes away but not the nature" (commenting upon 1 Cor. 7:31, quoted in *CCF*, p. 350). Those who focus upon the end of the world without a new beginning distort the text. Those who rejoice in a new beginning without awareness of an end diminish the text. It is both a consummation and a new beginning. "Behold, I make all things new" (Rev. 21:5, KJV). "Then I saw a new heaven and a new earth, for the first heaven and the first earth had passed away, and there was no longer any sea. I saw the Holy City, the new Jerusalem, coming down out of heaven from God, prepared as a bride beautifully dressed for her husband. And I heard a loud voice from the throne saying, 'Now the dwelling of God is with men, and he will live with them. They will be his people, and God himself will be with them and be their God. He will wipe every tear from their eyes. There will be no more death, or mourning or crying or pain, for the old order of things has passed away'" (Rev. 21:1–4).

The Brightness of His Glory. If in this age there is "nothing new under the sun" (Eccles. 1:9), in the age to come "things belonging in the state of glory are not 'under the sun'" in the former sense (Tho. Aq., *ST* supp., Q91.1, III, p. 2950).

The radiant beauty of the heavenly bodies consists chiefly in light. "The moon will shine like the sun, and the sunlight will be seven times brighter" (Isa. 30:26). "All the elements will be clothed with a certain brightness, not equally, however, but according to their mode: for it is said that the earth on its outward surface will be as transparent as glass, water as crystal, the air as heaven, fire as the lights of heaven. . . . Whatever remains after the world has been renewed will remain for ever, generation and corruption being done away" (Tho. Aq., *ST* supp., Q91.4–5, III, pp. 2955–56).

The Dross Consumed. The mode of the destruction is portrayed in scripture as fire. "The heavens will disappear with a roar; the elements will be destroyed by fire, and the earth and everything in it will be laid bare" (2 Pet. 3:11; Tho. Aq., *ST* supp., Q74.3, III, p. 2867). There is a moral connection between this verse and the next: "Since everything will be destroyed in this way, what kind of people ought you to be. You ought to live holy and godly lives as you look forward to the day of God" (2 Pet. 3:12).

Thomas argued that "the consumption of the things which ought not remain in the future state will most suitably take place by fire" which purifies, which is the most active of all the elements, and which "tends to consume the corruptible"

(Tho. Aq., *SCG* IV, p. 348). Do not miss the humor of Gerhard's conclusion: "Whether the fire be truly corporeal, material and visible, or incorporeal, immaterial and invisible, we leave unsettled (although we incline to the latter), and we earnestly pray God not to reveal this to us by knowledge gained from experience" (Gerhard, in Jacobs, *SCF,* p. 536)!

Not Annihilation but Purification and Transformation.   As the first destruction of the world came by flood, the final purification will occur by fire (Isa. 66:15; Commodianus, *Instructions* LXV, *ANF* IV, p. 212). To say that the world was "destroyed" by the flood, however, means not that all life ended but that a new beginning was made—similarly in the case of the "new earth." "By these waters also the world of that time was deluged and destroyed. By the same word the present heavens and earth are reserved for fire, being kept for the day of judgment and the destruction of ungodly men" (2 Pet. 3:7). What is destroyed is ungodliness, not creation as such.

Fire is the consistent biblical symbol of the cleansing, purifying, sanctifying power of God's holiness and justice. The fire of God's holiness against sin is not to be quenched (Matt. 23:33; Mark 9:48). Fire is appointed for cleansing and renewing the world, not merely for annihilation (Irenaeus, *Ag. Her.* V.36.1, *ANF* I, p. 566). "Combustion does not annihilate but only redistributes and rearranges particles of matter" (Jacobs, *SCF,* p. 534). Thus "through physical metaphors the prophets strike us with fear, although they employ no exaggeration to match our sluggishness" (Calvin, *Inst.* 3.12.2).

11 The Communion of Saints and the Life Everlasting

The symphony of theology is poised to celebrate its last reprise. The drama of history, having reached its resolution, is quickly drawing to a certain kind of close, which is itself a new age, remembering, "The Maker of time . . . is not subject to Time" (Gregory Nazianzen, *Orat.* XXXIX.12, *NPNF* 2 VII, p. 356).

THE COMMUNION OF SAINTS

The church is a fellowship not only among those living, but also with those who have died, as well as those yet unborn.

> One family we dwell in Him,
> One Church, above, beneath,
> Though now divided by the stream,
> The narrow stream of death.

> (C. Wesley, quoted by M. Hughes, *CF,* p. 179)

The Continuing Celebration

Eternal life with God brings an incomparable interpersonal blessing: communion with God amid the communion of the saints with God and with all who mirror God's holiness (Luke 23:43; John 12:26; Phil. 1:23; Rev. 14:4). This celebrating community embraces both the living faithful and the faithful departed who already enjoy eternal life with God.

The article on "the communion of saints" (*hagion koinonian*) is found in the received form of the Apostles' Creed and in those texts of the rule of faith passed on by Faustus of Riez (d. c. 490) and Caesarius of Arles (d. 542; *SCD* 6, p. 7). "Saints" refers to all baptized believers whose walk attests their faith in the power of the resurrection. *Sanctorum communio* leaves open the question of whether *sanctorum* is the genitive of *sancti* (saints) or *sancta* (that which makes holy or holy things) or of the Sanctifier, God the Spirit. These nuances flow together in the doxology of the community of celebration.

Communion with Whom?   The community or fellowship (*koinonia*) of the saints is a recurrent theme of the New Testament that points both to communion with God and communion with all who share God's life: "We proclaim to you what we have seen and heard, so that you also may have fellowship *with us*. And our fellowship is *with the Father,* and *with his Son,* Jesus Christ" (1 John 1:3, italics added; cf. 2 Cor. 13:14; Ambrose, *Of the Holy Spirit* I.XII.131, *NPNF* 2 X, p. 110). The Son prayed to the Father that the whole community of faith "may be one, as we are one" (John 17:11).

From Christ "the whole body, joined and held together by every supporting ligament, grows and builds itself up in love, as each part does its work" (Eph. 4:16). Those being regenerated and sanctified form a society, a "people" (*laos*, Rev. 19:4; 21:3; cf. Rom. 9:25; 2 Cor. 6:16; 1 Pet. 2:9, 10), a kingdom (Matt. 25:34; Rev. 1:6), a city (Heb. 11:10, 16; 12:22; Rev. 3:12; 21:2), a bonded community that lives in communion with those of all ages who hunger for righteousness (Ps. 118:63; Tho. Aq., *ST* supp., Q21.2, III, p. 2641; Pieper, *WCB*, p. 52).

Inclusive of Past, Present, and Future Faithful.   The Westminster divines summarized, "All saints that are united to Jesus Christ their head, by his Spirit and by faith, have fellowship with him in his graces, sufferings, death, resurrection and glory: and being united to one another in love, they have communion in each other's gifts and graces" (Westminster Conf. XXVI.1, *CC*, p. 223). There is a special union between the faithful on earth and in heaven, enabled by their mutual communion with the one Head, and with each other, a communion sustained by prayer, faith, hope, and love (*Longer Catech.,* Eastern Orthodox Church, 262, *COC* II, p. 485).

The communion of saints is not coterminous with the church triumphant, nor does it speak simply of the church on earth. It designates the common bond uniting all members of Christ's church in heaven and earth, Christ's mystical body within and beyond history, in a real communication of spiritual riches (Irenaeus, *Ag. Her.* V.27, *ANF* I, p. 556; Pearson, *EC* X; W. Rede, *Communion of Saints*). It includes the living faithful and all celebrant voices of the celestial city. Some remain pilgrims in history, while others having died in the Lord are already joyfully beholding "clearly God Himself triune and one, as He is" (Council of Florence, *Decretum pro Graecis, DS* 693, 1305).

Whether Pilgrims and Saints Share in a Single Communion.   Whatever unity is possible within the limits of history is best understood by eschatological reference. The unity that was manifest at Pentecost is "the first fruits of that perfect union of the Son with his Father, which will be known in its fulness only when all things are consummated by Christ in his glory. The Lord who is bringing all things into full unity at the last is he who constrains us to seek the unity which he wills for his Church on earth here and now" (New Delhi Message, *WCC, CC,* pp. 583, 589). One baptism unites all the faithful in their diversity of callings. All are baptized into one body (1 Cor. 12:13).

If the union between the saints in heaven is complete and unalloyed, the pilgrim union of saints on earth is mixed, flawed, and imperfect, hence "there is an union, partly perfect and partly imperfect, between the Saints in heaven and the Saints below upon earth" (Joseph Hall, *A Treatise of Christ Mystical* XXIV, *Works,* ed. Peter Hall, 1837, VII, p. 261, *Angl.,* p. 334).

While the spiritual combat of the pilgrim church continues on earth, the church triumphant "already set at liberty, is now in heaven, and triumphs over all those things overcome, and rejoices before the Lord. Yet these two churches have, notwithstanding, a communion and fellowship between themselves" (Second Helvetic Conf., *CC,* p. 142).

The *communio sanctorum* beyond history unites and shares in Christ's intercession for the church militant within history. On this premise, the recollection of saints in an annual cycle of celebration is a continuing expression of this article of faith (Gregory I, *Moralia* XII, XVII; *Dialogues* II; Tho. Aq., *ST* supp., Q71–73, III, pp. 2843–62).

Eucharistic Communion.   The communion of saints is portrayed as an already present heavenly community of angelic worshipers with the assembly of the spirits of just men and women made perfect: "But you have come to Mount Zion, to the heavenly Jerusalem, the city of the living God. You have come to thousands upon thousands of angels in joyful assembly, to the church of the first-born, whose names are written in heaven. You have come to God, the judge of all men, to the spirits of righteous men made perfect, to Jesus the Mediator" (Heb. 12:22–24a). It is this eschatological celebration that is received anticipatively at the Lord's Table.

For this reason the Eucharist is called a holy communion. There the faithful commune with Christ and with each other. "Because there is one loaf, we, who are many, are one body, for we all partake of the one loaf" (1 Cor. 10:17), feeding on Christ's body and blood by which vital communion with him enables the faithful to be vitally united with each other. "For the bread of God is he who comes down from heaven and gives life to the world" (John 6:33). From the outset the disciples are portrayed as continuing in the apostles' teaching and in fellowship with each other, breaking bread, and in prayer, confessing their faults, exhorting one another, sharing all things and most of all themselves (Acts 2:42–44; Rom. 12:4, 5; 1 Cor. 12:12; Eph. 4:15, 16).

A Community of Full Disclosure.   Full disclosure of all things characterizes this community. In this world and flesh, we now depend upon frail words to reveal partly yet partly conceal our thoughts and feelings. Then we will not need words to let ourselves be known, for the full clarity of our being will simply shine forth and achieve direct understanding (1 Cor. 8:3; Gal. 4:9).

If to know is to love, then we will fully love, for we will fully know, knowing even as we are known (1 Cor. 13:12b). The Eucharist prepares us for this uniting and knowing by bringing us all into unity with Christ and the neighbor. "Brother lives within his brother, none have secrets to conceal; Heart and mind and will and purpose, one throughout and one within" (Peter Damian, *Ad perennis vitae fontem,* Jacobs, *SCF,* p. 549; cf. *LH,* p. 299).

Life in Community.   Death does not destroy human relationships, but raises them to a higher sphere of communion in which the praise of God is the focal event. The redeemed are not separated from each other because they are not separated from Christ. This is a real and enduring communion of each one with Christ, and of each one with all who share life in Christ. Each one has fellowship with the one who has bound himself to sinful humanity on the cross. This unity binds each member of the body to every other member of the body (Eph. 3:6; 4:25).

The blessed do not live solitary lives, but share in a joyful union with the whole communion of saints (Matt. 8:11; Luke 13:28, 29; Heb. 12:23). "I say to you that many will come from the east and the west, and will take their places at the feast with Abraham, Isaac and Jacob in the kingdom of heaven" (Matt. 8:11). The kingdom of heaven is compared to "a wedding banquet" (Matt. 22:2). "Most pleasant will they be, when one loves another as himself, and both rejoice together, and the gaiety of one is the happiness of all" (Tho. Aq., *Exposition, Apostles' Creed, TATT,* p. 411). Solitary, hermetic Christianity is finally unthinkable, though the disciplines of solitude are needed along the way to the unalloyed community (Dame Juliana of Norwich, *RDL,* pp. 105–19).

Whether Eternity Is Endless Time.   That is eternal which transcends time, which is everlasting, without beginning or end, ceaseless, interminable. Eternity is duration or continuance without beginning or end. God's eternity is God's infinity in relation to time. God who is without beginning produces beginning (Clement of Alexandria, *Stromata* V.14, *ANF* II, p. 476). God is "before all time, now and for evermore" (Jude 25, NIV). God's wisdom was "before time began" (1 Cor. 2:7).

God is exalted above all temporal limits (John 17:24; Eph. 1:4; 2 Tim. 1:9). God transcends temporal duration and possesses his life in one indivisible present. God knows all events in a single cohesive act of consciousness, in contrast to the forms of finite knowing possible for creatures under the conditions of time. Divine omniscience implies that God grasps all time as if it were a single whole: "With the Lord a day is like a thousand years, and a thousand years are like a day" (2 Pet. 3:9). God's way of experiencing time is in radical simultaneity in which past, present, and future coinhere without being imprisoned as finite minds are in the succession of moments from past to present to future.

Unlike mortals who live in time, God always was (Gen. 21:23) and will be (Deut. 5:23). God's constancy "does not change like shifting shadows" (James 1:17). The constancy of God is his unchanging, utterly responsive faithfulness in time as covenant God. God has time in the fullest sense, whereas we experience time only in its fleeting mode of constant disappearance (Cullmann, *Christ and Time;* Padgett, *God, Eternity, and the Nature of Time*).

Time belongs to the created order, as distinct from the divine essence. With the world, time was created. Before time, nothing was but God. "There was no time, therefore, when thou hadst not made anything, because thou hadst made time itself" (Augustine, *Conf.* XI.14, *LCC* VII, p. 254). The world was created with time, not in time. There was no time "before" creation, since the "before" implies time. The notion of a time before time is self-contradictory (Augustine, *Conf.* XIII.48 ff., *LCC* VII, pp. 330 ff.).

Eternity is not abstract timelessness, but the most embracing temporal and transtemporal term—not merely unending time, but God's own time. God's life is not nontemporal, but transtemporal, while being always fully engaged in the exquisite details of the flow of time. In contrast to human beings, who experience time as fleeting, God enjoys time in an incomparably complete way (Ps. 90).

Aiōn (age, aeon), in the sense of the time of the world, is used for the duration of the world. In due course, *aiōn* came to mean the world itself (Matt. 13:22; 1 Cor. 1:20; 7:33). The faithful are redeemed from this aeon (Gal. 1:4) and share in the power of the future *aiōn* that has already begun in Christ's resurrection (Heb. 6:5). Eternal life points qualitatively to a regenerate life fit for life in the presence of the eternal, living God (John 5:24).

Whether Those Unaware of the Gospel May Share Life Eternal

It is fitting in this connection to assess the difficult arguments concerning those utterly ignorant of Christian teaching, unbaptized infants, and those unaware of the gospel, as to whether or in what sense they may have a share in life eternal.

The Hard Cases of "the Benighted Heathen and the Invincibly Ignorant." Are there undisclosed possibilities that might await those of distant cultures who may have never had adequate chance to hear the gospel? What of those utterly ignorant of God's coming? An oversimple answer is unambiguously to consign them to abandonment. Compassionate Christian teaching has often searched for insights into scripture texts by which their plight might be fairly understood. God takes "no pleasure in the death of the wicked, but rather that they turn from their ways and live" (Ezek. 33:11).

It is well to remember that the New Testament was written primarily for those who have had a reasonable chance to hear the gospel. It does not often focus speculatively on what might be the possible destiny of those who never have had such an opportunity. The judgment of which it speaks concerning the unjust is presumably based upon those who heard and rejected the gospel. If so, that judgment may not be directed in the same clear and absolute way against those who never knew of God's mercy. Those who have not heard the gospel and have not been baptized do not obtain obvious admittance to the Kingdom, but that in itself does not settle the question of their destiny under the merciful providence of God.

That God antecedently wills the salvation of all (2 Tim. 2:4) at least should motivate one to look for a way of grasping God's deeper intention for them. It is not contrary to orthodox teaching to hypothesize that God seeks continually to offer forgiveness and life, "if the fundamental disposition which they develop in their earthly probation has not nullified the moral possibility of their benefiting by it" (Hall, *DT* X, p. 50; cf. Origen, *De Principiis* I.6, *ANF* IV, pp. 260–61). Their salvation, like our own, can only be grounded in Christ's atoning work received in faith, because according to Scripture, no other basis is offered.

The elect are those called to receive the grace of repentance, faith, and baptism in this life. The elect may by their obduracy negate their baptism and fall away from their calling. The nonelect are those not effectively called to the grace of repentance, faith, and baptism in this life. "We certainly dogmatize beyond valid warrant, whether scriptural or other, when we understand the 'non-elect' to be necessarily doomed" (Hall, *DT* X, p. 50).

There is evidence that some outside the covenant (the centurion, the woman of Syrophoenicia, Mark 7:26; Matt. 8:5) showed a quality of life and faith of which Christ himself approved. "It would not be unchristian to feel that such lives as show a following, though far off, of the gleam that shines from Zion's hill may one day be led beyond all shadows into the full light of eternal love" (Church of Scotland, *Draft Catechism,* pp. 78, 79).

The Sufficiency of Prevening Grace. Those who lived before Christ will be judged according to their responses to the preparing and common grace given them. Abraham, Isaac, and Jacob will be present in the same heaven with Christian saints (Luke 16:19–31). The same may be said of pious Jews of every generation who remain faithful to the covenant (Rom. 11). Gentiles who have not heard of God's coming will be judged equitably according to the light given them (Rom. 2:6–16). All humanity is offered sufficient prevenient grace to enable each to respond rightly to probational opportunities. The crucial question is whether in meeting these situations they might have developed a general or inchoate predisposition for faith such as the Letter to Hebrews ascribes to Abel (Heb. 11:4).

If one wholly ignorant of the gospel displays an attitude profoundly congruent or analogous to that which the faithful exercise in justifying faith, that would stand as evidence in favor of one's salvability, or one's good predisposition toward faith, which, if one had been offered the chance, would have borne fruit. By good predisposition is meant one that the merciful God would accept as a token of faith, such that if that person had been able to hear the gospel, he or she would have accepted it (Tho. Aq., *ST* I–II, Q19.7–10, I, 676–80; Hall, *DT* X, pp. 52 ff.; Rahner, *RR,* pp. 211–14). Though such an argument is speculative, venturing beyond clear scriptural definition, at the very least it provides a way by which Christian teaching may keep the question open as to the destiny of the benighted.

The Hard Case of the Death of Unbaptized Infants. A similar line of reasoning is found in the thought that the unbaptized infant, though unready to enjoy the beatific vision, is nonetheless not punished for actual sin, according to orthodox teaching, but on the contrary has some capacity to enjoy a natural beatitude (Tho. Aq., *ST* III, supp., Q71, III, pp. 2843–58). "That Christ will not condemn to punishment those who have died in innocent infancy without being baptized, appears certain in the light of divine justice, which surely confines punishment to those who personally sin" (Hall, *DT* X, p. 183; Ezek. 18; John 9:2). Having "called a little child and had him stand among them," Jesus said: "See that you do not look down on one of these little ones. For I tell you that their angels in heaven always see the face of my Father in heaven" (Matt. 18:10).

It is a house of "many mansions" that the Lord is preparing for the faithful (John 14:2, KJV). As there is great diversity in the histories of persons who hear the gospel, and variety in the levels of capacity that various cultures and personal dispositions allow, and as there is not a simple equality of opportunity to hear the gospel, we may conclude that there may be many mansions of God's eternal care for the varieties of response (John Chrysostom, *Hom. on John* LXXIII, *NPNF* 1 XIV, pp. 267–70; Augustine, *Comm. on John,* tractate LXVII, *NPNF* 1 VII, pp. 322–24).

THE FINAL STATE OF THE UNJUST

Eternal Retributive Justice

It is only with tears that hell is contemplated by those who reach out daily in love for sinners (Lausanne Covenant).

What Is Hell?   Hell is the eternal bringing to nothing of corruption and ungodliness. Hell expresses the intent of the holy God to destroy sin completely and forever. Hell says not merely a temporal no but an eternal no to sin. The rejection of evil by the holy God is like a fire that burns on, a worm that dies not (Heb. 12:29; Mark 9:44–48; Aphrahat, *Demonstrations, Of Death, NPNF* 2 XIII, p. 409).

Hell is especially for those who think they are too good to be helped by God. Hell is to be forever without God, against God. This is why the good news carries with it a stern warning: If you chose in time to live without God, you thereby choose eternally to be without God. Hell is where the unjust get their just deserts (Hippolytus, *Ag. Plato* 1, *ANF* V, pp. 221, 222). Hell is the final state of those who are not in the book of life (Rev. 20:11–15), where "the light of the world does not shine" (*Ag. Plato* 1, *ANF* V, p. 221). Hell receives those who imagine themselves good; Jesus receives those who know themselves sinners.

Whether the Duration of Future Separation Is Determinable.   One who perpetually has chosen the settled disposition of unfaith against faith, and the godless love of self instead of the selfless love of God, lacking works of mercy, will continue after death in a similar self-chosen condition of radical, final separation from the divine presence. Exclusion from the presence of God is the central meaning of hell. Whoever "disowns me before men, I will disown him before my Father in heaven" (Matt. 10:33). "The teaching, in brief, is that unrepented sin is a fatal barrier to eternal life" (Hall, *DT* X, p. 195).

In Matthew's version of the parable of sheep and goats, Jesus concluded with these words to those who remained unresponsive to grace and love: "Depart from me, you who are cursed, into the eternal fire prepared for the devil and his angels." "Then they will go away to eternal punishment" (Matt. 25:41, 46). The words "eternal punishment" and "eternal fire" have withstood numerous attempts at generous reinterpretation, but they remain obstinately in the received text (Jerome, *Ag. Rufinus, FC* 53, pp. 109–15). The text remains resilient against our attempts to soften it. Every false theory is wrecked on these words, which are "not as doubtful or ambiguous as represented; and even if they were, the rule is to interpret the obscure by the plain" (Banks, *MCD,* p. 362). The problem is not that the words are obscure, but that they are all too plain (Augustine, *CG* XXI.23, *NPNF* 1 II, p. 469; S. Kierkegaard, *On Self-examination*).

Depart from Me.   Those who reject the way of the Son suffer the penalty of having no share in fellowship with the Father (Matt. 25:41; Calvin, *Inst.* 3.23). Scriptures describe the eternal condition of the ungodly as one of infinite distance from God (Fourth Lateran Council, *SCD* 429, p. 168). Those who die in original sin or grave personal sin, being separated from God's righteousness, have chosen to be permanently isolated from God's goodness. This is hell—the nonblessedness of life without God, against God (Quicunque Creed, *SCD* 40, p. 16; Council of Valence III, *SCD* 321, p. 128).

"Our merciful Lord never pronounced, nor ever will pronounce, a sentence more terrible than this: to be without God in eternity is Hell. 'Depart from Me'. . . . No profounder mystery is in the Apocalypse than the hallelujahs which are uttered over the demonstrations of the Divine wrath as they proceed from judgment to judgment in their direful procession" (Pope, *Compend.* 3, pp. 420, 422).

Jerome stated the consensual teaching on clemency: "Those who wish the punishments to come to an end eventually, and the torments to have a limit, even if after long ages, call upon this evidence: 'When the full number of the nations have entered, then all Israel will be saved' [Rom. 11:29 f.]. . . . We believe that there will be eternal torments for the devil, for all deniers of God and the impious, who have 'said in their heart: God does not exist' [Ps. 13:1]; while in the case of sinners, and the impious who are yet Christians, whose deeds are to be tested and purified in the fire, we think that the sentence of the judge will be moderate, and mingled with clemency" (Jerome, *Hom. on Isa.* 66:24, *LCF,* p. 190; 1 Cor. 3:13; 1 Pet. 1:7).

Hell as a Question of Justice.   Sin matters to God. The holy God detests injustice and evil. Creation is a moral order in which by breaking God's laws, oneself is broken. Those who persist in sin find themselves eternally alienated from the divine goodness, bringing "upon themselves the penalty of having no share in that everlasting life of love and joy of those who dwell together with Him" (Church of Scotland, *Draft Catechism* 68, pp. 79, 80).

Every creature finally either receives and welcomes the glory of God's presence or rejects it and passes into outer darkness. "All of us—Greeks and Jews, heretics and Christians—acknowledge that God is just. Now many who sinned have passed away without being punished, while many others, who led virtuous lives, did not die until they had suffered innumerable tribulations. If God is just, how will He reward the latter and punish the former, unless there be a Hell and a Resurrection?" (John Chrysostom, *Hom. on Phil.* 6; Pohle, *DT* XII, p. 480; cf. *NPNF* 1 XIII, p. 212). "The face of the Lord is against those who do evil, to cut off the memory of them from the earth" (Ps. 34:17).

Speaking of Hell

Due to speculations over an extended history, mischievous ideas have attached themselves to popular notions of hell. Because many have been repulsed by

Christianity as a result of these false assumptions, it is a worthwhile irenic task to try to correct them.

Common Misjudgments About Hell.   There is no ecumenically received scriptural authority for the view that God simply or absolutely or pretemporally predestines persons to hell without their choice or cooperation or without common or prevenient grace.

There is no scriptural-ecumenical authority for the view that metaphors like the fire and the worm must be taken literally; it would be indeed impossible to take both of those metaphors literally, since one would cancel out the other (E. B. Pusey, *What Is of Faith as to Everlasting Punishment?* pp. 18–21).

There is insufficient scriptural-ecumenical authority for the debatable assertion that those who have not had a fair chance to hear the gospel are consigned peremptorily and immediately to eternal punishment, for all who miss the joy of heaven will have had plausible opportunity to have chosen a better life, yet willfully refused it. They will be fairly judged according to how they have responded to the light received.

There is limited authority for the view that hell is a physical fire that works directly upon the physical body. Such views are speculative or dubious, and may be cast in ways abhorrent to the character of God. Those who assert them as orthodox are challenged to show that they have been received classically by a consensus of historic exegetes (Thielicke, *EF* III; Ladd, *The Presence of the Future*).

The Constructive Intent of Sobering Analogies.   Luther wryly commented that no picture of hell could be as bad as the reality (*Sermon on John 2:3*, 1526, *WLS* 2, p. 626; *WA* 19, 225 f.). We are spared by the use of metaphors. Though unpleasant, they only point toward the more final and serious reality.

Though analogies fail, they continue to be pressed to service to attempt to account for this future condition that no one yet knows how rightly to express. The analogies come from bodily experiences that seem to express despair and horror over evil—the burning of flesh, the "blackest darkness" (Jude 13), "weeping, and gnashing of teeth" (Matt. 8:12; 22:13), "unquenchable fire" (Matt. 3:12; Mark 9:43), an undying worm gnawing at the heart (Isa. 66:24). "By such expressions the Holy Spirit certainly intended to confound all our senses with dread" (Calvin, *Inst.* 3.25.12, p. 1007). If such metaphors sicken the stomach, that is their intended purpose—to spur to repentance, faith, and holiness. If the rhetoric comforted the hearer, it would not fulfill its intended function (Thomas Browne, *Religio Medici* I, p. 58; *Angl.*, p. 324). It seeks to bring a sense of ultimate accountability to all human decisions (Clementina, *Recognitions* V.28, *ANF* VIII, p. 150).

The teaching of hell rightly calls to mind the dignity of human freedom and the high cost of its abuse. Voluntarily, "they perish because they refused to love the truth and so be saved" (2 Thess. 2:10). "They never are free from punishment who in this life did not wish to be free from sin" (Hugh of St. Victor, *SCF*, p. 469). Those who ascribe their crimes constantly to the demonic powers tend to "free men from fault, and take away the freedom of the will" (Jerome, *Apology Ag. Rufinus* II.7, *NPNF* 2 III, pp. 503–4). God is willing to go to the great length of seeming to "frustrate all His Own purposes and practices upon me, and leave me, and cast me away, as though I had cost Him nothing," when he "could not get into me by standing and knocking, by His ordinary means of entering, by His Word,

His mercies, hath applied His judgements and hath shaked the house, this body, with agues [fevers] and palsies, and set this house on fire with fevers and calentures [delirium], and frighted the master of the houses, my soul, with horrors and heaven apprehensions, and so made an entrance into me" (John Donne, *Sermons* LXXVI, 1640, p. 776, *Angl.* p. 336).

Whether Fire Is a Metaphorical Reference.   This general observation on sobering analogies leads toward a specific application: burning by fire, one of the most intense kinds of pain one may experience, as nurses in hospital burn units will testify. If the metaphor is intended to disturb, it reaches its mark (Luke 17:29; James 3:6). It calls us to live so that we need not fear it (Luke 12:5; Rom. 13:3).

Though figurative, these metaphors intend accurately to convey truthful ideas and meanings, especially the dreadful reality of loss of God as an irreversible consequence of sin. The goodness of God guarantees that scripture would not unnecessarily "alarm his moral creatures with groundless fears, or to represent the consequences of sin as more dreadful than they really are" (Wakefield, *CT* 2, p. 642).

There has been a wildly disproportional emphasis on the literal interpretation of figurative expressions in some periods of the history of these problems, implying a flood of vindictiveness on the part of God. Undisciplined fantasies of the zealous have ended in exaggeration and caricature (Irenaeus, *Ag. Her.* V.9–17, *ANF* I, pp. 534–45).

The overreaction of modernity to these descriptions is to some degree understandable, even if undiscriminating. Hell has been seized upon by demythologizers as a cheap ploy for discrediting all ancient cosmology. Yet in no period more than the modern period, with its addicted babies, genocides, and weeping forests, does the concept of hell retain its special existential significance. When unwarranted speculations are taken away from it, the idea of hell has much to say to modern consciousness.

Such Fire as God Would Know.   Fire (Gk. *pur,* Lat. *ignis*) was used as a metaphor to point to the destruction of all that is inconsistent with the holiness of God. If salvation is analogous to light, then darkness serves as its antonym. Fire suggests an eternal casting away of sin. God hates sin. The destiny of sin is to burn and to be completely cast away from the presence of God. Fire will consume the adversaries of God (Isa. 26:11; Heb. 10:27; Jude 7).

These hellish images were not intended to be taken as physiological or empirical descriptions, but as expressive of the final reduction of evil and the eternal distance between God's holiness and sin (Council of Lyons II, *SCD* 464, p. 184). Hell is "neither a gnashing of the bodily teeth, nor a perpetual bodily fire, nor a bodily worm" (Ambrose, *Comm. on Luke* VII.204, in Pohle, *DT* XII, p. 58), but "a quality known to God." The everlasting fire of scripture could not be a "material fire like our fire, but such fire as God would know" (John of Damascus, *OF* IV.27, *NPNF* 2 IX, p. 101). It is less a material than a spiritual fire. We know little of it except that it exists (Augustine, *CG* XX.16, *NPNF* 1 II, pp. 435–36).

Lactantius distinguished physical from eternal fire: "The nature of that everlasting fire is different from this fire of ours, which we use for the necessary purposes of life, and which ceases to burn unless it be sustained by the fuel of some material. But that divine fire always lives by itself" (Lactantius, *DI* VII.21, cf. *ANF*

VII, p. 217; Augustine, *Literal Comm. on Gen.* XX.32). God, whose holiness is un-derived, who is incomparably alive, outlasts all challenges.

Gehenna.   The name Gehenna comes from the valley of Hinnom (Neh. 11:30), a desolate valley near Mount Zion long associated with idolatrous rites such as passing children through the fires of Moloch (Jer. 7:31; 32:35; 2 Kings 23:10; 2 Chron. 28:3; 33:6). There "perpetual fires were kept burning in this valley for consuming dead bodies of criminals and carcasses of animals and the refuse of the city," hence "Gehenna came to signify *a place of corporal and spiritual punishment for all the wicked in the presence of the righteous*" (Hughes, *CF,* p. 210; cf. 2 Esdras 7:36).

One gets the impression that the holiness of God is consuming sin, burning it away forever, as in a holocaust, a completely burned offering (Heb. *olah kalil,* Gk. *holokautōma*). The fire of hell to which Jesus referred in his saying about causing the little ones to sin is a fire that "never goes out" (Mark 9:43; cf. Matt. 5:18). The rejection of sin by the holy God appears to be complete and never ceasing. "On any theory of universalism or annihilation Christ's words are not true, for then there is termination, the fire is not eternal, not unquenchable, the worm does not die, the fire is quenched" (Banks, *MCD,* p. 363). Yet even these theories have the intent of exalting the sovereign holiness of God whose will is finally to overcome sin utterly.

The Metaphor of Exclusion.   The note of exclusion prevails as the most solemn aspect of the judgment of the wicked. "Just as heaven is God himself, won for ever, so hell is God himself as eternally lost. The essence of hell is *final exclusion from communion with God* because of one's own fault" (Kasper, *CCF,* p. 347, italics added). Damnation "consists in the loss of the sight and presence of God" (John Donne, sermon LXXVI, *Sermons,* 1640, p. 777; *Angl.,* p. 337). "As heaven means *God,* so hell means *no God*" (Rickaby, *EP,* p. 10). Those who have freely chosen to "go their own way" will be "baptized with fire in that last baptism which is more painful and longer, which devours wood like grass, and consumes the stubble of every evil" (Gregory Nazianzen, *Orat.* XXXIX.19, *NPNF* 2 VII, p. 359).

Correlated with these images is the metaphor of imprisonment: when the an-gels fell precipitously from grace to spread gloom in the created order, God "sent them to hell" [*tartarus*], "putting them into gloomy dungeons to be held for judg-ment" (2 Pet. 2:4).

Metaphors of Spatial Location and Descent: Is Hell a Place Down Some-where?   The impression that hell is down is derived from passages such as Isaiah 14:11: "pomp is brought down to the grave" (cf. Ps. 55:15; Ezek. 31:15), from the theme of Christ's descent into the netherworld, and from poetic expressions such as Dante's Inferno. Cosmas Indicopleustes's *Christian Topography* (c. A.D. 547) pic-tured hell in the center of the earth. John Chrysostom long ago had advised, "Do not inquire where Hell is, but how to escape it" (John Chrysostom, *Hom. on Rom.* 31.5, *MPG* 60, p. 674; in Pohle, *DT* XII, p. 51). With the loss of the geocentric conception of Ptolemaic science, the metaphors of above and below had to be recast in less spatially oriented terms.

If there is to be a body, it would seem to require a place, or something analo-gous to a place. Yet there can be a place only within time. We are now talking not simply about time, but about eternity. Hades is not merely the location in which this eternal distancing takes place, but more so the condition of distance itself: exclusion from the presence of God (Luther, *WLS* 2, pp. 626–28).

Moral Difficulties in Retributive Justice

It is hard to think of any Christian teaching that has stronger biblical precedent and greater traditional consensus than the teaching of eternal punishment (Jude 7; 2 Thess. 1:9; Mark 9:43; Matt. 13:42; Ignatius of Antioch, *To the Ephesians* 16.2; Justin Martyr, *Apology* II.9; Fourth Lateran Council, *DS* 429), yet it remains controversial and widely debated. It is not without its problems of exegesis. Several persistent issues have vexed the consensual tradition in the teaching of eternal punishment.

Whether Hell Is Compatible with Divine Justice.   Is eternal separation from God compatible with the justice and mercy of God? However difficult the questions that follow may be, it is well to remember that most of the core of the teaching of final separation came from Jesus himself and cannot easily be set aside as if it were not divine revelation. It does little good to condemn the teaching of hell if the consequence is to ignore the depth of the problem of sin, which has such horrible effects in human history.

Consensual teaching argues that final separation is necessary because moral justice cannot finally condone or allow the victory of the unjust or the prosperity of the wicked. It is largely those who persist in an optimistic account of human sin who "do not clearly apprehend the enduring effect of unremedied sin, and therefore cannot perceive the justice of everlasting punishment" (Hall, *DT* X, p. 195).

It is sometimes argued that eternal punishment is incompatible with key moral attributes of God: justice, goodness, and mercy. Can the final judgment be viewed not only as a purgative or curative act on behalf of God's holiness and mercy, but also as a retributive act on behalf of justice? Objectors argue that it cannot logically be viewed as having a corrective or disciplinary intent, because it is final and endless. The alternative is to suppose that there is no final retribution for sin on the last day, a premise that serious moral agents find implausible. Would not it be much more unjust if wickedness were permitted without any retribution?

Whether a Briefly Committed Sin Might Be Punished Endlessly.   Is it not unfair that an unrepented sin committed in a short time could result in separation from God eternally? Some argue that an endless punitive act would be incompatible with the justice and love of God, for it would be unjust for God to allow endless punishment for crimes or offenses committed under conditions of finitude. It seems disproportional to mete out eternal punishment for sins committed in time.

Augustine answered by noting the precedent of criminal law: If a robbery takes place in a few minutes, should one only have a few minutes' punishment? A rape that takes minutes may have consequences for a lifetime. A murder that takes only an instant is an irreparable damage (*CG* XX, *NPNF* 1 II, pp. 435 ff.; Hugh of St. Victor, *SCF*, p. 468). "The fact that adultery or murder is committed in a moment, does not call for a momentary punishment" (Tho. Aq., *ST* I–II, Q87.3.1, I, p. 975). So it is with the disobedience of humanity, as typified in Adam and Eve, whose wages were death for the entire ensuing history of sin. Remember that all sin is finally against not only creatures but the Creator, not only against oneself and one's neighbor but against the giver of freedom (Ps. 51:4).

If the consequences of sin extend beyond one's finite life, then it is not morally scandalous for the punishment of sin also to extend beyond one's finite life. Contrary arguments sometimes tend to try to settle the question of retributive justice by an emotive appeal to human sympathies. God's moral order prevails even where human emotions resist it. The permitting of suffering as a penalty for irresponsible self-determination is not inconsistent with God's goodness and mercy. If one hypothesizes the opposite, how could the moral order cohere? However much our natural sympathies or reasoning may resist it, the biblical testimony remains that God has seen fit to separate himself completely from sin in eternity, so that the final condition of the sinner is infinite distance from God (Matt. 7:23; 2 Pet. 2). "Will not the Judge of all the earth do right?" (Gen. 18:25).

Whether Hell Implies That God's Purpose Has Failed.   To some, the premise of hell seems to imply the failure of the redemptive purpose of God, who primordially "desires everyone to be saved and to come to the knowledge of the truth" (1 Tim. 2:4, NRSV). This conclusion, however, may fail to recognize the difference between God's antecedent will to save all and the consequent will of God to deal justly with the ramifications of free human choices (*LG,* pp. 92–95).

In this way the premise of hell is seen as an expression of the completion of the purpose of God, not an expression of the failure of that purpose (Cyprian, *Letters, FC* 51, pp. 171–76; Calvin, *Inst.* 3.25). God foreknew, but did not predetermine the choices of the unjust that lead to separation (Council of Quiersy, A.D. 853, *SCD* 316, 317, p. 126).

Satan

Eschatological reasoning is incomplete lacking reference to Satan (the adversary, accuser, hater) or the Devil (Gk. *diabolos,* calumniator, accuser, *daimonion,* demon), Lucifer, the supreme embodiment of evil, the superpersonal adversary of humanity (Lactantius, *DI* III.29, *ANF* VII, p. 99; Tertullian, *On the Soul* 20, *FC* 10, p. 227; Jerome, *Ag. Rufinus, FC* 53, pp. 109–14). He is the "creditor" for human sin, who became wounded by his own bite, whose power is renounced in baptism (Ambrose, *Letters* XLI.7, *NPNF* 2 X, p. 446, cf. 317, 339–40).

The Deceiver.   Satan is the ultimate adversary to God. The root meaning is one who plots against another. In the Old Testament, Satan is an angelic being hostile to God, the chief of the fallen angels (Calvin, *Inst.* 1.14.15–18). The devil fell by pride and envy and became determined to corrupt the world by deception (Barnabas, 19–21, *FC* 1, pp. 219–22; Gregory of Nyssa, *The Great Catechism* VI–XXVI, *NPNF* 2 IV, pp. 480–95).

This deceiver seeks to destroy truth while seeming to defend it (Athanasius, *Life of Antony, NPNF* 2 IV, pp. 196–207; Tertullian, *Ag. Praxeas* I, *ANF* III, p. 597). Satan has become through deception the god of this world, who is "designated god to those who believe not" (Irenaeus, *Fragments* 46, *ANF* I, p. 575), and remains the author of countless idolatrous imitations of faith (Tertullian, *Prescrip-*

tion Ag. Her. 38–40, *ANF* III, pp. 261–63) and innumerable pretensions to divinity (Tertullian, *Of the Crown* 7, *APT,* p. 172).

The serpent that seduced Eve is consensually interpreted as an embodiment of the devil, through whom "death entered the world" (Wisdom 2:24). Satan was tormentor of Saul (1 Sam. 18:10), deceiver of the prophets (1 Kings 22:21–23), and tempter of Job permitted by God to test the faithful (Jerome, *Ag. Jovinianus* II, *NPNF* 2 VI, pp. 388–91). In the pseudepigraphical literature, the ideas of Satan mushroomed so as to strongly affect the New Testament images of evil and theodicy.

The devil is portrayed as tempting Jesus from the outset of his ministry (Mark 1:13; Luke 4:1–13), pretending to be the master of the world (Matt. 4:8, 9). The enmity between the coming reign of God and the demonic powers is dramatically seen in the response of demoniacs to the Son. Satan tempted Peter, for whom the Lord prayed that he might overcome temptation (Luke 22:31–32).

Purveyor of Lust and Envy. Satan deceives the world and draws the faithful toward despair (Rev. 12:10–12; Tertullian, *Spectacles* 23, *FC* 40, pp. 96–97). Sexual brokenness remains evidence of his deceptiveness: "And the angels who did not keep their positions of authority but abandoned their own home—these he has kept in darkness, bound with everlasting chains for judgment on the great Day. In a similar way, Sodom and Gomorrah and the surrounding towns gave themselves up to sexual immorality and perversion. They serve as an example of those who suffer the punishment of eternal fire" (Jude 6; 7). "For the demons, inspired with frenzy against men by reason of their own wickedness, pervert their minds, which already incline downwards, by various deceptive scenic representations, that they may be disabled from rising to the path that leads to heaven." If it were possible, "they would without doubt pull down heaven itself with the rest of creation. But now this they can by no means effect, for they have not the power" (Tatian, *Address to the Greeks* XVI, *ANF* II, p. 72).

The Fall from Heaven. The power of Satan is already being broken by the Son, who "saw Satan fall like lightning from heaven" (Luke 10:18). The success of the seventy-two over the demons was taken as evidence of his impending demise (Luke 10:17; John Cassian, *Conferences, NPNF* 2 XI, pp. 280–81).

The more explicit account of the angels' fall is in Revelation 12, which describes the devil's persecution of the church under the metaphor of a woman "clothed with the sun" (Rev. 12:1). "And there was war in heaven. Michael and his angels fought against the dragon, and the dragon and his angels fought back. But he was not strong enough, and they lost their place in heaven. The great dragon was hurled down—that ancient serpent called the devil, or Satan, who leads the whole world astray. He was hurled to the earth, and his angels with him" (Rev. 12:7–9). Satan is "filled with fury because he knows his time is short" (Rev. 12:12; Tertullian, *Spectacles* 16, *FC* 40, pp. 84, 85).

The devil is not evil by created nature but by choice. He is called apostate because he was not wicked from the outset but became so by self-determination. Though many human wills may be wicked, "he alone is called wicked by preeminence," yet not so as to imagine that he is wicked by nature (John Chrysostom, *Hom. on Power of Demons* II.2, *NPNF* 1 IX, pp. 187–88; cf. pp. 197–98).

At least by the Fourth Lateran Council it had become consensually defined that the "Devil and other wicked spirits were created by God good by nature, but they became evil of their own accord" (*CC*, p. 57). "God created the angels to serve him. They are ministering spirits sent by God to help those who are heirs of salvation" (Batak Conf. XVII, *CC*, p. 565). Because fallen angels are posited as rational creatures, they too are destined to be judged (Matt. 8:29; 1 Cor. 6:3; 2 Pet. 2:4).

The Strong Man Bound: The Judgment of Fallen Angels.   A murderer from the beginning (John 8:44), the Deceiver is able temporarily to play the role of prince of this world (John 14:30), yet his power is already being overcome and judged by Christ (John 16:11; Luther, *Answer to the Goat, LW* 39, pp. 123–24). At the last judgment he will depart with the unjust into a lake of fire (Matt. 25:41).

The believer's sure defense is in attesting the merit of Christ's death, an attestation itself willing to die (Rev. 12:11). The apostles urged sobriety in resisting the devil (1 Pet. 5:8, 9; Cyprian, *The Lapsed, ACW* 25, pp. 13–21).

Classic exegetes thought it impossible to imagine a disordered angelic host or one lacking intentionality. Dionysius speculated that the princes of good angels have charge over collective peoples, angels have charge over individual persons, and the archangels announce affairs pertaining to the salvation of all (*De coelesti hierarchia* IX.1, *MPG* 3.257; Tho. Aq., *Compend.* 126, p. 132). The evil angels are usually portrayed as being arrayed under a single arch deceiver. It is this one who is bound.

The tempter's binding has present moral consequences in the combat with temptation. Hildegard prayed, "When the Evil One brandishes his sword against you, [Lord,] you break it in his own heart. For so you did to the first lost angel, tumbling the tower of his arrogance to hell" (Hildegard of Bingen, *Symphonia,* p. 145).

Parables of Separation.   A series of parables—the tares, the net, the marriage feast, the wise and foolish virgins, the talents, the pounds—focuses upon opportunities forever lost, trust finally abused, final exclusion and rejection. Without the exclusion theme, these parables lose their point. It is not merely later church teaching but Jesus himself and the apostle Paul who constantly remind hearers that there are sins that exclude one from the kingdom of God (Matt. 5:29–30; 10:28; 23:15, 33; 1 Cor. 6:9–10; Gal. 5:20, 21; Eph. 5:5). What this means is well expressed by Thomas Aquinas: having become by self-determination those who continually say no to God, "their disordered will shall never be taken away from them" (*SCG* IV, chap. 93, p. 341). God does not primordially desire that any creature should be lost, but consequent to their own choice, God gives creatures the radical freedom to send themselves to oblivion, or freedom that has the consequence of complete separation from the joy of the presence of God (1 Thess. 1:9; 1 Tim. 6:9).

Scripture repeatedly teaches that God finally rejects sin and permits the complete demise of the agents of unrepented sin. The vision is unrelenting: exclusion from God (2 Thess. 1:9); a bottomless pit (Rev. 9:1, 2); torment (Rev. 14:10–11); the wrath of God (Rom. 2:5); eternal punishment (Matt. 25:46). "If we are left in doubt as to the extent of the duration of the punishment, we may be content that the issue is in the hands of One whose righteousness and love are inseparable" (Hughes, *CF*, p. 232).

LIFE EVERLASTING

The last phrase of the creed concludes victoriously by confessing "I believe in the life everlasting [*zōon aiōnion;* Lat. *vitam aeternam*]" (*SCD* 6, pp. 7, 9). Life is called everlasting in the sense that "whilst it has a beginning, it will have no end" (Ursinus, *Comm. Heid. Catech.*, p. 319). "When that which is perfect is come, then that which is in part shall be done away" (1 Cor. 13:10 KJV).

"God always was, and always is, and always will be. Or rather, God always Is. For Was and Will be are fragments of our Time . . . what time, measured by the course of the sun is to us, that Eternity is to the Everlasting" (Gregory Nazianzen, *Orat.* XXXVIII.7, *NPNF* 2 VII, pp. 346, 347).

The Final State of the Righteous

The destiny of the righteous is eternal life in and with God forever freed from sin, able to enjoy the divine glory. The prevailing scriptural term for the final state of the blessed is "eternal life."

Eternal Life.   The destiny of the just is called simply "life," or "eternal life," "the life which is life indeed" (1 Tim. 6:19, KJV; Matt. 18:8; 7:14; Calvin, *Inst.* 4.16–17). "Whoever hears my word and believes him who sent me has eternal life and will not be condemned; he has crossed over from death to life" (John 5:24). The living God brings to endless presentness the new life, the work of transformation begun in baptism. Eternal life brings to completion the work of grace begun in this life, wherein one is utterly delivered from sin, its roots and consequences, fulfilling God's purpose in creation, redemption, and consummation (Hilary, *Trin.* VI.43–49, *NPNF* 2 IX, pp. 114–16; Calvin, *Inst.* 4.16, 17).

Eternal life is the consummation of the spiritual life begun in baptism, imparted in regeneration, which grows by sanctifying grace. This life is transmuted into a future life of glory that does not reach full expression until the general resurrection, final judgment, and final destiny (Cyril of Jerusalem, *Catech. Lect.* XVIII.28–32, *NPNF* 2 VII, p. 141). The eternity of eternal life is not an infinitely long duration of historical time, which would suggest a kind of unfulfillment still awaiting completion. Rather it is a fulfillment, the complete and unending enjoyment of life with God.

Eternal Life in the Present.   The best clue to the future of life with God is the life that has come from God in the Son and the life with God already enjoyed in the celebrating community. "Dear friends, now we are children of God, and what we will be has not yet been made known. But we know that when he appears, we shall be like him, for we shall see him as he is" (1 John 3:2; Tho. Aq., *ST* supp., Q92, III, pp. 2957–60).

Eternal life is already enjoyed (John 3:36; 1 John 5:11, 12). It is in full measure what is already experienced as the life of faith, hope, and love. "As I now feel in my heart the beginning of eternal joy, I shall after this life possess complete bliss, such as eye hath not seen, nor ear heard" (*Heid. Catech.* Q58, *COC* III, p. 326).

If the gifts of grace received in this life are firstfruits, the full harvest is to come abundantly in eternity (Rom. 8:23; Eph. 1:13, 14). "Eternal life begins here, in our hearts; for when we begin to believe in Christ, after we have been baptized, then, according to faith and the Word, we are liberated from death, from sin, and from the devil. Therefore we have the beginning of life eternal and its first fruits in this life, a sort of mild foretaste; we have entered the lobby; but soon, divested of this flesh, we shall fully appreciate all" (Luther, *Sermons on the Psalms*, Ps. 45:6, 1533; *WLS* 2, p. 620; *WA* 40 II, 517). "In short, as Christ begins the glory of his body in this world with manifold diversity of gifts, and increases it by degrees, so also he will perfect it in heaven" (Calvin, *Inst.* 3.25.10).

The Abode of the Righteous

To lift up is to heave or raise something upward. The Hebrew *shamayim* as well as the Anglo-Saxon *heaven* comes from this picture of that which is uplifted, or "heaved up" as the highest, beyond all that remains below. The Greek root word for heaven (*ouranos*) meant vault or ceiling or air, the expanse of sky lifted up above the earth.

Defining Heaven.   Biblical words for heaven (Heb. *shamayim,* Gk. *ouranos*) may be used to refer to the heavens (the sky, the upper atmosphere), to the invisible spirit world of both good and evil, and to the abode of God. In Christian teaching, heaven is both a place and a state of eternal rest and joy in the Lord. It is "to be present with the Lord" (2 Cor. 5:8). Heaven is where the blessed clearly see God and incomparably enjoy the blessings of divine glory (Matt. 5:12; 6:20; Luke 6:23; 1 Pet. 1:4). Our English word comes from the Anglo-Saxon *hebban* (to heave)— that life which is finally heaved upward or uplifted to God's presence.

Heaven is a place of unutterable glory, joy, and peace. Its most prominent features are tranquillity, holiness, light, beholding, happiness, and the presence of the Lord. Heaven is full and endless participation in God's own goodness and happiness. Those "whose names are written in heaven" have "come to God." They are "the spirits of righteous men made perfect" (Heb. 12:23), whose every redeemed power and capacity is reaching its goal.

Heaven is not an immanental elevation of finitude to an absolute natural happiness (John XXII, *SCD* 510, p. 196) but a divine gift of supernatural happiness that cannot be described or discovered by natural means or rational inquiry alone (1 Cor. 2:9–10; Council of Vienne, *SCD* 474 ff., p. 188; Pius XI, *SCD* 1669, p. 420). It is the destiny of the just in the future (Council of Toledo XI, *SCD* 287, p. 111). Heaven is the life willed for us originally in creation by God the Father, lived for us by the Son, and finally enabled by the Spirit.

Beholding God.   The faithful will see God's face (Rev. 22:4). "Now I know in part; then I shall know fully, even as I am fully known" (1 Cor. 13:12). "Blessed are the pure in heart, for they will see God" (Matt. 5:8). Christ prayed that the faithful would "behold my glory" (John 17:24, KJV). This is what the angels do constantly, as Jesus said of the guardian angels of children, who "in heaven always see the face of my Father in heaven" (Matt. 18:10). "Rightly is this blessedness promised to purity of heart. For the brightness of the true light will not be able to be seen by the unclean sight" (Leo, *Sermons* XCV, *NPNF* 2 XII, p. 205).

In heaven there is eternal communion between God and those who love God, where the faithful behold God "face to face" (1 Cor. 13:12; Clement VI, *SCD* 570, 574a, p. 206). There is an intimacy in these images, like the joy of the child looking into her or his father's eyes. God is beheld not merely as reflected by created vestiges (*SCD* 1928 f.) but as God is (Benedict XII, *SCD* 530, p. 197).

To see God is to be infinitely happy. The essential beatitude of the blessed consists in the vision of God and full contemplation of God's attributes (Clement of Alexandria, *Stromata* VII.10, *ANF* II, p. 539). The saints, seeing God, do not see all that God sees (Tho. Aq., *ST* supp., Q92.3, III, p. 2966), but behold the One who beholds all.

Sister Macrina taught Gregory of Nyssa that the blessed will be like God insofar as they will contemplate the beautiful in him, without regret or inordinate desire or unfulfilled expectation. "The Deity is in very substance Beautiful; and to the Deity the soul will in its state of purity have affinity, and will embrace It as like itself." The soul will "know herself accurately what her actual nature is, and should behold the Original Beauty reflected in the mirror and in the figure of her own beauty" (Sister Macrina, *On the Soul and the Resurrection*, *NPNF* 2 IV, p. 449).

The Illuminator of the City of Light.   This beholding takes place through the light of glory (Council of Vienne, *SCD* 475, p. 188) and is sustained eternally without interruption (*Faith of Damasus*, *SCD* 16, p. 10; Quicunque Creed, *SCD* 40, p. 16; Leo IX, *Symbol of Faith*, *SCD* 347, p. 141; Fourth Lateran Council, *SCD* 429, p. 169). The city is "full of light" (Hippolytus, *Ag. Plato* 1, *ANF* V, p. 222). The faithful live in the light of God's countenance (Num. 6:25, 26; Ps. 67:1).

The faithful are set apart for holiness not only "while on their pilgrimage" but "especially after their death, when all reflective vision being done away, they behold clearly the Holy Trinity, in whose infinite light they know what concerneth us" (Creed of Dositheus, VIII, *CC*, p. 491). "No eye has seen, no ear has heard, no mind has conceived what God has prepared for those who love him" (1 Cor. 2:9, in reference to Isa. 64:4).

The metaphors are ecstatic: "The city does not need the sun or the moon to shine on it, for the glory of God gives it light, and the Lamb is its lamp. The nations will walk by its light, and the kings of the earth will bring their splendor into it. On no day will its gates ever be shut, for there will be no night there" (Rev. 21:23–25). "There will be no more night. They will not need the light of a lamp or the light of the son, for the Lord God will give them light. And they will reign for ever and ever" (Rev. 22:5).

Knowing and Seeing Fully.   The blessed behold in heaven what they believed by faith on earth. A deeper knowing of God will be given to the saints, greater than the fragmentary knowing of this life (John 17:3; 1 Cor. 13:12) where they must "walk by faith, not by sight" (2 Cor. 5:7, KJV).

Faith is transformed into knowledge by meeting God face to face. "Now this is eternal life: that they may know you, the only true God, and Jesus Christ, whom you have sent" (John 17:3). The intellect is directly illumined by the light of glory (Gregory of Nyssa, *The Life of Moses*, *CWS*, pp. 111 ff.).

This beholding has already begun in the faithful, "who with unveiled faces all reflect [KJV: as in a mirror] the Lord's glory, are being transformed into his likeness with ever-increasing glory" (2 Cor. 3:18). If Paul could say that of this life, what will it be when we behold not as in a mirror but face to face? If Peter could write to God's elect, "Though you have not seen him, you love him; and even though you do not see him now, you believe in him and are filled with an inexpressible and glorious joy, for you are receiving the goal of your faith, the salvation of your souls" (1 Pet. 1:8, 9), what sustained or intensified form will this beholding take in eternity? In ways beyond present knowing, the glorified body will be adapted to this beholding, "I say they shall *in* the body see God; but whether they shall see Him *by means of* the body, as we now see the sun, moon, stars, sea, earth, and all that is in it, that is a difficult question" (Augustine, *CG* XXII.29, *NPNF* 1 II, p. 507, italics added).

The End of Homelessness. Jesus referred to the final rest as a "place" (*topos):* "I am going there to prepare a place for you. And if I go and prepare a place for you, I will come back and take you to be with me that you also may be where I am" (John 14:2, 3). The Almighty dwells in "a high and holy place" (Isa. 57:15; 33:5). "From heaven the Lord looks down and sees all mankind; from his dwelling place he watches all who live on earth" (Pss. 33:13, 14; 24:3; 91:1). The pilgrim people look "forward to the city with foundations, whose architect and builder is God" (Heb. 11:10).

Yet this place is different than any other place finitely known. Scripture portrays heaven as entirely beyond the limits of the visible creation, as Paul suggested when he said that Christ "ascended higher than all the heavens, in order to fill the whole universe" (Eph. 4:10; Origen, *Ag. Celsus* VII.25–31, *ANF* IV, pp. 621–23). So "place" should be thought in quotation marks, reminding us that it is not simply another time-space historical location.

God has not left the blessed homeless in the future life. Scriptures speak of a home for the faithful after the final judgment, a new heaven and a new earth (2 Pet. 3:13; Rev. 21:1; Isa. 65:17; 66:22). In the New Jerusalem the glorified saints will dwell in the bodies restored to them at the resurrection (Rev. 21:2; Irenaeus, *Ag. Her.* V.35, *ANF* I, pp. 565–66). The moral imperative remains presently to "learn upon earth that knowledge which will continue with us in heaven" (Jerome, Letters, 53, *NPNF* 2 VI, p. 102).

The Lord Is the Temple. The gaze is no longer directed toward the temple, in this heavenly Jerusalem, but toward the Lord himself: "I did not see a temple in the city, because the Lord God Almighty and the lamb are its temple" (Rev. 21:22). The leading motif in the heavenly vision in Revelation is the presence of the slain lamb. The throne is described as the throne of God and of the Lamb (22:1) to whom unceasing celebration is addressed (5:13).

The Blessed Employments of Heaven. The blessed are united in worship (Rev. 4:8; 5:9, 10; 7:4–11) and service (Rev. 22:3). The saints "serve him day and night in his temple, and he who sits on the throne will spread his tent over them. Never again will they hunger; never again will they thirst. The sun will not beat upon them, nor any scorching heat" (Rev. 7:15, 16). They sing God's praise. Heaven is a very musical place (Hildegard of Bingen, *Symphonia*, p. 143). The righteous are "hymned by the angels" (Hippolytus, *Ag. Plato* 1, *ANF* V, p. 21).

No happiness can be complete if constantly dogged by the awareness that it might soon end; hence perfect happiness must be eternal happiness (Augustine, *CG* XII.20, *NPNF* 1 II, pp. 239–40). "Here is possession displacing hope's desire, even as vision displaces faith's belief. . . . Then is our happiness complete, for the highest delight rises from our being united with what fits us best" (Tho. Aq., *Sentences* I.I.1, *TATT*, p. 404).

The Eternal Happiness of the Redeemed Will.   Those who perfectly behold the life of God eternally will also experience perfect enjoyment of the will. "Therefore, whoever is happy seeks nothing which does not belong to that in which true beatitude consists" (Tho. Aq., *SCG* IV, chap. 92, p. 340). If a joy could be imagined in which one is completely and permanently delivered from all evil, so as to share fully in the abundant good of the One who is incomparably good, that is the joy of heaven (Leo, *Sermons*, XXI–XXII, *NPNF* 2 XII, pp. 128–30).

Only an eternal happiness that cannot end is absolute felicity, for all other modes of happiness are prone to be morosely aware of their impending finite ending. The enjoyment of oneself in the presence of God is a "joy unspeakable and full of glory" (1 Pet. 1:8, KJV), where joy is raised to its highest expression (Cyprian, *Letters*, *FC* 51, pp. 315–17). The Revelation of John presses every analogy available to express the joy of this communion—everything that can delight the eye or energize the imagination.

Though analogies are used that imply that the joys of heaven resemble the pleasures of earthly life, all hedonic analogies are inadequate. For all earthly joys can be enjoyed only for a time, and are followed by satiety and depletion (John Chrysostom, *Baptismal Instructions*, *ACW* 31, p. 108). Heaven is a treasure that does not fail, that moth and rust cannot corrupt (Luke 12:33), a "crown of glory that will never fade away" (1 Pet. 5:4). "The future happiness of the saints will be more pure, more spiritual, and of an infinitely higher nature, than anything that earth can afford" (Wakefield, *CT* 2, p. 633), for heaven is alone the dwelling that is eternal (Gregory of Nyssa, *The Life of Moses*, *CWS*, pp. 100 ff.). The psalmist celebrated the One who "will not abandon me to the grave" and who ultimately "will fill me with joy in your presence, with eternal pleasures at your right hand" (Ps. 16:11).

Eternal happiness is "a happiness of whose excellence the minutest part would scarce be told if all were said that the tongues of all men can say. For though we very truly hear that the kingdom of God will be filled with splendor, joy, happiness, and glory, yet when these things are spoken of, they remain utterly remote from our perception, and as it were, wrapped in obscurities, until that day comes when he will reveal to us his glory" (Calvin, *Inst.* 3.25.10).

The glorified will of the blessed was described by Hippolytus: "There the righteous dwell from the beginning, not ruled by necessity, but enjoying always the contemplation of the blessings which are in their view, and delighting themselves with the expectation of others ever new, and deeming those ever better than these" (*Ag. Plato* 1, *ANF* V, p. 222).

The Absence of Obstacles

With final resurrection and judgment, the body of the just finally shares in the blessedness promised to the faithful. Final redemption restores what had been lost in the fall, the full exercise of the free will to celebrate and reflect the divine good endlessly (John of Damascus, *OF* IV.27, *NPNF* 2 IX, p. 101).

The blessings of the blessed are sometimes divided into privative and positive blessings. Under "privative blessings" are considered all that is absent from heaven.

Privative Blessings: Freedom from Evil. From what limitations are the blessed eternally relieved? "The *privative blessings* are the absence of sin and of the causes of sin, viz., the flesh inciting, the devil suggesting, and world seducing" (Quenstedt, *TDP* I, 553; Schmid, *DT*, p. 661). In heaven there is neither inordinate desire, nor sin, nor the consequent pain, sorrow, sickness and death that come from them. Absent from heaven will be mental aberrations, neuroses, moral depravity, all influences of the wicked, who "shall cease from troubling" (Job 3:17, KJV). The just will be separated completely from "those who practice magic arts, the sexually immoral, the murderers, the idolaters and everyone who loves and practices falsehood" (Rev. 22:15).

The Absence of Temptation. Absent from heaven is the temptation that characterizes the body-soul *compositum,* with finite freedom now no longer made vulnerable to anxiety and guilt. Because there is freedom from temptation, there is freedom from the possibility of sinning. In heaven it is no longer possible to sin. An hypothesized happiness would remain incomplete if not free from sin (Augustine, *Contra Julian* V.61, in Pohle, *DT* XII, p. 33). The glorified bodies of the celestial city are promised immunity from the drivenness of sex, hunger and thirst, and anxiety over the old body (Rev. 7:16; 1 Cor. 6:13; Matt. 22:30; 1 Cor. 15:42, 43).

Rest from Struggle. The Letter to the Hebrews described the final state of the just as "entering their rest" (Heb. 4:1–6) from the warfare of the struggle to be accountable under the conditions of embodied time. It is a rest from the contradictions of human existence under bondage to sin. This tranquillity is not inaction, but unfettered vitality, being raised in spiritual energy, being free of sin, more a rest of singing than sleeping (Rev. 14:3; 1 Cor. 12:9; Jacobs, *SCF,* p. 552).

After final judgment the consequences of sin can no more affect the faithful, who will have been freed from all that might detract the soul from God, without the tears or pain or limitations that come from sin. God will "wipe every tear from their eyes. There will be no more death or mourning or crying or pain, for the old order of things has passed away" (Rev. 21:4). "There the weary are at rest" (Job 3:17). There are "no toils" in Abraham's bosom (Hippolytus, *Ag. Plato* 1, *ANF* V, p. 222).

In this rest there is neither "pain, nor corruption, nor care, nor night, nor day measured by time . . . no numerous wanderings of stars, no painfully-trodden earth, no abode of paradise hard to find; no furious roaring of the sea, forbidding one to touch or traverse it; but this too will be readily passable for the righteous" (Hippolytus, *Ag. Plato* 2, *ANF* V, p. 223). "For then the outer man will be the peaceful and unblemished possession of the inner man; then the mind, engrossed in beholding God, will be hampered by no obstacles of human weakness" (Leo, *Sermons* XCV, *NPNF* 2 XII, p. 204).

The soul, which is restless until it finds its rest in God, desires two things above all: to "uninterruptedly enjoy the unchangeable good which is God; and that it be delivered from all dubiety, and know certainly that it shall eternally abide in the same enjoyment" (Augustine, *CG* XI.13, *NPNF* 1 II, p. 212; Dame Juliana of Norwich, *RDL*, pp. 88–89).

Positive Blessings

The privative blessings of freedom *from* sin are complemented by "positive blessings" of freedom *for* life in the presence of God, and all that is uniquely present to the glory of God's holiness.

Freedom for *Life.*   Each human faculty is incomparably blessed in God's presence: The soul is blessed with eternal life. The knowing capacity of the rational mind is blessed with enlightenment (1 Cor. 13:9–12). The will is blessed with rectitude and happiness (Ps. 17:15; Eph. 4:25; 5:27). The glorified body is blessed by the right ordering of appetitive powers. The imagination is blessed with the thought of the complete security of future blessedness without interruption (John 16:22; Tho. Aq., *Exposition, Apostles' Creed, TATT*, p. 411). This is a happiness that none can take away, for it is eternal union with God (*Longer Catech.*, Eastern Orthodox Church, 380, *COC* II, p. 505).

The spiritual body risen into eternal life will experience the full recovery of the condition of humanity prior to the fall: "To him who overcomes, I will give the right to eat from the tree of life, which is in the paradise of God" (Rev. 2:7). The awesome fact of death that had appeared to be so overwhelming becomes itself the transition into incomparable freedom, victory, and the eternal happiness of the just (1 Cor. 15:54–57). The souls of the faithful would be withered by the holiness of God were it not that the grace of God gives strength to endure the happiness that lives eternally in God's presence.

The Glorified Bodies of Saints: 1 Corinthians 15:42–53.   The key text describing endowments of the risen body: "The body that is sown is perishable; it is raised imperishable; it is sown in dishonor, it is raised in glory; it is sown in weakness, it is raised in power; it is sown a natural body, it is raised a spiritual body" (1 Cor. 15:42, 43; these are systematically discussed by Thomas Aquinas, *ST*, supp., Q83–88; Schmid, *DT*, pp. 661–63; Hodge, *ST* III, pp. 780–85; cf. 1 Cor. 4–5).

The glorified body, free from death, is characterized by incorruption (*aphtharsia*). The perishable has become clothed "with the imperishable, and the mortal with immortality" (1 Cor. 15:53), now beyond any feeling of discomfort or death, having put on incorruption (Rev. 21:4). Even the scars of the martyrs will enhance, not mar, the glory of their risen bodies (Augustine, *CG* XXII.19; Tho. Aq., *ST*, supp., Q82.1.5, III, p. 2906).

The risen body, freed from darkness, is characterized by clarity, brightness, *glory* (*doxa*), by which the "righteous will shine like the sun in the kingdom of their Father" (Matt. 13:43) because they fully reflect the glory of God. This same glory was anticipatively beheld by the disciples in the transfiguration (Mark 9:2).

The risen body, freed from infirmities, is characterized by agility and *power* (*dunamis*), by which the body will move with complete ease wherever directed by the soul, as typified by Christ's body in the resurrection (Tho. Aq., *ST,* supp., Q84.1, III, p. 2919).

Freed from time-space encumbrances, the risen body is to empirical eyes invisible, spiritual (*pneumatikos,* spirit-empowered), now characterized by subtility, by which the soul, being filled with the divine *pneuma,* "assumes into itself the life of the body and raises it to its own level," so that "the body becomes absolutely subject to the spirit" (Tho. Aq., *ST,* supp., Q83.2). This characteristic is sometimes referred to as impalpability or illocality. When these changes occur, "then the saying that is written will come true: 'Death has been swallowed up in victory'". (1 Cor. 15:54).

Whether Heaven Is Rightly Viewed as a Reward. It is not adequate to say that the just receive heaven as a reward, if by reward is meant that upon which one has a claim, for the just have no claim upon final blessedness by which they might assert that it is just that they receive it. Yet heaven is promised and given the faithful as the gracious consequence of their repentance, faith, and responsive works of love, and in this sense is called a reward (Luke 6:23; 35; 2 Tim. 4:14; Cyprian, *Letters, FC* 51, pp. 78–81; Calvin, *Inst.* 3.18). Rewards *in* heaven are distinguishable from the rewarding of heaven (or the heavenly reward of the faithful—*misthos en tō ouranō,* Luke 6:23; cf. 2 Tim. 4:14, 18; Heb. 6:4: "heavenly gift").

That there will be differences in heavenly rewards appears to be taught in the parable of the talents (Matt. 25:21–23) and of the pounds (Luke 19:16–19). The principle is, "From everyone who has been given much, much will be demanded, and from the one who has been entrusted with much, much more will be asked" (Luke 12:48). Some apparently will be saved barely, "but only as one escaping through the flames" (1 Cor. 3:15).

Whether There Are Degrees of Glorification—Gradus Gloriae. Each celestial celebrant will reflect the divine goodness in a different way (Irenaeus, *Ag. Her.* V.36.2, *ANF* I, p. 567; Clement of Alexandria, *Stromata* VI.13, *ANF* II, p. 504; *SHD* I 135). Though each individual shares in the same salvation, the refracted glory will not be monotone, but varied (John Chrysostom, *To the Fallen Theodore, NPNF* 1 IX, pp. 99 ff., 111). "The sun has one kind of splendor, the moon another and the stars another, and star differs from star in splendor. So will it be with the resurrection of the dead" (1 Cor. 15:41, 42; Clement of Alexandria, *Stromata* VI.14, *ANF* II, pp. 505–7; Cocceius, *Summa Theologica,* xcvii, 4, 5, in Heppe, *RD,* p. 709). The martyr is victorious over the hostile world in a different way than the virgin over lust or the teacher over the power of deception (Matt. 5:11; Rev. 14:3; Suarez, *De Fine Ultimo;* Bellarmine, *De Sanctorum Beatitudine*).

"So there will also be many degrees of splendor and glory in yonder life, as St. Paul teaches in 1 Cor. 15:40; and yet all will be alike in the enjoyment of the same eternal blessedness and delight, and there will be but *one* glory for all, because we shall all be the children of God" (Luther, *Sermons on Romans,* Rom. 8:18–23, 1535; *WLS* 2, p. 622; *WA* 41, 306). "The more one will be united to God the happier will one be. Now the measure of charity is the measure of one's union with God. Therefore the diversity of beatitude will be according to the difference of charity" (Tho. Aq., *ST,* supp., Q93.3, III, p. 2971).

If God is just, there are no injustices positable in heaven. Where seeming discrepancies or inequities appear when interpreted temporally from the vantage point of human egocentricities, they are not to be explained by human merits, but by the free grace of God (*Decretum Unionis* of Florence, *SCD* 693, p. 219). Each receives the recompense appropriate (Matt. 16:27), for "the man who plants and the man who waters have one purpose, and each will be rewarded according to his own labor" (1 Cor. 3:8). "Whoever sows sparingly will also reap sparingly" (2 Cor. 9:6; *Martyrdom of Polycarp* 40; Ignatius of Antioch, *To Polycarp* I.3; Tertullian, *Scorpiace* 6; Jerome, *Ag. Jovinianus* II.33, 34, *NPNF* 2 IV, p. 413).

The glory each one reflects is measured by the strength of the love one has for God (Tho. Aq., *ST* 1a, Q12, art. 6). "But just as small vessels can be as full as larger vessels (though the latter contain more), so everyone in heaven will be wholly fulfilled and wholly at peace" (Kasper, *CCF*, p. 345). "There will be no envy on account of unequal glory, because one love will govern all" (Augustine, *Tractate on John* 67.3, in Pohle, *DT* XII, p. 42; cf. *NPNF* 1 VII, pp. 338–40). "And thus one will have a gift less than another in such a way that he has the gift also, that he does not wish for more" (Hugh of St. Victor, *SCF*, p. 475).

In the celestial sociology, the variable status of blessed spirits does not prevent them, "even the lowest, from seeing the divine essence. Even though each of the blessed spirits sees God in His essence, some may behold Him more perfectly than others. . . . However, the more perfectly a cause is known, the more numerous are the effects discerned in it" (Tho. Aq., *Compend.* 126, p. 133).

The *Amen* to the Glory of the Lord

Marriage Feast of the Lamb. All who are members of Christ's body are being gathered from around the world (Mark 13:27). The dross having been burned away, and unworthy members having been removed, the church will receive her completed form (Matt. 13:41, 42) and will celebrate her marriage "prepared as a bride beautifully dressed for her husband" (Rev. 21:2), being welcomed into the city of God (Rev. 21:8–10). "The Spirit and the bride say, 'Come.' And let everyone who hears say, 'Come'" (Rev. 22:17, NRSV). As dowry precedes marriage, so does Christ provide gifts (*dotes beatorum,* the dowry of the blessed) to enable the spouse to enjoy eternal life and to enhance and beautify that enjoyment (John Chrysostom, *Baptismal Instructions, ACW* 31, pp. 27–30). The key event of the Revelation of John is the marriage supper of the Lamb (Rev. 19:6 ff.), a messianic banquet in which the bride, the church, is dressed in a spectacular wedding garment, clothed in the righteousness of the bridegroom, Christ (Tho. Aq., *ST*, supp., Q95, III, pp. 2974–80; G. R. Beasley-Murray, *Revelation*). The other symbolic figure, Babylon, gaudily dressed, clothed in unrighteousness, is brought to nothing (17:4). The wedding feast ends spectacularly with the destruction of the existing heaven and earth and the creation of a new heaven and earth (Rev. 21:1), a new Jerusalem (21:9–11), where God and the Lamb are worshiped, and where "the dwelling of God is with men, and he will live with them. They will be his people, and God himself will be with them and be their God. He will wipe every tear from their eyes. There will be no more death or mourning or crying or pain, for the old order of things has passed away" (21:3, 4).

Triune Praise. The echoes continue eternally in the celebration of the triune God. Nothing brings more delight to the communion of saints. God is one, indivisible, the giver of all and redeemer of all. The work begun in creation, having fallen and been redeemed, is being consummated according to God's promise.

That God the Father is Creator does not prevent the faithful from celebrating of the Son that "through him all things were made, and without him nothing was made that has been made" (John 1:3), and that the Spirit is the Eternal One through whom the creative Word speaks. The Father has called us out of darkness into the light of his love. The Father is truly God.

The work of redemption is the proper work of the Son, who is sent by the Father's will and empowered by the Spirit to do all things necessary for the work of redemption. Before all ages the Son was begotten of the Father as light comes from light. The Son has come to save us from sin. The Son is truly God.

The work of consummation, completion, and sanctification upon which we have focused in this volume is the work of the Spirit, of whom Christ said that this is the One "whom the Father will send in my name" (John 14:26). The Spirit dwells within us to enable us to conform to Christ's likeness. The Spirit is truly God.

The mystery of the triune God is that God is Father, God is Son, and God is Spirit, and that God is one. Yet we do not say that there is one Person in God, but three Persons, and we do not say that there are three gods, but one God. "Now this is the Catholic faith, that we worship one God in Trinity and Trinity in unity" (Quicunque vult, *CC*, p. 704). "What the Father is to us and gives to us, He is and gives through the Son, in the Holy Spirit; no one has the Father except in the Son, and no one confesses the Son except in the Holy Spirit" (Pieper, *WCB*, pp. 56–57; cf. Gregory Nazianzen, *Orat.* 31, *NPNF* 2 VI, pp. 318–28).

Systematic theology, like catechetics, is offered sacrificially in order rightly to enable baptism and communion, that we may know "for what purpose each of the holy mysteries of Baptism is performed, and with what reverence and order you must go from Baptism to the Holy Altar of God, and enjoy its spiritual and heavenly mysteries; that your souls being previously enlightened by the word of doctrine" may receive the gifts offered by God (Cyril of Jerusalem, *Catech. Lect.* XVIII.32, *NPNF* 2 VII, p. 142).

From Credo *to* Amēn.   The ancient prayer of the church embraces and sums the whole range of systematic theology: "Glory be to the Father, and to the Son, and to the Holy Ghost; as it was in the beginning, is now and ever shall be, world without end. Amen" (*Divine Liturgy of James, Early Liturgies, ANF* VII, p. 550; *BCP;* cf. Rev. 21:6; 22:13; Augustine, *Trin.* VII.4–6, *NPNF* 1 III, pp. 109–14; Eph. 3:21).

The *amēn* (truly, certainly) to which we come in the ancient baptismal creed is more than a period (*SCD* 2, p. 5). It is an act of whole body-soul affirmation, of trust, of confirmation. As the creed begins with "I believe" (*credo*), it ends with, "Yes, so be it," "verily," "I confirm it" (*amēn*). Jesus Christ himself is personally God's own "Amen" (Rev. 3:14). "For no matter how many promises God has made, they are 'Yes' in Christ. And so through him the 'Amen' is spoken by us to the glory of God" (2 Cor. 1:20).

Postscript

The gospel points simply to the love of God on the cross. The process by which this simple word has been culturally transmitted involves a complex history.

Considered as divine mystery, the subject matter of the simple gospel, God's holy love, is intrinsically "hard to explain" (*dushermēneutos*, Heb. 5:11) insofar as it is addressed objectively as a problem of human knowing. The rational clarification (*hermēneia*) of the meaning of divine mystery becomes an almost comic, circuitous, complicated exercise. The result is that the simplest points of theology have come to seem exceedingly dense, requiring considerable historical reflection and verbal precision and logical analysis to sort out. The inquiry into God, the most engaging of all subjects, has been inadvertently turned by theologians into a yawning bore.

Must the study of God, the most beautiful of all that is, be fated to be stuffy and tiresome? Is there some demonic censor who hiddenly consigns theology to the back pages of the newspaper, and keeps the subject insufferably dull? Two factors collude to make Christian teaching dense: the profundity of the divine Subject, and the stubborn resistance of hearers.

Whether Modern Chauvinism Is Irreversible.   The celebration of the atoning Word and life in the Spirit has been received by and transmitted through a hundred premodern generations. Now it is being heard by a postmodern generation who, having been taught to assume its out-of-dateness, is coming once again under the divine address. The very substructures of languages are shifting like earthquakes under the communities that guard and bear this testimony.

I have used the term *modern chauvinist* to describe those who have already decided that there is precious little worth learning from any premodern voice. They assume the intrinsic inferiority of all premodern texts and the intrinsic superiority of all modern methods of investigation of those texts. Though a serious affliction, the condition is not irreversible.

Whatever their academic credentials, modern chauvinist hearers of the gospel are exceedingly slow learners, having carefully constructed inward defenses against taking seriously any premodern teaching. Those who have already decided they must earn their salvation and make life better on their own resources find the premise that God has mercifully done it for them hard to hear and harder to trust. Deep inner blocks to prevent listening are carefully built and defended, and determined resistance given to hearing the Word.

It is the height of narcissism for moderns to think that they are the first to be scandalized by evangelical orthodoxy. Celsus beat them to it eighteen centuries ago, and the Corinthian pagans nineteen (1 Cor. 1:18–31).

On Hardness of Hearing.   While laboring with a strained analogy, the author of the letter to the Hebrews reflected on just these resistances. Midway in the letter he struggled to show how Christ is a unique priest forever "in the order of Melchizedek" (Heb. 5:8). Because Jesus was not born of the tribe of Levi, he reasoned, he could never be that sort of priest. If a priest, he would have to be of a different order, like Melchizedek, both king and priest, appointed directly by God, called "King of peace," as was Jesus (Gen. 14:18; Zech. 6:12, 13; Heb. 7:2, 21; Isa. 11:5–9).

At this sticky point the writer may have sensed his reader growing impatient. This labored analogy sparked a stunning throwaway reflection about the study of God—as if to shrug in exasperation: "We have much to say about this, but it is hard to explain because you are slow to learn. In fact, though by this time you ought to be teachers, you need someone to teach you the elementary truths of God's word all over again. You need milk, not solid food! Anyone who lives on milk, being still an infant, is not acquainted with the teaching about righteousness. But solid food is for the mature, who by constant use have trained themselves to distinguish good from evil" (Heb. 5:11–14).

Needed in this after-modern context: "someone to teach you the elementary truths of God's word all over again"—*stoicheia tēs archēs ton logion tou theou* ("the rudiments of the beginning of the oracles of God," Heb. 5:12; "the first principles," KJV). This is why this kind of study has become once again necessary for both clergy and laity, and why it has stretched to the length required. What the theologian has to give, let him give with simplicity (*haplotēs*, Rom. 12:8; 2 Cor. 12:3). Only by serious searching of scripture and its consensual tradition of interpretation, with earnest daily application, will postmodern persons become active hearers of the word.

Hilary's Apology for Theological Precision.   Hilary of Poitiers's second book, *On the Trinity,* written in exile (A.D. 356–360), began with a brilliant excursus on why precise language in theology was in his time required. He conceded that the believer already has in scripture all that he or she needs for faith. Moreover, the essential tenor of holy writ is concisely brought together in the baptismal formula of the great commission: "Therefore go and make disciples of all nations, baptizing them in the name of the Father and of the Son and of the Holy Spirit" (Matt. 28:18). All the theology one would ever need is already embedded in this passage. The theologian who would travel light may travel with this verse alone. "What element in the mystery of man's salvation is not included in those words? What is forgotten, what left in darkness?" (Hilary, *Trin.* II.1, *NPNF* 2 IX, p. 52).

Why then must theology travel so heavy? In answering, Hilary offered a profound apology for theological precision while at the same time showing its limited role: *"The error of others compels us to err in daring to embody in human terms truths which ought to be hidden* in the silent veneration of the heart." If skewed and malevolent distortions had not repeatedly muddied the waters, the *ekklēsia* would not have been forced to do so much detailed, defensive theological definition. Assuming a different world without these deceptions, Christians might simply celebrate the faith received in scripture without divisive detractions, merely "worshiping the Father, reverencing with Him the Son, abounding in the Holy Ghost."

Neither Hilary nor we live in such an uncluttered world. The challenges of false teachers have continually forced the *ekklēsia* to "scale perilous heights, to speak unutterable words, to trespass on forbidden ground"—by defending and interpreting scripture, showing its internal cohesion, comparing unclear passages with those that are clear. It is only because we must meet determined challenges that "we must strain the poor resources of our language to express thoughts too great for words" (Hilary, *Trin.* II.1, *NPNF* 2 IX, p. 52, italics added).

Whether Heresy May Forever Remain Unanswered.   It normally takes more time to correct than to make a mistake. This is why a simple, straightforward book on the consensual teaching of the Holy Spirit turns out to be so long: the more heresy, the more theology. It feels like an accumulated intergenerational punishment for decades of unanswered sloppy thinking. The more confusions sown, the more recastings are required, even generations later. "For there have risen many who have given to the plain words of holy Writ some arbitrary interpretation of their own, instead of its true and only sense" as celebrated consensually by the mind of the believing church. "Heresy lies in the sense assigned [by *hairesis,* by arbitrary interpreters], not in the word written; the guilt is that of the expositor, not of the text" (Hilary, *Trin.* II.2, *NPNF* 2 IX, p. 53).

If Hilary is correct, the reason our theological books grow thicker with time is that we face ever-new challenges to classic, consensual exegesis that must be corrected and brought into the ecumenical whole without unbalancing it. Without such challenges we could settle down to the simple celebration of the triune God at the Lord's Table.

Echoing from the fourth century, Hilary's voice seems to admonish guild scholarship of our time: "Since, therefore, they cannot make any change in the facts recorded, they bring novel principles and theories of man's device to bear upon them." This is precisely what happened in form-criticism—having found the premodern text itself so irritating and unacceptable, the modern critics scramble to imagine some fantasized oral tradition underlying the text that says something quite opposite from what the text says. This is the special burden of Christian scholarship in this century: to answer false teaching by setting forth rudimentary consensual Christian truth. Hilary's description of his motivation closely parallels my own reason for entering this conflicted arena.

Whether Silence Is the Profoundest Theological Act.   Why not play it safe and ignore the challenges? In measured tones, Hilary responded, "We must set a limit to their license of interpretation. Since their malice, inspired by [the Adversary's] cunning, *empties the doctrine of its meaning, while it retains the Names which convey the truth,* we must emphasize the truth which those Names convey" (italics added).

Those who stand in the apostolic tradition cannot pretend a wise silence in the face of blatantly false interpretations. Someone must at some point attempt to set a limit to license. This is why I have entered the fray, and why the contest has gone to so many rounds.

It may seem to critics as if it were "a light thing to tear up Perfection, to make laws for Omnipotence, to limit Infinity." In facing the duty of response, it is easy to sympathize with Hilary: "As for me, the task of answering them fills me with anxiety; my brain whirls, my intellect is stunned, my very words must be a confession, not that I am weak of utterance, but that I am dumb." Hilary knew that the subject was inexhaustible, yet the circumstances required that he answer, yet to answer would be to venture to speak "concerning God in terms more precise than He Himself has used" in scripture!

He chides both students and teachers of systematic theology: "Gird up your intellect to comprehend Him as a whole; He eludes you. God, as a whole, has left something within your grasp, but this something is inextricably involved in His entirety. Thus you have missed the whole, since it is only a part which remains in your hands" (Hilary, *Trin.* II.2, *NPNF* 2 IX, p. 53; cf. Clare of Assisi, *Rule, CWS,* pp. 216–18).

Whether Truthful Teaching Requires Rhetorical Skill. The weight of argument is not more easily carried by adding to it rhetorical ornament. Leo argued that "Christ's Gospel needs not this art [of rhetoric]; for in it the true teaching stands revealed by its own light: nor is there any seeking for that which shall please the ear, when to know Who is the Teacher is sufficient for true faith."

Those clever in debate tend to "make their chief boast in this, that in doubtful matters which are obscured by the variety of opinions they can induce their hearers to accept that view which each has chosen for his own genius and eloquence to bring forward." This is just why Christ chose disciples "not from among philosophers or orators, but took humble fishermen as instruments by which He would reveal Himself, lest the heavenly teaching, which was of itself full of mighty power, should seem to need the aid of words" (Leo, *Letters* CLXV, *NPNF* 2 XII, p. 106).

Theologians are warned not only against "saying in any way what is wrong, but against uttering even what is right overmuch, and inordinately; since the good effect of things spoken is often lost when enfeebled" by loquacity (Gregory the Great, *Book of Pastoral Rule, NPNF* 2 XII, p. 12).

Whether Theology Ever Comes to an Ending Point. The obvious place to end theology is with the end—God's own promised consummation of redeemed history—yet even then loose ends are destined to remain dangling.

The order and arrangement of topics we have followed is found generally in the baptismal formula and the rule of faith that formed around it, and more specifically from the tradition of triune teaching of the rule of faith found in Irenaeus, Gregory Nazianzen, Augustine, John of Damascus, Peter Lombard, and Calvin—from whether language can be attributed to God, and whether God is, to the triune God, creation, and providence, to all the questions surrounding God the Son, and then God the Spirit, salvation, the church, and eschatology.

The careful reader will note certain themes skirted in these three volumes that some might have expected to be fully treated. It is not out of simple neglect or ignorance or avoidance that certain noncreedal themes have been temporarily set aside or dealt with only in a cursory fashion. I wish to be explicit about the deliberate absence of several sets of issues that have been saved for further treatment in separate studies: anthropology (including detailed treatment of the doctrines of sin, soul, body, and freedom), liturgical theology, and Christian ethics. None are articles of the creed. They do not appear in any of the standard *regulae fidei,* hence are not chapters of this study, though they have all been frequently referenced. I have intentionally held these noncreedal loci until they could be dealt with more completely in subsequent investigations that remain in my mind in the form of long-range planning, awaiting to be attended if I am given sufficient time. This does not imply that these are less important, but that I hope to treat them more adequately in due course.

Epilogue

GENERAL CONSENT OF THE LAITY
AS THE PRINCIPLE OF LEGITIMACY

An Unembellished Account of How I Have Attempted to Assess Proximate Consensus

I owe it to my reader to try to explain just how I have struggled to identify a proximate consensus even while there remain many dissenting voices.

Scripture is the primary source, ground, and criterion of Christian teaching. All that any secondary interpreters can serve to do is help the reader of scripture to hear its address. Any secondary source that presumes to lord it over holy writ so as to become the criterion of scripture's authenticity has already ceased being useful to Christian teaching.

The Work of Listening.   The first order of importance for me has been listening carefully to the ecumenical councils (*NPNF* 2 XIV; *SCD; COC*). In addition to the seven general ecumenical councils, I have studied especially carefully those regional synods that appear to have gained wide, sustained, intergenerational consent (*SCD, COC*). I have listened intently to those teachers who have repeatedly and for many generations and cultures been received as expressions of the mind of the believing church (the recognized eight great doctors). In addition, I have listened for consensual interpreters of scripture both ancient and modern, those relatively more aware of the varied interpretations of a text in different cultural-historical situations, and those who have some sense of the enormous flexibility and variability of orthodoxy, and of the unique ability of orthodoxy to transform various cultural traditions and languages. These exegetes have formative, not normative value. Scripture alone is received as normative authority.

The Irenic Intent.   Because ecumenical theology is reconciling theology, I have tried to approach my task irenically, as a quiet, trudging peacemaker. Here the working theologian becomes something like a negotiator among parties in conflict. Peacemaking is often a very gradual and sometimes discouraging process.

I have tried to listen carefully to Baptists and Catholics, Lutherans and Eastern Orthodox, charismatic Christians and those formed by the Gregorian liturgy. I sought to see where they share the one body of Christ, yet with mutated languages and varied symbols and social forms and cultural formations and class consciousness. On every page I have attempted to make peace between Christians of different languages, periods, and moral orientations who yet share the same faith in the same Lord and the same baptism by the same Spirit. Some conflicts that seem to reflect recalcitrant differences, when examined amount only to verbal differences. This effort tends to engender a spirit of relative toleration in the study of classic ecumenic Christianity.

The Risk of Mistaken Identity.   The result is odd: Among evangelicals I experience myself as a very Catholic evangelical; among ecumenists I seem to be an old-fashioned antiquarian sort of ecumenist; among pietists I appear to be a very orthodox, bookish pietist. Among liberation theologians I seem to be a narrowly scriptural sort of liberationist; among neoconservatives I appear to be at various times a rather archaic or Thomistic or classic liberal critic. Among liberal mainliners I am likely to be perceived as a liturgically conservative Anglo-Catholic Evangelical. Among holiness tradition teachers and sanctificationists I come out as a very odd-looking Eastern Patristic sanctificationist. Among charismatics and Pentecostals I appear to be a very traditional Protestant believer in the witness of the Spirit. Among Arminians I may appear at times to be an old Reformed Protestant scholastic. To secular postmodernists I am reactionary; to reactionaries I am ultramodern. Among Christians I am a very pro-Jewish, pro-rabbinic Christian. Among Jews I have received a respectful hearing, with less confusion than among Christians. To those who allow me to define myself, I experience myself as an orthodox ecumenical evangelical.

There should be a lesson in all this: In trying to listen to the ancient ecumenical consensus, one should be prepared, ironically, to bear the burden of being pigeonholed into whatever slot the puzzled modern critic finds convenient. It is a yoke to be borne joyfully while being comically resisted, in hopes that the unity of Christ's body may become more manifest by being beheld historically.

The Critical Task of Postmodern Paleoorthodoxy.   In early phases of this research I have sought to function as a kind of sponge for all Christian voices, chiefly the luminous centrist ones, yet attentive to the graying peripheries. This early absorptive stage would then be followed by a tougher critical stage in which the true and false were winnowed in and out. The assessing of texts alleging to be consensual Christian teaching must not be uncritical, so as to fail to distinguish apostolic from quasi- or counterapostolic voices. When one hears a voice that pretends to be the biblical faith but remains substantially alien to it, one must listen all the more intently to the centrist interpreters of the received tradition for correctives.

How does one know where it is not peace to be made but combat? How does one recognize heresy? Only by first knowing and sharing deeply in the language, worship, ethics, and ethos of the ecumenical testimony of many cross-cultural generations of apostolic testimony. Nothing is more pathetic than a self-righteous presumed orthodox theologian who has failed to listen carefully to the varieties of orthodoxy and thus has prematurely written off orthodoxies that differ from his own local dialect or ethnocentrism.

Those who pretend to be able to recognize the catholic consensus without ever having been profoundly introduced to Athanasius or Vincent or John Owen or Roman canon law or Southern Baptist preaching or holiness hymnody are soon found out. The pretense can hardly sustain credibility for long among its relevant audiences. The only reliable corrective is to go back and study one's subject more carefully—the apostolic mission in its beautiful bimillennial varieties—East-West, African-Asian, Roman and Antiochene and Genevan—of cultural experience, exegesis, and pastoral care.

The Danger of Hypertolerance.   Suppose in the effort one becomes too tolerantly uncritical, and functionally latitudinarian. Suppose one begins to concede orthodox intent for all possible brands of Arian, Pelagian, Universalist, pseudo-Origenist, atheist, psychological reductionist, Marxist, and materialist mischief. One would thereby have lost the capacity to discern the difference between orthodoxy and heresy and would cease being a Christian theologian. One might seem temporarily successful as a no-boundaries mediator but could not expect to serve as an ecumenical theologian to be taken seriously by lay Christian consent over any long term.

The hard truth is that the irenic task can go on properly only if accompanied by a realistic, calm, nonhysterical, reasoned polemical effort—a disclaiming and discerning spirit, a constant vigilance, a rigorous attentiveness to faith being distorted, where scripture is often superficially quoted on behalf of spurious tendencies. False teachers, "feigning faith," may offer "something like a deadly drug" steeped in "honeyed wine" (Ignatius, *Trallians* 6, *AF,* p. 94).

We should not be surprised to find heresy mixed inconspicuously with orthodoxy, false with true teaching side by side in the same pew singing the same hymns. Unblemished and polluted fish are caught in the same net. As long as the church remains a soupy gray *corpus mixtum,* then we should not be surprised to find persons who come to church, partake of its sacraments, hear its word, and even are paid salaries to provide its leadership, being duly ordained to preach its word and administer its baptism and communion, who yet have not learned its most simple and generally received consensual teachings such as triunity, incarnation, atonement, resurrection, and the indwelling of the Spirit. Thus it behooves the irenic theologian committed to the apostolic faith to remain attentive to where the true word is being made false by twisted interpretations, however well intended (Hippolytus, *Refutation of All Her., ANF* IV, pp. 9 ff.; Simon Patrick, *A Brief Account of the New Sect of Latitudinarians*).

Whether Consensual Teachings Are Identifiable.   Those ancient teachers deserve our closest attention who have been recognized over generations as rightly assessing the word of truth, who, having been attentive to the Spirit's address through the written word, best represent the broadest consent of the *laos* of God of all times. These are the exegetes to be listened to most carefully, though not uncritically.

This is why I have listened most often to the eight designated voices most generally received by the whole church for the longest period of time as ecumenical interpreters of the apostles—persons with well-known names and recognized gifts—the four great doctors of the East: Athanasius, Basil, Gregory Nazianzen, and John Chrysostom; and of the West: Ambrose, Augustine, Jerome, and Gregory the Great. Augustine had the distinction of being cited by one of the Ecumenical Councils as "among the best teachers" (Ephesus, *SCD* 128, p. 52).

There are many others that speak the same voice of reliable consensual teaching, but these eight are known to seldom lead one astray. What I have found is what so many others have found: these eight are with few exceptions consensually reliable clarifiers of the mind of the believing church. That does not mean that they never made mistakes or misjudgments. One may occasionally find in Augustine an idea that has not been consensually received, such as the fixed number of the elect or a traducian view of the transmission of the human soul by parents to children. At times one may find in these eight a testy spirit, such as in Athanasius and Jerome, to whom we owe so much even amid their testiness. But we are more indebted to these eight exegetes than any since the apostles. All assumed the prior conciliar decisions that have been repeatedly accepted as received orthodox scriptural teaching.

The tradition of recognition of these and several other figures established itself early. By A.D. 495, the Gelasian decretal universally commended as ecumenical teaching not only the canons of Nicaea, Ephesus, and Chalcedon "to be received *after* those of the Old or New Testament, which we regularly accept. Likewise the works of blessed Caecilius Cyprian . . . *and in the same way* the works of Gregory Nazianzen, Basil, Athanasius, John Chrysostom, Theophilus, Cyril of Alexandria, Hilary, Ambrose, Augustine, Jerome and Prosper. Also the epistle of the blessed Leo" and "the decretal epistles" (*SCD* 165, p. 69). That early list included all the then extant ecumenical councils and the great doctors of the church, plus others whom we have quoted often.

Vincent of Lérins noted that the Council of Ephesus (A.D. 431) had quoted as ecumenically reliable witnesses the four leading bishops of Alexandria: Peter, Athanasius, Theophilus, and Cyril, plus the "stars of Cappadocia" (Basil, and the two Gregorys), and among Western bishops Cyprian, Felix I, Julius I, and Ambrose (*Comm.* 30, *FC* 7, pp. 326–27). Amid doctrinal challenges, the faithful were to be fortified by "the public reading aloud of quotations from the Fathers" such as Athanasius, Theophilus, and Cyril. "Let the standard of antiquity be maintained throughout" (Leo, *Letters,* CXXIX, *NPNF* 2 XII, p. 96).

The fifth ecumenical council (Constantinople II, A.D. 553) determined to "hold fast to the decrees of the four councils, and in every way follow the holy Fathers, Athanasius, Hilary, Basil, Gregory the Theologian, Gregory of Nyssa, Ambrose, Theophilus, John Chrysostom of Constantinople, Cyril, Augustine, Proclus, Leo and their writings on the true faith" (Session I, *NPNF* 2 XIV, p. 303). These are precisely the teachers I have most often referenced. Their own intent is abandoned, however, when their own word is preferred to scripture. What characterized them all was steady attentiveness to the written word.

Whether Consensual Teaching Authority Can Be Legitimated. How does the *laos* know that these are consensual teachers and teachings? It would be unreasonable to fail to take seriously the experiential authority of others who have earnestly pointed to them so repeatedly. But I figure my readers will trust me less if I function merely on the basis of accepting others' authority. So I have personally tested these voices again and again in my own reading. This has required years of study and comparative reading. There is no other way to make such a test. Those who doubt that such a consensus can exist must go through that lengthy learning process before a judgment can be made. Lacking a decade of meditative reading would be like a judge rendering a verdict without ever reading the brief.

Legitimate authority needs to be tested repeatedly to regain its legitimacy. It is always proper to ask the toughest questions to presumed authorities. But when these voices repeatedly radiate the spirit that comes from the center of the worshiping community, one gradually begins to trust them on most points and becomes surprised only when they occasionally misstep. These doctors understood themselves to be strongly guided by the previous prevailing ecumenical consensus. "The Church is taught indeed by the Life-giving Spirit, but through the medium of the holy Fathers and Doctors whose rule is acknowledged to be the Holy and Oecumenical Synods" (Conf. of Dositheus XII, *CC,* p. 496). They assumed that the Spirit was guiding the church into all truth, and that such guidance was occurring not merely individualistically, immediately, privately, or directly, but rather through the media of the written word and the consensual teaching tradition, reasonably assessed, corporately celebrated, and experientially tested.

The Intrinsic Fallibility of Finite Assessments of Consensuality.   Am I forever fallible in my best studied judgment of this supposed consensuality? Of course. This is precisely why I have written this book: I am specifically asking my reader to test my own fallibility. I solicit your admonition as to where I may have misperceived the gist of the broadest classic consensus. I expect to learn from those who respond, who each will be due a thoughtful reply. I hope you will help me to see more clearly where my own cultural assumptions or historical myopias or class biases may have misguided me or allured me into some affirmation that in fact has not been received broadly enough to be a serious statement for consensual celebration. This is what you can teach me, and what I need to be taught. We need each other to balance and amend private judgment, hoping that those to whom are given the guardianship tasks of teaching and testimony in the church do not lead the church astray. Those who fail to be specific in undertaking this admonition, who too readily dismiss consensual teaching, however, tend to rule themselves out of the sphere of orthodox criticism.

Whether Doctrinal Continuity Is a Projection.   The steady preoccupation of modern historical theology has been how Christian teaching has constantly been modifying, not how it has remained stable and centered. Much more is known of the development of doctrine than of the continuities within those developments. A huge literature exists on the varieties of Christian teaching, and a very small literature on centrist orthodox consent. My task in writing a systematic theology has been intentionally limited, wishing to speak primarily, insofar as possible, of continuities embracing apostolic Christian teaching of all periods and cultures. It is less how theology has changed than how it has remained the same that I find intriguing.

Are there not so many tortuous qualifications and subtle differences among developing views of Christian teaching that it is futile even to try to come up with an alleged consensus? Such highly qualified disclaimers are indeed expressions of honest historical study. Yet to fail to search for that which unifies the variety is just as egregious an error as to fail to acknowledge differences within the developing traditions—differences that I have never denied.

Is such catholic consent and continuity actually there, or merely a despairing projection of the minds of those who wish it to be there? If a projection, can there be any unity in a theological system? By the many references in the embedded notes I have tried to show that it is actually there textually and not merely an imagined projection. Each reference remains open to challenge as to its context and interpretation. That is where the future dialogue will best proceed, either by validating, correcting, or proposing alternatives.

The Unity Sought in a Theological System.   The deeper, cohesive unity of Christian teaching is the unity of the triune God, from whom and through whom and to whom are all things. The form of unity most worth celebrating in Christian teaching is that which the triune God offers to his gathered people through the gift of his Son, who by his death and resurrection binds us together in him in his Sonship to the Father. The only unity of the systematic task worth seeking is the unity given the people of God through the Holy Spirit whose varied gifts quicken and empower the new humanity in Christ. Our union with God is "a mystery which passes our understanding and defeats our efforts to express it" (New Delhi, *World Council of Churches Message, CC,* p. 585).

The unity of theology is not that of any theologian's invention, but the unity known at the Lord's Table, the unity shared in baptism, the unity embodied by those who receive the varied gifts of the one Spirit. This unity is being made visible in fragmented ways, and refracted in beautiful variegated forms and cultures, through varied efforts at consensual definition of Christian teaching of all ages. Baptized into this one baptism, confessing one faith in the one Lord, these attestors are being brought into one company of the faithful of all ages to confess the apostolic faith and to break the one bread (Eph. 4:3–5).

Christian teaching elicits action according to our knowing, keeping "before our eyes the fearful judgment threatened for disobedience" (*Longer Catech.,* Eastern Orthodox Church, 609, *COC* II, p. 541). "Now that you know these things, you will be blessed if you do them" (John 13:17). Meanwhile we are cautioned, "So you also, when you have done everything you were told to do, should say, 'We are unworthy servants; we have only done our duty'" (Luke 17:10).

The Conciliar Tradition of Consent

The principle of general lay consent does not ignore or circumvent cultural differences. Rather it celebrates those differences and the unity of the body of Christ that embraces them. The following section sets forth the textual authority upon which I have proceeded to speak of consensual exegesis amid vast diversity of personal and cultural expression.

Apostolic Consensus in the First Generation of the Ekklēsia.   The apostles themselves had a fully formed and sufficient vision of the Lord's teaching. But that did not prevent Peter and Paul from serious disagreement, or Paul and Barnabas. These differences were in due time mediated and melded into a more fully formed apostolic consensus. There indeed were tensions between the proclamations of Mark and John and between James and Paul that have required all subsequent proclaimers of apostolic teaching to search for their common ground. An assumption of common apostolic consent was already beginning to take shape in the earliest generations after the writing of the New Testament, so as to begin to form a shared understanding of varied scriptural motifs (Simon Patrick, *A Discourse About Tradition,* 1683).

It was not the unique or peculiar features of any one apostle's teaching (such as the justification teaching of Paul or the priestly Christology of the letter to the Hebrews) that most decisively shaped the consent of the primitive Christian *laos,* but rather those teachings that were most generally shared by all the apostles. Apostolic consensus did not develop out of an autonomous "group-think" process seeking the best available humanistic solutions to problems, but out of a bonded community freely and generally consenting to the Lord's teaching under the guidance of the Spirit.

Emergence of Key Loci of Consent.   By the time of the second-century Christian writers, there was a relatively unified consensual testimony to God's saving activity based upon the apostolic witness. Key points commonly shared by second-century interpreters of the apostolic teaching were these:

the Old Testament canon was essential to the interpretation of the New;

the words of Christ were accurately recalled by the Apostles by the power of the Spirit and had binding authority;

faith was attached to the Son, who being of the very nature of God, became flesh, sharing our human condition even unto death, was raised from the dead and ascended into heaven to intercede for sinners in the presence of the Father;

the indwelling Spirit was enabling the mission of the Son, distributing gifts for the upbuilding of the community of faith;

and the Son would come again in the last days. (*CC,* pp. 1–19; *COC* II, pp. 3–16; C. H. Dodd, *The Apostolic Teaching and Its Developments*)

The Primitive Rule of Faith.   Is there a brief way of accurately stating these common points of consent? Is there a textual norm or rule of faith by which the mass of material in scripture was by common consent thought to be brought together, rightly organized, and reliably understood? Already by the time of the second-century writers, and probably earlier, the baptismal formula (Matt. 28:19b) was thought to summarize the essence of faith (Ignatius, *Philadelphians* 7–9, *ANF* I, pp. 83–85, Irenaeus, *Ag. Her.* III.17, pp. 444–45).

What we know as the Apostles' Creed is the received text of the later consensual memory of the earliest baptismal confession, which developed as a summary exposition of the baptismal formula of Matthew 28:19 (*Didache* 7.1; Justin Martyr, *Apology* I.61). Tertullian credited the rule of faith to Christ himself (*Prescription Ag. Her.* 9, 13, 37, 44, *ANF* III, pp. 244, 249, 261, 265). Irenaeus regarded the rule of faith as the "canon of truth which he received in his baptism" (Irenaeus, *Ag. Her.* I.9.4, *ANF* I, p. 330; cf. I.10.1; Tertullian, *On Baptism* 11; *Prescription Ag. Her.* 14; Clement of Alexandria, *Stromata* VIII.15; Cyprian, *Epistles* 69.7; 70.2). Although variously stated and interpreted, this symbol, grounded in triune teaching, has remained the central norm of Christian teaching in every subsequent century (*Longer Catech.*, Eastern Orthodox Church, *COC* II, p. 456).

Baptism from the outset was intrinsically connected with triune teaching. The Council of Arles I in A.D. 314 "decided that, if anyone from a heretical sect come to the Church, he should be asked his creed, and if it is perceived that he has been baptized in the Father and the Son and the Holy Spirit, only the hand should be imposed upon him, in order that he may receive the Holy Spirit" (*SCD* 53, p. 25). There is no baptism without the triune name (*Longer Catech.*, Eastern Church 290, *COC* II, p. 491). As early as Ignatius (*Magnesians* 11; *Eph.* 7; *Trallians* 9) and Justin (*Apology* I.13, 31, 46; *Dialogue with Trypho* 85), and even earlier dating to Matthew and Paul, there appears to be a fixed formula of baptismal confession. By the middle of the second century a fixed form of the rule of faith or creed appears to have been in use at Rome. The twelve spare phrases of the Old Roman Symbol appear to be direct descendants of the easily memorizable original baptismal confession that must be hypothesized in the earliest decades of the *ekklēsia*. Though the oldest form of the baptismal confession cannot be reconstructed with absolute certainty, the oldest positively attested is the Old Roman Symbol, whose most ancient text is that of Marcellus (A.D. 337 or 338), but there can be little doubt that this rendering understood itself to be apostolic in origin and already long received as such by universal consent, hence antedating Marcellus by faithful memory toward the ten momentous generations stretching back toward Peter and Paul. If something was to be misremembered, it seems unlikely that it would have been the concise baptismal formula assumed to be the core of apostolic tradition-ing (*COC* II, pp. 45–56). The burden of proof is on those who hypothesize changes in the baptismal formula to offer plausible reasons why such changes might have been necessary (Hippolytus, *The Apostolic Tradition;* Tertullian, *Prescription Ag. Her.* 12–23, *APT,* pp. 462–77; cf. Prosper of Aquitaine, *Grace and Free Will, FC* 7, pp. 352–57).

Irenaeus and Tertullian regarded the baptismal confession as ecumenically received by universal consent of the *laos* of all generations, locating its origin in the apostolic age. Consent to apostolic teaching as defined by the baptismal rule of faith has been from the outset virtually synonymous with Christian orthodoxy of all ages (Tertullian, *Ag. Praxeas* 2, *CC,* p. 22).

The Conciliar Tradition of General Consent to the Rule of Faith. Though a competitive apocryphal literature emerged, it was thought especially heinous to lie about the authorship of pseudoapostolic writings, or pretend that they were truly written by the apostles (Council of Braga II, A.D. 561, *SCD* 245, p. 94; cf. Duns Scotus, *Sentences,* Prologue Q1.6 ff.; Q2.14). The apostolic testimony was ecumenically considered to have been reliably delivered through the guidance of the Spirit to the church and consensually received as true, and remains sufficient for salvation (Second Antiochean Formula, *COC* II, pp. 27–28; Creed of the 150 Fathers, *COC* II, p. 59, Orthodox Confession of 1643, 96, p. 373; Conf. of Dositheus, 2, *CC,* pp. 486–87).

It is this rule of faith that had to be reliably interpreted by the ecumenical councils, especially the first against Arius, who taught unworthily of the Son, and the second against Macedonius, who taught unworthily of the Spirit (*Longer Catech.,* Eastern Orthodox Church, *COC* II, p. 457). Later Leo would write, "For no one may venture upon anything in opposition to the enactments of the Fathers' canons which many long years ago in the city of Nicaea were founded upon the decrees of the Spirit, so that any one who wishes to pass any different decree injures himself rather than impairs them. . . . What is universally laid down for our perpetual advantage can never be modified by any change" (Leo, *Letters* CV, CVI, *NPNF* 2 XII, pp. 76, 78).

The Creed of Caesarea of A.D. 325 concluded with the striking assertion that "we have thought all this in heart and soul ever since we knew ourselves, and we now so think and speak in truth, being able to show by evidence and to convince you that we in past times so believed and preached accordingly" (Eusebius, in Socrates, *CH* I.8, *COC* II, p. 30; cf. Theodoret, *CH* I.12).

By A.D. 431 it was consensually defined that no one within orthodox catechesis is "allowed to declare or at any rate to compose or devise a faith other than that defined by the holy fathers who with the Holy Spirit came together at Nicea" (Third Ecumenical Council, Ephesus, *SCD* 125, p. 51).

The Ecumenical Council of Constantinople III, A.D. 680–681, warned against anyone who might presume to "introduce or to teach or to pass on another creed . . . [or] introduce a novel doctrine or an invention of discourse to the subversion of those things which now have been determined" by conciliar consent (*SCD* 293, p. 115). The Seventh Ecumenical Council, Nicaea II, A.D. 787, roundly condemned those who "invent perversely and cunningly for the overthrow of any one of the legitimate traditions" of the church, and those who reject "all ecclesiastical tradition either written or not written" (*SCD* 303, 308, pp. 122, 123).

Gelasius articulated in A.D. 495 the central issue of authority in orthodoxy: "What pray permits us to abrogate what has been condemned by the venerable Fathers, and to reconsider the impious dogmas that have been demolished by them? . . . If in our ignorance we desire to learn something, how every single thing to be avoided has been prescribed by the orthodox fathers and elders, or everything to be adapted to Catholic truth has been decreed, why are they not approved by these? Or are we wiser than they, or shall we be able to stand constant with firm stability, if we should undermine those [teachings] which have been established by them?" (*SCD* 161, p. 67).

Conciliar Orthodoxy. Seven ancient ecumenical councils are generally recognized by Orthodox, Catholic, Lutheran, Reformed, Anglican, and free church Protestant traditions as representing the mind of the believing church: Nicaea, A.D. 325; Constantinople I, 381; Ephesus, 431; Chalcedon, 451; Constantinople II, 553; Constantinople III, 680–681; Nicaea II, 787 (scattered minority voices receive only the first three or four). To these seven the Western medieval consensual tradition regarded as ecumenical five Lateran councils (1123, 1139, 1179, 1215, 1512–17), Lyons I and II (1245, 1274), Vienne (1311–12), Constance (1414–18), and Ferrara-Florence (1438–39), and the post-Reformation Roman tradition recognizes Trent (1545–63), Vatican I (1870), and Vatican II (1962–66).

Coptic and Armenian traditions recognize only the first three. "If it be asked who is to decide whether the decrees of a Council can be proved from Scripture, we can only reply that this is for the whole Church, clergy and laity, throughout the world, to decide; and that in the case of the first six Councils, the whole Church has decided. (The refusal of the Armenian and other churches to accept the fourth and sixth Councils, and of the Assyrian Church to accept the fifth Council, seems to be due to misunderstanding, and not to any real denial of the truth for which those Councils stood)" (Moss, *CF*, pp. 228, 229).

Conciliar Authority Grounded in General Lay Consent. The authority of these councils is grounded in general lay consent under the guidance of the Spirit through the written word. What makes the general councils reliable is the presence of the Holy Spirit assisting in the interpretation of the apostolic witness. The *episkopoi* are not to "do anything without the *consent of all;* for so there will be unanimity, and God will be glorified through the Lord in the Holy Spirit" (Apostolic Canons 34, Synod of Trullo, *NPNF* 2 XIV, p. 596, italics added; cf. Council of Constance, *COD*, pp. 379 ff.; Marsiglio of Padua, *Defender of Peace*).

Upon the ground of this consent, the council decisions were regarded as "immutable" (Council of Nicaea II, canon 1, *NPNF* 2 XIV, p. 555; Dietrich of Niem, *LCC* XIV, p. 160). The Council of Ephesus prohibited composing "a different (*heteran*) Faith as a rival to that established by the holy Fathers assembled with the

Holy Ghost in Nicaea" (Ecumenical Councils, *NPNF* 2 XIV, p. 231). The human agency that remained in the councils and their history of interpretation, however, leaves the exposition of their decrees ever subject to potential distortion, even when they speak the truth (Calvin, *Inst.* 4.9.10–11).

Since Gregory I the formula has been received that one is orthodox who accepts what the ecumenical councils (*sanctae universales synodi*) accepted and rejects what they rejected (Gregory the Great, *Letters*, book I.25, *NPNF* 2 XII, pp. 81–82; book V.51–54; VI.66; cf. *SHD* II 350 ff.). Since the ancient ecumenical councils were *"constituted by universal consent*, he overthrows not them but himself, whosoever presumes either to loose those whom they bind, or to bind those whom they loose" (Gregory, *Letters* I.25, *NPNF* 2 XII, p. 82, italics added). At the time of Gregory's writing, there had been only four synods of general lay consent, which he summarized so neatly as to be reminiscent of a schoolboy formula, "The Nicene, in which Arius, the Constantinopolitan, in which Macedonius, the First Ephesian, in which Nestorius, and the Chalcedonian, in which Eutyches and Dioscorus, were condemned" (Gregory I, *Letters* IV.28, *NPNF* 2 XII, p. 159).

The ecumenical council that gathered at Chalcedon was determined to "make no new exposition" but merely to take away all ambiguity by the consent of the whole church in a "united exposition and doctrine"—"further than this we can say nothing." "This is the orthodox faith; this we all believe; *into this we were baptized*, into this we baptize," (Ecumenical Councils, Chalcedon, session II, *NPNF* 2 XIV, p. 249, italics added). It is not as though the council fathers "were introducing any thing that had been lacking in their predecessors, but in order to explain through written documents that faith concerning the Holy Ghost against those who were seeking to destroy his sovereignty." No one shall "bring forward a different faith [*heteran pistin*]" or "deliver a different Creed [*heteron sumbolon*]" (Ecumenical Councils, Chalcedon, Definition of Faith, *NPNF* 2 XIV, p. 263).

The councils were pledged to "not move an ancient boundary stone set up by [our] forefathers" (Prov. 22:28). For it was not merely human ingenuity that spoke in the councils but "the Spirit himself of God" confirmed by general lay consent (Ecumenical Councils, Ephesus, *Letter of Cyril to John of Antioch, NPNF* 2 XIV, p. 253; Duns Scotus, *Sentences*, III.24 Q1.4; IV.43 Q1.11).

The Ancient Conciliar Tradition Received in the Reformation.   This tradition of general lay consent continued and was received in the Reformation by the acceptance of the three creeds (Apostles', Nicene, and Athanasian [*Quicunque vult*]) as evidenced in the Augsburg Apology, the Smalcald Articles, Melanchthon's Thesis of 1551 (*The Three Chief Symbols, BOC*, pp. 17–23; cf. 287 ff.; *SHD* II, p. 352), and the Thirty-nine Articles (*CC*, p. 269). "The three creeds, Nicene Creed, Athanasian Creed, and that which is commonly called the Apostles' Creed, ought *thoroughly* to be received and believed; for they may be proved by most certain warrants of holy scripture" (Thirty-nine Articles, *COC* III, p. 492).

Melanchthon believed that Protestant teaching was grounded in a genuinely "Catholic association, which embraces the common consensus of prophetic and apostolic doctrine, together with the belief of the true church. Thus in our Confession we profess to embrace the whole doctrine of the word of God, to which the church bears testimony, and that in the sense which the symbols show" (*CR* XXIV.398; cf. XXI.349). He condemned as novel whatever might clash with the three ancient consensual symbols of the church (*symbola accepta; Loci, LCC* XIX, pp. 19–20). He refused to alter the ancient formulae, for "often a change of words begets also new beliefs" (*CR* XXIV.427; cf. XII.399, 568; V.582; III.826).

The Consenting Process

Insofar as irenic Christian teaching appeals to consensual exegesis, it is necessary to define carefully the principle of ecumenical consent and the nature of the consenting community, and to clarify how it makes judgments—whether regional synods have come to express general ecumenical consent, and to what extent Protestant teaching accepts the principle of catholic consent, whether contemporary consent may reject historic consensus, whether the deposit of faith may change with time, and whether following the apostolic tradition requires critical reasoning.

The Principle of Ecumenical Consent.   The problem of heresy is precisely this: the pliable metaphors of scripture may be perversely skewed by the sophistries of human wisdom, confounding what ought to be distinguished (Tertullian, *Prescription Ag. Her.* 1–6, *APT*, pp. 451–56). If there is no corrective effort accurately to identify the apostolic witness as classically interpreted, then each person every day would be invited to hold entirely different and even contradictory senses of scripture as true. The process of interpretation would in time become entirely balkanized and individualized, hence trivialized.

Rather than pit consensual tradition against scripture, the classic exegetes have viewed the Spirit as working within the process of the recollection, accurate transmission, and fit interpretation of scripture, not merely as inspiring the writing of scripture so as to have the effect of abandoning each reader to his own private, egocentric interpretation. Some may find it objectionable that in irenic theology the recurrent appeal seems to be not directly to truth or historical accuracy or correctness of interpretation, but to consensuality of interpretation. There is a truth claim embedded in consensual argument. The ecumenical assumption is that consensuality under the guidance of the Spirit comes closer to the truth of Christ than independent, individualistic rationality. The goal is the truth of irenic understanding through listening to the historic-exegetic consensus.

There is an analogy to this in science: the general consent of the community of experimenters is more reliable than the particular judgment of one experimenter. The consensus of the body politic or scientific community or *ekklēsia* is less likely to be tilted, hence closer to truth, accuracy, and consistency, than is individual insight (Vincent of Lérins, *Comm.* XXVII–XXXIII, *NPNF* 2 XI, pp. 152–56).

Laos as Consenting Community in Time.   The Spirit and the written word are constantly resisting and counteracting whatever ill effects may have been left as residues of errant teachers. Even though some church bodies have clung to partially unscriptural teachings or imbalanced exegesis that appears sporadically in their confessions, such errors are in the long run being tested by general lay consent, and in hard cases by documentary conciliar ecumenical definition, as in the case of Arianism. In this way the Holy Spirit continues to guard and oversee the church's teaching.

When a consensual council or regional synod seeks to clarify or better articulate the faith once for all delivered to the saints, it in effect is proposing an interpretation to the remembering church and humbly asking the church of subsequent generations for confirmation of that interpretation. Some symbols have been so widely and repeatedly reaffirmed (such as the Apostles', Nicene, and Quicunque Creeds) that they have gained uncontested prestige as truly expressing the mind of the believing church for all times and places. They cannot be overturned by an alleged future consensus without a radical denial of the faith of ancient Christianity and an absurd claim that the ancient church was irreversibly apostate.

Laos as Jury. The whole *laos* remains in effect the jury for the councils. Their verdict may take decades or even centuries to render and reaffirm. This process, says Paul, must "not use deception," nor "distort the word of God. On the contrary, by setting forth the truth plainly we commend ourselves to *every man's conscience* [*pasan suneidēsin anthrōpōn*] in the sight of God. And even if our gospel is veiled, it is veiled to those who are perishing" (2 Cor. 4:2, 3, italics added). This appeal to conscience lies "open unto all that they may test our actions" (John Chrysostom, *Hom. on 2 Cor.* VIII, *NPNF* 1 XIII, p. 318).

The "subsequent consent" of the church reserves for the whole *laos* the right and duty critically to review any alleged Christian teaching as to its apostolicity. If the freedom of the church to criticize is limited, the Spirit grieves. Even a modern council claiming to be ecumenical must stand under this critical judgment. This is why no teaching is catholic unless at the same time apostolic.

The Proximate Role of Regional Synods and Confessions. It has often happened that local or regional councils or crucial synodal decrees have gradually become ecumenically recognized as expressing accurately the mind of the believing church. A regional council, the Third Council of Carthage (397), for example, finally defined the canon of scripture in a way that in time became universally accepted, and similarly with the Council of Arles (475) on predestination and the Second Council of Orange (529) on gracious ability and the Eleventh Council of Toledo (675) on the incarnation. These regional councils have provided definitions generally recognized as ecumenical teaching, by their being reverenced and quoted authoritatively over many centuries of consensual reference.

Hence a local or regional body can attempt to define ecumenical teaching, but not without the subsequent consent of the whole church. Yet one must not assume that absolute unanimity is required for ecumenical consent; otherwise no question would ever be closed, and a single heretic or tiny cadre of objectors would be an absolute obstacle to ecumenical teaching and unity in Christ.

The Second Council of Orange and the Eleventh Toledo, like the Augsburg, Heidelberg, and Westminster Confessions within Protestantism, have come to receive wide affirmation, not because of the particular individuals who wrote or signed them, but because they have recurrently been affirmed by this broader lay jury as expressing the mind of the believing church as consistent with the apostolic witness. When errors like Nestorianism survive for many centuries, it is because a certain amount of truth resides hiddenly even in their error (Jacobs, *SCF,* p. 409). The errors of the Second Creed (The Blasphemy) of Sirmium, A.D. 357, had to be corrected by a longer conciliar process (Hilary, *De Synodis* 11; cf. Athanasius, *De Synodis* 28; Socrates, *CH* II.30; *CCC,* p. 35).

The conciliar process has the advantage of allowing certain questions to be open for further discussion that are not clearly defined in the confession. Meanwhile the language of the *regulae fidei* indicates the outer edges of toleration of viewpoints considered foreign or inimical to the communion of saints (Formula of Concord, *COC* III, pp. 93–95; Thirty-nine Articles VIII, *CC*, p. 269; Beveridge, *Synodikon*).

Lay Consent a Protestant Principle.   The principle of general lay consent is firmly embedded in the confessions of the Protestant Reformation. According to the Augsburg Confession, "nothing is taught in our churches concerning articles of faith that is contrary to the Holy Scriptures *or what is common to the Christian church*" (Augsburg Conf., *CC*, p. 79). This is supported by frequent reference to consensual teachers such as John Chrysostom, Augustine, and Jerome, and to the ecumenical creeds and councils. Augsburg cautioned against ecclesial burdens "introduced contrary to *the custom of the universal Christian church*" (Augsburg Conf., *CC*, p. 105, italics added).

The objection of the Reformers to medieval Catholicism was not that it had grown too old, but that it was too new—that it had invented "an unprecedented novelty" in relation to apostolic testimony (Augsburg Conf., *CC*, p. 85). Sadly, the novelty was introduced precisely through leaders appointed to guard the tradition, who "under pretext of the power given them by Christ, have not only introduced new forms of worship and burdened consciences with reserved cases and violent use of the ban, but have also presumed to set up and depose kings" (Augsburg Conf., *CC*, p. 98).

The congregational tradition more self-consciously assumed a due process of consent that is entered into "not only expressly by word of mouth, but by sacrifice; by hand writing, and seal; and also sometimes by silent consent, without any writing, or expression of words at all." "The ordinary power of Government belonging only to the elders, power of privilege remaineth with the brotherhood (as power of judgment in matter of censure, and power of liberty, in matters of liberty)," so that *legitimated church teaching assumed consent* of both leaders and laity (Cambridge Platform, *CC*, pp. 391, 394).

Baptist doctrinal statements strongly embraced the principle of lay consent, as in the case of the Baptist consensual statement of 1925, cast in the context of congregational polity. It argued that Baptist statements of faith "constitute a consensus of opinion of some Baptist body, large or small, for the general instruction and guidance of our own people and others concerning those articles of the Christian faith which are most surely held among us. They are not intended to add anything to the simple conditions of salvation revealed in the New Testament," and they are "not to be used to hamper freedom of thought or investigation" (*CC*, p. 345).

Whether One May Rely Solely on Contemporary Consent Without the Consent of Historical Christianity.   The classic Vincentian method of multigenerational consent differs from that of Schleiermacher, where consent depends upon contemporary monogenerational consent alone. Schleiermacher was too ready to focus upon the current consent of the believing community as if it could be separated from the cross-cultural historical testimony of the general consent of the laity over many generations.

Classic irenic theology runs against the stream of both pietistic and liberal theology insofar as both tend to seek out a constructive theology on the basis either of personal experience or the social context of the contemporary church. The hermeneutic of orthodoxy struggles constantly against willful distortions of historical consent, asserting the classic ecumenical historical consensus over against modern diminutions and reductionisms.

Whether the Deposit of Faith Changes in Time.   The notion finally must be rejected that there is a substantive change of Christian teaching through time by which the basic deposit of faith changes from one meaning to an entirely different meaning contradictory to that offered by the apostles. The church remains guardian of the Word made flesh in Jesus Christ as handed down to each succeeding generation with the same sense and meaning throughout the apostolic tradition, beheld through its movement into and through varied cultural experiences.

By now we know that human history has not finally brought the gospel to more perfect clarity than that grasped by the apostles and by Jesus himself. Nothing modernity can offer is able to transcend or make dated the apostolic testimony. Nothing the culture of this age creates is an improvement upon the truth made known in the deposit of faith (Newman, *Essay on the Development of Doctrine*).

Greater light is yet to be shed by the written word upon present and future generations, and clearer conceptions of its truth are always possible and prayed for, but the light and truth that will thereby come will not be shining directly from the historical situation but from the truth of the written word addressing that historical situation.

Nor is it possible to divide ourselves as contemporary readers of scripture in two, one a modern person and the other a Christian believer. For Christian belief is not incompatible with living today, though it resists the illusions of modernity.

When held accountable to classic criteria, much recent theology has become expert in lying, skirting the truth—with the adversary appearing as an angel of light, appearing to bear apostolic testimony while actually propagating the illusions of modernity. The ancient writers could lie too, but not with form-criticism or psychoanalysis or computer data bases. Those who have been through modernity and come to postmodern paleoorthodox consciousness can celebrate with the Chalcedonian teachers that the true faith is "defended with the best results, when a false opinion is condemned even by those who have followed it" (Ecumenical Councils, Chalcedon, *Tome of Leo, NPNF* 2 XIV, p. 258), which means: Those who have come through and beyond modern heterodoxies are those best able to defend against them.

Apostolic Truth Received, Not Invented.   Paul instructed Timothy to guard what had been committed to him (1 Tim. 6:20)—Vincent commented, Christian teaching consists in "what you have received, not what you have thought up; a matter not of ingenuity, but of doctrine; not of private acquisition, but of public Tradition; a matter brought to you, not put forth by you, in which you must be not the author but the guardian, not the founder but the sharer, not the leader, but the follower." The *ekklēsia* is not seeking to discover a new word but proclaim the ancient gospel ever anew, so that "by your expounding it, may that now be understood more clearly which formerly was believed even in its obscurity" (Vincent of Lérins, *Comm.* XXII.27, *FEF* III, 2173, p. 264). It is tampering with the evidence to pretend to improve upon apostolic testimony.

This does not imply that there can be no progress in church teaching. Vincent argued that there is progress, but true progress is not change. True progress is an advance in understanding of that which has been given fully in the deposit of faith (*Comm.* XXIII.28, *FEF* III, 2174, p. 265). An analogous principle had been ably set forth by Ambrose: The Holy Spirit, being of the very nature of God, "works in others a change to grace, but is not changed Himself," for "how is He capable of change Who is always good?" (Ambrose, *Of the Holy Spirit* V.65, *NPNF* 2 X, p. 102; John of Damascus, *OF* I.9, *NPNF* 2 IX, p. 12; Tho. Aq., *SCG* I.13, pp. 86–89).

Apostolic Tradition and Critical Reasoning.   To whom is the reasonable believer to listen? To one who has detailed knowledge of the historical conditions surrounding the contexts of the writing of scripture, yet who may have gained little understanding of the transmission of the exegetical tradition through its centuries of apostolic mission? Or one who has assimilated the tradition of exegetical memory without much historical critical sophistication? Or to one who has experienced directly the power of the Holy Spirit in a redeemed life? Better to hear all fairly and without ruling out learning from any.

Are we to listen more to one who has been grasped by the poetry and rhetorical beauty and aesthetic joy of theological reasoning and the sheer joy of Christian celebration, or to one whose mind is analytical and logical and who is unwilling to buy into sloppy thinking, and who is ready to cut to pieces wherever is evasive, who can spot a non sequitur a mile away? The laity has a right to expect teachers able to do both in the same sentence. The irenic theologian is afraid of none of these voices and learns to listen to all.

The reason the consenting community has listened so often to Augustine and John Chrysostom is that they do all of the above exceptionally well. The remembering church has tested and known this for a long time. These minds were not without either critical acumen or humility or joy or logical precision. This is what has made them perennially plausible and reliable theological interpreters.

Each of the great eight doctors stood as daily overseers of the church's liturgy and pastoral care and preaching at a particularly crucial time of its early formation, just after the first two ecumenical councils had winnowed away much dross, when the early vitality of the church of martyrdom had not waned, and when the ascetic spirit was still vital. We listen to them because the more we know scripture, the more we realize that they understood how the consenting community reads and compares the texts of scripture.

Whether Consensus Clarification Is Possible

The purpose of this section is to answer a series of objections about the possibility of discerning ecumenical consensus. At first it may seem doubtful that anyone can with confidence say anything about how the consenting community as a whole is reading scripture. If the laity is stretched out over twenty centuries, doesn't that encompass too many different interpreters to pretend that there is a consensus? Moreover, may opportunists use consensus as an unjust tool for special interests or political leverage?

How Does the Consenting Community Read Scripture?   Within the vast fields of orthodoxy there is time and room for many colors of permissible interpretation, provided the *regula fide* is not diminished. Orthodoxy is not looking for a single interpretation that would bind up the written word and make the Spirit strictly subservient to a passing culture or economic class or political interpretation.

Wherever consensual exegesis is attempted, there lurks the temptation prematurely to impose a presumed consensus that is not there. This study risks being presumptuous in that sense. The greater risk is to make no attempt and accede to indifferentism.

The temptation of modern critics is to give up prematurely in despair of saying anything at all about general consent. We remain always tempted to say either too much or too little about the quality of catholic consent.

Am I to conclude, because I do not see a fully formed consensus on millennialism, that I will be silent about it? No—I can and must say something, even though I must not try to say everything, because there is so much that has been consensually received, though many questions remain open for continuing exegetical debate.

The Scandal of the Cultural Particularity of Each Observer.   I am not unaware that I see the world as does a middle-class academic, a white, male middle American. My black, Third-World, feminist, and nonacademic friends, to their credit, give me frequent reminders of the myopic temptations that collect around this social location. That in itself should give pause to anyone who is listening to me from the Third World or as a woman, or as impoverished, or as black or Asian. Though I learn constantly from my African and Asian mentors and students, my exposure to their cultures has been far too limited to be able to incorporate the experience of African and Asian Christianity sufficiently. This I acknowledge as a serious weakness. Though I cannot overleap structural limitations of my consciousness, I pray that some who have lived in Africa and Asia with deep roots in ancient ecumenical teaching will in due time provide needed correctives.

This is not a show of humility but the simple awareness that I lack experience. But in principle isn't everyone similarly limited? Yes, but not everyone equally. To say that everyone lacks sufficient experience to search for an irenic ecumenical theology may become an excuse to evade the task altogether. I am a male trying to write for both women and men in the faith, a white, middle-class American attempting to articulate a consensus of Christian teaching that embraces persons of all races, classes, and nations. I would cease being catholic and evangelical if that were not my aim. That calls for genuine, not false, humility.

That means that I must listen all the more empathically for the lost accents, trying especially to hear the neglected and silenced voices of the Christian past and present. If I wrote an allegedly consensual theology without listening to Phoebe Palmer or Sister Macrina or Clare of Assisi or Teresa of Avila or Teresa of Calcutta, I would be more likely to be misled than if I had studied and listened to them carefully. So with the great African tradition of Christian teaching from Clement of Alexandria and Origen and Cyprian through Athanasius and Augustine. So with the great early Eastern tradition from Nemesius and Aphrahat to John of Damascus. The classic Christian tradition would have been immeasurably impoverished without African and Asian voices.

Do we risk calling ecumenical what is actually a very class-bound, race-bound, politically interested statement? Marxist criticism has for decades dismissed Christian theology as ideologically motivated to sustain the status quo. Here I must be judged by my critics, not by myself. If I have fixated upon my own culture and class or the North American continent or the European cultural heritage, I would indeed be guilty of the very uncatholicity and counterecumenicity against which I have protested. From my own self-perception, I feel myself to be a critic of my American culture and European culture on the ground of values that predate both, and far more indebted to classic African and Asian voices than to later European teachers.

Pre-European Christianity: The Older East and Younger West. The classic ecumenical consensus was maturely formed well before the formation of Europe. There was not even anything called or looking like Europe in any meaningful cultural sense when Athanasius was writing in Africa or John Chrysostom was preaching in Antioch or Nemesius in Syria.

It is worth noting that the majority of the eight doctors of the church were from Africa and Asia: Athanasius and Augustine were African, not European. Basil, Gregory of Nazianzen, and John Chrysostom were all from the ancient Near East, not Europe. That leaves Jerome, who though born at Strido, spent much of his adult life in Palestine, and Gregory the Great, who as a Roman diplomat was more of a world Christian than any of the other seven, who served for an extended time in Constantinople and who earnestly desired to go as a missionary to England, and Ambrose, who spent most of his life in Milan, first as governor, then bishop. Only the credulous can imagine that these eight teachers were primarily European when Europe had not even been invented, and would not palpably emerge until long after their passing.

Consider the non-European locations of all the seven ecumenical councils: Constantinople, Nicaea, Ephesus, and Chalcedon—all beyond the pale of what we today call Europe. Not one met on European soil or with European hegemony of leadership. Who attended? Europeans? Europe was not yet conceived. Rather the predominant leadership was largely African (notably Alexandrian) or Antiochene or Cappadocian, along with some who came from the southern edges of what would later be called Europe. Except for the Romans and proto-Europeans, the vast majority of key players in the ecumenical councils were African and Asian. The churches of the western Mediterranean and along the Danube, Rhône, and Rhine rivers were marginally represented but were by no means major influencers. Their cultures were only beginning to exercise modest influence upon the more powerful East and South.

So how can it be said that ecumenical Christianity in its formative period was predominantly Western or European in orientation? The "West" was its outcome, not its premise. This is no small point. Christianity in its early ecumenical formation was clearly shaped more by the East and Africa than by Europe and the West, assuming the straits of Bosphorus as the accepted dividing line between East and West. Little decisive happened in the history of salvation west of Palestine until Paul's mission took him from Antioch to Troas and finally to Philippi, when "during the night Paul had a vision of a man of Macedonia standing and begging him, 'Come over to Macedonia and help us'" (Acts 16:9; Irenaeus, *Ag. Her.* III.14, *ANF* I, pp. 437–49).

The Blending of Voices. A single language of faith was formed by mutual consent and dialogue, yet translatable into many languages. At first that unity of consent was a remarkable linguistic event called Pentecost. Only gradually did general consent become a broadening historical fact in the consensual language of the councils. The language of the apostolic tradition moved from its original Aramaic to the two great international language streams of that period, Greek and Latin, and in due time to Armenian, Coptic, Syrian, and much later many others. Note that English, German, and French were all extremely late arrivals in the classic ecumenic tradition. Relatively little Christian teaching is available in these languages prior to the sixteenth century—only a quarter of the span of the two millennia of ecumenical teaching.

No one is claiming that all agreed on every specific point. Rather the claim is that there was mutual general consent on key points of interpretation of the rule of faith and on most texts of canonically received holy writ. The general consent of the *laos* never meant that everything could be stuffed uniformly into a single language pattern or liturgy so as to disallow all other local or native forms of expression. Only those words were rejected that were thought to mislead the body of Christ into false premises or conclusions.

Did Political "Winners" Eliminate "Losers"?   The claim of consensuality is not that everyone got an equal vote, as if the making of dogma might occur in a way analogous to a modern popular election. It was, after all, the Holy Spirit who was forming the consensus. Rather, the claim of consensuality is that all who stood in the circle of celebration of God's coming consented to the apostolic testimony, and that testimony was received in a constrained way so as not to admit alien interpretations contrary to its intent.

Questions abound as to the extent to which Christianity was taken over by oppressors and unfair winners of political and economic battles: If so, what of the legitimate interests of all the heretics who lost? What about those who had deeply moving experiences of the Holy Spirit but never wrote them down? What about the women who never got to speak? What about the slaves who never had power and those classes and nations and cultures alienated from centers of power? What about the laity whose voices were supposedly expressed by the clergy—were they adequately represented in the ecumenical councils? What about those who were more humble and less politically skillful who had less influence on emperors and prelates? What about those whose voices we never heard?

Most of the answers to these questions hinge on a single point: the scandal of particularity in the history of revelation. Having treated this theme at several points I do not now need to rehearse it thoroughly again, but the gist of it is this: If God is to become known personally in human history, God must become human, enter our historical sphere, being born as we are born, being tempted as we are, dying as we die. This cannot by definition happen at all times and places, but only at some particular nexus of time. Hence revelation in history is deeply enmeshed in a particular history. It does not emerge out of an abstract idea of humanity in general. If the incarnation occurs in history rather than in the realm of abstract ideas, it must be remembered and transmitted through the hazards of historical change.

It is particularly misleading to talk about early Christianity as an oppressive history of "winners." It is implausible to think of the martyrs of the Decian persecution as winners, or Athanasius, who was exiled a half dozen times and chased all over the Mediterranean world as a winner, or John Chrysostom, who was exiled and died in political oblivion as a winner, or Jerome, who lost his struggle in Rome and went to the far country of Palestine to live the monastic life—were any of these on the winning side of the controversies of their day? No. Only the slow, populist, long-range general consent of the *laos* would recognize them as the great doctors of the church. Was Antony in the desert a winner? Or Amma Theodora? Were Polycarp or Felicitas or Perpetua or Cyprian or Ignatius—all of whom were killed for their faith?

If we imagine that the articulators of consensus were all upper-class, comfortable elitists, we have failed to read carefully the biographies of Justin Martyr and Benedict, or Lawrence of Rome, or Gregory of Nazianzus, who served in such a tiny village that it can hardly be found on any map. Think of Dame Juliana of Norwich, who literally lived in a hole in the wall of a church, or Francis of Assisi, who lived in a mud hut or slept outdoors, or Paracelsus, who was a vagabond physician most of his life.

There indeed were some who, like Gregory the Great, were born to wealth, but in his case he voluntarily gave away all his wealth to the poor and entered monastic life, as did Ambrose, who resigned his gubernatorial office when he was baptized. Augustine and Jerome, who were arguably the most learned, lived most of their lives under conditions that most today would regard as poverty and ascetic deprivation beyond description. Few early Christian writers spent more time in jail or hiding or being hunted and hounded than did Athanasius.

So are we really talking seriously about elitist winners who somehow formed a consensus that was coercively imposed upon the masses and the poor and oppressed laity? Hardly. They would have had no voice at all if they did not express the voice of the poor and the whole variegated symphony of the laity. All Athanasius was trying to do in the *homoousion* struggle was to articulate the mind of the believing church, its *laos* and its people, not his own private notions, against the politically elitist intrusion of those determined to twist it beyond all recognition.

The "winner-loser" distinction applies an oversimple modern competitive sports metaphor to complex historical processes. Fair-minded persons will look deeper before allowing such a generalization to become a general putdown of patristic wisdom.

Whether Lay Consent Is Ever-Broadening.   Is it possible to seek a further democratization, internationalization, demasculinization, and cultural pluralization of the process and base of ecumenical consensus? Yes. Though all too gradual, these correctives are already occurring. One could also add dehellenization, de-Europeanization, de-Westernization, and postmodernization to the list of correctives already at work.

But if my hunch is right, the poor and the women and the despised Cretans were also given voice in the early ecumenical councils. Such councils could not have happened or been received without the consent of the poor or without women or without the dispossessed or without the slaves, bond servants, and second-class citizens of the world, who were at the same time citizens of the holy city manifesting itself already through Word and Sacrament.

To whom did the leaders of the Council of Ephesus report? Only to God and select leaders? They were accountable to God and to diocesan leaders, but they were also accountable to a consenting *laos,* without whose consent they had no power to construe apostolic teaching. Hence it was never a sure bet whether a particular council would be accepted or not. Some were not. It often took a century or more for consensus to be established by general lay consent. Sometimes local synods made bad judgments and had to be rescinded. In those cases the larger *laos* was saying to the leaders of those regional councils, Sorry, you got it wrong—that was not the one mind of the believing church.

The Providential Contribution of Heretics. More must be said of the positive contribution of heretics to the formation of orthodox consensual exegesis. Within orthodoxy, it was remembered with gratitude that the Holy Spirit worked through and beyond heterodoxies to clarify consensual teaching. More so we to-day have good reason to reexamine the ancient heresies attentively in order to grasp anew the fragmented elements of truth that they were seeking awkwardly or insufficiently to bring forth, without losing sight of their distortions. Heresy should be studied as carefully as orthodoxy, and orthodoxy cannot be studied without the examination of heresy.

Those who falsely claim to have a right to the apostolic witness while distorting it must be shown to be self-destructively undermining that very right, as Tertullian argued (*Prescription Ag. Her. APT*, pp. 465, 488–93). It is perennially the nature of heresy to exaggerate some aspect of the truth into ultimacy or false proportion so as to neglect the appropriate balance of apostolic teaching; hence there is by definition always some fragment of truth even in the worst heresies (Cyprian, *Letters, FC* 51, pp. 176–92, 237 ff., 259–312).

Is it possible that some of these heretical voices have something distinctly new to teach us that they could not, under the politicized and polemical circumstances of their times, teach? What for example is the enduring contribution of the so-called Semi-Pelagianism that was consensually rejected as heretical? It had a grain of truth, though in particular emphases it was dead wrong. What is the basic contribution of the Montanists and Novatians and Donatists who were trying to purify the church, even though they went too far? What were the Subordinationists and Adoptionists and Eutychians trying to say that we still need to hear, even though they spoke in an objectionable way at crucial points? These are questions that remain open for legitimate debate within irenic ecumenical orthodox Christianity.

The Spirit and Lay Consent

The Spirit found ways of hearing and making known the voices of the underclass and women and the oppressed in the deliberative process leading to the ecumenical councils. This is an a priori argument: the Spirit finds ways to awaken general lay consent, even when worldly power or hierarchical organization seem to override it (Athanasius, *Defence of the Nicene Definition;* Calvin, *Inst.* 1.6.12–13).

The Spirit Did Not Discriminate. Any hierarchy is powerless without general consent, and there can be no general consent in early Christianity without taking into consideration the masses of poor people, the disinherited, widows, political aliens, and bond servants. Hence it is necessary to posit general lay consent even and precisely amid the hierarchical order that offends modern sensibilities (Cyprian, *Epistles* 32, *ANF* V, p. 312; Nemesius, *On the Nature of Man, LCC* IV, p. 226).

It seems fatuous to argue that women were so powerless or immobilized or despairing or lacking in identity and influence that they failed wholly to affect that general consensus. This would be to neglect the important role of women in several obvious points of ecumenical consensus formation. One case in point is the decisive influence of the empress Irene in the iconoclastic controversy leading to the judgment of the last Ecumenical Council of Nicea. And think of the vast influence of Monica upon Augustine, of Paula upon Jerome, of his mother Nonna upon Gregory Nazianzen, and of his sister Macrina upon Gregory of Nyssa.

The principle of lay consent requires the a priori premise of the intention of God the Spirit to awaken faith in the whole body. It is the Spirit who finally guarantees the valid transmission of the apostolic tradition through the general consent of the laity, not by popular vote. Popular vote at times flowed contrary to orthodoxy, as in the Robber Synod of Ephesus. The Spirit did not collapse or fail in resistance to such misinterpretations, which eventually were repudiated. The laity found that they could count on the Spirit over time to bring the gospel to light and to remember rightly and guide the church into all truth.

The well-formed ecclesial leader does nothing without the consent of the community of faith, lay and clergy, nothing on private cognizance or autonomous judgment. Cyprian made up his mind "to do nothing on my own private opinion, without your advice and without the consent of the people" (Cyprian, *Epistles* 4, 5, *ANF* V, pp. 282–83, 410).

The Meek Inherit.   It is the meek who inherit the earth. The laity is filled with meekness. This general consenting community is the final singer of praise in the celestial city. Prelates come and go, not all admirable. Only those teachers are recalled over centuries in the memory of the faithful who themselves were faithful to apostolic testimony (Tertullian, *Prescription Ag. Her.* 20–44, *ANF* III, pp. 252–65; Dame Juliana of Norwich, *RDL*, p. 96).

Lay consent is a reliable guide, but not in a year or decade, only over centuries. Only time winnows away the chaff. Whether the leaders were politically skillful (like Ambrose and Gregory the Great) or politically inept (like Jerome and John Chrysostom) seems to have made little difference. The people saw through the facade to the reality.

It remains a fact that these eight great doctors and seven ecumenical councils and three venerable creeds spoke in a way that the *laos* knew was true, and remembered as true over many generations of historical crisis, and as substantially consistent with each other. Hence their joint testimony has become celebrated, not because they were politically skillful or shrewd manipulators of power, but because the Spirit accompanied their testimony in the recollections of the faithful *laos* of subsequent times and places (*Longer Catech.*, Eastern Church, intro., *COC* II, pp. 445–55). Hence Augustine is quoted far more often than Pelagius in this company, Cyprian more than Novatian, Athanasius more than Arius, Cyril more than Nestorius, and Gregory Nazianzen more than the Anomoeans and tritheists.

The Power of the People.   There is thus a resilient populist element in the Christian structure of authority that, though it must not be overstated, should not be neglected. The people must finally vote on the views of the theologians and councils. They do this with their feet and bodies, by general lay consent. It is hardly a perfect instrument of political expression. But it works over time. There is no received apostolic tradition without an intergenerational community of recipients.

Herein lies the power of the people in the Christian structure of authority. It is not a formal vote taken at particular intervals. But it is a vote, even if by the pocketbook or by the silent withholding of consent.

Does the search for irenic consensus risk making of Christian teaching merely a populist nose-count of archaic sources, so as to leave out the active, present work of the Holy Spirit? Insofar as it does run that risk, the search for catholicity needs the corrective of apostolicity and the search for unity the corrective of holiness. No vision of the work of the Spirit is more present-oriented or historically grounded than that of the ancient apostolic testimony.

Whether Ecumenical Consent May Err

Whether Consent May Remain Ill Informed over Many Generations. Lay consent may become skewed and ill informed, needing the correction of an emerging generation of reform. Sadly the examples are many of a poorly formed regional consensus of Christian opinion that is ill corrected by another poorly formed consensus. Here this principle applies: one extreme or false expression of lay consent is not rightly or fully corrected by the assertion of another extreme.

History abounds with regrettable illustrations: the false consensus of the German Christians during the Nazi period was not corrected by the false consensus of pacifists who opposed all efforts at resistance to aggression. Thank God that amid these extremes were Christians of the evangelical Confessing Church of the Barmen declaration who were trying to bring sanity to the situation within Germany, and many who died to stop Nazi tyranny from spreading.

The defensive consensus of Massachusetts Puritans who drove out the Quakers was not rightly corrected by the countersacramental consensus of the Quakers, who rejected all visible means of grace. A reconciling ground was needed to mediate the best aspects of each, and complement them with other lost evangelical and catholic insights.

The false consensus of the medieval scholastic preachers who sold indulgences was not corrected by the false consensus of purist Protestant iconoclasts who overthrew the entire system of sacramental grace because of its abuses. Nor was the false consensus of Protestant enthusiasts who killed Socinian Unitarians corrected by the false consensus of the Unitarians, who would abandon the teaching of the triune God.

The false consensus of males in the church that eliminated too much of the effective influence of females for centuries is not corrected by a limited consensus of radical feminists who regard all expressions of maleness as oppressive. The false consensus of ultramontanism that led to the captivity of the state by the church is not corrected by the equally false ultranationalist captivity of the church to a particular national state.

These examples serve to show how often the popular consensus has been temporarily ill formed or misunderstood, how often the unity of the church has been battered, how often heresy has paraded as orthodoxy, and supposed orthodoxy mistaken itself for immediate revelation. Correctives are often needed for a false expression of general lay consent, but they are not secured by creating new excesses.

Consent Vindicated Eschatologically.   If such examples abound, how is it possible
to assert a viable long-term victory of general lay consent? Only eschatologically,
when wheat and tares are separated.

The unity, holiness, catholicity, and apostolicity of the church remains more an
a priori argument grounded in scripture and an eschatological argument grounded in Christology than an empirical argument based on finite evidences. Whatever
the limits of human argument, they have not led the attesting tradition to despair
over the truth of revelation, but rather to revel paradoxically in its meekness, concreteness, vulnerability, and historicity.

The Vulnerability of Consent.   How is the unity, holiness, catholicity, and apostolicity of the church to be defended when the process of popular consent risks
going so far awry? What are we to say when a temporary consensus becomes an
excuse for the perpetuation of unjust political interest? Any historical expression of apostolic consensus itself leads the faithful to pray for the forgiveness
of the distorting church, its vulnerability to egocentricity, racialism, sexism,
and nationalism.

Can one point to any time or place in which the consensus was utterly unblemished, or when challengers to the consensus were thoroughly demonic? One
might think of the period of the Decian persecution or of Chalcedon or of the
Franciscans or of the early Protestant Reformation or of the Wesleyan societies or
of the second great awakening. But all these are vulnerable examples. In each case
they involve specific historical ambiguities and the kinds of particular follies and
contingencies that occur in ordinary historical situations. Even the best expressions of the living *ekklēsia* in history continue to be a *corpus mixtum* of good and
bad fish, and wheat and tares to be winnowed only on the last day.

Tradition as the History of Exegesis

Whether Oral Tradition Antecedes Scripture.   The primitive oral tradition
should not be considered inferior to the written word. The preaching of the apostles was oral before it was written. From Adam to Moses there appears to be little
known written word of God, yet God's speech was being remembered and traditioned orally.

Jesus chose to teach his disciples not by writing but primarily by his life. His
words, which interpreted his life, were only later recalled and in due time written
down. The oral tradition took precedence over the written.

The same method of oral communication was received and traditioned by the
apostles, who spread the word to the world first by oral preaching and only later
by writing. Scripture became written down in order that the events attested might
be preserved accurately and teaching remembered precisely.

Paul valued highly and commended earnestly both the received oral tradition
and the received written tradition. Among the New Testament's earliest written
documents was Paul's dual appeal that the Thessalonians might "stand firm" and
"hold fast to the *traditions [paradoseis]* which you have learned from us *by word or
by letter*" (2 Thess. 2:15, NEB, italics added), that is, orally or by writing.

The concept of "holy tradition" has come to refer to the teaching handed down
by general lay consent to the apostolic teaching from generation to generation. All
the faithful, by general consent to this testimony, are united in one body, the

church, "the pillar and ground of the truth" (1 Tim. 3:15, KJV). One need not seek elsewhere for "the truth which we may have for asking from the Church; for in her, as in a rich treasure-house, the Apostles have laid up in its fulness all that pertains to the truth" of salvation (Irenaeus, *Ag. Her.* III.4; *COC* II, p. 449).

Whether Persecution Required an Oral Tradition. The written word of canonical scripture is to be openly proclaimed to all, but in addition to this Basil assumed that the church had received a reliable oral apostolic tradition guarded through centuries of persecution by silence and mystery. Protestants offer only grudging attention to this hounded, threatened, molested, countercultural tradition of martyrdom that was so persecuted and despised that it could not even write things down but had to commit them to memory.

Among numerous examples of holy unwritten tradition mentioned by Basil are triune immersion, common prayer on the first day of the week, bending knees in prayer and rising anew as an analogue of death and resurrection, and the sign of the cross. In all these cases there is no residue of written apostolic tradition, but that absence did not for the first five centuries diminish their authority, since these practices were received consensually as unwritten traditions from the apostles shrouded in silence "out of the reach of curious meddling and inquisitive investigation. Well had they learnt the lesson that the awful dignity of the mysteries is best preserved by silence. What the uninitiated are not even allowed to look at was hardly likely to be publicly paraded about in written documents" (Basil, *On the Spirit* XXVII.66, *NPNF* 2 VIII, p. 42).

By analogy, Moses did not make all parts of the tabernacle open to all. Unbelievers did not enter at all, and the faithful were admitted only to its outer precincts. The Levites alone were allowed to serve in worship offering sacrifices. Only one priest was allowed to enter the holy of holies, and that only once each year. In this same tradition of awe, and under conditions of state persecution, the apostles passed on certain matters from the beginning guarding "the awful dignity of the mysteries in secrecy and silence" (Basil, *On the Spirit* III.27, *NPNF* 2 VIII, p. 42).

Basil applied this analogy: "If, as in a Court of Law, we were at a loss of documentary [written] evidence, but were able to bring before you a large number of [oral] witnesses, would you not give your vote for our acquittal?" On this basis Basil cherished the phrase "with the Spirit" in the doxology "as a legacy left me by my fathers"—specifically citing Irenaeus, Clement, Origen, Dionysius of Rome, Gregory Thaumaturgus, Firmilian, Eusebius, and Africanus. "Thus I apprehend, the powerful influence of tradition frequently impels men to express themselves in terms contradictory to their own opinions." "How then can I be an innovator and creator of new terms when I adduce as originators and champions of the word whole nations, cities, customs going back beyond the memory of man, men who were pillars of the church and conspicuous for all knowledge and spiritual power?" Thus he argued that memories and practices evidently familiar to those generations immediately following the apostles and "continued by long usage" should remain highly valued in Christian teaching (*On the Spirit* III.29, *NPNF* 2 VIII, pp. 45–47; cf. Augustine, *Letters*, *FC* 12, pp. 252–53).

Yet oral tradition, however precious, is always subject to abuse and uncertainty, as we have found in form-criticism. Thus the focus of orthodox Christian teaching remains fixed upon the written word and the early written documents exegeting that word. Meanwhile Basil still calls the *ekklēsia* to listen attentively to those known oral and hagiographic traditions widely received as apostolic memory and practice, and not dismiss them peremptorily as if they had no value, as if modern readers could look only to documentary written evidences recognized under the rules of the game of reductionistic historical methods.

Scripture Awakens Tradition, Tradition Guards Scripture. Scripture is best read devoutly, as the direct address of God, with a sincere desire that faith may become active in love in a way that is not dissonant with consensual Christian teachers and councils. That interpretation of scripture is thought to be consensually received, hence "orthodox and genuine which, being taken from the Scriptures themselves (that is, from *the spirit of that tongue in which they were written*, they being also *weighed according to the circumstances* and expounded according to the proportion of places, either of like or of unlike, also of more and plainer), accords with the rule of faith and charity" (Second Helvetic Conf., *CC*, p. 135, italics added). The creed charitably received is thus the guide for Reformed hermeneutics. Ancient Christian writers "all, with one consent, will not have their writings matched with the Canonical Scriptures, but bid us allow of them so far forth as they either agree with them or disagree" (Second Helvetic Conf., *CC*, p. 135).

"The Holy Scriptures being recognized as the primary rule of Faith, we agree that the genuine tradition, i.e., the unbroken transmission—partly oral, partly in writing—of the doctrine delivered by Christ and the Apostles, is an authoritative source of teaching for all successive generations of Christians. This tradition is partly to be found in the consensus of the great ecclesiastical bodies standing in historical continuity with the primitive Church, partly to be gathered by scientific method from the written documents of all centuries" (Fourteen Theses, Old Catholic Union Conference, *CC* II, p. 548).

The Plain Sense of Scripture and Spiritual Interpretation. When conflicting interpretations of scripture arise, the classic rule of hermeneutics may be appealed to: "Ask your father and he will tell you, your elders, and they will explain to you" (Deut. 32:7). And the proverb: "Do not move an ancient boundary stone set up by your forefathers" (Prov. 22:28; Vincent of Lérins, *Comm.* 21, 27, *NPNF* 2 XI, pp. 146–47, 152). These boundary stones were consensually assumed to be firmly established in the early ecumenical councils and consensual exegetes, so that subsequently those who "rashly seek for novelties and expositions of another faith" were found wanting by general lay consent of "all the people" who say to these councils, "So be it, so be it [Ps. 105:48]" (The Lateran Council, A.D. 649, *SCD* 274, p. 105).

The Synod of Dort exhorted both universities and churches "to regulate, by the Scripture, according to the analogy of faith, not only their sentiments, but also their language, and to abstain from all those phrases which exceed the limits necessary to be observed in ascertaining the genuine sense of the Holy Scriptures" (*COC* III, p. 597). As "witness and keeper of holy Writ" the church is not free to "so expound one place of Scripture that it be repugnant to another" (Irish Articles, 75, *COC* III, p. 539).

Where a text has a plain sense or literal meaning, it is not to be stretched symbolically or tampered with. But where a text has multiple meanings and layers of potential interpretation, its spiritual meaning is sought and often adequately defined by the classic exegesis.

The earliest exegetes, Irenaeus, Clement, Origen, and Tertullian, while leaving room for varied interpretations of scripture, assumed a position of basic subordination of all legitimate interpretations to the rule of faith—the baptismal confession. Where one text of scripture appeared contradictory to another, they reasoned by analogy from clear passages, looking for spiritual insight consistent with the rule of faith, assuming that the Holy Spirit had veiled the outward expression for some purpose. As the person has body, soul, and spirit in union, so does the interpretation of some texts of scripture have not only a literal and moral, but also a spiritual or anagogic or mystical meaning (Irenaeus, *Ag. Her.* III; Clement, *Stromata;* Origen, *Principles* IV; *Ag. Celsus* V.60; VI.7; Tertullian, *Ag. Praxeas* 18–21). If an alleged spiritual meaning is projected upon the text, only bad exegesis can result; but when the spiritual meaning is itself embedded in the text as remembered in the light of the resurrection (as in the case of the testing of Abraham), true and reliable spiritual exegesis is possible, especially when repeatedly confirmed consensually (Vincent of Lérins, *Comm.* 24–28, *NPNF* 2 XI, pp. 149–52).

Text, Context, and Order: Against Proof-texting Quotes Contrary to Their Context. Some may charge that the method of classical Christian exegesis condones noncontextual proof-texting. The traditional hermeneutic allows that *a text may be quoted apart from its context provided it is not quoted against its context,* or used in some way contrary to that which is implied or assumed in its context. This assumes that the context is always open for further inquiry.

This distinction protects Christian teaching from being reduced simply to a detached historical exercise of investigating the contexts of the written word, a valuable activity but not identical with Christian preaching or teaching. It also protects Christian teaching from the tendency to overapply the text apart from its context anywhere and everywhere, uncritically, without attentiveness to the author's intent or meaning.

The classic exegetes developed a highly refined pattern of referencing. From apostolic times the privilege to cite scriptural loci has belonged to the freedom to preach. One cannot preach without quoting or in some way referencing scripture. It is precisely the attempt to preach without scripture that has undermined preaching in our time. Peter at Pentecost did not turn his sermon into historical inquiry into the root word for repent. Each time a text was quoted by the apostles it was assumed that further inquiry would be pertinent and possible that might challenge the application of that text or view it differently in a different context.

Traditional hermeneutics requires rigorous exegetical study to grasp the flow of events within which holy writ became spoken, recalled, written, and transmitted. This requires serious philological and historical investigation, which itself is complementary to theology but not substitutable for preaching or irenic theology. The recollection and transmission process is also subject to detailed historical investigation. The careful study of the transmission of the tradition often freights deep meaning for the contemporary hearer.

Ecumenical orthodoxy unapologetically makes reference to texts of holy writ without the tedious necessity of detailing their context. There remains another legitimate arena of inquiry in which each of these texts may under other circumstances be studied in their varied contexts. The fullness of this inquiry requires much more time than most persons have available, if they are daily involved in the real responsibilities of family and vocation. Hence God has provided an ordered sacred ministry distinguishable from and representative of the general ministry of the laity, which is being freed and supported in order to study all these matters in sufficient detail to make them clear to the whole *laos* of God. This is the very purpose for which ministers are freed from other vocational burdens, to engage in this daily study of holy writ, including its historical context, the social location of writers and speakers, the history of its transmission and interpretation, and the array of cultural differences through which the address of God the Spirit moves.

The freedom to cite texts without detailed historical inquiry into their context must not become an excuse for failing to engage in the exegetical inquiries that are presupposed in systematic theology. If this freedom is taken away, there is no place to begin, no first step to take, in systematic theology. If this freedom is abused by those who use it, there are problems at every hand in each instance of irresponsible proof-texting.

My reasons for rejecting a simplistic form of proof-texting have been repeatedly made clear both in this study and previously in *After Modernity . . . What?—Agenda for Theology*. Proof-texting without exegetical study tends to demean and distort the text itself by forgetting its context. I solicit correction in instances where I may have misapplied a text reference. This is one of the reasons I am writing—to welcome the opportunity to receive this correction—for how could it be received if I never took the risk of revealing my ignorance, so that my caring critics could never give me that gracious admonition I so truly need? So "smite me friendly" (J. Wesley, *Earnest Appeal, WJW* VIII, pp. 1–457).

An Invitation to Critics

Lactantius held Plato responsible for leading Ambraciotes to suicide by his errant counsel (Lactantius, *DI, FC* 49, pp. 214–15). The unclear or ambivalent writer remains partly responsible for inadvertent but understandable misinterpretations of his sentences, for each instance of which he will be accountable on the last day. I expect to be held accountable for this work, if not by human auditors, then by the divine auditor.

Now this work is virtually done, except for a sincere invitation to critics: Nothing would please me more than that this modest study be followed by a rigorous phase of criticism that would argue for or against its principal thesis that there is indeed a consensus of classic Christian teaching, and a distinct method of consensual exegesis. This would invite others to do a more thorough job than I have done in attempting to show that there is. I am much more confident of my basic thesis than of specific and detailed ways I have sought to apply and defend it in numerous particulars. A serious round of searching criticism would give the next generation of scholars something better to do than retrack my generation's prodigalities of attempted pseudotheological innovations.

Professional historians of the patristic period will know in detail what I have briefly acknowledged from the outset, that at every turn of this walk there were challenges made to the consensus I have sought to identify. There will be respected partners in dialogue who will identify the consensus in different ways. Many alternative options claimed consensuality and exegetical truthfulness. On what basis does one take an amalgam of these views and assert them as consensual?

Were it not for consensually received texts, and consensual received exegetes working over two millennia, the task would be out of reach. Happily we are not without received texts in making such a determination. I expect to be held accountable to these consensual texts. My attempt has been accurately to attempt to identify that general ecumenical consent that has been repeatedly confirmed concerning the whole course of Christian teaching, its discrete doctrines, and their connection. Admittedly this is one person's attempt seen from one historical and social location and not another. I welcome into this arena others who have wider experience and better skills to achieve these aims more precisely and fittingly. I hope it will not be too long before many misjudgments and imbalances of the preceding argument will be rightly pruned and duly amended.

Saying Too Much or Too Little.   In this study I have offered my opinion about what is consensual, and I look to critics for its correction. The other road that might have been taken is that of withholding judgment about what is consensual so as to avoid potential conflict with those skeptical of any hint of consensuality.

It would be misleading were I at length to concede that my effort to identify consensus is merely a matter of subjective opinion, for I have tried to set my personal preferences aside as much as possible. It would be claiming too much if I pretended to have identified the consensus absolutely and without bias. It would deny my most basic intention if I inadvertently communicated to my reader that my particular view of this consensus is a final or absolutely accurate one, or that my view could be substituted for the complicated multigenerational process of general lay consent, or that it could be treated as if it needed no further amendment or development.

Such disclaimers are not made out of despair of consensuality, but out of hope for its clearer identification. The laity have waited too long for unapologetic classic Christian orthodoxy, however vulnerable to criticism. Protestants have too long neglected early Christian writers, and too long pursued exegesis on an antitraditional, counterhistorical basis. The modern ecumenical movement remains dominated by the liberal Protestant *Aufklärung,* while post–Vatican II reforming Catholic theology remains overenamored of its own innovativeness.

The classic consensus has been silently waiting through a series of tedious modernities to become better identified. If the above effort is a faulty one, we can at least thank God that some rough start is being made on the road to a more fully formed postmodern orthodoxy grounded in irenic, ecumenical consensual exegesis. I hope this effort is not so badly flawed that it cannot serve as the basis for some better-conceived efforts by succeeding generations of orthodox scholars. We have good reason to hope that many bright young scholars will be working on these issues in the transitional decades into the third millennia.

Requisites of Theological Temperament.   Consensual theology cannot be done without much historical sweat, daily prayer for guidance, rigorous philosophical and philological research, sufficient meekness in expression and humility of judgment, constant exegetical searching, acute cross-cultural perception, steady love for the body of Christ, and readiness for the Spirit.

All these aspects go into trustworthy judgments of proximate consensuality. A supposed irenic teacher who lacked any of them would in that measure tend to lack reliable judgment. One expects from a judge a well-formed judicial temperament. So one has a right to expect of a theologian a well-formed theological temperament. This implies rigorous exegetical work, philological awareness, historical understanding, logical consistency, moral integrity, and a wide data base of perceptions of the current *Zeitgeist*. This is why balanced irenic theology is so rare. Few are ready to do this work.

The best theological reasoning (such as that seen in Gregory Nazianzen or Leo) is a work of sanctifying grace, not merely of convicting or prevenient grace, and surely not of autonomous freedom alone. It is a mature work of the Spirit. It seeks to articulate something that can be spoken only after much lived human experience, study, prayer, and historical listening. These qualities make it clear why young theologians need to take time to be well fitted for this life of labor. When I was a young theologian, my energy and imagination were matched by enormous deficits of historical depth, exegetical mellowing, and personal maturing. Had I attempted a systematic theology at age thirty-five (in 1966! God help us) it would have been an even greater disaster than the uneven work you hold in your hands. What slender threads we would have had of Augustine, Luther, Wesley, or Barth had their careers ended at age thirty-five. When I began at age fifty to write this study, I felt inadequate at every step along the way. Now as I draw it to a close I continue to feel that my life experience has been far too limited, my linguistic skills too thin, my historical knowledge too narrow, my knowledge of the tradition too fragmentary. I can only say with the father of the convulsive child, "Lord I believe, help my unbelief" (Mark 9:24), and with the publican, "God, have mercy on me, a sinner" (Luke 18:13).

Abbreviations

AAS Acta Apostolicae Sedis, official record of papal statements.

Acc. According to

ACC An American Catholic Catechism. Edited by G. J. Dyer. New York: Seabury, 1975.

ACE Stephen M. Merrill. *Aspects of Christian Experience.* Cincinnati: Walden and Stone, 1882.

ACW Ancient Christian Writers: The Works of the Fathers in Translation. Edited by J. Quasten, J. C. Plumpe, and W. Burghardt. 44 vols. New York: Paulist Press, 1946–.

AEG Ante-Nicene Exegesis of the Gospels. 6 vols. Edited by Harold D. Smith. London: SPCK, 1925.

AF The Apostolic Fathers. Edited by J. N. Sparks. New York: Thomas Nelson, 1978.

Ag. Against

AHS Edmund J. Fortman. *Activities of the Holy Spirit.* Chicago: Franciscan Herald Press, 1984.

AMW Thomas C. Oden. *After Modernity . . . What?—Agenda for Theology.* Grand Rapids: Zondervan, 1989.

ANF Ante-Nicene Fathers. 10 vols. Edited by A. Roberts and J. Donaldson. 1885–1896. Reprint. Grand Rapids: Eerdmans, 1979. References include book (in Roman numerals) and chapter or section number (usually in Arabic numerals), followed by volume and page number.

Angl. Anglicanism, the Thought and Practice of the Church of England. Edited by P. E. More and F. L. Cross. London: SPCK, 1935.

Apost. Const. Apostolic constitutions

APT Tertullian, Apologetic and Practical Treatises. Edited by C. Dodgson. Oxford: J. H. Parker, 1854.

Ari. The Arians. In *Works of John Henry Cardinal Newman,* edited by Joseph Rickaby. Westminster, MD: Christian Classics, 1977.

Aspects F.S.B. Gavin. *Some Aspects of Contemporary Greek Orthodox Thought.* Milwaukee: Morehouse, 1923.

Ath. St. Athanasius. 2 vols. In *Works of John Henry Cardinal Newman,* edited by Joseph Rickaby. Westminster, MD: Christian Classics, 1977.

BCP Book of Common Prayer (1662). Royal Breviar's edition. London: SPCK, n.d.

BDC William Robinson. *The Biblical Doctrine of the Church.* St. Louis: Bethany Press, 1946.

BHT Walter Wink. *The Bible in Human Transformation.* Philadelphia: Fortress, 1973.

Bk. Book

BOC The Book of Concord (1580). Edited by T. G. Tappert. Philadelphia: Muhlenberg Press, 1959.

BOConf. Book of confessions

Catech. Catechism or catechetical

CC Creeds of the Churches. Edited by John Leith. Richmond, VA: John Knox Press, 1979.

CCC Creeds, Councils and Controversies. Edited by J. Stevenson. London: SPCK, 1966.
CCF German Bishop's Conference. *The Church's Confession of Faith.* Edited by Walther Kasper. San Francisco: Ignatius Press, 1987.
CD **1** Karl Barth. *Church Dogmatics.* 4 vols. Edited by G. W. Bromiley, T. F. Torrance, et al. Edinburgh: T. & T. Clark, 1936–1969. **2** Shirley Guthrie. *Christian Doctrine.* Atlanta: John Knox, 1969. **3** Johannes Jacobus van Oosterzee. *Christian Dogmatics.* London: Hodder & Stoughton, 1874.
CDG G. H. Joyce. *The Catholic Doctrine of Grace.* London: Burns & Oates, 1920.
CDH Anselm. *Cur Deus Homo.* Translated by S. N. Deane. LaSalle: Open Court, 1966.
CDisc. S. Kierkegaard. *Christian Discourses.* Oxford: Oxford Univ. Press, 1952.
CD&ST Augustus Schultze. *Christian Doctrine and Systematic Theology.* Bethlehem, PA: Times Publishing Co., 1909.
CER M. Luther. *Commentary on the Epistle to the Romans.* Translated by T. Mueller. Grand Rapids: Zondervan, 1954.
CF **1** *The Christian Faith.* Edited by J. Neuner and J. Dupuis. New York: Alba House, 1982. **2** Henry Maldwyn Hughes. *Christian Foundations.* London: Epworth Press, 1951. **3** Claude Beaufort Moss. *The Christian Faith.* New York: Morehouse-Gorham, 1944. **4** Olin Curtis. *The Christian Faith.* Grand Rapids: Kregel, 1971.
CG Augustine. *City of God. NPNF* 1 II.
CH Church History. Eusebius of Caesarea. *NPNF* 2 I. *FC* 19, 29.
Ch. Dogmatic Constitution on the Church (Lumen Gentium), Doc. Vat. II.
ChF Friedrich Schleiermacher. *The Christian Faith.* Edinburgh: T. & T. Clark, 1928.
Chr. Christian
ChrF Olin A. Curtis. *The Christian Faith.* New York: Methodist Book Concern, 1905.
Clem. II "An Anonymous Sermon, Commonly Called Clement's Second Letter." *LCC* I, pp. 183–90.
C&M Charles Gore. *The Church and the Ministry.* 4th ed. London: Longmans, Green, 1910.
CMM The Catechism of Modern Man: All in the Words of Vatican II. Boston: St. Paul Editions, 1967.
COC Creeds of Christendom. 3 vols. Edited by P. Schaff. New York: Harper & Brothers, 1919.
COD Conciliorum Oecumenicorum Decreta. Freiburg: Herder, 1962.
C of E Church of England
Comm. **1** Commentary. **2** *Commonitory.* Vincent of Lérins, *NPNF* 2 XI. **3** John Calvin. *Calvin's Commentaries.* 22 vols. Edinburgh: The Calvin Translation Society. Reprint. Grand Rapids: 1981.
Common Catech. The Common Catechism. Edited by Johannes Feiner and Lukas Vischer. New York: Seabury, 1975.
Compend. **1** Compendium. **2** Thomas Aquinas. *Compendium of Theology.* New York: Herder, 1947. **3** William Burt Pope. *Compendium of Christian Theology.* 3 vols. New York: Phillips & Hunt, n.d.
Conf. Confession or Confessions

CPHS J. Moltmann. *The Church in the Power of the Holy Spirit.* San Francisco: Harper & Row, 1967.

CR Corpus Reformatorum: Huldreich Zwinglis sämmtliche Werke; Johannis Calvini Opera; Philippi Melanchthonis Opera. Edited by C. G. Bretschneider and H. E. Bindseil. Halle: Halis Saxonium, 1834–1860.

CSEL Corpus Scriptorum Ecclesiasticorum Latinorum. Vienna: Tempsky, 1866.

CT **1** Johannes Henricus Heidegger. *Corpus Theologiae.* Zurich: 1700. **2** Adam Clarke. *Christian Theology.* Salem, OH: Schmul, 1990. **3** Millard J. Erickson. *Christian Theology.* Grand Rapids, MI: Baker, 1983. **4** John M. Shaw. *Essentials and Non-essentials of the Christian Faith.* Edinburgh: T & T Clark, 1928. **5** Samuel Wakefield. *A Complete System of Christian Theology.* New York: Carleton & Porter, 1862. **6** Jonathan Weaver. *Christian Theology.* Dayton: United Brethren Publishing House, 1900.

CTC Johannes Wollebius. *Christianae Theologiae Compendium.* Edited by Ernst Bizer. Neukirchen, 1935. (English translation by John Beardslee, in *RDB.*)

CUP S. Kierkegaard. *Concluding Unscientific Postscript.* Translated by David Swenson. Princeton: Princeton Univ. Press, 1944.

CVL The Commonitory of Vincent of Lérins. With an Appendix by Bishop Beveridge on Consent of the Church. Baltimore: Joseph Robinson, 1847.

CWB Matthew Henry. *Commentary on the Whole Bible.* 6 vols. Iowa Falls, IA: World Bible Publishers, n.d.

CWEI Edward Irving. *Collected Writings.* 5 vols. 1864–1865.

CWI Charles Journet. *The Church of the Word Incarnate.* London: Sheed & Ward, 1954. References are to vol. 1 unless otherwise noted.

CWMS Complete Writings of Menno Simons. Edited by John C. Wenger. Scottdale, PA: Herald Press, 1956.

CWS Classics of Western Spirituality. 30 vols. to date. Edited by Richard J. Payne et al. Mahwah, NJ: Paulist Press, 1978–.

CWST St. Teresa of Avila. *Complete Works of St. Teresa of Avila.* 3 Vols. Edited by E. A. Peers. New York: Sheed & Ward, 1950.

DF Johannes Braun. *Doctrina Foederum sive Systema Theologiae didacticae et elencticae.* Amsterdam, 1588.

DI Lactantius. *Divine Institutes.* FC 49. ANF VII.

Dir. Ec. Directory on Ecumenism. Secretariat for Promoting Christian Unity, 1967.

DNF George Bull. *Defensio Fidei Nicaenae.* 1685. 2 vols. Oxford: J. H. Parker, 1851.

Doc. Vat. II W. M. Abbott, ed. *Documents of Vatican II.* New York: America Press, 1966.

Dogm. **1** Dogmatic, Dogmatics. **2** Emil Brunner. *Dogmatics.* Philadelphia: Westminster Press, 1962. (*The Christian Doctrine of the Church, Faith, and Consummation,* unless otherwise indicated.)

DS Enchiridion Symbolorun, Definitionum et Declarationum de Rebus Fidei et Morum. Compiled by H. Denzinger, 1854, continued by C. Bannwart et al. Berlin: Herder, 1922.

DSWT Thomas C. Oden. *Doctrinal Standards in the Wesleyan Tradition.* Grand Rapids: Francis Asbury Press, 1988.

DT **1** Joseph Pohle. *Dogmatic Theology.* 12 vols. Edited by Arthur Preuss. St. Louis: B. Herder, 1922. **2** Heinrich Schmid. *Doctrinal Theology of the Evangelical*

Lutheran Church. 3d ed. Minneapolis: Augsburg, 1899. **3** Francis Hall. *Dogmatic Theology.* New York: Longmans, Green, 1907–1922.

DUCC Dictionnaire universel et complète des Conciles. Translated by J. P. Migne. Paris: Aux Ateliers Catholiques du Petit-Montrouge, 1847.

EA D. Martin Luthers sämmtliche Werke. Frankfurt and Erlangen, 1826–1857, Erlanger Ausgabe, volume number followed by page number.

Ec. Decree on Ecumenism (Unitatis redintegratio). Doc. Vat. II.

EC John Pearson. *An Exposition of the Creed.* Oxford, 1659.

ECD J. N. D. Kelly. *Early Christian Doctrines.* New York: Harper, 1959.

ECF Early Christian Fathers. Edited by H. Bettenson. London: Oxford Univ. Press, 1969.

ECW Early Christian Writers: The Apostolic Fathers. Translated by Maxwell Staniforth. London: Penguin Books, 1968.

ED Thomas N. Ralston. *Elements of Divinity.* New York: Abingdon, 1924.

EDQ Augustine. *Eighty-three Different Questions. FC* 70.

EF Helmut Thielicke. *The Evangelical Faith.* 3 vols. Grand Rapids: Eerdmans, 1974–1982.

EP Joseph J. Rickaby. *The Epistle of St. Paul to the Colossians.* London: n.p., 1921.

Epist. Epistle or Epistles

ERD Daniel Whedon. *Essays, Reviews, and Discourses.* New York: Phillips & Hunt, 1887.

ET English translation

ETA David Hollaz (or Hollatz). *Examen Theologicum Acroamaticum.* 1707. Leipzig: B. C. Brietkopf, 1763.

Evang. Evangelical

EVO Darwell Stone. *Episcopacy and Valid Orders in the Primitive Church.* London: Longmans, 1926.

Expos. Exposition

FC The Fathers of the Church: A New Translation. 80 vols. to date. Edited by R. J. Deferrari. Washington, DC: Catholic Univ. Press, 1947–.

FEF The Faith of the Early Fathers. 3 vols. Edited by William A. Jurgens. Collegeville, MN: Liturgical Press, 1970–.

FGG From Glory to Glory: Texts from Gregory of Nyssa's Mystical Writings. Translated by H. Musurillo. Crestwood, NY: St. Vladimir's Seminary Press, 1979.

F&T S. Kierkegaard. *Fear and Trembling and Sickness unto Death.* Translated by W. Lowrie. Princeton: Princeton Univ. Press, 1968.

FTCT Leonardus Riisen. *Francisci Turretini Compendium Theologiae.* Amsterdam, 1695.

Gk. Greek

GLNT J. H. Thayer and C. Grimm. *Greek-English Lexicon of the New Testament.* Grand Rapids: Zondervan, 1965.

HC K. J. von Hefele. *History of the Councils.* 5 vols. Edinburgh: T. & T. Clark, 1872–1896.

HCCC Eusebius. *The History of the Church from Christ to Constantine.* Translated by G. A. Williamson. New York: NYU Press, 1966.

HCS J. T. McNiell. *A History of the Cure of Souls.* New York: Harper & Brothers, 1951.

HCT Benjamin Field. *The Student's Handbook of Christian Theology.* New York: Methodist Book Concern, 1887.

Heid. Heidelberg

Her. Heresies

Hom. Homilies or Homily

HPEC Hymnal, The Protestant Episcopal Church. New York: Church Pension Fund, 1916.

HS **1** Alasdair Heron. *The Holy Spirit.* Philadelphia: Westminster Press, 1983. **2** G. T. Montague. *The Holy Spirit: Growth of a Biblical Tradition.* New York: Paulist Press, 1976. **3** John F. Walvoord. *The Holy Spirit.* Grand Rapids, MI: Zondervan, 1958.

IBC Interpretation: A Bible Commentary for Teaching and Preaching. Louisville: John Knox Press, 1987–.

IBHS Yves Congar. *I Believe in the Holy Spirit.* 2 vols. New York, 1983.

IC Joseph Ratzinger. *Introduction to Christianity.* New York: Herder & Herder, 1970.

ICD T. E. Jessop. *Introduction to Christian Doctrine.* New York: T. Nelson, 1960.

ICNT Paul S. Minear. *Images of the Church in the New Testament.* Philadelphia: Westminster, 1960.

Inst. John Calvin. *Institutes of the Christian Religion. LCC,* vols. 20, 21. References are by book and chapter number, at times followed by section number.

ITE Francis Turretin. *Institutio Theologiae elencticae.* Utrecht and Amsterdam, 1701.

ITLC Gulielmus Bucanus. *Institutiones Theologicae seu Locorum Communium Christiane Religionis.* Geneva: Torunes, 1658.

JJW The Journal of the Reverend John Wesley. 8 vols. Edited by Nehemiah Curnock. London: Epworth, 1909–1916.

JWO John Wesley. Edited by Albert C. Outler. *LPT.* New York: Oxford Univ. Press, 1964.

ĸjv King James Version of the Bible, 1611.

LACT Library of Anglo-Catholic Theology. 83 Vols. Oxford: J. H. Parker, 1841–1863.

LC A Compend of Luther's Theology. Edited by H. T. Kerr. Philadelphia: Westminster Press, 1943.

LCC The Library of Christian Classics. 26 vols. Edited by J. Baillie, J. T. McNeill, and H. P. Van Dusen. Philadelphia: Westminster, 1953–1961.

LCF The Later Christian Fathers. Edited by H. Bettenson. Oxford: Oxford Univ. Press, 1970.

LCHS Athanasius. *Letters of St. Athanasius Concerning the Holy Spirit, To Serapion.* Translated by C. R. B. Shapland. New York: Philosophical Library, 1951.

Lect. Lecture or Lectures

LEP Richard Hooker. *Of the Laws of Ecclesiastical Polity.* 2 vols. New York: E. P. Dutton, 1960–1963.

LG Thomas C. Oden. *The Living God.* Vol. 1 of *Systematic Theology.* San Francisco: Harper & Row, 1987.

LH S. W. Duffield. *The Latin Hymn-Writers.* New York: Funk & Wagnalls, 1889.

Lit. Constitution on the Sacred Liturgy (Sancrosantum Concilium). Doc. Vat. II.

LLA Library of Liberal Arts. Indianapolis: Bobbs-Merrill, 1960–.

Loci Melanchthon. *Loci Commumnes Theologici. LCC* XIX, pp. 18–154.

LT John Gerhard. *Loci Theologici.* 1610–1621. 22 vols. Tubingen: n.p., 1762–1787.

Luth. Sym. J. L. Neve. *Introduction to Lutheran Symbolics.* Burlington, IA: German Literary Board, 1917.

LW Luther's Works. 54 vols. to date. St. Louis: Concordia, 1960–.

Mand. Pastor of Hermas. *Mandates. ANF* II.

MCD John S. Banks. *A Manual of Christian Doctrine.* 1st American ed. Edited by J. J. Tigert. Nashville: Lamar & Barton, 1924.

MCT **1** Nathaniel Burwash. *Manual of Christian Theology.* 2 vols. London: Horace Marshall, 1900. **2** Matthias Joseph Wilhelm. *A Manual of Catholic Theology.* Edited by T. B. Scannell. New York: Benzinger, 1908–1909.

Med. Johann Heinrich Heidegger. *Medulla Theologiae Christianiae.* Tiguri: D. Gessner, 1696.

MH Methodist Hymnal. Nashville: United Methodist Publishing House, 1966.

MHD Bernhard John Otten. *A Manual of the History of Dogma.* 2 vols. London: Herder, 1917–1918.

Mis. Decree on the Church's Missionary Activity (Ad Gentes). Doc. Vat. II.

MLS Martin Luther: Selections from His Writings. Edited by John Dillenberger. New York: Doubleday, 1961.

MMIS Reinhold Niebuhr. *Moral Man and Immoral Society.* New York: Scribner, 1960.

MPG Patrologia Graeca. 162 vols. Edited by J. B. Migne. Paris: Migne, 1857–1876. Volume number followed by column number.

MPL Patrologia Latina. 221 vols. Edited by J. B. Migne. Paris: Migne, 1841–1865. Volume number followed by column number. *General Index,* Paris, 1912.

MS A. J. Gordon. *The Ministry of the Spirit.* Philadelphia: American Baptist Publication Society, 1894.

MTEC Vladimir Lossky. *Mystical Theology of the Eastern Church.* London: J. Clarke, 1957.

NA J. M. Campbell. *The Nature of the Atonement.* Cambridge: Macmillan, 1856.

NB John Wesley. *The New Birth.* Edited by T. Oden. San Francisco: Harper & Row, 1984.

NDM Reinhold Niebuhr. *Nature and Destiny of Man.* 2 vols. New York: Scribner's, 1941, 1943.

NE A New Eusebius. Edited by J. Stevenson. London: SPCK, 1957.

NEB New English Bible

NLG Alvin F. Kimel, Jr. *A New Language for God?* Shaker Heights. OH: Episcopalians United, 1990.

NPNF A Select Library of the Nicene and Post-Nicene Fathers of the Christian Church. 1st Series, 14 vols. 2d series, 14 vols. Edited by H. Wace and P. Schaff. New York: Christian, 1887–1900. References are by title, book or chapter, and subsection, and *NPNF* series number, volume, and page number.

NR Declaration on the Relation of the Church to Non-Christian Religions (Nostra aetate). Doc. Vat. II.

NRSV New Revised Standard Version

NT New Testament

NTT **1** W. Beyschlag. *New Testament Theology.* 2 vols. London, 1893. **2** Donald Guthrie. *New Testament Theology.* Downers Grove, IL: Intervarsity Press, 1981.

NUNT John Wesley. *Explanatory Notes upon the New Testament.* Naperville, IL: Allenson, 1958.

NUOT John Wesley. *Explanatory Notes upon the Old Testament.* Salem, OH: Schmul, 1975.

OCD Darwell Stone. *Outlines of Christian Dogma.* New York: Longmans, Green, 1900.

OCT William Newton Clarke. *An Outline of Christian Theology.* Edinburgh: T. & T. Clark, 1913.

OED Oxford English Dictionary.

OF John of Damascus. *On the Orthodox Faith. NPNF* 2 IX. *FC* 37.

OFP Origen. *On First Principles.* Translated by G. W. Butterworth. Gloucester, MA: Peter Smith, 1973.

OFP, CWS On First Principles. In *Origen: Selected Works,* translated by Rowan Greer. *CWS.* New York: Paulist Press, 1979.

OO Francisco Suarez. *Omnia Opera.* 29 vols. Paris: Ludovicum Vivès, 1856–1878.

OOT Archibald Alexander Hodge. *Outlines of Theology.* Grand Rapids: Eerdmans, 1928.

Orat. Oration or Orations

PACP J. Wesley. *Plain Account of Christian Perfection.* London: Epworth Press, 1952.

PCMT A. M. Fairbairn. *The Place of Christ in Modern Theology.* New York: Scribner, 1900.

PF S. Kierkegaard. *Philosophical Fragments.* Princeton: Princeton Univ. Press, 1962.

Philok. Philokalia. 3 vols. Edited by G. E. H. Palmer et. al. Boston: Faber & Faber, 1979.

PJC H. R. Mackintosh. *The Doctrine of the Person of Jesus Christ.* New York: Scribner, 1931.

PPS Parochial and Plain Sermons. In *Works of John Henry Cardinal Newman.* Edited by Joseph Rickaby. 8 vols. Westminster, MD: Christian Classics, 1977.

PPSW Phoebe Palmer: Selected Writings. Edited by Thomas C. Oden. Sources of American Spirituality Series. Mahwah, NJ: Paulist Press, 1988.

PS Wilbur Tillett. *Personal Salvation.* Nashville: Barbee & Smith, 1902.

PW Richard Baxter. *Practical Works.* 23 vols. London: James Duncan, 1830.

RAH Wolfhart Pannenberg, ed. *Revelation as History.* New York: Macmillan, 1968.

RD Heinrich Heppe. *Reformed Dogmatics.* Translated by G. T. Thomson. London: George Allen & Unwin, 1950.

RDL Julian of Norwich. *Revelations of Divine Love.* Edited by Francis Beer. Heidelberg: 1978.

RDB Reformed Dogmatics: Seventeenth-Century Reformed Theology Through the Writings of Wollebius, Voetius, and Turretin. Edited by John W. Beardslee III. Grand Rapids: Baker, 1965.

RMWC H. Richard Niebuhr. *Radical Monotheism and Western Culture.* New York: Harper, 1960.

RR Karl Rahner. *A Rahner Reader.* Edited by G. A. McCool. Greenwich, CT: Seabury, 1975.

SA Thomas C. Oden. *The Structure of Awareness.* Nashville: Abingdon, 1968.

SCD Sources of Christian Dogma (Enchiridion Symbolorum). Edited by Henry Denzinger and translated by Roy Deferrari. New York: Herder, 1954.

SCDoc. Isaak A. Dorner. *System of Christian Doctrine.* Edinburgh: T. & T. Clark, 1898. References are to volume four if not otherwise indicated.

SCF **1** Henry E. Jacobs. *A Summary of the Christian Faith.* Philadelphia: General Council of Publications, 1905. **2** Hugh of St. Victor. *On the Sacraments of the Christian Faith.* Cambridge, MA: Mediaeval Academy of America, 1951.

SCG Thomas Aquinas. *Summa Contra Gentiles.* 5 vols. Edited by Anton Pegis. Garden City, NY: Image Books, 1955–1957.

SD Søren Kierkegaard. *The Sickness unto Death.* Princeton: Princeton Univ. Press, 1954.

Sent. Sentences of Peter Lombard. Commentaria in Quator Libros Sententiarum. In *Works of Bonaventure,* 5 vols., translated by Jose de Vinck. Patterson, NJ: St. Anthony Guild Press, 1960–1970.

SHD Reinhold Seeberg. *Textbook of the History of Doctrines.* Grand Rapids: Baker, 1952. Unless otherwise noted, all references are to volume one.

Sim. Pastor of Hermas. *Similitudes. ANF* II.

SL Luis M. Bermejo. *The Spirit of Life.* Gujarat, India: Gujarat Sahitya Prakish, 1987.

SML Sermons of Martin Luther. 8 vols. Edited by J. N. Lenker. Grand Rapids: Baker, 1988.

ST **1** Thomas Aquinas. *Summa Theologica.* 3 vols. Edited by English Dominican Fathers. New York: Benziger, 1947. References include part, subpart, question number, and volume and page number of Benziger edition. **2** Louis Berkhof. *Systematic Theology.* Grand Rapids: Eerdmans, 1962. **3** S. Gamertsfelder. *Systematic Theology.* Harrisburg, PA: Evangelical Publishing House, 1952. **4** C. Hodge. *Systematic Theology.* 3 vols. Reprint. Grand Rapids: Eerdmans, 1986. **5** J. Miley. *Systematic Theology.* Reprint. Peabody, MA: Hendrickson, 1989. **6** Miner Raymond. *Systematic Theology.* 3 vols. Cincinnati: Hitchcock & Walden, 1877–1879. **7** Lewis Sperry Chafer. *Systematic Theology.* 8 vols. Dallas: Dallas Seminary Press, 1947. **8** A. H. Strong. *Systematic Theology.* **9** Thomas O. Summers. *Systematic Theology.* 2 vols. Edited by J. J. Tigert. Nashville: Methodist Publishing House South, 1888. **10** P. Tillich. *Systematic Theology.* 3 vols. Chicago: Univ. of Chicago Press, 1951–1963.

STCC Ernst Troeltsch. *Social Teachings of the Christian Churches.* 2 vols. New York: Macmillan, 1931.

STCR James O. Buswell. *Systematic Theology of the Christian Religion.* Grand Rapids: Zondervan, 1962.

SW John Calvin, Selections from His Writings. Edited by John Dillenberger. Missoula, MT: Scholars' Press, 1975.

Syst. Systematic

TAAAL John Calvin. *Treatises Against the Anabaptists and Against the Libertines.* Edited by B. W. Farley. Grand Rapids: Baker Book House, 1982.

TATT St. *Thomas Aquinas' Theological Texts.* Edited by Thomas Gilby. London: Oxford Univ. Press, 1955.

TC **1** Søren Kierkegaard. *Training in Christianity.* Princeton: Princeton Univ. Press, 1941. **2** Benedictus Pictet. *Theologia Christiana.* Geneva, 1696. **3** Hans Küng. *The Church.* New York: Doubleday, 1976.

TCI Amos Binney, with Daniel Steele. *Theological Compend Improved.* New York: Phillips & Hunt, 1875.

TCNT Twentieth-Century New Testament

TDNT Theological Dictionary of the New Testament. 9 vols. Edited by G. Kittel and translated by G. W. Bromiley. Grand Rapids: Eerdmans, 1964–1974.

TDP Freidrich Quenstedt. *Theologia Didactico-Polemica.* 4 parts in 1 vol. Wittenberg: J. L. Quensted, 1691.

TF Thomas F. Torrance. *The Trinitarian Faith.* Edinburgh: T. & T. Clark, 1988.

TFR Hulreich Zwingli. *Commentary on True and False Religion.* WZ III, pp. 43–343.

TGS Theology of God—Sources. Edited by K. Kehoe. New York: Bruce, 1971.

Tho. Aq. Thomas Aquinas

TI **1** Richard Watson. *Theological Institutes.* 2 vols. Edited by John M'Clintock. New York: Carlton & Porter, 1850. **2** Karl Rahner. *Theological Investigations.* London: Darton, Longman & Todd.

TM John Harries. *A Handbook of Theology: Homiletical Manual of Christian Doctrine.* London: C. H. Kelly, 1903.

TNC Martin Chemnitz. *The Two Natures in Christ.* Translated by J. A. O. Preus. St. Louis: Concordia Publishing House, 1971.

TNT **1** George E. Ladd. *A Theology of the New Testament.* Grand Rapids: Eerdmans, 1974. **2** George B. Stevens. *The Theology of the New Testament.* Edinburgh: T. & T. Clark, 1908.

Trent The Canons and Decrees of the Council of Trent. Edited by H. J. Schroeder. Rockford, IL: TAN, 1978.

Trin. Trinity

TSD J. H. Alsted, *Theologia Scholastica Didactica.* Hanover, 1618.

TWS Albert C. Outler. *Theology in the Wesleyan Spirit.* Nashville: Tidings, 1975.

UTS Caspar Brochmann. *Universae Theologiae Systema,* 1633.

Vat. Vatican

Vis. Visions. Pastor of Hermas. *ANF* II.

Vlg. Vulgate

WA Weimarer Ausgabe. Dr. Martin Luthers Werke. Kritische Gemsamtausgabe. Weimar: Hermann Boehlau, 1883–. References are to volume number followed by page number.

WCB Josef Pieper. *What Catholics Believe.* New York: Pantheon, 1951.

WCC World Council of Churches

Werke Huldreich Zwingli's Werke. 8 vols. Edited by M. Schuler and J. Schulthess. Zurich: Schulthess, 1828.

WHNS A Collection of Hymns for the Use of the People Called Methodists, with a New Supplement. London: Wesleyan Conference Office, 1876. Referenced by hymn number.

WHS Abraham Kuyper. *The Work of the Holy Spirit.* New York: Funk and Wagnalls, 1900.

WJE The Works of Jonathan Edwards. 2 vols. Carlisle, PA: Banner of Truth Trust, 1974.

WJW Works of the Rev. John Wesley. 14 vols. Edited by Thomas Jackson. London: Wesleyan Conference Office, 1872.

WJWB The Works of John Wesley. Bicentennial ed. Edited by Frank Baker. Nashville: Abingdon, 1975–. (Formerly published by Oxford Univ. Press.)

WL Thomas C. Oden. *The Word of Life.* Vol. 2 of *Systematic Theology.* San Francisco: Harper & Row, 1989.

WLS What Luther Says. 3 vols. Edited by E. Plass. St. Louis: Concordia, 1959.

WML Works of Martin Luther: An Anthology. Philadelphia ed. 6 vols. Philadelphia: Muhlenberg Press, 1943.

WNUUD *Webster's New Universal Unabridged Dictionary.* 2d ed. New York: World Publishing, 1983.

Works **1** *Complete Works of John Bunyan.* 4 vols. London: Virtue & Yorston, n.d. **2** *Works of John Fletcher.* 4 vols. Salem, OH: Schmul, 1974. **3** *Works of John Owen.* 16 vols. Reprint. Carlisle, PA: Banner of Truth, 1965. **4** *Works of Thomas Goodwin.* 12 vols. Edinburgh: J. Nichol, 1861–1866.

WZ *The Latin Works of Huldreich Zwingli.* 3 vols. Translated by S. M. Jackson. Philadelphia: Heidelberg Press, 1929.

Name Index

Subject Index

Scripture Index

New Testament

92, 160, 228, 286, 353, 384, 484; **4:2, 3,**
484; **4:4,** 92; **4:5,** 286; **4:6,** 160; **4:10, 11,**
228; **4:13,** 16; **4:16, 17,** 384; **5:1,** 116, 386,
388, 393; **5:1–8,** 386, 393, 400; **5:1–21,**
116; **5:2,** 81; **5:5–10,** 143, 200, 394; **5:7,** 10,
131, 205, 220, 461; **5:8,** 396, 460; **5:10,** 388,
392, 394, 436, 440, 439; **5:14,** 80, 91, 379;
5:15, 379; **5:17–21,** 127, 168, 253; **5:17,**
157, 160, 168, 176, 206, 267; **5:18,** 23, 127,
160, 251–53; **5:19–21,** 118; **5:19,** 118, 123,
251–52; **5:20,** 79, 356; **5:21,** 113, 123, 212,
319; **6:16,** 56, 166, 199, 296, 297, 445; **6:17,**
18, 199; **7:1,** 222, 227, 242; **7:4,** 247; **7:7, 8,**
9, 96; **7:10,** 86, 96; **7:11,** 96; **7:15,** 69; **8,**
257, 353; **8:1,** 257; **9:6,** 467; **9:8,** 221; **9:10,**
221; **9:13,** 142; **10:4, 5,** 74, 138; **10:15,** 150,
152; **11,** 67, 239, 295, 331; **11:13, 14,** 67;
11:14, 15, 239; **11:16,** 331; **12:2,** 395; **12:3,**
395, 470; **12:4,** 66, 395–96; **12:7–10,** 19,
189, 321; **13:1,** 242; **13:5,** 202; **13:9,** 227,
243; **13:11,** 227, 242–43; **13:13,** 279; **13:14,**
16, 257, 396, 445

Galatians **1:1–10,** 356; **1:1,** 143, 353, 356; **1:2,**
305; **1:4,** 370, 448; **1:6–9,** 304, 311; **1:8, 9,**
vii, 351, 353; **1:13–20,** 353; **1:13,** 270, 271,
353; **1:15,** 174; **1:18,** 361; **1:19, 20,** 352;
2:2, 353; **2:7–14,** 322, 361; **2:7,** 353, 361;
2:11–21, 362; **2:11,** 311, 322, 362; **2:16,**
110, 112, 120; **2:18,** 245; **2:19, 20,** 162;
2:20, 85, 143, 205–6, 210, 243, 247, 286; **3,**
21, 82, 89, 94, 110, 115, 118, 160, 173, 177,
182, 196–97, 199, 203, 214, 227, 248, 253,
277, 296–97, 370, 383; **3:1–5,** 82; **3:2,** 21,
177; **3:3,** 21, 227; **3:8, 9,** 118; **3:13,** 248,
383; **3:16–29,** 296; **3:23,** 89, 370; **3:24,** 94,
115, 118; **3:26–4:7,** 277; **3:26,** 182, 197,
199, 277; **3:27,** 160, 173, 182; **3:28,** 196,
253; **4,** 297; **4:3,** 5; **4:4–7,** 196; **4:4,** 26, 194,
196, 350; **4:5,** 26, 194–95; **4:6,** 4, 165, 200;
4:6, 7, 196, 200; **4:9,** 447; **4:10,** 295; **4:19,**
211, 290; **4:20,** 269; **4:21,** 302; **4:26,** 271;
4:31, 302; **5,** 4, 5, 56, 82, 125, 134, 142,
146–47, 149, 163, 165, 176, 179, 187, 192,
206, 222, 224, 240, 246, 264, 276, 306, 311,
323, 342, 370, 401, 458; **5:1,** 142, 163; **5:5,**
370; **5:6,** 125, 146–47, 149, 179; **5:13,** 187,
246; **5:16–26,** 82; **5:16, 17,** 246; **5:17,** 165,
222, 224, 240, 306, 401; **5:18,** 180, 240,
246; **5:19–23,** 4, 56, 192, 264, 311, 458;
5:22–25, 192; **5:22,** 176, 192, 264; **5:23,**
342, 264; **5:24,** 176, 206; **5:25,** 134, 176,
276; **6:1,** 187; **6:2,** 69, 187; **6:7, 8,** 440; **6:8,**
381; **6:10,** 295; **6:14,** 206, 215; **6:15,** 49,
157, 160; **6:16,** 39, 50, 269

Ephesians **1:1,** 157, 229; **1:3,** 212; **1:4–11,** 38,
169, 217, 447; **1:5,** 31, 38, 217, 288; **1:6, 7,**
122; **1:7,** 32, 53, 121, 257; **1:8,** 195; **1:9,** 31;
1:10, 157, 411, 441; **1:11,** 33; **1:13,** 81, 118,

173, 177, 183, 460; **1:14,** 118, 183, 296,
460; **1:17,** 15–16; **1:18,** 217; **1:19, 20,** 161;
1:22, 40, 278, 289, 308; **1:23,** 40, 289, 308;
2:1, 37, 85, 113, 162, 170, 254; **2:1–10,** 37,
85, 147, 162, 254; **2:3,** 199; **2:4–10,** 99;
2:5–8, 80; **2:5,** 80, 161, 257; **2:7,** 122, 370;
2:8, 92, 122, 125, 128, 143, 293,; **2:8–15,**
92, 293; **2:9,** 128; **2:10,** 160; **2:11–21,** 194,
283, 415; **2:12,** 22, 51, 194; **2:13,** 51; **2:14–**
16, 252; **2:14,** 252, 270, 308; **2:18,** 23;
2:19–22, 290, 295; **2:19–3:6,** 291, 353;
2:19, 54, 194, 252, 290, 291, 295, 353; **2:20,**
267, 354, 355; **2:21,** 56, 166, 279, 292, 296;
2:22, 17, 56, 191, 296; **3:2,** 15, 19, 22, 32,
56, 85, 99, 124, 205; **3:6,** 268, 447; **3:8, 18,**
217; **3:12,** 95, 140; **3:14–19,** 56, 207, 243,
295; **3:16,** 56, 94, 141, 207, 243; **3:21,** 468;
4, 157, 160–61, 179, 182–83, 185–86, 188–
89, 217–18, 221, 224, 227, 237, 242–43,
246, 254, 264, 276, 290–91, 305, 307–8,
332, 335, 342, 350, 402, 408, 445–47, 462,
465, 478; **4:1,** 218; **4:1–16,** 283; **4:2,** 218,
342; **4:2–15,** 304; **4:2–4,** 218; **4:3–6,** 305.
308, 478; **4:4,** 15, 182, 307–8; **4:5,** 182,
218, 276, 307; **4:6,** 218; **4:7–16,** 218; **4:10,**
462; **4:11–16,** 242–43; **4:11,** 186, 188–89,
242; **4:12,** 186, 189, 218, 221, 227, 243;
4:13, 218, 221, 227, 408; **4:15–5:20,** 217,
221; **4:15,** 124, 218, 221, 237, 291, 446;
4:16, 182, 237, 291, 335, 305, 445–46;
4:17, 18, 19, 217; **4:22–26,** 160, 168, 243,
246; **4:22,** 217, 246; **4:23,** 99, 157, 160;
4:24, 99, 157, 160–61, 224; **4:25–29,** 217,
402; **4:25,** 217, 290, 447, 465; **4:30,** 19, 22,
56, 85, 179, 183, 185; **4:31,** 217, 185; **4:32,**
342, 185; **5:1, 2,** 236; **5:3,** 217, 236; **5:5,**
217, 458; **5:8,** 117, 160; **5:13–16,** 51; **5:15,**
378; **5:18,** 66, 226; **5:18b–20,** 180; **5:19,**
284, 287; **5:20,** 226, 287; **5:21–33,** 295;
5:22–6:9, 218; **5:25–7,** 217, 242, 273, 316;
5:26, 171, 229, 300; **5:27,** 229, 304, 307,
335, 420, 437, 465; **5:28–32,** 210; **5:30,**
267; **6:10–12,** 51, 143; **6:10,** 51, 306; **6:12–**
16, 51; **6:17,** 165; **6:18,** 276, 56; **6:23,** 125

Philippians **1:1,** 229, 331; **1:6,** x, 85, 164, 413;
1:11, 226, 228; **1:15–17,** 322; **1:19, 20,** 394;
1:20–23, 381; **1:21,** 206; **1:23,** 381, 393,
395–96, 445; **2,** 65, 68, 92, 126, 144, 189,
205, 218, 228, 256, 279–80, 291, 293–94,
325, 331, 356, 432; **2:1, 2,** 280; **2:2–11,** 56,
68, 291–93; **2:5,** 228, 293; **2:10,** 279, 432;
2:10, 11, 279; **2:11,** 65; **2:12,** 92, 126, 144,
205, 218, 325; **2:13,** 31, 92, 144, 205, 218;
2:27, 189; **2:30,** 331; **3:2–4,** 297; **3:3,** 56;
3:7, 9, 145; **3:9,** 123, 149, 206, 439; **3:10,**
157; **3:12–17,** 151, 214, 237, 245; **3:12,**
151, 214, 245, 430; **3:15,** 227, 243, 245;
3:18, 323; **3:19,** 381; **3:20,** 250, 269, 323,
405, 419, 427; **3:21,** 250, 269, 405, 427; **4:3,**

Apocrypha